Contemporary Business Report Writing

Shirley Kuiper

Moore School of Business

University of South Carolina

THOMSON

SOUTH-WESTERN

D1534560

Australia · Brazil · Canada · Mexico · Singapore · Spain · United Kingdom · United States

THOMSON
SOUTH-WESTERN

Contemporary Business Report Writing, Third Edition
Shirley Kuiper

VP/Editorial Director:
Jack W. Calhoun

Senior Publisher:
Melissa S. Acuña

Developmental Editor:
Erin Berger

Senior Marketing Manager:
Larry Qualls

Production Project Manager:
Margaret M. Bril

Manager of Technology, Editorial:
Vicky True

Technology Project Editor:
Kelly Reid

Web Coordinator:
Scott Cook

Senior Manufacturing Coordinator:
Diane Lohman

Production House:
Interactive Composition Corporation (ICC)

Printer:
Webcom Toronto, Ontario

Art Director:
Stacy Shirley

Internal Designer:
Lou Ann Thesing

Cover Designer:
Lou Ann Thesing

Cover Images:
© Getty Images

Library of Congress Control Number: 2005937606

For more information about our products, contact us at:

Thomson Learning Academic Resource Center

1-800-423-0563

Thomson Higher Education
5191 Natorp Boulevard
Mason, OH 45040
USA

Brief Contents

Contents

Preface

Contemporary Business Report Writing, 3rd edition, is a flexible teaching and learning tool designed to help students develop business research and reporting skills. The text contains general guides for report writing; specific guides for a variety of common business reports; illustrations and examples of the guides presented; and an abundance of application exercises that encourage students to practice their research, writing, and speaking skills. The text can be used for seminars or for courses ranging from a few weeks to a full quarter or semester. Instructors may also use parts of the text to complement other teaching materials by requesting custom publication of desired chapters.

PURPOSE, SCOPE, AND STRUCTURE

The primary purpose of *Contemporary Business Report Writing* is to enable students to approach their reporting responsibilities with confidence. Guides for effective reports emphasize the importance of all steps in the report planning, writing, and presentation processes. Guides are also given for completing those processes effectively in collaboration with team members when a person is assigned to a research or writing project that requires the joint efforts of individuals who possess varied talents and skills. In addition, ethical concerns are addressed.

The book contains 18 chapters. Those chapters observe the pedagogical practice of moving from the simple to the complex. They may be characterized as follows:

- Chapters 1 through 5 orient the students to business reports. These chapters define a business report, discuss business report characteristics, present a process for planning and writing the report, help students understand and implement appropriate writing styles, alert writers to frequently occurring writing lapses, and give guides for formatting and illustrating the report. Each chapter includes a discussion of ethical issues report writers will confront and techniques for collaborative writing.
- Chapters 6 and 7 present guides for and illustrations of typical simple reports. Simple reports are defined as those which address a relatively uncomplicated reporting situation. The report may not require extensive research; nonetheless, it is an important communication medium used in the decision process. Some reports are classified as routine (for example, a trip report or a meeting report); others are classified as nonroutine (for example, a feasibility report or an exception report). These chapters continue to expose students to ethical considerations.

- Chapters 8 through 13 focus on business research, which often culminates in a lengthy, comprehensive report. Techniques for planning the research, including writing a research proposal, are presented first. This discussion is followed by chapters focusing on selecting data sources, with detailed discussions of using secondary and primary data sources; analyzing data; and documenting data sources. Again, ethical considerations are presented.
- Chapters 14 and 15 help students develop skills in presenting the results of their business research, both in written reports and in oral presentations. Both chapters include ethical considerations related to the communication of research results.
- Chapters 16 through 18 present guides for special-purpose writing—types of writing that are not common occurrences in business but may be vital to some students' career success. Specific topics covered are business plans, policies and procedures, and promotional and persuasive writing for non-profit organizations. Again ethical issues are included.

SPECIAL FEATURES

Contemporary Business Report Writing has several strong features to help students become competent report writers.

- Contemporary business examples and illustrations reinforce traditional principles for effective writing and speaking. Guides are immediately reinforced with examples of good and bad practices.
- The ethical aspects of reporting are integrated with instruction about the research, writing, and speaking processes. Chapter 1 presents a model of routes to moral judgments and questions to direct moral decision making. Throughout the text, students are asked to apply the model and answer the questions as they apply to their research and writing responsibilities.
- Each of the first four chapters presents techniques for successful collaborative writing. These chapters include applications that require collaboration. Chapter 5 presents a summary model of pre-writing tasks, writing tasks, and post-writing activities that will help students succeed in a collaborative writing environment.
- A variety of end-of-chapter activities ("Topics for Discussion" and "Applications") reinforce the concepts and guides presented in each chapter. Each chapter includes applications relevant to the global business environment. Chapters 6, 7, and 8 include applications contributed by native Thai academics and business people.

As a package, the book provides instruction in the fundamental requirements for preparing effective business reports as ethical individuals working in a collaborative, global business environment. Through reading, discussion, and application of knowledge, students are led through the essential stages for production of effective simple and complex reports.

Acknowledgments

Several people have influenced the production of this edition of *Contemporary Business Report Writing*. To name some runs the risk of omitting others. But I shall take that risk.

- Erin Berger, Assistant Editor, has marshaled this book through the publication maze, from earliest teleconferences through unveiling of the final product. Thanks, Erin, for your loyalty and attention to detail.
- Cheryl M. Luke, former colleague, hammered out the first edition with me. Her influence is still felt in this edition. Thanks, Cheryl, for friendship and professional stimulation.
- Earl A. Dvorak, one of my graduate school mentors, taught me most of what I know about business research and reporting. Thanks, Earl, for teaching me to stick to a task and always aim for the highest goals.
- Morris P. Wolf, with whom I coauthored three editions of *Effective Communication for Business*, also taught me much about communication and the effectiveness of precise language. His confidence in me on that first collaboration made me think I could write another book.
- Dorinda Clippinger, William Sandberg, and Lulis del Castillo-Gonzalez wrote chapters or parts of chapters. Nongluck Sriussadaporn Chareonngam, along with her friends and colleagues, contributed applications. Thank you, friends and colleagues, for adding dimensions to the book that I could not have contributed.
- Thomas H. Fitzpatrick, my husband of more than 20 years, has stood by me through the production of more books than he wants to count. Thanks, Tom, for your patience, your culinary skills, and your constant support and love.
- Schatzie and Liebchen, our two Miniature Schnauzers, communicate unconditional love no matter how stressed or irritable I may be. Sit! Wait!

During my 40-year-plus teaching career, students, too numerous to mention, and many colleagues have influenced my thinking about communication and education for business. I owe a huge debt to them. In particular I thank these colleagues whose critical comments and helpful suggestions have improved the quality of this book:

Dr. Linda Cresap
  Minot State University
Dr. Patricia Mandia
  Kent State University Stark Campus

Dr. Glynna Morse
    Georgia College and State University
Joan Ryan
    Clackamas Community College
Sandra Valensky
    Baker College of Auburn Hills
Beverly Neiderman
    Kent State University
Donna M. Carlon, Ph.D.
    University of Central Oklahoma
Laurie Ribble Libove
    Dominican University of California

I invite you, the users of *Contemporary Business Report Writing,* to share your suggestions and recommendations with me.

SHIRLEY KUIPER, Emerita Professor
Moore School of Business
University of South Carolina
skuiper@bellsouth.net

Report Characteristics

What do a bank manager, a retail store manager, a vice president of a manufacturing company, and an executive director of a nonprofit organization have in common? Although their job descriptions may show considerably different duties, one task is common to all: preparing reports.

FUNCTIONS OF BUSINESS REPORTS

Business reports are organized, objective presentations of observations, experiences, or facts used in the decision-making process. Some reports supply information necessary for decision making; others convey information about decisions that have been made and must be implemented. Some reports provide information only; these are often called *information* reports. Other reports also analyze the data and supply conclusions and recommendations; these may be referred to as *analytical* reports.

Since people at all levels of an organization must make or carry out decisions, reports are used in every kind of job. For example, a report may be as simple as a bank manager's oral reassignment of a teller from an inside workstation to a drive-up window after the manager observes that cars are lining up at the window. Or a report may be as complex as a retail store manager's written analysis of the store's operations, competition, and goals, concluding with a recommendation that the business be relocated.

For many students, the word *report* suggests a term paper, a book review, or a case analysis. But those documents differ from on-the-job reports in many respects. Whereas you may write a term paper to demonstrate your knowledge of a subject, you will write business reports to influence actions of other people. Although school reports usually flow upward (from student to instructor), business reports move up, down, and across the formal organizational structure. You may use the Internet or books and journals from your university library as the major data sources for a term paper; but your business reports will frequently contain data drawn from company files or your experience and observations as well as from print and electronic media. The quality of a term paper may affect your course grade, but the quality of a business report can determine the success or failure of your career—and that of your company.

The role of reports in the decision-making process is shown in Table 1-1. The illustration suggests several reports related to one business situation, entering an international market. The first report is an informal oral report by a J Pac sales associate to the Vice President for Marketing. Assume that J Pac is a major United States manufacturer of gas grills. The sales associate recently returned from a vacation in Brazil, which is a significant regional producer and consumer of meats. While in Brazil, the sales associate noticed that many restaurants serve meats to order—including lamb, beef, pork, fish, and fowl—and those foods are often grilled. Many families also enjoy outdoor grilling. However, the grilling is done primarily over charcoal. Although gas is readily available to homes and restaurants, the use of gas grills is minimal at this time. The sales associate thinks there is a potential opportunity to enter the Brazilian market with J Pac's top-of-the-line gas grills.

As Table 1-1 shows, the initial oral report by the sales associate could lead to a series of reports related to the feasibility of marketing gas grills in Latin America. Those reports may be simple or complex, oral or written, formal or informal. Moreover, reporting occurs at every level of the organizational structure. Reports perform many functions in the organization, but the primary function is to improve the decision-making process and the quality of actions based on those decisions.

CHARACTERISTICS OF EFFECTIVE REPORTS

Effective reports are understood by the reader as the writer intended, and they influence the reader to act as the writer desired. The writer's objectives are most likely to be achieved if they correspond with the needs and objectives of the reader. An effective report is accurate, clear, empathetic, and concise. Above all, an effective report presents information ethically.

Accuracy

Effective decisions can be made only if they are based on accurate information. Consequently, the first criterion for effective reporting is accuracy. The effective

TABLE 1-1	REPORTS AND DECISIONS			
Sender	**Receiver**	**Report Content**	**Report Characteristics**	**Decision/Action**
J Pac sales associate	J Pac sales manager	Consumers in Brazil enjoy grilled meats; most use charcoal; potential market for our gas grills	Oral; informal	Sales manager does preliminary research; relays information to vice president for marketing
Sales manager	Vice president for marketing	Burgeoning consumer market is attracting many U.S. companies to Brazil; several of our competitors are already selling gas grills in Latin America	Written; semi-formal; supplemented by oral summary	Vice president for marketing asks director of market research to conduct further research about feasibility of entering Latin American market
Vice president for marketing	Director of market research	Summary of previous reports; request to study feasibility of entering Latin American market	Written; semi-formal	Director of market research assigns task to research staff; requests research proposal
Director of market research	Research staff	Summary of vice president's reports; requests research proposal	Oral; informal; part of weekly staff meeting	Staff begins work on research proposal
Research staff	Director of market research	Proposed plan for feasibility study	Written; formal	Director approves plan; staff conducts study
Research staff	Director of market research	Findings, conclusions, recommendations of feasibility study	Formal; written; perhaps supplemented by oral presentation	Director asks staff to present report to management committee
Research staff and director of market research	Management committee	Background; summary of preliminary studies; findings, conclusions, recommendations of feasibility study	Oral/visual presentation; written summary of key findings and recommendations	Management authorization of budget for marketing division to begin efforts to establish distributorships in Brazil

reporter attempts to gather accurate, objective data; verifies data when necessary; and presents the data accurately. Correct data are conveyed through accurate number use, word choice, spelling, grammar, and punctuation. Careful use of visual aids also promotes correctness. Compare the following examples of incorrect and correct portions of reports.

Incorrect: The projector cost $49.50; $30.00 for labor, $9.50 for materials, and $20.00 for indirect costs.

Correct: The projected cost is $59.50 per unit: $30.00 for labor, $9.50 for materials, and $20.00 for indirect costs.

OR

The projected unit cost:

Labor	$30.00
Materials	$9.50
Indirect costs	$20.00
Total	$59.50

Completeness is another aspect of accuracy. Incomplete messages that omit essential data are likely to be inaccurate. Senders of incomplete messages tend to assume that the reader knows or will "fill in" certain details that the reader, in fact, may not know or cannot supply. Consequently, receivers of incomplete messages often interpret them quite differently from the sender's intention. Compare the following incomplete and complete presentations of information. Which versions are more effective?

Incomplete: The editorial staff will meet at 8 on Tuesday.

Complete: The editorial staff will meet at 8 a.m. on Tuesday, March 1, in Conference Room A.

OR

Editorial Staff Meeting
When: Tuesday, March 1 at 8 a.m.
Where: Conference Room A

Incomplete: Orders from Oxford Tool and Supply Co. have declined during recent months. Please let me know soon what you plan to do to revive this account.

Complete: Orders from Oxford Tool and Supply Co. for saw blades and router bits went down 10 percent each month during August, September, and October.

Please give me a detailed action plan for that account before November 15. Include in your plan the number of calls you have scheduled, whom you will contact, what questions you intend to ask, and what special offers, if any, you will make to revive that account.

Clarity

Since communication is an extremely complex process, the risks of misunderstanding are always present. A general guide for clarity is to use simple rather than complex words, sentences, and paragraphs.

Simple words are those that are familiar to both the sender and receiver. For example, most users of American English understand the words *dog* and *cat*, but fewer understand their synonyms *canine* and *feline*.

The relative simplicity of words is also related to the context in which they are used. Jargon, the technical or special language of a specific group, may simplify communication within that group; but when used with persons outside that group, jargon becomes a communication barrier. Among computer users, for example, terms like SDRAM, gigabyte, and media accelerator are simple. To people who are not familiar with computers, those terms may be meaningless. Study the following examples of sentences using complex and simple words.

Complex: Subsequent to perusing the vendor's missive, Austin declaimed his opposition regarding the egregious proposition.

Simple: After reading the seller's letter, Austin loudly rejected the extremely bad offer.

Another guide for clear writing is to use concrete, vivid words and descriptions rather than abstractions. Concrete words permit a narrow range of interpretation, but abstract words may be interpreted in many ways. For example, the abstract term *writing instrument* may suggest objects as diverse as pencils, pens, typewriters, and computers. But the concrete terms *pencil* and *typewriter* are not likely to bring to mind images of pens or computers. The following examples illustrate abstract and concrete language.

Abstract: Please return the questionnaire as soon as possible. Your responses are valuable to us and other consumers.

Concrete: Please complete and mail the questionnaire to 123 Blake Street, Citizen, OH 00000-0000, before April 30, [year]. Your responses will help us determine whether our customers would benefit from Saturday banking hours.

Sentence structure also contributes to or distracts from clarity. The simplest sentence follows the subject–verb–complement structure. That structure clearly identifies the actor, the action, and the receiver of the action, leaving little possibility of misinterpretation. However, excessive use of simple sentences can result in a choppy, nearly childlike writing style. An appropriate balance of simple sentences and longer, more complex sentences contributes to clear, interesting writing. Compare the following examples.

Complex: Because there was insufficient evidence of carrier responsibility, the carrier refused the damage claim that was filed by the customer only three days after the shipment arrived.

Too simple: The shipment arrived. Three days later the customer filed a damage claim. There was no evidence of carrier fault. The carrier refused the claim.

Appropriate balance: The customer filed a damage claim three days after the shipment arrived. The carrier refused that claim because there was no evidence of carrier fault.

Clear writing also requires correct use of pronouns. Indefinite pronoun reference—using a pronoun without a clear antecedent—destroys clarity because the reader or listener is not sure what noun is replaced by the pronoun. Compare the following examples.

Indefinite reference: After customers return the questionnaires to the company, they will analyze them.

Clear reference: After customers return the questionnaires to the company, the research staff will analyze the responses.

Indefinite reference: Ignoring customers' comments about unsatisfactory service will soon affect the bottom line. That is something we must correct immediately.

Clear reference: Ignoring customers' comments about unsatisfactory service will soon affect profits. We must respond to customers' comments promptly, and we must correct the service problems immediately.

A final aspect of clarity is grammatical, structural, and logical consistency. Grammatical consistency (parallelism) exists when a writer uses the same grammatical structure for equivalent sentence or paragraph components. Compare the following examples of nonparallel and parallel grammatical structures.

Nonparallel: The survey revealed that our customers want evening shopping hours, free delivery, and to be able to consult an interior decorator.

Parallel: The survey revealed customers' desires for evening shopping hours, free delivery, and interior decorating advice.

Nonparallel: Harter, Monk, and Ms. Adamson are analyzing the customer survey.

Parallel: Mr. Harter, Mr. Monk, and Ms. Adamson are analyzing the customer survey.

OR

Harter, Monk, and Adamson are analyzing the customer survey.

Structural consistency is achieved by maintaining the same structure for parallel units of a report. For example, the wording and placement of headings in a report contribute to, or distract from, structural consistency. Compare the following examples of inconsistent and consistent report headings.

Inconsistent:

1. Performance of Model A2C500
   1.1. Start-up Costs
   1.2. Operating Costs
   1.3. Revenue
   1.4. Return on Investment
2. Model B3B400
   a. Initial Costs
   b. Costs of Operation
   c. Investment Return

Consistent:

1. Performance of Model A2C500
   1.1. Start-up Costs
   1.2. Operating Costs
   1.3. Revenue
   1.4. Return on Investment
2. Performance of Model B3B400
   2.1. Start-up Costs
   2.2. Operating Costs
   2.3. Revenue
   2.4. Return on Investment

Effective writers also strive to achieve logical consistency. Logic is a form of reasoning that imposes order on information. Logical reasoning contributes to truth, but fallacies (false or invalid arguments) distract from truth. Four common fallacies that report writers should avoid are *post hoc, ergo propter hoc* ("after this, therefore, because of this"), *non sequitur* ("it does not follow"), begging the question, and hasty generalization.

The *post hoc, ergo propter hoc* fallacy confuses passage of time with cause and effect. A writer guilty of this fallacy assumes that if one event occurred before another, the first event caused the second. Compare the following example of a *post hoc, ergo propter hoc* fallacy with the logical statement that follows it. Notice that the complete, correct logical statement is longer than the fallacy. Logical consistency should not be sacrificed for conciseness.

Post hoc, ergo propter hoc: District A sales have increased 1 percent each month since Wilson became district manager. Wilson has turned that territory around.

Logical statement: Although economic conditions have not changed in District A, its sales have increased 1 percent each month since Wilson became district manager. Wilson has personally helped each sales representative develop a sales plan. That management technique appears to have improved the district's performance.

A *non sequitur* states a conclusion based on faulty or insufficient evidence. The following sentences contrast a *non sequitur* with a logical statement.

Non sequitur: We received 200 calls in response to Sunday's newspaper advertisement. Our sales are sure to pick up this month.

Logical statement: We received 200 calls in response to Sunday's newspaper advertisement. If only 10 percent of those respondents order by February 28, February's sales will be 2 percent above January's.

Begging the question is a fallacy in which an assumption or conclusion is restated instead of being supported by logical reasons or evidence. "I should be more assertive because I need to assert myself" merely repeats the need to be assertive but does not supply a reason. "I need to be more assertive because people often take advantage of me" supplies a reason for the conclusion. The following examples further contrast begging the question with a logical statement.

Begging the question: I rejected this proposal because I cannot accept it in its present form.

Logical statement: I rejected this proposal because the cost data were incomplete.

In a hasty generalization, a person reasons that because something is true in some instances it is true in the case under discussion. Compare the following examples.

Hasty generalization: Sandy has more education than any other applicant. Sandy is the best person for this position.

Logical statement: Sandy scored higher than any other applicant on all selection criteria. Sandy is the best applicant for this position.

Grammatical, structural, and logical consistency tends to improve report clarity. Moreover, presenting data and conclusions logically makes a report and its writer believable, whereas fallacies tend to cast doubt on the report content and its writer. Another way to improve credibility is to demonstrate empathy for the reader.

Empathy

Empathy is being sensitive to and vicariously experiencing the needs or feelings of another. A successful report writer attempts to understand the reader's needs and to fulfill those needs through report content, structure, and tone. Empathy is demonstrated by supplying all necessary information in an easily comprehended structure. Thus, coherent paragraph structure, logical organization of a report, and use of headings to guide the reader become evidences of empathy. Similarly, a courteous and respectful tone demonstrates empathy. Compare the following examples of nonempathetic and empathetic writing.

Nonempathetic: After reviewing the Airgo Corporation passenger questionnaire carefully, I have concluded that the corporation should do four things to improve the questionnaire. First, including a brief transmittal message explaining why the passenger's responses to the questionnaire are needed would give the passenger justification for completing the questionnaire. Second, all of the time questions could be avoided because that information could be obtained from other sources. Third, the question that asks about the rating of the service should have been open ended. This would allow the passenger to respond to specific aspects of the service that were or were not satisfactory. Finally, the question that asks for the name, address, and telephone number of the passenger could be avoided because that information is likely not relevant.

Empathetic: Airgo Corporation can improve its customer-service questionnaire in four ways:

1. Include a brief transmittal message explaining why the passenger's responses are needed. Such a message may increase the response rate.
2. Delete the questions about flight times. That information can be obtained from company records.
3. Provide an open-ended response mode for rating the service. This mode will let passengers comment about different aspects of the service.
4. Delete the request for passenger's name, address, and telephone number. The information seems irrelevant and may discourage some passengers from completing the form.

A final characteristic—conciseness—complements accuracy, clarity, and empathy.

Conciseness

An effective writer uses the least number of words necessary to convey information accurately, completely, clearly, consistently, and empathetically. Concise writing is characterized by lack of trite expressions, redundancies, or unnecessary words. Compare the following examples.

Trite, commonplace expressions:

I look forward to serving you soon.
Let us supply all your hair needs.
Thank you in advance for your business.

Concise, relevant language:

I'll service your copier each Friday morning.
Hair Trimmers carries a complete selection of Head Turners shampoos
and conditioners.
I would be pleased to provide your tax service during this new year.

Redundant: This report presentation provides the necessary information essential for reaching an informed decision regarding your plans and prospects for success in a profitable venture in that part of the city, that is, a new branch office.

Concise: This report provides information about the potential profitability of a branch office in the Shady Grove area.

Conciseness does not mean brevity above all; conciseness means to avoid unnecessary words. Compare the following examples of accurate, clear, empathetic, and concise writing with those that violate one or more of those criteria.

Concise but incomplete, nonempathetic: Call me tomorrow.

Concise, complete, empathetic: Please call me (555-5974) between 8 a.m. and 11:30 a.m. tomorrow.

Concise but incomplete: Amy's fee is less.

Concise and complete: Amy's fee is $500 less than Matt's.

Wordy, unclear, incorrect modification: Keeping in mind the objective of facilitating timely processing of rebate requests, it appears that a personnel increase in the neighborhood of 10 percent of our current staff will be essential.

Concise, clear, correct modification: To fulfill rebate requests promptly, we will need 20 additional employees.

As you compose reports, evaluate your writing by the criteria of correctness, clarity, empathy, and conciseness. Each of those qualities contributes to another major dimension of reporting: the ethical dimension.

ETHICAL CONSIDERATIONS

Individuals, organizational leaders, and government agencies do not always agree about what constitutes ethical behavior. Most people agree that persons or organizations that are in a position to influence the lives of others ought to behave ethically—they should do "the right thing." But "oughts" or "shoulds" are themselves ethical judgments, indicating the complexity of the ethical arena.

Since the objective of a report is to bring about good decisions, the writer has an ethical responsibility. Ethical considerations apply to all aspects of reporting: timing, content, structure, word choice, illustrations. Two strategies that will help you through ethical pitfalls while writing are to avoid manipulative language and to be guided by an ethical model as you make writing decisions.

Avoid Manipulative Language

Language can be manipulated to modify or mask reality. Awareness of manipulative techniques should help you avoid using potentially unethical communication and being a victim of such messages.[1]

FALSE IMPRESSIONS

Creating a false impression is implying that certain conditions exist when they do not. For example, promoters of a time-share resort invite potential buyers to spend three free days at the resort. The only obligation is to listen to a sales presentation about the resort. Although the brochure accompanying the invitation shows luxurious rooms, the visitors are in fact housed in a run-down motel near the resort. The false impression created by the brochure is that the guests would enjoy the luxury of the resort for three days.

IMPRECISE LANGUAGE

Imprecise language, such as abstractions, euphemisms, and generalities, can mislead readers. When a restaurant offers free toys with children's meals and encourages children to collect the entire set, many children and parents mistakenly assume that all toys are available and the child may choose a preferred toy, in fact, limited numbers of some toys are available and the children often are given no choice.

MISSING OR OMITTED INFORMATION

Omitting information that a reader needs to make an informed decision can be misleading. An airline that was experiencing severe financial problems issued a news release saying that the carrier had experienced a 17 percent increase in the number of passengers carried the previous month. The release did not include the fact that during that month the airline had run a "2 for 1" promotion, by which two passengers could fly for the price of one. The unanswered question: Did revenues increase in proportion to the increase in passenger miles? Apparently not; three months later the carrier went into bankruptcy.

FALSE OR INACCURATE INFORMATION

Some writers may knowingly or unwittingly present false or inaccurate information. One writer reporting on the feasibility of entering the heating and air conditioning market in Poland erroneously reported that the exchange rate was $1 U.S. = 14 Zloty, when in fact the rate at that time was approximately $1 U.S. = 14,000 Zloty. Had the error not been caught, the potential exporter could have suffered serious losses from underpricing its product.

De-Emphasizing or Suppressing Important Information

Unfavorable information is often de-emphasized by page layout, print size, or use of less-dominant color. For example, most customer-reward programs promoted by airlines and hotels have restrictions about how and when awards can be used. Promotional materials typically show those restrictions in smaller print and in more obscure positions than the positive features of the program. A related suppressing practice is to put important information on an Internet website while making the path to that information so complicated that many web users give up the search before finding the information.

Emphasizing Misleading or Incorrect Information

Illustrations, color, and print size can be used to emphasize information inappropriately. Prominent pictures of optional equipment in an automobile brochure may give the impression that such equipment is standard on most models.

No-Fault Writing

No-fault writing does not identify the person or persons responsible for an action. Ethical writers and decision makers are willing to take responsibility for their words and actions. "It has been decided . . ." or "Your request cannot be granted at this time . . ." avoids placing responsibility for the decision. Moreover, no-fault writing rarely supplies the reader with adequate feedback to take corrective action.

Answering the questions shown in Illustration 1-1, in addition to using ethical models to direct judgments made during the communication process, can improve the quality of your writing.

ILLUSTRATION 1-1 QUESTIONS FOR ANALYZING THE ETHICS OF COMMUNICATION

1. Is the communication honest and truthful?
2. Am I acting in the company's best interest? in the public's best interest? in my own best interest?
3. What if everybody acted or communicated in this way? If the action or communication is right in this situation, is it right for everyone else in the same situation?
4. Am I willing to take responsibility for the action or communication publicly and privately?
5. Does the action or communication violate the rights of any of the people involved?

Source: Sims, B. R. (Summer, 1993). Linking ethics and language in the technical communication classroom. *Technical Communication Quarterly, 2(3),* 285–299.

Be Guided by an Ethical Model

To achieve some degree of consistency and consensus about what is good, people and organizations develop ethical systems or frameworks. One ethicist, R. C. Chewning, proposes that human beings judge behaviors of themselves and others in terms of "being" and "doing."[2] Moral being refers to intentions, motives, or character traits. Moral doing refers to human behavior and its consequences.

That framework for moral judgments is diagrammed in Illustration 1-2. As the diagram suggests, when faced with a moral issue, a person may take one of several routes to decide upon an action. Two persons may arrive at entirely different conclusions about good behavior; or as circumstances vary, an individual may arrive at different conclusions.

For example, two U.S. laws (the Pregnancy Discrimination Act, 1978; the Family and Medical Leave Act, 1993) make it illegal for employers to discriminate against pregnant women. Subsequently, many U.S. firms, whether trying to develop a family-friendly culture or merely trying to comply with the law, have developed family-leave policies. Firms that are truly trying to develop a family-friendly culture could be operating in the "moral being" realm—valuing the virtues of kindness in itself, and sensing that the virtue leads to good consequences. Firms that merely try to comply with the law appear to be operating in the "moral doing" realm—taking action based on rules or laws that will result in good consequences; or, at least, avoidance of bad consequences.

Despite the existence of family-friendly policies, however, many women feel their careers may be threatened if they take full advantage of stated policies. In

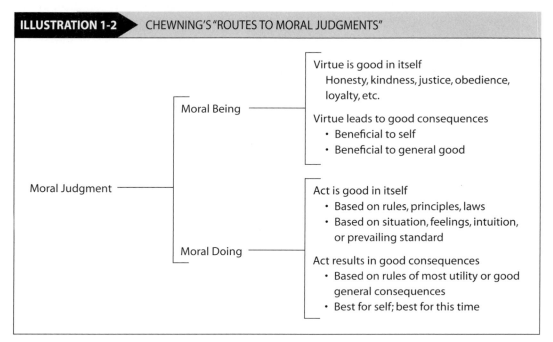

ILLUSTRATION 1-2   CHEWNING'S "ROUTES TO MORAL JUDGMENTS"

Moral Judgment

Moral Being
- Virtue is good in itself
  Honesty, kindness, justice, obedience, loyalty, etc.
- Virtue leads to good consequences
  - Beneficial to self
  - Beneficial to general good

Moral Doing
- Act is good in itself
  - Based on rules, principles, laws
  - Based on situation, feelings, intuition, or prevailing standard
- Act results in good consequences
  - Based on rules of most utility or good general consequences
  - Best for self; best for this time

Source: Chewning, R. C. (1983). *Business ethics in a changing culture*. Richmond: Robert F. Dame, Inc., 112–113.

those cases, a woman must choose between two good values: retaining a job to help support her family or her concept of self; or following health practices that will protect the baby and/or her own physical and psychological needs.[3]

More often than not, ethical questions concern right vs. right rather than right vs. wrong. Right vs. right questions vary in complexity and cannot be resolved with easy solutions such as "do the right thing." J. L. Badaracco proposes that some ethical issues involve responsibility to self alone; others include responsibility to self and for others; and still others concern an added responsibility—that which is shared with other groups in society.[4] In each category, a person who wants to act ethically and wisely should answer a series of questions to promote a well-reasoned decision, as opposed to a simplistic or impulsive decision. (See Illustration 1-3.)

ILLUSTRATION 1-3 ▶ QUESTIONS TO DIRECT MORAL DECISION MAKING

PERSONAL ASPECTS—RESPONSIBILITY TO SELF

1. How do my feelings and intuitions define the dilemma for me?
2. How deep are the moral roots of the conflicting values that are creating the right-versus-right conflict? Which of the responsibilities and values in conflict have the deepest roots in my life and in communities I care about?
3. Are these the values by which *I* want to shape *my* future, as opposed to *others* who may want to shape my future?
4. What will work in the world as it is? How can expediency and shrewdness, imagination and boldness, move me toward the goals about which I care most strongly?

ORGANIZATIONAL ASPECTS—RESPONSIBILITY TO SELF AND FOR OTHERS

1. What is truth? What are the other strong, persuasive, competing interpretations of the situation or problem? What kind of interpretation is most likely to win a contest of interpretation inside the organization and influence the thinking and behavior of others?
2. What is the cash value of this situation and of my ideas for the people whose support I need?
3. Have I orchestrated a process that can make the values I care about become the truth for my organization?
4. Am I playing to win?

SOCIETAL ASPECTS—RESPONSIBILITY SHARED WITH OTHERS

1. Have I done all I can to secure my position and the strength and stability of my organization?
2. Have I thought creatively and imaginatively about my organization's role in society and its relationship to stakeholders?
3. Do I have the strength and power to act boldly (like a lion) or should I act more craftily (like a fox)? What allies do I have, inside and outside my company? What allies do I need? Which parties will resist or fight my efforts? Have I underestimated their power and tactical skill or overestimated their ethics? Can I respond quickly and flexibly, thereby seizing opportunities?

Source: Summarized from Badaracco, Joseph L., Jr. (1997). *Defining moments: When managers must choose between right and right.* Boston: Harvard Business School Press, p. 147.

For example, when offered a position as office manager for an accounting firm, rather than as a member of the audit staff, a woman who has passed the CPA exam may face this dilemma: Should I accept this offer because it provides secure employment near my home? Should I reject it because it seems to be a case of sexism? When a manager is asked to dismiss a young man whose wife recently lost her job, should the manager consider the needs of the company above the needs of the employee? When a company president who enjoys attending ballet performances proposes that the company make a generous contribution to a local ballet company, the president's individual values must be balanced against the values of the stockholders and the community as a whole.

Understanding frameworks for moral judgments, such as those proposed by Chewning and Badaracco, will help you understand how and why your decisions sometimes differ from those of other well-meaning, moral, rational persons. Ideally, a behavior satisfies four criteria laid out by Chewning: The act is good in itself, the act results in good consequences, the act is prompted by a virtue that is good in itself, and the virtue leads to good consequences. But when all these ideals cannot be met, moral compromises must be reached. By answering the questions posed in Illustration 1-3, you should become more skilled in making ethical decisions that result in the greatest good for yourself, for those to whom you have a responsibility, and for the larger society—a responsibility that you may share with others.

COLLABORATIVE WRITING

Many reports are produced through collaboration, the process whereby a group of people works together to produce a finished product such as a report. The first step in producing a collaborative report is understanding and following these guides for effective collaboration.

- Have empathy for the other collaborators. See their point of view. Do not assume you know what they are saying or are going to say. Actively listen and hear what they are saying.
- Be considerate of others. Support the other members of the group with compliments and friendliness. Motivate, rather than pressure, people to act by being supportive.
- Be loyal to the group without agreeing to everything. Tactfully assert yourself when you have a contribution to make or when you disagree.
- Invite criticism of your contributions and be ready to criticize your own ideas. Detach yourself from your ideas and try to see them objectively, as you hope others will. Never attack people personally for their ideas. The criticism should be directed to the idea, not the person.
- Understand that communication often breaks down. Do not be shocked when you are misunderstood or when you misunderstand others.
- Remember that most ideas that are not obvious seem strange at first, yet they may be the best ideas.

Reviewing these guides each time you begin a collaborative project will get you off to a productive start and bring you to a satisfying end of the project. Further guides for effective collaboration will be given in subsequent chapters.

SUMMARY

Reports are organized, objective presentations of observations, experiences, or facts. Their basic function is to provide information for effective decisions and actions at all levels of the organization. Effective reports contribute to personal career success as well as to the success of the organization.

To prepare an effective report, evaluate your work for accuracy, clarity, empathy, and conciseness. Also evaluate the ethical implications of your report: Will it contribute to good or bad decisions and actions? Have you avoided manipulative language? Have you tested your writing decisions against an ethical model?

As you undertake your report-writing activities, you will often be required to work collaboratively. Following basic guides for collaboration—empathy, consideration, loyalty, and openness to criticism and new ideas—should get you off to a good start in any collaborative effort.

TOPICS FOR DISCUSSION

1. Business reports are defined as *organized, objective* presentations of *observations, experiences, or facts* used in the *decision-making process.* What is your understanding of each of the italicized terms? Why should you keep each of those ideas in mind as you prepare reports in any organization? What problems could arise if you neglect any one of those factors?

2. In what ways do business reports differ from a typical college term paper?

3. Give examples (other than those in the textbook) to demonstrate your understanding of each of the following characteristics of effective reports:
   - Accuracy
   - Clarity
   - Empathy
   - Conciseness

4. Explain each of the following forms of consistency. Provide examples of violations of these types of consistency that you have observed in the print media or business writing:
   - Grammatical
   - Structural
   - Logical

5. Define and give examples (other than those in the textbook) of these fallacies:
   - *post hoc, ergo propter hoc*
   - *non sequitur*
   - begging the question
   - hasty generalization

6. Define empathy; give an example of how nonempathetic writing can be changed to demonstrate empathy.

7. Explain this statement: "Conciseness does not mean brevity above all."

8. Identify five examples of ways in which some writers manipulate language to modify or mask reality. Give examples of each. Find examples in the print media or business publications to share with your class.

9. Following an accident in which Rachel George's car was totally destroyed, the insurance company provided for a rental car. The first car that Ms. George got from the rental agency was a subcompact, which had been authorized by her local insurance agent. Since Ms. George had been driving a luxury sedan, she told her agent that she did not feel safe in the rental vehicle. He replied, "Rachel, get whatever car you want. We'll settle the details later." Although the sedan she then rented exceeded the daily amount stipulated in her insurance contract, Ms. George assumed that her agent's words meant that he would cover at least part of the difference. When time came to settle the insurance claim, the insurance company paid only the amount stipulated in the policy. The local agent (who had enjoyed Ms. George's insurance business for over 25 years) did not offer to pay any of the additional cost; instead he suggested that she buy a higher level of rental car coverage when she insured her new automobile.
   - Were the agent's words to the insured client accurate, clear, empathetic?
   - Did the agent act ethically toward the client?
   - Did the client act ethically toward the agent?
   - What ethical routes (cf. Chewning) did the agent and the client take?
   - What questions (cf. Badaracco) might have helped the agent and policyholder avoid the misunderstanding?

10. Discuss ways in which you can contribute to effective collaboration. If you have had experience producing a report collaboratively, describe that experience to your classmates. Was it successful? If so, what contributed to its success? If not, what contributed to its failure?

APPLICATIONS

1. Find an example of a message (report, announcement, business letter, advertisement, etc.) that violates one or more of the characteristics of an effective report presented in Chapter 1. As directed by your instructor, share

your findings with your classmates in a brief oral presentation, or write a report in a format specified by your instructor. Explain how the item has failed to meet one or more of the criteria.

2. Select the item that best demonstrates accuracy. Explain your choice by identifying the errors that appear in the remaining items.
   a. Of 480 questionnaire respondents, 40 percent, or 129 people, had seen the Tyler Company TV commercials.
   b. Of 480 questionnaire respondents, 40 percent, or 190 people, had seen the Tyler Company TV commercials.
   c. Forty percent (192) of the 480 questionnaire respondents had seen the Tyler Company TV commercials.

3. Select the item that best demonstrates completeness. Explain your choice.
   a. WBI's Flight 319 is 10 minutes faster than 535.
   b. WBI's Flight 319 is 10 minutes faster than its Flight 535.
   c. WBI's flight is faster than SAC's.

4. Select the item that best demonstrates clarity. Explain your choice.
   a. Sales declines were registered by two departments in a recent month.
   b. Housewares showed a 5 percent sales decline in March, which was two percentage points better than Home Furnishings, which also showed a decline compared with a year ago.
   c. Compared with a year ago, Housewares sales in March were down 5 percent and Home Furnishings sales were down 7 percent.

5. Select the item that best demonstrates correct modification. Explain your choice.
   a. Arriving ahead of schedule, it was necessary to store the cartons.
   b. Arriving ahead of schedule, John asked me to store the cartons.
   c. Arriving ahead of schedule, the cartons had to be stored.

6. Select the item that best demonstrates grammatical consistency. Explain your choice.
   a. Unless you plan your messages, you waste time and money.
   b. Unless you plan your messages, it wastes time and money.
   c. Saving time and to not waste money are reasons to plan your messages.

7. Select the item that best demonstrates logical consistency. Explain your choice.
   a. In a recent customer survey, 90 percent of our repeat customers reported that our policy of filling orders within one day of receipt influenced their purchases. We should continue that service.
   b. This report shows that we filled 96 percent of our orders within a day of their receipt. That's why we have so many repeat customers.
   c. With our computerized inventory-control system, we can determine instantaneously the exact quantity of any item in stock. Therefore, we can fill customer orders promptly.

8. Select the item that best demonstrates empathy. Explain your choice.
   a. Margaret, get me the report of yesterday's sales calls.
   b. Margaret, I need the report of yesterday's sales calls. Where is it?
   c. Margaret, I need the report of yesterday's sales calls for my meeting with Dr. Jameson at 1 p.m. today. Will you find it for me, please?

9. Select the item that best demonstrates conciseness. Explain your choice.
   a. We project a 10 to 15 percent gain.
   b. At this point in time we are projecting an approximate gain in the range of 10 to 15 percent.
   c. We expect a reasonable gain.

10. Rewrite each of the following sentences, correcting expressions that are not grammatically parallel.
    a. This job includes scheduling mechanical maintenance and also that you should dispatch the delivery vans.
    b. The job requires good communication skills and also someone who enjoys working in a busy environment.
    c. Writers should always write clearly, concisely, and with accuracy.
    d. Ellen enjoys writing sales copy and to design sales brochures.

11. Identify the fallacies present in the following quotations. Write logical revisions.
    a. "... In 1963, a case was brought before the U.S. Supreme Court claiming that prayer in public schools violated the Constitution, and the left-wing justices banished God from our schools.

       "What has happened since that fateful day in 1963? We have seen violence grow as never before. Children without this moral guidance have grown up and become lawbreakers in ever-increasing numbers. ..." (*The State,* January 17, 2005, p. A8.)
    b. "(XXX) Corp.—a pioneer in the development of data protection software and products—will receive $8.1 million in venture capital that company officials say will double the company's employment and annual revenues." (*The State,* January 18, 2005, p. B6.)
    c. "Fresher, local food means better health" (*The State,* January 20, 2005, p. A11.)
    d. "When (the governor's) budget is passed and we add more Highway Patrol troopers to the force, we will have ample law enforcement officers to see that (the seatbelt) law is enforced." (*The State,* January 20, 2005, p. A10.)
    e. In response to speculation that a restructured organization would be weaker: "Everybody is doing a good job. ... We have new people in positions. They're still feeling their way in those positions." (*The State,* January 21, 2005, p. C4.)

12. Flora Garcia has received an oral offer for a position as volunteer coordinator with Save Our Pets, a nonprofit organization devoted to rescuing abandoned animals. The position was originally advertised with an

annual salary of $40,000; but during a job interview, the executive indicated that the position carries an annual salary of $40,500 and benefits equal to those in Ms Garcia's current position. Garcia currently earns $37,500 annually. To accept the offer, she will have to move to a new location approximately 500 miles from her current home. After some thought, Ms. Garcia decided to decline the offer because the salary increase will barely pay for moving expenses and the increased cost of living at the new location. She notified Samantha Hayes, Executive Director of Save Our Pets, of her decision by telephone. Since Hayes could not offer a higher salary, she offered to pay all moving expenses. Garcia verbally accepted that offer, and Hayes told her a formal job offer would be mailed within a few days.

Two weeks later, Garcia received the following letter. Identify the communication problems that appear to have occurred in this situation.

SAVE OUR PETS

1705 Millwood Rd.,   TELEPHONE: 352-555-5957
Gainesville, FL 32608-4665

February 13, <year>

Ms. Flora Garcia
2209 Rena Drive
Lafayette, LA 70503

Dear Ms. Garcia

We are pleased to offer you the position of Director of Volunteer Services beginning March 15, <year>, at an annual salary of $40,000. You will be eligible to participate in our benefits package, which is explained in the enclosed brochure.

We would like to have your written acceptance of this offer before February 25. We look forward to having you on our staff.

Sincerely

Samantha Hayes
Executive Director

Enclosure

As a guide, ask yourself, "What characteristics of effective report writing were lacking?" Write an improved version of the message.

13. Jim Thomas received the following e-mail message from his supervisor at the investment firm where he works.

    Jim, I just got a call from a man who is 65 years old. Although he retired from real estate sales when he was 62, he has been working part-time since then at Salene's department store and participating in its retirement program. Salene's requires that part-time employees withdraw their retirement funds in a lump sum when they reach 65 or roll the money over into an IRA account. He wants to open an IRA with us and roll the retirement funds into it.

    This account isn't going to be worth much. He clearly is not interested in other kinds of investments—doesn't have much money to spare. I don't want to bother with him, so I gave him your name. He'll probably call you. Please handle it.

    Using the criteria for effective reports in Chapter 1, critique the message. Write an improved version of the message.

14. Select a recent controversial action by a national or local business or nonprofit organization. (Such names as Ken Lay, Martha Stewart, Sam Waksal, Richard Scrushy, and Armstrong Williams can get you started in your search for an example.) Use the Chewning and Badaracco guides to analyze how the persons involved may have reached the decision to act as they did. Present your analysis in a brief report to your instructor. Include a brief description of the action, why it is controversial (what value conflicts are evident), the route the organization's managers seem to have taken to justify the action, and whether you think the action was ethical. Write the report in a format specified by your instructor. As directed by your instructor, begin a file on the topic of corporate ethics or corporate fraud for use in later assignments.

15. Obtain a copy of a family-leave policy in effect at a local business or nonprofit organization. Using the Chewning and Badaracco guides, analyze possible routes that both management and employees would use to decide whether the policy is just or unjust. Present your analysis in a brief report to your instructor. Use a format specified by your instructor and attach a copy of the policy to your report. As directed by your instructor, begin a file on the topic of family-leave policies for use in later assignments.

REFERENCES

1. This discussion of manipulation is based on Sims, B. R. (Summer, 1993). Linking ethics and language in the technical communication classroom. *Technical Communication Quarterly, 2(3)*, 285–299.

2. Chewning, R. C. (1983). *Business ethics in a changing culture.* Richmond: Robert F. Dame, Inc., 112–113.

3. For an insightful discussion of this issue, see Liu, Meina and Buzzanell, Patrice M. (October, 2004). Negotiating maternity leave expectations: Perceived tensions between ethics of justice and care. *Journal of Business Communication, (41)4*, 323–349.

4. Badaracco, Joseph L., Jr. (1997). *Defining moments: When managers must choose between right and right.* Boston: Harvard Business School Press, 18–19.

Planning and Writing the Report

LEARNING OBJECTIVES

After you have read this chapter, you should be able to:

1. Identify the purpose, audience, and context for a report.
2. Select appropriate report content.
3. Choose an appropriate medium.
4. Choose a report structure that complements its purpose, audience, context, and content.
5. Apply outlining strategies and electronic technology to develop your report structure.
6. Draft, revise, and edit your report.
7. Collaborate effectively to write a report.
8. Consider ethical implications that arise during the writing process.

A well-planned report contributes to effective communication, whereas a hastily written report frequently leads to misunderstanding. Some reports require only brief, informal plans. Consider, for example, a one-page memo to employees reporting that management has approved an extra holiday, January 2, for all employees. A manager could easily write this report after reviewing notes made in a managers' meeting; but the effective writer would take time to consider the audience, desired effect of the report, exact information to be included, and order of presentation.

In contrast, consider a report from a market researcher to a management committee about a recently completed market survey. Before writing the report, the researcher would develop a formal plan that would likely be presented to a supervisor for evaluation, suggestions, and approval. That plan would include such factors as the intended audience for the report, the purpose of the study, a full description of how the research was conducted, and the results. As a general guide, the formality and length of the report plan are directly related to the complexity of the information to be reported.

PLANNING THE REPORT

Effective report writers follow a six-step plan before beginning to write, as shown in Illustration 2-1. Although report writers sometimes follow those steps in the order listed, the dotted lines in the illustration indicate that the process is recursive, not linear. The elements are interdependent. For example, identification of the context may help to identify the audience, identification of purpose may help to define the content, and identification of the content and audience should contribute to selection of the appropriate medium.

Identify Purpose

In some instances the motivation for the report is that your job description requires you to submit such a report. For example, a sales representative may be required to present a weekly report of calls made, contracts acquired, and plans for the following week. Whether the report is prompted by your job description or by special circumstances, the report will be most effective if you define your purpose in terms of what you want your reader to do or think after reading it. If you do not define the desired outcome, the report may become nothing more than a presentation of data; you will place the burden of interpretation on the reader. The reader may well conclude that action is necessary, but the action may not be what you expected.

Reports can be classified according to their general purposes: production, innovation, or maintenance.[1] Production messages relate to getting the job done. Assigning an employee a new area of responsibility and reporting a deviation from production standards are examples of production messages.

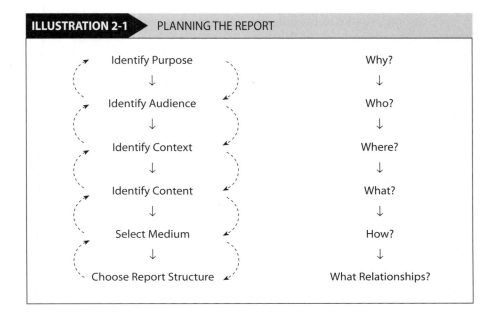

ILLUSTRATION 2-1   PLANNING THE REPORT

Identify Purpose	Why?
Identify Audience	Who?
Identify Context	Where?
Identify Content	What?
Select Medium	How?
Choose Report Structure	What Relationships?

Innovation messages relate to initiating change in an organization. A proposal to split an operating division into two operating units and a memo explaining a company's newly adopted telecommuting policy are examples of innovation messages. Maintenance messages relate to maintaining the goodwill and morale of the people in the organization. Reports about employee accomplishments or plans for the company picnic are examples of maintenance messages.

Most short, simple reports are production messages. Each deals with a single, clearly definable topic and an objective that relates directly to accomplishing the organization's tasks. A sales representative's weekly production report, for example, tells a sales manager about the progress the representative is making toward achieving sales goals, and a policy statement about drug use tells employees what can, must, and will be done to maintain a productive working environment.

By its very nature, innovation often requires review of a problem or presentation of a rationale that requires or justifies an organizational change. For that reason, a well-structured message that will persuade a reader to accept change may require greater length and formality than is typically associated with many short reports. However, context and audience could also justify a relatively short report for an innovation message. For example, a complete analysis of the benefits and disadvantages of telecommuting might be presented in a lengthy, formal report to management. But management's report to employees about the new telecommuting policy could be written in a page or two.

Managers also write short reports for maintenance purposes. A report about employees' volunteer activities with local hospitals or a report identifying and congratulating top sales associates for the month would be written primarily to reinforce the employees' sense of self-worth and worth to the organization—to maintain employee morale.

As you plan your report, it is useful to identify the general purpose as production, innovation, or maintenance. This identification will help you determine the specific purpose (for example, to report last week's sales; to gain approval for a new policy; to congratulate employees for participation in the United Way campaign), as well as the appropriate content, structure, writing style, and tone for the message.

Assume, for example, that your company, which develops computer software for the insurance industry, has a sick leave policy. This policy specifically requires employees to inform their supervisors before 8:30 a.m. if they are ill and unable to come to work. The policy allows 1.5 days of leave per month, which may be accumulated to up to 36 days of sick leave. If employees are suspected of misusing the benefit, they may be required to submit medical proof of illness. One of your employees, Janice Widener, has recently taken a part-time job with a start-up software firm that has been somewhat secretive about the type of software it is working on. The job requires her to work from 6 p.m. until 10 p.m. on Tuesday and Thursday. Since taking that job, Widener has frequently called in "sick" on Wednesday or Friday. She has averaged one sick day per week, sometimes two mornings. You have also observed that she often seems sluggish on days following her evening work hours. You have spoken with her about her absences and her lackluster performance, but the pattern persists. When you questioned her about the frequency of "sick" days, she said there should be no problem because she had accumulated 15 days of leave.

You now plan to report the situation to the director of human resources. Before preparing the report, you must define what you want the director to do: Counsel Widener? Make an entry in Widener's personnel records? Advise you about ways to motivate Widener to stop that behavior? Your decision about the report's purpose will influence other reporting steps, such as identification of content and selection of medium.

Identify Audience

Before preparing your report, you must identify your audience, both primary and secondary. In the Widener case, the primary receiver is the human resources director to whom you will send the report. Secondary readers may be current and future HR staff or higher-level managers—and perhaps Widener herself.

Audience identification requires more than merely identifying who will receive the report. After identifying the primary receiver, try to empathize with that person and identify her or his information and ego needs. If your purpose complements those needs, your writing task is relatively easy. But if your purpose contradicts the receiver's needs, your task becomes more difficult. In such a situation, before you state the main point of your report, you will have to give enough information to overcome possible objections in the receiver's mind.

Consider again the Widener example. One need of the human resources director is to be well informed about all personnel issues. You may also know that the director is altruistic (that is, desires to help others); and as a busy manager, the director likely prefers clear, concise, complete messages that permit immediate action without further clarification. As an effective report writer, you will satisfy all of those needs by indicating clearly what you want the director to do, including all necessary information to support that request and excluding unnecessary details. Knowing the director is altruistic, you might word the request to show that the desired action will help you, Widener, or other employees.

Although your first concern is to address the primary reader, recognize also that others may read the report. Even if you and the human resources director are well acquainted, considering the possible secondary readers should prevent you from using an excessively personal or casual tone in the report. The possibility that Widener herself may have access to the report or that it may become evidence in a disciplinary action should also prompt you to avoid emotional or abstract terms. The report must be objective and unambiguous.

Identify Context

The report context includes the physical and psychological environment of the communication exchange. Many reports are transmitted routinely with little thought about the context in which the message will be received. But effective communicators send their reports to arrive at a time and place that will encourage the reader to give full attention to the message.

If, for example, you know that the human resources director always has a management meeting on Monday morning, you might be wise to ensure that the director receives the report about Widener on Wednesday or Thursday. That timing would permit the director to dispose of tasks related to the previous Monday's management meeting and give full attention to the report. Appropriate timing would allow the director to consider appropriate action, including what—if anything—about the case should be discussed at the next management meeting. Or assume you decide to give Widener a final oral warning before reporting her absences and erratic performance. The appropriate place and time for that warning would be privately in your office or at Widener's workstation immediately after you observe her breakdown in performance—not at her annual review several months later.

Identify Content

Identifying purpose, audience, and context will help you determine appropriate content for your report. You must include all information the receiver requires to fulfill your purpose, and you must include details that motivate the receiver to act. Fully as important, however, is to exclude unnecessary details that may obstruct understanding. Include all the receiver must know, not necessarily all you know or all the receiver may want to know.

If, for example, your purpose is to stimulate the human resources director to discipline Widener, you must provide all information justifying such action: a record of Widener's infractions, what you have done to correct the situation, Widener's responses to your actions, the effects of her behavior. You should not, however, include comments about your personal dislike of Widener or rumors about her plans to leave your company and work full-time for her current part-time employer.

Another critical part of your report-writing plan is to choose a medium to transmit the report.

Select Medium

Media differ in their ability to transmit information. Lengel and Daft[2] classify media as "rich" or "lean" on the basis of three criteria: ability to transmit multiple cues, to facilitate rapid feedback, and to provide a personal focus. (See Illustration 2-2.)

The richest medium is face-to-face communication, because it meets all three criteria. Impersonal media, such as flyers or bulletin-board announcements, are lean. They can accommodate few cues, allow for delayed feedback only, and have no personal focus. Memos, letters, and reports tailored for a specific receiver are richer than bulletins because they have a more personal focus even though they do not permit immediate feedback. E-mail is somewhat

---

ILLUSTRATION 2-2	EXAMPLES OF MEDIA RICHNESS

Media Richness

Least Rich ————————————————————————————————➤ **Richest**

Physical Presence	**Interactive Media**	**Personal Static Media**	**Impersonal Static Media**
(face-to-face discussion; oral presentation with Q/A session)	(telephone, e-mail, electronic conferencing)	(memos, letters, reports in personal style)	(flyers, bulletins, posters, printout of spreadsheet, generalized reports)

Source: Adapted from Lengel, R. H. & Daft, R. L. (1988). The selection of communication media as an executive skill. *The Academy of Management EXECUTIVE, 2(3),* 226.

richer than printed letters or memorandums; while permitting a personal focus, it also enables more rapid feedback than does a printed letter or memorandum. Interactive media, such as the telephone or online conferences, are richer than memos, letters, or e-mail; they permit both a personal focus and immediate feedback. Although some interactive media (for example, videoconferencing) can accommodate both visual and vocal cues, others (for example, the telephone) cannot do so. No interactive medium is as rich as face-to-face communication, which can accommodate the full range of vocal and visual cues.

Research has shown that using lean media for communicating about routine management problems and richer media for nonroutine problems contributes to communication effectiveness. In contrast, using a lean medium for a nonroutine problem contributes to communication breakdown. Lean media provide too few cues for the message receiver, resulting in information shortage. Similarly, using a rich medium for a routine problem tends to cause communication breakdown because the message provides excess cues, resulting in information overload or noise. (See Illustration 2-3.)

Consider again Janice Widener's absences and lackluster performance on days following her night job. The first time you approach Widener to report that this behavior must change, you would probably use face-to-face communication for this nonroutine message. To post a notice on the bulletin board reminding employees of the sick leave policy would likely have little effect on Widener because the medium is too impersonal. On the other hand, a memo (or e-mail, if that medium is preferred by the director) would be an effective medium to report Widener's behavior to Human Resources. Neither you nor the director needs immediate feedback, but the memo can be personalized and can become part of Widener's personnel file. A telephone call or a face-to-face conversation could result in miscommunication. The richness of those media could overemphasize the significance of a problem that is routine to most human resources directors who handle such situations as one of their normal

ILLUSTRATION 2-3	MEDIA SELECTION

Media Richness	Management Problem	
	Routine	**Nonroutine**
Rich ↓	*Communication Failure* Rich medium used for routine situation • Too much data. • Excess cues cause confusion and distort meaning	*Communication Success* Rich medium used for nonroutine situation • Allows sufficient data • Number, kinds of cues signal significance of messages
Lean	*Communication Success* Lean medium used for routine situation • Sufficient data • No excess cues to distract receiver	*Communication Failure* Lean medium used for nonroutine situation • Insufficient data • Number, kinds of cues downplay significance of messages

Source: Adapted from Lengel & Daft.

duties. Moreover, although those media permit immediate feedback, they provide no immediate record of the communication.

Choose Report Structure

The appropriate structure for a report depends on the specific purpose, content, and context of the report. That fact will be demonstrated as you consider nine commonly used structures for entire reports or for parts of reports. These structures may even be applied at the paragraph level.

To help you understand the relationship of report structure to purpose, a specific objective is given in parentheses before each example of structure.

Deductive (Direct)

The deductive structure begins with the main point, which is followed by supporting data. This style is appropriate when the reader needs little psychological preparation for the main point because it is an expected or easy-to-accept message. Since this structure provides no preface to the main topic, it is also called the direct structure.

The following message demonstrates the direct (deductive) structure. The main point or general statement ("Arriving on time . . . and we intend to ensure that you do.") precedes the detailed facts about how World Wings has changed flight schedules to and from Atlanta.

(**Objective:** To reinforce customer loyalty.)

Arriving on time is important to you, and we intend to ensure that you do.

Our goal at World Wings is to deliver fast and reliable service. One of the ways we hope to achieve this is by adjusting flight schedules to and from Atlanta, the world's busiest passenger airport. Beginning January 31, 2006, our new schedule will offer more than 1,000 daily nonstop flights to nearly 200 domestic and international destinations from Atlanta. The new schedule will give you:

- More on-time arrivals and departures
- More flight choices
- Less congestion and smoother check-in and security processes

For more information about these changes and other World Wings news, please visit www.worldwings.com.

Thank you for flying World Wings.

INDUCTIVE (INDIRECT)

Inductive structure provides specific facts before generalizations based on those facts. Inductive structure is appropriate when the reader requires background details before being able to understand or accept the thrust of the message. Since the main point follows supporting details, this structure is also called the indirect structure.

The following message demonstrates indirect (inductive) structure. The generalization or conclusion (fewer flights to and from Atlanta) follows the facts that justify the changes.

(**Objective:** To maintain customer loyalty and goodwill in spite of schedule reductions.)

During 2005, several commercial airlines announced reductions in their flight schedules. Knowing that people who spend much of their time flying with us are a key to our success, we at World Wings maintained the number of flights to and from Atlanta, while other carriers were cutting their programs.

To demonstrate our appreciation for your loyalty, we will continue to offer all current early morning and early evening flights. This means you will continue to be able to attend business meetings on a timely schedule and easily make connections to and from most international flights.

Security issues, airport congestion, and spiraling fuel costs, however, require that we curtail the less frequently used flights. Therefore, beginning in 2006, we will reduce the number of flights arriving at and departing from Atlanta during the hours of 10:30 a.m. and 5:30 p.m.

For more information about these changes and other World Wings news, please visit www.worldwings.com.

Thank you for flying World Wings.

CHRONOLOGICAL

Chronological structure uses time as the central organizational component of the message. This structure is appropriate when time is an essential ingredient for understanding the basis of a request or for fulfilling that request. Any time units—minutes, hours, days, weeks, months, years, eras—relevant to the report may be used. The following example illustrates chronological structure.

(**Objective:** To stimulate conference participation and clarify target dates for successful participation.)

You are invited to participate in the 2008 Association for Human Resource Management Annual Conference. You are especially encouraged to share some of your experience—successful or otherwise—with other human resource managers by presenting a paper or a symposium at the conference in New Orleans, LA, on October 20–22, 2008.

Please note these important dates:

April 15, 2008:	Deadline for submission of proposal for paper or symposium
April 25, 2008:	Acceptance notification
August 1, 2008:	Final copy due at Association Headquarters
September 17, 2008:	Deadline for conference registration
October 20–22, 2008:	Conference in New Orleans, LA

The chronological structure may be appropriate for part of a report but not necessarily for the entire report. Chronological structure may also record events by exact time of occurrence; this type of structure is called log structure. The following example illustrates log structure.

(**Objective:** To ensure that convention volunteers fulfill their duties completely and accurately.)

To ensure that all convention participants have an enjoyable experience, we ask all volunteers to adhere to the following schedule on the first day of the convention, October 20, 2008.

- 6:30 a.m. Report to Room 398 (Convention Headquarters) in the Super View Hotel; receive post assignment and all materials needed at that post.
- 7:00 a.m. Report to post; set up materials.
- 7:30 a.m. Be prepared to greet visitors to your post.

- 7:30 a.m.–1:00 p.m. Answer questions posed by visitors; ask each visitor to complete a visitor's survey.
- 1:00 p.m. Close post; return to Room 398; deposit visitor surveys in box labeled "Surveys"; report any unusual incidents to R. J. Conway, convention chair, who will be on duty in Room 398.

Please remember: You are the "face" of AHRM. Please help convention registrants feel welcome when they arrive and be proud of this organization when they leave.

PROBLEM–SOLUTION

As the name implies, the problem–solution structure presents a problem, followed by a proposed solution. This structure is effective when the problem and proposed solution can be stated concisely and are likely to receive little objection. When dealing with a complex problem, you may find the inductive style more effective because it allows you greater latitude to describe the details of the problem and the reasons for the proposed solution.

Here is an example of the problem–solution structure. Notice how this structure directs the reader's attention to the major elements of the report.

(**Objective:** To stimulate the reader to resolve a production problem.)

Problem: Recently our department has experienced several production delays because of inefficient service from Information Technology Support. Here's one example:

On May 15 an important project was delayed by more than two hours because a technician did not run all tests after installing a new memory chip on May 14. At 9:00 a.m. my assistant was unable to retrieve a file stored the previous day. Work on the project was delayed until 11:15 a.m. when ITS finally corrected the difficulty.

Solution: We should request a meeting with the Director of ITS. At that meeting we should provide evidence of IT inefficiencies that have impaired our productivity. Let's assure the director that we will support her efforts to obtain and train additional staff for her area, but let's also insist that she provide plans to improve service to our department.

CAUSE–EFFECT

When using the cause–effect structure, the writer identifies and discusses conditions (causes) and a predicted outcome (effect) of those conditions. This structure is similar to the inductive structure since it moves from specific facts to generalizations based on those facts. The structure is appropriate when you want to report your perception of a direct relationship between two or more events. Here is an example of cause–effect structure.

(**Objective:** To justify an investment in equipment and employee training.)

Three months ago we upgraded the computers in the claims department and authorized cross-training so that each examiner is able to process a broader range of claims. Examiners received 10 hours of training on their new computers and new responsibilities. With no increase in personnel, monthly output in the claims department is now 10 percent above what it had been before these changes. Upgrading the computers and retraining our claims processors increased productivity in the claims department.

SPATIAL

The spatial structure is appropriate any time your data can be presented logically in terms of geographic units. Those units may be as large as continents or nations or as small as areas of a parking lot or a room. You may, for example, wish to analyze the layout of an office, parking lot assignments, productivity by sales districts, or market potential by countries. The spatial structure would be appropriate for presentation of data analysis, conclusions, or recommendations for each of those reports. The following example demonstrates spatial structure in the presentation of recommendations.

(**Objective:** To meet customer-service needs effectively in all areas of the city.)

As you requested, I have analyzed customer assistance calls, complaints about customer assistance, and potential needs for customer assistance in our market area. Based on that analysis, I recommend the following changes in service personnel.

Central City: Add one service consultant.
Northeast: Add two service consultants and one technician.
Northwest: Add two service technicians.
Southwest: Reassign one technician from this district to the Southeast district.
Southeast: Assign one technician from the Southwest district and add one service consultant.

TOPICAL

In topical structure, information is organized around major topics of discussion. A report divided into Findings, Conclusions, and Recommendations is organized topically. To be more meaningful, however, topical headings should identify the factors or elements of analysis. For example, a report presenting the results of a survey to determine preferences for employee benefits could be structured effectively in terms of the major categories of benefits, such as medical insurance, retirement, child or elder care, and profit sharing.

The following example contains headings from a credit union report that was arranged by topic.

(**Objective:** To present credit union performance on major measures of operating success.)

Subject: Credit Union Performance, 2005

Distribution of Consumer Savings

Xxxxxxxxxxxxxxxxxxxxxxxxxxxxxxxxxxxxxxxxxxxxxxxxxxxxxxxxxxxxxxxxxxxxx

xxxxxxxxxxxxxxxxxxxxxxxxxxxxxxxxxxxxxxxxxxxxxxxxxxxxxxxxxxxxx

Composition of Savings

Xxxxxxxxxxxxxxxxxxxxxxxxxxxxxxxxxxxxxxxxxxxxxxxxxxxxxxxxxxxxxxxxxxxxx

xxxxxxxxxxxxxxxxxxxxxxxxxxxxxxxxxxxxxxxxxxxxxxxxxxxxxxxxxxxxx

Share of Installment Credit Outstanding by Selected Lenders

Xxxxxxxxxxxxxxxxxxxxxxxxxxxxxxxxxxxxxxxxxxxxxxxxxxxxxxxxxxxxxxxxxxxxx

xxxxxxxxxxxxxxxxxxxxxxxxxxxxxxxxxxxxxxxxxxxxxxxxxxxxxxxxxxxxx

Share of Auto Loans Outstanding by Selected Lenders

Xxxxxxxxxxxxxxxxxxxxxxxxxxxxxxxxxxxxxxxxxxxxxxxxxxxxxxxxxxxxxxxxxxxxx

xxxxxxxxxxxxxxxxxxxxxxxxxxxxxxxxxxxxxxxxxxxxxxxxxxxxxxxxxxxxx

Average Loan Rates by Credit Union Asset Size

Xxxxxxxxxxxxxxxxxxxxxxxxxxxxxxxxxxxxxxxxxxxxxxxxxxxxxxxxxxxxxxxxxxxxx

xxxxxxxxxxxxxxxxxxxxxxxxxxxxxxxxxxxxxxxxxxxxxxxxxxxxxxxxxxxxx

---

COMPARISON OR CONTRAST

Comparison or contrast structure examines two or more items in terms of common criteria. Comparison implies examining the qualities of items to discover similarities and differences. Contrasting focuses primarily on differences.

Assume, for example, that you must prepare a report for college seniors who are thinking of pursuing an MBA degree. The purpose of your report is to provide an objective tool for comparing three MBA programs. You would determine the criteria by which the programs should be evaluated, such as admission standards, cost, availability of financial aid, program requirements, quality of faculty, and placement of graduates. Your report could be structured effectively around those criteria, showing how the programs are similar or different on each criterion. One organizational pattern would evaluate each college on all criteria, as shown in the following example.

(**Objective:** To compare three MBA programs.)

Program A
    Admission Standards
    Cost
    Financial Aid
    Requirements
    Faculty
    Placement of Graduates

Program B
    Admission Standards
    Cost
    Financial Aid
    Requirements
    Faculty
    Placement of Graduates

Program C
    Admission Standards
    Cost
    Financial Aid
    Requirements
    Faculty
    Placement of Graduates

Another organizational pattern would compare all colleges on each criterion, as shown in the following example.

Admission Standards
    Program A
    Program B
    Program C

Cost
    Program A
    Program B
    Program C

Financial Aid
    Program A
    Program B
    Program C

Requirements
    Program A
    Program B
    Program C

Faculty
  Program A
  Program B
  Program C

Placement of Graduates
  Program A
  Program B
  Program C

COMBINATION

As you may have inferred, few reports adhere to a single structural pattern. The combination structure employs two or more of the patterns discussed. Returning again to the Widener case, assume that you have decided to ask the director to suspend Widener for one day without pay. You could use an inductive structure that begins with a description of the problem and ends with the requested action. Your description of the problem itself could be written in a cause–effect structure, as shown in the following example.

Current problem: Widener's frequent absence and poor performance on days following her evening job.

History

- Previous observations of absences and lackluster performance
- Previous corrective action
- Most recent incident

Effects

- Decline in department morale
- Occasional misuse of sick leave benefit by other employees

Requested action: Suspend Widener without pay for one day

If you know, however, that the director prefers that reports requesting action begin with the request, your report should be written in the direct structure, and the essential details to support your request could be presented in cause–effect structure.

Requested action: Suspend Widener without pay for one day

Previous observations of absences and lackluster performance

- Previous corrective action
- Most recent incident
- Effects of Widener's behavior
- Decline in department morale
- Occasional misuse of sick leave benefit by other employees

An outline will help you plan the structure of your report. The outline should indicate the relative importance of the facts and their relationships to one another.

Outlining the Report

As you develop your outline—whether it is formal or informal—always keep the reader's needs uppermost in your mind. What does the reader already know about the problem? What does the reader look for first? What supporting data does the reader need? What order of presentation best contributes to reader comprehension of the problem and the solution? How will the reader use the information? The final outline of your report reflects your choice of report structure, which in turn reflects your understanding of the reader's needs and the purpose for the report.

Informal Outlines

An informal outline is a list of topics to be included in the report. It often consists of words, short phrases, or combinations of those elements. Such an outline is primarily an idea-generating tool. For many short reports, the informal outline may be the first and final stage of planning before you draft your report. For longer reports, however, the outline should be expanded to provide you with more detail about content and structure.

After preparing an informal outline, you should examine it carefully to verify that all essential topics have been listed (or present it to a colleague or supervisor for review). Then organize and reorganize the topics until you generate a structure that will help you achieve your objective with your audience.

To illustrate how you would prepare an informal outline, assume the following facts.

Context: Your company, BestMeters, specializes in the manufacture and service of flowmeters, which are used in many industries that transport a liquid product and must measure the flow of that product during delivery.

The Situation: The company wishes to expand its business by marketing its BESTFLO meter in the South American market. This meter is an electronic unit that is mounted on a truck and measures the flow of liquefied petroleum gas (LPG) at point of delivery. Preliminary research showed that demand for the product would likely be strongest in Argentina, Brazil, and Venezuela. However, management needs extensive information about the nature of the market before deciding whether to launch a South American venture.

The Report Objective: You were asked to evaluate the potential market for the BESTFLO meter in Argentina, Brazil, and Venezuela. Specifically, you attempted to answer four questions for each of the three countries:

1. What economic conditions influence the development of the LPG industry?
2. What is the general sales potential for BESTFLO?
3. Who are the primary customers and the largest companies distributing LPG?
4. What are the optimal means of distributing and promoting BESTFLO?

Status: You have completed your research and are about to write the report.

Primary Audience: Your report will be presented to the vice president for marketing, Robert Montero. Mr. Montero is familiar with the purpose of the research and he discussed it at length when he authorized you to conduct the study. You gave Montero periodic progress reports as you worked on the project. He is eager to learn your findings, conclusions, and recommendations and has asked you to give him a written analytical report at the conclusion of your research.

The process of preparing your informal outline would be similar to the steps shown in Illustration 2-4. The process requires that you:

1. List the topics to be included in the report.
2. Edit the list to be sure it contains all essential topics and no unnecessary topics. Since Mr. Montero is the primary reader and is familiar with the problem, you could perhaps omit much of the background information, as indicated by the deletion mark in the left column of Illustration 2-4.
3. Arrange the topics into a sequence that shows relationships of key points and satisfies the communication needs of your readers. Since Mr. Montero is eager to learn the outcome of your research, the direct structure—presenting your recommendations first—will likely be effective.

A slight change in the facts about the audience could result in a substantially different outline. Assume the following facts in addition to those already considered.

Secondary Audience: Mr. Montero will present your report to the executive committee. He wants you to include full background information and details about how you conducted your study so that all members of the committee can understand the situation fully.

Since Montero has specifically requested background information for the committee's use, you must include it in your topic list. Moreover, the committee members, who are not familiar with the entire situation, may appreciate an inductive structure. That structure will lead the reader through the problem-solving stages you experienced: recognizing a problem, planning a way to analyze the problem, gathering and analyzing data, drawing conclusions, and formulating recommendations. The process of outlining a report for this situation would be similar to the steps shown in the right column of Illustration 2-4.

ILLUSTRATION 2-4   DEVELOPING AN INFORMAL OUTLINE

Informal Outline: Deductive Structure

1. **List of topics**
   - Background
     Problem
     Purpose
     Scope
     Method
   - Findings
     Economic conditions
     Sales potential
     Primary customers
     Distribution and promotion strategies
   - Conclusions
     Growing market for flowmeters
     Few LPG distributors; focus marketing
     Few competitors, but market is price sensitive
     Company has good reputation
   - Recommendations
     Respond quickly to needs of growing market
     Concentrate on five LPG distributors
     Educate potential customers about price/product superiority

2. **Edit the list**
   - Background
     Problem
     Purpose
     Scope
     Method
   - Findings
     Economic conditions
     Sales potential
     Primary customers
     Distribution and promotion strategies
   - Conclusions
     Growing market for flowmeters
     Few LPG distributors; focus marketing
     Few competitors, but market is price sensitive
     Company has good reputation
   - Recommendations
     Respond quickly to needs of growing market
     Concentrate on five LPG distributors
     Educate potential customers about price/product superiority

Informal Outline: Inductive Structure

1. **List of topics**
   - Background
     Problem
     Purpose
     Scope
     Method
   - Findings
     Economic conditions
     Sales potential
     Primary customers
     Distribution and promotion strategies
   - Conclusions
     Growing market for flowmeters
     Few LPG distributors; focus marketing
     Few competitors, but market is price-sensitive
     Company has good reputation
   - Recommendations
     Respond quickly to needs of growing market
     Concentrate on five LPG distributors
     Educate potential customers about price/product superiority

2. **Edit the list**
   - Background
     Problem
     Purpose
     Scope
     Method
   - Findings
     Economic conditions
     Sales potential
     Primary customers
     Distribution and promotion strategies
   - Conclusions
     Growing market for flowmeters
     Few LPG distributors; focus marketing
     Few competitors, but market is price sensitive
     Company has good reputation
   - Recommendations
     Respond quickly to needs of growing market
     Concentrate on five LPG distributors
     Educate potential customers about price/product superiority

continued

ILLUSTRATION 2-4 CONTINUED

3. Arrange topics into sequence for report

- Recommendations
  Respond quickly to needs of growing market
  Concentrate on five LPG distributors
  Educate potential customers about price/product superiority
- Review of Problem, Scope
- Conclusions
  Growing market for flowmeters
  Few LPG distributors; focus marketing
  Few competitors; but market is price-sensitive
  Company has good reputation
- Findings
  Economic conditions
  Sales potential
  Primary customers
  Distribution and promotion strategies

3. Arrange topics into sequence for report

- Background
- Research
  Problem
  Purpose
  Scope
  Method
- Findings
  Economic conditions
  Sales potential
  Primary customers
  Distribution and promotion strategies
- Conclusions
  Growing market for flowmeters
  Few LPG distributors; focus marketing
  Few competitors, but market is price sensitive
  Company has good reputation
- Recommendations
  Respond quickly to needs of growing market
  Concentrate on five LPG distributors
  Educate potential customers about price/product superiority

An informal outline will readily communicate necessary information to you, the writer, and will help you to compile the report. That outline may not, however, effectively communicate your report content and structure to someone else who may be responsible for approving your work or helping you with it. For that purpose you need a formal outline.

Formal Outlines

A formal outline uses phrases or sentences to describe the content of each division and subdivision of the report. A formal outline also employs a structured numbering system to show the various levels into which the report is divided.

A formal outline is a useful communication tool both before and after you write the report. If you wish to discuss the structure of your report with a supervisor or a colleague before you begin writing, you can use the outline as a guide. If you follow the outline faithfully when writing, it can become the table of contents for the report. You will only have to add page numbers for the report divisions. Illustration 2-5 shows one example of a formal outline that corresponds to the final informal outline in Illustration 2-4.

To number the sections of a formal outline, you may use either the traditional outline system or a decimal system. Whether to use the traditional

ILLUSTRATION 2-5 A FORMAL OUTLINE

The Feasibility of Marketing BESTFLO in South America

I. Background: BestMeters wants to expand its market for BESTFLO.

II. The Research Question: Is it feasible to promote BESTFLO to the South American LPG industry?
    A. The purpose of the study
    B. The scope of analysis
    C. The method of study
        1. Data sources
        2. Data collection
        3. Data analysis

III. The findings
    A. Economic conditions
        1. Argentina
        2. Brazil
        3. Venezuela
    B. Sales potential for LPG flowmeters
        1. Argentina
        2. Brazil
        3. Venezuela
    C. Primary competitors
        1. Argentina
        2. Brazil
        3. Venezuela
    D. Distribution and promotion strategies

IV. Conclusions
    A. Growing market for flowmeters in the three countries
    B. LPG distribution controlled by few companies
    C. Few competitors in the market
    D. Unique characteristics of each country require country-specific adaptations

V. Recommendations
    A. Respond quickly to growing market
    B. Establish BESTFO as industry standard
        1. Adapt meter for needs of specific countries
        2. Target nine specific LPG suppliers
    C. Educate potential customers
        1. Quality of BESTFLO
        2. Competitive price of BESTFLO

system or the decimal system for your outline depends largely on the preferences of your report readers.

The traditional system consists of Roman numerals to indicate first-level divisions, uppercase letters for second-level divisions, Arabic numerals for third-level divisions, and lowercase letters for fourth-level divisions. Few outlines progress beyond fourth-level divisions; but when you need such divisions, continue the numbering system by alternating Arabic numerals and lowercase letters. The *Chicago Manual of Style*[3] recommends that the divisional numerals or letters for the first three levels be set off by periods, and that those for the lower levels be set off by single or double parentheses.

The decimal system, used by many engineering companies, law firms, and government agencies, uses Arabic numerals and decimals to indicate main topics and subtopics. The numbering begins with a single digit (1, 2, 3, etc.) to mark first-level divisions. For each subdivision, a decimal is added and the parts of that subdivision are numbered consecutively (1.1, 1.2; 2.1, 2.2; 2.2.1, 2.2.2; etc.).

Illustration 2-5 demonstrates the traditional system, and Illustration 2-6 shows the decimal system. You can check the accuracy of your decimal numbering system by comparing the numbers with the division level. Notice that every first-level division is marked with a single number; every second-level division has two numbers, separated by a decimal; every third-level division has three numbers, separated by decimals; etc. Both systems, traditional or decimal, require that you observe basic outlining guides.

Outline Guides

To communicate report content effectively, your outline must be clear and coherent. Observing the following guides will help you achieve those qualities.

1. Every division and subdivision must have at least two parts. Logically, nothing can be divided into less than two parts. Therefore, every topic that is divided must have a minimum of two subtopics. The following examples contrast ineffective, illogical outline divisions with effective, logical divisions.

Illogical; Ineffective	**Logical; Effective**

A. The current system
  1. Inefficient
	A. The current system
	  1. Inefficient
	  2. Error-prone
	  3. Costly

B. The proposed system
  1. Efficient
	B. The proposed system
	  1. Efficient
	  2. Accurate
	  3. Cost-effective

ILLUSTRATION 2-6 ▶ PARALLELISM IN OUTLINES

Improving Organizational Effectiveness

1. Define organizational mission

2. Identify organizational goals
    2.1 Unit goals
        2.1.1 Short term
        2.1.2 Long term
    2.2 Department goals
        2.2.1 Short term
        2.2.2 Long term
    2.3 Division goals
        2.3.1 Short term
        2.3.2 Long term
    2.4 Organization goals
        2.4.1 Short term
        2.4.2 Long term

3. Determine performance criteria
    3.1 Unit level
    3.2 Department level
    3.3 Division level
    3.4 Organization level

4. Assess organizational effectiveness
    4.1 Select indicators
    4.2 Select samples
    4.3 Collect data
    4.4 Apply criteria
    4.5 Interpret findings

5. Use assessment findings
    5.1 Identify strengths and weaknesses
    5.2 Modify goals
    5.3 Allocate resources

---

2. Divisions should be balanced. All divisions need not have the same number of topics and subtopics; but if any section of your outline is considerably longer or shorter than other sections, you should reevaluate the outline. Lack of balance may suggest the need to regroup information for a more coherent report structure. The following examples contrast unbalanced, ineffective sections with balanced, effective sections.

Unbalanced; Ineffective	**Balanced; Effective**

A. The current system
   1. Inefficient
	A. The current system
	   1. Inefficient
	   2. Error-prone
	   3. Costly

B. The proposed system
   1. Easily learned
   2. Fast
   3. Accurate
   4. Desired by employees
   5. Easy to correct errors
   6. Inexpensive to install
   7. Inexpensive to operate
   8. Can use some of old equipment
	B. The proposed system
	   1. Efficient
	   2. Accurate
	   3. Cost-effective

3. Divisions and subdivisions should help the reader focus quickly on significant report content. When any part of an outline contains more than four division levels, you may be focusing the reader's attention on minor rather than major points. The following examples show how the previous outlines can be improved by clarifying major and minor points.

Major/Minor Points Unclear	**Major/Minor Points Clear**

The proposed system:
   Easily learned
   Fast
   Accurate
   Desired by employees
   Easy to correct errors
   Inexpensive to install
   Inexpensive to operate
   Can use some of old
     equipment
	The proposed system:
	   Efficient
	     Fast
	     Accurate
	     Easy corrections
	   Cost-effective
	     Inexpensive to install
	     Inexpensive to operate
	     Use some old equipment
	   Acceptable to employees
	     Desired
	     Easily learned

4. Division headings should be stated concisely. Topic headings, such as those often used in a tentative outline, may be too concise to communicate report content to the reader. If the outline in Illustration 2-6 were a topic outline, the first-level headings might be single words or short phrases, such as *mission, goals, criteria, assessment*, and *use*. Although such an outline may guide the report writer, it conveys little to the reader.

Talking headings, written in parallel phrases or short sentences as in Illustration 2-6, provide more information about the report content. Lengthy talking headings, however, may distract from effective communication. Assume, for example, that Heading 2 in Illustration 2-6 were written in this way: "Identify goals by getting input at all organizational levels." Such a heading burdens the reader with unnecessary words, particularly since the subtopics listed under the heading indicate that goals must be identified at all levels.

5. Division topics must be expressed in parallel grammatical structure. Appropriate parallelism is demonstrated in Illustration 2-6. Notice that first-level divisions (1 through 4) are grammatically parallel; second-level divisions, such as 2.1 through 2.4, are parallel within the division but not necessarily parallel with other second-level divisions, such as 4.1 through 4.5.

Computer-Assisted Outlining

Most word-processing software permits the user to create an outline that is later used as the basic structure for the report. To use such an outline effectively for planning a document, you must first compose the outline in the outline feature, also called outline view. To subsequently use that outline to guide your drafting of the document, you switch to a page view or format and write the report narrative for each section.

Writers who use outline software often insert the main ideas to be developed under each outline heading and subheading. This process is known as capsuling. Report composition then becomes a relatively easy task of supporting those ideas with data and visual aids. Many writers have found that this technique helps them to write clearly and concisely.

Using the outline feature has several advantages when you revise, edit, and format your report. With most word-processing outline options, you can easily restructure a document by merely moving outline headings. When outline headings are reorganized, the corresponding sections of the report are automatically moved to reflect the new organizational structure. You can move easily from outline format to report format and vice versa. When you view the document in outline format, you can easily see whether your headings and subheadings are logically consistent and complement the content of each section. Another advantage is the related ability to easily generate a table of contents for a document that has been composed from outline to full document in the same software.

DRAFTING, REVISING, AND EDITING THE REPORT

After writing an informal or a formal outline, you are ready to write the first draft of your report. The steps for drafting, revising, and editing a report are diagrammed on the inside front cover of this book. As the diagram indicates, these steps in the writing process differ, depending on the complexity of the report. For example, when you must prepare a complex report, such as a study of the feasibility of moving your office to a new location, and you do not yet know all that should be included, you should begin at Step 1 of Stage 1, Preliminary Draft. A report presenting your comparative evaluation of three properties considered for the new office location could well begin at Step 1 of Stage 2, Review Draft. Finally, if you must write a simple report announcing that the office will be closed on Monday so that commercial movers can move all furniture and equipment to the new location, you could begin at Step 1 of Stage 3, Near Final Draft.

Drafting the Report

With your outline as a guide, you can draft the report by major sections. Do not, however, feel that you must draft the report in the exact sequence in which it will finally appear. Attempting to write the report from beginning to end as indicated by the outline may create writing barriers that delay the production of the report.

A key to successful writing is to recognize writing barriers and develop strategies for overcoming them. Some writers, for example, begin by writing the easiest sections of the report. This technique provides a sense of accomplishment and stimulates them to move on to the more difficult sections. Other writers begin with the sections that they think will be most difficult to write. They prefer to complete the hard tasks early in the writing process so that they will not feel pressured toward the end. Many writers move among sections of the document. For example, when you have difficulty with one part of the report, you may find it helpful to work on another section. After some time has passed, you will often find that you have subconsciously removed the writing block and can think more clearly and write more easily about the difficult topic.

One useful technique is to prepare all visual aids—tables, charts, graphs—before writing the report narrative. Your primary writing task then is to explain those aids. After writing the explanatory narrative, your next task is to write the transitions between report parts. Your final task is to write introductory and summary sections.

Revising and Editing the Report

Before preparing a final copy of your report, read it carefully to evaluate all aspects of the report: content, structure, diction, tone, overall style, and impact. The drafting guide inside the front cover encourages you to review your draft carefully and to subject your work to another person's critical review. The Writing Review Checklist inside the back cover provides a systematic guide that you and your reviewer can use as you attend to specific parts of your report.

Critical revision and editing often mark the differences between an effective and an ineffective report. Revising a report consists of rewriting sentences, paragraphs, or entire sections of a report or moving them to different locations. Adding or deleting information may also be part of the revision process. Editing consists of locating and correcting errors in writing mechanics, such as spelling, punctuation, word use, subject–verb agreement, pronoun references, and sentence structure. Chapter 3 provides guides to improve the style, tone, and grammatical precision of your reports.

The final draft should be a coherent document that flows smoothly from start to finish, always giving the reader a sense of forward movement. Your summaries and transitions should help the reader understand the relevance of what has been said and anticipate what will be said next. Avoid vague references such as *this*, *that*, and *it* without a clear antecedent. Similarly, avoid comprehensive references like "as stated above" or "the previously mentioned facts." Such statements often require readers to move backward in the document to be sure they understand the reference.

The following examples contrast a style that moves forward with a style that disrupts the message flow. The first example disrupts the flow by requiring readers to return to previous sections of the document if they do not recall the criteria. In the second example, the writer briefly recalls previous information as a transition to a discussion of empathy, thereby moving the reader forward in the document.

Disrupted: In addition to the characteristics already discussed, your reports should demonstrate empathy for the reader.

Forward Movement: Accuracy, clarity, and conciseness will help the reader understand your message. In addition, your writing should demonstrate empathy for the reader.

After revising and editing your report, you are ready to prepare the final copy in an appropriate format. Chapter 4 presents guides for document design and commonly used report formats.

COLLABORATIVE WRITING

As documents and the techniques used to produce them become more complex, the degree of collaboration is likely to increase. The final product should be seamless. That is, the reader should not be able to tell where Joan's work leaves off and Mark's work begins.

In reality, collaborative writing often consists of a combination of collective and independent work, depending on the stage of the project. (See Illustration 2-7.)

| ILLUSTRATION 2-7 | A PROCESS FOR COLLABORATIVE WRITING |

Planning the Report—Collective Work

- Clarify task—identify audience, purpose, and scope of project.
- Develop preliminary outline.
- Identify possible data sources.
- Select writing style, format.
- Make data-gathering assignments.

Collecting and Analyzing Data—Independent Work

- Fulfill data-gathering assignment.
- Evaluate adequacy of data.
- Prepare to present your data and its assessment to the group or continue working until you have met the assignment.

Evaluating Data—Collective Work

- Evaluate data.
- Return to data-gathering stage if data are inadequate.

Drafting and Revising—Independent and Collective Work

- Draft your part of the report.
- Revise and edit until that section is as good as you can make it.
- Review each member's contribution for adequacy and style; provide constructive criticism.
- Revise your section of the report, based on suggestions of team members.
- Deliver final, corrected version of your section to group.

Producing Final Document—Collective Work

- Assist in merging parts of document, placing visuals, etc.
- Review entire report for accuracy, completeness, and consistency.

Planning the Report

During the planning stage, the writing team should collectively identify the audience, purpose, and scope of the project. At this stage the team should review the overall project to be sure everyone understands the expected outcome. After the scope of the project has been identified, the group may assign specific data-collection responsibilities to individual team members.

At this stage the team could also develop a preliminary outline for the final report to ensure that all necessary topics are covered and to guide the team members as they gather data. Team members should always allow for revisions in the outline as new perspectives arise during the data collection and analysis stages.

Another collective task during the planning stage is to agree on a general writing style, formal or informal. The team should also make formatting decisions or select a standard template so that all writers use the same software for their drafts; within that software they should use the agreed-upon margins, font, typeface, type size, and type style for the report body and headings. These decisions will ease the process of merging individual documents into a master document.

Collecting and Analyzing Data

Collectively, the team should identify possible data sources. If the research requires use of primary data, one or two members of the team might be responsible for designing the questionnaires or interview guides, but all members should participate in a critical review of those instruments before they are used. During the data-collection phase it may be efficient for team members to function independently, each person collecting and interpreting data for the segment of the study for which he or she is responsible.

After the data are collected and analyzed, the group should again work together as they plan to draft the report. Members should discuss the data, evaluate its adequacy, and agree on its interpretation. At this time the team should also review the report outline and adjust it as necessary.

Drafting and Revising

During the drafting stage, individuals may again work independently. Each person should draft the part of the report for which he or she is responsible. Each writer should write and revise until satisfied that the section is as polished as the individual author can make it.

Then the group again shifts into a collective mode. Every team member should review all parts written by other members; in a group setting, reviewers should provide constructive criticism and the group should give directions for final revision to the individual authors.

The individual authors should then evaluate the suggestions of the group and incorporate the best of their advice into the final revision.

Producing the Final Document

All writers should participate in the production of the final document. Each writer should bring the final, corrected version of her or his draft to a group meeting and be prepared to assist with the merging of parts, preparation and placement of visual aids, and final review of the document. Individual responsibilities include checking the writer's own section to ensure that it is correct and evaluating the entire report for consistent writing style and format.

Checking the entire document is a particularly important step when the drafting work has been divided among the group members. Even with agreements beforehand about format, inconsistencies will no doubt occur. Differing word-processing skill levels can be a great factor in consistency. Be alert for them. Fonts, headings, margins, and spacing should be consistent; footnotes or references should all be in the same style; and so on.

ETHICAL CONSIDERATIONS

Ethical issues may arise as you plan reports. When deciding upon the purpose, audience, context, content, and medium for a report, ethical individuals would ask why each decision is made. Does each decision promote the sender's good only, or does it contribute to the well-being of others also?

Assume, for example, that you have observed safety violations in the manufacturing plant in which you work. You decide to prepare a report in which you will identify each violation and recommend corrections. Is your purpose to improve working conditions or to expose lax management? Will you present both sides of the issue? Should your audience be upper management or should it include employees and the press? What tone should you use? Should the report be released if your analysis of context reveals that an environmental interest group in the community is attempting to have the plant closed—even though many community members would lose their jobs? Should the report disclose all violations you have observed or only selected ones? Which medium—oral or written—would yield greater "good"?

A growing ethical issue is the tendency for people to act as though information on the Internet is in the public domain (that is, not subject to copyright laws). In reality, most information contained on websites is copyright protected. When you obtain copyrighted information from a website, it must be documented as meticulously as information obtained from other publications. Subsequent chapters will discuss data collection and how to acknowledge data sources. At this point, it is important to remember that ethical writers always give proper credit to information and ideas obtained from another source, whether primary or secondary. Appropriate documentation establishes your credibility as well as your honesty.

With increased use of collaborative writing teams, writers should also consider the ethical issues that may arise under such working conditions. An ethical obligation that would seem obvious is to honor your commitments to others. When you are tempted not to fulfill your share of the assignment, answer these basic questions about your responsibility to yourself and for others.

- Is keeping a promise one of your core values?
- Are you acting as the person you want to be?
- Are you acting in the group's best interest?
- Are you willing to take public responsibility for your action?
- Does the action violate the rights of any other people?

SUMMARY

Following the six steps for a report plan—identify purpose, audience, and context; select content and medium; and choose a structure—will keep you on target as you write your report. Writing a clear, coherent report begins with a logical outline. A well-constructed outline can reveal strengths and weaknesses in the proposed report structure. If weaknesses are evident, you can correct them before you write the report. Outline software permits you to reorganize a report quickly and easily.

At each step of the planning process, an ethical writer evaluates the potential effect of the planning decisions: Do they promote the well-being of others as well as of the writer and the writer's organization?

Effective collaborative writing consists of a purposeful balance of collective and independent work throughout the writing process. Effective collaboration also requires that all writers act ethically toward one another and fulfill the obligations they have accepted.

TOPICS FOR DISCUSSION

1. When is an informal report plan justified?

2. Describe the steps to be included in a report plan. Why are the steps called *recursive?*

3. Explain each of these message classifications: production, innovation, maintenance.

4. What is a primary audience? a secondary audience?

5. What are the characteristics of a lean medium? a rich medium? How does knowledge of these characteristics affect your choice of a medium? Into which classification(s) do most short, simple reports fall?

6. Compare or contrast inductive and deductive report structure. Give examples of appropriate uses for each.

7. Give examples of appropriate uses for these structures:
   - Chronological
   - Problem–solution
   - Cause–effect
   - Spatial

8. Compare or contrast topical and comparison structures. Give examples of appropriate uses for each or combinations of the two.

9. Describe appropriate collective and independent activities for a team that must collaborate to produce a report.

10. Identify ethical issues that may arise as you work independently or collaboratively to produce a report.

11. If you have had a collaborative writing experience, share information about that experience with your classmates. Was it successful or unsuccessful? What contributed to its success or failure?

APPLICATIONS

1. In a small-group discussion, plan a report for each of the following scenarios. In each situation:

   - Clarify the context of the report. Then identify the audience; the sender's purpose; the receiver's needs; and appropriate content, structure, and medium for the report.
   - Prepare an outline for the report.
   - Select a member of your group to present to the class an oral summary of the group's decisions, along with reasons for those decisions.

   a. While representing her company at a business exposition in Vienna, Austria, Jun Wong arrived at the hotel at which she thought the exposition participants would be lodged. The hotel had no reservation for her, nor did it have a block of rooms reserved for exposition participants. The hotel front-desk clerk, Hans Schoenberg, called several hotels in the city and located the one at which the participants were lodging. He confirmed that Wong had a reservation at that hotel, called a cab, and explained Wong's situation to the driver. Wong wants to report this exceptional service to Schoenberg's manager.

   b. Dan Sullivan, a benefits consultant with Gibbs and Associates, helped Mr. and Mrs. McCants apply for long-term care insurance. After the underwriting company had reviewed the applications and the medical information obtained from the clients' doctors, the company offered Mrs. McCants the coverage she had applied for but rejected Mr. McCants because of certain health conditions. Sullivan thinks he can get another company to underwrite Mr. McCants with slightly less coverage and a 10 percent higher premium. He thinks Mrs. McCants should accept the plan that was approved and that Mr. McCants should apply to the second company. Mr. Sullivan must report this information to Mr. and Mrs. McCants.

   c. Assume you are the Executive Director of Food for Families, a nonprofit agency that provides food to individuals and families in need. Potential food recipients enter a reception area where they participate in an intake interview. After legitimate need is determined, the applicants for food are given a voucher, which they redeem at the adjacent warehouse where your food supplies are stored. You have hired a cleaning company to clean your facility twice a week. The task includes cleaning the office and the reception area. Although the cleaning crew has not been asked to clean the warehouse in which you store the food, you have noticed "inventory shrinkage" after some of their visits. The missing inventory has ranged from as little as a case of sodas to as much as several cases of canned fruits and vegetables. You want to report the food loss, along with your suspicions that the cleaning crew may be responsible. Since you know the owner of the cleaning service as a friend and supporter of the agency, you do not want to offend him. Yet you cannot afford continued inventory shrinkage.

d. Three years ago, the director of the Career Center at Metro College arranged to have a faculty member accompany interviewers to lunch, with the lunch billed to the Center. Both the interviewers and the professors who participated reported that the lunches provided an opportunity for mutually beneficial exchanges of information. Moreover, interviewers who had a positive lunch experience tended to schedule return recruiting visits to the campus. Because of budget limitations, that program was discontinued. Now the director wants to reinstate the program and will ask the college dean to approve up to $4,000 to fund the lunches.

e. Assume that the dean has approved the request for $4,000 to host recruiter–faculty lunches (Application 1-d). Now the Career Center director must encourage professors to volunteer to take a recruiter to lunch. Plan and write a memo asking professors to volunteer for the "There is a Free Lunch" program. Include the following details:

- The Career Center will try to match recruiters and professors who have common interests (for example, accounting recruiters with accounting professors).
- Professors will be invited a week in advance to accompany the recruiter to lunch.
- The Career Center will make reservations at a local restaurant and give the professor a form to authorize billing the Career Center.
- The Career Center director will remind the professor the day before the scheduled lunch and indicate when and where he or she should meet the recruiter.

f. Three employees under Rick Kattreh's supervision have each volunteered to spend two weeks of their vacation time working with the local Habitat for Humanity. Simona Kelly worked with a prospective homeowner to select paint, wallpaper, and window coverings for the house and scheduled additional volunteers to complete the interior decorating. Ty Lathrop helped frame three houses. Glen Miner helped the local Habitat director contact businesses to ask for monetary or in-kind (lumber, nails, etc.) contributions. Kattreh wants to commend the employees for their volunteer work. He also wants to encourage other employees to participate in the program.

g. The director of the motor pool for a large state agency has been criticized for the vehicle purchase/retention plan in use at the agency. The current plan includes replacing vehicles after three years of use or at 80,000–90,000 miles, whichever occurs first. Typically, this has resulted in replacement of about one-third of the fleet each year. Requests for bids are issued in September, with purchases made in November. In the past, the agency has used only gasoline-powered vehicles; the director wonders if the time has come to consider hybrid vehicles for at least part of the fleet. He asks you to determine the cost savings, if any, to be obtained if the agency splits this year's anticipated purchases between hybrid and gasoline-powered vehicles.

2. Using the outlining feature in your word processor, develop an outline for one of the following topics:

   - A comparison of two printer/scanner/copier/fax units to use in your home office or dormitory room
   - Reasons for the increase in the number of computer viruses
   - Major arguments for and against copying software
   - Methods to block spam from your e-mail mailbox

REFERENCES

1. Farace, R. V., & MacDonald, D. (Spring, 1974). New directions in the study of organizational communication. *Personnel Psychology, 27,* 115.

2. Lengel, R. H., & Daft, R. L. (1988). The selection of communication media as an executive skill. *The Academy of Management Executive, 2(3),* 225–232.

3. *The Chicago Manual of Style,* (14th ed.). (1993). Chicago: The University of Chicago Press, 314–315.

Writing Style and Lapses

After you have read this chapter, you should be able to:

1. Choose a writing style that complements the audience, content, and context of your report.

2. Recognize and revise an inappropriate writing style.

3. Identify these common writing lapses and avoid or correct them in your own writing:

   - Lapses in noun/pronoun and subject/verb agreement
   - Errors in the use of nouns and pronouns
   - Errors in sentence structure
   - Problems with punctuation
   - Errors in word choice

4. Work effectively with team members to produce a document that is professional in all aspects of writing style and mechanics.

5. Demonstrate responsibility in style choices and language usage while working alone or with others.

Style is a distinctive manner of expression or a technique by which something is done or created. Accuracy, clarity, empathy, and conciseness are qualities that should be demonstrated in all reports—long or short, simple or complex. To achieve those qualities you must choose a writing style purposefully.

CHOOSING A WRITING STYLE

Style involves an element of choice—you can select a style for your report that is appropriate for its content, context, and desired outcome. As you choose a writing style for a particular report, you should empathize with your readers. Consider their needs—both information needs and ego needs. Information needs are the data that will enable the receiver to understand and fulfill your wishes. Ego needs are desires for recognition and acknowledgment of worth. A report may provide all the information a receiver needs; but unless the report also satisfies ego needs, it may not motivate that person to act.

The content, context, and desired outcomes for simple and complex reports may differ considerably. The overall style of simple, relatively short reports such as a trip report, a production report, or minutes of a meeting differs from the style of complex, specialized reports, such as a business plan or a business research report. The decisions you make about report tone, level of formality, and objectivity will define your report style.

Choosing Report Tone

Tone is evidence of the sender's attitude toward the message and the receiver. Some descriptors of tone are personal, impersonal; formal, informal; positive, negative; courteous, curt; passive, forceful; conciliatory, defensive. In written reports, tone is conveyed by word choice and message structure. In oral reports, tone may be conveyed additionally by vocal pitch or emphasis, posture, and gestures.

The following examples demonstrate how a sender might plan to accommodate the receiver's needs by carefully selecting tone, structure, and presentation mode as well as content. Notice that the sender's objective in both cases is to get the receiver to act. The first example demonstrates a plan for a relatively simple, informal report.

Sender's objective: A bank teller will move to a station that will enable more effective customer service.

Receiver's needs: Information—To know when to move, where to move. Ego—to be respected as a valued member of the organization.

Report structure: Direct—main point followed by brief explanation, if any.

Report tone: Courteous, informal.

Presentation mode: Oral; no written supplement (for example, "Juan, please close this window and take over the drive-up window. Cars are beginning to line up out there.")

In contrast, a store manager's more complex report to company officers about relocating the business might include these planning considerations:

Sender's objective: Upper management will move the store to a new location so that profits may increase.

Receiver's needs: Information—Justification for, likely benefits of, and estimated costs of moving the store. Ego—Recognition of status and decision-making authority; respect for value of reader's time.

Report structure: Direct—Recommendation to move the store to a new location followed by supporting details: profitability of current location, problems associated with current location, goals for store, cost of move to new location, benefits of move.

Report tone: Formal, respectful, yet forceful and confident.

Presentation mode: Written, supplemented by oral; both enhanced by visual aids.

Choosing Degree of Formality

When you write a report, you must choose the degree of formality you want to convey. Formality is conveyed by language and by inclusion or exclusion of certain parts of a report. You can decide what formal parts to include with your report after you have written the report body. You must, however, decide about the formality of language before you write the body of the report.

Some contexts may justify informality. That style is most often reserved for situations in which the writer knows the primary reader well or frequently works with that person. Even under those circumstances, however, informal style may not be appropriate because secondary readers must also be considered. If a report is to pass among many readers, some of whom the writer does not know, a formal style is generally preferable. Similarly, when the primary reader files the report for future use by other people, a formal style is often used.

Assume, for example, that two cities are trying to annex a residential area known as Winslow Hills. You are a member of the Winslow Hills Homeowners Association, and its officers have asked you to determine the homeowners' attitudes and preferences with respect to annexation. The officers will circulate the summary of your final report to all homeowners and will present the full report to the competing city councils. In such a situation, an informal style is appropriate for a progress report to the officers of the homeowners association, whom you know well and with whom you share common concerns. The final report, however, would likely be written in a formal style. That formal style will show respect for the elected officials while impressing them with the seriousness of the annexation issue.

No sharp distinction exists between formality and informality in reports. Consequently, no one can define exactly what constitutes formal or informal language. Nonetheless, the language we tend to use with peers or individuals whom we know well is often characterized as informal language. Informal language includes frequent use of first names, contractions, and first- and second-person pronouns: *I, me, my, mine, we, us, our, ours, you, your, yours*. In addition, colloquial expressions tend to connote informality. Colloquialisms are words and phrases commonly used in conversation (for example, *OK, thumbs up, go-ahead* as equivalents for *agreement, approval*) or those common to certain regions (for example, *crack the window* for *open the window; cut on the light* for *turn on the light*).

In contrast, the language we tend to use with someone who holds a high-status position or individuals whom we do not know well is characterized as formal language. The major difference between formal and informal language is the presence or absence of words that suggest how well the writer and reader (speaker and listener) are acquainted. Absence of first- and second-person pronouns, use of courtesy or position titles with full names or last names, and avoidance of contractions and colloquial expressions characterize a more formal style. For example, the author of this book met a relatively young college professor from an Asian country at a professional conference. In conversations at the conference and in subsequent e-mail correspondence, the younger woman always addressed the older woman as Doctor or Professor. She even expressed discomfort with using the older person's first name. Such factors as age, professional experience, and cultural practices prompted her to use a more formal style.

You should not confuse formality with wordiness, unwieldy sentences, and overuse of passive verbs. Even formal writing can be concise, clear, and vigorous.

The following examples contrast features of informal and formal writing.

First- and Second-Person Pronouns

Informal: I interviewed your Information Technology managers and technicians. Your IT crew is eager to have a Tai Chi class offered on your premises during the lunch hour.

Formal: Interviews with Information Technology managers and technicians revealed their eagerness to participate in an on-site Tai Chi class.

Informal: Your employees are pumped; you should have a good turnout if you offer a Tai Chi class during lunch hour.

Formal: Information Technology personnel have strong motivation to support an on-site Tai Chi class.

Names, Titles

Informal: Jean said that IT support increased 12 percent in February.

Formal: Ms. Jean Herriot, IT Support Coordinator, reported a 12 percent increase in support requests during February.

Informal: If you need additional information, Alex, please let me know.

Formal: If you need additional information, Mr. Padgett, please let me know.

Contractions

Informal: What's your reaction? I'm eager to hear from you. You can reach me at 555-8765.

Formal: Please direct questions or comments about this proposal to Ms. Marlow at Extension 109.

Informal: Your IT guys said they're concerned about the increase in support requests.

Formal: Information Technology managers and technicians expressed concern about the volume of support requests.

Colloquialisms

Informal: Your designers are computer savvy. They are chomping at the bit to get updated hardware and software.

Formal: Product-design personnel have enough computer expertise and interest to realize that their production is hampered by outdated hardware and software.

Informal: Let's look at the numbers. The bottom line is that your crew wants and you can afford a better system.

Formal: The data show two important facts:

1. Washtenaw Electric employees want a more efficient system.
2. Washtenaw Electric can afford a more efficient system.

To summarize, informal reports project a more personal tone. They may use first- and second-person pronouns as well as near-conversational language. Many informal reports are presented orally or in memorandum format. Study the scenario diagrammed in Table 3-1. The sales associate's report to the sales manager and the research director's report to the research staff are informal reports.

In contrast, a formal report typically uses impersonal language and tone. Although formal reports may be written in memorandum or letter format, they are often presented in manuscript form. The format frequently includes headings to guide the reader through the report content; and if presented in manuscript format, the report generally includes a title page and perhaps a transmittal message. As report length increases, other preliminary pages may be included to accommodate reader needs, such as a table of contents and an executive summary. Some lengthy formal reports also contain supplements such as a bibliography or source list and an appendix. The feasibility study referenced in Table 3-1 would likely be prepared as a formal report because

TABLE 3-1 DEGREES OF FORMALITY

Sender	Receiver	Report Content	Report Characteristics	Decision/Action
J Pac sales associate	J Pac sales manager	Consumers in Brazil enjoy grilled meats; most use charcoal; potential market for our gas grills	Oral; informal	Sales manager does preliminary research; relays information to vice president for marketing
Sales manager	Vice president for marketing	Burgeoning consumer market is attracting many U.S. companies to Brazil; several of our competitors are already selling gas grills in Latin America	Written; semi-formal; supplemented by oral summary	Vice president for marketing asks director of market research to conduct further research about feasibility of entering Latin American market
Vice president for marketing	Director of market research	Summary of previous reports; request to study feasibility of entering Latin American market	Written; semi-formal	Director of market research assigns task to research staff; requests research proposal
Director of market research	Research staff	Summary of vice president's reports; requests research proposal	Oral; informal; part of weekly staff meeting	Staff begins work on research proposal
Research staff	Director of market research	Proposed plan for feasibility study	Written; formal	Director approves plan; staff conducts study
Research staff	Director of market research	Findings, conclusions, recommendations of feasibility study	Formal; written; perhaps supplemented by oral presentation	Director asks staff to present report to management committee
Research staff and director of market research	Management committee	Background; summary of preliminary studies; findings, conclusions, recommendations of feasibility study	Oral/visual presentation; written summary of key findings and recommendations	Management authorization of budget for marketing division to begin efforts to establish distributorships in Brazil

it would go not only to the staff's immediate supervisor, but also to upper management. Moreover, the report will contain much technical market information, requiring a table of contents, a source list, and perhaps some appendixes. The writer may also provide an executive summary to give readers a concise preview of the report content. These parts, which differentiate formal from informal reports, are discussed and illustrated in Chapter 14.

Some situations call for a combination of formal and informal style. For example, a lengthy, complex analysis of a business problem may be presented in formal style and format, but it may be accompanied by a transmittal message that is written in an informal tone and supplemented by a semiformal oral summary. The marketing research staff's report to the management committee (Table 3-1) is such a situation.

Whether you choose a formal or an informal style, all of your reports must meet the criteria for effective writing: accuracy, clarity, empathy, and conciseness. Moreover, all data must be presented objectively, not emotionally.

Writing Objectively

Objectivity requires that all available, relevant data be presented. Moreover, you should focus on the data, not on what you think or feel about the situation. Each step in data analysis—presenting data, interpreting data, drawing conclusions, and making recommendations—takes you further from the original facts, experience, or observation. To maintain credibility, you must discipline yourself to keep the analysis free of your biases or emotions and express your conclusions and recommendations in objective language.

For example, a bank loan officer may observe that the number of applications for home equity loans increased substantially after Christmas. But to conclude that borrowers use home equity loans to pay for Christmas debts is an improper conclusion. Such a conclusion may be drawn only if information obtained from customers consistently shows they intend to use the equity loan to pay for holiday purchases. Likewise, to conclude that borrowing on home equity is irresponsible financial management is the expression of an opinion based on a writer's values, not an objective conclusion.

The following examples contrast emotional language with objective language.

Emotional: I was not surprised to find that the vast majority of your product-design personnel strongly favored getting state-of-the-art hardware and software rather than continuing to use the grossly inefficient technology currently in use. Therefore, you should honor their preferences and scrap the present system immediately.

Objective: Eighty-five percent of the product-design personnel said they could be more productive if they had state-of-the-art technology. Moreover, all employees have the necessary computer expertise to adapt to updated hardware and software. Therefore, a transition from the current system to the proposed system can be accomplished with minimum employee orientation and training.

Although your writing should not contain unjustifiable expressions of opinion or emotion, you should demonstrate confidence in your findings, conclusions, and recommendations.

Expressing Confidence

Confidence does not mean brashness or impudence. Instead, it means that when the data are sufficient, you will not hesitate to state your objective findings, conclusions, and recommendations, even if they are contrary to the outcome your reader might have preferred. If, on the other hand, the data are insufficient to support any logical and objective conclusions and recommendations, you will also state that fact confidently.

To demonstrate confidence, many writers use imperative sentences when stating recommendations that are clearly supported by the data. The following examples contrast impudent, hesitant, and confident styles.

Impudent: The company has obviously neglected to use its available resources to provide an efficient drafting system. That error can be corrected simply by doing two things.

1. Buy new computer hardware and software for the drafting department.
2. Establish a much-needed electronic network for product-design employees.

Hesitant: The company might want to consider buying new computers for the drafting department. If that were done, the company could probably also connect the computers to create an electronic network for product-design employees.

Confident: The recommendations are that Washtenaw Electric should:

1. Purchase and install new computer hardware and software in the drafting department.
2. Connect the available computers to create an electronic network for product-design employees.

Unjustifiably confident: Approximately 50 percent of the design engineers are eager to use an integrated design network. With their enthusiasm, they should be able to convert the others to the concept. I recommend that you install the new system.

Justifiably hesitant: Approximately 50 percent of the design engineers expressed reluctance to transfer to an integrated design network. Conversion to that system at this time appears to be unwise. Further study to determine how to overcome objections to the proposed network may be necessary to ensure eventual success of such a system.

Ideally, choices about writing style are made before you begin writing your first draft. It is not unusual, however, for the style to evolve as you experience various stages of drafting and revising your report. As you draft and revise the report, you should also be alert to frequently occurring writing lapses.

Frequently Occurring Writing Lapses

Whereas choice enters into writing style, the mechanical aspects of writing involve little choice. Following generally accepted standards for grammar and word usage marks the writer as a literate, well-educated individual. Ignoring such standards may tag the writer as either careless or uneducated.

Some writing lapses are minor; others are irritating; but all become distractions when a knowledgeable reader encounters them. To avoid being labeled as a FOWL writer, learn to identify—and avoid—the *frequently occurring writing lapses* (FOWLs) discussed in this chapter.

The items are categorized and numbered for easy reference and to allow your instructor to indicate by number the types of FOWLs that appear in your writing. The following groups of FOWLs are discussed:

- Agreement lapses
- Problems with nouns and pronouns
- Sentence errors
- Punctuation problems
- Language lapses

Agreement Lapses (A1–A2)

Lack of agreement between subject and verb or noun and pronoun may result in reader confusion, misinterpretation, or irritation.

A1: Mixed Singular and Plural Nouns and Pronouns

A pronoun must agree in number with its antecedent. Mixtures of singular and plural pronouns occur most frequently in reference to companies or organizations.

FOWLs

A. Boulware, Inc. has launched an intensive effort to penetrate the Eastern European market for central heating and air conditioning. *They* intend to be the first with the best in that region of the world.
B. Management must commit to an extensive advertising campaign. *They have* little time to lose.

Corrections

A. Boulware, Inc. has launched an intensive effort to penetrate the Eastern European market for central heating and air conditioning. *It* (or *The company*) intends to be the first with the best in that region of the world.
B. Management must commit to an extensive advertising campaign. *It has* little time to lose.

A2: Mixed Singular and Plural Subjects and Verbs

Subjects and verbs must agree in number. Mixtures of singular and plural nouns and verbs occur most frequently when modifying words or phrases are inserted between the subject and verb.

FOWLs

A. Accounting *knowledge* of trainees *were* determined by an analysis of scores on a standardized accounting examination.
B. Communication *skills*, as well as accounting knowledge, *is* expected of all accounting trainees.
C. *This type* of problems *are* seen often.

Corrections

A. Accounting *knowledge* of trainees *was* determined by an analysis of scores on a standardized accounting examination.

OR

The trainees' accounting *knowledge was* determined by an analysis of …

B. Communication *skills,* as well as accounting knowledge, *are* expected of all accounting trainees.

OR

All accounting *trainees are* expected to have accounting knowledge and communication skills.

C. *These types* of problems *are* seen often.

OR

This type of problem *is* seen often.

Problems with Nouns and Pronouns (PN1–PN6)

Incorrect use of nouns and pronouns also tends to confuse or distract the reader. Avoid the noun and pronoun errors discussed here.

PN1: Possessive Noun Error

Because many possessive forms of nouns (*company's, employee's*) sound like the plural forms (*companies, employees*), correct punctuation of the possessive forms is essential for clarity. Mastery of possessives requires application of the following four guides:

- Recognize the correct spelling of the singular and plural noun forms.
- Form the possessive of the singular noun by adding *'s*, no matter how the noun ends.
- Form the possessive of a plural noun that ends in *s* by adding an apostrophe only.
- Form the possessive of a plural noun that does *not* end in *s* by adding *'s*.

FOWLs

A. Many company's offer benefits that differ from this companies benefits.
B. Those companie's benefits differ from others in the industry.
C. Because our companies benefits package allows employee's to make choices, each employees' package may be designed to fit her or his needs.
D. Ms. Thomson-Hass' employer provides on-site child care.
E. An employees minor childs' dental care is covered by our plan.
F. Employee's spouses are included in the family plan.
G. The first years coverage for your child includes all well-baby care.
H. The first five years coverage for your child includes all inoculations.
I. Childrens' benefits end when children reach age 21.

Corrections

A. Many companies offer benefits that differ from this company's benefits.
B. Those companies' benefits differ from others in the industry.
C. Because our company's benefits package allows employees to make choices, each employee's package may be designed to fit her or his needs.
D. Ms. Thomson-Hass's employer provides on-site child care.
E. An employee's minor child's dental care is covered by our plan.
F. Employees' spouses are included in the family plan.
G. The first year's coverage for your child includes all well-baby care.
H. The first five years' coverage for your child includes all inoculations.
I. Children's benefits end when children reach age 21.

PN2: CONFUSION OF CONTRACTIONS AND POSSESSIVE PRONOUNS

Possessive pronouns have no apostrophes. A contraction requires an apostrophe to indicate the omission of one or more letters. *It's* is a contraction for *it is; they're* is a contraction for *they are; who's* is a contraction for *who is. Its, their,* and *whose* are possessive pronouns.

FOWLs

A. If a company does not communicate quickly during a crisis, *it's* reputation may suffer severe damage. *Its* difficult to recover from loss of goodwill.
B. Employees should be notified immediately when *their* in potential danger.
C. Investigators try to determine *whose* at fault when an industrial accident occurs.

Corrections

A. If a company does not communicate quickly during a crisis, *its* reputation may suffer severe damage. *It's* difficult to recover from loss of goodwill.

OR

If a company does not communicate quickly during a crisis, *it's* possible that the company's reputation will be damaged.

B. Employees should be notified immediately when *they're* in potential danger.

OR

When *their* work environment is dangerous, employees should be notified of potential hazards.

C. Investigators try to determine *who's* at fault when an industrial accident occurs.

OR

Investigators try to determine *whose* error caused the accident.

PN3: Reflexive Pronoun Error

Reflexive pronouns serve two purposes: to emphasize (for example, Joe *himself* is responsible for this error); to reflect the action of the verb toward a noun or pronoun already used in the sentence (for example, Joe asked *himself* how he could have avoided the error). Errors in the use of reflexive pronouns typically occur in the first person when an individual makes a mistakenly modest attempt to avoid using *I* or *me*.

FOWLs

A. Lee and *myself* conducted interviews with the clients.
B. The subjects expressed their opinions openly to Lee and *myself*.

Corrections

A. Lee and *I* conducted interviews with the clients.

OR

I conducted the interviews *myself.*

B. The subjects expressed their opinions openly to Lee and *me.*

PN4: Relative Pronoun Error

Relative pronouns refer to nouns that immediately precede them. The most common relative pronouns are *who* (for persons), *that* (for persons and things), and *which* (for things). Relative pronouns introduce adjective clauses; in those clauses, the pronouns act as subjects or objects and must be in the appropriate case. Most contemporary writers reserve *which* for nonrestrictive clauses and *that* for restrictive clauses.

FOWLs

A. Is Joan the person *which* shipped this box?
B. Joan is the person *who* I saw.
C. This is the third box *which* I've delivered today.
D. This box *that* Joan sent is heavy. I wonder what's in it.

Corrections

A. Is Joan the person *who* shipped this box?
B. Joan is the person *whom* I saw.
C. This is the third box *that* I've delivered today.
D. This box, *which* Joan sent, is heavy. I wonder what's in it.

PN5: Confusion of Conjunctions and Relative Pronouns

The linking verb *is* should be followed by a noun or adjective form to complete the sentence. A noun clause introduced by *that* may be used as the complement. The conjunction *because* should be reserved to introduce an adverbial construction and should not follow a linking verb.

FOWL

The *reason* is *because* bond yields are more uncertain as they are projected further into the future.

Corrections

> The *reason* is *clear:* Bond yields are more uncertain as they are projected further into the future.
>
> The *reason* is *that* bond yields are more uncertain as they are projected further into the future.
>
> We may have difficulty finding an underwriter for this issue *because bond yields are more uncertain as they are projected further into the future.*

PN6: Indefinite Reference

An antecedent is the noun for which a pronoun substitutes. A pronoun should refer unmistakably to its antecedent; otherwise, the antecedent should be repeated, or the entire sentence should be rewritten for clarity.

FOWLs

A. Competition in capital markets determines the appropriate tradeoff function between risk and return for different classes of securities. *This* occurs when ...
B. The increased return on investment in 2006 buoyed investors' optimism. *It* soared to a level never before experienced.
C. We successfully closed the Conrad contract, *which* pleased us.

Corrections

> A. Competition in capital markets determines the appropriate tradeoff function between risk and return for different classes of securities. *This tradeoff* occurs when ...
> B. The increased return on investment in 2006 buoyed investors' optimism. *ROI* soared to a level never before reached.
> C. Successfully closing the Conrad contract pleased us.
>
> OR
>
> The Conrad contract, *which* pleased us, was successfully closed yesterday.

Sentence Errors (S1–S7)

A third class of FOWLs includes seven errors in sentence construction.

S1: Dangling and Misplaced Modifiers

A modifier must be structurally and logically related to a word or clause in the sentence. Dangling and misplaced modifiers frequently occur when the writer begins a sentence with a verbal phrase and follows the phrase with a noun that the phrase cannot logically modify. Misplaced modifiers frequently occur when a sentence contains too many modifying words and phrases.

FOWLs

A. *After completing the audit,* a *report* was prepared for the client.
B. Raising EPS to $5.79, the *annual report* shows diversification has paid off.
C. For a family of four with a teenage driver, *which drives 15,000 miles per year,* the 4 Runner is a more economical vehicle than the Suburban.

Corrections

A. *After completing the audit,* the *accountant* prepared a report for the client.
B. The annual report shows that diversification has paid off, *raising EPS to $5.79.*
C. For a four-member family that drives 15,000 miles per year, the 4 Runner is a more economical vehicle than the Suburban.

S2: Excessive Use of Expletives

An expletive is a word or phrase used to fill out a sentence or to provide emphasis. Unless emphasis is desired and can be achieved in no other way, expletives should be avoided. In fact, a more direct style may strengthen the impact of the sentence.

FOWLs

A. *There are* several conclusions that might be drawn from the study.
B. *It is* apparent that hiring overqualified workers may be a costly practice.

Corrections

A. Several conclusions might be drawn from the study.
B. Hiring overqualified workers is a costly practice.

S3: Excessive Use of Parenthetical Expressions

Parentheses or dashes may be used to show a sudden interruption or shift of thought, to provide a supplementary explanation, or to show emphasis. However, excessive use of parentheses or dashes may obstruct the main idea of the sentence. Using shorter sentences, you can often work the qualifying information into the discussion.

FOWL

Annual fuel costs based on $3 per gallon (a fair estimate for this area) would be $2,255 for the 4 Runner and $3,469 for the Suburban based on 15,000 miles of driving—a reasonable average for a family of four (including a driving teenager).

Correction

> A fair estimate for gasoline in this area is $3 per gallon. Annual driving mileage for a family of four with a teenage driver is estimated at 15,000 miles. Based on these figures, the family could expect fuel costs of $2,255 for the 4 Runner and $3,469 for the Suburban.

S4: NONPARALLEL CONSTRUCTIONS

Parallelism indicates equality of ideas. To achieve parallelism, balance nouns with nouns, adjectives with adjectives, verbs with verbs, adverbs with adverbs, prepositions with prepositions, conjunctions with conjunctions, and verbals with verbals.

FOWLs

A. The company's net income differed from its projections because of random events, ignoring relevant assumptions, and when interest rates fluctuated.
B. This job requires skills in accounting, management, and the ability to communicate well.
C. An employee manual should be revised when:
New laws are enacted.
The company changes benefit plans.
Changes in company goals and philosophies.

Corrections

> A. The company's net income differed from its projections because of random events, omission of relevant assumptions, and fluctuations of interest rates.
> B. This job requires skills in accounting, management, and communication.
> C. An employee manual should be revised when any of these events occur:
> Laws change.
> Company benefits plans change.
> Goals and philosophies change.

S5: FRAGMENTED SENTENCES, CLAUSES, AND PHRASES

Every sentence must contain a subject and a verb and express a completed thought. Although a subordinate clause contains a subject and a verb (for example, the first clause of this sentence), it does not express a completed thought. The most common fragmentation error is separating a subordinate clause from the independent clause to which it is related. Another fragmentation error is separating a phrase (which contains no subject and verb) from the item that it is intended to modify.

FOWLs

> A. Some employees elect not to participate in the medical insurance plan. Although that is a rare occurrence.
> B. Even if they think they already have enough life insurance. Employees should never reject the free life insurance offered by the company.
> C. Foolishly conservative. Some employees elect not to participate in the medical insurance plan.

Corrections

A. Some employees elect not to participate in the medical insurance plan, although that is a rare occurrence.
B. Even if they think they already have enough life insurance, employees should never reject the free life insurance offered by the company.
C. Foolishly conservative, some employees elect not to participate in the medical insurance plan.

S6: Run-On or Spliced Sentences

A run-on sentence is one that combines two or more independent clauses without appropriate punctuation or conjunctions. The major punctuation error, in addition to lack of any punctuation, is the use of a comma when a period or semicolon should be used. This is called a comma splice.

FOWLs

> A. When you have made a complete statement, and are ready to move on to the next statement, you must make one of four decisions: to end the sentence and begin a new one, to link the two clauses with a semicolon, to link the two clauses with a comma and a coordinating conjunction, or to link the two clauses with a semicolon, a conjunctive adverb, and a comma.
> B. Some writers have difficulty determining when one sentence should end and another should begin, they just keep going on.

Corrections

A. When you have made a complete statement and are ready to move on to the next statement, you must make one of four decisions: to end the sentence and begin a new one; to link the two clauses with a semicolon; to link the two clauses with a comma and a coordinating conjunction; or to link the two clauses with a semicolon, a conjunctive adverb, and a comma.

OR

When you have made a complete statement and are ready to move on to the next statement, you must take one of four actions.

- End the sentence and begin a new one.
- Link the two clauses with a semicolon.
- Link the two clauses with a comma and a coordinating conjunction.
- Link the two clauses with a semicolon, a conjunctive adverb, and a comma.

B. Some writers have difficulty determining when one sentence should end and another should begin. They just keep going on.

OR

Some writers have difficulty determining when one sentence should end and another should begin; they just keep going on.

OR

Some writers have difficulty determining when one sentence should end and another should begin, and they just keep going on.

OR

Some writers have difficulty determining when one sentence should end and another should begin; therefore, they just keep going on.

S7: Long and Complex Sentences

Some writers mistakenly think that long, complex sentences will impress the reader. Quite the contrary is true. A reader will not be impressed by a sentence if he or she must struggle to extract its meaning.

FOWL

Most investor-owned utilities (IOUs) are vertically integrated, which means that they do not specialize in any of the aspects of the electricity industry, generation, transmission, or distribution; however, three major types of utilities (municipal systems, federal agencies, and state agencies) fall under the broad category known as publicly owned utilities (POUs), which, unlike IOUs, are not vertically integrated but, instead, specialize in either generation or distribution.

Correction

Electric utilities fall into one of two categories: investor-owned utilities (IOUs) or publicly owned utilities (POUs). POUs include municipal systems, federal agencies, and state agencies. Most IOUs are vertically integrated; that is, they generate, transmit, and distribute electricity. In contrast, most POUs specialize in either generation or distribution.

Punctuation Problems (P1–P4)

Punctuation marks are communication signals that improve message coherence. Consider these examples:

- Send this report to Jorge Ray.
- Send this report to Jorge, Ray.
- Raise the gear-release lever.
- Raise the gear; release lever.

The few rules included here should help you avoid the most common punctuation problems.

P1: Comma Omitted or Misused

Use commas for these purposes:

- To punctuate a long introductory phrase, an introductory phrase containing a verbal, or an introductory adverb clause
- To set off a *nonrestrictive* clause or appositive. *Do not* use commas to set off a *restrictive* clause or appositive. (A *nonrestrictive* clause or appositive describes but does not limit its antecedent; a *restrictive* clause or appositive limits its antecedent to a particular group or category.)
- To set off parenthetical words or phrases, including terms of direct address
- To punctuate independent clauses joined by a coordinating conjunction (that is, *and, but, for, or, nor*)
- To separate whole numbers into groups of three digits (except items such as room numbers, policy numbers, and telephone numbers)

Space once after a comma, except when it is used to divide numbers into three-digit groups ($4,329).

FOWLs

A. After completing the employee survey the human resources division developed a new policy about making personal cell phone calls on company time.
B. Employees, who make personal cell phone calls on company time, will be disciplined.
C. Michael who rarely uses his cell phone at his desk is not worried about the new policy.
D. Michael do you approve of the new cell phone policy? Consider if you will the consequences of this policy.
E. Michael approves of the general policy but he thinks some exceptions should be allowed.
F. Your bonus is $4329, because you signed up more than 1500 new clients.

Corrections

A. After completing the employee survey, the human resources division developed a new policy about making personal cell phone calls on company time.
B. Employees who make personal cell phone calls on company time will be disciplined.
C. Michael, who rarely uses his cell phone at his desk, is not worried about the new policy.
D. Michael, do you approve of the new cell phone policy? Consider, if you will, the consequences of this policy.
E. Michael approves of the general policy, but he thinks some exceptions should be allowed.
F. Your bonus is $4,329 because you signed up more than 1,500 new clients.

P2: SEMICOLON OMITTED OR MISUSED

Although the semicolon is a useful mark of punctuation, many writers avoid it because they are unsure about its use. Others use it often, but incorrectly. The semicolon should be used in the following ways:

- To punctuate independent clauses of a compound sentence when no coordinating conjunction links the clauses
- To separate independent clauses or items of a series when at least one of those items already contains a comma
- To punctuate independent clauses of a compound sentence when a conjunctive adverb (for example, *nonetheless, however, therefore, consequently*) is used to link the clauses
- To punctuate transitions (for example, *such as, for example, i.e., e.g.*)

Always use a comma after a conjunctive adverb or transition that is preceded by a semicolon. Space once after the semicolon; do not space before the semicolon.

FOWLs

A. Employees must sign and complete FORM B-290 before December 1 of each year, all changes will become effective on January 1 of the subsequent year.
B. To change benefits options employees must sign and complete FORM B-290 before December 1 but changes will not become effective until January 1 of the subsequent year.
C. Follow these procedures: Pick up FORM B-290, Election of Benefits, at the Human Resources Office, complete and sign the form, give the form to the benefits administrator before December 1.

D. The Medical Spending Account applies to this year only, therefore any money not spent during the current year will be forfeited.
E. Olmstead Manufacturing has a flexible benefits plan, that is the company lets employees choose from an array of benefits.

Corrections

A. Employees must sign and complete FORM B-290 before December 1 of each year; all changes will become effective on January 1 of the subsequent year.
B. To change benefits options, employees must sign and complete FORM B-290 before December 1; but changes will not become effective until January 1 of the subsequent year.
C. Follow these procedures: Pick up FORM B-290, Election of Benefits, at the Human Resources Office; complete and sign the form; give the form to the benefits administrator before December 1.
D. The Medical Spending Account applies to this year only; therefore, any money not spent during the current year will be forfeited.
E. Olmstead Manufacturing has a flexible benefits plan; that is, the company lets employees choose from an array of benefits.

P3: Colon Omitted or Misused

The colon is used for these purposes:

- To present a sentence element emphatically
- To introduce a series or list within a sentence (do not use a colon if the list is preceded by a linking verb or a preposition)
- To introduce a vertical list
- To introduce a long or formal quotation
- To separate hours, minutes, and seconds when time is stated in figures
- To punctuate the greeting of a business letter in the mixed punctuation style

Space twice after a colon in a sentence; do not space after a colon in a time notation; never space before a colon.

FOWLs

A. I have just one word to say to you, Congratulations!
B. The traditional management functions are: planning, organizing, activating, and controlling.
C. I have proofread everything except: Chapter 13, Chapter 14, and the Appendix.
D. The second paragraph of our agreement states you are obligated under this contract to return unused items.
E. The conference began at 8 :30 a.m.
F. Dear Ms. Rossi,

Corrections

A. I have just one word to say to you: Congratulations!
B. The traditional management functions are planning, organizing, activating, and controlling.

OR

We will study these traditional management functions:

- Planning
- Organizing
- Activating
- Controlling

C. I have proofread everything except Chapter 13, Chapter 14, and the Appendix.
D. The second paragraph of our agreement states: "You are obligated under this contract to return unused items."
E. The conference began at 8:30 a.m.
F. Dear Ms. Rossi:

P4: HYPHEN OMITTED OR MISUSED

A hyphen should be used:

- To join two or more adjectives (compound adjective) that *precede* a noun and define a single concept (for example, *up-to-the-minute* report; *first-class* work; *five-room* suite). Generally, hyphens are not used when a compound adjective *follows* the noun it modifies (for example, These data appear to be *up to date*)
- In compound numbers written as words (for example, *ninety-eight; twenty-nine; seventy-seven,* etc.)
- To clarify intended meanings (for example, They are junior *high-school* students; They are *junior-high* school students)

Do not use a hyphen between an adverb and the adjective that it modifies (for example, a *highly effective* presentation).

FOWLs

A. *Hard earned* sales growth appeared in the third quarter.
B. The customer expected the delivery to be *on-time*.
C. *Twenty eight* associates got *well deserved* salary increases.
D. A *debt reducing* action appears to be essential.
E. These *highly-toxic* materials must be labeled clearly.

Corrections

A. *Hard-earned* sales growth appeared in the third quarter.
B. The customer expected *on-time* delivery.

OR

The customer expected the delivery to be *on time*.

C. *Twenty-eight* associates got *well-deserved* salary increases.
D. A *debt-reducing* action appears to be essential.
E. These *highly toxic* materials must be labeled clearly.

Language Lapses (L1; L2a–s)

Take care to avoid two common language errors: biased language and use of wrong words. Both types of errors can jar readers and diminish their respect for and confidence in the writer.

L1: BIASED LANGUAGE

In today's increasingly diverse workplace, sensitive writers avoid language that can be interpreted as exclusionary (that is, excludes one or more members of your audience because of inappropriate word choice). Nonexclusionary language avoids references to gender, age, racial, or physical characteristics unless they are relevant to the context.

FOWLs

A. Our young female African-American Secretary of State maintains a grueling travel schedule.
B. William Raspberry, a noted black *Washington Post* columnist, won the Pulitzer Prize for Distinguished Commentary in 1994.
C. The girls in Printing did a fine job on this brochure.
D. Every manager must ensure that his employees accurately report time taken for sick leave.

Corrections

A. Our Secretary of State maintains a grueling travel schedule.
B. William Raspberry, a *Washington Post* columnist, won the Pulitzer Prize for Distinguished Commentary in 1994.
C. The Printing staff did a fine job on this brochure.
D. Managers must ensure that their employees accurately report time taken for sick leave.

L2: Wrong Word

Many word-use errors occur when writers confuse words that sound alike or nearly alike but have different spellings and meanings. Other word-use errors involve selection of an incorrect part of speech, such as adverb–adjective or noun–verb confusion. You can improve your writing by mastering this list of frequently misused words.

L2a: Affect–Effect

Use *affect* as a verb, meaning *to influence or to produce an effect*; as a noun, meaning a *feeling, emotion,* or *desire*. Use *effect* as a noun, meaning a *result* or *impact*; as a verb, meaning *to bring about* or *accomplish*.

The hurricane had a devastating *effect* on the state's economy.

In what ways did the hurricane *affect* the economy?

Have you ever measured a hurricane survivor's *affect* about the *effectiveness* of emergency aid programs?

We must *effect* a better way to distribute emergency aid.

L2b: Among–Between

Both words mean *in company with*. Use *between* when referring to two; use *among* when referring to more than two.

Rewards should be distributed equitably *among* employees.

The bonus was distributed equally *between* Ms. Evans and Mr. Kay.

L2c: Amount–Number

Use *amount* with reference to things in bulk or mass; use *number* for things that can be counted as individual items.

The *amount* of money needed for this project is more than we anticipated.

The *number* of employees who elected to participate in the medical savings account is encouraging.

L2d: Complement–Compliment

A *complement* is something that *completes* (notice the *comple . . .* spelling of both words). A *compliment* is an expression or act of praise or courtesy. Each word can be used either as a noun or in an adjective form (complementary/complimentary).

> Hollandaise sauce is a tasty *complement* to steamed asparagus.
>
> Jed blushed when he received profuse *compliments* about his musical talent.
>
> The *complimentary* close of a letter should *complement* the tone of the letter.
>
> Many restaurants offer customers over age 60 a *complimentary* beverage with a food order.

L2e: Compose–Comprise

Compose means *to create* or *to make up the whole*. Both the active and the passive forms are appropriate. *Comprise* means *to contain, to embrace, to include all parts*, or *to be composed of*. Comprise is generally used only in the active voice; consequently, *comprised of* is considered nonstandard usage.

> The seven department heads *compose* the advisory committee.
>
> The advisory committee *is composed of* seven department heads.
>
> The advisory committee *comprises* [not *is comprised of*] the seven department heads.

L2f: Economic–Economical

Economic means of or relating to economics; *economical* means sparing in the use of resources. Although *economic* is sometimes accepted in lieu of *economical*, *economical* should not be substituted for *economic*.

> Current *economic* [not *economical*] conditions require that we use our resources sparingly.
>
> *Economical* use of our resources is necessary at all times.
>
> Your plan appears to be an *economical* [or *economic*] approach to resource management.

L2g: Fewer Than–Less Than

Use *fewer than* in reference to items that can be counted; use *less than* in reference to bulk or mass.

> We have *fewer* sales associates in the field this year *than* last year.
>
> It is not surprising that this year's sales revenue is *less than* last year's.

L2h: Incidence–Incidents–Incidences

Incidence is rate of occurrence; *incident* is a *single* occurrence; and *incidents* is the plural of *incident*. *Incidences* is often used incorrectly in place of *incidents*. (If you practice pronouncing the words—*incidence, incident,* and *incidents*—you will likely remember their appropriate uses.)

> The *incidence* of shoplifting has declined dramatically this year.
>
> This is the first shoplifting *incident* we have experienced this year.
>
> We have had fewer *incidents* of shoplifting this year than last year.

L2i: Insure–Ensure–Assure

Each of these words means *to make secure or certain*. However, they have slightly different connotations and uses. Use *insure* only with reference to guaranteeing the value of life or property. Use *assure* with reference to people, meaning to set their minds at ease. Use *ensure* in other situations.

> You should consider replacement value when you *insure* your property.
>
> Let me *assure* you, your property is well protected.
>
> I will send the policy by overnight delivery to *ensure* that it arrives tomorrow.

L2j: In to–Into

In colloquial language, *in to* is used with a verb to suggest the action of submitting or transmitting something from one person to another person or place. *Into* is used to express motion or direction to a point or within, direction of attention or concern, or a change of state.

> We must turn this report *in to* our professor tomorrow morning. [Saying you turned your paper *into* your professor suggests an act of magic.]
>
> Unprepared students walked *into* the room apprehensively.
>
> I'll look *into* that matter for you.
>
> Please break *into* groups of three.
>
> The magician appeared to turn the belt *into* a stick.

L2k: Its–It's–Its'

Its is a possessive pronoun; *it's* is the contraction for *it is*. *Its'* is not a standard English form. To avoid the *its–it's* error, always read *it is* when you see *it's*. If that reading doesn't make sense, it's the wrong word.

The Hoboken office has surpassed *its* sales goals.

It's about time to set new goals for all of our regional offices.

L2L: LOOSE–LOSE

Loose is an adjective meaning *not bound or confined,* or a verb meaning *to untie, free, relax,* or *slacken; lose* is a verb meaning *to cease to have.*

If you carry too much *loose* change in your pocket, you may *lose* some of it.

Loosing the constraints on sales territories may provide an incentive for expansion.

This division has been *losing* money steadily for the past year.

L2M: MANUFACTURE–MANUFACTURER

Manufacture is a verb meaning *to make a product; manufacturer* is a noun used in reference to *a person or organization that manufactures something.* (If you practice pronouncing the words, you will likely remember their appropriate uses.)

IBM is a long-time *manufacturer* of computers. However, at some points in its history, the company did not *manufacture* what the market demanded.

L2N: PERSPECTIVE–PROSPECTIVE

Use perspective as a noun meaning the apparent relation between visible objects or the mental view of the relative importance of things; use prospective as an adjective meaning expected or future.

From this *perspective* the building looks like a pyramid.

How many *prospective* clients do we have in Cincinnati?

What is your *perspective* on the *prospective* sales for January?

L2O: SITE–SIGHT–CITE

Use *site* as a noun, meaning a *place or location;* as a verb, meaning *to locate.* Use *sight* as a noun, meaning *something that is seen;* as a verb, meaning *to get a view of* or *to take aim.* Use *cite* as a verb meaning to *quote* or *refer to.*

Meg *cited* a Internet *site* on which she caught *sight* of the auto she wants to buy.

While visiting the building *site,* we thought we *sighted* a pine marten.

When you prepare a report, always *cite* the sources of your information.

L2P: THEIR–THERE–THEY'RE

Their is a possessive pronoun, *there* is an adverb, and *they're* is a contraction for *they are*.

> *Their* house is over *there*, but it looks like *they're* not home.

L2Q: THEN–THAN

Use *then* to mean at that time; use *than* as the second term in a comparison.

> *Then* it became evident that Willie's Filly was faster *than* Harry's Horse and would win the race.

L2R: TO–TOO–TWO

Use *to* as a preposition introducing a noun or pronoun or with a verb to form an infinitive; use *too* as an intensifier or to replace *also*; use *two* to represent a number or quantity.

> After you have completed the form, please return it *to* me.
>
> I hope I will not have *to* wait *too* much longer for a response.
>
> Please check this column *too*.
>
> *Two* employees volunteered *to* organize a softball team.

L2S: WHOSE–WHO'S

Whose is used as a possessive or relative pronoun; *who's* is the contraction for *who is*.

> I wonder *whose* book this is.
>
> Gerry, *whose* book was stolen, will have difficulty studying for the exam.
>
> *Who's* going to help her?

COLLABORATIVE WRITING

When a report is written collaboratively, matters of style and avoidance of FOWLs must be attended to. The overall style should be agreed upon before individuals begin writing their parts of the report. If decisions about tone, degree of formality, objectivity, and confidence are addressed early in the writing stage, the process of merging parts of the document will be simplified. There should be few style differences among the group's writers.

The issue of writing lapses is somewhat more complex. Few people choose to make the errors enumerated in this chapter, and writers come to the group with different skill levels. Some groups assign the proofreading and editing task to the person most skilled in detecting writing lapses. However, even if one person accepts the task of final editing and proofreading, each writer has a responsibility to present the best copy he or she is capable of.

If you know you are weak in the mechanical aspects of writing, a first useful step is to use the spelling and grammar tool in your word processing program. Be aware, however, that those programs are not infallible. You must have enough knowledge about the writing standards presented in this chapter to be able to make a correct choice from the options offered by the spelling and grammar program. Another strategy is to seek help from outside the group so that you do not unfairly burden the group members with your weaknesses. A useful technique is to pair up with someone, exchange copies of your writing, and critique style and mechanics. Even strong writers use this technique, because an independent eye often is able to detect errors that you do not notice in your own writing.

ETHICAL CONSIDERATIONS

Since writing style involves choice, it is not farfetched to say that choosing a style may have ethical implications. For example, if you use a curt or excessively informal tone in a sensitive situation, you may offend associates or clients, and ultimately the health of your company. Is it ethical to say, "Well, that's just my style, and they'll have to get used to it"? Or should you demonstrate enough concern for the company and your associates to try to modify your style? As a manager, what is your responsibility to assist a person who has difficulty choosing and using an appropriate tone?

Another ethical issue that may arise is the legitimacy of asking another person to proofread and edit your work. If you question the honesty of such a practice, you may reach an ethical decision by answering these questions: Is asking someone to review one's work an accepted practice in this organization? Why am I doing this? Am I trying to conceal one of my weaknesses? Have I done all I can to overcome that weakness? Am I exploiting the goodwill of a fellow employee? Will a document with writing lapses negatively affect this organization? Ultimately, the question is: Does this practice yield good results for others or only for me?

SUMMARY

This chapter has juxtaposed two important aspects of writing: style, in which you have a range of choices; and the technical aspects of writing, in which you have few choices.

As you write you must make choices about tone, formality, and objectivity. You must also decide how much confidence you should demonstrate in your writing. Ideally, your choices will reflect an understanding of the possible impact on readers and, ultimately, on your organization.

This chapter has also presented several frequently occurring writing lapses (FOWLs). If you find that you lapse into some of these errors, you should not become discouraged; neither should you become complacent. The lapses presented are some of the most common errors made even by competent, intelligent writers. An occasional lapse is forgiven. However, the writer who does not learn from and correct those lapses runs the risk that all of her or his work will be devalued to some extent.

Although students sometimes devalue the matters discussed in this chapter, mastering this content may ultimately make or break your career, as is shown in the following anecdote.

An MBA graduate returned to reminisce with his former report writing professor. He related his experience in a highly competitive training program. The program required each trainee to give five presentations; a single lapse, including the kinds presented in this chapter, would result in a failing assessment for that presentation. Three failures would result in expulsion from the program.

How did this man pass the test? He remembered that his professor had urged the students to know their weaknesses and to submit all writing to a trusted critic before releasing it to his ultimate audience. That audience included readers and listeners who could "make or break" his future with the company. Although some persons might question the ethics of this practice, others would say that it demonstrated appropriate awareness of his strengths and weaknesses and the wisdom to use a strategy to overcome the weaknesses.

TOPICS FOR DISCUSSION

1. What is the role of style in planning and writing a report?

2. What is meant by report or message *tone?* What are some ways to describe tone?

3. Contrast formal and informal writing style, using examples of the following:
   * First- and second-person pronouns
   * Names, titles
   * Contractions
   * Colloquialisms

4. Define and give an example of objective writing style.

5. Give examples to contrast confident and hesitant writing styles.

6. What is the value of learning or reviewing the grammatical rules presented in this chapter?

7. Which of the FOWLs appear most frequently in your writing? Discuss ways to overcome those writing lapses.

8. Which of the rules do you find most confusing? Discuss ways to remember and apply those rules.

9. How do you react when any of the lapses are demonstrated by one of your classmates? a professor? a business or professional person whom you admire?

10. Do you know of a situation in which a person experienced negative reactions when he or she used nonstandard written or spoken English in connection with work responsibilities? If so, share that information with your classmates.

APPLICATIONS

For each of the following applications, write the message in the format requested by your instructor. Examples of letter, memo, and manuscript format are given in Chapter 4.

1. Sacred Words Bookstore is a small church-sponsored bookstore located on the church property. Its sales have declined approximately 10 percent during the past fiscal year. The store manager, Ann Singletary, is convinced that the lack of convenient parking has contributed to the sales decline. The parking lot tends to be filled with church employees' cars, leaving little space for visitors. Although a parishioner has offered free parking in a garage located one block from the church, the church's employees continue to use the limited space in the church lot. Ms. Singletary has asked the church's administrative manager, Eddie Victor, to require all who work at the church in any capacity to use the garage that is available, leaving the parking lot open for visitors. Church employees include ordained clergy, business office personnel, bookstore personnel and volunteers, building and grounds staff, and the child-care center staff. Mr. Victor has asked Ms. Singletary to compose a message that he can send to the staff asking (directing?) them to park in the garage.

   Acting as Ann Singletary, write the message. Be prepared to justify the message content, structure, and style to your classmates. Answering these questions should help you as you plan the message:
   - What is the purpose of the message? (Hint: What action do you want?)
   - Who is the primary audience? the secondary audience?
   - What is the context?
   - What is the content?
   - What is an appropriate structure?
   - What is an appropriate tone? level of formality?
   - How much emotion should you inject into the message?
   - How confident should you be about your request?

2. Pair up with one of your classmates to review the work each person did for Application 1. Use the following procedures:
   - Exchange copies of your messages. Read one another's work.
   - Provide constructive criticism of the content, structure, tone, formality, objectivity, and level of confidence demonstrated by the writing style. Also examine the messages for possible FOWLs.

3. The Executive Director of a small nonprofit agency thinks the Director of Development is not bringing in enough revenue and wants to discontinue the position entirely. The Director of Development's major responsibility is to find new revenue sources for the agency. The job includes planning and executing fundraising events, writing and sending two general fundraising letters each year, and soliciting donations from local businesses. Her current salary is $45,000 per year; during the past year she brought in about $60,000 in new money. The Executive Director has made an oral request to the Board president to bring the matter before the Board. There has been no action on that request.

   In a small group, do the following:
   - Discuss this question: What communication barriers may account for the Board president's failure to respond to the Executive Director's request?
   - Plan the message to be sent to the president. Identify the purpose, audience (primary and secondary), context, content, medium, structure, and style for the report. Ask your instructor to review the plan and authorize you to write the message.
   - After your instructor approves the plan, each member of the group should draft the message. Assume you are the Executive Director.
   - Share your draft with the group. Critique all aspects of the messages: awareness of audience, content, structure, style, mechanics. Submit the best message (or combined elements of the best messages) to your instructor to represent your group's work.

4. Using word processing software, write a message to your instructor identifying and describing the computerized reference sources in your school library. After you draft, revise, and edit your message, use the spelling/grammar check to locate any misspelled words or other writing errors. Be prepared to defend your writing style by answering the questions listed in Application 1.

5. Find examples of three writing lapses presented in this chapter. (Hint: Use newspapers, business signage, posters on campus, letters you receive, etc., as sources.) In a message to your instructor, identify the type of lapse, tell where you found it, and present a corrected version.

6. Review at least two pages of writing you have done for this class, another class, or at your workplace. Circle any FOWLs that you can now identify. Exchange papers with a classmate. Review her or his paper and circle any additional FOWLs that you detect. Together write appropriate corrections for all errors detected. Present these corrections, along with the original documents, to your instructor for review.

7. Correct all FOWLs appearing in the following sentences. Each sentence contains at least one error; many contain more than one error. More than one revision may be acceptable. Be prepared to defend your revisions. If classmates come up with revisions that differ from yours, discuss the effectiveness of each version.

   a. The collection procedure is customary. Although you can modify them when necessary.

   b. Your work is excellent, therefore you will receive a bonus.

   c. There is many routes which a tourist can use (if they are so inclined) to get to Cincinnati (if that's where they want to go).

   d. Entering the classroom 10 minutes late, the professor asked Gerrit if he had overslept, sarcastically.

   e. Tired from a long day of work, the bed looked good to me.

   f. These guides are useful for coherence and to enhance clarity.

   g. There cite is more appropriate then ours.

   h. Kelly, a person that enjoys Saturday garage sales excursions said that the reason David and herself bought an antique chest at a sale in a neighbor's garage was because it was offered for an unbelievably-low price.

   i. Management must retire when they reach age 70.

   j. When was those circuits tested?

   k. Unless you plan your day's work, it may omit some important tasks.

   l. Here is the contract and my expense report.

   m. There's good reasons why a writer should avoid biased language in his memos.

   n. ABC Corp. announced their merger with XYZ.

   o. When Van Dorn discussed the production schedule with Gates, he emphasized critical deadlines.

   p. Analyzing your companies needs and your customers needs are necessary if you don't want to loose market share.

   q. Its hard to determine what affect the advertising campaign had on year end sales.

   r. The IRS treats incidences of tax fraud seriously, however its' tax assistance division generously answers individual's questions about legitimate deductions.

   s. Your prospective on the importance of each topic will effect the organization of your report.

   t. Cathy, a typical female engineer, was surprised by the affects of her tirade but their was no excuses for that kind of behavior.

   u. To regain trust she will have to come in early tomorrow review her work schedule with her supervisor and submit an outline a bibliography, and a draft for the exception report—even if its rough—before noon.

   v. Her supervisor expects the report to be: complete, accurate, coherent and on-time.

   w. Whitney Corporation a major manufacture of home appliances offer attractive career opportunities.

x. Kelsey who's business plan won the entrepreneurship award sites his fathers influence and his own hard-work as the thing that has helped him succeed.

y. Hunter said that Jordan and himself had found a location for they're new business.

z. The perspective cite which they had located was turned in to a parking lot before they had a chance too make an affective offer.

Formatting the Report

LEARNING OBJECTIVES

After you have read this chapter, you should be able to:

1. Apply current business protocols for formatting memorandums, letters, and manuscripts.
2. Plan an effective, readable design for a simple or complex document.
3. Use computer technology to improve the appearance of your reports.
4. Work effectively with team members to plan and produce an appropriate, effective format for a report or other document.
5. Demonstrate ethical responsibility with respect to accessing and disseminating data electronically.

After planning, writing, revising, and editing your report, you may feel confident that you have prepared an effective message. However, you must also consider how to "package" that fine product. An effective format will entice the receiver to read the report; lead the reader effortlessly through the information presented; maintain the reader's interest; and, ideally, stimulate the reader to respond to the report as you had hoped.

You can produce professionally formatted reports by mastering three commonly used report formats (letter, memo, and manuscript) and following a few basic guides for document design.

FORMATTING THE REPORT

Most business reports are written in memorandum, letter, or manuscript format. Whichever of those formats you choose, you should apply the following general guides.

General Guides

Applying these guides will help your reader scan the document, quickly determine its content, and focus attention on specific information.

SPACING

Since most printed business documents are single spaced, standard spacing for memorandum and letter reports is single spacing. The trend is also to use single spacing for manuscript reports, although some organizations still use double spacing.

A blank line (one extra stroke of the computer's Enter or Return key) separates paragraphs of single-spaced documents from one another. Most single-spaced documents have no paragraph indentions. Double-spaced documents have no extra blank line between paragraphs, but have a paragraph indention of approximately one-half inch.

TYPOGRAPHY

Typography—your selection of typeface, type style, and type size—affects the appearance and readability of your report. The primary goal of typography is to create a document that is consistent, harmonious, and balanced. Too much variety can be distracting to the reader.

Typeface refers to the shape or design of letters and characters. NOTE: Another word for typeface is *font*. As the typefaces shown in Illustration 4-1 demonstrate, some typefaces are considerably more intricate—and often less readable—than others. Typefaces are also identified as serif or sans serif. *Serif* refers to the fine lines that cross the main stroke of a letter. *Sans serif* typefaces do not have the lines at the ends of letters. A third way to classify typefaces is by spacing characteristics. Monospaced typefaces allocate equal space to each letter; proportionally spaced typefaces allocate more space to wide letters, such as W, and less space to narrow letters, such as *l*. Although some offices may still have typewriters with monospaced characters, most computer typefaces are proportionally spaced.

Along with choosing a typeface, you must consider type size and type style. The majority of the report text should be produced in regular or plain type. Bold, italic, and bold italic may be used sparingly for emphasis or to clarify the text. For example, bold is often used for headings and subheadings and italics for names of publications or for emphasis. Avoid underlining. Readers recognize words by their shapes; underlining tends to obscure the descending portions of letters like *g*, *j*, *p*, and *y*.

Type size is measured in points (1 inch = 72 points) from the top of the typeface's ascenders (letters like *k* and *l*) to the bottom of its descenders (letters such as *p* and *q*). Font size for report text should be between 10 and 14 points. Size 10 may be too small for some readers, but it is sometimes used when the writer wants to limit the pages in a document or shrink a document to one page. Any size larger than 14 points is considered display type and should be reserved for headings and subheads. Using anything larger than 12 points for the main text may give the impression that you are trying to pad the report. You may use a hierarchy of sizes, with headings larger than the text.

Restrict your use of full capitalization to report titles or first-level headings when the report contains several division levels. Text set entirely in uppercase type is harder to read and takes up significantly more horizontal space than text that is set in a combination of upper- and lowercase. Moreover, using all

ILLUSTRATION 4-1 COMPARATIVE TYPEFACES, TYPE SIZES, AND TYPE STYLES

Serif Typefaces

Times New Roman, 12 point, regular

Times New Roman, 14 point, bold

Times New Roman, 16 point, italics

Times New Roman, 18 point, underlined

Century Gothic, 12 point, regular

Century Gothic, 14 point, bold

Century Gothic, 16 point, italics

Century Gothic, 18 point, underlined

Palatino Linotype, 12 point, regular

Palatino Linotype, 14 point, bold

Palatino Linotype, 16 point, italics

Palatino Linotype, 18 point, underlined

Sans Serif Typefaces

Tahoma, 12 point, Regular

Tahoma, 14 point, bold

Tahoma, 16 point, italics

Tahoma, 18 point, underlined

Century, 12 point, regular

Century, 14 point, bold

Century, 16 point, italics

Century, 18 point, underlined

Comic Sans MS, 12 point, regular

Comic Sans MS, 14 point, bold

Comic Sans MS, 16 point, italics

Comic Sans MS, 18 point, underlined

uppercase letters has come to be equated with shouting. E-mail protocols, for example, discourage use of all capital letters except for headings or occasional emphasis within the message.

Finally, leading and kerning are factors that affect the appearance and readability of text. *Leading* is the adjustment of vertical space between lines of type, and *kerning* is the adjustment of space between characters to produce a better type fit. Text tends to appear crowded and difficult to read when leading or kerning is too small, and it appears somewhat disjointed when either factor is too large.

EMPHASIS TECHNIQUES

When you want to emphasize certain information in a report, you may use one of several emphasis techniques, such as enumeration, bulleted lists, or special fonts.

Grouping and numbering or bulleting closely related items focuses attention on that information. To group items effectively, follow these guides:

- Use an introductory sentence or phrase to unify the group. The sentence immediately preceding this list is an example of such a sentence.
- Include at least two items in your list. Logically, you cannot have a group of one.
- Write all items in parallel grammatical structure. Each item in this list begins with an imperative verb and is followed by an explanation.

Bold or italicized type may be used to emphasize words, headings, sentences, or even full paragraphs. Use such techniques sparingly, however. Overuse of emphasis techniques can be distracting. When too many things are emphasized, nothing receives appropriate emphasis.

HEADINGS

Headings should represent the outline of your report and guide the reader through its content. When you use headings, the type style must convey the relationships of report sections. All first-level headings, which indicate major divisions of the report, must be printed in uniform style; and all second-level headings, which identify subdivisions of the major divisions, must be printed in a uniform style that clearly distinguishes them from first-level or third-level divisions. One acceptable style for headings is shown in Table 4-1. In that illustration, first-level headings are centered, second-level headings are placed at the left margin, and third-level headings are placed at the beginnings of paragraphs.

As you study the illustrations of reports throughout this book, notice how the general guides for spacing, typography, headings, and emphasis are applied. In addition, observe the following specific guides for memorandum, letter, and manuscript reports. When you apply those guides, you not only enhance readability; you also demonstrate your knowledge of contemporary business writing protocols that accommodate differences in the content and context of messages.

TABLE 4-1	LEVELS OF HEADINGS IN REPORTS

Title	**Organizational Effectiveness**
First-Level	Determining Criteria for Effectiveness
	Xxxxxxxxxxxxx xxx xxxxxxxxxxx xxxxx xxxxx xxxxxx. Xxxxx xxxxxxxxxxx xxxx.xxxxx xxxx. Xxxxxxxxxxxxxx. x…
First-Level	Assessing Effectiveness
	Xxxxxxxxxxxxx xxxxxxxxx xxxxxx xxxxxxx. Xxxxxxxxx xxxxxx xxxx…
Second-Level	Setting Standards
	Xxxx xxxxxxx xxxxxxxxx xxxxxxxx xxxxxxxx xxxxxxxxx xxxxx. Xxxxxxxxx xxxxxx xxx xx xxxxx xxx…
Second-Level	Selecting Indicators
	Xxxxxxxxxxxxxx xxxxxx xx xxxxxxx xxx xxxx xxx xxxxxxxxx xx xxxxxxxx. Xxxx xxxx xxxx xxxxxxxxxxxxx xxxxxx x xxxx xxxxx xxx…
Third-Level	Outcomes. Xxxxxxxxxx xxxx xxxx xxxxx xx. Xxxxxxx xxxxx xxxxxx xxx xxx…
Third-Level	Processes. Xxxxx xxxxxxxxx xx xxxxx xxx xxxx. Xxxxxxxxx xxx xxxxx xxx xxxxxxxxx…
Third-Level	Structures. Xxxxxxx xxx xxxxxxxxx xxx xxxx xxx. Xxxxxxxx xx xxxxx xxxxxxx xxxxxx…
Second-Level	Selecting Samples
	Xxxxxxxxxxxxxx xxxxx xxxx xxx. Xxxx xxx xxxxxx xxxxxxx xxxxx xxxx…
Second-Level	Applying Measurements
	Xxxxxxxxx xxxxxx xx xxxxx xxxx. Xxxx xxx xx xxxxxxx xxxxx xxx…
First-Level	Explaining Effectiveness
	Xxxxxxxxx xxxxxxxxxxxx xxxxx xxxxxxxxxxxxxxxxxxxx xxxxxxx xxxxxxxxxxxxx xxxxxxxx xxxxxxxxx xxxxxxxxx xxxx xxx xxxxx xxxxxxxxxx xxxxx…

Memorandum Formats

Most relatively brief internal reports are written in memorandum (memo) format. A commonly used memorandum format is shown in Illustration 4-2. The memo heading includes the guidewords *To, From, Date,* and *Subject.* Those items may appear in different sequence and locations in the heading, but the standard memo format includes all four items as identifying information. Illustration 4-3 shows the simplified memorandum format, which is widely

ILLUSTRATION 4-2 ▸ STANDARD MEMORANDUM FORMAT

To: Report Writing Students

From: Report Writing Instructor

Date: September 17, <year>

Subject: Standard Memorandum Format

This illustration demonstrates standard memorandum format. Please notice these features of memo format.

1. The standard heading consists of the captions *To, From, Date,* and *Subject.* Those captions may be arranged in different ways, but either *Date* or *To* should be the first item, and *Subject* should immediately precede the memo body (message).

2. The subject line must be a brief, meaningful summary of the memo's content.

3. The memo body is single-spaced. Use double spacing between the heading and the first paragraph of the body; also use double spacing between paragraphs.

4. Left and right margins should be at least one inch wide.

5. Enumerations focus the reader's attention on specific information. Numbered items also permit a reader to identify specific items for response. If a memo contains only one major point, do not number it.

6. The memo sender frequently places her or his initials after the typewritten name to indicate approval of the message. Some writers sign or initial the memo at the end of the message. However, do not use a closing line (such as Sincerely or Yours truly) at the end of the memo.

Please follow these guides or the guides for the simplified memorandum format as you prepare memo reports. Other illustrations of memo reports appear throughout this book.

ILLUSTRATION 4-3   SIMPLIFIED MEMORANDUM FORMAT

September 27, <year>

Report Writing Students

SIMPLIFIED MEMORANDUM FORMAT

This illustration demonstrates the simplified memorandum, which is growing in popularity. Observe these features of the simplified format.

- The guide words *To, From, Date,* and *Subject* are omitted.

- The date appears first on the memorandum; the name of the receiver is entered two or three lines below the date; the subject line—in all capital letters—is placed a double space below the receiver's name.

- The message is single spaced, with double spacing between paragraphs.

- Items may be enumerated or bulleted for clarity, but this technique is not required.

- The signature and the writer's typed name appear at the end of the message.

The simplified memorandum format is efficient when forms or templates with guide words are not available. Because the format is relatively new, you should obtain approval from your supervisor before you use it consistently.

R. W. Instructor

R. W. Instructor

used today and is easily adapted for e-mail use. In this format the guidewords are omitted and the writer's name is placed at the end of the message.

Courtesy titles (Mr., Mrs., Ms., Dr., etc.) are usually omitted in intra-company memos, but position titles (Vice President, Supervisor, etc.) are sometimes included. When you begin a new job, it is wise to check the organization's office manual or files to determine the preferences within that organization.

Letter Formats

External reports of one to three pages may be written in letter format. If the report is longer than three pages, it should be written in manuscript format, accompanied by a letter to the receiver.

Three standard letter formats—block, modified block, and simplified block—are shown in Illustrations 4-4, 4-5, and 4-6. Notice that the body of each letter explains specific features of its format.

As you study the illustrations of letters, notice also the following features that apply to all letters.

1. Identity of sender. Every letter must include a letterhead or return address to identify the sender. A well-designed letterhead presents the organization favorably and provides all information needed to communicate with that organization, such as address, telephone number, and fax number. Many companies today also include their e-mail or World Wide Web addresses.

   If the sender has no letterhead, the sender's return address appears first. Depending on letter length, the return address should be placed one to two inches from the top of the page. The return address includes everything but the writer's name, which always appears in the signature lines at the end of the letter.

2. Date of letter. A letter should always contain the date on which it was written and/or mailed. When letterhead is used, the date appears one or two lines below the letterhead. However, when a return address is used, the date is placed immediately below that address. Here are examples of return addresses and dates.

1610 Castle Drive	Rt. 1, Box 50
Byron Center, MI 49315	Edgerton, MN 56128
January 11, <year>	May 18, <year>

3. Address of receiver. The letter address (receiver's address) is placed approximately four lines below the date. Since messages going outside the organization tend to be more formal than those moving within an organization, etiquette calls for using a person's courtesy title if it is known. Do not, however, include a title if you do not know the person's gender, marital status, or title preference. A position title, placed after the name or on the next line, may also be included. The letter address governs the envelope address—the two must be identical.

ILLUSTRATION 4-4 ▶ BLOCK LETTER FORMAT, OPEN PUNCTUATION

Communications Design Associates

801 JACKSON STREET, WEST   CABLE: COMDA
CHICAGO, IL 60607-5511   TELEPHONE: (312) 555-9753

<Date>

Return/Enter 4
(R/E) {

Ms. Maria Pettas
Communications Director
Pettas Fine Foods
1849 N. Halifax Avenue
Daytona Beach, FL 32018-4421

R/E 2 {

Dear Ms. Pettas

R/E 2 {

This letter demonstrates block letter format. In block format, all lines begin at the left margin. No letter parts or paragraphs are indented.

Single
Space
all
paragraphs.
R/E 2
between
paragraphs.

The block format is used extensively in business today. Its efficiency and crisp appearance are pleasing to contemporary business writers.

This letter also demonstrates open punctuation, with no punctuation marks after the greeting and the complimentary closing. This style is becoming increasingly popular. Mixed punctuation, with a colon after the greeting and a comma after the closing, may also be used. However, use of that punctuation style is declining.

I think you will find the block letter format useful for your business reports and correspondence, Ms. Pettas. If you have other questions about report formats, I will be happy to discuss them with you and provide illustrations.

Sincerely

R/E 4 {

Jerri Martino

Jerri Martino
Staff Consultant

ILLUSTRATION 4-5 MODIFIED BLOCK LETTER FORMAT, MIXED PUNCTUATION

Communications Design Associates

801 JACKSON STREET, WEST   CABLE: COMDA
CHICAGO, IL 60607-5511   TELEPHONE: (312) 555-9753

<Date>

Return/Enter 4 {
(R/E)

Ms. Maria Pettas
Communications Director
Pettas Fine Foods
1849 N. Halifax Avenue
Daytona Beach, FL 32018-4421

R/E 2 {

Dear Ms. Pettas:

R/E 2 {

Single
Space
all
paragraphs.
R/E 2
between
paragraphs.

This letter demonstrates modified block letter format. In modified block format, the date line and the complimentary closing begin at the approximate center of the page. The inside address and greeting are placed at the left margin. Paragraphs are usually blocked at the left margin. Paragraphs may be indented five to ten spaces, but contemporary business writers rarely use that style.

The modified block letter format is a more traditional style than is the block format. Companies that wish to project a somewhat conservative image to their clients might consider this style.

This letter also demonstrates mixed punctuation, which uses a colon after the greeting and a comma after the complimentary closing. Open punctuation, with no punctuation marks after the greeting and closing, may also be used.

If you have questions about the modified block format, Ms. Pettas, please call me at 1-800-555-7777. I will be happy to discuss it with you by telephone or in your office.

Sincerely,

Jerri Martino

R/E 4 {

Jerri Martino
Staff Consultant

ILLUSTRATION 4-6   SIMPLIFIED BLOCK LETTER FORMAT

Communications Design Associates

801 JACKSON STREET, WEST   CABLE: COMDA
CHICAGO, IL 60607-5511   TELEPHONE: (312) 555-9753

January 19, <year>

Ms. Maria Pettas
Communications Director
Pettas Fine Foods
1849 N. Halifax Avenue
Daytona Beach, FL 32018-4421

SIMPLIFIED BLOCK LETTER FORMAT

This letter demonstrates the simplified block letter format, Ms. Pettas. The format has these features:

- All lines begin at the left margin.

- A subject line replaces the traditional salutation. The subject line may be keyed in all capital letters or in upper- and lowercase letters. Double space above and below the subject line.

- The letter body is single-spaced with double spacing between paragraphs.

- Major points may be bulleted or numbered, but such emphasis techniques should be used only when they complement the message content.

- The complimentary close is omitted. The writer's name is placed on the fourth line below the letter body. The writer's title or department may be included. The signature block may be keyed in all capital letters or in upper- and lowercase.

Although the simplified block style may be used for any correspondence, it is especially useful when you do not know the courtesy title of your receiver. On such occasions, use no title in the inside address.

Please let me know what you think of this format, Ms. Pettas. Many of our clients have adopted it as a standard letter format.

Jerri Martino

JERRI MARTINO - STAFF CONSULTANT

4. Greeting. The letter address also governs the greeting. When a courtesy title appears in the address, it is used in the greeting, without the individual's first name. For example, the standard greeting for a letter addressed to Ms. Kimberly Hagood is "Dear Ms. Hagood," not "Dear Kimberly Hagood." An exception to that rule is appropriate when the letter writer knows the reader very well. Then a first-name greeting, such as "Dear Kimberly," or even "Dear Kim," is appropriate. When the address has no courtesy title (for example, K. Hagood) or has only a position title (for example, Marketing Director), you must choose an alternative to the standard greeting. Popular choices today include:

- The person's name as given in the address (Dear K. Hagood)
- The position title used in the address, when no name is given (Dear Marketing Director)
- The simplified block format, which omits the greeting (Illustration 4-6)

Sometimes the first line of the letter address is a company name rather than an individual's name, or a letter may be addressed to a company, followed by an attention line that names a person. This is an ideal situation in which to use the simplified block format. Although some writers use an impersonal greeting such as "Ladies and Gentlemen" or "Gentlemen and Ladies," that language seems excessively formal for contemporary business writing. Considerate writers avoid "Dear Sir" or "Dear Sirs" because those words convey an exclusionary, sexist tone. Avoid, also, the excessively impersonal "To whom it may concern"; that greeting may connote that you do not care who reads the message. Moreover, it shifts the responsibility of determining an appropriate reader from you, the sender, to the receiver.

Manuscript Formats

Internal or external reports that exceed three pages are generally written in manuscript format. A cover letter or memorandum almost always accompanies such a report, and the report usually has a title page. Illustration 4-7 shows the title page and the first page of a report in manuscript format. Notice that the report discusses and demonstrates the general guides for spacing, typography, emphasis, and headings.

In specialized reporting situations, several additional preliminary or supplementary parts are included in the manuscript. Those components will be discussed in the chapter on research reports. Other publications, such as brochures, newsletters, and annual reports, also require careful attention to document design.

PRINCIPLES OF DOCUMENT DESIGN

You have already studied general guides for spacing, typography, emphasis techniques, and the use of headings in reports. As you design any document, you must attend also to page layout and graphics.

ILLUSTRATION 4-7 MANUSCRIPT REPORT

FORMAT FOR MANUSCRIPT REPORT

Prepared for

Mountain View Industries
13666 E. Bates Avenue
Aurora, CO 80014

Prepared by

KK&L Communication Consultants
Suite 116, Castle Complex
1218 Fairview Road
Denver, CO 80202

January 19, <year>

ILLUSTRATION 4-7   Continued

FORMAT FOR MANUSCRIPT REPORT

This illustration explains one commonly used format for business reports. Notice these features of the report format: title page, margins, typography, report headings, and spacing.

Title Page

A title page may be used to orient the reader to the report and its writer. The title page should include the report title, for whom it is written, by whom it is written, and the transmittal date. Optional items are the company logo and other design elements that suggest the report content or the nature of the organization.

Although a title page may be optional in some situations, a creative design can create a positive first impression. Therefore, choose a format that conveys your professionalism.

Margins

Place the title approximately 1 1/2 inches from the top of the first page of the report. Use a 1-inch top margin for all remaining pages. If the manuscript is unbound or stapled in the upper left corner, use a 1-inch left margin. For a left-bound manuscript, use a 1 1/2-inch left margin. Right and bottom margins should be approximately 1 inch on all pages.

Typography

Use no more than two typefaces in your report. This illustration, for example, uses a sans serif font (Arial) for the headings and a serif font (Times New Roman) for the report text. It would also be appropriate to use the same typeface, preferably a serif font, for headings and report text. You may use bold and italic type sparingly for emphasis.

Spacing

This single-spaced, blocked format is used extensively by contemporary business writers. All paragraphs are single-spaced. Use triple or quadruple spacing after the title, with double spacing before and after headings and between paragraphs.

Since some readers prefer double-spaced format, always determine reader preference before completing the final copy of your report.

Report Headings

Use headings in any report containing more than one major section. Headings should orient the reader to the report content.

Type style and placement must indicate the relationship of headings and subheadings. Notice that the headings in this report are centered and keyed in identical style. If subheadings were used in any section, they would be keyed and placed to distinguish them from the main headings. For example, subheadings might be placed at the margin.

Guides for Page Layout

The design of a document should reflect its purpose, content, and intended audience. The annual report of a small nonprofit agency will differ considerably from the annual report of a major for-profit corporation. Likewise, a brochure highlighting the services of a nonprofit may differ considerably from a brochure promoting the services of a computer service business. Since the design of a document will be influenced by funds budgeted for the project and the perceived reading level of the recipients, many experts suggest that you plan a document before you compose the contents. You must decide how many pages will be included, the size of paper you will use, and how the document will be bound or folded.

You should begin with a sketch of how you want the finished document to appear. A useful technique is to sketch the contents on paper by blocking areas for headings, text, and visuals. This sketch will help you plan page layout for effective visual impact. Illustration 4-8 contains a sketch for a four-page newsletter to be printed front and back on a 17- × 11-inch sheet of paper that will be folded in the center, creating an 8 1/2- × 11-inch finished document.

Criteria for effective page design include balance, consistency, contrast, focus, and proportion.

- Balance—visual harmony of top, bottom, and side margins as well as placement of text and graphics on a page. To achieve visual balance and compensate for optical illusion, the bottom margin should be slightly larger than the top margin.
- Consistency—harmony of typefaces, type styles, type sizes, heading structure, and graphics. You can mix these elements sparingly and still achieve consistency in appearance.
- Contrast—use of white (blank) space, shaded areas, and graphics in documents. Use contrast techniques to relieve visual tedium.
- Focus—methods used to attract reader attention. Focusing techniques include placement of graphics, modifications of typeface, and use of color.
- Proportion—relationship of type size in headlines and text, the size of a graphic to surrounding text, and the amount of space assigned to content. The most important information should have more space assigned to it than the least important information.

As you plan your page layout, follow these guides:

- Allow sufficient white space. Some experts suggest 20 to 25 percent of the page should be reserved for white space.
- Keep the design simple. Too much clutter distracts a reader.
- Use text lines that are comfortable for the eye to follow. Aim for 40 to 50 characters per line. Lines that are too short or too long are difficult to read. This guide suggests that on a sheet of paper that is 8 1/2 inches wide, two or three columns will be more readable than one or four columns.
- Use uneven right margins. Uneven right margins are easier to read than justified right margins and create a "friendly" appearance. With justified

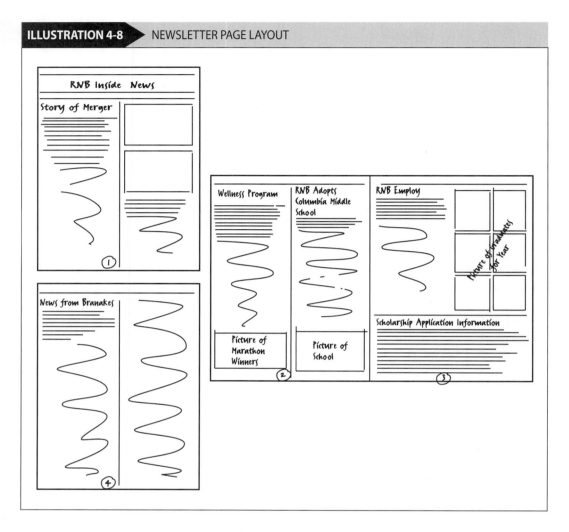

ILLUSTRATION 4-8 NEWSLETTER PAGE LAYOUT

right margins, extra spaces are placed between some words; those spaces tend to distract readers and may disrupt the sentence flow.

■ Rank the importance of each article. This ranking will help you place material effectively. The most important article or lead story should be placed at the dominant center of visual interest, usually the top left corner of a page. The next most important article should be placed at a secondary center of visual interest, such as at the top right corner, bottom left corner, or bottom center of a page.

Guides for Text

In addition to the guides for typography given earlier in this chapter, here are some guides to help you plan attractive, readable text.

■ Use *serif* typefaces for text. Serif typefaces are more legible because the serifs visually link letters into words.

- Use *sans serif* typefaces for headings. Those typefaces tend to attract the reader's attention.
- Use special typefaces purposefully to achieve desired emphasis. A useful guide is to use only one or two typefaces on a page.
- Use a type size from 9 to 12 points for text in brochures and pamphlets. Smaller type sizes are acceptable for footnotes and explanatory comments; larger type is recommended for titles and headings.
- Use leading equal to the size of the font plus 1 to 3 points.
- Use uppercase and lowercase characters (not all uppercase) for text and most headings. When a document has more than one level of heading, some writers use all uppercase characters for the first-level heading.
- Limit the different type sizes on one page to six or fewer.

Guides for Graphics

Most desktop publishing or word processing software enables you to integrate graphics with text. In formal written reports, writers often use the introduce-display-discuss technique of incorporating visual aids into reports. With that technique, you would first write a statement that highlights a major point the reader should see in the visual, then display the visual, and follow it with an interpretive discussion. That strategy is effective for many documents. However, some kinds of writing, such as brochures, newsletters, and annual reports, may benefit from other placement techniques. In those documents, a graphic should be placed where it is most likely to attract reader attention. Graphics can be displayed above, in the middle of, or below related text.

Choose visuals purposefully. The graphic should complement the text message, not clutter it. Here are some guides for using visuals effectively in promotional materials.

- Avoid visual clutter. Keep the number of graphic elements small enough to stand out. A good guide is to use no more than two visuals on an 8 1/2- x 11-inch page.
- Use sufficient white space around the visual to optimize impact.
- Keep the hierarchy of importance clear. Place the most important visual where it will gain the most attention.
- Consider eye movement when placing visuals on the page. For instance, a profile picture of a person should be placed so that the person is looking into the page rather than off the side of the page.
- When a picture is too large for the space, cut (crop) unnecessary parts from the visual. For example, a picture of a person standing may be cropped to show only the person's head and shoulders.
- When a visual such as clip art or a chart is too large or too small for the space allotted, scale the visual in both height and width. Scaling the visual in one direction only will distort the appearance and sometimes the meaning conveyed by the item.

Illustration 4-9 contrasts cluttered, inappropriate use of visuals with balanced, purposeful, focused use of visuals.

Attractively designed and correctly formatted reports contribute to the readability and, thereby, the effectiveness of your reports. Using your computer efficiently will help you prepare readable, attractively formatted reports.

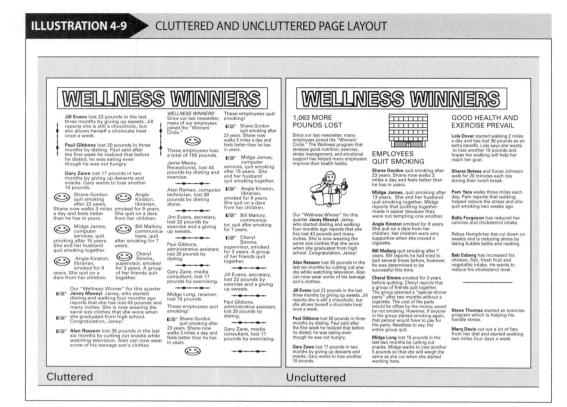

ILLUSTRATION 4-9 CLUTTERED AND UNCLUTTERED PAGE LAYOUT

USING COMPUTER TECHNOLOGY TO IMPROVE REPORT FORMATS

Composing reports on the computer can eliminate some of the time-consuming activities of gathering data and drafting reports. You can enhance your efficiency by resolving some aspects of report format before you begin writing. Five guidelines can help you successfully format your report.

- Use features that are available in your computer software. Most word processing software has default standards that are preset for the most commonly used margins, type styles, and type sizes. You can use the defaults or customize the settings. You can also change the format for a portion of a document; for example, a double-spaced report may have a single-spaced section or vice-versa. Once these formats have been made, they will be stored in the document until they are changed.

- Know what decisions you can or may make. Your company, for example, may already have a standard format for memos, letters, and manuscripts. Many software programs come with standard templates, which are formatting instructions that can be used repeatedly so that documents in a series look alike. Most templates can be modified to satisfy the writer's formatting preferences. If someone has built a template for reports like the one you are writing, you may be expected to use it.

- Select a simple, functional format. You will impress readers most by providing just the information they need in a way that makes it easy for them to find and understand it. An overly elaborate design may give readers the impression that you did not pay enough attention to the content. Weigh the value of additions such as a glossary of terms carefully. Add something only if you can justify it on the basis of functionality. For example, if your report contains only a few words that need to be defined, put the definitions in the text. On the other hand, if you use many terms that may be unfamiliar to some of your readers, a glossary is a helpful addition.
- Plan for visuals. While planning your report, look for places where visuals can help explain the points. Instead of giving an array of statistics in your text, turn them into simple tables and graphs. Software programs now make it easy to integrate tables, charts, and graphs into your text. Word processing software can also automatically renumber figures and references to these figures.
- Keep the format consistent. Consistency in spacing, typography, and headings shows readers how each section fits into the report. Using predefined styles helps considerably with consistency, especially when you are collaborating with other writers.

COLLABORATIVE WRITING

Early planning efforts for a group project typically focus on group processes and task requirements. Group members must become acquainted with one another and identify individuals' strengths, weaknesses, work styles, and so on. The group must also clarify the objective of the group project, the kinds of tasks that must be completed to reach a successful conclusion, and individual responsibilities for those tasks. Decisions about the "deliverable"—the document that must be delivered—are often postponed until late in the collaborative process.

However, postponing decisions about matters related to writing style and format—spacing, typography, emphasis techniques, headings, page layout, and use of visuals—tends to lead to extra work or inferior quality when individual contributions must be merged. If everyone begins "on the same page" with respect to these matters, the task of finalizing the document will be simplified considerably. It is especially helpful for all group members to share their knowledge of formatting and computer tools that will help the group design and produce a professional-looking document.

ETHICAL CONSIDERATIONS

Computer technology assists you with more than document design and format. As you progress in your report-writing responsibilities, you will use the computer increasingly to acquire and disseminate data. The capability of technology to provide access to vast amounts of information and to transmit it to a large number of people creates ethical responsibilities in four areas: privacy, ownership, accuracy, and accessibility.[1]

Privacy

Knowledgeable technicians can freely access large amounts of confidential data. Some writers may be tempted to invade another person's privacy to get information, share it, or tamper with it.

Of particular concern today are the vast amounts of employee and customer information maintained in corporate data banks. In fact, identity theft has become a major privacy and security concern. Communicating private or confidential information over electronic mail or the Internet could be extremely damaging to individuals and organizations. For example, many U.S. colleges have discontinued use of Social Security numbers for student identification because of the risks associated with unauthorized use of such numbers.

Ownership

Laws are relatively clear about taking someone else's copyrighted material, but the issue of how much electronic modification may legally occur is still being decided. Entering a database or electronic file to obtain, manipulate, or change information that does not belong to you or for which you do not have authorization is equivalent to theft or burglary. The unauthorized copying or pirating of commercial software is illegal, as well. In addition, intentionally damaging an electronic file by introducing a virus is a federal offense.

The issue of who owns software, text, images, sound, and video has caused many organizations to take an aggressive stance when protecting themselves and their products. Surprise visits by "software police" representing the industry's trade association have increased as the battle over piracy has intensified.

Accuracy

Legal rulings have upheld that the publisher of material, whether hard copy or electronic, is responsible for the accuracy of the content. However, an inexpensive scanner can duplicate images from a variety of sources at minimal cost. Photographs, drawings, and designs can be scanned easily and quickly into a computer, modified slightly, and claimed as one's own work. The effect of appropriating and modifying the work of other people has the potential for profound personal and corporate damage. If the data are altered, the potential for damage increases because responsibility for accuracy may be hard to pinpoint.

Accessibility

Because computers allow storage of vast amounts of information, it becomes increasingly important to consider the types of information to which organizations are entitled, the conditions under which they might obtain information, and the safeguards in place to protect all individuals' rights. Access to databases, whether internal or external to the organization, must be protected to prevent access by information hijackers or software viruses.

Other accessibility issues arise. For example, should employees be able to use their company computers for personal benefit or to access other employees' computer files that are not password protected? The city manager of Columbia, SC, lost her job in 2003 after another city employee accessed one of her computer files that contained potentially offensive comments about certain employees whom she supervised. She asserted the file was merely her form of brainstorming about a personnel matter. Should she have been protected from the employee who accessed her file? Should she have used the office computer for recording her unique, personal way of thinking through a personnel issue? Did she violate the privacy of the individuals mentioned in her file?

A final issue involves cost. Since organizations pay a fee to access databases or the Internet, should everyone have access to the information or only those whose work is deemed to require it? Should employees be permitted to use those resources for personal benefit during "off" hours?

Clearly, the arguments involving privacy, ownership, accuracy, and accessibility have yet to fully unfold. Competent communicators use their technical knowledge and ability to access information to achieve their goals while acting in an ethical manner.

TOPICS FOR DISCUSSION

1. What spacing guides should you apply to your reports?

2. What typography guides should you apply to your reports?

3. What cautions about emphasis techniques should you observe in your reports?

4. What should guide your use of headings in reports?

5. Identify three commonly used formats for written reports and indicate circumstances in which each would be used.

6. Explain how the standard and simplified memorandum formats differ.

7. Compare and/or contrast the block, modified block, and simplified block letter formats with respect to these letter parts:
   - Date of letter
   - Letter address
   - Greeting
   - Letter body
   - Complimentary close
   - Punctuation of greeting and complimentary close

8. Give an appropriate formal and informal greeting (or other option) for each of these letter addresses:
   - R. S. French, III, 187 Ocean Drive, Jacksonville, FL 32217-1234
   - Director, Office of Consumer Affairs, State of Arizona, P.O. Box 16650, Tucson, AZ 85732-5678
   - Mrs. Jennie Wilson, 755 Camille Lane, Chicago, IL 60643-0910
   - Kites for Tikes, Attn. Customer Services, 808 Dayton Street, Indianapolis, IN 46204-1112
   - Mr. and Mrs. Jeremy Dreise, 1112 Prairie View, Sioux Center, IA 51250-1314
   - Dori Carter and Will Jordan, 227 Esplanade Drive, Dallas, TX 75220-1516

9. Identify guides to follow as you design a page layout.

10. Identify guides to follow as you plan placement of pictures and graphics in a document.

11. Describe word processing features that will help you achieve an effective report format.

12. Discuss ways in which you can contribute to a group's decisions about document design and format.

13. Discuss the ethical responsibilities you should exercise as you use electronic technology in the reporting process. Add issues you perceive in addition to those presented in this chapter.

APPLICATIONS

1. Study the format and typography of the following letter. Identify inconsistencies and explain necessary changes to bring it up to contemporary standards.

2. Return to Chapter 2, Application 1, in which you were asked to plan reports. As directed by your instructor, write one or more of those reports, using an appropriate structure, style, and format.

3. Assume that the laptop (notebook) computer you use in your work-related travel no longer meets your needs. The computer performs well for word processing, spreadsheet, and presentation applications as well as for dial-up Internet connections. However, it is relatively heavy, has a battery life of only 1.5 hours, and does not have an Ethernet port for broadband and network connections. Determine features you would prefer in a laptop computer. Consult the World Wide Web, a current newspaper, or a computer catalog to determine the specifications and price of a computer that meets your requirements. Write a memo to your supervisor, H. J. Cooper, requesting a new computer. Be prepared to justify your message content and structure, writing style, and format.

ILLUSTRATION FOR APPLICATION 4-1

July 3, <year>

Teranne Babcock
Vice President
Integrated Management Systems, Inc.
P. O. Box 10
Charlotte, NC 28223-0010

Dear Mrs. Babcock,

As you requested in our initial meeting, we have researched the feasibility of introducing IMSI products into the Canadian life insurance market. Our macro and micro analyses were based on your initial specified parameters: environment, market potential, and competition.

As a result of our analysis, we offer these conclusions:

- Canada's strong economy and current market trends justify IMSI's entry into the Canadian market.

- IMSI should target medium and large life insurance companies with a single product, IMSI-Life.

- Initial market strategy should focus on developing partnerships with two Canadian life insurance companies to minimize cost of market entry.

The research team will present a full oral report to you on July 10 at 10:00 a.m. in your Charlotte office. At that time we will also give you a comprehensive written report of our research.

Igor Jakovich, Team Leader

4. Bonnie Gregory drives a company car, which is replaced every two years. At replacement time, the employee has the option of buying the car at 50% of its current book value. The limitation is that the car must be purchased for use by the employee or someone in the employee's immediate family. Bonnie wants to buy a car for her 16-year-old son. Although her car has been maintained well, it has nearly 95,000 miles on it; and Bonnie is unsure she wants to buy that one. Her colleague, Gerry Barber, is also due to get a new company vehicle; but he is not interested in buying his old one. Bonnie wants to buy Barber's car instead of hers. As Bonnie Gregory, determine the book value of her current company vehicle (make reasonable assumptions about make, model, year, and condition) and her co-worker's

(again make appropriate assumptions, but make it a better vehicle). Write a report to her supervisor, A. L. Cain, providing the details about each car and requesting that Bonnie be permitted to buy Gerry Barber's car. Be prepared to defend your choice of content, structure, style, and format.

5. As owner of Beauty Ideal Day Spa, you want to sponsor a benefit for a local nonprofit agency. (Choose a local nonprofit agency that interests you.) Your plan is to give the agency 50 percent of all revenues you take in on September 29. That percentage represents your entire profit; the balance goes to cover supplies, overhead, and salaries. You want to suggest that your staff (massage therapists, aestheticians, nail technicians, hair stylists, etc.) make a contribution also. Write a memo to the staff suggesting that they donate all tips received that day. Include enough information about the agency to stimulate the staff to comply with your suggestion. Be prepared to defend your choice of content, structure, style, and format.

6. Your local Chamber of Commerce, which is revising its tourism brochure, has asked your instructor for help. Your instructor convinced the Chamber CEO, Ike Voehringer, to sponsor a contest in which students will write and prepare the brochure. The writer(s) of the winning entry will receive $500 and be honored at the Chamber's annual awards banquet.

   The first phase of the contest is to write descriptions of three major attractions in your city. Limit the description of each attraction to a maximum of 350 words. You are allowed a total of 1,000 words. The Chamber will provide pictures to supplement the winning copy.

   Collect appropriate information, outline, draft, and revise your description. Remember, at this time you do not have to prepare the brochure, only the text that will be used in a brochure. Prepare the report in manuscript format. Include a title page and a cover letter, addressed to Mr. Voehringer (assume an appropriate address).

   With your instructor's permission, you may collaborate with one or two classmates to complete this application and Application 7.

7. Assume that the content for the brochure (Application 6) has been approved. Now plan and write the brochure. Remember: You are trying to win a $500 prize.

8. Obtain a copy of a corporate annual report. Critically analyze the style and format of the report, using the guides presented in this chapter. Present your analysis in a report prepared in manuscript format.

REFERENCE

1. Hershel, R. R., & Hayes, P. H. (April, 1997). Ethical implications of technological advances on business communication. *The Journal of Business Communication, 34*(2), 160–170.

Illustrating the Report

Have you ever tried to follow complex written task instructions, such as those for assembling a bicycle, and wished the author had included pictures or diagrams to guide you? Have you noticed that some manufacturers now supply only visuals as directions for use or assembly of their products? Have you ever listened to a detailed explanation of statistical information, such as an insurance salesperson's description of the rate structure, and wished the person would summarize the data in a table? If so, you can appreciate the complementary value of visual aids to words, either written or oral.

PURPOSES OF VISUAL AIDS

Although many writers readily think of using visual aids in long reports, such aids can also increase the effectiveness of short reports. You should use visual aids to emphasize, clarify, simplify, reinforce, and summarize information in both simple and complex oral or written reports. Further, visuals may be used to add interest, improve credibility, and increase the coherence of written messages.

Emphasize

Newspaper reporters and advertising copywriters are well aware of the value of pictures, diagrams, or charts to emphasize an important fact. For example, a picture of people milling about and waving placards in front of a government building emphasizes the number of people involved in a protest far more effectively than a verbal report that "1,500 people demonstrated before the State House." Similarly, a line chart showing steadily increasing sales emphasizes the increase more effectively than does a written narrative alone.

Reports often cover many points, but not all are of equal importance. Visual aids can be used effectively within reports to emphasize specific information. In addition, a visual aid on the report cover can draw the reader's attention to the main point of that report. Assume, for example, that you must prepare a report to employees to show that health insurance claims have increased dramatically while employee contributions to the health insurance plan have increased minimally during the past ten years. For emphasis, you could prepare line charts showing claims and contributions as percentages of total wages for ten years. Those charts could be placed strategically within the report. As an alternative, however, you could place a multiple line chart on the report cover showing the relationships of employee claims and contributions, thereby emphasizing a significant fact to readers as soon as they pick up the report.

Clarify

A second purpose of visual aids is to clarify something that may be difficult to express clearly in words alone. Assume you wish to explain to your employees how payments for insurance benefits have been distributed among various benefit categories. Although you could provide that information in narrative form, the same data could be conveyed more clearly in a visual aid, such as a pie chart.

Simplify

Another purpose for visual aids is to simplify data. Simplification involves breaking a complex whole into its component parts while preserving the essential nature of the whole. The previous example of a pie chart used to clarify information is also an example of simplification. The pie chart presents the essential components (amount in each benefit category) while retaining the whole (total benefit payments).

A flowchart is another example of a visual aid often used to simplify a complex process. The flow diagram you studied in Chapter 2 (Illustration 2-1) simplifies the complex process of planning a report by identifying essential parts and sequences in that process.

Reinforce

To reinforce is to make stronger or more pronounced. Repetition is one form of reinforcement that helps people remember something important; but reinforcement is usually most effective when information is presented in more than one way, rather than through mere repetition.

You can increase reader retention and recall of important facts by using visual aids to reinforce your report narrative. For example, if you were asked to present a case for your company's participation in a major contract, your visual aids would probably include information about the company's past performances with projects similar to the one being considered. You would show charts reflecting the creative methods used by the company to keep costs down, performance statistics to indicate your high-quality standards, and your best idea-to-production times to show the audience how adept you are at meeting target dates.

To be most effective as reinforcers, visual aids should be used selectively. If minor as well as major verbal information is supplemented by a visual aid, the visuals become commonplace, and their reinforcing value is reduced.

Summarize

Visual aids can effectively summarize detailed information. A summary covers main points succinctly without providing all details. A good summary presents a reader with essential information and minimizes the amount of reading required to obtain that information. If constructed accurately, a single visual aid, such as a table or chart, can summarize several pages of narrative.

As a summary, the visual aid cannot fully replace the narrative. The visual aid provides major points, but the narrative may describe fine points that cannot be included in the summary.

Add Interest

When you pick up a magazine or newspaper, do you immediately begin to read the narrative or do you first look at pictures or charts in that publication? If you are like many people, you are first attracted to the visuals. Similarly, after reading several pages of narrative in a textbook, you probably welcome the sight of a picture or diagram.

Visuals are effective tools to create interest and to relieve the tedium of a lengthy narrative. They make a report more attractive. Even in short reports, visual devices such as bullets (•), squares (□), or pointers (→) can provide interest.

Improve Credibility

Visual aids tend to add a sense of credibility that cannot be conveyed through words alone. The statement that profits have "increased dramatically" during the past five years may be interpreted as self-serving puffery. But that same statement may seem credible if it is accompanied by a line chart that shows sharply rising profits.

Graphics and pictures create a sense of preciseness. Many readers tend to believe that a writer who uses well-designed, accurate visual aids is a confident, credible information source.

Increase Coherence

Effective reports are coherent—that is, all parts come together in logical relationships. The report writer may understand the relationships because of extensive exposure to the data, but the report will not be effective unless those relationships are also made clear to the readers. Visual aids such as flowcharts, summary tables, or diagrams can show the relationships among different parts of a report.

As you study the examples of visual aids in this chapter, consider which of the purposes—to emphasize, clarify, simplify, reinforce, summarize, add interest, improve credibility, and increase coherence—each aid would serve if it appeared in a report.

CRITERIA FOR EFFECTIVE VISUAL AIDS

To use visual aids effectively in reports, you must be familiar with certain principles of graphics that apply to all visuals. In addition, you should follow guides for identification and placement of visuals in reports and adhere to criteria for ethical representation of information.

Principles of Graphics

Well-constructed visuals meet four standards for effective graphics: simplicity, contrast, unity, and balance.[1]

SIMPLICITY

The most effective graphics are simple. Regardless of how complex the subject, the visual itself should include no more information than absolutely necessary to support the author's message. Each visual aid should focus on one main point. A complex, cluttered visual presents too many stimuli to the viewer, thereby diverting the reader's attention rather than focusing it on the main point to be conveyed. Moreover, as the number of stimuli increases, the possible interpretations of the visual aid also increase, adding to the probability of misunderstanding.

Consider, for example, the simplicity and effectiveness of international traffic symbols. Even when people cannot read or understand the local language, they can interpret those traffic signs. In effect, the simplicity of the signs helps to overcome a language barrier.

CONTRAST

The second principle that you should demonstrate in your graphics is contrast. To be effective, a visual must be noticed. Therefore, it must first of all stand out from its field. In written reports that field is the page of the report. Contrast is achieved by visually separating the graphic from narrative. This separation can be accomplished by using additional white space or a line between the text and the visual or by boxing the visual off from the text.

Secondly, contrast must be achieved within the visual itself to clarify the comparisons or relationships that are presented. Contrast within the visual is achieved by solid and dotted lines; plain, crosshatched, shaded, or colored bars; and different shapes to represent contrasted items, as shown in the following examples.

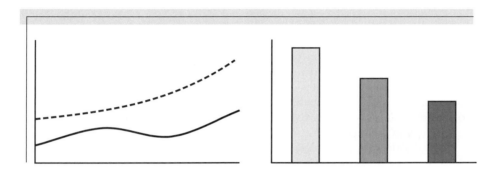

UNITY

The third principle to observe is unity. An effective visual aid gives the impression that all parts belong and fit together. A unified chart or table shows the logical relationship of the parts to one another.

A sense of unity can be achieved by proximity, grouping, connecting lines, common shape, or common base. Some of those techniques are shown in the following examples.

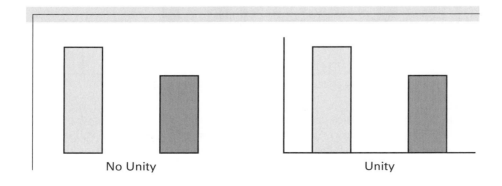

No Unity   Unity

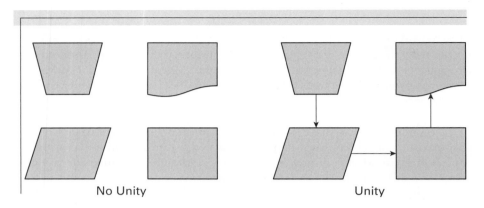

No Unity   Unity

BALANCE

The fourth principle for graphics construction is balance. Balance refers to a sense of equal weight among the components of the visual aid. When two or more equal things are being described, balance is relatively easy to achieve. Each item can be presented in exactly the same size, shape, or plane of the visual. That type of balance is called symmetrical balance. In business reports, however, you must often present factors that are not equally weighted. Then you must achieve asymmetrical balance by planning and controlling the location, size, and arrangement of the symbols and labels used in the visual.

In the following examples, symmetrical balance and asymmetrical balance are contrasted with unbalanced presentations. Notice that the balanced presentations are more aesthetically appealing. An unbalanced arrangement may be justified under some conditions. For example, the unbalanced bar chart shown in the example would be justified if the bars are arranged chronologically. But if the bars represent discrete data, such as sales by region, the balanced presentation is preferable.

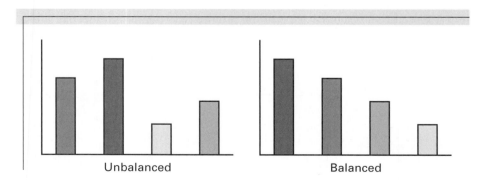

Unbalanced   Balanced

In pie charts, balance can be achieved by beginning the largest segment at the 12 o'clock position on the circle. The other segments should follow in a clockwise direction, by size, ending with the smallest. Again, rationale may exist for an unbalanced presentation. If the two pies, for example, show contributions of parts to the whole for two different years, logical arrangement would be to place the segments of the first pie according to the principles of balance and the segments of the second pie in the same sequence.

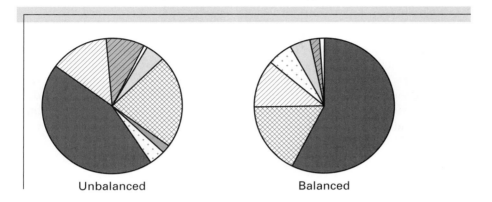

Unbalanced   Balanced

Identification and Placement

When your report contains several visual aids, identify each by a label, number, and title. For simplicity, some writers label all visual aids as illustrations (for example, Illustration 1, Illustration 2, etc.). An alternative practice is to differentiate tables from other visual aids, usually referring to charts, diagrams, maps, etc., as figures or illustrations (for example, Table 1, Table 2, Figure 1, Figure 2, etc.). Some writers are beginning to use the word *Table* for tables and the word *Figure* for all illustrations except tables. Current practice is to use Arabic, not Roman, numerals in the identification labels.

A title must be descriptive but concise. A well-written title answers the *what* and *when* questions about the data, and in many cases the title should also answer *who* and *where*. For example, "Microcom Sales by District, 2005 and 2006" is a more meaningful title for a chart than "Microcom Sales" or "Sales by District." Titles of tables are usually placed above the table, whereas titles of charts or figures may be placed at either the top or bottom. However, because most readers in the Western world read from the top to the bottom of a page, it is reader-friendly to place the number and title at the top of all visual aids so that the reader sees that identifying information before studying the visual. Remember to be consistent with your placement of titles.

In addition to identifying the visual aid by label, number, and title, you should identify the data source. If you used secondary data, the source may be identified in a shortened form, assuming that full identification is provided in the report bibliography or endnotes. An example of noting a secondary source is "Source: Statistical Abstract of the United States, 2004–2005." If the data are from a primary source, the simple notation "Source: Primary" is adequate. As you study this chapter, notice the identification techniques used in the illustrations.

The most effective placement of visual aids is within a report, not in a report appendix, unless you know that your primary reader prefers that the visuals be grouped in an appendix. Visuals should be placed where they are needed for emphasis, clarity, simplification, reinforcement, summary, interest, credibility, or coherence. A visual aid should be placed as near as possible to the accompanying narrative. An effective three-step process for incorporating a visual aid into a report is to introduce the aid, display it, and then discuss it.

INTRODUCE

In the introductory statement, mention a primary fact that the visual illustrates. Focus on the information contained in that visual, not on the visual aid itself. Following the introduction, identify the aid by number or title to help the reader locate it in the report. If the aid is on another page, also include the page number in the identification. The following examples contrast less effective and more effective introductions.

Less Effective: Illustration 1 shows sales for Oat Bran, Rice Bran, and Wheat Bran in 2006.

More Effective: Oat Bran substantially outsold both Rice Bran and Wheat Bran in 2006. (See Illustration 1.)

Less Effective: As Figure 1 shows, a research plan contains 12 parts.

More Effective: Planning research is a 12-part process, as demonstrated in Figure 1, page 12.

DISPLAY

Following the introduction, display the visual aid as soon as possible. Separate the visual from the narrative with additional white space or lines to achieve contrast.

If space permits, place the visual on the same page as the introduction. If the visual does not fit on the same page, do not leave a large patch of white space at the bottom of the page; just continue with your discussion and place the visual at the top of the next page. Visuals must fit within the margins of the report narrative and should not be so large that they distract from the narrative. If necessary, reduce the visual so that it will fit attractively within the report margins.

When large visuals must be used, they may occupy a full page and may be placed vertically or horizontally. Whenever possible, display full-page visuals on the page immediately following the one on which the visual was introduced.

DISCUSS

A visual aid can add interest to a report or summarize essential information, but it is your responsibility as the report writer to interpret the data in that aid. After introducing and displaying the visual aid, discuss it in an interpretive manner. Interpretation requires more than merely repeating the data presented in the visual. Your discussion must clarify data or add details that cannot be captured visually.

ILLUSTRATION 5-1 PLACEMENT OF VISUAL AIDS IN REPORT

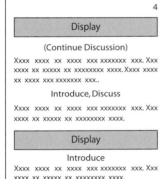

TITLE PAGE OR COVER 1

2

TITLE

Xxxx xxxx xx xxxx xxx xxxxxxx xxx. Xxx xxxx xx xxxxx xx xxxxxxxx xxxx. Xxxx xxx xxxxx xx xxxxxxxx xxxx.

Introduce

Xxxx xxxx xx xxxx xxx xxxxxxx xxx. Xxx xxxx xx xxxxx xx xxxxxxxx xxxx.

Display

Xxxx xxxx xx xxxx xxx xxxxxxx xxx. Xxx xxxx xx xxxxx xx xxxxxxxx xxxx. Xxxx xxx xxxxx xx xxxxxxxx xxxx.

Discuss

Xxxx xxxx xx xxxx xxx xxxxxxx xxx. Xxx xxxx xx xxxxx xx xxxxxxxx xxxx.

3

Xxxx xxxx xx xxxx xxx xxxxxxx xxx. Xxx xxxx xx xxxxx xx xxxxxxxx xxxx. Xxx xxxx xx xxxx xxx xxxxxxx xxx. Xxx xxxx xx xxxxx xx xxxxxxxx xxxx. Xxxx xxx xxxxx xx xxxxxxxx xxxx.

Introduce

Xxxx xxxx xx xxxx xxx xxxxxxx xxx. Xxx xxxx xx xxxxx xx xxxxxxxx xxxx. Xxxx xxxx xx xxxx xxx xxxxxxx xxx. Xxx xxxx xx xxxxx xx xxxxxxxx xxxx.

Discuss

Xxxx xxxx xx xxxx xxx xxxxxxx xxx. Xxx xxxx xx xxxxx xx xxxxxxxx xxxx. Xxxx xxx xxxxx xx xxxxxxxx xxxx.

4

Display

(Continue Discussion)

Xxxx xxxx xx xxxx xxx xxxxxxx xxx. Xxx xxxx xx xxxxx xx xxxxxxxx xxxx. Xxxx xxxx xx xxxx xxx xxxxxxx xxx..

Introduce, Discuss

Xxxx xxxx xx xxxx xxx xxxxxxx xxx. Xxx xxxx xx xxxxx xx xxxxxxxx xxxx.

Display

Introduce

Xxxx xxxx xx xxxx xxx xxxxxxx xxx. Xxx xxxx xx xxxxx xx xxxxxxxx xxxx.

5

Display

6

Xxxx xxxx xx xxxx xxx xxxxxxx xxx. Xxx xxxx xx xxxxx xx xxxxxxxx xxxx.

Discuss

Xxxx xxxx xx xxxx xxx xxxxxxx xxx. Xxx xxxx xx xxxxx xx xxxxxxxx xxxx. Xxxx xxx xxxxx xx xxxx xx xxxxxxxx xxxx. Xxxx xxxx xx xxxx xxxxxxxx xxx.

Xxxx xxxx xx xxxx xxx xxxxxxx xxx. Xxx xxxx xx xxxxx xx xxxxxxxx xxxx. Xxxx xxxx xx xxxx xxx xxxxxxx xxx. Xxx xxxx xx xxxxx xx xxxxxxxx xxxx. Xxxx xxx xxxxx xx xxxxxxxx xxxx. Xxxx xxxx xx xxxx xxx xxxxxxx xxx. Xxx xxxx xx xxxxx xx xxxxxxxx xxxx.

When your discussion requires only one paragraph, you may combine the introduction and discussion. In such a situation, display the visual after the discussion. If the discussion is lengthy, however, the introduce-display-discuss sequence is more effective. Acceptable patterns for introducing, displaying, and discussing visual aids are demonstrated in Illustration 5-1.

CHOOSING AND CONSTRUCTING VISUAL AIDS

Although visual aids serve many purposes in reports, those purposes are achieved only if the appropriate aid is chosen. Knowing the characteristics of each type of visual aid will help you choose graphics to achieve your purposes. Following are specific guides for constructing five types of visuals to increase the effectiveness of your reports: line charts, bar charts, pie charts, relationship charts, and tables. Three other visual aids—pictures, pictographs, and statistical maps—also are discussed briefly.

Bar Charts

A *bar chart* is a simple graphic that uses two or more rectangles along with vertical and horizontal axes to represent information. When the rectangles are placed vertically, the chart is sometimes called a column chart, but the more common term is vertical bar chart. When the rectangles are placed horizontally, the chart is called a horizontal bar chart.

USES

Bar charts are used to compare discrete (noncontinuous, distinct, unconnected) quantitative information, such as the numbers of females and males in a training program, sales volume of two or more products in a stated time period, or distribution of time among several activities. The bar chart provides a quick visual impression of the relationships between or among the components that are being compared.

CONSTRUCTION GUIDES

Following these guides will help you construct effective bar charts:

- Plan size and page location carefully. Allow sufficient space so that the chart, including its title and source notation, will not be crowded. Locate the chart according to the introduce-display-discuss criterion.
- Achieve balance in length and width of bars. All bars must be the same width, and the space between bars should be no less than half the width of the bar itself. For readability, vertical bars should be no longer than seven inches, and horizontal bars should not exceed five inches. Unless it is logical to do otherwise, arrange bars in ascending or descending order by length.
- Draw axes and scale units accurately. Units of measurement must be uniform; that is, all steps of a scale must represent the same unit size and must be placed equal distances from one another. Place the unit of measurement on the horizontal (x) axis for horizontal bars chart and on the vertical (y) axis for vertical bar charts.
- Label the chart. For each axis identify scale units and categories of comparison. In multiple bar charts, use shading, color, or crosshatching to differentiate categories. Provide a key or legend within the chart to interpret those items. Observe how those guides are applied in Illustrations 5-2 through 5-5.

VARIATIONS

A simple *bar chart* compares two or more variables on one dimension, as shown in Illustration 5-2. That chart compares five variables or categories on one dimension—by percent of respondents who participated in each.

A multiple bar chart compares two or more variables on two or more dimensions, as shown in Illustration 5-3. That chart compares two variables

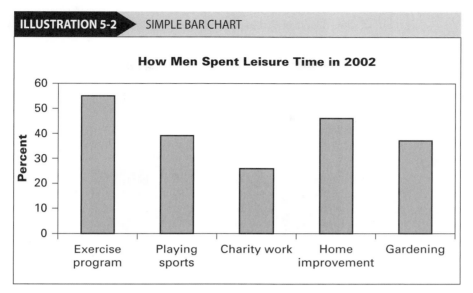

ILLUSTRATION 5-2   SIMPLE BAR CHART

How Men Spent Leisure Time in 2002

Source: *Statistical Abstract of the United States: 2004–2005*, p. 769.

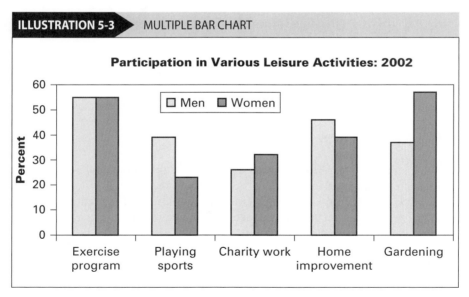

ILLUSTRATION 5-3   MULTIPLE BAR CHART

Participation in Various Leisure Activities: 2002

Source: *Statistical Abstract of the United States: 2004–2005*, p. 769.

(men and women) on five dimensions (leisure time activities). A segmented bar chart adds another dimension to a comparison, as shown in Illustration 5-4. The parallel segmented bars clearly show changes in revenue sources and permits ready comparison of those sources in the two years.

Another variation of the bar chart is the bilateral bar chart, which permits display of positive and negative values. (See Illustration 5-5.) Notice that this

| ILLUSTRATION 5-4 | SEGMENTED BAR CHART |

Independent Sector: Sources of Revenue 1987 and 1997

	1987	1997
Other income	8	11
Private contributions	28	20
Government contracts and grants	23	31
Private payments for dues and services	41	38

☐ Private payments for dues and services   ☐ Private contributions
■ Government contracts and grants   ■ Other income

Source: *The New Nonprofit Almanac and Desk Reference, 2000,* p. xxxii.

chart dramatizes differences in salary changes, but does not show actual dollar amounts in either year.

Bar charts are effective aids to compare amounts and percentages. When you wish to emphasize the parts of which a factor is composed, a pie chart is an effective tool.

Pie Charts

A *pie chart* is a circle divided into segments. The circle represents the whole amount (100 percent), and each segment represents a proportion of the whole. Pie charts are also called circle charts or circle graphs.

Uses

A pie chart is effective when you want to emphasize relative proportions. Pie charts permit comparisons of parts that make up a whole but may be less effective than bar charts in comparing absolute amounts. Two or more pies can also be placed side by side to compare factors at different times, such as

ILLUSTRATION 5-5 BILATERAL BAR CHART

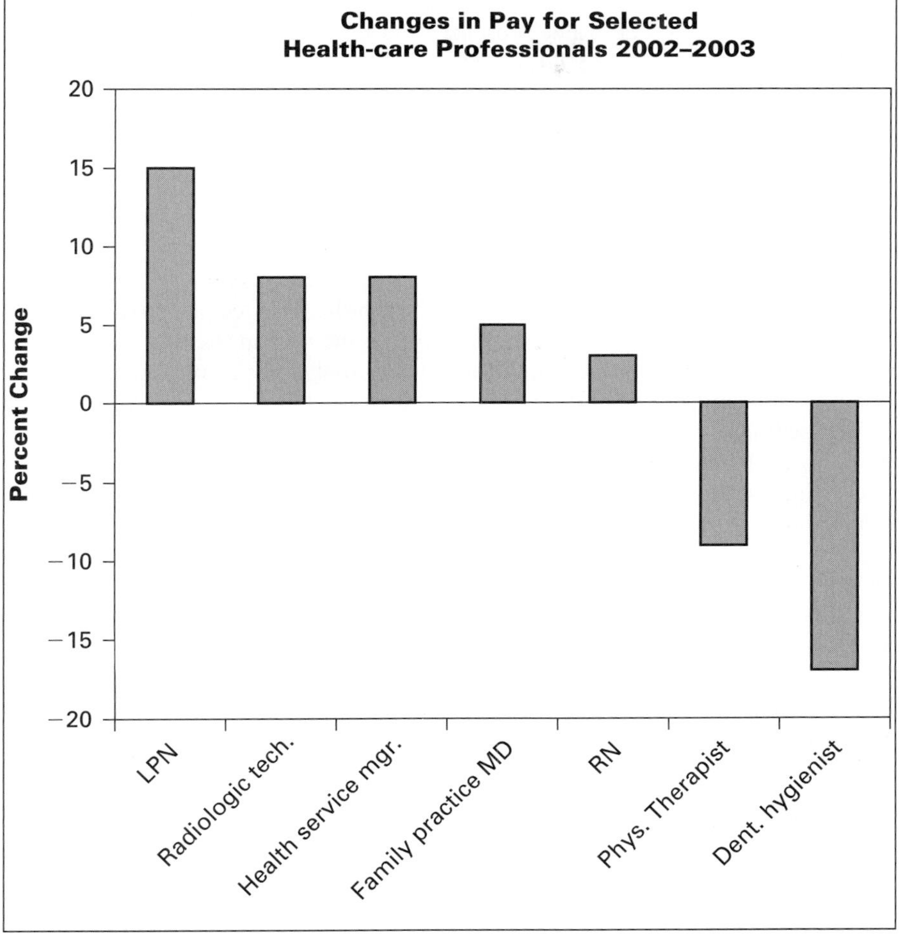
Changes in Pay for Selected
Health-care Professionals 2002–2003
Percent Change
20
15
10
5
0
−5
−10
−15
−20
LPN
Radiologic tech.
Health service mgr.
Family practice MD
RN
Phys. Therapist
Dent. hygienist

Source: *The State,* March 11, 2005, p. B6.

expenditures in two years, or to compare two related factors, such as sources and uses of funds.

Construction Guides

To construct effective pie charts, follow these guides:

- Keep the number of segments to a minimum. When a pie chart contains too many segments, the comparisons are difficult to comprehend. Some graphics experts recommend that you use no more than eight segments.
- Balance the segments. Because people in the Western world tend to read pie charts in a clockwise direction, graphics designers recommend that

you place the largest segment first, beginning at the 12 o'clock position. Place other segments around the circle in descending order of size unless logic requires some other arrangement. For example, the data presented in Illustration 5-4 could be presented in two pie charts placed side by side. If that were done, the largest-to-smallest clockwise sequence for 1987 would be Private payments for dues and services, Government contracts and grants, Private contributions, Other income. It would then be logical to use that same sequence for 1997, even though the segments would not be in the largest-to-smallest arrangement.

- Label the chart. Appropriate labeling includes a title, a source notation, and identification of the segments. The title must include the factor being analyzed and the time represented by the chart. Clearly name each segment and identify its proportion of the whole. If space permits, place that identifying information on the face of the pie within the appropriate segments. If space is limited, the identifying labels may be placed around the perimeter of the pie and you may use a short line to connect each label to its segment.

- Show segment values accurately. When segment values are stated in percentages, the segments must always total 100 percent. Draw each segment accurately to represent true proportions. Although pie chart units are most often in percentages, units may also be in absolute numbers. If you state units in absolute numbers, be sure that each segment size still represents its accurate proportion of the pie.

- Keep the chart simple. Although color, shading, or crosshatching may be used to add interest to the chart, use those techniques sparingly. If it is labeled correctly, a pie chart is quite effective without such additions. Excessive use of interest techniques can impair readability of the chart.

VARIATIONS

Pie charts are either one-dimensional or multidimensional. A one-dimensional pie chart is a simple circle cut into segments, as shown in Illustration 5-6.

Multidimensional pie charts employ various graphics techniques to emphasize certain segments or to increase interest. Common multidimensional techniques are to separate segments or "explode" one segment. Only the segment that is being referred to should be exploded. Another technique is to draw the circle with a shaded or crosshatched area to suggest the factor being discussed or to add a bar to explain one of the segments. Those techniques are demonstrated in Illustration 5-7.

Bar and pie charts permit comparison of discrete, independent items. When you wish to show relationships between or among continuous, dependent variables, a line chart is an appropriate tool.

Line Charts

A line chart consists of a vertical axis, a horizontal axis, and two or more plotted lines. Each axis contains a measurement scale that identifies the factors of

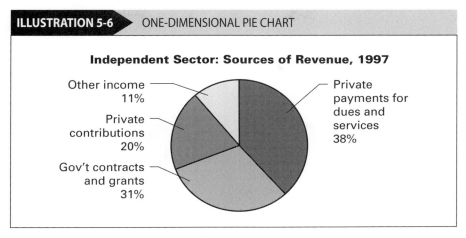

ILLUSTRATION 5-6 ▷ ONE-DIMENSIONAL PIE CHART

Independent Sector: Sources of Revenue, 1997

Other income
11%

Private
contributions
20%

Gov't contracts
and grants
31%

Private
payments for
dues and
services
38%

Source: *The New Nonprofit Almanac and Desk Reference, 2000,* p. xxxii.

comparison: income, age groups, time periods, percents, rates, amounts, etc. Traditionally, the horizontal dimension represents time and the vertical dimension represents values. There are underlying assumptions of continuity and equal intervals in the measurement scales. For example, a time scale is based on the assumption that time is a continuous variable and all scale points represent equal intervals of time.

USES

Line charts show the relationship between the variables plotted on the vertical and horizontal axes. In business reports one of the most commonly used line charts is a time chart, which shows trends or changes in a variable over time. Another frequently used line chart is a frequency distribution, which shows the relationship between two factors (excluding time), such as anticipated sales at various unit prices or unit costs at various production levels.

Line charts should not be used to compare obviously independent items, such as sales in each of several districts. A bar or pie chart appropriately compares that kind of data.

CONSTRUCTION GUIDES

The following guides, which are applied in Illustrations 5-8 through 5-14, will help you construct effective line charts:

- Plan the chart size for readability. The maximum size should occupy less than a full page of the report so that there will be enough space for the title and other identifying information. If you are tempted to use a chart that is larger than a full page, reconsider. You are probably trying to present too much data in a single chart. The minimum width and height should be 2 to 3 inches so that the title, scales, and labels are legible.

ILLUSTRATION 5-7   MULTIDIMENSIONAL PIE CHARTS

Independent Sector: Sources of Revenue, 1997

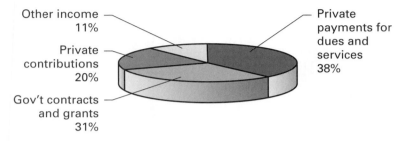

Pie Chart with 3-D Visual Effect

Independent Sector: Sources of Revenue, 1997

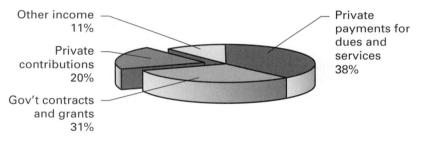

Exploded Pie with 3-D Visual Effect

Independent Sector: Sources of Revenue, 1997

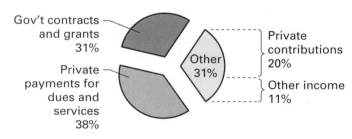

Pie with Value Extracted and Combined into Stacked Bar

- Follow standard plotting protocols. Use the horizontal axis to designate the independent variable or the method of classification (for example, time, scores, age groups). Use the vertical axis to show the dependent variable, amounts, or frequency (for example, sales volume, numbers in classification ranges).

- Use accurate, nondistorting scale proportions. To avoid distortion, follow the "three-quarter rule" whenever possible. That rule, observed by many statisticians, states that the height of the vertical axis should be about three-quarters the length of the horizontal axis. The distances between markers on each axis must be the same. Although the distances on the x- and y-axis do not have to match, a good guide is to attempt to make them approximately the same. Vastly different scale units can distort the data. For example, reducing distances on the vertical scale of a time chart tends to minimize differences across time, whereas expanding the distances tends to maximize differences. The vertical scale must begin at zero. If the entire plotted line lies considerably above zero, you may break the vertical scale to show omission of unnecessary data. This technique is appropriate only when the entire line can be plotted above the scale break.

- Label the chart. Identify the x-axis and y-axis scale units. In multiple-line charts use one solid line along with dotted or broken lines to differentiate the variables and provide a legend within the chart to interpret those lines. As with all charts, full identification includes an appropriate title and source notation.

VARIATIONS

A basic line chart contains one plotted line showing the changes of the variable plotted on the vertical axis as the variable on the horizontal axis changes. In a basic time chart, that line represents the changes in a variable over time. (See Illustration 5-8.) A multiple line chart permits comparison of both trends and relationships. For example, two types of charitable contributions can be compared with a multiple line chart, such as the one shown in Illustration 5-9.

A band chart or belt chart is another variation of the line chart. In this chart the factors that contribute to a total are identified. A line is plotted for each factor. The areas between the plotted lines represent the respective contributions of the factors to the total, and the top line represents the sum of all factors. The data plotted in Illustration 5-9 could also be plotted as a band chart, as is done in Illustration 5-10.

Notice that the band chart effectively demonstrates total contributions and the proportion attributed to each giving category, but the amount of each category is somewhat difficult to determine. The multiple line chart (Illustration 5-9) more effectively displays the actual amounts contributed by each.

A bilateral line chart permits plotting of both positive and negative values. To accommodate negative values, the vertical scale must continue below the zero point, as is shown in Illustration 5-11.

ILLUSTRATION 5-8 LINE CHART (TIME CHART)

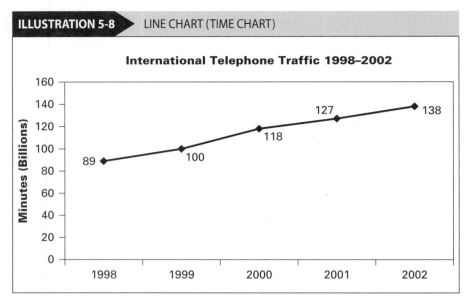

International Telephone Traffic 1998–2002

Source: *Statistical Abstract of the United States: 2004-2005*, p. 870.

ILLUSTRATION 5-9 MULTIPLE LINE CHART

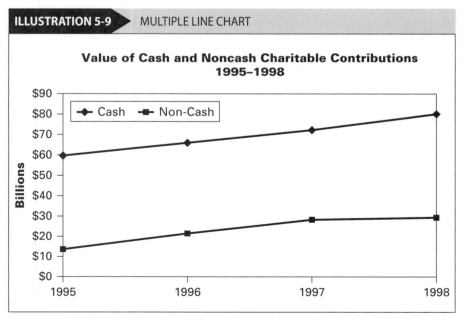

Value of Cash and Noncash Charitable Contributions 1995–1998

Source: *The New Nonprofit Almanac and Desk Reference, 2002*, p. 66.

ILLUSTRATION 5-10 BAND CHART

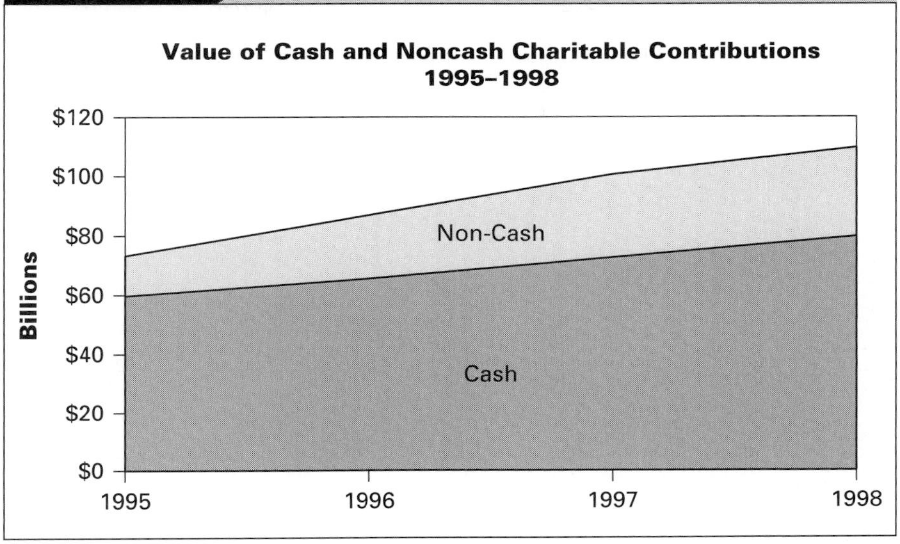

Value of Cash and Noncash Charitable Contributions
1995–1998
$120
$100
$80
$60
$40
$20
$0
Billions
Non-Cash
Cash
1995
1996
1997
1998

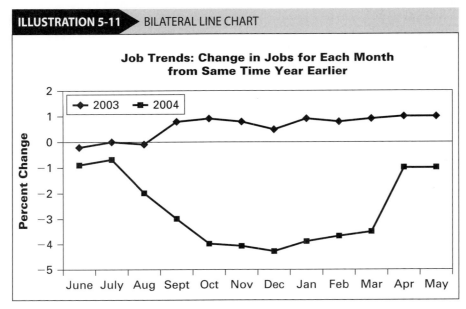

Source: *The New Nonprofit Almanac and Desk Reference, 2002*, p. 66.

ILLUSTRATION 5-11 BILATERAL LINE CHART

Job Trends: Change in Jobs for Each Month
from Same Time Year Earlier
2003
2004
2
1
0
−1
−2
−3
−4
−5
Percent Change
June July Aug Sept Oct Nov Dec Jan Feb Mar Apr May

Source: *The State, Columbia Business Journal,* July 12, 2004, p. 40.

ILLUSTRATION 5-12   HIGH-LOW CHART

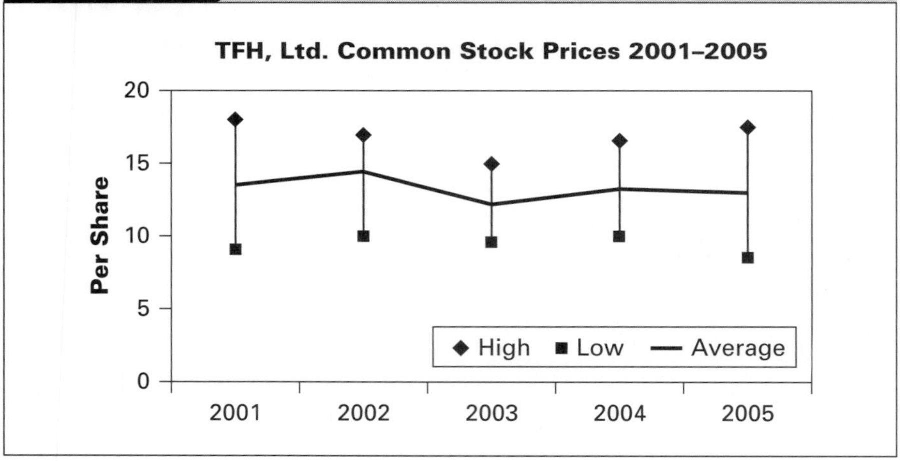

TFH, Ltd. Common Stock Prices 2001–2005

Source: Primary

The high-low chart is an interesting variation of the line chart. This chart permits you to show variations in values for a factor during a time period as well as the average value of the factor. A bar marks the high and low values, and a line is plotted through the bars to show the average values. Quarterly stock prices for a hypothetical company are shown in the high-low chart in Illustration 5-12.

A final line-chart variation that you may find useful is the cumulative line chart. (See Illustration 5-13.) In this chart, each plot point on the horizontal scale represents the total for that unit plus the previous amounts. To avoid misrepresentation, always label a cumulative line chart as such. Otherwise the reader may rightly assume that the chart is a basic line chart.

Whereas line charts show quantitative relationships, the next section presents two charts used to show nonquantitative information.

Relationship Charts

A *relationship chart* shows how several non-numeric factors act together. Two relationship charts that you may find useful in reports are the flow chart and the factor relationship chart.

FLOWCHARTS

A *flowchart* shows pictorially how a series of activities, operations, events, and other factors fit together to accomplish a full cycle. Complex flowcharts are often used as engineering or systems analysis tools. But simple flowcharts also can be used effectively in business reports to condense, clarify, or simplify a description of a series of activities.

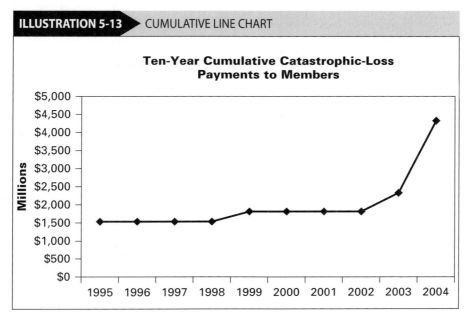

ILLUSTRATION 5-13   CUMULATIVE LINE CHART

Ten-Year Cumulative Catastrophic-Loss Payments to Members

Source: *2004 USAA Report to Members,* p. 11.

A flowchart consists of a title, shapes (squares, rectangles, triangles, etc.) to represent various elements in the process, labels to identify each element, and lines or arrows to connect the shapes and show the direction of flow. Although simple flowcharts may use a rectangle or a square for each element, many flowchart designers use the standard flowchart symbols shown on page 134.

A flowchart describing how to process a credit card statement is shown in Illustration 5-14.

FACTOR RELATIONSHIP CHARTS

A factor relationship chart is useful to describe nonlinear relationships. Such a chart shows how a primary factor and secondary factors interact with one another. The chart consists of a title, shapes to represent various factors that interact with one another, labels to identify those factors, and multiple arrows to show how the factors interact. The layout of this chart should draw the eye to the primary factor and clearly indicate how other factors interact with one another and with the primary factor. A relationship chart (Illustration 5-18) near the end of this chapter summarizes the collaborative writing process. That chart shows how various tasks and activities should interact for successful collaboration.

Although bar charts, pie charts, line charts, and relationship charts effectively summarize and simplify information, the amount of information that

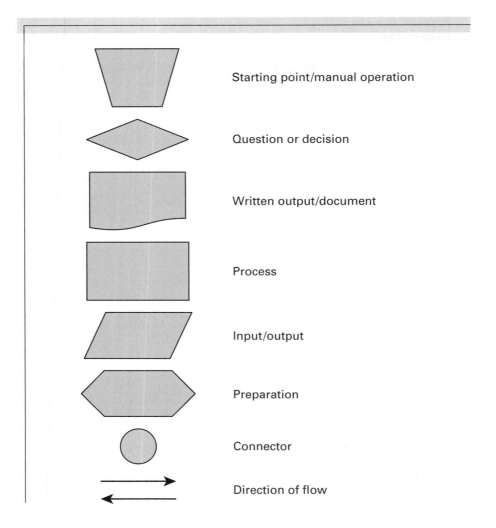

	Starting point/manual operation
	Question or decision
	Written output/document
	Process
	Input/output
	Preparation
	Connector
	Direction of flow

can be shown in such charts is limited. When greater detail is desired, a table is the best visual aid.

Tables

Both formal and informal tables are used in reports. A table consists of columns and rows of quantitative data, along with labels to identify the data. A formal table also has a title and generally has more identifying information than does an informal table.

A table surpasses all charts in ability to present detailed information. Consequently, you should use a table when you want the reader to compare exact figures. As the number of dimensions to be compared increases, the need for identifying labels also increases. Therefore, formal tables are required for presentation of complex data.

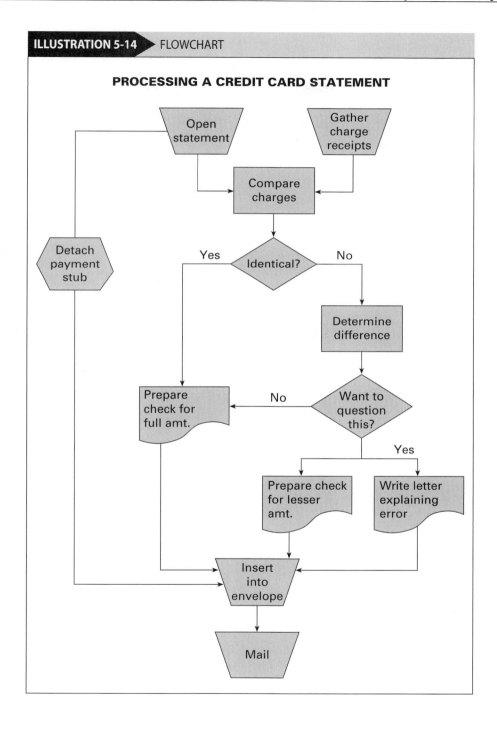

ILLUSTRATION 5-14 FLOWCHART

PROCESSING A CREDIT CARD STATEMENT

ILLUSTRATION 5-15 FORMAL TABLE

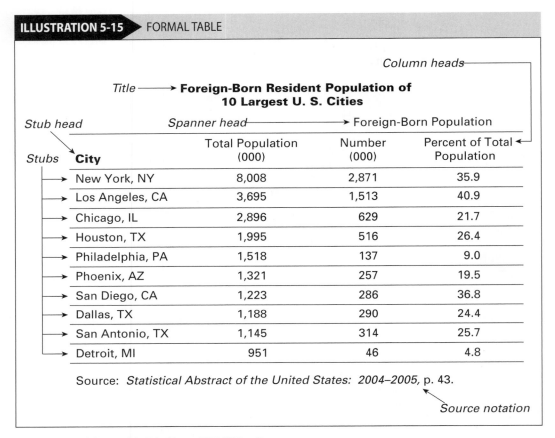

Column heads

Title → **Foreign-Born Resident Population of 10 Largest U. S. Cities**

Stub head

Spanner head → Foreign-Born Population

City	Total Population (000)	Number (000)	Percent of Total Population
New York, NY	8,008	2,871	35.9
Los Angeles, CA	3,695	1,513	40.9
Chicago, IL	2,896	629	21.7
Houston, TX	1,995	516	26.4
Philadelphia, PA	1,518	137	9.0
Phoenix, AZ	1,321	257	19.5
San Diego, CA	1,223	286	36.8
Dallas, TX	1,188	290	24.4
San Antonio, TX	1,145	314	25.7
Detroit, MI	951	46	4.8

Stubs

Source: *Statistical Abstract of the United States: 2004–2005*, p. 43.

Source notation

Source: *Statistical Abstract of the United States: 2004–2005,* p. 43.

FORMAL TABLES

As with charts, a formal table is separated from the report narrative and is identified by title. A formal table may also be numbered and show a source notation. In addition to columns and rows of numbers, other features of a formal table include column heads, stubs to identify rows, and stub heads. Some formal tables also contain a spanner head, which unifies the column heads. For clarity, you may use horizontal and vertical lines to separate heads. In long tables you can improve readability by inserting an extra line space about every five rows. Features of a formal table are identified in Illustration 5-15.

INFORMAL TABLES

An informal table is a brief tabulation inserted directly into the text. This type of table has no title, and column and stub heads may also be omitted if the text clearly identifies the table's contents. The following examples demonstrate techniques for including informal tables in a report.

Between 1994 and 2004, Lexington County showed the largest percentage increase in population, but its increase in bank deposits fell behind Richland County's.

County	Deposits in 2004	Change Since '94	Residents in 2004	Change Since '94	Per-Person Deposits, 2004
Lexington	$1,938,820	67%	231,057	23%	$ 8,388
Richland	$4,881,475	75%	334,609	11%	$17,577

(Source: *The State,* June 6, 2005)

Phoenix EPS has nearly doubled during the past five years in spite of unfavorable market conditions.

2005	$0.93
2004	.77
2003	−.62
2002	.26
2001	.58

Although charts and tables are the most common visual aids in reports, other visual aids are also used to add interest.

Other Visual Aids

Three visual aids that are especially effective to add interest to a report are pictures, pictographs, and statistical maps.

PICTURES

Because of their universal appeal, pictures effectively capture reader attention. That fact prompts many corporations to use pictures extensively in annual reports. You may also find opportunities to use pictures effectively in other business reports. Many report writers, for example, incorporate pictures into an oral presentation that supplements a written report.

Pictures tend to add a sense of reality to a report. With digital cameras, high-quality pictures are easy to take and integrate within reports. Although viewers know that pictures can be posed and that good photographers compose a picture, nonetheless many perceive pictures as truth. Because of that fact, an ethical obligation exists to ensure that pictures represent accurately the conditions they are intended to portray. For example, a picture of employees at work should accurately portray the environment in which the majority of employees work. Picturing the most favorable working conditions that perhaps only a few enjoy would present a distorted view of reality.

PICTOGRAPHS

A *pictograph* or pictogram is a diagram representing statistical data in pictorial form. Pictographs often portray quantitative data that might be presented in bar, pie, or line charts, but pictorial variations of those charts add interest and emphasis. Notice how the pictograph in Illustration 5-16 emphasizes the goal of Women to Women International, which is to help women around the world improve their economic well-being.

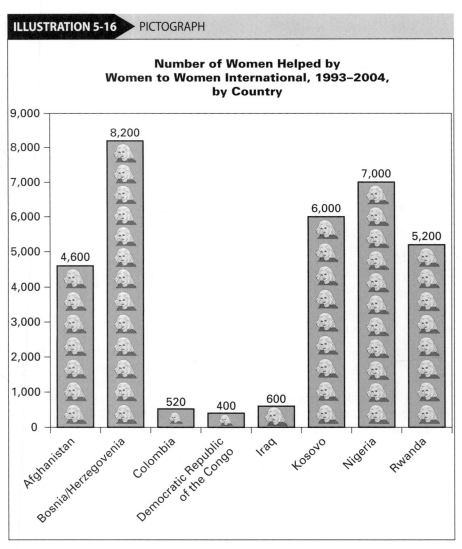

ILLUSTRATION 5-16 PICTOGRAPH

Number of Women Helped by Women to Women International, 1993–2004, by Country

Source: *Women to Women International Newsletter,* Summer 2005.

STATISTICAL MAPS

A statistical map presents numerical data superimposed on a map of the geographical units to which the data are related. Although the same data could be presented in a table or a bar chart, the map image helps the reader associate the data more directly with specific geographic areas.

Many variations of statistical maps can be designed, including separating and enlarging or exploding part of the map. One statistical map technique is demonstrated in Illustration 5-17.

ILLUSTRATION 5-17 STATISTICAL MAP

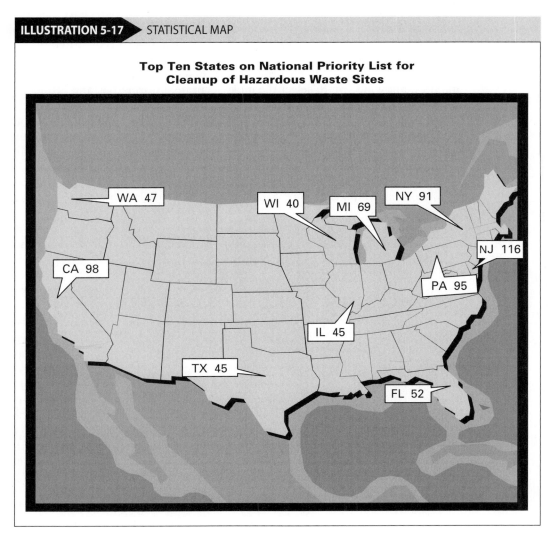

Top Ten States on National Priority List for Cleanup of Hazardous Waste Sites

Source: *Statistical Abstract of the United States: 2004–2005*, p. 225.

All visual aids discussed in this chapter can be constructed with the traditional tools of a pen and pencil, ruler, template, graph paper, camera, etc. Many corporations have graphics departments to help report writers prepare visual aids. However, with the advent of personal computers, graphics software, and digital cameras, many report writers now design visual aids efficiently and effectively with their own computers.

COMPUTER GRAPHICS

Computer graphics is a broad term that refers to computer-generated charts, diagrams, drawings, etc. The term refers to line charts, bar charts, or pie charts that can be produced from most spreadsheet software. It also applies to images made with computer graphics software and to sophisticated drawings generated by computer-assisted design (CAD) programs. Many of these user-friendly systems can plot numerous versions of the same data within minutes, allowing you to select the most accurate, informative, and attractive version.

Unlike the hand-drawn visuals of the past, computer graphics allow you to experiment with scales, formats, colors, perspectives, and patterns. Many systems use a WYSIWYG (What You See Is What You Get) approach, in which the on-screen display is virtually identical to the hard-copy image that will be printed out. Thus, by testing various format options on-screen, you can revise and enhance your visual repeatedly until it achieves your exact purposes.

Producing effective graphics by computer requires compatible software and hardware. A discussion of all options and technical standards is beyond the scope of this textbook. What you must know, however, is that to produce high-quality graphics you need a computer equipped with an appropriate graphics board, a graphics software package, and a compatible printer or plotter.

The job of the graphics software is to let you generate readable charts, diagrams, etc. Most spreadsheet applications such as Microsoft Excel, Lotus 1-2-3, and QuattroPro, and presentation graphics programs such as Microsoft PowerPoint, Lotus Freelance Graphics, and Harvard Graphics, permit even nontechnical people to generate quality line, bar, and pie charts from the data contained in the spreadsheet. Most business graphics software permits you to import data from a spreadsheet or enter quantitative data for the preparation of charts. In addition, graphics software usually contains a library of templates (ready-to-use shapes) and permits freehand drawing. With minimal practice, business report writers often master basic graphics production techniques and have at their disposal a wide range of options for illustrating their reports.

To prepare computer graphics, begin by assembling your data, usually in table form. Next, you must decide what type of visual you want to develop. For example, to make a pie chart showing sales of software by type, enter the data or select the data from an existing file. Add a title for the chart, as well as any necessary labels. Most programs will automatically generate legends for visuals. If you wish, however, you can easily customize titles and legends. The finished visual, in this case, the pie chart, can be printed on paper or imported into your word processing document to be printed with your finished report.

Graphics must be integrated strategically into the report narrative. The "import" or "insert" function in most word processing applications permits the writer to move visuals from a graphics application into the text composed in the word processing environment. Also available are integrated software packages that contain word processing, graphics, and other applications. With an integrated software package, a report writer can move easily from one application to another, and merge the work being done in more than one application. Thus, a writer can prepare the report narrative in word processing, go to a database to locate information, transfer that information into the graphics application to prepare a chart, and move that chart into the report narrative. Another useful feature of most word processing programs involves linking and importing tables. The table can be linked to the spreadsheet program so that the most current changes made in the worksheet will be reflected automatically in the table as it appears in the word processing document.

Although computer graphics applications can facilitate preparation of visual aids, you still are obligated to evaluate the effectiveness of the aid. Some report writers get carried away with the many options available, and they overload their reports with charts and diagrams. To use computer graphics effectively you must decide what data should be illustrated; then select the most appropriate aid to achieve your purpose, and follow the principles for effective graphics discussed earlier in this chapter. Avoid the temptation to demonstrate your computer graphics skill. Instead, demonstrate your total reporting skill. Here are some guidelines for creating computer graphics.

- Designate the visual as a figure, table, or illustration and assign it a number.
- Use the introduce-display-discuss technique to incorporate the visual into the most advantageous location within the text.
- Select patterns that are easily differentiated from one another. For example, for crosshatching a bar chart, use vertical lines to contrast with horizontal lines rather than with a diagonal pattern.
- Group related elements by color.
- Include white space around the visual so that it will stand out.
- Include a legend when there are two or more variables in the chart. When only one variable is present, use the title and axes to identify it.
- Label the axes so that they can be read without rotating the visual.
- Ensure that the title accurately states the desired message.
- Remove any unnecessary decorations or chart clutter.
- Cite the source, if applicable, using proper bibliographical form.

The major advantage of using computer graphics is that you can produce professional-looking reports if you have the right configuration of software and hardware and take time to learn graphics techniques. Benefits include near-professional quality visuals, shorter preparation time, and substantial savings in preparation costs. The major disadvantage is that some users have little graphics knowledge and do not know how to design visually effective displays. Following the guides for visual aids presented in this chapter should help you to avoid that disadvantage.

ETHICAL CONSIDERATIONS

A final criterion for effective visual aids is that all visuals must be ethical representations of data. Although you may use visuals effectively to emphasize, summarize, etc., you should avoid distortion of data. Visuals can sometimes have more impact than their accompanying text for three reasons.[2]

- Visuals have an emotional impact that words lack.
- Skimmers of items will see visuals even when they do not read the text.
- Readers remember visuals longer.

A report narrative may present comprehensive and accurate data, but readers tend to gain first impressions of information from visual aids. Those first impressions and visual images often influence the reader more strongly than does the verbal narrative.

You can avoid distortion by attending carefully to scale dimensions and sizes of symbols (bars, circles, boxes, etc.) used in your visual aids. Line charts are especially vulnerable to distortion. When improperly drawn or when a scale is collapsed, they can exaggerate growth or minimize problems. The distance between all units of measurement on each axis must be equal, except for proportional-line charts, which are too complex for inclusion in this discussion. Although the units of measurement on the vertical axis (y-axis or ordinate) of a line or bar chart need not be the same size as the units on the horizontal axis (x-axis or abscissa), making them approximately the same can avoid distortion. Further, if you use symbols to compare items, draw those symbols to an accurate scale so that relative size represents appropriate comparisons. Charts can also mislead if they are incomplete. Remember that a key element for preparing effective reports is completeness.

The following examples demonstrate the distortion that may result from changing the size of scale units or of objects used in comparisons. Notice that changing the horizontal scale units makes the rise in expenses appear more gradual, and showing expenses with a smaller circle makes expenses appear to be considerably smaller than revenue, even though no data about amounts are given.

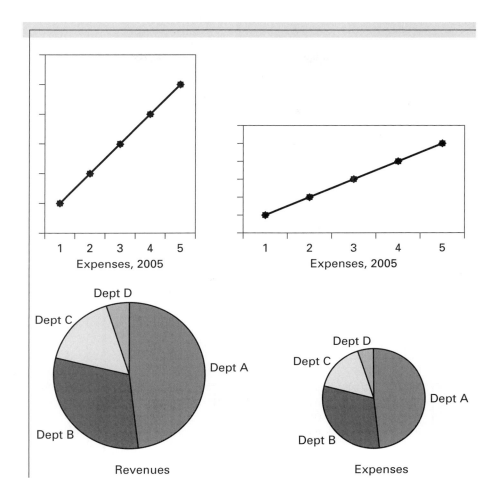

COLLABORATIVE WRITING

Previous chapters have introduced you to collaborative writing (CW) and ways to improve the collaborative process. You have probably come to realize that effective collaboration includes many kinds of activities that occur before, during, and after the actual writing activity. In a work setting (and in many classrooms) some of the pre-writing tasks are undertaken by someone in a supervisory position. For example, a supervisor or instructor defines the goal of a project and sets up the conditions that will foster collaborative work. (See Illustration 5-18, Pre-CW task.) After the group members have been notified of the task, they must first form a team, as opposed to a mere collection of people. Only after team formation can they effectively move on to planning the task and producing the document. After the document has been produced, perhaps in its near-final version, the effective team engages in

ILLUSTRATION 5-18 COLLABORATIVE WRITING TASKS AND ACTIVITIES[3]

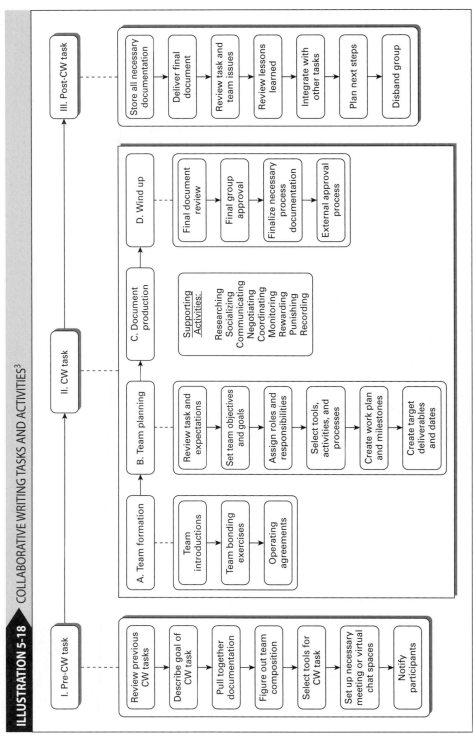

Source: *Lowry, Curtis, and Lowry, p. 73.*

purposeful wind-up work. (See Illustration 5-18, CW task.) If the collaborative writing task is to be a learning experience with benefits for both the team members and the organization, the task-related activities extend beyond the point at which the document is approved. In addition to delivering the document to appropriate recipients, the team and its supervisor can benefit from reviewing the process and lessons learned from working together. (See Illustration 5-18, Post-CW task.)

Whenever you are assigned to a collaborative writing group, the model shown in Illustration 5-18 can serve as a guide to ensure that essential tasks are not omitted. Awareness of all aspects of collaborative writing should improve your CW experiences.

SUMMARY

Visual aids may be used to emphasize, clarify, simplify, reinforce, or summarize report data. In addition, effective visual aids add interest to a report, improve the credibility of the report and its writer, and increase report coherence.

Effective visual aids demonstrate simplicity, contrast, unity, and balance. All parts of the aids are identified fully, and the aid itself is identified by title and keyed into the report. The most effective placement of visuals is in the report narrative, preferably immediately after a brief introductory statement. Effective visual aids are also ethical representations of data; that is, they are accurate "pictures," not distortions of reality.

Useful visual aids consist of bar, pie, line, and relationship charts; formal and informal tables; pictures, pictographs, and statistical maps. Computer graphics software and appropriate computer hardware help contemporary report writers construct those aids. Designers must apply all principles for effective graphics when using computer graphics as well as when constructing visuals manually.

During your career, you will likely be part of a collaborative writing team or a supervisor who requests that a team produce a document. Whether you are a supervisor or a team writer, attention to the wide array of pre-writing, writing, and post-writing tasks will contribute to successful collaboration.

TOPICS FOR DISCUSSION

1. Identify and explain the eight purposes of visual aids in reports.

2. Explain the significance of each of the following principles of graphics:
   a. Simplicity
   b. Contrast
   c. Unity
   d. Balance

3. Explain what is needed in a well-written title for a visual aid.

4. Improve the following introductory statements for visual aids:
   a. Table 1 shows the net profits for Company 1, Company 2, and Company 3 in <year>.
   b. As Figure 1 indicates, collaborative writing tasks can be grouped into three stages.
   c. The following bar chart shows peach production by county in Georgia for <year>.

5. Describe the three-step technique for incorporating visual aids into a report.

6. Compare and contrast the following visual aids:
   - Simple bar chart, multiple bar chart, and bilateral bar chart
   - Bar chart and pie chart
   - Basic line chart, multiple line chart, band chart, and cumulative line chart
   - Flowchart and factor relationship chart
   - Formal table and informal table
   - Picture and pictograph

7. Give guides for constructing each of the following visual aids:
   - Bar chart
   - Pie chart
   - Line chart

8. Identify potential benefits and problems of using computer graphics in reports. If you have had experience using computer software to develop graphics, describe that experience for your classmates. What was easiest to master? What was most difficult to master?

9. Discuss ways in which data may be misrepresented in visual aids.

10. Identify two techniques for avoiding distortion in visual aids.

11. Explain the three major stages of collaborative writing. What special challenges may arise if a writing team must incorporate several visual aids into its report?

APPLICATIONS

1. Which visual would be the most appropriate to illustrate the following types of information? Be prepared to support your decision while recognizing that for some items, several alternatives may be possible.

   a. A comparison of sales volume, customer volume, and number of employees of the top eight worldwide restaurant systems
   b. A comparison of the sales of a Fortune 500 company for two product lines for the last three years
   c. The mean, maximum, and minimum temperatures for your city for each month of the year
   d. The profits for a company for the past five years

e. The percentage breakdown of employees by gender and ethnic background for an organization

f. The relative market share for the top three software producers in the U.S.

g. An explanation of how to assemble a gas barbecue grill

h. Sales, profits, and assets of the five largest U.S. industrial corporations

i. A breakdown of auto production by country (four countries) and model types (three types)

j. A breakdown of your monthly budget

2. Locate a visual that needs improvement. You may want to look in newspapers, magazines, textbooks, brochures, newsletters, or computer manuals. Revise and enhance the visual. Submit to your instructor a copy of the original, along with a memo explaining your improvements.

3. Compare and contrast the visuals used in two corporate annual reports. Critique those visuals, applying criteria you have learned while studying this chapter. Present the criteria and your critique in a three-page manuscript report to your instructor.

4. Conduct research and develop a visual to illustrate one or more of the following sets of data. Incorporate the visual into a short memorandum report, applying the introduce-display-discuss technique presented in this chapter.
   - How managers spend time during a typical day
   - Number of auto registrations in your state (or county), by these vehicle types: SUVs, vans, pickups
   - Amount (percent) of time you spend on various activities during a week
   - Number of violent crimes in your city during each of the past six months
   - Increase in Medicare Part B premiums since 2000

5. Prepare a visual showing how selected occupations ranked in terms of the public's perception of honesty and ethical standards: Nurses, 79%; Grade school teachers, 73%; Druggists, 72%; Military officers, 72%; Medical doctors, 67%; Policemen, 60%; Clergy, 56%; Judges, 53%; Day care providers, 49%; Bankers, 36%; Auto mechanics, 26%; Local officeholders, 26%; Nursing home operators, 24%; State officeholders, 24%; TV reporters, 23%; Newspaper reporters, 21%; Business executives, 20%; Members of Congress, 20%; Lawyers, 18%; Ad practitioners, 10%; Car salespersons, 9%. Source: Gallup Poll, Nov. 19–21, 2004.

6. Devise a pictograph that shows the composition of LifeStyle decorative paint products. Each gallon of paint contains the following percentages of ingredients:

Titanium Dioxide	18.4%
Silicates	10.4%
Calcium Carbonate	5.0%
Tinting Colors	1.0%
Water and Synthetic Rubber Emulsion Base	65.2%

7. In 2004, Nobuko Company (hypothetical) had sales of $1.9 million. Broken down, the revenue came from the following product lines: Jewelry, 39%; Personal Care Products, 34%; Food Products, 21%; Novelties, 4%; Other Products, 2%.

   The company's pretax profit totaled $319,000 and came from the same lines as above, but in the following percentages: Jewelry, 47%; Personal care products, 29%; Food products, 14%; Novelties, 6%; Other products, 4%.

   - Incorporate the data into an illustration to show the relationship between the sales of each product line and the pretax profits from the same lines.
   - Convert the sales and pretax profit percentages into dollar amounts, and construct an illustration to show those amounts for each product division.

8. You are a sales manager for Santiago and Son's, Inc., a large local furniture store in your area. You must report to your supervisor, the owner, about the annual efforts of your sales area and of the individual efforts of your sales force. In one section of your report you decide to show the percentage of change from last year's sales for each of your sales associates. These are your data (name of associate, percentage of change): Jose Ruiz, +3.5; Sophie Davis, +3.7; Jean March, −7.3; Victor Heldago, −10; Amy Wilson, +15.3; Thom Profit, −1.5; James Cummings, −6.2; Teresa Davis, −13.1; Arlis Jamison, +7.1; Harrison Toomey, +11.2.

   Prepare only this section of the report; write the sentence that will precede the illustration; prepare the illustration and insert it into the narrative; and write the discussion that will follow it. Remember to interpret the data; don't merely repeat it.

9. You work as the Wellness Director for the Human Resources Division of a large insurance company. You want to publish information in your monthly newsletter that will stimulate employees to think about their weight and the potential need to lose weight. Here are some data you will use in your newsletter. (Source: *AARP Bulletin*, June 2005, p. 15.)

Weight Ranges (in pounds)

Height	Normal	Overweight	Obese	Extremely Obese
5'0"	97–127	128–152	153–203	204–276
5'3"	107–140	141–168	169–224	225–304
5'6"	118–154	155–185	186–246	247–334
5'9"	128–168	169–202	203–269	270–365
6'0"	140–183	184–220	221–293	294–397
6'3"	152–199	200–239	240–318	319–431

Construct an appropriate visual to present this information. Incorporate it into a page of text that can be used in the newsletter.

10. A major state university released the Grade Point Averages of its athletes, overall and by team. Here are the data: Overall, 2.886; Baseball, 3.005; Men's basketball, 2.910; Women's basketball, 2.992; Equestrian, 2.980; Football, 2.217; Men's golf, 3.502; Women's golf, 3.671; Men's soccer, 2.703; Women's soccer, 3.356; Softball, 3.266; Men's swimming and diving, 2.850; Women's swimming and diving, 3.303; Men's tennis, 3.538; Women's tennis, 3.369; Men's track and field, 2.831; Women's track and field, 3.265; Volleyball, 2.769. Construct an appropriate visual aid to represent some or all of the data (depending on the main point you want to convey). Incorporate that visual into a memorandum report sent from the Director of Athletics to all Academic Department Heads. Remember to use the introduce-display-discuss technique.

11. A state retirement system sends an annual report to each person insured by that program. Part of the report compares benefit expenses and revenues received for a period of five years. Here are the data by year, expressed in millions of dollars. Benefit expenses: *2000, 973; 2001, 1,126; 2002, 1,369; 2003, 1,493; 2004, 1,655.* Revenues received: *2000, 1,868; 2001, 2,547; 2002, 1,274; 2003, 2,937; 2004, 3,077.*

    Some lawmakers and pensioners have expressed concern about the solvency of the system. Prepare a visual aid to represent the data. Incorporate the aid into one page of text that can be used in the annual report. Be sure to discuss the data in an interpretive manner.

12. The pension fund mentioned in Application 11 held the following investments as of June 30, 2004. Here are the data, shown by investment category, in thousands of dollars: Common trust funds, 5,293,944; Common stocks, 4,967,547; Corporate bonds, 4,441,928; Short-term investments, 3,339,280; Financial & other, 2,322,343; U.S. gov't agencies, 2,006,362; U.S. gov't bonds, 1,711,502; Convertible bonds, 3,227; Convertible preferred stock, 408. Construct an appropriate visual aid to represent the data. Incorporate it into a short memo report from the fund manager to the legislative Budget and Control Board.

13. You have been asked to improve a brochure intended to attract entering students into your department or college of business. The text of the brochure looks intimidating, sounds confusing, and could actually drive students away from majoring in business. After reading the following statement, develop a visual that could follow the narrative and add clarification.

    Entering students must have a minimum of a 2.5 GPA (A=4.0); then they, in their chosen majors, work through several modules of courses. First there are the introductory courses like Introduction to Business (BUS 240), Personal Finance (FIN 220), and Careers in Business and Industry (BUS 230). Then there are the skills courses like Business Writing (BUS 260), Statistics (MAT 150), and Business Law (BUS 270). Next come the core courses like Management Concepts (BUS 340), Principles of Marketing (MKT 310), Principles of Accounting (ACT 350), and Foundations of Economics (ECO 325). Finally, the capstone course, Business Policy (BUS 480), should be completed. Students must also select four courses in their selected majors. Please see your department for an updated list of major courses.

14. You work as a research associate for a major publisher. Your company wants to capture more of the leisure dollar by stimulating people to read more books. You have been asked to find out how much U.S. citizens currently spend on various categories of entertainment. This is what you have found (Source: *Statistical Abstract of the United States: 2004–2005*, p. 766.).

Expenditures per Consumer Unit for Entertainment
(annual averages, in dollars)

Region of Country	Fees and Admissions	TV, Radio, and Sound Equipment	Other Equipment and Services	Reading
Northeast	657	725	905	165
Midwest	538	688	917	149
South	419	643	643	103
West	644	747	1,044	162

Construct an appropriate visual aid to represent some or all of the data (depending on the main point you want to convey). Incorporate that visual into a memorandum report sent from you to the Director of Marketing. Use the introduce-display-discuss technique.

REFERENCES

1. Lefferts, R. (1981). *How to prepare charts and graphs for effective reports.* New York: Barnes and Noble Books.

2. Kienzler, D. D. (April, 1997). Visual ethics. *The Journal of Business Communication, 34,* 171–187.

3. Lowry, P. B., Curtis, A., & Lowry, M. R. (2004). Building a taxonomy and nomenclature of collaborative writing to improve interdisciplinary research and practice. *Journal of Business Communication, 41(1),* 66–99.

Writing Routine Reports

You will write and receive many kinds of simple reports during your career. A simple report (sometimes called a short report) does not require an extensive search for the necessary information. In many instances you will recall from memory the principal data for the report. In other situations you may refer to minutes of meetings, data from files, notes written during an experience or observation, or messages given to you by other employees or clients.

Although the data-gathering method may be relatively simple, the resulting report is still a significant element in your organization's decision process. Your job performance and career advancement will certainly be influenced by simple reports—those written by others and those that you write.

Simple reports can be further classified as routine and nonroutine reports. A *routine report* is one that you will be expected to prepare as a part of your normal work assignment. Its purpose is to keep people informed of how you are accomplishing your regular duties. A weekly production report is an example of a routine report. That report and others are demonstrated in this chapter.

In contrast, a *nonroutine report* deals with an occurrence that is an exception to your daily activities and responsibilities. For example, you may be permitted to grant a potentially lucrative customer a larger-than-normal discount on an initial order. However, since that is not the normal sales procedure, you would likely write an exception report to notify your supervisor of your actions. Chapter 7 presents that type of report and other nonroutine reports.

TYPICAL ROUTINE REPORTS

To illustrate every kind of report you will encounter is impossible; but the examples that follow illustrate the most common routine reports used in contemporary businesses: form reports, trip reports, production reports, progress reports, and meeting reports.

Form Reports

When an organization requires frequent reporting of the same categories of information, efficiency may be gained by developing a standard form for that report. For example, most health insurance companies send reports to the insured parties indicating how a claim for payment of medical services has been processed. Since an insurance company processes many such claims each day and reports standard categories of information to its customers, using a standard form expedites the reporting process. Illustration 6-1 demonstrates such a form report. Other kinds of reports that may be simplified by the use of a well-designed form are reports related to sales and production, repairs or use of equipment and vehicles, and activity on delivery routes.

Trip Reports

Your career responsibilities will often require that you travel away from your home base for a number of reasons: to attend a convention or trade show, to observe activities at another work site, to interview a potential employee, to sell your company's products or services, etc. When your supervisor authorizes your travel, that person will be accountable for your time and expenses. Therefore, the supervisor needs information to evaluate whether the company benefits from your travel. The purpose of a trip report is to provide that information.

A trip report should be brief and factual. Although you may comment about the value of the trip, do not clutter the message with personal reflections about the good—or bad—time you had. Provide complete, clear, well-organized information that will permit the supervisor to draw conclusions or take action. Appropriate style and structure for a trip report are demonstrated in Illustration 6-2. Notice that the report uses a concise but complete subject line, topical structure, headings that clearly identify the topics, and a concrete request for response. Other structures, such as a chronological or log structure, could also be appropriate in some circumstances. Many companies use a standard form for reporting trip activities and requesting reimbursement for travel expenses.

Production Reports

Most jobs require periodic reports about individual or group performance—production reports. Sales representatives, supervisors of manufacturing units, service technicians, and some office employees may be required to submit daily or weekly production reports. Other employees, such as insurance claims examiners, college professors, librarians, or loan officers may prepare production reports less frequently—monthly, quarterly, or annually. The closest that some

ILLUSTRATION 6-1 ▶ FORM REPORT TO INSURANCE CLIENT

HEALTH INSURANCE, INC.
4361 STATE STREET
MARION, IN 46952
(317) 555-6580

I.D. Number: 371-14-2209
Patient Name: Thomas Svenson
Relationship: Spouse
Group Number: 002036590
Claim Number: 718941593
Date of Notice: 07/14/<year>
Date of Service: 07/08/<year>

Policyholder:

Lorraine Svenson
116 Varsity Drive
South Bend, IN 46322

Explanation of Benefits   THIS IS NOT A BILL

Service Provider	Date of Service	Amount Charged	Noncovered Amount/Reason	Covered Amount	Copayment	Amount Paid
Bailey Phys. Partners Medical Services	10/11/<year>	846.00	471.00 01	375.00	75.00	300.00

Total health benefits paid for this person this benefit period:	797.80	The payment for this claim has been sent to the provider	300.00
Lifetime Health Benefits Paid for this person to date:	9,338.10	Balance due to provider	546.00

Remarks:

01 This amount exceeds the maximum allowable benefit for this service

ILLUSTRATION 6-2 ▸ TRIP REPORT IN MEMO FORMAT

DATE: April 13, <year>

TO: Michael Dreyer

FROM: Noah Isaacs

SUBJECT: Inspection Trip, McNabb Project, April 12, <year>

As you requested, I went to Chesapeake yesterday to inspect the McNabb project and investigate why it has fallen behind schedule. Here is what I learned.

Construction Quality

All completed phases of the project meet our quality standards. Invoices and samples of materials indicate that building materials meet the specifications set forth in our RFPs. Files in the construction office contain reports from local building inspectors showing that requirements of local codes have been met.

Construction Delays

Several factors contributed to construction delays during the past two months:

1. The supplier who was awarded the contract for plumbing supplies initially delivered substandard materials. The construction chief, David Bowen, insisted on the quality specified in the contract. Those materials were delivered two weeks later.

2. Since our policy is to pay skilled-labor crews only when they are actually on the job, Bowen could not pay the plumbing crew while waiting for the materials. Consequently that crew moved to another construction project.

3. Because of the high demand for and low supply of skilled-labor crews in the Chesapeake area, we lost another week while Bowen tried to hire a new plumbing crew. Naturally, some phases of construction could not be completed until the basic plumbing system was installed.

Requests

Bowen asks that he be authorized to pay skilled-labor crews for up to one week of waiting time when delays are caused by shortages of materials. He acknowledges that weather-related delays are normally considered an occupational hazard for which construction crews are not compensated. But in today's tight labor market, we risk losing good crews if we refuse to pay them for other delays.

ILLUSTRATION 6-2	CONTINUED

Michael Dreyer — 2 — April 13, <year>

Additional Information

I have reminded Bowen that he must report failure of suppliers to meet bid specifications immediately. If he had reported the supplier's actions earlier, we perhaps could have transferred plumbing materials from other projects or put pressure on the supplier to fulfill the contract terms promptly.

I also asked Bowen to submit a monthly progress report detailing what has been completed, problems encountered, and any other information needed that will help us help him meet project goals.

Request for Response

I promised Bowen that I'd give him an answer before April 30 about paying crews for waiting time. Please let me know your decision.

employees come to preparing a production report is the completion of a self-evaluation before a formal performance appraisal; nonetheless, that is also a production report.

A production report is important employee-to-manager feedback. The purpose of such a report is to let a manager or supervisor know whether individual employees or work units are meeting performance goals. The report usually identifies quantities and units of production (for example, customers contacted, items manufactured, loans closed, claims processed, etc.) during an identified time period. Comments about the production experience, such as difficulties encountered or successes enjoyed, are also appropriate. Many production reports also include a work plan or objectives for the next period. Those kinds of information help managers evaluate an individual employee's contributions to the organization's success. The report may tell the manager that all is well and no intervention is needed, or the report may provide evidence that potential or immediate problems require the manager's intervention or assistance.

A typical production report is demonstrated in Illustration 6-3. Notice that the report form clearly identifies the kind of information the manager needs. The report could have been prepared in memo format if the company had not designed a form. A production report in memo format is shown in Illustration 6-4.

Although most production reports flow from subordinates to superiors, supervisors or managers may also send production reports to their subordinates. These reports are often summaries of the unit's production and may be sent to bolster the morale of a unit with evidence of its accomplishments. An

ILLUSTRATION 6-3 FORM PRODUCTION REPORT

FAST TRACK DELIVERIES

Sales Representative: _____Powell Henderson_____

Rep. Number: _____103_____   District: _____7_____

Month: _____April_____   Date Submitted: _____5/1/<year>_____

New Clients

Prospects contacted	63
New clients from those contacts	19
Total pickups	123
Total deliveries	51
Total revenues related to new clients	$2,740.50

Current Clients

Total pickups	326
Total deliveries	215
Total revenues from current clients	$8,520.75
Total revenue for month	$11,261.25

Plans for Next Month (Use additional pages if needed.)

The increasing volume of pickups and deliveries restricts the amount of time I can spend calling on prospective clients. I plan to hire a driver to handle most of the pickup and delivery work. I hope to have someone on the job by May 15.

My goal for May is to add a minimum of 30 new clients and retain those currently using our services. With an assistant to handle the pickups and deliveries, I will have more time to contact potential clients and make follow-up calls on current users.

ILLUSTRATION 6-4	PRODUCTION REPORT IN MEMO FORMAT

Date: May 1, <year>

To: Kira McKimson

From: Powell Henderson, Agent No. 103

Subject: Sales and Delivery Activity, April <year>

By targeting new clients and providing prompt service to established clients, I have been able to increase revenues in my territory by approximately 33 percent in April. Here is a summary of my activity:

New Clients

Prospects contacted	63	
New clients from those contacts	19	
Total pickups	123	
Total deliveries	51	
Total revenues related to new clients		$2,740.50

Established Clients

Total pickups	326	
Total deliveries	215	
Total revenues		$8,520.75

Total Revenue $11,261.25

Plans for May <year>

The increasing volume of pickups and deliveries restricts the amount of time I can spend calling on prospective clients. I plan to hire a driver to handle most of the pickup and delivery work. I hope to have someone on the job by May 15.

My goal for May is to add a minimum of 30 new clients and retain those currently using our services. With an assistant to handle the pickups and deliveries, I will have more time to contact potential clients and make follow-up calls on current users.

ILLUSTRATION 6-5 ▶ E-MAIL PRODUCTION REPORT

Mail Server

From / To

REPLY

Fast Track Agents

Subject

April Revenue: Up 25%

Message

Forward

Thanks to your diligent sales and service efforts, Fast Track revenues for April increased 25% over last month.

You are doing a great job of promoting the same-day delivery concept and providing the service our clients have a right to expect. Keep up the great work.

Delete

Kira McKimson

example of a supervisor-to-employees production report is shown in Illustration 6-5. Since the primary purpose of the report is to enhance morale, the relatively informal medium—e-mail—and style are appropriate.

Progress Reports

A progress report is similar to a production report. However, a progress report is related to a major, usually one-time, project. In some organizations, this report is called a status report.

Progress reports must include all information needed by the manager to evaluate whether the project will be completed as planned. Such information could include the current status and projected completion dates of the entire project or parts of it. Accomplishments since the last report, difficulties encountered (if any), difficulties anticipated (if any), and budget data are also appropriate content for a progress report. Some contracts for major projects provide that a penalty will be assessed if the project is not completed as scheduled. In such instances a progress report is an important tool to ensure that penalties are not incurred for failure to meet scheduled completion dates.

Progress reports are production messages that must be written in a style, structure, and format that permit the manager to learn quickly what is happening on a project for which that person is accountable. Study the content, style, structure, format, and tone of the progress report in Illustration 6-6. That report demonstrates the combined structure: direct (deductive), topical, and chronological.

Meeting Reports

Much of an organization's business is conducted in face-to-face or electronically mediated meetings. These sessions may range from the meeting of a project team, a standing committee, or an *ad hoc* committee within a company to a major assemblage of members of a professional or trade association. In all cases, the meeting organizer or chairperson is responsible for informing participants—and often company managers—of upcoming activities and results of the meetings. The most common tools for communicating such information are the agenda and minutes.

MEETING AGENDA

An agenda provides potential participants with the information needed to prepare effectively for the meeting. A complete agenda includes the name of the person or agency calling the meeting; the date, time, and location of the meeting; and a schedule of business to be conducted. The schedule of business is often structured as follows:

1. Call to order
2. Correction and approval of minutes of <date> meeting
3. Reports of standing committees or subcommittees (identify each that will report)
4. Reports of special committees or subcommittees (identify each that will report)
5. Unfinished business (include appropriate details)
6. New business (include appropriate details)
7. Announcements (may include "good of the order," an opportunity for members to bring information or concerns to the group)
8. Adjournment

Although some meetings may not require all elements listed, an effective agenda includes everything that will enable participants to come to the meeting prepared to conduct business efficiently.

Many organizations today find that the speed and efficiency of e-mail makes it an ideal medium for transmission of a meeting agenda. An example of such an agenda appears in Illustration 6-7.

MINUTES OF MEETING

To ensure accurate records of its accomplishments, every group that conducts meetings should appoint or elect a recorder or secretary. That person's task is to take notes during the group's deliberations and provide minutes, a written record of the group's decisions. The minutes are sent to meeting participants and other persons who have an interest in that work.

ILLUSTRATION 6-6 ▶ PROGRESS REPORT IN MEMO FORMAT

DATE: May 31, <year>

TO: Frederick Cox, City Manager

FROM: Chao-chen Yang, Systems Coordinator

SUBJECT: Progress on Implementation of Geographic Information System (GIS)

After overcoming some initial problems, we are well on the way to an operational GIS that will improve productivity for many areas of Orlando city government.

Tasks Completed

During the past four months we have established the working base for an effective Geographic Information System. Specifically, this is what we did:

- Held meetings with key members of each department in city government to explain the objectives, functions, and benefits of GIS.

- Identified with those key members the kinds of geographic information their departments need for effective operations.

- Identified the kinds of information each department should supply to establish the initial data-base.

- Ran sample reports for each department to demonstrate the speed, accuracy, and versatility of the GIS.

Problems Encountered

The primary problems were lack of knowledge and lack of trust. We resolved both problems in these ways:

- Held small-group discussions in each department.

- Assigned one systems analyst to a full-time consulting position to help departments identify their needs and potential uses for GIS.

- Demonstrated specific ways each department could use the system.

ILLUSTRATION 6-6 ▶ CONTINUED

Frederick Cox — 2 — May 31, <year>

Target Dates for Remainder of Project

We plan to have the GIS in full operation by September 1. The following target dates have been set for completion of major parts of the project:

June 15   Collection of data from each department for database

June 30   Entry of data

August 30   Training of potential GIS users

Additional Information

The next two months are critical to the success of the Geographic Information System. Collecting and entering data can become routine, and people who could benefit from a successful system may get discouraged. I suggest we arrange several trips for key employees to observe the GIS operation in Miami. That city has had an effective system in operation for three years. The police, zoning, business licensing, tax, and traffic planning departments are especially enthusiastic about the kinds of maps the system can generate to help them with their work.

Minutes are summaries of actions taken, not verbatim transcripts of the deliberations. Minutes should include only objective data and actions, not subjective generalities. For example, although members of a committee may comment about the superior quality of a subcommittee's work, the minutes should report only the facts presented by the subcommittee and the action taken by the full group. Unless the group passes an official resolution that includes descriptive words (such as *brilliant, outstanding, superb;* or *faulty, inefficient, ineffective*), the recorder should avoid descriptive adjectives. Those terms could be problematical if they are considered to reflect the group's opinion when in fact they represent only the recorder's interpretation of something that occurred in the meeting.

Minutes usually include the following data:

1. Identification of group
2. Classification of meeting (for example, regular, monthly, quarterly, special, emergency)
3. Location, date, and time of meeting
4. Identification of people in attendance and the person presiding
5. Identification of absentees along with reasons for the absences or excused/ unexcused notation

ILLUSTRATION 6-7   E-MAIL AGENDA FOR MEETING

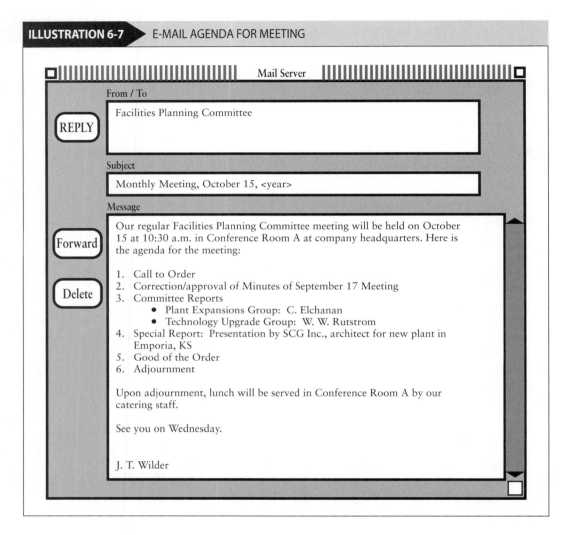

Mail Server

REPLY

From / To

Facilities Planning Committee

Subject

Monthly Meeting, October 15, <year>

Message

Forward

Delete

Our regular Facilities Planning Committee meeting will be held on October 15 at 10:30 a.m. in Conference Room A at company headquarters. Here is the agenda for the meeting:

1. Call to Order
2. Correction/approval of Minutes of September 17 Meeting
3. Committee Reports
    - Plant Expansions Group: C. Elchanan
    - Technology Upgrade Group: W. W. Rutstrom
4. Special Report: Presentation by SCG Inc., architect for new plant in Emporia, KS
5. Good of the Order
6. Adjournment

Upon adjournment, lunch will be served in Conference Room A by our catering staff.

See you on Wednesday.

J. T. Wilder

6. Reference to minutes of previous meeting: accepted as presented or amended and then accepted
7. Reports of action on matters previously presented to the group (old business)
8. Reports of action on matters currently presented to the group (new business)
9. Reports of "good of the order" information
10. Place and time of next meeting
11. Time of adjournment
12. Identification of person responsible for preparing the minutes

Formats for minutes vary among organizations, but the format should enable each reader to focus easily on any item that may be of special interest to that person. An example of such a format appears in Illustration 6-8.

ILLUSTRATION 6-8 MINUTES OF MEETING

NORCAL TEXTILES, INC.
Minutes of Facilities Planning Committee Meeting
(regular monthly meeting)

Time/Date/Place	10:30 a.m., October 15, <year>, corporate headquarters
Presiding Officer	J. T. Wilder
Members Present	D. C. Blackburn, G. E. Bradley, C. Elchanan, S. K. Leung, W. W. Rutstrom
Member Absent	J. L. Palij (representing the company at the Fiber Manufacturers Association Meeting in New Orleans)
Minutes Approved:	Minutes of the September 15, <year>, meeting were approved as distributed
Committee Reports	Plant Expansions: Elchanan reported that expansions of the plants at Bartlesville, OK, and Hutchinson, KS, are proceeding as planned. Production schedules have slowed slightly during this building program, but all orders have been filled on schedule. The expansions should be completed early next year.
	Technology Upgrade: Rutstrom presented proposals from two rapid access ISPs, NETlink and USA-World. After reviewing the proposals, the committee voted to accept NETlink and authorized Rutstrom to sign the contract with that company.
Special Report	C. D. Heilmann from SCG, Inc., presented the architectural plans for the Emporia, KS, plant. Modifications to the shipping and receiving areas and the fitness facility were discussed. Heilmann was instructed to incorporate the desired changes into the plans and present the modified drawings at the November meeting.
Next Meeting	The next regular meeting of the committee will be held at 1:30 p.m. on November 19. The location will be announced when the agenda is distributed.
Adjournment	The meeting was adjourned at 12:15 p.m.

Respectfully submitted

W. W. Rutstrom

W. W. Rutstrom

ETHICAL CONSIDERATIONS

A major ethical challenge that arises during the preparation of routine reports is the need to maintain objectivity. Because the primary data sources for many routine reports are the writer's memory or notes made during or after an observation or experience, the writer must constantly separate her or his feelings and opinions from the objective facts.

For example, as you write a report about your trip to a trade show, you may recall the pleasant experiences you had—building your professional network, eating in fine restaurants, seeing some of the sights of a city you had not visited before. Although you would enjoy attending another show of this type, you must objectively evaluate the benefit your company receives from sending you to such an event. If, in fact, you learned little or made few contacts that you can use to benefit your organization, your report should include those facts. The report then might end with a recommendation that the company should re-evaluate or discontinue its practice of sending a representative to that event.

Similarly, as you write a report about the status of a major project, you must include objective statements about what has been accomplished and any difficulties encountered. If the project is behind schedule, you should include factual statements about what can or cannot be done to bring it back on schedule, not your "feelings" that you can inspire everyone to work hard and get the job done.

SUMMARY

The most common routine reports are form, trip, production, progress, and meeting reports. Although the reports are routine in the sense that they are prepared regularly, they are nonetheless significant to the success of the organization. To ensure effectiveness, consider purpose, audience, context, content, medium, and structure as you plan your reports. Also use an appropriate writing style and format for each report, as illustrated in this chapter. Remember: Your goal is to help the reader comprehend the message easily, quickly, and accurately.

TOPICS FOR DISCUSSION

1. In what ways are routine and nonroutine reports similar? How do they differ from one another?

2. Identify the purpose and characteristics of each of the following routine reports:
   a. Form report
   b. Trip report

    c. Production report

    d. Progress report

    e. Meeting agenda

    f. Minutes of meeting

3. What is the relationship of a progress report to a project's budget?

4. Why are meeting agendas often sent by e-mail?

5. In your judgment, what conditions would justify the use of e-mail for other reports described in this chapter?

6. Identify a major ethical challenge that may arise as you prepare routine reports. If you have had experience preparing such reports, share with your classmates other ethical issues, if any, you have had to resolve.

APPLICATIONS

1. Assume you are a consultant to two young men who want to start a "same-day" delivery service. These enterprising young men have seen the success of overnight delivery companies, and they hope to apply some of the principles those companies have followed. Their plan is to guarantee same-day delivery to anyone located within a 250-mile radius of their hub location. The men plan to begin with one hub, located in Greenville, SC. They want to gather accurate information about each delivery so that they can use that information for billing purposes and to determine when and how to expand the business. They ask you to prepare a form that will help route drivers report what they do each day. The form should enable drivers to report the time they left the terminal, each stop during the day, the number of parcels delivered and/or picked up at each stop, and the time they returned to the terminal. In addition, the form should contain spaces to record identifying information such as route number, driver's name, vehicle number, and total miles driven. Remember, the form must be easy to handle and complete so that drivers will provide all information each day.

2. As office manager for Pet Rescue of the Midlands, you must prepare a Monthly Activity Report to present to the Board of Directors. Each month you ask employees in your nonprofit organization to report their activities to you, after which you merge the information into a single report for the Board of Directors. In addition to you, the office manager, Pet Rescue employs an executive director, a director of animal adoptions, and a director of volunteer services. The executive director is primarily responsible for general management of the agency, fundraising, and promotional activities, including presentations to community groups. The director of animal adoptions is primarily responsible for determining a pet's readiness for adoption, screening of adoptive families, and follow-up contacts with adoptive families. The director of volunteer services is responsible for

recruiting, training, and managing all volunteers, including veterinarians who monitor animal health and conduct spay-neuter clinics as well as volunteers who feed and exercise the animals each day.

Prepare a form that will help your employees report to you in an efficient, timely manner and will help you compile an easy-to-read report for the Board. Since not all categories apply to every employee, design the form in a way that allows each employee to complete those parts most relevant to her or him. The kinds of information needed include the following:

- Active volunteers who worked during the month; total volunteer hours
- Types of volunteer service
- Volunteer training sessions
- Number of volunteers trained
- Donations: total amount, number of new donors, number of repeat donors
- Animal placements: number, category, new adoptive families, repeat adoptive families
- Client Satisfaction Questionnaires: number distributed, number returned
- Presentations: number, audience, etc.
- Meetings attended by staff
- Spay-neuter clinics:
  - Number of clinics
  - Number of surgeries
- Promotional activities:
  - Public Service Announcements
  - News releases
  - TV appearances
  - Newsletters
  - Other promotional activities

3. As Riley Corp's Vice President for Human Resources, you (T. Holmgren) recently sent your training director, Shelley Kennedy, to visit your juice-processing facility in Siedlce, Poland. The purpose of the trip was to gather information that would help Riley Corp. develop a training program to prepare your employees more effectively for assignments in Poland. After Kennedy had returned, you received the trip report shown in Illustration for Application 6-3 (page 168). You were not pleased with the report; you decide to rewrite it and instruct your training director how to write an effective trip report.

   Revise the trip report and attach it to a memo to your instructor in which you explain your decisions about content, structure, style, and format.

4. Holmgren has approved a $1,500 travel allowance (Application 3) for your U.S. nationals in Poland, not the $3,000 they had suggested. Write a message that you can send by e-mail to announce the plan to the five employees who qualify for it. Be sure to indicate how much each may spend and the reporting requirement.

5. As assistant to the circulation manager for your local newspaper, you recently attended the annual conference of the Newspaper Association of America. The major focus of the conference was an analysis of the drop in circulation experienced by most newspapers during the past decade and ways to counteract that drop. You must now write a trip report to the circulation manager Thad Mille, who typically wants a summary of what you learned at the conference as well as other pertinent information that will help him assess the value of such conferences.

Select pertinent information from the following notes and write the trip report. Use a structure and a format that demonstrate your understanding of the editor's communication preferences.

- We are not alone in experiencing declining circulation. Average weekday sales for NAA members were down 1.9 percent during the last six months compared with the same period last year. Sunday sales dropped 2.5 percent. Our declines for that time were 2.1 percent (weekday) and 2.0 percent (Sunday)

- Forty percent of 18- to 34-year-olds read a weekday newspaper in 2004 compared with 60 percent in 1984.

- Many young people get their news about current affairs from other sources, including cable news channels and the Internet.

- U.S. federal law limiting telemarketing has cut into sales.

- Some newspapers are trying to cut back on total circulation, targeting well-to-do readers that advertisers want to reach. Some participants questioned the ethics of that approach, saying the news profession has a moral obligation to inform lower-income citizens of current events.

- Some publishers focus on total readership rather than circulation figures. This figure includes people who access the paper's website and spin-off publications, such as free editions targeting certain groups (for example, issues focusing on employment, health, religion, newcomers to community, etc.). Our readership figures would look better if we counted these readers.

- Several publishers reported increased circulation following sponsorship of a community event or linkage with a nonprofit agency. Successful linkages included sponsoring a health fair with the local hospital and providing free daily papers to college freshmen enrolled in a "transition to college" type of course. Perhaps we could gain goodwill and publicity by partnering with local charities—providing free or reduced-rate promotion of fundraising events.

- The two-day conference (four days away, including travel time) was held in New York City. Total cost to attend was $1,440.27: $375.63 for round-trip discounted coach airfare; $ 450.77 for three nights of hotel lodging; $463.87 for food; $150 registration fee. You charged all costs to your personal credit card and have submitted the receipts, along with Form TR 101, to the business office for reimbursement.

- You were able to attend a Broadway show while in New York, and enjoyed that experience, along with the opportunity to eat at some of New York's fine restaurants. But you had to work extra-long hours after your return to catch up on the work that had piled up on your desk.

ILLUSTRATION FOR APPLICATION 6-3   ▶   TRIP REPORT TO BE REVISED

Date: June 1, <year>

To: T. Holmgren, Vice-President for Human Resources

From: Shelley Kennedy

Subject: Siedlce, Poland

As you requested, I left to visit our facility in Siedlce, Poland, on May 15. After a long delay in the Atlanta, GA, airport, I was finally on the way. I had to change planes in Frankfurt, Germany; but since you had permitted me to fly first class (thanks!!!), I was able to spend the waiting time in the Top Class Lounge. There I enjoyed comfortable chairs, fine foods, and a variety of beverages before continuing on the journey.

When I arrived in Warsaw, I was surprised at how long it took to go through customs. You'd think I was a terrorist! But after that ordeal, I finally got my bags and found an English-speaking cab driver who delivered me to my hotel. By then it was late afternoon, so I called "Doc" Jones at our Siedlce operation and asked him to meet me at the hotel for dinner.

As you know, Siedlce is located in a lush apple-growing region approximately 80 kilometers east of Warsaw. We buy apples from the local orchards, process them into juice at the Siedlce facility, and sell the finished product primarily in Poland, Austria, Germany, and the Czech Republic. Up to this time we have depended upon the local economy for production workers, but we have used U.S. nationals to supervise the purchasing, manufacturing, and marketing functions. "Doc" has identified several Polish nationals who have been working the production line but are ready for promotion to production supervision and, perhaps, sales positions. Our problem is that he has not yet developed a program to train Polish nationals for these positions.

I spoke with "Doc" and the four other U.S. nationals who have been largely responsible for recruiting and training Polish nationals, for purchasing the apples from local producers, and for marketing the processed juices. They spoke openly about the kinds of information they should have been given before arriving in Poland—most notably more information about the country's history and culture. They also indicated the kinds of technical and supervisory training the Polish nationals will need before they assume supervisory duties. Our U.S. nationals think the greatest need is to help Polish nationals "buy into" the free-market system so that they can motivate their workers to perform.

ILLUSTRATION FOR APPLICATION 6-3   Continued

T. Holmgren   – 2 –   June 1, <year>

I plan to use the input gained from my interviews as I revise the current training program for U.S. nationals and develop a new training program for Polish nationals.

One additional benefit the U.S. nationals requested was a travel budget that they could use for weekend and holiday trips to learn more about the country. Most of the U.S. nationals feel they received inadequate information about the history and culture of the region; that lack of information has sometimes hampered communication between them and the Polish nationals they have contact with, both in business and social settings. The U.S. nationals think that travel to learn about the country should be considered an ongoing training expense. They suggested that each U.S. national be given a $3,000 (US) allowance annually for travel in Poland. Each person would be required to account for how the money is spent and the benefits received from the travel.

So, Tim, I think the trip was a success. I have filed my travel reimbursement request for $6,369.89 with the accounting department. I'd appreciate approval of the travel allowance plan for the U.S. nationals so that I can notify them to get "ready to roll."

6. Quick-Action Loan Company is experiencing an increase in residential mortgage loan applications. When Karen Gibson, manager of the mortgage loan department, reviewed the departmental activity at the end of June, she found the number of mortgage loan applications in June was 10 percent higher than the number of applications received in May; and the number of applications in May was 12 percent higher than the number received in April. Ms. Gibson wants to include this information in her quarterly production report. She also wants to inform management that her employees handled the increased number of loan applications without additional staff. Moreover, since April 1, 98 percent of loan applications were processed and approved within a two-day period, the new goal that the department has set for processing applications. The previous processing time was three to four days. This production level is commendable because one employee took a week's vacation in May and one took two weeks of vacation in June. Ms. Gibson attributes this productivity in part to the changed processing procedures recently adopted and the training program that the regional office developed to familiarize the staff with those procedures.

    Acting as Ms. Gibson, write a production report in memo format. Direct the report to J. P. Houston, Regional Manager.

7. Ms. Gibson (Application 6) wants to inform her staff about the department's productivity and express her appreciation for their efforts. The report should not be identical to the one presented to management, but it may contain much of the same information.

   In a memo to your instructor, answer the following questions:
   - What content must be included? What content is optional?
   - What structure do you recommend? Why?
   - What tone do you recommend? Why?
   - What medium do you recommend? Why?
   - What is the best time to transmit the message? Why?

   Write the message and attach a copy to your memo.

8. You have been asked to chair a committee to plan your department's annual December holiday party. Two of your co-workers, Jo-Ann Brinkley and Jerry Gluzman, are also on the committee. Your job is to plan a party that will accommodate the cultural differences that exist in your unit. Religious faiths that you are aware of in your unit include Christianity (Eastern Orthodox, Protestant, and Roman Catholic), Islam, and Judaism. Some employees also celebrate Kwanzaa. Racial/ethnic heritages include first- to fourth-generation linkages to Brazil, England, France, Germany, Poland, Korea, and the African continent. The department has 28 employees (13 females and 15 males), and their ages range from 19 to 55 years. Your department supervisor has authorized up to $1,000 in company funds for the party, but you may charge each participant a fee if you think it is necessary.

   Your first task is to prepare an agenda for a meeting of the committee. In a memorandum to your instructor, answer the following questions:
   - What content must be included? What content is optional?
   - What structure do you recommend? Why?
   - What tone do you recommend? Why?
   - What medium do you recommend? Why?
   - What is the best time to transmit the message? Why?

   Prepare the agenda and attach a copy to your memo.

9. With your instructor's approval, complete this application with two of your classmates. Each is to assume the role of one of the committee members referred to in Application 8.

   Hold a meeting to reach decisions concerning the holiday event. Write the minutes of the meeting. You may assume any actions that would be appropriate to your task of planning the event.

10. Benacells Co., Ltd. is a biotechnology company that leads in production of cutting-edge products for treating patients with degenerative diseases such as heart disease and cancer. Benacells is currently conducting its first product promotion to a group of cardiologists in Thailand. Dr. Johnson Carmen, expatriate Marketing Director from the U.S. headquarters has assigned his marketing team to begin the promotional program by giving a luncheon presentation to 50 top cardiologists in Thailand during the next month.

As an assistant to the Marketing Director, you must report the progress made in planning this event. To date, you have assigned the following tasks to Ms. Chalida and Mr. Pravit:

- Confirmation of date and venue for the presentation—Ms. Chalida
- Invitation cards sent to participants and follow up for confirmation—Ms. Chalida
- Cooperation with PR Agency, Lion Communications Co., Ltd., for inviting press and media—Mr. Pravit
- Design the printed advertisement for the event—Mr. Pravit
- Coordinate with the guest speaker, Dr. Dena Watts, for the data of the presentation—Ms. Chalida

You will be able to give details of their accomplishments in next week's report. Dr. Carmen has asked you to write these weekly progress reports in e-mail format and to send copies of them to everyone in your team as well.

Application 10 written by Chonthicha Ungkanungdecha, Senior Marketing Officer at KPMG Phoomchai Holding Co., Ltd, a subsidiary of KPMG International.

11. The Town Council of the Village of Lake Lure has asked the Lake Lure Chief of Police to give a summary report of Police Department activities each month. In August <year>, the police department had the following information to report:

> Arrests: 14, driving while impaired; 12, marijuana possession; 11, drug paraphernalia possession; 1, cocaine possession; 1, carrying a concealed weapon.

> Calls/Incidents: 21, bank escort; 67, security check; 53, traffic offense, warning; 12, traffic offense, citation; 29, citizen requested assistance; 38, suspicious person/vehicle/incident.

> Promotions: Hester Eric to Lieutenant; Peggy McWhorter and Roger Schultz to Sergeant; Sean Owens and Robert Humphries to Corporal. Chief Mike Butner says these personnel changes should enhance the overall performance of the department and ensure the professional level of service the citizens of this great community expect and deserve as the area continues to grow.

> Write the activity report in memo format. Use a structure and tone that are appropriate for presentation to the town council members at their monthly meeting.

Writing Nonroutine Reports

The need to write or read reports differs for each individual almost daily. As you carry out your work, you will sometimes confront circumstances, make decisions, or take actions that deviate from your normal routine yet fall within your range of responsibility. These situations often require that you report your actions or decisions to management, to your supervisees, or even to the public or stockholders. Those reports may be classified as *nonroutine* reports.

EXAMPLES OF NONROUTINE REPORTS

It is impossible to illustrate all nonroutine reports that you will encounter. However, among the nonroutine reports that you will send and receive are interview reports, exception reports, justification reports, feasibility reports, staff reports, policy statements, press releases, and business proposals.

Interview Reports

An *interview report* can be thought of as a special form of a production report. Although you may not interview people regularly in your job, you may on occasion be assigned to a special project that requires you to interview people to obtain critical information. Rather than provide verbatim transcripts of your interviews, you will likely be expected to summarize the information you obtained in a report to your project leader or the members of your project team.

Appropriate content for an interview report would include a statement about when, where, and how the interviews were conducted; a summary of the information obtained; and relevant comments about the experience, such as problems encountered or recommendations related to the interview experience. Illustration 7-1 demonstrates one form of an interview report. It provides the information necessary for others to evaluate the interviews and take action based on those interviews.

Exception Reports

An *exception report* conveys information about deviations from the normal operations of the organization. Exception reports are production-related messages. In fact, some businesses operate under the philosophy of "management by exception." That is, managers are expected to spend their time and attention on matters that require their particular expertise. In such organizations, individuals are not required to file periodic production reports; but they must prepare an exception report if something occurs that is contrary to expectations, policies, or standards.

An exception report may present facts about the deviation only; or the report may include additional information, such as how the exception was handled, suggestions for handling or avoiding future occurrences, or a request for advice or assistance. Suggested style, structure, content, and format for an exception report are shown in Illustration 7-2. Notice the informative subject line, direct style, and numbered items—all appreciated by busy managers because those techniques simplify and clarify a message.

Justification Reports

A *justification report* describes or proposes an action and the reasons for that action. For example, a notification from an automobile manufacturer to auto owners that they should take their cars to a dealership to check for a possible defect in the steering mechanism is a justification report: The manufacturer requests a specific action and provides reasons for it. Justification reports are similar to exception reports when they describe an exception to a policy or practice and justify that exception. They may also be similar to proposals (discussed later in this chapter) when they propose adoption or rejection of a policy, procedure, or plan.

A typical justification report appears in Illustration 7-3. Notice the courteous, personal, confident tone that is appropriate when a district manager writes to a regional manager. Notice also the subject line, direct structure, and headings, all of which help the reader process the message quickly and respond to the writer's request.

Feasibility Reports

Feasibility report is the term often used to identify a special type of justification report, which analyzes the potential success of a major undertaking. Feasibility studies are often conducted before a company commits itself to a large capital investment, a new product or service, or a new plant location.

Although most feasibility studies result in lengthy, analytical reports, some feasibility reports are presented as short reports. For example, analyzing the

ILLUSTRATION 7-1 ▶ INTERVIEW REPORT

To: R. J. Lin

From: C. G. Gardner

Date: July 22, <year>

Subject: Prospective Mothers' Attitudes About Bucky Bear

Here are the results of the marketing interviews you requested during our staff meeting on June 15. The objective of the interviews was to sample prospective mothers' attitudes toward the new cartoon-like character, Bucky Bear, that we are testing as an imprint on children's bedding and clothing.

Interview Procedures: The market survey team conducted the interviews from 10:30 a.m. until 4:00 p.m., Monday through Friday, during the week of June 14. With the manager's permission, we set up a display table inside Baby's World, about 30 feet from the entrance. The table contained a banner inviting prospective mothers to ask about a free gift. When a woman stopped to inquire, we offered her a free Bucky Bear crib sheet if she would answer a few questions about the Bucky Bear figure.

Respondents: During the week, we interviewed 83 women. Twenty-four were expecting a first child; 43, a second child; and 16, a child beyond the second.

Reactions to Bucky Bear: The first question asked the shopper to describe the character in one word, using the first word that came to mind. Seventy-five percent of all interviewees described Bucky Bear with words such as "sleepy," "inactive," "sad," or "uninteresting." Only 10 percent of the women described Bucky as "cute," "lovable," or "cuddly."

When asked to suggest how to make the bear more appealing, 73 percent of the respondents suggested showing the bear in more active poses, 41 percent suggested using more brilliant colors, and 62 percent suggested showing the bear in scenes with other characters. (Totals equal more than 100 percent because several interviewees made more than one suggestion.)

Conclusion: These interviews suggest that our current depiction of Bucky Bear does not appeal to the majority of expectant mothers.

Recommendation: Bucky Bear should be sent back to Textile Design for modifications that make it look like a more lively, sociable creature.

ILLUSTRATION 7-2   EXCEPTION REPORT IN MEMO FORMAT

TO: Ron Ahrendts, General Manager

FROM: Richard Bast, Sales Representative

DATE: March 20, <year>

SUBJECT: Exception to Standard Price, Replacement Windows

Yesterday I approved a special price reduction on an order for seven replacement windows. Here are the details:

1. On March 3, I met with the customer in her home and gave an estimate for replacing all windows in the house. Approximate cost of replacing all windows was $15,000.

2. On March 17, the customer ordered five No. 755 windows, one No. 775, and one No. 739 in white frames, for a total price of $5,770 installed. The customer indicated plans to replace the remaining windows in 12 to 18 months.

3. On March 19, the customer called to say she preferred brown frames. I told her the order could be changed but that brown frames cost 10 percent more than white. She insisted I had not previously mentioned the additional charge, became emotional, and threatened to cancel the entire order.

4. To assure her that we do not use "bait-and-switch" tactics and to improve the chances of getting the order for the rest of the house, I told her I would order the brown frames this time at the price quoted for white frames. However, I indicated she would have to pay the additional charge when she ordered the remaining windows.

I understand your policy is that sales reps must absorb price reductions from commissions if we do not get your prior approval. However, this customer was on the verge of canceling the contract within the 48-hour period allowed by law. I had no time to locate you before making a decision. Since I gave the customer an allowance of $577 to secure a potential $15,000 order, I trust you will not charge that allowance against my commission income.

Please call me (555-1010) if you need further information about this transaction.

ILLUSTRATION 7-3   JUSTIFICATION REPORT IN BLOCK LETTER FORMAT

WORLD-VIEW WINDOWS

201 Leventis Drive
Columbia, SC 29209-1989

March 22, <year>

Mr. Rivers E. Williams
Regional Manager
World-Wide Windows
P.O. Box 1039
Atlanta, GA 30340-1039

Dear Rivers

Subject: Override of commission policy

I recommend that Richard Bast, one of our Macon, GA, sales representatives, be paid full commission on contract No. 31789, even though he gave the customer a special price on the windows. He should not be required to cover the price differential from his commission in this case.

Justification

This exception is justified for four reasons:

1. Bast made the contract adjustment in good faith, attempting to salvage a sizable account.

2. The evidence is unclear. Bast insists he told the customer that brown window frames cost 10 percent more than white; the customer insists he did not.

3. I have reviewed the sales closing procedure with Bast, and he has demonstrated it to a group of trainees. I am convinced he will not repeat the error nor compromise prices unnecessarily in the future.

4. Bast has experienced excessive medical expense related to his child's illness. The commission is significant to him, but relatively insignificant to the company. This is an opportunity to demonstrate our faith in him and build the morale of a potentially excellent sales representative.

ILLUSTRATION 7-3 CONTINUED

Mr. Rivers E. Williams — 2 — March 22, <year>

Request for Action

Please call me before April 15 if you have any questions. If I do not hear from you by that date, I will notify Bast that he will receive the full commission in his April 30 check.

Sincerely

Ron Ahrendts, General Manager
Southeast District

feasibility of opening a textile manufacturing plant in the Republic of Korea would surely require considerable research and analysis and would result in a lengthy report. In contrast, analyzing the feasibility of changing the hours of operation of a local restaurant would require considerably less data collection and analysis, and the result could be presented in a short-report format.

A feasibility report must identify the project that is being analyzed, provide an unequivocal recommendation about the potential success or failure of that project, and supply data to support that recommendation. Feasibility reports usually present the recommendation at or near the beginning of the report because the person requesting the report is primarily interested in the recommendation—whether positive or negative. A short feasibility report appears in Illustration 7-4. Notice its structure, content, style, and format.

Staff Reports

The term *staff report* may be used to identify any report produced by a manager's staff for the manager. A staff report frequently analyzes a problem about which the manager must take action, make a recommendation, or formulate a position. Assume, for example, that a homeowners' association objects to rezoning an area bordering its neighborhood from a residential to a commercial designation. The head of the zoning board would likely ask the board's staff to investigate the positions of proponents and opponents and to recommend what action the zoning board should take.

A staff report may be prepared in any format suitable for the nature of the problem and content presented. Managers assign such reports to staff

ILLUSTRATION 7-4 ▶ FEASIBILITY REPORT

MARKET SCOPE, INC.

P.O. Box 1584
Madison, WI 53713-1584

April 24, <year>

Ms. Heather Bonnifield
107 Marlene Drive
Marshall, MN 56258

FEASIBILITY OF MAIL-ORDER BUSINESS: WOMEN'S FASHIONS

In January you asked that I conduct a study of the feasibility of your beginning a mail-order business to market fashionable clothing to career women in the 30–45 age range. You planned to operate that business from Marshall, MN, with an initial investment of not more than $1 million.

Recommendation

I recommend that you **not** launch the mail-order business you proposed. If successful, you should reach the break-even point after three years, after which you can anticipate a 10 percent annual pre-tax profit. But you will likely have an accumulated loss of over $4 million during the first three years.

Furthermore, industry figures show that 90 percent of new mail-order businesses fail. The competition for catalog sales is growing, with the number of small mail-order companies up 50 percent in the last five years. Therefore, the very real risk exists that at the end of three years you will not be looking at a 10 percent pre-tax profit but at the loss of your $1 million investment.

You can currently invest your money in a risk-free money market account and earn approximately 3.5 percent annually. At the end of three years, your investment will grow to more than $1,109,000. Here are the findings that justify my recommendation.

Projected first-year costs and revenues

The first year of operation will require that you conduct marketing tests to establish your customer base; locate and buy appropriate merchandise; develop, print, and mail catalogs; pay salaries; and cover bad debts. If you send out 500,000 catalogs, you can anticipate that 1 percent of the recipients will respond with an average order of $90, generating $450,000 in sales.

ILLUSTRATION 7-4 CONTINUED

Ms. Heather Bonnifield   – 2 –   April 24, <year>

Your costs to generate those sales are projected as follows:

Catalog development	$ 60,000
Printing and mailing	270,000
Salaries (marketing, merchandising,	
customer service, telemarketing)	500,000
Cost of merchandise (45–55% of sales)	225,000
Bad debt allowance (2% of sales)	9,000
Total	$1,064,000

As you can see, your first-year investment would be more than your specified maximum of $1 million, with a likely income of $450,000.

Projected second-year costs and revenues

If you increase distribution to 3 million catalogs, catalog development costs will remain about the same; but your printing, mailing, and personnel costs will increase proportionate to sales. If the response rate holds, you can anticipate revenues of $2,700,000. To earn that revenue you will incur the following expenses:

Catalog development	$ 60,000
Printing and mailing	1,620,000
Salaries	3,000,000
Cost of merchandise	1,350,000
Bad debt allowance	29,000
Total	$ 6,059,000

Projected third-year costs and revenue

You should increase your catalog distribution to 5.5 million in the third year to remain competitive. As the customer base develops, you may expect a 3 percent to 6 percent response rate. I am projecting a 3.5 percent response rate with an average purchase of $90. That will bring in revenue of $17,325,000. Related cost projections follow:

Catalog development	$ 60,000
Printing and mailing	2,970,000
Salaries	5,500,000
Cost of merchandise	8,662,500
Bad debts allowance	346,500
Total	$ 17,539,000

ILLUSTRATION 7-4 ▶ CONTINUED

Ms. Heather Bonnifield   – 3 –   April 24, <year>

Summary

To summarize, here is what you can expect during the first three years if marginally successful.

Year	Revenue	Expenses
1	$ 450,000	$ 1,604,000
2	2,700,000	6,059,000
3	17,325,000	17,539,000
Total	$20,475,000	$25,202,000

Those projections result in a net loss of approximately $4,727,000 over three years. In contrast, if you were to invest your $1 million in a money market account earning 3.5 percent, you would see net income of approximately $109,000.

Additional Comments

I have enjoyed doing this study for you. If you are interested in an analysis of another entrepreneurial opportunity, please call me.

Heidi Fitzpatrick

HEIDI FITZPATRICK
ENTREPRENEURIAL CONSULTANT

members because they are too busy to do the investigation themselves. Therefore, the report should be designed to help the manager extract the essential information quickly.

Notice the structure and format of the staff report shown in Illustration 7-5. That report is presented in direct structure because, although the message is negative, the president surely remembers requesting the analysis and is awaiting the results.

Press Releases

A *press release* is a report that is released by an organization for distribution by the mass media: newspapers, magazines, radio, and television. Although large

ILLUSTRATION 7-5   STAFF REPORT IN MEMO FORMAT

TO:	Edward W. McGill, President
FROM:	Community Service Staff, Human Resources Division
DATE:	April 25, \<year\>
SUBJECT:	Removal of Over-the-Counter Cold Medications from Shelves

As you requested, we have analyzed the current problem related to home-based production of methamphetamines and the role our company may be playing in that problem.

Staff Recommendations

We recommend that all over-the-counter medications containing pseudoephedrine be removed from our shelves and be made available to customers only at the pharmacy. We also recommend that Quality Drugs run a series of newspaper announcements informing the public of this decision.

The Problem

Evidence exists that criminals have been stealing these medications and using them to produce the dangerous and addictive drug methamphetamine. "Meth" is often produced in crude home labs. Production in such facilities is especially dangerous to the community, not only because of the addictive qualities of the drug being produced, but also because the production itself is highly dangerous. Explosions have been known to occur during production. In addition, children have been known to be subjected to an extremely toxic environment in homes in which the drug is produced.

Current Market

During the past year, our company has sold approximately $3.8 million in O-T-C cold remedies. However, these are not impulse purchases. Our customer research shows that most customers needing the medication go to a drugstore specifically for the purpose of purchasing that product when needed. That research also shows strong consumer support for making the drugs less easily available to people who will misuse them. Customers indicated they would be willing to ask for the drugs at the pharmacy if a sign were posted in the store directing them to that location.

Financial Impact

Since cold medications are generally destination purchases, there will likely be little impact on our bottom line if we place them in the pharmacy instead of on open shelves. In fact, we may well suffer no revenue loss because we will have fewer thefts of the products.

Benefits

By removing these drugs from the open shelves, Quality Drugs can contribute to the control of a growing crime problem and gain community support with a minimal sacrifice of profits, if any.

companies typically have a corporate communication division that is responsible for press releases, if you work for a small business or nonprofit organization, you may be asked to write a press release. An effective press release contains the following information:

- Name of organization releasing the news
- Target date for publication of the news
- A headline that states the core of the story
- The information source, when applicable
- Answers to the basic communication questions: Who? What? When? Where? Why? How?
- Name of person to contact for further information, along with telephone or fax numbers or e-mail address

The body of the press release should be organized in inverted pyramid form: Answers to basic questions appear first, followed by supporting details. This structure permits the editor to cut the story without deleting vital facts. The news should be written in a style that will appeal to a broad audience. To accommodate the editors of the agencies to whom the release is sent, the news release should be double-spaced, preferably with extra space between paragraphs. Illustration 7-6 demonstrates effective structure and format for a written press release.

Today many companies also use the *video news release* (VNR) as part of their media outreach. A VNR is a professionally produced medium that is sent free of charge by satellite link or videocassette to television newsrooms. VNRs can be used to cover product innovations, company milestones, and current consumer issues. Professional associations, such as the National Association of Life Underwriters, have used VNRs to educate the public about the various segments of the industry and to combat misunderstandings.

Networks and local television stations are free to air the tapes or not. Some stations air them as they are presented; others use parts of the presentation or take its ideas and build their own stories. To increase the probability of having the tape aired, companies should produce the tapes in an objective, newsworthy fashion. To attract the interest of the news media, the story must capture the interest of the average consumer in the viewing audience.

Executive Summaries

Another nonroutine report that you may be required to prepare is an *executive summary*. An executive summary often accompanies a lengthy analytical report, but executive summaries are also used in other circumstances. For example, your state legislature may be proposing more stringent pollution-control requirements. Upper management in your company needs an analysis of the proposed legislation and its potential impact on your company. You may be asked to study the issue and prepare an executive summary. Another use for executive summaries is to help the executive keep up with current trends or issues in the industry. You may also be asked to skim several professional or trade journals and write an abstract of pertinent articles or a summary of what you learn about a particular trend.

ILLUSTRATION 7-6 PRESS RELEASE

Press Release

Contact: Jeremy Grant
616-555-5588; Ext. 8
Fax: 616.555.5587

Release Date: Immediate

BOE plans to relocate branch

One of BOE's busiest branches will soon have more operating space.

BOE's Northeast branch will move across the street from its present site on Polo Road into a new five-story building that is under construction, BOE spokesperson Katherine Canady said. BOE will occupy the first floor of the building at 8950 Polo Road. The rest of the space will be rented for professional offices.

At a cost of $10 million, the building is testimony to BOE's confidence in the growth of northeast Howell County. "We're going from 1,500 to 4,500 square feet," Canady said. "We'll be adding services that our customers in this part of the county have requested. We will be the first bank in northeast Howell County to offer a full range of trust, investment, and mortgage services, along with commercial and retail lending."

Booming residential and commercial development during the past few years have made northeast Howell County an attractive location for related professional services. BOE expects to occupy the first floor of the building. Roe and Roe Architects has already contracted to occupy the entire fifth floor. The remaining floors will be rented to other financial services companies.

Canady is confident BOE will have no difficulty leasing the space. "The difference between here and downtown is that we can offer ample parking near the building. The rent will also be lower than downtown. We'll have no difficulty attracting the kinds of clients we want."

X X X END X X X

> **ILLUSTRATION 7-7** WRITING AN EXECUTIVE SUMMARY[1]
>
> **An Effective Executive Summary**
>
> - Emphasizes key points of the report or journal article
> - Represents the author's view accurately
> - Is written in your own words
> - Is concise, specific, and clear
> - Is presented in a format that enhances readability
> - Is free of spelling, grammar, and sentence errors
>
> **How to Prepare an Executive Summary**
>
> 1. Read the report or each journal article to determine the main idea(s).
> 2. Write each main idea in a single sentence, using your own words.
> 3. List key facts or assertions that support the main point(s).
> 4. Write brief sentences containing the supporting facts or assertions.
> 5. Reread the report or article for background information needed to understand the main idea(s).
> 6. Write sentences to present the background information.
> 7. Combine your sentences describing the background, main idea(s), and supporting information.
> 8. Revise and edit your summary: Eliminate unnecessary words and sentences; evaluate structure (should it be direct? indirect?); check accuracy of spelling, grammar, sentence and paragraph structures.
> 9. Produce the final report in an appropriate format.

Whether you are writing an executive summary of a report you wrote, an abstract of a business article, or a summary of several documents pertaining to a single issue, you should write clearly, concisely, and in your own words. An executive summary should include only the most essential information that its readers need to make informed decisions and act wisely. Such a summary typically includes identification of the issue or problem that is addressed, major findings about the matter, and concise conclusions and recommendations. The guides shown in Illustration 7-7 will help you develop a complete, concise executive summary, whether it is an abstract of a trade journal article or a summary of a major report.

As Illustration 7-8 shows, executive summaries are often presented in direct structure. Because the readers already have some knowledge about the general problem, they are eager to know what you recommend.

Business Proposals

A *proposal* offers a plan of action. The objective of a proposal is to influence others—to persuade someone to act in a way that the proposer considers good or desirable. Business proposals share that general purpose, even though they have many different specific purposes.

ILLUSTRATION 7-8 ▸ EXECUTIVE SUMMARY

Promoting FARMCO via Video News Releases

Executive Summary

This report summarizes the current status of Video News Releases (VNRs) as reported in several trade journals.

Recommendation. The literature review supports the following recommendation:
Farmco should contract with a professional video producer, such as TOP-10, to prepare a VNR package about the minimal environmental impact of our pesticides.

Conclusions. Within the past 10 years, the VNR has become an increasingly effective tool in a company's media mix. This increased effectiveness can be attributed to the following developments:

- The increasing cost-effectiveness of satellite delivery
- The trend toward content that serves to educate the public
- The push by the Public Relations Society of America to develop a code of good practice for VNR production and use
- The reduced resistance of television news executives to VNR packages that provide flexibility in how the station will use the information

Summary of Findings. Journalists are still debating the ethics of using VNRs. If the station does not control the content of the video, it is considered a breach of ethics to air it. However, today's technology permits stations to exercise a good bit of control over what is used: video only with a stations' reporter doing voice-over, video clips, story line supplemented by the station's own reporting, and so on. Members of the Public Relations profession have worked to establish a quality control program that will guarantee formats and content that will be acceptable to broadcasters.

A VNR can get considerable airing, which is essentially free air time, if it addresses a consumer interest. For example, a VNR prepared for the Irish Tourist Board successfully promoted tourism by tying into St. Patrick's Day. The video was distributed by cassette to 240 stations nationwide, was aired 160 times by 125 different stations, and was viewed by an estimated audience of nearly 8 million.

PURPOSES OF PROPOSALS

A proposal may be solicited or unsolicited. A solicited proposal is presented in response to a request for proposal (often abbreviated RFP). In the RFP, the requesting person or agency indicates its needs, and the proposal writer attempts to show that the proposed action can satisfy those needs.

An unsolicited proposal is initiated by the proposer. That individual perceives a need or problem and offers a research plan, a product or service, or an action to satisfy the need. The proposal may be submitted to someone who is unaware of the situation. The writer's purpose is twofold: to convince the reader that a need or problem exists and to show how the proposed action will result in benefits to the reader.

KINDS OF PROPOSALS

Business proposals fall into three categories: proposals to investigate or conduct research, proposals to provide a product or service, and proposals to change a policy, procedure, or organizational structure. Each may be independent of the others, but the three may also be related to one another. For example, assume that as a human resources director you recognize that rising worker-compensation costs require the company to find alternatives to losing trained employees who have been injured on the job. You first write a proposal to investigate the feasibility of implementing a rehabilitation program for injured employees. Upon receiving approval for the proposed research, you ask one of your associates to conduct the research. Perhaps the research plan calls for a survey of employees to determine their attitudes about rehabilitating injured employees and integrating them into the work force. You decide that you want an external agency to conduct that employee survey, and you request that a professional testing agency submit a proposal to provide that service. If the completed research shows that an employee rehabilitation program is a cost-effective way of returning injured employees to the workplace, you will write an operational proposal to management recommending immediate adoption of such a program.

The investigative or research proposal is a formal version of a research plan. This kind of proposal will be discussed in a later chapter of this book. This chapter illustrates a product/service proposal and an operational proposal.

Product or service proposals (sometimes called bids) offer to provide something for the recipient. Such proposals are often solicited. The RFP frequently specifies the exact content and format desired by the receiver. To increase the probability that your proposal will be considered, you must adhere to those specifications.

Some organizations use relatively informal procedures to solicit product or service proposals. For example, a training director may telephone a consultant, describe a training need, and ask for a proposal. In such a situation, the consultant chooses the proposal's content and structure. Both must convince the training director that the consultant understands the need and can satisfy it. Illustration 7-9 demonstrates a service proposal. Notice that it includes

ILLUSTRATION 7-9 ▸ SERVICE PROPOSAL

IOWA TESTING ASSOCIATES

859 RIVER DRIVE
IOWA CITY, IA 54441

TELEPHONE: 319-555-4961

February 15, <year>

Ms. J. B. McCarthy
Director of Human Resources
Empire Industries
158 Hawkeye Boulevard
Iowa City, IA 52240

Dear Ms. McCarthy

In response to your February 12 telephone request, I submit this proposal for a survey to determine your employees' attitudes toward a corporate rehabilitation program.

Background

My understanding is that you have authorized one of your human resources associates, D. W. Singleton, to conduct a study of the feasibility of a corporate rehabilitation program. One element of that study is a survey of employee attitudes toward such a program. To ensure objectivity, you have advised Mr. Singleton that you wish to contract with an independent testing agency for this aspect of the study. Mr. Singleton agrees that employees are likely to respond more candidly to a neutral party than to someone inside the company.

Procedure

I propose to follow these steps for the survey:

1. Design a questionnaire to assess employee attitudes. You will be given the opportunity to review the questionnaire, and I will test it in an independent focus group before it is distributed to your employees.
2. Administer the questionnaire to your employees during their 8:00 a.m. to 5:00 p.m. working hours.
3. Tabulate and interpret the data.
4. Present to you a written report summarizing the findings.

ILLUSTRATION 7-9 CONTINUED

Ms. J. B. McCarthy — 2 — February 15, <year>

Cost

The cost for this service will be $10,000 to survey a maximum of 250 employees. This sample size is adequate for reliable results. I request an initial payment of $5,000 upon acceptance of this proposal; the final payment of $5,000 will be made upon completion of the report.

Completion Date

The final report will be presented to you no later than April 30. Completion by this date will allow Mr. Singleton to correlate the data with other data he is collecting for his study. Interim goals:

March 30	Questionnaire ready for your review
April 10–12	Questionnaires distributed to employees
April 13–18	Analysis of data
April 19–20	Completion of report

Qualifications

You are aware of Iowa Testing's reputation for conducting reliable surveys. References of satisfied clients will be provided upon your request.

Request for Approval

Please call me if you have any questions about this proposal. Your approval before February 28 will ensure completion of the survey in accordance with your research schedule.

Sincerely

Carlota Flores

Carlota Flores, Project Coordinator

everything the reader requires for an informed decision: a general description of the reader's problem or needs; a description of the service that the writer can provide; cost of the proposed service; proposed completion date; and qualifications of the provider. Notice also that the proposal requests a specific action: approval to proceed.

ILLUSTRATION 7-10   OPERATIONAL PROPOSAL

To: Executive Committee

From: J. B. McCarthy, Director of Human Resources   *J.B.M.*

Date: May 30, \<year\>

Subject: Corporate Rehabilitation Program Proposal

I recommend immediate implementation of a corporate rehabilitation program for disabled employees.

Justification

D. W. Singleton recently completed a study of the feasibility of a corporate-funded employee rehabilitation program. Major findings of that study follow:

1. Current employees strongly favor such a program.

2. Other companies have found that training disabled employees for new jobs is less costly than training new employees for similar jobs.

3. Rehabilitating disabled employees should reduce worker-compensation costs by 70%.

4. A full-fledged rehabilitation program can be implemented within six months.

Additional Information

A copy of Singleton's full report is in my office. I have also asked him to attend our June 10 executive committee meeting to present an oral summary of the report. I will gladly provide any substantiating information you request before that meeting.

Request for Approval

You can contribute to cost reduction and improved employee morale by approving this proposal. Your approval at the June 10 meeting will assure the program's operation before the end of the year.

Organizational or operational proposals set forth suggestions or plans for changes in organizational structure or operations. In some organizations, such proposals are called justification reports. The proposal presents a plan or suggestion and provides objective information to justify it. This kind of proposal is often accompanied by an oral presentation that contains more of the detailed data that constitute the justification.

An example of an operational proposal appears in Illustration 7-10. Notice that the report structure and content complement the readers' needs. The busy members of the executive committee will appreciate the direct, clear statement of the proposed action and the brief, easy-to-read justification for that action. Again, the proposal ends with a clear, concrete statement of the desired action.

ETHICAL CONSIDERATIONS

As demonstrated by the illustrations in this chapter, the writer of a nonroutine report may face an ethical dilemma. In many instances, the problem is not that you must choose between a good or bad action; instead, you must choose between two good actions or outcomes. Should a sales representative seek approval for an action that deviates from a standard operating procedure when the outcome will have a short-term cost to the company, or should the sales representative accept the related cost of her or his action? What is the potential good—or bad—result of a manager's attempt to justify a subordinate's actions? How should a consultant report data to a client when he or she knows the client will be disappointed by the information? Should a staff member recommend an action that will have a negative impact on company employees but will eventually benefit the company and its stockholders? What kind of "spin" should you put into a press release? How do you draw the line between blatant product promotion and news in a VNR? When you respond to a request for a proposal, can you demonstrate that you have the ability to meet the expectations of the potential client—that you have the necessary expertise to provide the requested product or service? A review of the ethical model and the questions presented in Chapter 1 will help you make some of these difficult decisions about message content and style.

Another ethical dilemma may also arise as you price your services. How should you value your services? Should you charge "what the market will bear" in all situations? Should you reduce your price for a nonprofit organization and consider part of the work a *pro bono* contribution? In February, 2005, *The State* (daily newspaper published in Columbia, SC) reported that a consultant had proposed to conduct a "summit on homelessness" for the city; the proposed fee: $78,000. Some citizens and city council members questioned whether that amount of money should be spent to study the issue and develop a long-term strategy for serving homeless residents of the city. The operations director of one facility that helps homeless people recover from drug and alcohol addictions reported that his annual budget is little more than $100,000.[2] Clearly, weighing right vs. right issues is not easy.

SUMMARY

Nonroutine reports address significant problems that are job-related yet not confronted daily. The ability to prepare effective nonroutine reports—such as interview reports, exception reports, justification reports, feasibility reports, staff reports, press releases, executive summaries, and business proposals—will have a significant effect on your career.

The content and structure of those reports must always complement the needs of the receiver and clearly identify the desired action. Because these reports deal with exceptions to normal operations, the writer often faces an ethical dilemma. The content and the style of nonroutine reports should always be scrutinized to ensure that they meet the ethical standards of the organization and its constituencies.

TOPICS FOR DISCUSSION

1. Describe the potential role of nonroutine reports in your business career.

2. Identify the purpose and characteristics of each of these nonroutine reports:
   a. Interview report
   b. Exception report
   c. Justification report
   d. Feasibility report
   e. Staff report
   f. Press release
   g. Video news release
   h. Executive summary

3. What is the general objective of all proposals?

4. Give an example of a solicited proposal and an unsolicited proposal.

5. What is the specific objective of each of the following proposals?
   a. Investigative/research proposal
   b. Product/service proposal
   c. Organizational/operational proposal

6. Identify ethical dilemmas that may arise as you prepare nonroutine reports. In your judgment, are you more or less likely to face ethical dilemmas as you write nonroutine reports than when you prepare routine reports?

7. If you have had experience writing any of the nonroutine reports described in this chapter, share your experiences with your classmates. Who determined that the report should be written? How did you plan the report? How did you obtain the necessary information? What ethical issues did you have to consider?

APPLICATIONS

1. Form a team composed of you and two or three of your classmates. You are to make an initial assessment of the need for child-care services on your campus by interviewing at least 20 students who have children under the age of 5. Use the following procedures for the interviews and report preparation:
   - Meet with your team members to determine the questions you should ask and the interview procedures (where, when, etc.).
   - Summarize your findings in a report to be submitted to the director of student services (or another appropriate administrator) at your school. Write the report in memo format.

2. Assume you work for a carpet-cleaning company. Your supervisor, Cate Peerbolte, sent you on a recent job to clean the carpet in the living room, hallway, and two bedrooms of a new customer. When you arrived, you inadvertently sprayed water into the kitchen while setting up your equipment. The customer was quite irritated by that action, but you vacuumed up the water and thought you had remedied the situation. However, a little later the customer slipped on the wet tile floor and nearly fell.

   As you started cleaning, the customer asked you to move the small furniture items out of the bedroom so that you could clean completely under them. You told her that moving furniture in the bedroom was not part of the deal. This made her so irate that she ordered you to leave the premises immediately. You did so and went on to your next job.

   Since you are paid only upon presentation of paperwork signed by the customer, you will not be paid for the time and mileage associated with this aborted job. You may also receive a poor performance evaluation if the customer reports the incident. Your opinion is that the problem was not your fault for two reasons: (1) The worker who used the cleaning equipment the previous day had left a valve open, which caused the water to spray when you were setting up the job; (2) The person who took the order by telephone should have told the customer about the policy to clean only traffic areas in the bedrooms and to move no furniture. You also think the company is in a better position than you to absorb the cost of your lost time and wasted miles.

   Write an exception report in memo format to Peerbolte. Explain what happened but also make a case for being paid for the time you would have spent on the job (about two hours) and your travel (25 miles) to get there.

3. Dennis Halkyard, student advisor at Westford Community College, counsels all business students when they enter the college, during their tenure at Westford, and prior to graduation. The college has a clearly defined curriculum that all business students are expected to complete to receive the Associate of Business Sciences degree. However, many students in the program have had considerable business experience and ask

that courses be waived when they think they have already mastered the knowledge by practical experience. Halkyard has leeway to grant such waivers at his discretion, which he does only after consulting extensively with the students and the professor teaching the course that is to be waived. When a course is waived, the student must take another course in its stead (that is, the student must still earn the required number of academic credit hours).

At the end of each semester Halkyard must file an exception report with the dean of the college to indicate how many waivers he has granted. During the past semester he granted three waivers for BUS 102, The Business Environment; five waivers for BUS 201, Managerial Accounting; and four waivers for BUS 250, Business Communication. He rejected ten requests to waive BUS 102; six to waive BUS 201; and nine to waive BUS 250.

Acting as Dennis Halkyard, write the exception report directed to Dean Ioana Tudor.

4. Sandi Kahn, a market researcher for Surf & Turf, an American-style steak and seafood restaurant, was sent to Kyoto, Japan, to research the feasibility of opening a Surf & Turf in that city. Although Surf & Turf allows up to $150 per day for lodging and $75 per day for meals when employees travel on company business, this allowance did not cover Sandi's expenses in Kyoto. When she submitted her expense reimbursement voucher to you, director of marketing, she explained that the hotel she had booked in advance had been unable to honor her reservation. Consequently, she got a room at another hotel, but it cost $200 US. Meals were also more expensive than anticipated, averaging $100 US per day. Therefore, her five-day stay in Kyoto exceeded the normal travel allowance by $375.

You thought the overage was justifiable and reimbursed Ms. Kahn in full. Now, however, you must explain your actions to the company comptroller, Brian Baker. Write a justification report. You may add appropriate details to justify your action.

5. C. D. Leonard's is a small, family-owned restaurant located at 335 State Street, Newton, IA. The restaurant features steaks, fried-to-order hamburgers, and broasted chicken. As complements to these menu items, the restaurant also offers baked and french fried potatoes, salads, a fresh vegetable (chef's daily choice), and a variety of nonalcoholic beverages, including milkshakes. The restaurant is currently open from 11 a.m. until 8 p.m., Monday through Saturday. The owner, C. D. Leonard, is considering expanding the business in one of two ways: opening at 6:30 a.m. and adding a breakfast menu to be served from 6:30 until 11:00 a.m.; extending the hours until 11:00 p.m. on Friday and Saturday evenings. He asked you to conduct a study to determine whether either of those options would be feasible.

To obtain data for your study, you prepared a short questionnaire, which the wait staff distributed to diners (one per table) after the customers had placed their orders. The diners were asked to complete the questionnaire while the orders were being prepared, and the wait staff collected the forms when they delivered the food to the tables. Here are the results of your survey.

- One hundred twenty-nine questionnaires were completed; these represented 69 families with children, 20 couples, and 40 individuals dining alone.
- Breakfast: 80 percent of the individual diners indicated an interest in eating breakfast at C.D. Leonard's at least once a week, with Friday and Saturday mornings being the preferred days; 20 percent of the families indicated an interest in breakfast, with Saturday as the preferred day; 99 percent of the couples indicated an interest, with Tuesday and Wednesday as the preferred days. Evenings: No families were interested in extended evening hours on Friday and Saturday; 98 percent of the couples and 96 percent of the individual diners were interested in extended evening hours on Friday and Saturday.
- Food Purchases: The average cost of food purchased during your survey was $25 total for families; $18 total for couples; and $10 total for individuals.
- Anticipated Sales: 89 percent of respondents indicated they would likely eat dinner one additional evening per week if the Friday and Saturday hours were extended; 50 percent of respondents said they would likely eat breakfast at least once a week if a breakfast menu were offered.
- Additional Comments: Ten individuals and five couples suggested that the restaurant offer a Sunday morning brunch; three individuals and one couple suggested offering live music by local talent on Friday and Saturday evening; two families and three couples suggested expanding the menu to offer more "heart healthy" items; one individual and two couples suggested adding beer and wine to the beverage menu.

Based on your interpretation of the data (you may make other reasonable assumptions), write a report for C. D. Leonard. Prepare the report in manuscript format and include a cover letter to Leonard. Draw a definite conclusion about the feasibility of expanding his business by one or both of the options that he is considering. Provide data to support your conclusion. You may make additional recommendations if you think the data support them.

6. PET Co., Ltd., is a frontline research-based international company that is keen on producing and distributing high-quality companion animal health products in both local and overseas markets.

Recently, PET Co., Ltd., and Yok University formed a cooperative educational venture. The venture was announced at a Memorandum of Understanding (MOU) Signing Ceremony held in the conference room of the Faculty of Veterinary Science, Yok University. Mr. Pete Derik, Managing Director of PET Co., Ltd., and Mrs. Ravi Uthai, Rector of Yok University, represented their organizations.

Under the MOU, PET Co., Ltd., demonstrates its role as a research and development supporter in the next five years by:

a. Providing scholarships annually for the best four innovative research and development proposals, specializing in the companion animal field, to master's and doctoral students. The scholarship covers all expenses related to an approved research project conducted by each scholarship winner.

b. Supplying use of the company's laboratory and lab consultation for scholarship winners.

c. Welcoming five undergrad students yearly as interns to gain hands-on research experience.

As a member of PET Co., Ltd.'s Corporate Communications department, you were assigned to attend the ceremony, produce the news release, and send it to local news outlets as soon as possible. A staff photographer accompanied you to take some photo shots of the signing ceremony. You recorded the following quotations made by the principal participants in the ceremony.

Mr. Derik: "This is a great chance for PET to reinforce the next generation's research capabilities. Today's students are a potential resource to lead our country to prosperity. We are interested in supporting other educational activities. With today's initiative, we are just at the start line."

Mrs. Uthai: "One of Yok University's duties, besides being a knowledge provider, is to push our students to apply their knowledge and practice their skills alongside experts in companies that hold high standards. The scholarship winners and interns will have a chance to experience what is best in the real world."

Write a news release about the MOU Signing Ceremony in appropriate structure and format.

Application written by Viraya Khunprom, Public Relations Officer at Bayer Thai Co., Ltd.

7. Byars Construction has provided its project managers with cellular telephones to enable them to communicate readily with the home office when they are out in the field. Several of those managers have requested that the company upgrade this service to "smart phones," the newest generation of mobile phones, which incorporate features of PCs, PDAs, and cell phones. Nokia, Motorola, and palmOne are some current marketers of this electronic device. In addition to the usual cell phone features, with appropriate software written specifically for the phones, the managers would be able to use the phone in place of their PDAs; stay in touch with architects and suppliers by e-mail; and gain access to blueprints, contracts, and other documents that currently can be accessed only at the office. Since the engineers who had company cell phones were also permitted to use them for personal calls, it is likely they will want to continue that practice.

Assume that Byars Construction is located in your city. Contact cellular service providers in your area to determine the cost of providing these state-of-the-art telephones for the engineers. Select the provider that best meets the needs of the Byars project managers. Write a proposal to the company operations manager, Mary Grasman, recommending that the company provide "smart phones" for all project managers.

8. Ms. Thara Suthirak is a Thai executive working as a senior consultant at Kommunika Management Consulting and Training Co., Ltd. in Bangkok. Her job is to visit clients, analyze clients' problems, and propose suitable workshops to solve those problems.

Last week Thara Suthirak and Mr. Damon Bond, the American Managing Director of Kommunika visited Mr. David Kahn, at ALPHA Pharma (Thailand) Co., Ltd., one of the biggest pharmaceutical companies worldwide, with headquarters in Germany. Mr. David Kahn is a German Managing Director who has been sent to the company's Bangkok station for a three-year assignment. After he had been there for five months, he found that ALPHA Pharma (Thailand) has a lot of political issues and needs to improve teamwork skills and create a better organizational culture.

Mr. Kahn has attended Kommunika's Managing Diversity workshop. He was happy with the course, so he invited Kommunika to discuss the possibility of providing a similar service for his team. After meeting with Mr. Kahn, Ms. Suthirak and Mr. Bond concluded that Kommunica should propose a teambuilding workshop called "**ALPHA Thailand—Team of Excellence**" to Mr. Kahn. They believe that this workshop will begin to solve some of ALPHA Pharma's problems.

The workshop details are as follows:

Objectives:
- Improve communication skills
- Increase the appreciation for the value and benefits of teamwork
- Create a better "ALPHA Thailand" organization culture

Training Methods:
- The workshop is a combination of teamwork and communication activities, including case studies, role-plays, and outdoor team games.

Participants:
- Maximum 24 people

Duration:
- Three days

Venue:
- To be announced by ALPHA Pharma (Thailand) Co., Ltd.

Fee:
- 250,000 baht

Deposit:
- 25% (62,500 baht) to be paid within 7 days after the date of receiving invoice

Balance:
- 75% (187,500 baht) to be paid within 7 days after the course is done

Condition:
- The deposit for the workshop is nonrefundable, if ALPHA Pharma (Thailand) Co., Ltd., fails to inform the cancellation of this course 30 days prior to the scheduled start of this course. NOTE: The above fees are exclusive of 7% VAT (value added tax).

Acting as Ms. Suthirak, write a proposal to Mr. Kahn, using the information provided. You may make other reasonable assumptions.

Application written by Mingkhwan Sinthuwong, Business Development Manager at Sun Bright Co., Ltd., her family-owned business in Bangkok, Thailand.

9. Read three newspaper, magazine, or journal articles on one of the following topics (or another topic assigned by your instructor). Present what you have learned from the articles in an executive summary directed to your instructor.
   - Should state development boards give tax incentives to induce businesses to establish a new plant (or other business entity) in your state?
   - Have state-operated lotteries resulted in significant increases in funding for elementary and secondary education?
   - How rigidly do airlines enforce their baggage limitations? Do they enforce the policies more rigidly for economy-class flyers than for first-class flyers?
   - What are the advantages and disadvantages of using a home equity line of credit to pay a child's college tuition.
   - What impact has digital photography had on film manufacturers, such as Fuji and Kodak, and film processing companies?

10. Riverbend is a private residential community consisting of approximately 1,500 acres of mountainous property. A river runs through the community, and two small lakes are within the community's confines. The property owners are responsible for maintenance of all roads and recreational facilities, such as the riverfront hiking trail, the picnic areas, and the lakes.

In recent years, people who do not own Riverbend property have used its amenities, and the residents have not objected. However, increased vandalism and maintenance costs have prompted some association members to request that the community be gated, with access given only to members.

As a member of the Riverbend Property Owners' Association Board of Directors, you recently chaired a committee that investigated the feasibility of installing security gates at the four entrances to the Riverbend Community. Based on your report, the Board has authorized installation of the gates. Some deciding factors were the statement by a property appraiser that security gates would immediately increase the value of each lot by as much as $5,000; the strong support from 75 percent of the current residents (however, the 25 percent that opposes the gates is an extremely vocal, sometimes troublesome group); and the fact that current homeowners' fees are sufficient to cover the cost and operation of the gates (the number of fee-paying homeowners has increased steadily during the past five years, resulting in a comfortable surplus in the operating budget).

The gates should be in full service by July 1. Here are some details about the installation and operation of the gates.

- The installation will include entry/exit gates at the main entrance on Highway 64 and the secondary entrance on Bob's Creek Road. Entry to Riverbend can be made only through those two entrances. The remaining secondary entrances will be changed to exit only.
- Entry gates will be operated by coded electronic entry card or electronic "clicker." Owners of each home site will be given two gate cards; additional gate cards may be purchased for $10 each; clickers, for $40 each. Cards and clickers must be picked up at the developer's office no later than June 30.
- An electronic registry of homeowners will be placed at the main entry gate. To gain entry, visitors must look up the name of the homeowner and enter that homeowner's number into the keypad. The telephone will ring in the homeowner's house; and, after speaking with the person who wants entry, the homeowner can enter a code to open the gate for the visitor. Homeowners should not open the gate to strangers.
- The U.S. Postal Service carrier and drivers for other delivery services who need frequent access to the community will be given an entry code.
- Homeowners may request a temporary card for visitors who will be spending more than one day on the site.
- A greeter will be on duty at the Main Entrance to assist anyone having difficulty with the gate system.

The Board has asked you to write the equivalent of a staff report to the homeowners, explaining the reasons for the board's decision, schedule for gate installation, plans for putting gates into operation, and operating procedures. Your report will be included in the community's monthly newsletter on May 1. Since some homeowners strenuously objected to the plan to gate the community, convey a positive tone in your report. You may add other information that you think will enhance the effectiveness of the report.

11. As a homeowner in the Riverbend community (Application 10), you want to make some improvements to your property. The by-laws of the property owners' association require that all home and landscape plans be submitted to the Board for approval; a $25 fee must accompany the plans. The purpose of the approval is to ensure that homeowners adhere to all restrictive covenants of the community, particularly those that affect the appearance of the property.

When you built your home seven years ago, you submitted the landscape plan, which included a semicircular driveway with a gravel surface. At the time, you thought the driveway would be adequate for your use, but you soon discovered that when you park more than one vehicle in the driveway, entry and exit are difficult. You need a parking area that will accommodate at least two vehicles. When you talked to a licensed contractor who specializes in this type of work, you were pleased that he was able to begin the job immediately. You authorized the work, even though you had not contacted the Board for approval. The work was completed within two days and had no negative impact on the roadway in front of the house. The finished gravel-surfaced area extends to the west of the existing drive, permitting you and your guests to park vehicles off the driveway.

Although you do not object to getting the Board's approval for major architectural or landscaping changes, you considered it unnecessary in this case because the parking area does not significantly alter your landscape, is not visible from the road, and does not impair road traffic in any way. For the same reasons, you think you should not have to pay the landscape review fee. You have always been supportive of Board policies and have paid all homeowner's fees on time, contrary to the behaviors of some of the residents.

Write a justification report to the Riverbend Board of Directors, telling them why you had the work done before gaining board approval. Also ask for a waiver of the landscape review fee. Caution: Plan the content, structure, and tone of this message carefully. You know you have violated a rule, but you want the board to approve an action already completed.

12. According to a survey conducted by the United Nations Conference on Trade and Development (UNCTAD) and the British magazine *Corporation Locations,* Thailand ranks fourth as an attractive country for foreign direct investment, after China, India, and the United States.

Assume you are a successful Thai businessperson working as Executive Director at *Matsukochi Corporation* in Thailand. You have had extensive experience working with Japanese expatriates for years. Professor Hiromi Itoh, Chairperson of the International Business Communication Program (IBCP) at Shuo University in Japan, has indicated that she would like to invite you as a guest speaker to deliver a one-day talk to Japanese business people who expect to be transferred to Thailand. These business people will be attending an intercultural training program organized by IBCP at Shuo University. The training program is designed to help the Japanese to be well-prepared for working in Thailand.

Professor Itoh requested that you prepare a proposal for a lecture to the trainees. She would like the content to be easy to understand, interesting, and inspiring enough to motivate the trainees to feel enthusiastic about working in Thailand. Eighty percent of the trainees possess only a threshold level of English proficiency; but you are proficient in Japanese, Thai, and English.

Write a proposal, addressed to Professor Itoh, that she will be able to submit to the Dean's office to request financial support for your trip. The following information will help you develop the proposal.

- Duration of presentation: six hours
  - Morning sessions: 9:00–10:30; 10:45–12:00
  - Coffee break: 10:30–10:45
  - Afternoon sessions: 13:00–15:00; 15:15–16:30
  - Coffee break: 15:00–15:15

- Content of presentation
  - Doing business in Thailand: general principles and practices
  - Getting to know Thai culture: customs and courtesies
  - Getting to know Thai people: personal attributes and attitudes toward Japanese people
  - Keys to success in working and communicating with Thai local employees
  - Major failures of expatriate managers in working and communicating with Thai local employees
  - Thai local employees' work-related expectations from foreign managers
  - How to deal with difficult Thai employees
  - Cases of successful and unsuccessful business communication and practices in Thailand
- Methods of presentation
  - Lecture with PowerPoint® presentation
  - Case study and discussion
- Fees
  - Round-trip airfare: Bangkok, Thailand, to Tokyo, Japan
  - Lodging in Shuo University guest house or nearby hotel
  - Honorarium of 50,000 Japanese yen

Application written by Nongluck Sriussadaporn Chareonngam, Assistant Professor, Department of Speech Communication and Performing Arts, Faculty of Communication Arts, Chulalongkorn University, Bangkok, Thailand.

REFERENCES

1. Adapted from Cox, P., Bobrowski, P. E., & Maher, L. (2003). Teaching first-year business students to summarize: Abstract writing assignment. *Business Communication Quarterly, 66(4),* 36–54.

2. Summit on homelessness carries $78,000 price tag. (2005, Feb. 24). *The State,* p. A1.

Planning the Research

Managers must often make decisions that will have a major impact on the success of their organizations. Should a would-be entrepreneur begin the business that he or she has long contemplated? Should an automobile manufacturer open an assembly plant in another country? Should an advertising agency give a substantial amount of money to a state university to establish a business communication center? Should an insurance company change its policy about who may be considered "family" for medical insurance benefits?

These and other questions require extensive research before they can be answered with confidence. The first step in the research process is to create a plan that clearly identifies the problem to be studied and its scope, as well as the purpose of the study and the audience to whom the information will be reported. All factors related to the study, including costs and time required, may be presented formally in a research proposal.

PLANNING THE RESEARCH

A report about a complex problem begins with a research plan, which becomes a guide for collecting data, analyzing data, and reporting the results of the analysis.

A *research plan*, as indicated in Illustration 8-1, includes twelve parts: obtain or review authorization, identify the audience, define the problem, clarify the purpose, narrow the scope, state delimitations and limitations, plan data

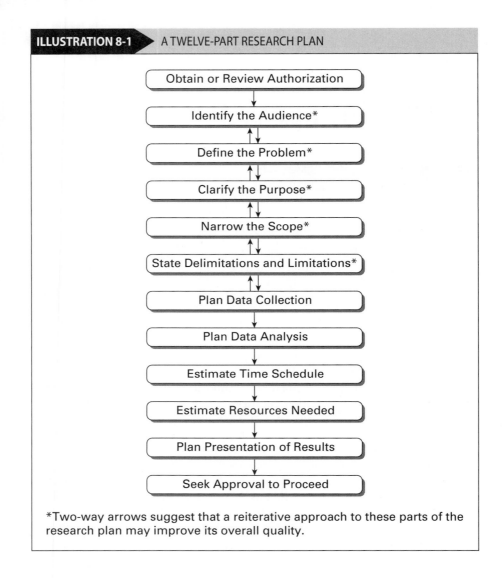

ILLUSTRATION 8-1 A TWELVE-PART RESEARCH PLAN

- Obtain or Review Authorization
- Identify the Audience*
- Define the Problem*
- Clarify the Purpose*
- Narrow the Scope*
- State Delimitations and Limitations*
- Plan Data Collection
- Plan Data Analysis
- Estimate Time Schedule
- Estimate Resources Needed
- Plan Presentation of Results
- Seek Approval to Proceed

*Two-way arrows suggest that a reiterative approach to these parts of the research plan may improve its overall quality.

collection, plan data analysis, estimate time schedule, estimate resources needed, plan the presentation of results, and seek approval to proceed.

Obtain or Review Authorization

When a project requires extensive research, you must be sure that you are authorized to spend time or money on the project. In some situations your job description will require that you prepare specific reports; then you need no additional authorization to initiate a research plan for that report. But you may also discover the need to analyze a unique problem related to your work; then part of your plan is to be sure you are authorized to do the research. In addition, your supervisor may ask you to work on a special project; then your research plan must include a review of the request to demonstrate that you understand what the supervisor wants you to do.

Identify the Audience

As when preparing a simple report, you must have a clear understanding of your audience, both primary and secondary. The authorization facts may tell you who the receivers are, or you may need to determine who they will be. When you initiate a research plan, decide whom you want to influence with the report. When asked to work on a project, clarify who is—and is not—to have access to the information.

Assume, for example, that you must prepare a report investigating the feasibility of relocating a branch bank currently located in an economically deprived neighborhood. The intended primary audience would likely be upper-level corporate managers, and releasing information prematurely to anyone not authorized to receive it could result in negative attitudes and behaviors among employees and customers. After deciding to relocate the bank, management may ask you to write a report to the employees, who become your primary audience. But—unless employees can be prevented from sharing this information with acquaintances—the potential secondary audience, such as neighborhood leaders, customers, and news media, must also be considered and may influence report content, structure, and tone.

Sometimes you cannot determine the full audience until you have clearly defined the problem. The definition of the problem may provide a clearer view of potential audiences for the report.

Define the Problem

The problem is the central focus of the research and the report. A clear, concise statement of the problem keeps the researcher on target. To conduct business research, you must distinguish between the managerial problem and the research problem.

The observable phenomena about which a decision must be made comprise the managerial problem. Such phenomena are also called the symptoms of the problem. For example, a manager may observe that the office support personnel often are tardy for work, turn in poor-quality work, and complain about eyestrain, wrist strain, and backache. These are all symptoms that something is amiss in the office support system. A manager who considers only one symptom at a time may decide that the resolution to the "problem" is to reprimand tardy employees, give negative work evaluations to employees who do inferior work, or buy new office chairs and wrist rests. But a manager who looks at several symptoms may decide that a deeper problem exists. Perhaps the question that must be addressed is: How can we improve the productivity of our office support staff? That question would become the research *problem* or research *question*.

Clarifying the purpose of the report frequently helps the researcher define the problem.

Clarify the Purpose

Whereas the problem defines *what* is to be investigated, the purpose identifies *why* the research should be conducted. When the research is completed, the *purpose* guides the formulation of recommendations.

In some situations the problem and purpose are nearly identical. For example, the purpose of investigating ways to improve office productivity would be to improve productivity. When the problem and purpose are similar, they may be stated as the objective of the study. The objective is the overall outcome or goal of a report.

In other cases, the problem and purpose must be differentiated from one another. Consider the following situation. The new administrator of Peaceful Village, a retirement center that has been in operation for three years, observes several phenomena.

1. The facility has averaged 90 percent occupancy during the past year, whereas the goal is 99 percent.
2. Three new facilities have opened during the past year in the Peaceful Village service area.
3. Three months ago Peaceful Village's dietician/cook took a job with a competing facility. Since then the residents have complained frequently that the meals served differ considerably from the posted menus. Although the menus sound appetizing, the food is not.
4. Although five potential residents toured the facility during the past month, only one became a resident. That person complained about the intake interview and procedures and almost refused to sign the contract.
5. The head nurse conducts the intake interviews in the medical office. Personnel who need supplies from the office or must ask the nurse a question frequently interrupt the interviews.

The phenomena suggest a major managerial problem. If the facility continues to operate at less than optimal capacity, it will lose money. If it cannot satisfy its residents, it will likely not operate at full capacity. Several approaches could be taken to solve the managerial problem. After some preliminary investigation, the administrator authorizes a study to investigate ways to attract and retain residents. That investigation is the research problem. The purpose of such a study is to enable the facility to reach its goal of 99 percent occupancy.

Having defined the problem and purpose, your next step is to identify the scope of the investigation.

Narrow the Scope

By narrowing the scope of the analysis, you identify the specific factors or elements to be analyzed. A perfect study would investigate all possible aspects of the research question. But time and money constraints require that you focus your study on the factors most likely to yield relevant data. Preliminary research often leads to the identification of those elements. After identifying the factors, you will concentrate the remainder of your research on those items.

In the Peaceful Village example, the scope could include these factors regarding attracting and retaining residents:

A. Advertising
   1. Cost/benefit analysis of current program
   2. Analysis of competitors' advertising
B. Intake Procedures
   1. Work-flow analysis of current procedures
   2. Analysis of procedures used in other facilities
   3. Residents' evaluation of current procedures
C. Services to Residents
   1. Food
   2. Recreation
   3. Entertainment
   4. Personal and medical services
   5. Maintenance of private rooms
   6. Maintenance of common facilities

Notice that the scope remains focused on the problem of attracting and retaining residents. It does not, for example, include looking at alternative uses for the building and grounds. That factor is outside the scope of this research problem.

State Delimitations and Limitations

Two concepts, delimitations and limitations, relate to narrowing the project's scope. *Delimitations* are additional boundaries or restrictions that you place on the study. For example, in the Peaceful Village study, a decision to interview only current residents is a delimitation. *Limitations* are potential shortcomings or inadequacies of the study. Some limitations arise from circumstances beyond your control; others derive from the way you define the scope and delimitations. Interviewing only current residents prevents you from knowing why former residents left and why people who toured your facility did not become residents. Failure to acquire that information may seriously limit the validity of your conclusions. If, however, you do not delimit your study in this way, you may find it extremely difficult and costly to locate those nonresidents. Practical constraints may make the delimitation necessary.

Delimitations and limitations are not required in all research plans. But effective planners include those items when they are relevant. Stating delimitations tends to clarify and refine the scope; stating limitations demonstrates that the researcher understands and is willing to acknowledge the weaknesses of the proposed study.

Having carefully defined the problem, purpose, and scope of the study, you are now ready to plan how you will collect relevant data.

Plan Data Collection

The first step in data collection is to identify potential sources. Researchers use two kinds of data: primary and secondary. Information that has been collected and published by others is secondary data. Books, magazines, journals, and corporate annual reports found in public or private libraries are examples of secondary data sources. Many traditional secondary sources are now available as online or CD-ROM services. Primary data consist of information that is collected at its origin. People and company files are major sources of primary data used in business research.

You will learn methods for collecting primary and secondary data when you study Chapters 9 through 11. Recognize now, however, that the scope of the research problem directs the selection of data sources. To ensure the validity of the data, sources must be chosen for their relevance, not their convenience.

Plan Data Analysis

Data analysis is the process by which researchers find meaning in the many facts and figures they have accumulated. Both quantitative and qualitative analysis procedures are used in business research. Quantitative analysis involves the use of statistics to derive meaning from numerical data. Qualitative analysis is the use of logical thought processes to discover relationships and meaning in data. You will learn more about data analysis when you study Chapter 12. At this time, observe that even before you collect data, you must decide how you will analyze them. (Please note that *data* is the plural form of *datum*. Always refer to *data* with a plural pronoun and accompany the word with a plural verb.)

Although some people consider quantitative analysis to be the more objective form of analysis, that method also has a subjective component. Selection of a statistical procedure and interpretation of the computations rest on subjective judgments. In both quantitative and qualitative analysis, the researcher must avoid faulty reasoning. For example, a researcher could make a hasty generalization about the interrupted intake interview referred to in the previous example of the retirement center. In a hasty generalization, the researcher concludes that something that was true in one instance is true in all cases. If the observed instance was an unusual situation resulting from unexpected events on that day, the researcher would be in error to design a study to determine how to improve intake interviews. The interview situation could also be a symptom of a larger management problem, such as lack of standard procedures for several aspects of the operation.

The manager must also know when the project will be completed. Therefore, the proposal should include a realistic estimate of time required for the work.

Estimate Time Schedule

The purpose of a time schedule is twofold. It ensures the manager that you have considered carefully the time required and are making a commitment to keep to that schedule. It also serves as a checklist for people working on the project to remind them of obligations at various stages. The terms of a proposal often become part of a formal contract; some contracts include penalties if the project is not completed on time or bonuses if completed ahead of schedule.

An effective time schedule includes target dates for completion of various segments of the project as well as a projected date for presentation of the results. It may also include dates on which interim or progress reports will be made. When a researcher has been given a deadline for a project, an effective method for developing a time schedule is to work backward from that date and allocate the maximum length of time that can be devoted to each phase of the project. If no deadline has been given, the proposal writer may work forward from the date of the proposal and project the amount of time required for each phase.

Estimate Resources Needed

Research always requires time; in addition, some research requires special equipment or supplies. Before approving a project, a manager must know how much of the company's resources the project will consume. A research plan should include realistic estimates of the costs of necessary labor (researchers and assistants), supplies, equipment, travel, etc. The manager can then evaluate the potential benefits against the projected costs of the research.

In many companies the accounting department has developed standard costs to apply when employees prepare proposals. For example, you would follow standard cost procedures for determining the value of the time that you and your associates will spend on the project. However, it is your responsibility to make a realistic estimate of the kinds of personnel and the number of hours the project will require. You can usually obtain costs for equipment and supplies from vendors, but it is your responsibility to assess realistically the quantities of such materials that will be required. You can get reasonably accurate estimates of costs for airfare and lodging from a travel agent or online services provided by airlines and hotels. Company policy may require that you use a company vehicle for land travel. If you are permitted to use your own vehicle, apply your employer's standard mileage allowance or the Internal Revenue Service's allowance.

Plan Presentation of Results

Research has no value until the results have been communicated. A complete research plan indicates how the findings, conclusions, and recommendations will be presented.

Since research deals with a nonroutine problem, a relatively rich medium must be chosen. That medium is usually a carefully designed, comprehensive written report, perhaps supplemented by an oral presentation. A tentative outline for the written report may be included in the research plan as evidence that the researcher has thought the project through to its completion.

Seek Approval to Proceed

By now you can probably appreciate that one more item must be included in a research plan: a request for approval. Since research addresses a nonroutine problem and may consume substantial resources, the researchers and managers must agree upon all items in the plan. Even when authorized to prepare the plan, effective researchers do not assume that it is automatically approved. They specifically request feedback and approval. That request opens the door for clarification, possible modification, and approval of the plan. Upon approval, the researcher can work confidently, knowing that carrying out the plan will contribute to both individual and organizational goals.

To obtain approval, most researchers write the research plan and present it in a formal document called a research or project proposal. The proposal may also be presented orally so that managers can ask questions immediately and clarify any ambiguities or request changes before giving their approval.

THE RESEARCH PROPOSAL

The objective of a business proposal is to persuade another person or persons to do something the proposer thinks will be beneficial for the organization and its stakeholders. In the case of a research proposal, the objective is to persuade the recipient to authorize the time and money required to carry out a significant research project.

The persuasiveness of the proposal will depend on your ability to show that you understand the problem and are capable of conducting the study. Additional persuasive elements are honest, realistic estimates of time and resources needed for the project and evidence that you have considered how you will present your results. Therefore, an investigative or research proposal is a formal version of your research plan.

As you prepare a research proposal, use the twelve parts of the research plan as a guide. Include all parts that are relevant to the proposed investigation. The situation may justify omission of certain parts. For example, stating delimitations or limitations is not necessary if the scope of the project is already stated very narrowly and no obvious limitations are foreseen. The order in which the parts are presented must contribute to the reader's understanding of what you plan to investigate. The presentation sequence should also lead the reader to appreciate the significance of the research.

Since a research proposal is a complex document, structural devices such as headings, enumerations, and columns can be used advantageously. Illustration 8-2 demonstrates effective format and structure for a research proposal.

Although Illustration 8-2 shows the proposal in memorandum format, that proposal could also be presented in letter or manuscript format. Manuscript format usually includes a title page and a transmittal message, which includes the request for approval. Illustrations 8-3 through 8-5 show the same proposal presented in manuscript format. Notice that most of the proposal could be identical to one presented in memo format. The introductory material might be changed slightly because some of those details would logically be included in the transmittal message. Similarly, the request for approval is excluded from the manuscript when that request is included in the transmittal message.

| ILLUSTRATION 8-2 | RESEARCH PROPOSAL |

INTEROFFICE COMMUNICATION

TO: J. B. McCarthy, Director of Human Resources

FROM: D. W. Singleton, Personnel Research Associate

DATE: February 9, <year>

SUBJECT: Feasibility Study—Employee Rehabilitation Program

Authorization and Background

At our staff meeting on February 7, you mentioned the need to reduce corporate costs for employee injuries. Although the company has made significant progress in reducing workplace hazards, you requested that I explore creative ways to reduce costs related to worker injuries. I submit this proposal in response to that request.

My preliminary study revealed that a number of firms have reduced worker-compensation costs by helping employees return to the workforce. A recent *Wall Street Journal* report cited the experience of two companies similar to ours. One company estimates that it has saved $8 million over five years by helping injured employees return to work. Another company reduced its worker-compensation costs by 83 percent in only four years with such a program.

Statement of the Problem

Rising worker-compensation costs require that we find alternatives to losing trained employees who have been injured on the job. I propose to study the feasibility of implementing a rehabilitation program for injured employees.

Purpose of the Study

The objective of this study is to reduce worker-compensation costs and improve employee self-esteem. Accomplishing these goals requires a cost-effective program that is acceptable to all employees.

ILLUSTRATION 8-2 ▶ CONTINUED

J. B. McCarthy   – 2 –   February 9, <year>

Scope of Analysis

To determine the feasibility of a rehabilitation program, the following questions must be answered:

1. What is the company's cost for employee disability?
2. What jobs can potentially be filled by disabled employees?
3. What training can be obtained for disabled employees?
4. What is the cost of retraining disabled employees?
5. What are employee attitudes about a rehabilitation program?

Delimitations

The research will be delimitated in the following ways:

1. Study of financial and personnel records will be confined to the last five years.
2. Study of available training will be restricted to programs available within a 100-mile radius of our plant.
3. Analysis of employee attitudes will be limited to attitudes of current employees.

Limitations

The attitudes of current able-bodied employees may not adequately reflect the significance of such a program to injured employees. However, current employees should be able to empathize with injured co-workers and project themselves into a "what if" situation.

Data Collection

Data will be gathered from company personnel and financial records to determine the number and cost of disabilities during the past five years. Supervisors in each major production area will be interviewed to identify potential jobs for disabled employees. Secondary data sources will be used to identify companies that have implemented rehabilitation programs. Those companies and government rehabilitation agencies will be contacted to evaluate the availability and cost of appropriate training. A sample of employees will be surveyed to assess employee attitudes toward a corporate rehabilitation program.

Data Analysis

Logical analysis of available jobs, available training, and employee attitudes will provide the basis for determining whether a rehabilitation program is functional. Cost/benefit analysis will be used to determine whether a program can be financially sound. Conclusions will be based on those qualitative and quantitative factors.

ILLUSTRATION 8-2 ▶ CONTINUED

J. B. McCarthy	– 3 –	February 9, <year>

Time Required

Since I will have other job responsibilities while working on this project, I will need approximately three months to complete the study. Target dates are as follows:

Complete Secondary Research	February 23
Design Employee Questionnaire	February 28
Test and Revise Questionnaire	March 7
Survey Employees and Analyze Results	March 21
Interview Supervisors	April 5
Identify Potential Training Options	April 19
Analyze Data	April 24
Complete Report	May 5

Resources Needed

I anticipate spending approximately 100 hours on this project. My research assistant will use approximately 60 hours to prepare questionnaires and letters, tabulate data, and edit the final report. Standard cost allocations for our respective job grades are applied. In addition, the project requires travel by company car to examine potential training programs and the use of office supplies. The total projected budget is $10,600.

Travel	$ 1,000.00
Supplies	300.00
Labor: Primary Researcher ($75/hr.)	7,500.00
Labor: Research Assistant ($30/hr.)	1,800.00
TOTAL	$ 10,600.00

Presentation of Results

I will present my findings, conclusions, and recommendations to you in a formal written report along with an oral summary. You indicated your plan to circulate the report first to the executive committee and then to others who may need access to the information.

Request for Approval

Approval of this proposal by February 13 will permit me to begin and end on schedule. If you have questions, please call me at extension 597.

ILLUSTRATION 8-3   TITLE PAGE OF RESEARCH PROPOSAL

A PROPOSAL TO STUDY
THE FEASIBILITY OF
AN EMPLOYEE REHABILITATION PROGRAM

Submitted to

J. B. McCarthy
Director of Human Resources

Submitted by

D. W. Singleton
Personnel Research Associate

February 9, <year>

| ILLUSTRATION 8-4 | TRANSMITTAL MESSAGE FOR RESEARCH PROPOSAL |

INTEROFFICE COMMUNICATION

TO: J. B. McCarthy, Director of Human Resources

FROM: D. W. Singleton, Personnel Research Associate

DATE: February 9, <year>

SUBJECT: Feasibility Study—Employee Rehabilitation Program

At our staff meeting on February 7, you mentioned the need to reduce corporate costs for employee injuries. Although the company has made significant progress in reducing workplace hazards, you requested that I explore creative ways to reduce costs related to worker injuries. I submit this proposal in response to that request.

The proposal includes a schedule of target dates for completion of parts of the project. I expect to be able to complete the research and report the results to you within three months.

Approval of this proposal by February 13 will permit me to begin and end on schedule. If you have questions, please call me at extension 597.

ETHICAL CONSIDERATIONS

Ethical issues may arise as you plan research and prepare proposals. At each step in the planning process, ethical individuals would weigh the possible impact of their decisions. Does each decision promote the researcher's good only, or does it contribute to the well-being of others also?

For example, what are the implications of narrowing the scope of analysis? Researchers are often confronted by the very practical constraint of not being able to analyze all possible elements of a problem. But the decision to include some elements and exclude others implies a judgment that one route of analysis will lead to "better" results than another—in essence a moral judgment. Discussing a research problem with a group of colleagues who can judge the work impartially may help you identify the "best" set of factors to include in the scope of analysis.

Again for practical purposes, researchers must sometimes accept data sources that are less than ideal, such as interviewing shoppers in Mall Y because the management of Mall X would not give permission to conduct the interviews. Because of such practical constraints, an honest statement of delimitations and limitations is a practice honored by ethical researchers.

ILLUSTRATION 8-5   RESEARCH PROPOSAL IN MANUSCRIPT FORMAT

A PROPOSAL TO STUDY

THE FEASIBILITY OF AN EMPLOYEE REHABILITATION PROGRAM

A number of firms have reduced worker-compensation costs by helping employees return to the workforce. A recent *Wall Street Journal* report cited the experience of two companies similar to ours. One company estimates that it has saved $8 million over five years by helping injured employees return to work. Another company reduced its worker-compensation costs by 83 percent in only four years with such a program.

Statement of the Problem

Rising worker-compensation costs require that we find alternatives to losing trained employees who have been injured on the job. I propose to study the feasibility of implementing a rehabilitation program for injured employees.

Purpose of the Study

The objective of this study is to reduce worker-compensation costs and improve employee self-esteem. Accomplishing these goals requires a cost-effective program that is acceptable to all employees.

Scope of Analysis

To determine the feasibility of a rehabilitation program, the following questions must be answered:

1. What is the company's cost for employee disability?
2. What jobs can potentially be filled by disabled employees?
3. What training can be obtained for disabled employees?
4. What is the cost of retraining disabled employees?
5. What are employee attitudes about a rehabilitation program?

Delimitations

The research will be delimited in the following ways:

1. Study of financial and personnel records will be confined to the last five years.
2. Study of available training will be restricted to programs available within a 100-mile radius of our plant.
3. Analysis of employee attitudes will be limited to attitudes of current employees.

ILLUSTRATION 8-5 CONTINUED

2

Limitations

The attitudes of current able-bodied employees may not adequately reflect the significance of such a program to injured employees. However, current employees should be able to empathize with injured co-workers and project themselves into a "what if" situation.

Data Collection

Data will be gathered from company personnel and financial records to determine the number and cost of disabilities during the past five years. Supervisors in each major production area will be interviewed to identify potential jobs for disabled employees. Secondary data sources will be used to identify companies that have implemented rehabilitation programs. Those companies and government rehabilitation agencies will be contacted to evaluate the availability and cost of appropriate training. A sample of employees will be surveyed to assess employee attitudes toward a corporate rehabilitation program.

Data Analysis

Logical analysis of available jobs, available training, and employee attitudes will provide the basis for determining whether a rehabilitation program is functional. Cost/benefit analysis will be used to determine whether a program can be financially sound. Conclusions will be based on those qualitative and quantitative factors.

Time Required

Since I will have other job responsibilities while working on this project, I will need approximately three months to complete the study. Target dates are as follows:

Complete Secondary Research	February 23
Design Employee Questionnaire	February 28
Test and Revise Questionnaire	March 7
Survey Employees and Analyze Results	March 21
Interview Supervisors	April 5
Identify Potential Training Options	April 19
Analyze Data	April 24
Complete Report	May 5

ILLUSTRATION 8-5 ▶ CONTINUED

3

Resources Needed

I anticipate spending approximately 100 hours on this project. My research assistant will use approximately 60 hours to prepare questionnaires and letters, tabulate data, and edit the final report. Standard cost allocations for our respective job grades are applied. In addition, the project requires travel by company car to examine potential training programs and the use of office supplies. The total projected budget is $10,600.

Travel	$ 1,000.00
Supplies	300.00
Labor: Primary Researcher ($75/hr.)	7,500.00
Labor: Research Assistant ($30/hr.)	1,800.00
TOTAL	$ 10,600.00

Presentation of Results

I will present my findings, conclusions, and recommendations to you in a formal written report along with an oral summary. You indicated your plan to circulate the report first to the executive committee and then to others who may need access to the information.

Similarly, the request for approval is more than a request for authorization of funds. Do you have (or can you acquire) the skills needed to carry out the research as proposed? The person who gives approval has an ethical responsibility to evaluate the quality of the proposed research, its value to the organization, and the competence of those who will conduct the research. For that reason some proposal writers include the qualifications of the person or persons who will conduct the study to demonstrate competence to fulfill the proposal.

The public is becoming increasingly concerned about invasion of privacy and identity theft. If primary data are to be used in the research, both the researcher and managers who authorize the research have a moral obligation to protect the confidentiality of the data and the safety of human and nonhuman subjects. Specific techniques for protecting confidentiality may be included in the proposed plan for data collection.

Individual rights and the good of others are always involved in proposal preparation. Whenever a person attempts to influence others, ethics are involved. When a proposal is solicited, ethical standards require that a person submit a proposal only if he or she is able to satisfy the requester's needs. When presenting unsolicited proposals, ethical individuals address only genuine, verifiable problems that they can competently analyze.

SUMMARY

A research plan guides the investigator toward completion of effective research. Content and context determine the formality of the plan. A complex project requires a research plan that includes these steps: obtain or review authorization, identify the audience, define the problem, clarify the purpose, narrow the scope, state delimitations and limitations, plan data collection, plan data analysis, estimate time schedule, estimate resources needed, plan presentation of results, and seek approval to proceed. A research or project proposal is a formal written version of such a plan.

Ethical issues may arise at each stage of project planning. The ethical researcher considers motives for and likely outcomes of decisions made in each planning step.

TOPICS FOR DISCUSSION

1. What is the function of a research plan?

2. What are the parts of a research plan?

3. What is the relationship of a research plan to a research proposal?

4. Differentiate these parts of a research plan: managerial problem, research problem, research purpose.

5. Why must you limit a project's scope?

6. What are delimitations and limitations? Why should these factors be considered when the research is being planned?

7. How do primary and secondary data differ from one another?

8. Why should data analysis be addressed in a research proposal?

9. Why should a research proposal include estimates of time and resources needed?

10. Why are both authorization of a research project and approval of the project proposal necessary?

11. If you have conducted business research, share with your classmates some of the ethical issues that you had to consider as you planned the research.

12. If you were asked to provide personal data for business research purposes, what concerns would you have about the use of the data? What evidence would you require to ensure that the researcher would use the data ethically?

APPLICATIONS

1. For each of the following situations, assume you are a researcher for Abrams, Beltzer, Cox, and Duoma, LLP, a business consulting firm to small businesses. Each scenario requires that you write a proposal to conduct research that will help the client resolve a problem. You do not have to conduct the research at this time. Just write the proposal, providing the kinds of information the client will need before authorizing you to proceed with the research. In each situation, identify the managerial problem, the research problem and purpose, the scope of your analysis, and possible data sources. Add other factors that will convince the client to hire you to do the research.

   a. Zack Pupchek has observed the growing popularity of resale, consignment, and thrift shops. Many astute consumers have learned to stretch their dollars by buying "nearly new" clothing, toys, and home furnishings in such shops, and they are becoming a growing force in retail markets. Pupchek has asked you whether opening a resale, consignment, or thrift shop in your city or a nearby town is a good business venture. NOTE: Check the National Association of Resale & Thrift Shops (http://www.narts.org) for distinctions among the three classifications and other information about this industry.

   b. Natural Fare is a supermarket that specializes in organically grown fruits, vegetables, and other grocery items classified as "natural" or "organic." Its shopping carts have become quite dilapidated and must be replaced. The owner, Hans Grossman, has read about new supermarket carts that are equipped with touch screens that can guide the shopper through the store and let the shopper order items from the deli or meat department without having to stand in line. Since many of Grossman's customers are busy professional people who don't want to spend a lot of time shopping for food, he thinks the "smart" carts may be the way to go when he replaces his old equipment. Grossman has asked you to study the advantages and disadvantages of "smart" carts. (IBM has test marketed its "shopping buddy" in Massachusetts, and Springfield Retail Networks has tested its Concierge in Canadian stores.)

   c. Lisa Carswell has completed a dog grooming course and has worked for three years with one of the busiest pet grooming businesses in your city. She thinks she wants to begin a mobile dog grooming business (no cats, please), in which she would take her fully equipped van to homes and groom dogs on their owners' premises. She thinks the service would appeal to retirees who may have difficulty taking their pets to the grooming parlor and busy professionals who often cannot find time to take their dogs out to be groomed. Carswell asked you to study the potential for such a business in your town.

   d. Obesity is surging among the affluent. In the early 1970s, fewer than 10 percent of those in the $60,000+ income bracket were obese compared with almost 25 percent of those earning less than $25,000.

But the University of Iowa College of Public Health reports that in 2001–02 over 26 percent of those in the $60,000+ bracket were obese compared with 31.5 percent of those earning less than $25,000 (incomes adjusted for 2000 dollars). (Source: Hellmich, Nanci. *USA Today,* May 3, 2005, p. 1A.) Karen Hosse, a registered dietician, has written a book featuring nutritious, simple meals along with a practical exercise plan that most people should be able to incorporate into their daily lifestyles. She asks you to research the potential market for such a book.

e. While visiting Japan, Brian Paschal and his wife Victoria were captivated by the rickshaw, a light, two-wheeled vehicle drawn by one or two persons. They currently own a gift shop in a beach resort community. Auto traffic is prohibited in the main shopping area of the town, an area covering four square blocks. Parking lots are located on the perimeter of the shopping square and customers must walk from their cars into the commercial area. Some shop owners think that the restricted access prevents potential customers from browsing in the shops. Brian and Victoria think that a rickshaw service, transporting people from their cars into the shopping area, could be profitable both for the operator of that service and for merchants who might gain more business by increasing customer traffic. They ask you to research the requirements for such a business and its potential success.

2. Several employees who are approaching retirement have asked you, Director of Human Resources for West Trust Bank, whether the company will allow them to continue to work part time when they reach retirement age. They have suggested that they should be allowed to work half time and draw part of their pensions at the same time. You would like to keep some of the better employees in part-time positions, but would be happy to see the less effective employees retire. You know the issue will require considerable research before you can bring a plan to the management committee. Write a research proposal that will address this issue. Address the proposal to Willard Dawson, Vice President for Administration.

3. According to International Spa Association–Europe, spa business can be classified into seven groups:
   1. Hotel and Resort Spa—located in a hotel or resort area; providing services to guests of that hotel or resort.
   2. Destination Spa—a standalone spa service; providing various spa packages, such as tension release treatment and body and mind revitalization.
   3. Medical Spa—usually located in a hospital; providing spa services together with medical treatments under supervision of medically licensed personnel.
   4. Day Spa or City Spa—usually located in the downtown area of big cities, providing 1– or 2–hour spa treatments without accommodation service.

5. Mineral Spring Spa—located in natural spring areas; providing services to tourists.
6. Club Spa—a membership spa service in sport clubs or fitness centers; providing services to exercise enthusiasts.
7. Cruise Ship Spa—a spa on a cruise ship; providing exercise courses and spa treatments, together with nutrition services.

The spa business in Thailand began to gain popularity among foreign tourists during 1993 and 1994, with a number of newly opened spas in five-star hotels around the country. With more than 5 million tourists in 1994 who reportedly were customers of Thai spas, Thailand foresaw a great business opportunity. Thai economic developers announced a plan to promote spa services as part of the country's strategy for bringing in foreign money.

Thai spa business stepped into a booming period in 2001. By the end of that year, there were around 200 registered spa service providers around the country. These were located mainly in Bangkok and other tourist destinations, including Phuket, Surathani (Koh Samui), and Chiengmai. Main patrons were foreign tourists and a growing number of local customers. The business looks very promising as most people are moving toward a self-pampering and healthy lifestyle.

The hotel and resort spa group is receiving a good share of the market in Thailand, targeting tourists with high purchasing power. In addition to Thailand's well-known hospitality and exotic cuisine, spa services have become major attractions for tourists staying at hotels and resorts. Most of the hotels and resorts report their investment in spa services ranges from 10 to 50 million baht, and they expect the payback period to be from 12 to 18 months.

The destination spa group in Thailand offers distinguished world-class spa services. Chivasom is the first of its kind in Thailand and well known among high-end customers, including the world's richest and most famous people. With its unique spa packages and services, Chivasom was named the world's best spa in 2002 by *Conde Nast Traveler*. Currently, there are only a few local players in the destination spa business.

Medical spa service is gaining in popularity among hospitals in Thailand as an alternative medical treatment. As the health care business is becoming more competitive, numbers of large private hospitals are spending big investments on developing medical spa services to differentiate themselves.

Day spa services are targeted mainly at the middle-level market and take advantage of lower price offerings with quality spa treatments and herbal aromatic products. The investment in a stand-alone day spa ranges from 3 to 5 million baht with a payback period of 8 to 12 months.

Various factors yield promising opportunities for the spa business in Thailand. First, there are many natural spring sites in the country, with more than 200,000 visitors a year. Moreover, Thailand is renowned for its impressive hospitality and magnificent natural tourist places. Thailand's delicate cuisine and traditional ways of life add a magic touch for those who have visited the country. The total number of foreign tourists was reported to be as high as 10 million in 2003, bringing in more than 340,000 million baht to the country. In addition, Thailand has strength in developing its own unique herbal products from local materials. These products are certified by nationally recognized organizations. Finally, the Thai government has displayed strong support for developing the country to become the center of the spa business in Southeast Asia. For instance, the government has cooperated with the private sector in establishing spa training institutes; promoting a tourist campaign, "Unseen Spa"; investing in many research projects on Thai local herbs; and offering special investment packages to both local and foreign business investors who want to invest in the spa business.

However, there are also some threats to the success of the spa business in Thailand, including:

- High competition among various spa investors in the country
- Competition with other countries in the region
- A lack of well-trained personnel as the demand is growing rapidly

Assume you are a member of the marketing research staff with a major U.S.-based hotel chain. (Select a major chain about which you will be able to obtain significant operating and financial information.) Supplementing the information provided here, you are to write a report on the feasibility for that hotel chain to enter the spa business in Thailand. Your first task is to write a research proposal to be presented to the Director of International Marketing for the hotel chain.

Application written by Wichai Utsahajit, Assistant Professor of the Graduate Program in Human Resource Development at the National Institute of Development Administration (NIDA), Thailand; part-time Lecturer at the Faculty of Commerce and Accountancy, Chulalongkorn University; and Training and Program Development Director at Toyota Motor Thailand.

4. Prepare a proposal to conduct a study related to a topic of your choice, to be approved by your instructor. Select a personal or organizational problem in which you have a special interest. You may choose a topic related to a significant personal decision (for example, options for a major consumer purchase, such as an automobile, a boat, or a house; feasibility of establishing a particular kind of business); a communication topic (for example, communication problems and needs of the elderly when dealing with health-care professionals, insurance companies, or social service agencies; effective ways for a nonprofit agency to inform the public of its services; communication problems between expatriate managers and foreign nationals whom they supervise); or an organizational problem (for example, environmentally responsible or irresponsible actions of X company; use of hybrid vehicles vs. traditional gasoline-fueled vehicles for pizza deliveries). Your instructor may discuss other options with you.

Include the following in your proposal:

- Background information that will identify the managerial (general) problem
- The research problem and its scope

- The purpose of the research
- Delimitations and limitations, if relevant
- A preliminary plan for data collection and analysis
- An estimate of the resources needed to complete the research
- A projected time schedule for completion of the project
- A statement of how you will report your research results
- A request for approval to proceed with your proposed project

After receiving feedback from your instructor and approval to conduct the research, use the proposal as your guide for data collection, data analysis, and preparation of a report. Chapters 9–13 will provide more details to guide your completion of this project.

Selecting Data Sources

LEARNING OBJECTIVES

After you have read this chapter, you should be able to:

1. Explain how to determine appropriate data sources for your research.
2. Discuss criteria for evaluating data sources.
3. Define the characteristics of a valid sample.
4. Identify general guides for determining sample size.
5. Identify kinds of samples used in business research.

The value of all research depends on the validity and reliability of the data acquired for the project. GIGO (garbage in, garbage out) is an acronym used often by systems analysts to remind themselves and system users to protect the quality of information that enters the system. That acronym is also an appropriate warning to report writers. The quality of a report can be no better than the quality of the data on which it is based. Therefore, report writers must master the skills of selecting appropriate data sources and using those sources accurately.

DETERMINING DATA SOURCES

Defining potential data sources is part of the development of a research plan, as discussed in Chapter 8. Two questions should guide you as you determine possible sources for research data:

- What kinds of information do I need to answer the research question?
- Should I use primary or secondary data sources—or both—to obtain that information?

Data Need

The research question, divided into appropriate elements or factors of analysis, must direct your search for data. After you have defined the research question clearly and have narrowed the scope, you must focus your attention on finding data directly related to those factors.

ILLUSTRATION 9-1 ▶ DETERMINING DATA SOURCES

Research Problem: To project market conditions for skilled construction labor in the Northwest United States during the next three years.

Research Purpose: To ensure that Benco has an adequate supply of labor to fulfill construction contracts.

ELEMENTS (SCOPE)	DATA NEEDED	POTENTIAL SOURCES
Projected demand for skilled construction labor	a. Sizes of projects under contract by major regional contractors b. Projects to be bid and contracted for during next three years	a. Regional contractors b. State economic development boards
Projected supply of skilled labor	a. Demographics of crews currently hired by major contractors in the Northwest b. Projected graduates from technical schools in the Northwest for next three years	a. Regional contractors; state employment service b. Registrars and placement officers of technical schools
Benco recruitment and employment practices	a. Methods currently used to locate skilled construction crews b. Benco employment practices that attract crews to Benco c. Benco employment practices that deter crews from working for Benco	a. Benco Director of Human Resources b. Members of current Benco crews c. Members of former Benco crews d. Benco Human Resource director

Keeping the scope of analysis in mind will make you an efficient, effective researcher. You will be efficient because you will target your data search toward the sources most likely to yield meaningful information rather than wasting time looking at unrelated data. You will be effective because you will be able to judge all data in terms of its relevance to the research problem and will not be tempted to include interesting but irrelevant data.

The chart in Illustration 9-1 shows how the research question guides the selection of information sources. After the research problem and purpose have been defined, the scope of analysis must be narrowed. Then specific kinds of data and specific data sources must be identified for each element in the scope. Note that more than one kind of data and more than one data source may be required to analyze a specific element adequately.

Primary Versus Secondary Data

Effective business researchers use both primary and secondary data to solve business problems. *Primary data* are data acquired at their sources through observation, experimentation, interviews, questionnaire surveys, and searches through company records. *Secondary data* consist of information that others have accumulated and made available through books, magazines, journals, and other published documents. Other important sources of secondary data include online services and information made available on microforms and CD-ROMs. Specific techniques for collecting secondary and primary data will be discussed in Chapters 10 and 11.

Some researchers mistakenly consider primary data to be better than secondary data. They assume that information "straight from the source" is better information than secondhand data. Others prefer to use primary data because they are stimulated by that data collection process and feel restricted when they must sit in a library searching through documents or scanning a computer for secondary information.

In contrast, some researchers—equally mistakenly—suspect the accuracy of primary data. They recognize that people can deliberately distort self-reported information, and researchers can make incorrect observations or lead people to report what the researcher wants to record. In addition, some researchers may feel uncomfortable with the primary data collection process but enjoy the sense of discovery that comes from searching out well-documented information in secondary sources.

Neither attitude can produce consistently effective research reports. When you recognize a problem and the need for research, you should first consult secondary sources. Secondary sources often provide information to help define the problem more clearly and to identify elements that should be investigated. After narrowing the scope of the analysis, you must determine whether primary or secondary sources will best answer each element of the problem, as was demonstrated in Illustration 9-1. When the problem you are investigating is unique to your organization, primary data may be the only usable information. But if adequate secondary data are available, you should use those data instead of spending the time and effort required to use primary sources effectively.

EVALUATING DATA SOURCES

Before using any data source, you should be sure the source meets three criteria: validity, reliability, and practicality.

Validity

Validity is a measurement concept that refers to the extent to which differences revealed with a measuring tool represent true differences among the people or objects being measured. For example, a test to determine prospective employees' knowledge of and skill in using spreadsheet software is valid to the extent that the test can differentiate among applicants who have various levels of spreadsheet knowledge and skill. The test has content validity if it tests or measures what it purports to measure. To have content validity, a test to determine employees' knowledge of spreadsheet software must test enough aspects of software use to be able to assess different levels of competence. A test has criterion-related validity if test scores can predict a relevant behavior. The spreadsheet test has criterion-related validity if it can successfully predict which applicants will use spreadsheet software efficiently and effectively as required in their job assignments.

In a broader sense, validity can apply to data sources and the data obtained from those sources, as well as to the instruments used to collect data. A data source is valid if it is able to provide objective, accurate information about the research topic. Some sources have greater degrees of validity than others. For example, assume your research requires information about the number of single-parent households in your county. The most recent U.S. Census (secondary source) has greater validity than would a heads-of-household sample in the county conducted by your staff (primary source), because the data come from a more extensive survey than you could conduct yourself. In contrast, assume your research requires data about average cost-of-living pay increases granted in your county last year. In that case, a survey of local businesses could be more valid than the census data because it is more current.

Reliability

Reliability is a measurement concept that refers to the consistency of results obtained with a measuring device. A reliable instrument is relatively free of random or unstable error; such an instrument helps the researcher get as close to the truth as possible. For example, a steel measuring rod is more reliable than a cloth measuring tape to measure distance or height. The steel rod itself changes little with variations in temperature, moisture, or pressure; but a cloth measuring tape may stretch or shrink in response to those conditions.

Two aspects of consistency—stability and equivalence—contribute to reliability. An instrument has stability if it gives consistent measurements of the same person or thing at different times; for example, your car odometer records nearly the same mileage each time you measure the distance of the route from your home to your campus or workplace. The instrument has equivalence if different people using the instrument at approximately the same time and for the same purpose get consistent results; both you and your spouse or a friend gets the same results when measuring distance by the odometer. To illustrate further, assume that two professors will rate your oral presentation. Such an evaluation can be somewhat subjective, but a reliable instrument can remove much of the subjectivity from the situation. The evaluation will be more reliable than it would be if the professors used no instrument to guide their ratings, because the rating guide directs both observers to focus on the same evaluation factors. If the two professors give you nearly equivalent scores, the instrument may be presumed to have equivalent reliability.

The concept of reliability extends to data sources and data obtained from them, as well as to data collection instruments. Assume you operate an upscale women's clothing store and you want to identify services that will attract more customers to your store. A sample of women in a specific income range within the geographic area you plan to serve would be a more reliable data source than would your current customers. Your current customers' perceptions are not representative of people who do not shop at your store.

Ideally, data sources and data collection techniques are both reliable and valid. Valid instruments and sources are also reliable, but reliable sources or instruments are not necessarily valid. Assume, for example, that survey participants mistakenly believe they have used a laundry detergent (Product X) that is similar to but different from the detergent they have actually used (Product Y). The participants may consistently report satisfaction with Product X (reliability), but the information is not valid because they have never used that product. They are clearly reporting satisfaction with something, but not with the test detergent.

Another example will illustrate the relationship between validity and reliability. Automobile odometers, which measure travel distance and speed, are calibrated to be used with certain tire sizes. If an auto owner installs a tire larger in diameter than that for which the odometer was calibrated, the odometer will consistently (reliably) register a speed that is slower than the auto is actually traveling. By using a reliable instrument that records incorrect (invalid) data, the driver may have an unpleasant experience with the highway patrol!

As you select data sources, always consider both the validity and the reliability of each source, especially when you use the Internet in a data search. Since few restrictions exist with respect to who may post information on the Internet and what may be posted, invalid information from unreliable sources exists on this valuable resource. Guides for evaluating Internet sources are provided in Chapter 10.

Practicality

A final criterion by which you must judge potential data sources is practicality. Although business researchers desire validity and reliability, some tradeoffs are usually needed between the ideal project and what can be achieved within time and budget constraints.

Practicality refers to both the cost and the convenience of using a data source. Assume, for example, that you are assisting the manager of a Bank of America branch who wants to investigate customer satisfaction with teller services. Bank customers are certainly a more valid data source than are bank tellers. Observation of customers interacting with bank tellers and face-to-face interviews with bank customers may be your preferred data-gathering techniques. The time and cost required to use those techniques, however, may force you to substitute a less expensive mail survey. As you prepare your questionnaire, you may recall that increasing the number of items is one way to improve questionnaire reliability. However, since survey participants often resist completing a long questionnaire, you may shorten the questionnaire, thereby trading a degree of reliability for practicality.

Another practical decision that you would likely make is that you cannot question all bank customers about their satisfaction with teller services. Most business researchers are confronted with the need to sample data sources rather than attempt to use the entire population.

Sampling Data Sources

To understand sampling concepts, you must understand five terms: population, element, sample, subject, and population frame.

Population refers to the entire group of people, events, or other items of interest that are the focus of a study. If the manager of Central City Club, a private club, wants to know members' opinions about the club's services, the population is all members of the club. An *element* is a single unit of the population, that is, one member of the club. The population, therefore, consists of the total collection of elements about which a researcher wishes to make inferences. A *sample* is a subgroup of the population composed of some of the elements, and a *subject* is a single member of the sample.

Before a sample can be drawn from a population, all members of the population must be identified. A *population frame* (sometimes called a sampling frame) is a list of all elements in a population from which a sample could be drawn. In some cases, devising that list is relatively easy; for example, an accurate list of Central City Club members should be relatively easy to obtain. In other cases, identifying all members of the population may be nearly impossible, and a list that reasonably approximates the population must be chosen. For example, if the school board of Central City wants to learn how the community rates its performance on major educational issues, identifying all members of the community would be prohibitive. Some researchers use a telephone directory as the population frame when they wish to sample the city population. However, with the current popularity of cell phones, many city residents have no land-based telephones and others have unlisted numbers. Therefore, the telephone directory is not a true representation of the population. To obtain valid data, a researcher working for the Central City school board would do well to avoid using that source as its population frame. A list of registered voters in the areas served by that school might be a better population frame for the school board research. That list would presumably include all people who show enough concern for civic matters to be involved, at least to some extent, in the electoral process.

In business research, an investigation may involve hundreds or thousands of potential subjects. Time and budget constraints often prohibit data collection from or about every element that could be studied; therefore, a sample is used. The basic idea of sampling is that elements in a population provide useful data about the characteristics of that population. When you judge the quality of a box of chocolate truffles, for example, you take a sample (one truffle), analyze the characteristics of that sample, and generalize that the entire population (all truffles in the box) has the same characteristics. Similarly, in Central City Club's member satisfaction survey, the researcher infers that the characteristics of a sample of those members represent the characteristics of the entire member population. Such inferences, however, are valid only if the sample is valid.

Characteristics of a Valid Sample

A valid sample is one that accurately represents its population characteristics. Sample validity depends on three factors: accuracy, precision, and sample size.[1]

ACCURACY

An accurate sample is free of bias; that is, it neither over-represents nor under-represents certain population characteristics. An accurate sample has no systematic variance, which is the variation in measurement due to some known or unknown influence that causes the scores to lean in a particular direction. For example, assume that a group of young professionals meets for breakfast at Central City Club every Tuesday, 7–8 a.m. If the club draws a sample from members who visit the club during those hours, the sample may be systematically biased toward attitudes of young professionals. The attitudes of retired members who use club services primarily during lunch hours or to entertain dinner guests would be systematically under-represented.

Inaccuracy sometimes results from use of an inaccurate population frame. Central City Club could use a list of all members as a population frame. However, if the member list is not updated daily to indicate new and discontinued accounts, the population frame would be inaccurate and could contribute to inaccuracy in any sample drawn from it.

PRECISION

No sample can be identical to its population in all respects. A sample statistic (such as the arithmetic mean of the sample) may be expected to vary from its corresponding population value (the arithmetic mean of the population) because of random fluctuations in the sampling process. Such fluctuations or variations are referred to as sampling error. A precise sample has little sampling error.

Assume, for example, that Central City Club wants information about its members who are retired. For practical reasons, the researcher may decide to take a sample of customers who come to the club between 11:30 a.m. and 1 p.m. because that is when many retirees visit the club. But a sample taken at that time would contain sampling error if it randomly included guests who accompanied members to the club for lunch that day.

ADEQUATE SAMPLE SIZE

Precision and accuracy are important sampling issues because a researcher wants to be sure that inferences about the population are justifiable. Sample size can affect the accuracy and precision of your inferences.

Generally, if the characteristics that are being studied are widely dispersed in the population, the accuracy and precision of inferences based upon the sample can be improved by increasing the sample size. For example, if the monthly expenditures of Central City Club's retired members range from $50 to $3,000, to gain the desired levels of precision and accuracy, the researcher will have to draw a larger sample than would be necessary if the monthly expenditures were $50 to $300. In contrast, if the characteristics are narrowly dispersed in the population, drawing a large sample size may be wasteful and costly. It may be possible to achieve the desired precision and accuracy with a relatively small sample. By following the guides given in the next section, you should be able to select an appropriate sample size for your research.

Guides for Determining Sample Size

Four rules of thumb guide researchers in determining sample size.

1. Sample sizes larger than 30 and less than 500 are appropriate for most research. Where samples are to be broken into subsamples (males/females, juniors/seniors, etc.), a minimum sample size of 30 for each category is necessary.
2. If several variables are used in the research, the sample size should be several times (preferably 10 times or more) as large as the number of variables measured in the study. For example, if you are measuring four variables, your sample size should be at least 40.
3. For simple experimental research with tight experimental controls, successful research is possible with samples as small as 10 or 20.

A final consideration in sampling is the kind of sample to use. Several options are available. The nature of your research problem and the desired degree of accuracy determine which sampling technique is appropriate.

KINDS OF SAMPLES

Sampling designs fall into two major categories: probability and nonprobability. In *probability sampling*, the population elements have a known chance or probability of being selected. In *nonprobability* sampling, the elements do not have a predetermined chance of being selected.

Probability Sampling

When representativeness of the sample is important, probability sampling is used. This type of sampling can be unrestricted or restricted. Unrestricted probability sampling is commonly called simple random sampling. Restricted or complex sampling designs have been developed to compensate for the inefficiencies of unrestricted sampling. Four of those designs—systematic, stratified random, cluster, and area sampling—are used frequently in business research.

SIMPLE RANDOM SAMPLING

In *simple random sampling*, every element in the population has an equal chance of being selected as a subject. Assume that Central City Club has 1,000 members and wishes to draw a sample of 100. If all names are thrown into a basket and a blindfolded individual draws 100, each depositor has an equal chance (100 in 1,000) of being drawn. Actually, to retain that 100 in 1,000 chance, each name must be returned to the basket after having been drawn, and the drawing must continue until 100 different names have been selected.

Simple random sampling has the least bias, but the technique can be cumbersome and expensive. In addition, bias can enter the sample if the population frame is not accurate and up to date.

SYSTEMATIC SAMPLING

The *systematic sampling* design involves drawing every *n*th element in the population, starting with a randomly chosen element. To draw a systematic sample of 100, the Central City Club researcher would randomly select a member number, such as 128, and then draw every tenth (if that is the chosen *n*) account thereafter (138, 148, 158, etc.) until 100 have been drawn.

Accuracy of this method depends upon an accurate population frame. In addition, researchers using this technique must be cautious to avoid systematic bias. For example, a researcher may decide to draw a systematic sample of 25 companies from the most recent list of the Fortune 500 largest industries, drawing every tenth firm after randomly selecting a starting point. Assume the starting number is 201. Although the population frame may be up to date, this design would systematically bias the sample toward the smallest firms. Number 1 on the list is the largest firm, but the sample would be drawn from Numbers 201 through 441. This problem could have been avoided by using a larger interval (such as 20) that would require returning to the beginning of the list after the number 500 was reached. This example illustrates that a researcher must be aware of the characteristics of the population frame before defining the *n* to use in systematic sampling.

STRATIFIED RANDOM SAMPLING

The *stratified random sampling* design requires stratification or segregation of the elements, followed by a random selection of subjects from the strata. To draw this type of sample, the Central City Club could stratify its members by age groups corresponding approximately to education and career stages, such as 21–30, 31–40, 41–50, 51–60, and over 60. Then the club would determine what kind of sample it requires from each age group to achieve the objectives of the study.

For proportionate sampling, the club would draw a number from each stratum that is proportionate to the percentage of the total population represented by elements in that stratum. The table in Illustration 9-2 shows the number of

ILLUSTRATION 9-2	PROPORTIONATE AND DISPROPORTIONATE STRATIFIED RANDOM SAMPLES			
Population Strata	N	%	Proportionate (N = 200)	Disproportionate (N = 200)
21–30	200	20	40	40
31–40	250	25	50	47
41–50	300	30	60	50
51–60	190	19	38	38
Over 60	60	6	12	25
Totals	1000	100	200	200

subjects to be drawn from each stratum if Central City Club wishes to draw a proportionate stratified random sample of 100 from its 1,000 members.

For disproportionate sampling, elements are drawn from each stratum based on the researcher's judgment. One factor that justifies disproportionate sampling is extreme imbalance in strata sizes warranting more or less than proportional representation of certain strata. That situation exists in the proportionate sample shown in Illustration 9-2. The disproportionate sample in that table shows how a researcher could adjust a sample to compensate for small numbers in certain categories. Disproportionate sampling is also used at times because it is convenient, simple, and economical to administer.

Cluster Sampling

A *cluster sampling* technique may be appropriate when a targeted population is already divided into groups or can easily be clustered. After defining the clusters, the researcher randomly selects some of those clusters and studies all elements in each cluster. Ideally, the clusters demonstrate heterogeneity (diversity) within and homogeneity (similarity) across groups. In the Central City Club case, for example, ideal clusters would contain many different kinds of members (that is, varied by age, gender, profession, years of membership, etc.) but all clusters would represent the "typical" club member.

Naturally occurring clusters, such as clusters of students or residents, are often used in business research. But those clusters typically are relatively homogeneous within and heterogeneous across groups. For example, homeowners clustered by neighborhoods tend to be similar within groups, but different across groups. For that reason, naturally occurring clusters, although convenient for some kinds of research, tend to lack the precision and accuracy desired in samples.

Area Sampling

When research can be identified with some geographic region, area sampling is appropriate. Area sampling is a form of cluster sampling in which a sample is drawn from a defined geographic area.

This technique is efficient and relatively inexpensive. Suppose, for example, that Belle's Day Spa wants to survey the adult residents of the northeast section of the city to determine the feasibility of opening a branch in that area. Obtaining a complete list of all adults in that area would be virtually impossible. But it would be relatively easy to look at a map, define the area commonly considered the "northeast section," and draw a sample of homes by street addresses.

Nonprobability Sampling

Nonprobability sampling is appropriate when a researcher's objective is to gather preliminary information in a quick and inexpensive way rather than to make generalizations about a larger population. There are also times when nonprobability sampling is the only feasible technique. For example, probability sampling could not be used for an analysis of the content of internal reports because it would be impossible to construct the population frame of all internal reports. Some reports would be too confidential to release for research purposes, some would have been misplaced or destroyed, and some, such as oral reports, would not have been recorded in a permanent form. Nonprobability sampling takes two forms: convenience and purposive.

CONVENIENCE SAMPLING

A *convenience sample* is unrestricted; the researcher is free to choose elements according to their availability. This technique is easy and relatively inexpensive, and it satisfies the demands of some research designs.

Assume, for example, Belle's Day Spa wants preliminary information about additional spa services that customers are interested in. The spa might draw a convenience sample by placing a set of questionnaires at the door of the spa with a sign saying "Tell us how we can serve you." Although the sample could not possibly represent the total customer population, the results of the survey would provide worthwhile clues about customer interests. Similarly, interviewing a convenience sample of people as they leave the opening performance in a new concert hall can provide valuable information to the hall manager about the positive and negative aspects of the building (acoustics, seats, restrooms, etc.) and identify needed adjustments.

PURPOSIVE SAMPLING

A purposive sample is a nonprobability sample that conforms to certain criteria. There are two major types: judgment and quota sampling.

In a *judgment sample* the researcher handpicks elements that conform to certain criteria. This technique is used when only limited numbers of people possess the information that is sought or when elements are chosen because of their predictive power in the past. For example, if you want to investigate what it takes for a female to become a partner in a Wall Street law firm, you might appropriately seek information only from females who have achieved that status. Political analysts use judgment sampling when they predict the outcome of an election by projecting from results of a few precincts whose voting records in the past have predicted election results.

In a *quota sample* the researcher tries to ensure that the sample is representative of the population from which it is drawn by specifying certain control dimensions. The dimensions selected must have a known distribution in the population and they must be relevant to the topic studied.

Assume, for example, that you wish to conduct a study at your school to determine student opinion about required drug testing for student athletes. You may hypothesize that differences in attitudes may be related to gender, athletic team membership, and class level. You could assume two categories for each dimension and determine what percent of the student population fits into each category, as follows:

Gender	Female	57 percent
	Male	43 percent
Athletic Team	Member	29 percent
	Nonmember	71 percent
Class Level	Undergraduate	87 percent
	Graduate	13 percent

You would then draw a convenience sample, choosing subjects until you have secured the same proportions of males and females, athletic team members and nonmembers, and undergraduate and graduate students that comprise the student population.

An obvious weakness of quota sampling is that the sample may not be representative of the population; hence, the researcher's ability to generalize (draw conclusions) from the findings is limited. For example, you could conceivably draw your entire quota from students enrolled in the humanities, whose opinions might differ widely from those of students enrolled in business or engineering. Researchers can protect the sample from such bias, however, by careful selection of relevant dimensions that define the quota. In this example, including the course of study as a dimension would have forced you to avoid selecting all subjects from one academic area.

ETHICAL CONSIDERATIONS

As you choose data sources, you may again confront ethical dilemmas. For example, what are the ethical implications of using a convenience sample rather than a stratified random sample? There is no absolute answer to that question, but you should always attempt to use the most powerful sampling techniques available to you within your time and monetary budgets. Doing less than that could lead to faulty conclusions based on the data, with potential damaging outcomes—loss of customers, loss of goodwill, etc.—to your organization.

The relative importance of your research problem should also influence your choice of a sampling procedure. For example, a convenience sample of individuals entering a store may be adequate to test consumers' initial reactions to a new perfume. Although that sampling technique is easy to apply and relatively inexpensive, a perfumer would be unwise to base a major marketing campaign on the outcome of such a survey. A more difficult and costly technique, the stratified random sample, would be a better choice for identifying the socio-economic group that should be targeted in a major marketing campaign.

SUMMARY

A report can be no better than the data on which it is based, and data can be no more valid or reliable than the sources from which they are obtained. Therefore, your choice of data sources is a critical step in research planning. Both primary and secondary data sources are selected for their validity (ability to provide data related to the factors of analysis) and reliability (consistency). In addition, data sources are chosen for their practicality.

The impracticality of using an entire population of interest often requires the researcher to select a sample of that population and draw inferences based upon data obtained from the sample. Accuracy and precision are desired in samples. When there is considerable variability in the population, sample accuracy and precision can be improved by increasing the sample size. When the population shows little variability, accuracy and precision may be possible with a small sample.

The research problem and purpose must be considered before deciding whether to use probability or nonprobability sampling. Probability samples include simple random, systematic, stratified random, cluster, and area samples. Nonprobability samples are either convenience or purposive samples. Two kinds of purposive samples are judgment and quota samples. To gather valid and reliable data, a researcher must choose the appropriate sampling technique.

TOPICS FOR DISCUSSION

1. Explain how a research question directs the choice of data sources.

2. Why should a researcher consult secondary data sources before primary sources?

3. Explain these terms: validity, content validity, and criterion-related validity.

4. Explain these terms: reliability, stability, and equivalence.

5. Explain the relationship of validity and reliability.

6. Why can validity and reliability not be the only criteria for selection of data sources?

7. Define these terms:
   a. Population
   b. Element
   c. Sample
   d. Subject
   e. Population frame

8. What are the characteristics of a valid sample?

9. Give four guides for determining sample size.

10. Compare and/or contrast the following sampling concepts:
    a. Probability and nonprobability
    b. Simple random, systematic, and stratified random
    c. Cluster and area
    d. Convenience and purposive
    e. Judgment and quota

APPLICATIONS

1. Plan the data collection for each of the following situations. Specifically, do the following:
   - Identify the kinds of information needed.
   - Identify the appropriate sources of data.
   - Identify the likely sequence for collecting the data.
   - Identity the best sampling technique for any necessary primary data.
   a. Carl Zumhoff, the manager of a large real estate firm, is concerned about the rising home prices, especially the potential impact on first-time home buyers. He has read about friends and families jointly buying a home to be shared by two families or two or more friends, and he wants to study the feasibility of promoting such joint purchases in his community. Elements of the problem include qualification processes (that is, determining what kind of financial burden the buyers can handle); changes required in contracts to protect buyers, sellers, and mortgage lenders; closing procedures; experience of real estate brokers in other cities; potential impact on the firm's sales.
   b. Stella Linden, manager of human resources for an insurance company, thinks many employees resign because of inadequate child care, and she knows some companies provide child care facilities on their premises. Ms. Linden wants to analyze the feasibility of providing child care for children of employees. Elements of the problem include methods of providing child care, success of other company-sponsored child care programs, costs, the company's responsibilities and potential liability when providing child care, government policies affecting child care centers, and the number of employees desiring child care on the company's premises.
   c. Letty Angler has learned that a newly organized national association of female college athletes is searching for an executive director. Ms. Angler has extensive experience in association management and has represented her current association effectively in promoting legislation that benefits its members. She is also an avid fan of female athletics, both amateur and professional. To prepare for an interview with the association, Ms. Angler has asked you to research this question: What opportunities exist for female athletes in college sports? Elements of the research include the history of college athletics for females, current status of college athletics programs for

females, changes in those programs during the past 10 years, availability of scholarships for female athletes, changes in scholarship funding during the past 10 years, revenue generated by athletics programs for females, athletic opportunities for females after college, and public perceptions of female athletes.

2. For each of the following situations, identify the elements or scope of the research project and plan the data collection. With your instructor's approval, you may benefit by doing this application in groups of three or four people. Specifically, do the following:
   - Identify the elements of the research problem.
   - Identify the kinds of information needed.
   - Identify the appropriate sources of data.
   - Identify the likely sequence for collecting the data.
   - Identify the best sampling technique for any necessary primary data.

   a. McDonald's has recognized the need to update its image. At its flagship restaurant in Oak Brook, IL, the company now offers digital-media kiosks where customers can burn CDs, download cell-phone ring tones, and print photos; plasma-screen TVs; Wi-Fi-Internet access; lighter menu items, such as new chicken sandwiches; and an adjoining McCafe with gourmet coffees, fancy pastries, and a fireplace. (*The State*, June 15, 2005, p. A12.) As the owner of Rusty's, a long-standing local restaurant that features prime beef burgers and fried chicken, you are aware that other restaurant "hangouts" such as Starbucks and Panera Bread have drained away some of your business. Now, if McDonald's repackages its fast-food image in your community, you may lose even more business. You want to determine how Rusty's can compete with this new restaurant concept.

   b. Analytic Graphics, Inc., in Exton, PA, provides a range of unusual employee benefits. Those benefits include free breakfast, lunch, and dinner (families included, if desired by employee); fully equipped playroom for children, who may be taken to the office at any time; flextime; exercise room with free personal trainer; oil changes for a competitive fee, done in the parking lot; weekly pickup and delivery from dry cleaner and shoe repair shop; shipping of personal packages at cost, through the company shipping department. AGI's CEO insists that spending money on employees pays off with greater productivity and loyalty. (*The State, Columbia Business Journal*, Aug. 2, 2004, p. 16.) As owner of a small but growing firm that offers Computer Assisted Design (CAD) services to a variety of businesses, you are aware that employees often work late into the night on projects so that they can meet deadlines, or they become so captivated by their work that they forget to eat lunch. You want to retain such dedicated workers, but you also know they can easily find work with competing companies. You want to evaluate the positive and negative aspects of offering your employees some additional perks similar to some of those offered by AGI.

c. Pioneer Insurance Company instituted a wellness program for its workers ten years ago. For the first four years of the program, employee participation increased each year, and during the fifth year 63 percent of the company's employees participated. Since that time, employee participation has decreased each year; and now it is down to only 15 percent of the employees. Pioneer Insurance wants to know the reasons for the decline in participation.

d. Wendy Harvey recently completed a culinary arts program and also has three years' experience working as a chef with a well-known restaurant in your community. She wants to begin a personal chef business. Her idea is to offer in-home cooking services to clients (for example, retirees, busy professional people, etc.) who have little time or ability to prepare nutritious meals daily. Her plan is to go into a home once a week to prepare meals that can be frozen and cooked at a later time. She will plan the meals, shop for the ingredients, cook the meals, and package them for freezing and reheating. She wants to know the potential for success of such a business in your community.

e. WorldView Productions is a privately held U.S. company specializing in the creation and production of educational supplements to major textbooks. Examples of past work are DVDs providing background information for high school literature classes, CDs with study guides used as the primary tools in lieu of textbooks for high school language classes, and DVDs promoting cross-cultural understanding for middle school students in the U.S. and Canada. WorldView is a full-service operation that handles all facets of the production process from determining the target audience and its needs to full production of the desired educational materials.

WorldView now wants to explore the market for corporate communication products in the United Kingdom and Japan. The company specifically wants to know whether a market exists for such products in either or both countries, potential customers, and existing competition. Ultimately, the company wants to be able to evaluate the potential for success in this market in the United Kingdom and/or Japan.

f. Because of the nursing shortage in your state, some hospitals have resorted to hiring nurses from the Philippines. Filipino nurses have done well on the national licensing exam. Since they learn English as part of their education in their homeland, most Filipino nurses have little difficulty communicating with patients and co-workers. As director of nursing at Health Help Hospital in your community, you want to determine the feasibility of hiring Filipino nurses to relieve the nurse staffing problem in your hospital.

g. A North Carolina company, BUZZ OFF Insect Shield, Ltd., has developed a process for putting an insect-repellant chemical into clothing. The process was approved by the Environmental Protection Agency in 2003, by the U.S. military, and by such retailers as L.L. Bean and the Orvis Co. (*The State,* July 2, 2005, p. B7.) Assume you want to open a sportswear store that will feature your personal brand products, including clothing that will be treated with BUZZ OFF.

3. After you have determined the appropriate data sources for items in Applications 1 and 2, as directed by your instructor, write a memo to report your recommendations regarding data collection for one or more of the studies.

4. If you wrote a proposal for any of the Applications in Chapter 8, continue with that project, focusing at this time on appropriate data sources.

Reference

1. This discussion explains general concepts related to accuracy, precision, and sample size. For further study consult books such as Kumar, V., Aaker, D. A., & Day, G. S. (1999). *Essentials of marketing research*. New York: John Wiley & Sons, Inc.; and Brace, I. (2004). *Questionnaire design*. London & Sterling, VA: Kogan Page.

10

Using Secondary Data Sources*

LEARNING OBJECTIVES

After you have read this chapter, you should be able to:

1. Identify secondary sources (printed and web) for business research.
2. Evaluate secondary sources and data.
3. Demonstrate techniques for extracting and reporting secondary data.
4. Use standard procedures to acknowledge secondary data sources.
5. Observe ethical standards for using secondary data.

A library is an exciting place. In a library, including the global library known as the World Wide Web (web), you can learn about the major current developments in business, science, education, politics, the arts, etc. Moreover, a library contains the accumulated wisdom and experience of many cultures, enabling you to link the past with the present.

Several types of libraries are prevalent today: online (web), public, academic, and business or trade. The web, huge in scope and less organized than other library types, houses vast collections of accessible information on virtually every imaginable topic. Public libraries, general in nature, collect information for a rather broad user population. Academic libraries, such as college or university libraries, contain strong research collections that support student and faculty research. Often these libraries maintain strong collections in certain areas but not in others. Business or trade libraries serve a specific clientele. Such libraries include those of companies, professional associations, trade associations, institutes, or research agencies. Narrow in focus, business or trade libraries offer depth in their specific areas. Many of these libraries, though not open to the public, offer advice and answer questions over the telephone.

The information accumulated in secondary sources can be valuable as you attempt to solve business problems. Secondary data constitutes information already gathered and recorded or posted by someone else. When you review *Consumer Reports* (printed or online) before buying a car, plasma TV, or DVD player, you use secondary data. The use of secondary data saves you time and

*Chapter contributed by Dr. Dorinda Clippinger, Lecturer in Management, Moore School of Business, University of South Carolina.

money by avoiding unnecessary duplication. Efficient business researchers usually consult secondary sources before attempting to obtain data from primary sources (see Chapter 11). Secondary sources are important in business research for two reasons:

1. Secondary data can help you gain perspective on the problem and identify and define what must be investigated.
2. Secondary sources may contain adequate data to solve the problem (and for the report), eliminating the need to collect primary data. In fact, some secondary sources contain more extensive and more valid data than you would be able to collect from primary sources.

To gather secondary data, you must be able to identify appropriate sources, use secondary sources efficiently and ethically, and apply standard procedures for acknowledging your data sources. Generally, any data-gathering process should start with secondary research. Whatever your problem, similar ones likely have occurred in other organizations or have been researched by others. The solutions to these problems may be reported in business publications. Although these problems will differ slightly from your own, your knowledge of what other individuals and organizations concluded in similar situations can help to answer your questions.

Collecting secondary data includes four steps: (1) locating the data, (2) evaluating the data source, (3) extracting the data from its source, and (4) keeping records.

LOCATING SECONDARY DATA

To locate secondary data for business research, you may consult the web, specialized databases, reference books, periodical indexes, and the catalog of holdings found in most libraries. Though online information services continually expand, you should expect to use a library's printed sources and CD-ROM and database subscriptions, as well as generally accessible websites.

Catalogs

Nowadays most libraries list books and periodicals and other items in an online catalog (electronic database), rather than in a card catalog. Thus users can search the catalog and produce a list of available items, along with full bibliographic information for each item, a brief description of its contents, and where and how to access it. Any of these terms can be used to search most online catalogs: author, title, library call number, subject, or keyword.

Keyword search, as you may know, is a technique to narrow the scope of your data search. Assume, for example, that you are conducting research on labor force impacts of bank mergers in the southeastern United States. A manual search would necessitate looking under several subjects, such as labor force, bank mergers, displacement, retraining, and outplacement; and within those subject areas, you would have to select items that discuss impact in the

Southeast. But by combining selected keywords in a database search—for example, labor force, bank mergers, and southeast—you would likely locate pertinent material quickly and eliminate irrelevant items.

Typically an online catalog has a catchy name, like The Cat (Penn State University), CDL (University of California Digital Libraries), CUNY UNION (City University of New York, all libraries), IUCAT (Indiana University catalog), Sterling (Howard University catalog), or USCAN (University of South Carolina Access Network). Typically, too, first-time catalog users need help in addition to the online help provided. Libraries generally offer printed or online tutorials, and librarians give assistance readily when asked.

Using the website titled Gateway to the Library of Congress (http://www.loc.gov/z3950/), one can search the immense Library of Congress collection and the library holdings of hundreds of other institutions.

A few libraries continue to maintain a card catalog. A card catalog generally indexes all library holdings by subject, title, and author. Therefore, for each item in the library, three cards appear in the card catalog. Each card contains full bibliographic information for the item, a brief description of its contents, and a call number identifying its location in the library.

To find a book whose title or author you know, you may locate its card in either the title or author section of the catalog; record the call number; and retrieve the book from its library location. In many situations, you will look for information on a particular subject. In such instances, you must search for the subject in the card catalog until you find items that appear to meet your needs.

Directories

Many directories can be accessed in a number of ways, such as by industry type or by geographic location. Some of the following business directories can be found on the web. Type the full title of a directory in your browser's search box to determine if it's available on the web.

America's Corporate Families and International Affiliates. Dun's Marketing Services, Inc. Two-volume set. First volume includes U.S. companies; second volume includes international affiliates. Several special indexes: alphabetical, industrial, and geographical.

Craigshead's International Business, Travel, and Relocation Guide to 90 Countries. Detroit: Gale/Thomson. Provides destination-specific business and relocation information. Includes information about doing business and living and working conditions in 90 countries most important to international business. Acquaints readers with business and cultural environments.

D&B Million Dollar Directory: America's Leading Public and Private Companies. Dun's Marketing Services, Inc. Cross-indexed volume provides access by SIC (Standard Industrial Classification) number of geographic location. List of major U.S. companies with address, telephone number, officers, and business type.

Directory of Corporation Affiliations. New Jersey: National Register Publishing. Includes directory information on parent companies and their subsidiaries and divisions, by table of contents.

Directory of Multinationals. New York: Stockton Press. Two-volume set gives up-to-date profiles of the world's 500 largest corporations. Now includes service, retailing and construction companies, reflecting today's high-technology and service-oriented environment. Identifies companies' key strategies at home and abroad. Reports directors, products, background and current situation, and five-year statistical summaries.

Japan Trade Directory. JETRO: Japan External Trade Organization. Annual guide to Japanese companies and organizations. Helpful to foreign companies interested in doing business with Japan. Gives details of specific products that Japanese companies look to import and export and services they want to provide. Extensive information about business conditions and locations. Much of this information is available on the web (http://www.jetro.go.jp/).

Macmillan Directory of Leading Private Companies. New Jersey: National Register Publishing. Basic directory information on leading private companies in U.S. Excellent alphabetical cross-referenced index in front of book, plus industry and geographic index in back.

Political Risk Yearbook. New York: The PRS Group, Inc. Eight-volume set reports extensively on political challenges (protests, general strikes, crime, civil violence, and outright war) that affect economic growth, inflation restraint, and maintenance of social order in 100 monitored countries.

Risk: A Country by Country Guide. London: Kogan Page. Divided into five regions (Southeast Asia, North Africa/Middle East, Latin America, CIS and Central/Eastern Europe, and Sub-Saharan Africa), this directory reports assets and weaknesses, conditions of market access, census data, and a risk assessment for more than 100 countries.

Thomas Register of American Manufacturers. New York: Thomas Publishing Company. Multivolume directory of manufacturers. Volumes 1–12 include companies listed by product; Volumes 13–14 provide company information; Volumes 15–21 include examples of company catalogs. Available on the web as ThomasNet (http://www.thomasnet.com/).

Ward's Business Directory of U.S. Private and Public Companies. Detroit: Gale Research, Inc. A comprehensive guide to 90,000 companies arranged alphabetically and geographically. Information includes rankings of top companies within the SIC. Volume 1 includes companies with over $11.5 million in sales; Volume 2 includes companies with $0.5 to $11.5 million in sales; and Volume 3 ranks companies by industry sales.

World Business Directory. Detroit: The Gale Group Four volumes profile global marketplace with data on 140,000 companies in 180 countries.

Includes top import/export companies, leading manufacturers, small and medium-sized firms, and forecasts, plus alphabetic, product, and SIC indexes.

Databases

Although directories may provide useful data for your research, you frequently require more current information than that found in these books. Periodicals (bulletins, journals, magazines, etc.) also contain much current business information and can be located with the help of a periodical index or an online database.

A *journal* is a periodical on a single topic published by an academic or association press. A journal, which contains original research, is more scholarly than a magazine. Journal articles are signed by the authors and include a bibliography. A *magazine* is a periodical produced by a commercial publisher and covering multiple topics in one issue. Magazine articles, often reporting on events or a person's work, are usually unsigned and omit a bibliography.

Most libraries, especially academic and business or trade libraries, subscribe to commercial databases delivered on the web and accessed by means of keyword search. Most databases today offer full-text articles and or entire journals. The following databases are widely used for collecting secondary business data. Some are *aggregated* databases: EBSCO, for example, includes several of the other databases on the list. (For you to access most databases on this list free of charge, your library must have subscribed to it.)

ABI / INFORM. A database covering approximately 500 journals in the broad area of business and management. About 300 journals are designed as "core journals," and all articles published in them are indexed and abstracted. Articles from the remaining journals are selected on the basis of their relevance to management practice and theory.

Business Source Premier. EBSCO database covering virtually all business-related subject areas and providing full-text for about 7,600 business magazines and journals, plus monographs, market research reports, industry reports, country reports, and company profiles. Additional journals are included with abstracts only.

Datastream. Contains detailed numerical data on corporations, bonds, and stocks.

Disclosure.® A database containing financial and management information for over 12,000 public companies. Data extracted from annual and periodic reports filed with U.S. Securities and Exchange Commission. Data indexed by subject, permitting search by single subject (for example, sales volume) or combination of subjects (for example, industry size, sales volume). Data can be captured and imported to a spreadsheet or word processing document. Available on CD-ROM and web databases, including Lexis/Nexis. Note: Disclosure® is a registered trademark of Disclosure Incorporated.

Economist.com/index.html. Electronic version of the weekly *Economist* journal. Features daily updates on reports in finance and economics, business, science, and technology.

EDGAR: Electronic Data Gathering, Analysis, and Retrieval System of the SEC (Securities and Exchange Commission). Includes searchable registration statements, periodic reports, and other forms required by the SEC (with some exceptions) from all domestic and foreign companies. This database may be accessed by anyone on the web (http://www.sec.gov/edgar.shtml).

EIU: Economist Intelligence Unit. Database providing analysis and forecasts on more than 200 countries and eight key industries.

Hoover's Online. Contains detailed public company information for both U.S. and overseas firms. Also contains many web links to industry, career, and investment data. Companies can be sorted by industry, location, and sales.

InfoTrac Searchbank. Varied database offering biographies, health and wellness resources, investment (Investext) information, legal documents, and full-text articles from over 100 U.S. and international newspapers.

Kompass. Database/global directory providing directory information for about 1.8 million companies in 75 countries.

Lexis-Nexis Academic. Database containing company, industry, and market news in the form of full text from newspapers, newswires, and journals. Also includes company financial data, corporate directory listings, annual reports, and country data.

Mediamark Reporter. Database contains Mediamark Research Reports, which offers exposure to all forms of advertising media. Includes comprehensive demographic, lifestyle, and product usage information.

Proquest Direct Web. Database of *The Wall Street Journal* articles from about early 1981 to the present. Includes daily updates.

PsychInfo. Database provides indexes to journals—as well as books, chapters, dissertations, reports, and other documents—from 1887 to the present on criminology, education, law, medicine, organizational behavior, psychiatry, social science, and social work.

Reuters Business Insight. Database containing full-text, in-depth research reports in multiple industries: consumer goods, energy, finance, healthcare, and technology.

STAT-USA. Full-text database of government reports on international business and trade. Includes National Trade Data Bank, Country Commercial Guides, Market Research Reports, and CIA World Factbook among others.

TDNet. Comprehensive database with links to electronic edition of full-text articles from journal, magazines, and newspapers.

Value Line Investment Survey Online. Includes stock surveys with performance charges and quarterly and three- to five-year earnings estimates.

Wilson Business Abstracts. Database that indexes and summarizes articles from 400 business, trade, and research journals.

Periodical Indexes

Mainly because of the high cost of database subscriptions, some small libraries maintain printed and bound copies of periodicals. In such situations you can use printed periodical indexes and abstracting services to locate the most current information on your subject. Some indexes and abstracts (summaries) cover specific subject areas; others serve as general guides to current literature. The list that follows includes both types.

Accounting & Tax Index. Index to books, pamphlets, government documents, and articles on accounting, auditing, data processing, financial management, financial reporting, investments and securities, management, and taxation.

Business Periodicals Index. Index of approximately 300 periodicals in business and management including accounting, advertising and public relations, banking, communications, economics, finance and investments, industrial relations, insurance, international business, labor, marketing, personnel, as well as specific businesses, some industries, and some trades. Those broad areas are further divided into relevant subtopics.

New York Times Index. A detailed index to *The New York Times*, arranged alphabetically with many cross-references.

Predicasts F&S Index United States. An excellent source for current U.S. company, product, and industry information. Indexes over 750 business, industrial, and financial periodicals.

Predicasts F&S Index Europe and Predicasts F&S Index International. Companion indexes to Predicasts F&S Index United States covering articles on foreign companies, products, and industries.

Public Affairs Information Service Bulletin and Public Affairs Information Service: Foreign Language Index. Indexes of selected articles about economic and social conditions, public administration, and international relations. Includes articles from journals, books, pamphlets, government publications, and public and private agency reports.

Each entry in a periodical index cites the author, article title, journal in which published, publication volume number and/or date, and page numbers. Most periodical indexes classify magazine, journal, or newspaper articles by author, subject, and title. Periodical indexes on CD-ROM or in a database may also allow for keyword searches.

Unless you are looking for an article by a specific author or title, begin your search by naming the subject(s) under which you are most likely to find relevant data. When doing a manual search, check all relevant subject headings for the time period to which you delimited your study. When doing a database search, try narrowing your search by combining keywords.

After locating specific journal or newspaper article citations, you must still locate the article itself. For citations located in a printed periodical index, obtain the call number of the journal or newspaper from the library catalog, locate that journal in the library, and then locate the specific pages cited in the index. For citations located by keyword search, you may need to obtain the call number from the online catalog; then locate the journal in the library. Often, though, you will be able to click a link in the citation to view a full-text rendering of the article.

Some libraries, especially those libraries that use a card catalog, list journals and newspapers in a separate serials index. And, often, a serials index is on microfiche—a sheet of film containing photographically reduced pages. The film is placed into a special fiche reader and moved manually until the desired pages or lines appear on the viewing screen. A typical microfiche in a serials index contains the names, call numbers, and holdings information for approximately 1,000 journals.

Special Issues of Business Periodicals

In addition to using periodicals for current information on a broad range of business and economic topics, you will find special issues of selected periodicals useful for specialized statistical data about the status of U.S. businesses.

Fortune. Annual rankings of companies by sales, assets, net income, stockholders' equity, employees, net income as percentage of stockholders' equity, earnings per share, and total return to investors. Last April or first May issue contains "The Fortune 500" list of U.S. industrial corporations; second June issue contains "The Service 500"; last May issue covers the 50 largest private companies; first August issue reports the 50 leading exporters; and second August issue presents the "Fortune World Business Directory," ranking the 50 largest industrial corporations, the 500 largest foreign industrial corporations, and the 100 largest commercial banks outside the United States. Fortune Magazine also publishes other lists, such as the Fortune 1000, the Global 500, the 100 Best Companies to Work For, and the 100 Fastest-Growing Companies. Lists also available on the web (http://www.fortune.com).

Forbes. Annual Directory Issue. Mid-May each year. Ranks the 500 largest U.S. corporations by sales, profits, assets, stock market value, and number of employees. Also ranks the Super 500—individual rankings of the firms that made one or more of the lists: sales, profits, assets, and market value. The Forbes 500 differs from the Fortune directories in that it includes industrial and nonindustrial corporations in one ranking. Also available on the web (http://www.forbes.com).

Forbes. Annual Report on American Industry. First January issue each year. Surveys 46 major industries, ranking leading companies in each industry on profitability and growth.

Guide to Special Issues and Indexes of Periodicals. Special Libraries Association. Focuses on the 1,750 U.S. and Canadian periodicals that publish recurring special issues. Includes classified lists of the periodicals and comprehensive subject index.

Sales & Marketing Management, Annual Survey of Buying Power issues. Second July issue includes Survey of Buying Power; second October issue includes Survey of Buying Power, Part II; second April issue includes Survey of Industrial & Commercial Buying Power; and second February issue includes Survey of Selling Costs. Provides detailed, current estimates of U.S. and Canadian demographic data, including statistics, such as population by age group and household categories; Effective Buying Index; retail sales by store groups; sales by merchandise line; television market; number of industrial and commercial establishments; and lodging, meals, taxi, and automobile rental rates. Data are given for metropolitan areas, counties, and cities, with some regional and national summaries. Considered a major data source for marketing and economic researchers. Also available on the web (http://www.salesandmarketing.com).

Sources for Statistical Data

The following statistical compilations will provide you with current social, political, and economic statistics.

Business Statistics of the United States. Maryland: Bernan Press. Contains historical information about the U.S. economy since World War II and interpretation of new economic data. Predominantly graphics.

County Business Patterns and ZIP Business Patterns. U.S. Bureau of the Census, Washington, DC. U.S. Government Printing Office. An annual with separate numbers for each state and a U.S. summary volume. Annual compilation of first-quarter employment and payroll statistics by county, detailed industry, and employment-size class. Valuable for analyzing market potential in a particular geographic location.

Global Competitiveness Report. (Series also covers Africa, Arab World, Latin America, and Europe.) Oxford University Press. Evaluates economic competitiveness of about 100 countries, using two sophisticated indexes— Growth Competitiveness Index (GCI) and the Business Competitiveness Index (BCI).

Handbook of Basic Economic Statistics. A compilation of current and historical statistics condensed from federal government data in American industry, commerce, labor, and agriculture. Some data series go back as far as 1913.

International Financial Statistics Yearbook. (IMF: International Monetary Fund.) Statistics on all aspects of domestic and international finance. Includes exchange rates, money and banking, interest rates, prices, production, government finance, and more. Information presented in tables for specific countries and for area and world aggregates.

Predicasts Forecasts. Short- and long-range forecast statistics for basic economic indicators and for individual industries and products. Includes date and page reference of the current journal, government report, or study from which the statistics are taken.

Statistical Service. (New York: Standard & Poor's Current Statistics.) Source of current and basic statistics in banking and finance; production indexes and labor statistics; price indexes (commodities, producer, cost of living); income and trade; building and building materials; energy, electric power, and fuels; metals; transportation; textiles, chemical, and paper; agriculture products; security price index record. Latest annual figures appear in white-page supplement, and latest monthly figures for the current year are in yellow-page supplement.

Statistical Abstract of the United States. (U.S. Bureau of the Census, Washington, DC: U.S. Government Printing Office.) Annual. A prime source for U.S. industrial, social, political, and economic statistics. Includes source notes at the foot of each table, "Guide to Sources of Statistics," and "Guide to State Statistical Abstracts." Late editions available on CD-ROM; also available on the Web (http://www.census.gov/statab/www/).

Reference Books

Reference books contain a wealth of current and historical business data. The reference section of the library contains, for example, several of the sources for company, industry, and statistical data, as well as atlases, telephone directories, dictionaries, and encyclopedias. The reference section typically contains general business information sources, such as books about business careers and business and social customs around the world. Becoming familiar with the reference section of a library will acquaint you with valuable sources of secondary data.

Sources for Company and Industry Data

The following reference books will help you find data about companies and industries in the U.S. and outside the U.S.

Dow Jones Investor's Handbook. (Homewood, IL: Dow Jones-Irwin.) Annual. Provides investment data for industrial, transportation, and public utility stocks traded on the New York and American Stock Exchanges and in over-the-counter transactions. Information includes daily closing Dow Jones averages for the most recent year; monthly closing averages for 20 years; quarterly earnings, dividend yields, and price-earnings ratios for 38 years.

Hoover's World Handbook. (Austin, TX: Hoovers Business Press.) Profiles 300 of the world's most influential companies outside the U.S. Gives overview, history, officers, locations, products/operations, competitors, historical financials, and employees. Other Hoover items include Handbook of American Business, Handbook of Emerging Companies, and Handbook of Private Companies.

Industrial Surveys. (New York: Standard & Poor's Corp.) Separate pamphlets for 33 industries, updated quarterly and annually. A basic analysis of about 40 pages for each industry is revised annually; a current analysis of about eight pages is published three times a year. A four-page monthly publication provides industry trends and projections; and a monthly "Earnings Supplement" gives revenue, income, and profitability data on over 1,000 leading companies in the 33 major industries.

Moody's Manuals. (New York: Moody's Investors Service.) Seven volumes and an index. Annual with semiweekly or weekly supplements. This set of financial manuals includes Moody's Bank and Finance Manual, Moody's Industrial Manual, Moody's International Manual, Moody's Municipal & Government Manual, Moody's OTC Industrial Manual, Moody's Public Utilities Manual, Moody's Transportation Manual, and Moody's Complete Corporate Index. The manuals contain information about companies listed on U.S. stock exchanges, usually including capital structure, brief corporate history, subsidiaries, business and properties, names of officers and directors, CEO's letter to stockholders, highlights from the annual report, seven-year income and balance sheet statistics, number of stockholders, number of employees, and other pertinent data.

Standard & Poor's Register of Corporations, Directors and Executives. (New York: Standard & Poor's Corp.) Three volumes. Annual, with three cumulative supplements. Volume 1 alphabetically lists about 40,000 companies. For each company, information is provided about its officers, line of business, SIC codes, sales range, number of employees, accounting firm, primary bank and law firm, and stock exchange symbol. Volume 2 provides brief biographical data about each company's executives and directors. Volume 3 includes an index to Volumes 1 and 2 as well as additional miscellaneous data about the companies and officers. One useful list in Volume 3 is a "corporate family" index, cross-referencing subsidiaries and parent companies.

Stock Reports. (New York: Standard & Poor's Corp.) Looseleaf with weekly supplement. Three separate stock report services: Standard ASE Stock Reports, Standard NYSE Stock Reports, and Standard OTC Stock

Reports. Each report gives a business summary; recent developments, income, balance sheet, and per share data; capitalization; dividends; and other relevant information.

Value Line Investment Survey. (New York: A. Bernhard & Co.) Looseleaf with weekly updates. The online version is Value Line Data Base II. Very current analysis of 1,700 companies in over 90 industries. One-page-per company summaries include 11-year statistical history of 22 key investment factors. Estimates three to five years into future; quarterly sales; EPS; dividends; Value Line ratings on timeliness, safety, and Beta; review of latest developments; and future prospects.

Who Owns Whom: North America. (London: Dun & Bradstreet, Ltd.) Annual. A directory of U.S. and Canadian parent companies and their subsidiaries and associates. Dun & Bradstreet publishes similar volumes for Australasia and the Far East, Continental Europe, and the United Kingdom and Ireland.

Company Annual Reports: In addition to the sources cited, you should consult the company's most recent annual report when researching a specific company. Many university and public libraries maintain files of company annual reports.

This list should help you get started on any search for secondary data. If the data you require cannot be located in the sources listed, consult a reference librarian. A reference librarian, a highly trained individual, can guide you to appropriate sources if you clearly define your research problem and the kinds of data you need.

SOURCES FOR INFORMATION ON THE WEB

The World Wide Web offers a rich source of information for the business researcher. This section focuses on the web, though much information can be derived from e-mail, discussion lists, and USENET newsgroups. Several search tools are available to the web user, some of which operate more efficiently and accurately than others. Begin your search by typing the keyword or phrase into the search text box and clicking the accompanying button. Find the tools that best fit your purposes; but generally, use more than one. For example, begin with a meta-search engine, such as Dogpile, or a general-purpose one, such as Google or Yahoo. Then follow up with an Alta Vista or Lycos search and end with a special-purpose engine, such as HighBeam, Pathfinder, or WWW Virtual Library. A list of popular search tools follow. For more options, go to the Search Engine Colossus website (http://www.searchenginecolossus.com/). It contains an international directory of search engines.

A9 (http://a9.com/)
Alta Vista Search (http://www.altavista.com/)

Dogpile (http://www.dogpile.com/)
Go (http://go.com/)
Google (http://www.google.com/)
Gopher (http://www.gophersearch.com/)
HighBeam Research (http://www.highbeam.com/)
HotBot (http://www.hotbot.com/)
Lycos (http://www.lycos.com/)
Pathfinder (http://www.pathfinder.com), a navigator for searching Time
Inc., websites
Thomas (http://thomas.loc.gov), for searching the Congressional Record
WWW Virtual Library (http://vlib.org/)
Yahoo (http://www.yahoo.com/)

The website Business.com (http://www.business.com/) serves as search engine and directory to business products, jobs, and services, case studies, company profiles, magazine articles, and academic and business journal articles.

Following is a list of specific business information sources that may be useful as you conduct research related to your college major and specific report topic.

Sources for Accounting Information

A variety of accounting-related sites currently exists on the web. These sites provide accounting students with a host of resources from which to examine career possibilities, research accounting technical issues, explore tax accounting issues, and examine financial statements, which are filed publicly with the Securities and Exchange Commission and posted by corporations for the benefit of prospective clients and customers.

American Accounting Association (*http://aaahq.org/*). The American Accounting Association is an academic association of educators, practitioners, and business professionals. This site provides access to accounting research, teaching tools, practice references, association activities, and recent publications.

Department of Treasury–Internal Revenue Service (*http://www.irs.gov*). The two main uses for this site are to get IRS tax forms and publications and to seek answers to frequently asked tax questions.

Internal Revenue Code (*http://caselaw.lp.findlaw.com/casecode/uscodes/26/toc.html*). This site is an index of the U.S. Internal Revenue Code as of January 1994. You might find that using this site is much faster than leafing through the code manually.

Corporate Financial Links (*http://www.kristelli.com/corporat.html*). This site provides references to web pages of particular interest to investors regarding corporate financial information.

Sources for Economic Information

The web has many economics sites, most of them sponsored by the U.S. government. These sites contain not only important statistical data, but also insightful data that may help you better understand economics.

BEA: Bureau of Economic Analysis (*http://www.bea.doc.gov/*). The BEA is responsible for integrating and interpreting economic data. BEA's economic accounts—national, regional, and international—provide information on economic growth, regional development, and the world economy.

DOC: Department of Commerce (*http://www.commerce.gov/*). The U.S. Department of Commerce maintains this website to carry out its mission to promote American business and trade. Available information includes statistics on U.S. population and housing and geographical breakdowns of the economy.

Federal Trade Commission (*http://www.ftc.gov/*). This site provides consumer alerts and notices and transcripts of hearings. It also collects public comment. One section, "Consumer Line," offers over 150 consumer and business publications on such topics as diet programs, mortgage servicing, and gas-saving products.

MAC: Market Access and Compliance (*http://www.mac.doc.gov/internet/aboutmac.htm*). This site provides country and regional information for American exporters. It includes information on the North American Free Trade Agreement (NAFTA), the independent states of the former U.S.S.R., and Central and Eastern Europe.

Rand Journal of Economics (*http://www.rje.org/*) . This site supports and encourages research in the behavior of regulated industries; the economic analysis of organizations; and, more generally, applied economics. It provides both theoretical and empirical manuscripts in economics and law.

World Bank (*http://www.worldbank.org/*). This site provides glimpses into activities of the World Bank and reveals research that economics students may find beneficial.

Sources for Finance Information

Finance information on the web is growing and covers topics from public finance policy to tax issues. Following are some helpful sites.

CME: Chicago Mercantile Exchange (*http://www.cme.com/*). This site—a rich resource for investors and students alike—includes daily closing settlement prices on such items as agricultural commodities, foreign currencies, interest rates, and stock indexes.

IIA: Institute of Internal Auditors (*http://www.theiia.org/*). Established in 1941, the Institute of Internal Auditors is an international professional association of more than 100,000 members. The IIA website offers varied information about the internal auditing profession and includes links to online resources.

Tenny's Banking/Financial Page (*http://www.mebbs.com/tenny/banking.htm*). This website, sponsored by The Wall Street Journal, lists more than 70 links to financial sites.

The Wall Street Journal Online (*http://online.wsj.com/*). This site provides financial news and analysis in both fee-for-service and free formats.

Zagury Financial Directory (*http://www.zagury.com/*). This site is a searchable database of sites pertaining to the finance industry, including investments, banking, and trade.

Sources for Global Business Information

Several websites, including two in the education domain, stand out as providers of information for students of international business.

globalEDGE™: Your Source for Global Business Knowledge (*http://globaledge.msu.edu*). Created by the Center for International Business Education and Research (CIBER) at Michigan State University (MSU). Partially funded by a U.S. Department of Education grant. Offers more than 5,000 global resources, a wealth of information on all countries, an interactive forum for business professionals, the latest issues in international business, research and teaching resources, and decision-support tools for managers. Note: globalEDGE™ is an MSU-CIBER trademark.

JETRO: Japan External Trade Organization (*http://www.jetro.go.jp/*). JETRO, a government-related organization, promotes foreign direct investment into Japan. Site provides wide range of information through news and press releases, publications, e-mail newsletter, current articles, and more.

VIBES: Virtual International Business and Economic Sources (*http://library.uncc.edu/display/?dept=reference&format=open&page=68*). Provides over 2,800 links to websites containing international business and economic information. Provides access to full-text articles and research reports, statistical tables and graphs, and numerous links to other sources. Includes only information written in English and available free of charge.

Sources for Marketing and Advertising Information

A wide assortment of sites await the student of marketing. Although each site has a slightly different take on marketing concepts, each provides valuable tools and ideas. A list of some marketing and advertising sites follows.

AdMarket International (*http://www.admarketintl.com/*). This site provides information about marketing, media, advertising, and public relations. It also provides access to various advertising agencies, media producers, marketers, and marketing organization home pages. In addition, it identifies and references web resources for advertisers.

Advertising Age (*http://www.adage.com/*). Advertising Age is a periodical devoted to marketing innovations. This site provides information in marketing, advertising, and media news along with coverage of marketing for consumers, businesses, and international clients.

AMA: American Marketing Association (*http://www.marketingpower.com/*). The American Marketing Association, an international nonprofit society, serves the educational and professional needs of marketing executives. The AMA's website provides information about the study, practice, and teaching of marketing.

Marketing Cases (*http://www.marketingpower.com/content16636C4596 .php*). This AMA-sponsored site allows students of marketing to review and analyze marketing strategies of various businesses on the web. The AMA home page includes links to additional marketing case studies.

Sources for Real Estate Information

Real estate activities thrive on the web. You can now view a potential purchase from the privacy of your home, whether the house is down the street or across the country. One-stop shopping centers, which can provide everything from financing alternatives to information on home site selection, are now available. Following are some useful real estate sites.

Fannie Mae (*www.fanniemae.com/*). Fannie Mae is American's largest supplier of conventional home mortgage funds. This site provides helpful information about refinancing mortgages, different mortgage programs, and two-step or asset integrated mortgages.

Homebuyer's Fair (*www.homefair.com/*). This site provides relocation and mortgage services, homebuyer information, and classified services. Its stated mission: to help homebuyers keep more of their money when they buy a house. The site includes links to real estate sites on the web.

HSH Associates (*http://www.hsh.com/*). HSH Associates is the world's leading publisher of mortgage and consumer loan information. At this site, HSH supplies current and accurate market information to consumers, real estate agents, lenders, the media, and other audiences.

Sources for Small Business Information

The five websites in the following list cater to the needs of entrepreneurs and small business owners.

BPlans (*http://www.bplans.com/index.cfm*). Site sponsored by Palo Alto Software; covers business planning and strategy. Offers large collection of free business plans. Includes answers to frequently asked questions, interactive tools, and practical planning advice.

Business Plans Index (*http://www.carnegielibrary.org/locations/downtown*). Provides numerous links to business databases and books; also, business resources and plans.

MOOT CORP® Competition (*http://www.businessplans.org/index.asp*). Site covers strategy insights, business plan software, and planning guidelines. Includes web resources, a list of consultants, and sample business plans. Note: MOOT CORP® is a registered trademark of Business Research Software, Inc.

Nolo.com—Small Business Legal Encyclopedia (*http://www.nolo.com/index.cfm*). Website designed to help consumers and small business people handle their own everyday legal matters. Includes employment, human resources, intellectual property, real estate, taxes, and starting and running a small business.

SBA: Small Business Administration (*http://www.sba.gov/*). This site provides information on many worthwhile topics, such as starting, financing, and managing your own business.

Sources for General Business Information

A number of general business topics such as business ethics, technology in business education, and business law are available on the web. Following are some useful sites.

DBIS: Dun & Bradstreet Information Services (*http://www.dnb.com/us/*). Dun & Bradstreet helps customers interpret and use D&B's information as well as D&B's own data. D&B charges for its individual company reports; however, extensive information is available free of charge.

U.S. Business Advisor (*http://www.business.gov/*). This site provides regulatory, financial, labor, trade, and domestic commerce information to U.S. businesses.

U.S. Code of Law (*http://straylight.law.cornell.edu/uscode/*). The Cornell University Law School placed the U.S. Code on the web. At this informative site, all text is dated; and new information issued by the House of Representatives is generally posted within 24 hours.

Although much valuable information can be derived from the preceding websites, you should adhere to the following guides to save time and money:

- Be aware that websites constantly change and move. Thus a site you visited yesterday may be moved today.
- Use specific, concrete search terms. Avoid using articles and prepositions in your searches. Search engines usually ignore such words.

- Most sites with a large picture file offer a text-based alternative to shorten loading time. When loading a large picture file at a site you visit, you can scroll down the page to avoid wasting time.
- Use several search engines for thorough research. Each search site has its own database resources. Some sites may have information that others do not.
- Bookmark (add to Favorites) any site to which you may return. You can use the history (Address) list to return to sites visited recently.

EVALUATING SOURCES

A researcher must evaluate source reliability and continue to search for data until satisfied that, within the time and budget constraints of the research project, the most valid and reliable sources have been found. The following five criteria will help you evaluate the reliability of secondary sources:

- Timeliness: Is the source current? If outdated, the source should not be used.
- Relevance: Does the source address the research problem? Even if extremely interesting and timely, sources should be used only if they address the problem specifically.
- Accuracy: Is the source reliable and unbiased? Is the author a recognized expert? Did the author use a reliable data collection method? Where and how were any statistics derived? Does the source include complete information? If any answer is "no" or "doubtful," the source should not be used. Be cautious of sources on the web, since that information constantly changes. Also keep in mind that website sponsors, unlike publishers of most print sources, rarely employ fact checkers. Furthermore, many websites serve sponsors' commercial interests.
- Quality: Is the information verifiable, consistent, and properly referenced? What discrepancies do you expect? For example, while expert opinions may differ, data discrepancies might result from differences in geography, population, or company size.
- Cost: Will the available data lead to an appropriate, cost-effective solution to the problem? If primary data would lead to a better solution, the data collection cost may be justifiable as opposed to using the lower-cost secondary data.

EXTRACTING DATA AND KEEPING RECORDS

After you have found relevant information, you must extract it from its source for use in your data analysis and report. To use data effectively, you must know when and how to record data verbatim (word for word, exactly as written) from sources and when and how to paraphrase information. You must also develop a system for recording data sources.

Keeping records of data sources is an essential part of the research process. Efficient researchers keep those records carefully and constantly while collecting data, avoiding the need to return to the source later to verify documentation details.

Verbatim Data

Record information verbatim when you must preserve the exact nature of the data. For example, when you attribute a controversial statement to an individual, it is wise to quote the statement exactly as it was written or spoken. Similarly, when reporting certain statistics, the exact numbers, even to two or three places beyond the decimal, may be significant in your research.

Two commonly used techniques for recording secondary data verbatim are notetaking and photocopying. Notetaking involves copying the exact information onto a note card or into a looseleaf notebook. (Use a word processing file only if it can be available constantly as you seek and find data.) To use the notetaking technique, follow these suggestions:

- Prepare a reference card or sheet for each source used. Include complete *who, what, where,* and *when* information. Number each source record as you prepare it. (If listing sources in a word processing file, include "Sources" in the filename; type only sources in the file; place each source on a separate page; and number each source.)
- Use a separate card or sheet for each quotation. Write the subject and number of the source (reference card) above the quotation. (Alternatively, open a separate word processing file named "Quotations." Type the subject and number of the source above each quotation; insert a page break below each quotation.)
- Copy material exactly as it appears in your source. Place quotation marks before and after the material to remind you that the material is directly quoted. Record the exact page reference beside the quotation. (In a word processing file, check your typed text word by word and correct even minor typing errors. When quoting from an online database or website, you may be able to copy and paste the text to your "Quotations" file. Then insert quotation marks before and after the material.)

Those suggestions, as well as suggestions for recording paraphrased information, are demonstrated in Illustration 10-1. Linking reference and note cards or sheets by numbers is a timesaving technique. It eliminates the need to write the full source on each note card, yet ensures that sources can be relocated if needed when preparing the report.

Many people prefer the convenience of photocopying pages containing desired data. Copyright law governs photocopying; but, generally, the law allows copying without the copyright owner's permission if the use is reasonable and not harmful to the owner's rights. (Copyright law also applies to printing or copying and pasting web pages.) Making a single copy for research purposes is considered fair use of the material. However, copying can become costly and inefficient if a person copies indiscriminately. (In academic libraries subscribing

ILLUSTRATION 10-1 REFERENCE AND NOTE CARDS

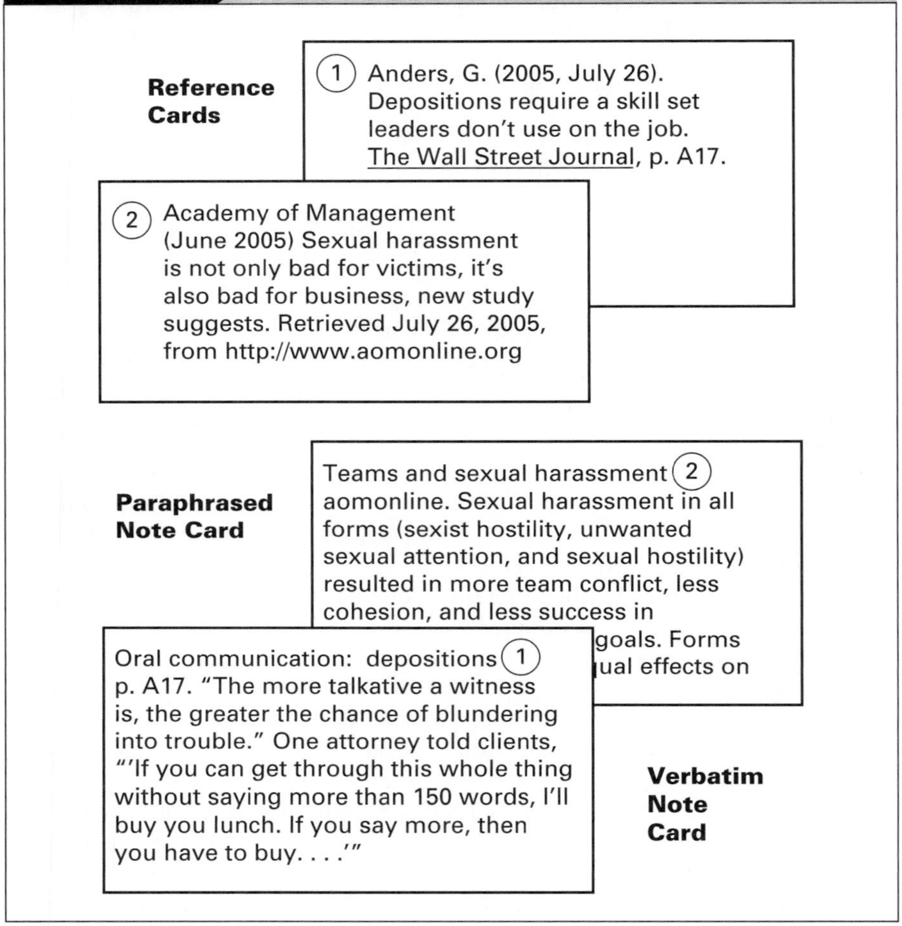

Reference Cards

(1) Anders, G. (2005, July 26). Depositions require a skill set leaders don't use on the job. <u>The Wall Street Journal</u>, p. A17.

(2) Academy of Management (June 2005) Sexual harassment is not only bad for victims, it's also bad for business, new study suggests. Retrieved July 26, 2005, from http://www.aomonline.org

Paraphrased Note Card

Teams and sexual harassment (2) aomonline. Sexual harassment in all forms (sexist hostility, unwanted sexual attention, and sexual hostility) resulted in more team conflict, less cohesion, and less success in goals. Forms ual effects on

Oral communication: depositions (1) p. A17. "The more talkative a witness is, the greater the chance of blundering into trouble." One attorney told clients, "'If you can get through this whole thing without saying more than 150 words, I'll buy you lunch. If you say more, then you have to buy. . . .'"

Verbatim Note Card

to full-text databases, students usually have a less costly alternative: e-mailing articles to their own e-mail address.)

When you photocopy material, immediately prepare a reference card or sheet as you would when taking notes, or record the full source on the copy itself. Also write the subject at the top of the copy. The technique shown in Illustration 10-2 will help you correlate your photocopied data with other data by subject and will ensure that you have essential information for your report's references.

Although some verbatim data may be appropriate in a business report, excessive use of such data tends to suggest that the report writer lacks the ability to analyze and synthesize information. Therefore, you must become proficient at paraphrasing data.

ILLUSTRATION 10-2 ▶ PHOTOCOPY AND REFERENCE CARD

Fortune Global
500 **Ranked by Performance**

③

Biggest
Oil companies once again spewed money, but so did banks and GE.

Fastest
The easiest way to boost revenues? Make a big acquisition, like Mittal.

Leanest
The top performers were banks on opposite sides of the world.

HIGHEST PROFITS

RANK	GLOBAL 500 RANK		2004 PROFITS $ millions
1	EXXON MOBIL	3	25,330.0
2	ROYAL DUTCH / SHELL	4	18,138.0
3	CITIGROUP	16	17,046.0
4	GENERAL ELECTRIC	9	16,819.0
5	BP	2	15,371.0
6	BANK OF AMERICA CORP	52	14,143.0
7	CHEVRON	11	13,328.0
8	TOTAL	10	11,955.0
9	HSBC HOLDINGS	36	11,840.0
10	PFIZER	75	11,361.0
11	TOYOTA MOTOR	7	10,898.2
12	WAL-MART STORES	1	10,267.0
13	AMERICAN INTL GROUP	19	9,731.0
14	SAMSUNG ELECTRONICS	39	9,419.5
15	ALTRIA GROUP	50	9,416.0
16	PETRONAS	133	9,356.9
17	ENI	33	9,047.1
18	CHINA NATL PETROLEUM	46	8,757.1
19	JOHNSON & JOHNSON	88	8,509.0
20	INTL BUS MACHINES	20	8,430.0
	THE GLOBAL 500 MEDIAN		1,052.3

INCREASE IN REVENUE

RANK	GLOBAL 500 RANK		% change from 2003
1	MITTAL STEEL	253	310.2
2	CAREMARK RX	204	184.6
3	WM MORRISON	252	172.5
4	ST PAUL TRAVELERS	240	159.0
5	MITSUBISHI	149	131.9
6	SANOFI-AVENTIS	321	105.4
7	ALCAN	214	82.3
8	MANULIFE	279	75.4
9	PREMCOR	395	74.2
10	PLAINS ALL AM PIPE	275	66.6
11	PWR CORP CANADA	323	66.2
12	AIR FRANCE—KLM	222	65.5
13	OFFICEMAX	466	60.9
14	RAG	232	59.7
15	AUSTRALIA & NZ	490	59.4
16	WILLIAM HILL	403	56.2
17	COMMONWEALTH	406	51.8
18	KOC HOLDING	389	51.1
19	HON HAI PREC IND	371	50.4
20	HILTON GROUP	260	49.3
	THE GLOBAL 500 MEDIAN		13.0

RETURN ON REVENUE

RANK	GLOBAL 500 RANK		2004 PROFITS as % of revenues
1	CHINA CON BNK	315	30.7
2	U.S. BANCORP	420	28.3
3	ENCANA	499	28.3
4	PETRONAS	133	25.9
5	MERCK	239	25.3
6	L'ORÉAL	336	24.9
7	NEXTEL COMM	463	22.4
8	BNK OF AM CORP	52	22.3
9	MICROSOFT	127	22.2
10	COCA-COLA	257	22.1
11	INTEL	141	22.0
12	GLAXOSMITHKLIN	122	21.7
13	PFIZER	75	21.5
14	ROCHE GROUP	209	21.2
15	MITTAL STEEL	253	21.2
16	BELLSOUTH	244	20.9
17	SABIC	331	20.7
18	WELLS FARGO	144	20.7
19	MIZUHO FINC GRP	184	20.6
20	NOVARTIS	186	20.4
	THE GLOBAL 500 MEDIAN		4.3

20 BIGGEST LOSSES

RANK	GLOBAL 500 RANK		2004 LOSS $ millions
1	VIACOM	196	17,462.2
2	VODAFONE	53	13,910.4*
3	AT&T	162	6,469.0
4	DELTA AIR LINES	408	5,198.0*
5	UFJ HOLDINGS	264	5,159.8
†6	DAIEI	353	4,744.7
7	SANOFI-AVENTIS	321	4490.0
8	MITSUBISHI MOTORS	304	4417.7*
9	MCI	247	4,002.0
10	HVB GROUP	195	2,833.3*
11	TENET HEALTHCARE	495	2,640.0
12	PEMEX	51	2,258.9
13	SUMITOMO MITSUI GROUP	147	2,179.2
14	FIAT	57	1,972.6
15	QWEST COMMUNICATIONS	451	1,794.0
16	UAL	366	1,721.0*
17	SANYO ELECTRIC	237	1,596.2
18	VISTEON	324	1,499.0*
19	WESTLB	460	1,441.8*
20	ALSTOM	348	1,088.7
	THE GLOBAL 500 MEDIAN		1,265.3†

INCREASE IN PROFITS*

RANK	GLOBAL 500 RANK		% change from 2003
1	MITTAL STEEL	253	7,022.7
2	ROYAL MILL HOLDGS	361	3,556.4
3	VOLVO	180	3,351.9
4	SNCF	190	3,126.9
5	OFFICEMAX	466	1,992.1
...			
20	ROYL PHILLIPS ELEC	116	348.4
	THE GLOBAL 500 MEDIAN		33.3

RETURN ON ASSETS

RANK	GLOBAL 500 RANK		2004 PROFITS as % of assets
1	MITTAL STEEL	253	24.5
2	GLAXOSMITHKLIN	122	18.7
3	L'ORÉAL	336	18.3
4	KARSTADTQUELLE	343	16.9
5	JOHNSN & JOHNSN	88	16.0
			15.6
			15.5
			15.2
			15.0
			15.0
			14.9
			14.9
			14.4
			14.3
			14.3
			14.3
			14.1
			13.9
			13.7
20	MERCK	239	13.7
	THE GLOBAL 500 MEDIAN		2.7

③ Fortune global 500 ranked by performance. Fortune Industrial Edition 25 July 2005: 140.

*Also lost $ in 2003. †For 38 companies with 2004 losses.   *Excludes companies that lost $ in 2003.

Paraphrased Data

Paraphrased data are data that you have restated in your own words. When you write a paraphrase, you capture the essence of the information by summarizing key facts and stating them in a way that is relevant to your topic of analysis. Paraphrased data are more desirable than exact quotations when the basic meaning is important, but specific wording is not. For example, if you are reporting a company's growth for a three-year period, it may be more meaningful to compute and report a percentage of increase in gross revenues for each year than to report the exact gross revenues. Computing and recording percentages of increase based on exact revenues that you find in a secondary source is a form of paraphrasing.

Even when information is paraphrased, you must cite your data source. Therefore, you should maintain reference and note cards similar to those kept for verbatim data. The reference cards will not differ from those kept for verbatim data, but the note cards will differ slightly. Since they will contain paraphrased data, you will use no quotation marks as you record information. The note card should contain a subject heading, the number of the related reference card, and the page number of the original data from which you wrote your paraphrase. (See Illustration 10-1.)

An abstract is a form of a paraphrase. The term abstract usually refers to a summary of the contents of a journal article, a special report, a book chapter, or an entire book. Whereas a paraphrased note summarizes one topic only, an abstract may include a summary of more than one topic covered in a particular publication. In some organizations, a report writer's duties may include abstracting current journal articles for managers or technical personnel. The duty of the person writing the abstract, also called an executive summary, is to capture the vital information in articles so that managers or technical personnel can be informed about current developments in their fields without having to read the contents of several journals. Guides for writing an effective abstract or executive summary are given in Chapter 7.

ACKNOWLEDGING SECONDARY SOURCES

Whether paraphrasing or directly quoting an author, you must credit the source in your report. Fully crediting sources, or documentation, consists of two parts:

- An alphabetical list of all references used, placed at the end of the report
- A citation in the report text wherever extracted data are used

Chapter 13 contains guides and examples for preparing a reference list and inserting citations.

ETHICAL CONSIDERATIONS

As you use secondary data sources, you may be confronted with ethical dilemmas, particularly with respect to selecting and acknowledging data sources.

Selecting Data

The quality of decisions based on a report can be no better than the quality of the data presented in the report. Therefore, as an ethical researcher, you must constantly evaluate the accuracy, balance, credibility, and documentation of the data you find. As you uncover secondary data, ask yourself the following questions, and take the time to answer honestly. To do less jeopardizes the validity of your research.

- Accurate: Are statements factual—containing few superlatives and exclamation points—rather than opinionated or emotional? Did the author give the "whole story," or only part of it? Did the author include precise details or only sweeping generalities? Is the source correct right now?
- Balanced: Are the data sensible and practical? Do the data square with your existing knowledge and experience? Are data presented objectively, or can you detect a biased tone? Does the author seem concerned with truth and fairness? For example, if advantages are listed, disadvantages appear also.
- Credible: Do you intuitively trust or distrust the data? What are the author's credentials? Is the author and/or publication a known, respected authority on the subject? Did an organization sponsor publication of the data? If so, what kind?
- Documented: Do the data include a list of sources and information for contacting the author or publisher? Are all claims supported by evidence and/or references? Can you find at least two other sources that support the data?

Acknowledging Sources

An ethical researcher acknowledges the sources that have contributed unique information to a research project. The ethical question usually concerns the uniqueness of the data and the degree to which one's credibility is affected by acknowledging sources.

Report writers generally do not cite the source of information that is common knowledge among the report readers; however, the more specific the data are, the greater is the need to cite sources. Data sources must be provided for two classes of secondary data:

- All direct quotations
- All paraphrased information that is not common knowledge among the report readers

Some writers erroneously think that their credibility is reduced when they recognize dependence on others for report data. However, in 2002, the careers of two popular historians, both best-selling authors and TV pundits, were defaced (independently) by their failure to put quotation marks around direct quotations and close paraphrases from secondary sources. Both writers had attributed the lifted material in footnotes or endnotes. A few years later, the plagiarism headlines have stopped, but not the controversy. The works of one author, now deceased, remain suspect in the academic community, while the other best-selling author strives to regain lost credibility from colleagues and readers alike.

In fact, a writer's credibility is enhanced by appropriate acknowledgment of sources. By citing sources that contributed unique information, you demonstrate integrity. Moreover, by inference all information in your report that is not attributed to another source may be attributed to you. Those parts of the report demonstrate your ability to analyze and synthesize information.

SUMMARY

Most researchers begin their research by consulting secondary data sources. Those sources help the researcher gain a perspective on the problem, and they often provide adequate data to solve the problem.

Appropriate use of secondary sources in research requires locating relevant, valid data; extracting that data from the source (either verbatim or paraphrased); and citing sources that contributed unique information to the report. The wide range of available secondary sources requires that you become proficient in the use of online or card catalogs, directories, online databases, periodical indexes, special issues of business periodicals, sources for statistical data, reference books, sources for company and industry data, and the World Wide Web.

TOPICS FOR DISCUSSION

1. Give five or more reasons why a businessperson would use secondary data sources in solving business problems.

2. Name four steps in collecting secondary data. Explain each step concisely (25 words or fewer).

3. Explain how directories, databases, and reference books help business people search for secondary data.

4. Cite five criteria for evaluating secondary sources. Briefly explain each criterion.

5. Name five search engines available for searching the Internet. Point out notable differences among those search engines you have used.

6. Define "keyword search." Explain how to search for data on the subject of taxing Internet sales.

7. Describe the record-keeping procedures for paraphrased data.

8. Explain how and why the record-keeping procedure for verbatim data differs from that for paraphrasing.

9. Name four characteristics of "good" secondary data. For each characteristic, give an example.

10. When must you acknowledge secondary sources in a written or oral report?

APPLICATIONS

1. You have been asked to write a feasibility report for opening a cut-rate natural and organic food store in Louisville, Kentucky. Answer the following questions using the latest information available. Provide a citation for each source.
   a. What is the population of Louisville, Kentucky? What percentage of this population is between the ages of 18 and 24, and what percentage is over 60?
   b. What is the per capita income of Louisville, Kentucky, residents?
   c. What is the outlook for natural and organic food stores nationwide?
   d. Locate and skim a current (past three years) journal, magazine, newspaper, or web article on the topic. (Hint: Look up the Texas-based company named Whole Foods.)

2. Choose a public company; then locate its SEC 10-Q filings for the most recent quarter. First, search the EDGAR database (http://www.sec.gov/edgar .shtml); then, locate the company's filings. Finally, print the consolidated balance sheet (Form 10-Q).

3. Select three stocks traded on a major exchange that are of interest to you and relevant to your course of study. Use either the NASDAQ or S&P 500 website to examine today's trading activity and activity for the past 12 months. Compare and contrast the three stocks in a three-page letter report to your instructor.

4. At the American Marketing Association's web page, see the list of AMA publications (Learn section). In a two-page memo report to your instructor, describe each publication. Identify two publications you might consult for your current work in school or business. Likewise, identify two publications for your instructor's use. Explain both choices.

5. As directed by your instructor, collect secondary data for one of the following situations. Identify the kinds of data needed. (Hint: List several questions to be answered.) Then locate and evaluate at least three data sources. Finally, extract the necessary data and record reference information.
   a. Voicemail, designed to save time and effort for callers and the person called, sometimes falls short of this goal. For example, most of us know the frustration of voicemail systems that loop endlessly, making it impossible for callers to speak with a person. And some of us

know the frustration of indecipherable voicemail messages. Make a list of voicemail advantages and disadvantages. Follow up with a set of guidelines for voicemail users (callers and person called).

b. In her 2004 *Orion* magazine article, "High-Tech Wasteland," Ellen Grossman wrote: "According to the Environmental Protection Agency (EPA), more than two million tons of high-tech electronics are dumped in U.S. landfills each year, and only about 10 percent of discarded personal computers are recycled. The EPA expects at least 200 million televisions to be discarded between 2003 and 2010, 250 million computers to become obsolete in the next five years, and 65,000 tons of used and broken cell phones to accumulate by 2005. And these numbers are for the U.S. alone." In your medium-sized organization, you are part of a team collecting data on electronic recycling. Your role: Identify U.S. businesses that methodically recycle electronics. In as much detail as possible, describe each company's electronic recycling plan.

c. Businesses in the United States voluntarily assist many educational institutions. They donate money or electronic equipment, and they provide cooperative training programs. You have been asked to examine articles on this subject, describe other ways that businesses help educational institutions, and describe benefits businesses gain by their efforts and contributions.

d. You are a part-time worker at a publishing company. Your supervisor, Jared Schaber, has asked you to research the topic of speech recognition technology (SRT). He wants to know how SRT is used by other businesses, the types of messages for which it is useful, and the potential increase in productivity SRT offers for manuscript production.

6. After you have collected the data requested in Application 5, write a memo report to your instructor. In the report, summarize the data and synthesize (blend) the ideas it contains. Also cite sources in your report. (Hint: Use Illustrations 10-1 and 10-2 as guides, or refer to Chapter 13.)

7. Visit three websites that list position openings in your major field and where you could post a scannable résumé. Browse each site thoroughly, becoming familiar with its features and user-friendliness. In a letter report to your instructor, identify and describe the potential usefulness of these sites in business education.

8. Prepare an annotated list of references on developments in communication as applied to one of the following fields. Include at least five journal articles published since 2000. (Hint: Articles may be located in print, in a database, or on the web.) An illustration of an annotated list appears in Chapter 13.
   - Accounting
   - Advertising
   - Business Law
   - Economics
   - Finance

- Global Business
- Human Resource Management
- Marketing
- Real Estate
- Small Business Management
- Your major, if not listed above
- Robotics
- Geographic Positioning Systems (GPS)

9. In Moody's Manual, Standard and Poor's Register of Corporations, or another source of company data listed in the chapter, find information about a large international corporation. Write a short memo (one full page or less) to your instructor describing the kinds of information available in the source.

10. Use secondary sources to locate and record the information for any six of the following items. Record a full reference for each source.
- Population of Vietnam
- Capital city of Malaysia
- Latest list of the Fortune 500
- Monetary unit in South Africa
- Population of your hometown
- Origin of the word "capitalism"
- Main cause of small business failures
- Estimated trade-in value of the car you drive
- Name of the first woman elected to the U.S. Congress
- Location of Cluj-Napoca, Romania, on world map
- Locations of the three most recent winter Olympics
- *The New York Times* headline on the day you were born
- Distance from New York City to Rio de Janeiro, Brazil
- Size of continental United States compared to Australia
- Name and location of world's five largest cities (population)
- Exact value of today's U.S. dollar in Euro dollars and Japanese yen
- Web address (URL) for a site dedicated to your hobby or interest
- Originator of this statement: "There's a sucker born every minute."

Using Primary Data Sources

LEARNING OBJECTIVES

After you have read this chapter, you should be able to:

1. Identify ways to acquire primary data.
2. Construct appropriate data collection instruments.
3. Explain ethical issues related to using primary data.
4. Maintain accurate records that will contribute to ethical acknowledgement of data sources.

When you determine that secondary data are not adequate to answer your research questions, you must use primary data. To use primary data effectively, your first tasks are to select appropriate sources and valid, reliable methods of collecting data from those sources.

ACQUIRING PRIMARY DATA

Primary data are data acquired at their source. Commonly used primary data sources for business research are company records; people, such as employees, customers, and suppliers; and phenomena, such as activities and processes. Methods to obtain information from those sources are either active or passive. *Passive data collection* involves observation of characteristics of the people or actions that are the elements of analysis; the person collecting the data does not actively interact or communicate with those subjects. *Active data collection* involves questioning the subjects; the person collecting the data interacts with the subjects who actively supply the data to the researcher.

Passive Methods

Passive data collection methods used by business researchers include searches of company records, observations, and some forms of experimentation.

SEARCH OF COMPANY RECORDS

Company records contain much information generated during daily operations. Personnel, production, marketing, credit, accounting, and finance records are accumulated and modified daily. Those records are often used in day-to-day decisions and subsequently stored for possible future use. Although some of the information may be made available to the public in an annual report or a publicity release, much of the material is never published and distributed externally. But as new problems or challenges arise within the organization, the data that have been accumulated in the files often provide a perspective on the problems and information to solve them.

Company records are often the first primary data source consulted by a business researcher. Some researchers consider company records to be superior to other primary data sources for two reasons:

- The data are objective. The data were generated for purposes other than the immediate report that is being prepared.
- They are economical to use. Collecting data from company files is generally the least expensive method of gathering primary data.

Company files are especially useful when the research requires historical data about some aspect of the company's operations. For example, data from personnel files will show changes in the composition of the company's labor force, data from customer service files can identify a possible flaw in product design, and data from files in the IT assistance center may be able to identify emerging user needs. When company records cannot provide adequate valid data, however, other strategies must be used.

Many companies store information about company activity in computerized databases and digitized files. A database is a collection of related records stored in a computer file. For example, a customer database might contain such information as name, street or post office address, city, state, zip code, telephone number, account number, and credit limit. A record is all of the information about one person or organization. Each category of information within the record is called a field. In this example there would be eight fields: name, street or post office address, city, state, zip code, telephone number, account number, and credit limit. A digitized file, on the other hand, usually consists of text and graphics. A proposal received via electronic mail, a sales report, a memo reporting the decisions at a meeting, and a status report of a project are examples of the types of documents stored as digitized files.

When information processing systems are integrated, personal computers are linked to other equipment so that information can be accessed by all authorized users. In an integrated system you can collect and process information stored in a database relatively easily. You must first obtain authority to use the file, then gain access to the appropriate file, identify the correct record, identify the categories of data desired, and direct the computer to find the data. You can then organize the data in many ways; alphabetically or numerically, ascending or descending order, or by any category of information stored in the file. Assume, for example, that as regional sales manager for Valdex Company you help sales representatives call on inactive customers, those who have not placed orders within the previous six months. While preparing to visit Ohio, you can access the database to identify customers in Ohio. Next, inactive accounts can be identified and arranged geographically by ZIP code so that your travel time is kept to a minimum. You can also sort the accounts alphabetically, by the date of the last order, or by the amount of the last order. If you desire, you can also insert this information in a letter report to Ohio sales representatives with a few simple keystrokes.

In contrast, if individual workstations are not linked, you must request the needed information from the division of the organization controlling that information. It is your responsibility to define what information is needed and how it is to be organized. After receiving the information, you must integrate it into the report, often by re-entering the data.

Report writers may also use digitized files to collect textual or statistical information. Documents stored digitally are coded with key words or phrases identifying the contents of the document. To locate information stored in files, you must first determine the appropriate criteria for the desired information and instruct the computer to locate files that match the criteria. You then select relevant documents from the list generated by the computer search. For instance, suppose you are the director of continuing education for a medical school. You know that many medical doctors practicing in rural communities find it difficult to leave their practices for a few days to travel to the medical school for the training needed to maintain their medical licenses. You want the medical school to develop online courses that will permit those rural doctors to participate in continuing education from their offices or homes. You think that several documents exist relating to this idea. To locate the documents, you would direct the computer to search for the keywords *medical, continuing education, rural*. After the document list has been generated, you would select those that will support your proposal for online continuing education.

OBSERVATION

A second passive method is observation. In this technique the researcher (or a mechanical or electronic device) watches the data sources and records information about the elements that are being analyzed.

Assume, for example, that productivity is lower than average among the employees of one supervisor in a computer tech support call center. You may decide to collect data about working patterns of those employees. Company records are not likely to contain that information, except to the extent that it has been recorded in performance reviews. Asking employees about working patterns is unlikely to yield valid data, because the technicians may be unwilling or unable to report how they work. Therefore, observation of the employees performing their tasks may be the best data collection method. In your observation you could record several behaviors: how quickly they begin work after arrival, how they organize their workstations, how much call time is spent on "chit-chat" with the customer and how much is spent on solving the technical problem, the degree of direct supervision they receive, how they respond to the supervisor's comments, the percentage of time they are away from the workstation, etc.

In some situations observation can be accomplished mechanically. For example, highway departments regularly use traffic counting devices to help determine whether to install a traffic signal at a particular intersection. A time clock used to record when employees check in and check out of work is another type of mechanical or electronic observation.

Observation is often an integral part of another method, experimentation. Experimentation may employ both passive and active data collection methods. Assume that, as part of a wellness program, a company's dietician wants to encourage employees to eat fresh fruits and vegetables. You are assigned the task of determining how to increase employee consumption of those foods in the company cafeteria. In cooperation with the cafeteria staff, you decide to conduct an experiment in which you manipulate the location of the fruits and vegetables in the cafeteria layout. Then you observe employee behavior (looking at fruits and vegetables, not looking at them, selecting, not selecting, etc.) as they go through the line. That observation is a passive method. But you may supplement it with an active method, asking employees why they did or did not choose a fresh fruit or vegetable.

A major shortcoming of observation is that the observer must interpret what he or she sees, and different observers may assign different meanings to events. Another weakness is the assumption that the characteristic being studied happens when it occurs. In the cafeteria experiment, for example, when an employee pauses in front of the fruits and vegetables, one observer may interpret that behavior as noticing the display. Another observer may interpret the behavior as a delay caused by other factors such as a slowdown somewhere on the line. When an employee selects an item from the display, the observer might be tempted to assume the decision was made at that time and was influenced by the attractiveness of the display. But the employee may have decided several hours earlier to eat an apple or a salad for lunch. Because of such potential shortcomings in observation, that method is often supplemented by an active method.

Active Methods

Active methods involve questioning subjects. Questioning is an appropriate data collection method when the information you need consists of knowledge, attitudes, opinions, or beliefs. In many situations, questioning is the only way to obtain necessary data. You can, for example, get data from personnel files about employee participation in a 401K plan; but you cannot determine employee attitudes toward the company's contribution to the plan from those files. Attitudes must be determined by questioning the employees. After the questioning, the results may be compiled and stored in company files; but those data then become historical data. Attitudes could change dramatically within a short time if company policy or economic conditions change.

Questioning can be accomplished by either personal or impersonal means. Interviewing is a personal means, whereas using questionnaires and electronic surveys tends to be impersonal.[1]

INTERVIEWS

In an interview, the researcher or an assistant orally presents instructions and questions to the subjects and records their answers. Interviews may be face-to-face or mediated.

The face-to-face interview is a rich communication medium that allows both the interviewer and respondent to interpret nonverbal cues as well as verbal questions. For example, the respondent can ask for clarification of a question he or she does not understand. Likewise the interviewer can use probes to encourage deeper thought if the responses seem superficial. Such richness may improve rapport between the researcher and the subject, thereby encouraging openness; but that same richness may stimulate the respondent to give socially acceptable answers, thereby biasing the data.

In a mediated interview, such as a telephone interview, the participants cannot see one another. Thus, trust and rapport must be established through verbal means. Telephone interviews are considered by some researchers to be equal or perhaps superior to other active primary data collection methods in obtaining valid data, particularly when the subject matter is sensitive. For example, respondents may be more willing to answer questions about personal health matters in the relative anonymity of a telephone interview than in a face-to-face interview. Telephone interviews have been particularly successful in business-to-business situations because respondents may be willing to give a few minutes of telephone time when they are not willing to schedule an appointment for an interview.

The inability to show prompts, display materials, or present a long list of options is a severe limitation of telephone interviews. Another major disadvantage of telephone interviews is the increasing consumer resistance to that method of home intrusion for marketing purposes.

Interviews may be structured or unstructured. In a structured interview, the interviewer follows a formal guide that provides the exact wording of instructions and questions as well as the exact sequence in which questions are to be asked. If interviewers follow the guide as written, all subjects will be questioned in essentially the same manner. In an unstructured interview, the interviewee uses either no formalized questions or very loosely structured ones. The objective is to get the respondent to talk freely about the interview topic.

Today, researchers use computer assistance in both face-to-face and telephone interviews. For example, in telephone surveys, questions may be presented by a voice recording; the subject is asked to respond by pressing designated digits on the telephone keypad. The computer may be set up to provide the interviewer with a questionnaire and a means of recording responses. A particular advantage is the ability to branch easily to different paths in the interview, depending upon a respondent's answer. Calculations can also be programmed into the questionnaire enabling the interviewer to ask a simple question, such as how many glasses of milk each family member consumes in a day, and immediately convert the answer into annual family consumption. Another advantage is the ability to randomize or rotate series of questions. In a face-to-face interview, the computer can also present visual stimuli.

FOCUS GROUP INTERVIEWS

Focus group interviews are often used to determine interest in a new product or service, the effectiveness of advertising and communications research, background studies on consumers' frames of reference, or consumer attitudes and behaviors toward an idea, organization, etc.

The standard focus group interview involves 8 to 12 similar individuals, such as male college students, female lawyers, or Toyota Camry owners, who are brought together to discuss a particular topic. The respondents are selected according to the relevant sampling plan and meet at a central location that has facilities for taping or filming the interviews. A moderator or facilitator is present to keep the discussion moving and focused on the topic, but otherwise the sessions are free-flowing. The competent moderator attempts to develop three clear stages in a one- to three-hour interview:

1. Establish rapport with the group, structure the rules of the group interaction, and set objectives.
2. Provoke intense discussion in relevant areas.
3. Summarize the group's responses to determine the extent of agreement.

Usually the moderator also prepares a summary of each session, after analyzing the session's transcript or recording.

Focus groups can generate much data in a relatively short period. When little is known in advance of an investigation, the focus group may provide a basis for formulating research questions and problems.

QUESTIONNAIRE SURVEYS

In a questionnaire survey (also called a self-completion survey), instructions and questions are presented to the subjects in a printed questionnaire, and the subjects record their answers on the questionnaire or another medium.

Questionnaire surveys are attractive to investigators for three reasons.

- The cost is low relative to the amount of data that can be collected in one survey.
- The large geographic area from which the researcher can draw the sample may improve data validity.
- The assurance of anonymity and lack of pressure while the respondent completes the questionnaire contribute to data validity.

Response rates to questionnaire surveys are relatively low, however. Response rates can be influenced by questionnaire design, which is discussed later in this chapter. To increase response rates—and, thereby, data validity—researchers often offer inducements to the subjects. Market researchers have identified the relative effectiveness of various inducements, as follows:[2]

Inducement	Influence
Pre-notification	Increase in response
Personalization	Increase in response
Monetary incentives	Increase in response
Follow-up	Increase in response
Return postage	Increase in response
Sources sponsorship	Increase if subject identifies with sponsor
Appeal in cover letter	Ego, science, or social utility appeals tend to be most effective
Specification of deadline	No influence on number of returns; may accelerate speed of returns
Typewritten vs. printed; color; length; pre-coding	No influence on returns

ELECTRONIC SURVEYS

The increasing number of people who have access to the Internet has made it a popular tool for self-completion surveys. Customer satisfaction surveys are commonly conducted by this medium, particularly after a major purchase. At time of purchase, the customer is encouraged to go to a website, enter identifying information, and answer questions about the purchase experience. These surveys often include an incentive, such as entry into a sweepstakes or receipt of a gift card. Some researchers have successfully used the technique of contacting potential subjects by e-mail to request that the recipient participate in the survey. The e-mail usually includes a link to a website containing the questionnaire. Individuals willing to participate in the research can easily access, complete, and submit the questionnaire.

Studies have shown that Web-based questionnaires, when skillfully designed, are completed more quickly than telephone, face-to-face, and paper questionnaire surveys. This medium also allows presentation of visual images, longer lists of options, and easy branching strategies. By involving the participant visually and manually, this questionnaire tends to maintain the respondents' attention and promotes good-quality data to the end of the questionnaire.[3]

Comparison of Primary Data Collection Methods

Your choice of a data collection method must be based on its ability to obtain accurate data and satisfy other relevant research criteria. Factors that often influence the success of a project are the ability to identify subjects or to assure subject anonymity, flexibility of the data-gathering technique, ability of the technique to tap sensitive data, protecting the data from researcher influence, scheduling requirements, time requirements, probable response rate, and cost. (See Table 11-1.)

As the table shows, if your research design requires that subjects be identified, a search of company records, observation, or personal interview would

TABLE 11-1 COMPARISON OF PRIMARY DATA COLLECTION METHODS

			Methods			
Dimensions	**Search of Records**	**Observation**	**Personal Interview**	**Focus Group Interview**	**Questionnaire Survey**	**Electronic Survey**
Subject identification/anonymity	Excellent	Excellent*	Excellent	Excellent*	Fair	Excellent*
Flexibility	Excellent	Good to Fair	Excellent	Excellent	Fair	Poor
Subject anonymity	Fair to Poor	Excellent*	Poor	Excellent*	Excellent*	Excellent*
Accuracy of sensitive data	Excellent	Fair	Fair	Fair	Good	Excellent
Control of researcher effects	Good	Poor	Poor	Poor	Excellent	Excellent
Flexibility of scheduling	Excellent	Fair	Poor	Fair	Excellent	Good
Time required	Good	Fair	Fair	Fair	Fair	Excellent
Probable response rate	Good	Good	Good	Good	Fair to poor	Good
Cost	Excellent	Fair	Poor	Fair	Good	Good

*Dependent on design of study; subject identification or anonymity can be planned.

be an excellent technique. On the other hand, if you wish to ensure subject anonymity, a search of company records or a personal interview would be a poor technique. Similarly, if you are concerned about the accuracy of sensitive data, you should choose the records search technique or a survey as opposed to observation or personal interviews. Some sensitive data, such as information about contributions to a political party or personal health practices, cannot be collected by observation and may be distorted in an interview. By weighing the relative importance of the nine dimensions, you can select a technique that best meets the requirements of your project.

After selecting your data collection method or methods, you must design a way to capture the data and make them available for analysis. The precision of your data collection instruments will influence the quality of your data.

Preparing Instruments to Collect Primary Data

Primary data collection tools consist of observation forms, questionnaires, and interview guides. To design those tools, you must understand some basic concepts about measurement and measurement scales.

Measurement and Measurement Scales

Measurement is the process of assigning numbers to an element or characteristic that is being observed or analyzed, and a measurement scale is any device used to assign numbers to the characteristic. Height—the distance from the bottom to the top of something standing upright—is a common measurement with which you are familiar. Height can be scaled in inches, feet, yards, centimeters, millimeters, or meters.

A primary purpose of measurement is to permit analysis and comparisons of relevant characteristics. For example, through measurement of an infant's height at birth and at age three months you can learn something about the child's growth. By comparing those measurements with the average measurements for children in your culture, you obtain additional information about the child's growth rate.

In business research you will frequently want to measure and compare behaviors, attitudes, desires, or other characteristics of a target group of people. Four scales are commonly used to measure or assign numbers to such data: nominal, ordinal, interval, and ratio.

Nominal

A *nominal* scale allows you to classify information and assign a number to each classification. The classifications used for nominal scales must be all-inclusive and mutually exclusive. For example, every survey respondent can be classified with respect to gender into one of two groups, female or male. In a customer survey, a private business/dining club may wish to categorize respondents by type of club services used:

1. Breakfast
2. Lunch
3. Dinner
4. Private Banquet Service
5. Private Meeting Rooms
6. Business Networking Events

A *nominal* scale merely permits assignment of numbers to the categories that are of interest to the researcher. Consequently, the statistics that can be computed from a nominal scale are limited to such descriptive items as the percentage of responses in each category and the mode, that is, which category has the greatest number of responses. A nominal scale provides no information about relative value of the items classified. A number does not indicate that items in that category are better or worse, weaker or stronger than items in another category.

Ordinal

An *ordinal* scale permits determination of a qualitative difference among categories. Assume the business-oriented club wants to know what proposed new services are most attractive to consumers. Respondents could be asked to indicate their preferences by ranking five services as shown in the following example. Assume the numbers in the "rank" column are one subject's responses, with 1 representing the most preferred and 5 the least preferred service.

Service	Rank
1. Half-price "Happy Hour" on Wednesday, 5–7 p.m.	4
2. "Quick Lunch" menu/service, Monday–Friday	3
3. Wireless Internet Service	2
4. Reduced-priced dinner on member's birthday	5
5. Free use of private rooms for business meetings	1

An *ordinal* scale helps the researcher determine the percentage of respondents who consider half-price "Happy Hour" most important, the percentage who consider a "Quick Lunch" most important, etc. Such a scale also shows that the individual who ranked the services as shown prefers Service 5 to all other services, Service 2 and Service 3 to Service 1 or 4; but the ranking does not indicate the relative strength of the preferences. The individual may consider the first-ranked item to be only slightly more important than the second-ranked item; but the respondent may think that the item given the second rank is considerably more important than the third-ranked service.

Interval

If the club wants to analyze the strength of differences in attitudes toward various services, the researcher must use an interval scale. Such a scale presents equally spaced (or equal-appearing) points on a continuum to represent order, differences, and magnitude of differences. Although five-point interval scales are common, any number of points may be used. On the basis of the research problem, the researcher must decide how refined the measure should be.

The following example illustrates how the club might use an interval scale to determine the strength of preferences for various services.

Indicate how important each of the following services is to you by circling the number on the scale that reflects your attitude:

1 = Very Unimportant
2 = Unimportant
3 = Neutral
4 = Important
5 = Extremely Important

Service	Rating				
1. Half-price "Happy Hour" on Wednesday, 5–7 p.m.	1	2	3	4	5
2. "Quick Lunch" menu/service, Mon.–Fri.	1	2	3	4	5
3. Wireless Internet service	1	2	3	4	5
4. Reduced-priced dinner on member's birthday	1	2	3	4	5
5. Free use of private rooms for business meetings	1	2	3	4	5

An *interval* scale permits calculation of an arithmetic mean for each variable. Such a scale also permits calculation of the variance and standard deviation to analyze how responses are distributed around the mean.

An interval scale begins at an arbitrary point other than zero. The scale in the foregoing illustration begins at 1, but it could have started with any number. Since the scale does not begin at zero, it cannot measure the proportions of differences. Although the distances between points on the scale are assumed to be equal, a value of 5 cannot be interpreted as five times greater than a value of 1. Considering a Fahrenheit thermometer will help you understand that characteristic of an interval scale. A thermometer's scale range may be from a point below zero, −50 degrees for example, to a point above zero, such as +150 degrees. After using the thermometer to record outdoor temperature every day at 12 noon for one month, you can compute the average noontime temperature for that month. But if the temperature is 80 degrees at noon one day and 60 the next day, you cannot say that the temperature has fallen 25 percent; you can only say that it has fallen 20 degrees.

Ratio

A *ratio* scale has an absolute zero point and equal intervals on the scale, making it the most powerful measurement scale. Some examples of ratio scales are income, age, height, and weight. This scale permits calculation of the magnitude of differences. For example, a $10,000 income is one-third of a $30,000 income; a 75-year-old person has lived three times longer than a 25-year-old person; a 90-foot structure is 50 percent taller than a 60-foot structure; and an object that weighs 260 pounds is twice a heavy as an object weighing 130 pounds.

Although the ratio scale is the most powerful scale, it cannot be used for some kinds of measurement. When measuring a behavioral characteristic, such as attitudes, it is rarely logical to assume that an individual completely lacks the characteristic that is being studied. For example, most club patrons have some attitude or opinion about the desirability of various services, even if the attitude is that a particular service is very unimportant. Logic requires, therefore, that a scale used to measure most behavioral dimensions begin at a point above zero.

The type of measurement scale—nominal, ordinal, interval, or ratio—determines what kinds of statistics can be used for data analysis. Any statistic that can be computed from less powerfully scaled data (that is, nominal or ordinal) can be computed on more powerfully scaled data (that is, interval and ratio). But many statistics that can be computed for interval or ratio data cannot be applied to nominal or ordinal data. You will learn more about analysis of scaled data in Chapter 12.

To design an effective instrument for primary data collection, you must first decide which measurement scale or scales will help you collect and analyze the necessary data needed to solve your research problem. After making that decision, you must design the instrument carefully and test it before beginning your actual collection. In addition, in some research, such as in questionnaire surveys, you must also prepare a transmittal message to stimulate potential respondents to participate in the study.

Criteria for Instrument Design

All primary data collection instruments must meet certain design standards. The overall objective is that the instrument must enable someone (the observer, interviewer, or subject) to record valid data in a manner that permits analysis. To achieve that objective, the tool must meet criteria related to content, language, format, and instructions. As you study the following criteria, notice their application in Illustration 11-1, Observation Form; Illustration 11-2, Interview Guide; and Illustration 11-3, Questionnaire.

CONTENT

The content of the data collection instrument must be justified in terms of its relevance to the research problem. Research time and money are wasted if irrelevant items are included. To determine relevance, ask yourself what purpose each item serves:

- **Is the information required for the data analysis plan?** Demographic data, such as gender or age of participant, may be relevant if data analysis calls for comparisons by gender or age. But if such comparisons are not planned, questions about gender or age should not be included.
- **Is the question required to establish rapport or to screen potential subjects?** Even though specific answers to such a question may not be part of the data analysis, the question may be relevant because it facilitates the

ILLUSTRATION 11-1 OBSERVATION FORM

OBSERVATION—TELLER SERVICE AT RNB

Instructions: Please observe the teller(s) at the window to which you have been assigned. On the date indicated on this form, make your observations at two randomly selected times. Because of the random time selections, you may be observing different tellers each time, or you may be observing the same teller twice. Do not identify the teller. Please sit or stand unobtrusively in a position that allows you to see the teller clearly. Observe teller behaviors and check the appropriate items on this form to record your observations. Write additional comments as needed.

Bank No. _____   **Teller Window No.** _____

Date of Observations _____   Observer _____

Observation 1. Time: _____   **Observation 2. Time:** _____

Greeted customer pleasantly _____	Greeted customer pleasantly _____
Handled documents/checks/ currency efficiently _____	Handled documents/checks/ currency efficiently _____
Operated computer efficiently _____	Operated computer efficiently _____
Did not converse with other tellers while handling transaction _____	Did not converse with other tellers while handling transaction _____
Listened attentively as customer spoke _____	Listened attentively as customer spoke _____
Appeared to be able to answer customer's questions _____	Appeared to be able to answer customer's questions _____
Did not leave window without giving customer an explanation _____	Did not leave window without giving customer an explanation _____
Ended transaction cordially _____	Ended transaction cordially _____

| ILLUSTRATION 11-2 | INTERVIEW GUIDE |

**Annual Physical Examination
Interview Guide**

_____   _____
Patient's Name   Date of Interview

Instructions to Nurses and Assistants

After you have accompanied the patient to an examination room and have taken the usual measures to make her or him comfortable, please take a few minutes to interview the patient about her or his attitude toward having an annual physical examination. Please sit in a comfortable position, near the patient. Do not stand above the patient in a "superior" position. Speak in a friendly tone, indicating your interest in the individual.

- **Address the patient courteously:** Mr./Mrs./Ms. _____, Dr. Kimm has asked me to get some information from you. We are trying to determine whether you actually need or want a full physical exam each year. Some patients and doctors have questioned whether an annual examination is necessary for people who are in generally good health. May I ask you a few questions about your annual physical exam?
- **If the response is "no," say:** That's OK. I'll tell Dr. Kimm that you prefer not to answer the questions. She will continue to serve you in the same manner she has up to this time. **(Discontinue the interview. Discuss schedules for exams, etc., if the patient has any questions.)**
- **If the response is "yes," proceed with the following questions.**

1. Were you aware that some doctors and researchers have questioned the need for annual physical exams?

   Yes _____   No _____

2. Do you feel strongly that you should have an annual physical exam?

   Yes _____   No _____

   If "yes," go to   **If "no," go to**
         ↓   ↓

3. In your opinion, what is the greatest advantage of having an annual physical exam?	4. How frequently would you prefer to have a physical exam?
	5. In your opinion, what is the greatest advantage of having a physical exam on that kind of schedule?
Go to closing statement	**Go to closing statement**

Closing statement: Thank you, Mr./Mrs./Ms. _____.

Dr. Kimm will be with you shortly to continue your exam.

ILLUSTRATION 11-3 ▶ QUESTIONNAIRE

WINSLOW HILLS
BANKING QUESTIONNAIRE

Instructions: Please select one adult (age 18 or older) from your household to complete this questionnaire. That person should have at least one account in a South Carolina bank. That person should answer each question as it applies to him or her.

1. Who is answering the questionnaire?

   Unmarried head of household ( )
   Wife ( )
   Husband ( )
   Other (specify) _____

2. What is your age?

   18 to 24 ( )   35 to 44 ( )   55 to 64 ( )
   25 to 34 ( )   45 to 54 ( )   65 or older ( )

3. How long have you lived in Winslow Hills?

   1 year or less ( )   Over 3, less than 5 years ( )
   Over 1, less than 3 years ( )   Over 5 years ( )

4. Where did you live before moving to Winslow Hills? _____

5. How many adults (age 18 or older) live in this household? _____

6. How many full-time wage earners live in this household? _____

7. In what city do you bank most frequently? (Please check only one.)

   Camden ( )   Florence ( )   Pontiac ( )
   Cayce/West Columbia ( )   Irmo ( )   Sumter ( )
   Columbia ( )   Lexington ( )   Other (specify) ( )

8. When do you usually do your banking? (Please check no more than two items.)

   Going to or from work ( )   While shopping ( )
   During working day (e.g., lunch hour) ( )   On a special banking trip ( )
   Other (specify) _____

9. What are your attitudes toward Automatic Teller Machines? (Check any that apply.)

   They are too impersonal. ( )   They are convenient and easy to use. ( )
   They often do not function correctly. ( )   Users risk being robbed. ( )
   It is safe to use them at any time. ( )   They record transactions accurately. ( )
   It is safe to use them during daylight but not after dark. ( )   They create traffic hazards. ( )
   We need more in my neighborhood. ( )

10. What banking services do you use? (Check any that apply.)

    Automatic Teller Machine ( )   Drive-Up Window ( )
    Certificate of Deposit ( )   Individual Retirement Account ( )
    Checking Account ( )   Loan ( )
    Credit Card ( )   Safe Deposit Box ( )
    Deposit by Mail ( )   Savings Account ( )
    Direct Payroll Deposit ( )   Trust Services ( )
    Other (specify) ( )

11. What would be your reaction to establishment of a 24-hour, 7-days-a-week automatic teller machine at the Winslow Hills entrance?

    Very pleased ( )
    Somewhat pleased ( )   } Go to Item 12.
    Indifferent ( )
    Somewhat displeased ( )   } Go to Item 13.
    Very displeased ( )

12. If you did not already have an account with the bank that established the automatic teller machine at Winslow Hills, how likely would you be to change your banking business to that institution?

    Very likely ( )
    Somewhat likely ( )   } Go to Item 15.
    Unsure ( )
    Would open a checking account but keep other business as it is. ( )
    Somewhat unlikely ( )   } Go to Item 14.
    Very unlikely ( )

13. Please explain why you would be displeased. _____

    Go to Item 15.

14. Please explain why you would be unlikely to change. _____

15. Thank you for completing this questionnaire. Please return the questionnaire in the enclosed envelope to:

    Ms. Erin Murrah
    P.O. Box 123
    Charleston, SC 29424-0123

data collection process. For example, the question "Approximately how long have you been a member of the club?" can establish rapport by providing an opening, nonthreatening question that stimulates conversation. That question can also be a screening device. If you wish to interview members who have patronized the club for more than two years, the answer indicates whether to continue or discontinue the interview.

- **Is this the best way to obtain the information?** If the information can be obtained in another way, the time of observers or respondents should not be wasted. For example, if club records show the date a customer joined the club, that information should not be sought unless it is used to screen participants or establish rapport.

- **Is this question (or observation) capable of generating valid data?** If a question is offensive or unduly taxes a respondent's memory, the person may refuse to answer or may fabricate an answer. If a question is biased or leading, the respondent may unknowingly provide invalid data. In some situations subjects will provide answers they think are acceptable rather than admit lack of knowledge or understanding. An observer may also record inaccurate or fictitious data if the observation form demands more than the observer can handle capably.

LANGUAGE

The overall effect of the language should be to encourage people to participate and provide accurate information. To achieve that effect, the language used in instructions and questions must be positive and confident, but not condescending; clear; unbiased; and neutral, or not leading. The following examples illustrate the effects of language.

Condescending: You may not know it, but the state legislature is debating whether to approve a state lottery to fund elementary, secondary, and post-secondary education.

Positive, Confident: The state legislature is debating whether to approve a state lottery to fund elementary, secondary, and post-secondary education. The primary issue is that a lottery may open the door to other forms of legalized gambling. What are your attitudes toward a state lottery to fund education?

Condescending: I'm sure you will agree that we all have an obligation to improve elementary and secondary education in this state. That's why I'm conducting this study.

Positive, Confident: You can help improve elementary and secondary education in this state. Your answers, along with those of others, will help to identify critical education issues for our legislators to consider during the coming legislative session.

Unclear: Where were you married?
(Respondent does not know whether to supply city, state, or exact site such as church, home, garden, county court.)

Clear: Where was your wedding ceremony performed?
Church or synagogue   _____
Judge's chambers   _____
Home or private club   _____
Other (specify)   _____

Unclear, leading: What additional services would you like the club to provide? (Assumes respondent knows all services that are currently provided; assumes respondent wants additional services.)

Clear: Which of the following club services, if any, would be useful to you? Check all that apply. (Follow the question with a list of services the club may offer.)

Biased: Do you support public financing for all federal elections to take back control from the special interests?
(Tends to lead toward "yes" because of negative publicity about "special interests.")

Unbiased: Do you support public financing for all federal elections?

Biased: What is your favorite Chinese restaurant in this city?
(If the question is followed by a list of restaurant names, many respondents will select one—probably the most familiar name—even if they rarely eat Chinese foods.)

Unbiased: Answer the following question only if you eat in a Chinese restaurant at least three times a year. What is your favorite Chinese restaurant in this city?

Leading: Should the Federal government ensure that no older Americans will have to sacrifice their homes to receive necessary health care?
(Is anyone so heartless as to answer "no"?)

Neutral: What health-care insurance, if any, do you think the Federal government should provide for older Americans?

Leading: Do you think there should be more public funding of the arts and arts education since private support of the arts has declined by more than 50% during the last 10 years?
(A "no" to this question could suggest that the respondent lacks an appreciation for the arts.)

Neutral: Under what conditions should the state legislature continue to fund arts education in elementary and secondary schools?

FORMAT

The format of observation forms, interview guides, and questionnaires must contribute to readability, ease of completion, and accuracy in completion. In addition, questionnaire format should encourage subjects to complete the questionnaire rather than discourage them. The following guides will help you achieve those objectives.

■ **Provide enough space to record information neatly and clearly.** If insufficient space is provided, respondents may become discouraged and decide not to provide all data, or they may enter the information illegibly.

- **Use white space advantageously.** All margins should be at least one inch and sufficient space should be placed between items to avoid a crowded, oppressive appearance.
- **Place spaces or boxes for responses near the items to be answered.** This practice contributes to accuracy. If the answer spaces are too far from the items, the respondent may accidentally use the wrong line or select an unintended answer.
- **Choose open and closed question formats wisely.** Open items state a question or make a statement to be completed by the respondent. No answer options are provided. Open items are appropriate when the researcher wants to probe for a range of responses or when the range is known to be so broad that it is impossible to list all options. Because the answers can vary considerably, responses to open items are difficult to process.

  Closed items provide a list of anticipated answers from which the respondent chooses. Closed items are appropriate when the range of responses can be anticipated or when the researcher wants to force responses into ranges that have been defined in the research problem. Options for closed items must be all-inclusive and mutually exclusive; that is, all possible answers must be included, and concepts or categories contained in the options must not overlap. The following example illustrates that criterion.

Incorrect:	Under $10,000
	$10,000–20,000
	$20,000–30,000
	$30,000–40,000
	$40,000–50,000
	Over $50,000
Correct:	Under $10,000
	$10,000–19,999
	$20,000–29,999
	$30,000–39,999
	$40,000–49,999
	Over $50,000
Incorrect:	Christian
	Jew
	Protestant
Correct:	Christian—Catholic
	Christian—Eastern Orthodox
	Christian—Protestant
	Jew—Conservative
	Jew—Orthodox
	Jew—Reformed
	Muslim
	Other

■ **Arrange questions logically; and use branching techniques, if necessary, to help respondents avoid irrelevant questions.** Branching techniques are demonstrated in Items 11 and 12 of the questionnaire shown in Illustration 11-3. The branch in Item 11 directs the respondent to Item 12 or Item 13, depending upon the person's answer. Similarly, Items 12 and 13 direct the respondents to appropriate items and helps them avoid irrelevant questions.

INSTRUCTIONS

The instrument must contain clear, complete instructions to the user. Instructions must indicate how to complete the instrument and what to do with it after completion. In addition, the researcher should define any terms or scale values that may be interpreted in different ways, as is demonstrated in Item 5 of Illustration 11-3 where *adult* is defined as a person age 18 or older. Ambiguity must be avoided in instructions as well as in questions.

If the instrument is complicated or lengthy, the instructions should be broken into understandable units. For each new section of the instrument, instructions related to that specific section should be provided. When a rating scale is used, it should be repeated at the top of each page to which it applies so that users need not turn back to check the scale values. Many respondents will not expend that effort; they may, instead, supply inaccurate responses.

To ensure that the instructions are not lost or misplaced, they should appear on the instrument itself, not in a separate letter or instruction sheet. Even when an addressed return envelope is provided, the instrument itself should show the address to which it must be returned. Envelopes can easily be lost, making response impossible.

Although instructions tell respondents what to do with an instrument, the instrument itself must be presented to potential participants in such a way that they are motivated to respond. An effective transmittal message accomplishes that objective. No survey instrument should be distributed without a transmittal message, either contained in a separate message or placed on the instrument itself.

Guides for Transmittal Messages

An effective transmittal message builds researcher-subject rapport and motivates subjects to participate in the research. A transmittal message may be written, as in a cover letter that accompanies a questionnaire; or it may be spoken, as in an opening conversation with interviewees. In both situations, the message must be planned so that it will reveal enough information to stimulate interest and motivation without biasing responses.

The following guides, which have been applied in the cover letter shown in Illustration 11-4, will help you develop effective transmittal messages.

■ **Use an interesting opening that focuses on the receiver, not on the sender, of the message.** When possible, identify a reader interest or need that may provide motivation to participate.

ILLUSTRATION 11-4 ▶ TRANSMITTAL MESSAGE

Researching Financial Markets Since 1960   (803) 555-7777

MURRAH & GORSAGE
P.O. Box 123
Charleston, SC 29424-0123

February 6, <year>

Dear Winslow Hills Resident

When you chose a home in Winslow Hills, you demonstrated your appreciation for a gracious yet convenient lifestyle. By sharing information about your banking practices and attitudes, you may be able to make life at Winslow Hills even more pleasing than it is now.

A major bank plans to expand its services, and its managers want to know if Winslow Hills residents need and want additional banking services. By answering the enclosed questionnaire, you may influence the managers' decisions.

If we receive your answers before February 28, they will be included in our analysis. Please take a few minutes now to complete the questionnaire and mail it in the enclosed envelope.

Sincerely

Erin Murrah

Erin Murrah
President

sk

Enclosures

- **Provide enough identifying information to legitimize your request.** That information may include the purpose of the study, the company or agency for which it is being conducted, how the information will be used, and potential benefits of the study.
- **Indicate the role of the participants and the protections that are extended to them.** Role definition may include explanation of how participants were selected and what is requested of them (for example, five minutes of your time, answers to ten questions, etc.). Protection usually includes assurance of confidentiality, particularly if sensitive information is sought.

- Specify exactly what is required (for example, complete the questionnaire and mail it before August 15), and make that action as easy as possible. Enclosing a stamped, addressed envelope with a mail survey or asking short, clearly worded questions in a telephone survey are ways to make response easy.
- Offer an inducement to participate, if possible. For example, enclosing a $1 bill and suggesting the recipient give it to her or his favorite charity has been known to induce response, even though the $1 does not adequately compensate the time spent on the questionnaire. If an inducement with material value cannot be offered, a realistic appeal to the individual's needs or interests may be sufficient inducement (for example, desire for recognition, sense of altruism, potential benefit to a group of which the person is a member).

After the instrument and transmittal message have been developed, one task remains before they are ready for use: testing and revision.

Testing and Revising Instruments

The objective of instrument testing is to detect errors or weaknesses in all aspects of the instrument before it is used. Instructions, questions, response modes, sequence of items, format, and level of language should be scrutinized. Ideally, two kinds of testing are used: in-house and field testing.

In-house testing involves presenting the instrument to colleagues or other impartial critics for their evaluation. To evaluate all aspects of the instrument, those critics should be knowledgeable about instrument design and about the kinds of data that are to be collected. Such evaluators can often detect shortcomings and provide suggestions for instrument revision.

Field testing involves presenting the instrument to a group of respondents typical of those with whom it will eventually be used. One way to do a field test is to ask potential participants to complete the instrument without informing them that they are a test group. After they have completed the instrument, the test group should then be asked to provide additional information about the effectiveness of the instrument—its clarity, format, time requirement, and so forth. Discussion of the respondents' reactions while completing the questionnaire will frequently yield valuable suggestions for instrument revision.

While planning and conducting primary research, you will confront ethical issues. The next section discusses some of those concerns.

ETHICAL CONSIDERATIONS

Much primary research requires gathering data from and about people. A major ethical issue concerns how people are used for the researcher's advantage. Three specific concerns that must be considered are invasion of privacy, protection of subjects, and confidentiality of information.

Invasion of Privacy

The right to privacy is a fundamental human right guaranteed by Supreme Court interpretations of the Fourth Amendment to the U.S. Constitution. Both passive and active data collection techniques have the potential to violate that right. An observation technique, for example, can be conducted in such a way that no rights are violated, as in observation of shoppers' responses to a store display. But observation may be a violation of the right to privacy when the observer secretly conducts an observation to which subjects would not likely consent. Is it ethical to place monitors in store dressing rooms to observe behaviors of shoppers without their knowledge or consent? Is it ethical to place secret recording devices on an employee's telephone to monitor communication practices or message content?

The invasion of privacy issue also relates to surveys conducted in homes. Is it ethical for a researcher to use the telephone to enter the privacy of homes primarily for the benefit of the researcher? The Federal Trade Commission's Telemarketing Sales Rule (TSR) requires that telemarketers disclose their identity and the purpose of the call promptly and restricts calls to the hours of 8 a.m. to 9 p.m.[4] This rule also covers such things as a consumer satisfaction survey if a sales attempt is intended to accompany the survey. Calls originating from a foreign location are also covered by the TSR, and most states have enacted similar protections. The South Carolina statute, for example, defines a consumer call to include a call "for the purpose of obtaining information that will or *may* (italics added) be used for the direct solicitation of a sale of consumer goods or services. . . ."[5] Under that definition, certain marketing surveys would be governed by the law.

Protection of Subjects

Humans also have the right to be free from injury to person or reputation—and to defend themselves against such harm. In experimental research, the researcher has an ethical obligation to protect subjects from harm. If the potential for injury exists, the researcher has an obligation to inform subjects and to give them the option not to participate. Is it ethical to test a new product on subjects when the full effect is not known? In the United States the federal government attempts to protect subjects from potentially harmful food and drugs by requiring extensive records of research on nonhuman subjects before approving research on humans.

An interesting related issue concerns the ethics of *not* testing a substance on humans when it has the potential to help those who need help. In 1989 some doctors decided to use a new drug with AIDS patients, even though its use had not been approved by the U.S. Food and Drug Administration. The moral judgment was that although the act was not good (illegal, in fact), it had the potential for good results—helping people who at that time had little hope of relief from their illness. In 1997 a major issue confronting the Food and Drug Administration was whether a popular antidepressant drug should be approved for use by children and adolescents. Although the drug had not specifically been banned for use by such patients, neither had the drug manufacturer submitted research to demonstrate the drug's safety and effectiveness for children and adolescents. Both the drug manufacturer and some doctors had apparently made the moral judgment that using the drug on a younger population was a "good" action. However, in 2005, the attorney for a teenaged boy who had killed his grandparents presented the defense that the boy's treatment with such antidepressants had caused his aberrant behavior.

Confidentiality and Acknowledgement of Primary Data Sources

The confidentiality issue is closely related to the invasion-of-privacy and protection-of-subjects issues. After obtaining data from and about subjects, the researcher analyzes the data and reports the results of the analysis. In that report the researcher has a continuing obligation to guarantee the right to privacy and to protect the subjects from injury to reputation, from reprisals by report readers, etc. Those protections are usually accomplished by maintaining confidentiality—not identifying data sources unless authorized to do so.

When a researcher accepts the moral obligation to maintain the confidentiality of data sources, questions may arise about the appropriate ways to acknowledge primary data sources. The following guides will help you deal with that complex ethical issue.

- **Confidential sources.** When confidentiality has been promised to participants, primary data sources can be acknowledged only in a general way. However, confidential sources must still be recognized in the report body and in the source list. In the report body, provide a general description of the data collection method. In the source list, give a brief description of the data collection facts. The following examples illustrate accepted techniques:

    Report body: Data about EXACTO employees' attitudes toward the company benefits plan were obtained by a mail survey. Questionnaires were mailed to employees' homes with the request that they send the completed questionnaire to the researcher. The researcher processed the data. No EXACTO managers had access to the data.

    Source list: EXACTO employees, mail survey conducted during April <year>.

- **Identified sources.** When subjects grant permission to be identified, source acknowledgements are similar to those used for secondary data, and should be recognized in both the report body and the source list. Essential facts include *who, what, where, when*. In the report body, use the same techniques that you use to cite secondary data sources (footnote with superscript, endnote with superscript, or internal citation). In the source list identify interviews, observations, and surveys as described here.

    Interviews: (Name of interviewee) in an interview with (name of interviewer) at (place) on (date).

    Observations: Observations of (describe people, activities) at (place) on (date).

    Surveys: Survey of (describe subjects) conducted (state applicable details of method, place, date).

More extensive guides for documenting primary and secondary data sources are presented in Chapter 13.

SUMMARY

You have several options for collecting data from primary sources: search of company records, observation, face-to-face and telephone interviews, and respondent-completed questionnaires. Many methods have been adapted for electronic surveys. To collect valid, reliable data, you must carefully design and test content, language, format, and instructions of all data collection instruments and protect the privacy of subjects participating in the research. When reporting data obtained from primary sources, the researcher must reconcile the obligation to cite data sources with the obligation to respect the subjects' desires for confidentiality.

TOPICS FOR DISCUSSION

1. Distinguish between active and passive data collection methods.

2. Identify two passive methods to collect primary data.

3. In what ways has computer technology made the collection of primary data more efficient? If you have conducted or participated in a computer-moderated survey, describe your experience.

4. Identify three active methods to collect primary data.

5. In what ways do structured and unstructured interviews differ?

6. Identify the advantages and disadvantages of each primary data collection method discussed in this chapter.

7. Identify and describe four measurement scales.

8. What questions must be answered as you evaluate the content of a data collection instrument?

9. What aspects of language must be considered as you evaluate a data collection instrument?

10. What characteristics of format should you look for as you evaluate a data collection instrument?

11. What purposes are served by instrument instructions? by a transmittal message?

12. What guides should be followed in preparation of a transmittal message?

13. Why and how should instruments be tested?

14. Identify three specific areas of ethics that must be considered when you use primary data sources.

APPLICATIONS

1. As directed by your instructor, develop the data collection tools for one or more of the research problems in the Applications in Chapter 9. Follow these steps to complete your assignment.
   - Identify the appropriate method for collecting primary data.
   - Prepare a data collection instrument.
   - Write a transmittal message.
   - Identify potential ethical issues and ways to resolve them.

2. As directed by your instructor, develop primary data collection instruments for one or more of the following situations. Follow these steps to complete your assignment:
   - Identify the information needed.
   - Identify the best sources of information.
   - Identify appropriate methods for collecting primary data.
   - Prepare data collection instruments.
   - Write a transmittal message.
   - Identify potential ethical issues and ways to resolve them.
   a. Snelling Wood Products has been making particle board for furniture manufacturers. Since the furniture industry has fallen on hard times, Snelling's market has declined; and the company was forced to diversify. It recently spent about $40 million to modify its plant and install machinery to make quarter-inch tongue-and-groove laminate flooring. Homeowners are buying more hardwood and laminate flooring, cutting into the market for carpet and sheet vinyl. The laminate floor market has been dominated by Pergo of Sweden and Wilsonart of the United States.

   Snelling is considering an additional investment of at least $100 million in machinery to make heavier-grade laminates in an attempt to capture a greater share of the U.S. market for laminate flooring. The company needs to know whether sellers of flooring materials would consider switching from Pergo or Wilsonart to a new U.S. supplier.
   b. The president of your college wants to evaluate the effectiveness of police protection on your campus. Determine facts about crime on your campus for the previous five years. Elements of the problem include types of crimes, campus locations where crimes occurred, times of day crimes occurred, rapidity of police response, and number of crimes that were solved. You may add other elements that seem especially relevant for your campus.
   c. In 2004 the University of South Carolina opened its first "green" dorm. This dormitory has been described as "the largest environmentally friendly residence hall complex in the world." (*The State*, November 6, 2004, p. B1.) Determine what early planning steps a business or educational institution should take to ensure the most cost-effective production and maintenance of a "green" building.

d. A group of investors is considering the restoration of a 19th-century opera house in Smalltown, a town with a population of approximately 11,000. The town is approximately 30 miles from a metropolitan area with a population of approximately 500,000. Although that larger city has a performing arts center, the investors believe that the residents of Smalltown, who are fiercely loyal to their town, would rather attend concerts in the restored opera house than drive 30 miles for performances in the larger city. Moreover, the investors, who are local residents, think that the restored opera house and its programs may attract tourists and residents of nearby towns and serve as a focal point for the revitalization of Smalltown's downtown area. Because the restoration is expected to cost about $5 million, the investors want to determine the potential success of the opera house.

e. All-American Bottlers has brought a new sport drink to the market. In an effort to promote the drink to the youth market, All-American has asked you to determine the effects of promotions on purchasing decisions in households that have youths between the ages of 8 to 12. More specifically, the company wants to know what sports the youngsters participate in, the kinds of snacks provided to the players during practice and at games, how promotions influence the youngsters themselves, and what influence they have on the person who purchases beverages for the home or the team.

f. In an attempt to raise money for an animal shelter, your local chapter of the Society for the Prevention of Cruelty to Animals (SPCA) has scheduled a "Bark in the Park" event. The event will be held on a Saturday morning in a local park. It will feature contests for the best-dressed dog as well as vendors of pet-oriented products and a booth promoting SPCA. Admission to the event is $10 per family, including dog. To get an idea of the level of support for an animal shelter, you will conduct a survey of those who attend. You want to know what prompted the participants to come to the event, attitudes about the admission fee, rating of the event's entertainment value, willingness to contribute money or volunteer services to the shelter, and suggestions for other community events for pet lovers. Add other factors that would be of interest to such an organization.

3. Technology has brought many supposed time-saving devices to the consumer market, such as automatic teller machines, self-serve gasoline pumps, and self-checkout stations in supermarkets and home improvement stores. Some consumers, however, are becoming increasingly frustrated with the loss of personal service in the self-service economy. Develop a questionnaire to evaluate consumer attitudes toward consumer service in a particular sector of the economy (for example, hospitality, industry, retail clothing sales, banking, etc.). Include at least 10 items in the questionnaire.

4. Using the guidelines for effective primary data collection instruments, critique the following questionnaire (on page 298). Write a memo to your instructor detailing your evaluation of the effectiveness of the questionnaire.

5. Using the guidelines for effective primary data collection instruments, critique the following questionnaire (on page 299). Write a memo to your instructor detailing your evaluation of the effectiveness of the questionnaire.

REFERENCES

1. For further discussion of active methods of data collection see Brace, I. (2004). *Questionnaire design.* London & Sterling, VA: Kogan Page.

2. Adapted from Davis, D. & Cosenza, R. M. (1985). *Business research for decision making.* Boston: Kent Publishing Company, p. 265.

3. Brace, I. (2004). pp. 37–42.

4. Federal Trade Commission (2003). Part 310-telemarketing sales rule (Electronic revision). *Federal register,* 68, 4669–4674. Retrieved November 25, 2005, from http://www.ftc.gov

5. Amendments (1988) to Article 7, Chapter 17, Title 16, Code of Laws of South Carolina, 1976, Relating to Offenses Against Public Policy.

SPORT UTILITY VEHICLE SAFETY QUESTIONNAIRE

Name _____ Address _____

Occupation _____ Age _____ Sex _____

Vehicles Owned _____

INSTRUCTIONS: This questionnaire contains several statements about the growing practice of installing air horns on sport utility vehicles (SUVs). Please indicate the degree to which you agree or disagree with each statement by writing the number that best expresses your feelings: (1) strongly agree, (2) agree, (3) neither agree nor disagree, (4) disagree, or (5) strongly disagree.

_____ 1. I don't like to be startled while driving my car.

_____ 2. I drive safely and am intimidated by large SUVs.

_____ 3. I feel nervous when an SUV driver honks a loud horn at me.

_____ 4. SUV drivers should not crowd other drivers on the road.

_____ 5. The city should enforce the anti-noise laws more stringently.

_____ 6. Drivers should be able to report the auto tag of an SUV whose driver has blasted a loud air horn.

_____ 7. SUV drivers who use loud horns should be ticketed for a traffic violation.

_____ 8. I would consider installing an air horn on one of my vehicles.

_____ 9. A law should be enacted to prohibit the use of air horns on passenger vehicles, including SUVs.

_____ 10. I rarely sound the horn on my vehicle.

_____ 11. I always drive cautiously and considerately.

ILLUSTRATION FOR APPLICATION 11-5

National Recreation and Parks Association

22377 Belmont Ridge Road, Ashburn, VA. 20148
703-555-0784   www. nrpa.org

> Instructions: Please indicate your answers with a checkmark in the appropriate box. Then return the form in the enclosed envelope. Your name, address, and responses will remain confidential. Results will be published in an upcoming issue of *P & R News*.

1. Have you visited a national park within the past two years?

   Yes _____   No _____

2. What park activities do you enjoy?

3. Would you be willing to make a reservation to enter popular parks during the peak season if reservations would reduce crowding and help protect park resources?

   Yes _____   No _____

4. In general, how well do you think natural resources in the national parks are being protected?

5. For its size, Minnesota's Voyageurs National Park has more land for snowmobile use than any other national park. Congress is considering opening the remainder of the park wilderness areas to snowmobiles. Should these wilderness areas be opened to the noise and pollution of snowmobiles?

   Yes _____   No _____

6. At national parks like Grand Canyon and Great Smoky Mountains, companies offer low-flying airplane or helicopter sightseeing trips. Do you think these noisy flights should be limited or banned?

   Yes _____   No _____

7. Would you be willing to make a financial contribution if it could help prevent a full-scale crisis in our National Park System?

   Yes _____   No _____

chapter 12

Analyzing Data for Complex Reports

LEARNING OBJECTIVES

After you have read this chapter, you should be able to:

1. Describe qualitative and quantitative data.
2. Explain the requirements for accurate data analysis.
3. Prepare data for analysis.
4. Select appropriate nonstatistical and statistical analysis techniques.
5. Draw appropriate conclusions and make justifiable recommendations.
6. Demonstrate ethical behavior with respect to data analysis.

In previous chapters you learned how to plan a research project and how to collect secondary and primary data. You learned that a thorough understanding of the managerial problem, a clear definition of the research question, and a comprehension of the purpose of the study must determine your data collection techniques.

As you collect relevant data from secondary and primary sources, you accumulate a mass of facts—your raw data. Perhaps the most crucial task of the entire research process remains. Since decision makers are rarely interested in the raw data, your duty as a researcher and report writer is to interpret those data, demonstrating their relationship to the project's problem and purpose and the context in which decisions must be made.

Data analysis is the entire process of converting raw data into meaningful information for decision makers. Analysis is a process of data reduction: the mass of raw data is reduced to classes or sets of information; those sets are reduced to major findings; and ultimately the findings are interpreted to yield conclusions and recommendations.

Assume, for example, that you are asked to conduct research to identify potential sites for a new FreshMart supermarket. Your data collection activities will yield many facts, which might include demographic data, responses to a consumer survey, and data about available building sites currently on the market.

Your data analysis will require classification of the data into meaningful groups that will permit you to compare the desirability of different sites. One category could be demographics of defined sections of the city. The many facts about each area—population growth, average household income, effective buying power, new home construction, etc.—can be reduced to major findings. Those findings would include the area that has shown the fastest growth in population, has the highest average household income, has the greatest effective buying power, and has had the most new home construction during a defined period of time. Those findings may be reduced further into a summary statement identifying one section of the city that demonstrates the greatest economic vitality. Similar data reduction would be required for the facts gathered in your consumer survey and the information about available building sites.

Conceivably, a data set containing hundreds of facts may finally be reduced to one recommendation. Assume your findings indicate that a revitalized section of the central city shows the greatest economic vitality, consumers in that area expressed the greatest desire for a conveniently located supermarket, and a building site is available in an appropriate location and at an affordable price. Your single recommendation would likely be that the company purchase the site for a new supermarket.

Data that you collect are either qualitative or quantitative. To analyze data effectively, you must first understand the nature of those general data classes.

QUALITATIVE AND QUANTITATIVE DATA

Qualitative data are non-numeric data; *quantitative data* are numeric data. Both kinds of data are useful in business research.

Resume your role as a researcher who has been asked to identify potential sites for a new FreshMart supermarket. You might consult a source such as the *Sales and Marketing Management* "Survey of Buying Power" issue for demographic data about various sections of the county, talk to a real estate agent about available commercial sites in the county, and survey a sample of residents to determine their grocery-buying habits and preferences.

Your data set will contain both quantitative and qualitative data. The demographic data are quantitative and objective if the data were originally collected in a valid and reliable way. These data can be analyzed statistically. The information about site availability, however, may be both quantitative and qualitative. Dimensions of lots and quoted prices are quantitative; one site can be mathematically described as larger or smaller than another and more or less costly to acquire. Other aspects of site description, however, are qualitative and require subjective interpretation. For example, is a square lot more or less desirable than a rectangular lot? Is a sloped lot more or less desirable than a flat one? Is a lot near other businesses more or less desirable than one near a residential area?

Data about consumer grocery-buying habits and preferences are largely qualitative; they are expressions of consumer qualities or characteristics, which generally are not numeric. An example of a specific qualitative fact is a consumer's expression that he or she would like to be able to shop for food on the way home from work or has recently moved to a central-city apartment and would like to be able to walk to the grocery. Interpretation of such data requires subjective judgment.

To improve objectivity when analyzing qualitative data, however, many researchers attempt to quantify the facts. Using a five-point ordinal scale, for example, for measuring consumer preferences would permit you to compute relative strength of various attitudes. You could also establish a set of criteria that a potential site must meet, assign weights to the relative importance of each criterion, and then evaluate each site by those criteria.

The following example illustrates such a weighting technique. In this example, three criteria are identified and their relative importance is determined. Location is the primary criterion and is given a weight of .60. Price and size are considered equally important, but considerably less important than location. Each of those criteria is given a weight of .20. Weights for all factors must total 1 (100 percent). The maximum points to be allocated to each criterion must also be determined. In this example a maximum of 50 was chosen. Then points for each criterion are assigned to each site. Criterion points are multiplied by criterion weight to get a weighted value. The total weighted values permit comparison of the two sites, with Site A scoring higher on the criteria than Site B.

Criterion	Weights	Site A		Site B	
		Points	Weighted Value	Points	Weighted Value
Location	.60	50	30	40	24
Price	.20	30	6	40	8
Size	.20	40	8	25	5
Total Weighted Value			44		37

Although such a procedure may improve objectivity, you must be aware that the choice of criteria, the weights given to each, and the values assigned to the criteria during site evaluation are all subjective judgments. Effective interpretation of qualitative data requires rational, logical, unbiased thinking throughout the entire process.

Interpretation of quantitative data also requires rational, logical, unbiased judgment. Although quantitative data are in themselves objective, their interpretation often involves subjective judgment. Your data may show that the average annual household income for a particular section of the city is $70,000. That figure is objective; but your interpretation that the neighborhood is a high-, middle-, or low-income community is subjective.

As the foregoing examples suggest, data analysis is never a completely objective process. You can, however, actively monitor the accuracy and objectivity of your analysis by observing the four requirements discussed next.

REQUIREMENTS FOR ACCURATE DATA ANALYSIS

To enhance the accuracy of your analyses, you must understand the research problem, maintain a critical mindset, apply logical thinking, and understand basic statistical procedures.

Understand Research Problem

Reviewing the research problem and purpose will remind you of what stimulated the research and of the objectives to be met by the study. Assume the following research problem and purpose.

> **Research Problem:** To evaluate potential sites for a new FreshMart supermarket.
>
> **Purpose:** To locate a site that will permit the company to serve a market that currently has inadequate supermarket service.

With that problem and purpose as guides, you will analyze all data (characteristics of available sites, demographic data, survey results) in terms of what they contribute to identifying an area of the county that needs additional supermarket service and identifying a suitable site in that area. The analysis must move toward a conclusion and recommendation that will contribute to achieving the stated purpose—even if you conclude that no suitable site is currently available. You may recommend that the company conduct further site analyses and delay opening a new store until a satisfactory site is found.

Maintain Critical Mindset

Maintaining a critical mindset requires that you constantly evaluate your data and your interpretation of the data. Assume that you are a resident of the central city, which currently has no supermarket. As you conduct your research on potential market sites, you might feel the need for a central-city market keenly and find an excellent site in that area. Knowing your preferences, you should ask yourself several questions: Have I used valid sources? Have I gathered enough data? Have I gathered the right kinds of data? Have I permitted my biases to affect the interpretation of the data? Will others agree with my interpretation? If so, why? If not, why not?

One way to maintain a critical viewpoint is to discuss your research with others who are authorized to review the data, particularly during the data analysis. It is natural to develop some proprietary tendencies after working on a project for awhile. You may become reluctant to discard data that are inadequate or irrelevant or to change tentative conclusions that are contradicted by the data. Individuals who have no vested interest in the project will be able to look at the data objectively and help you maintain your capacity to criticize your own work.

Apply Logical Thinking

Both qualitative and quantitative data must be interpreted logically. You can improve the quality of your analysis by understanding two basic styles of logic: induction and deduction.

Induction involves reasoning from specific facts, examples, or cases to generalizations based on those specifics. Assume that, in our FreshMart example, you look at specific data about population, family income, number of groceries, and locations of groceries in the central city. Based on those specific data, you generalize that the potential customers and the competitive environment are favorable for establishment of a FreshMart. That is inductive reasoning. When using induction you must be especially careful to avoid such fallacies as the hasty generalization (reasoning that something true in one case is true in all cases), and the *non sequitur* (generalization based on inadequate data).

> **Example:** The FreshMart in central-city Charlotte has exceeded sales projections for its first year; a FreshMart is bound to succeed in central-city Asheville. (Have you gathered enough data? Do the data show that the conditions are similar?)

In deduction you reason from general concepts or principles to specific facts or cases. Deduction is based on the logical syllogism, which has three parts.

1. A major premise—a large assumption or primary fact
2. A minor premise—a small assumption or secondary fact
3. A conclusion—a logically inescapable inference based on the premises

In deductive reasoning, the major premise is broader than the minor premise, the minor premise is broader than the conclusion, and a specific fact is inferred from the more general premises. When using deduction, you must always test the accuracy of your premises, as demonstrated in the following examples.

If either the major or the minor premise is false, the conclusion is false.

False Major Premise; False Conclusion

Major Premise: Central-city residents are dissatisfied with current grocery services in their area. (False premise; possibly a hasty generalization.)

Minor Premise: You are a central-city resident. (True premise.)

Conclusion: You are dissatisfied with your grocery services in your area. (Logically correct, but false conclusion.)

False Minor Premise; False Conclusion

Major Premise: The FreshMart in central-city Charlotte has exceeded sales projections for its first year. (True premise.)

Minor Premise: Central-city Asheville is similar to central-city Charlotte. (False premise unless backed by sufficient data.)

Conclusion: A FreshMart is bound to succeed in central-city Asheville. (Logically correct, but false conclusion.)

If both the major and minor premises are true, the conclusion is valid.

True Major and Minor Premises; Valid Conclusion

Major Premise: The ratio of households to supermarkets in the central city is 2,000 to 0. (True premise.)

Minor Premise: Industry statistics indicate that the ideal ratio is 1,500 to 1. (True premise.)

Conclusion: There are enough households in the central city to support a FreshMart supermarket. (Logically inescapable inference.)

In addition to using accurate induction and deduction, you can sometimes improve the accuracy of your analysis by subjecting all or some of the data to statistical analysis.

Understand Use of Statistics

Statistics are the tools by which meaning is extracted from quantitative data. Through statistical computations, for example, you could determine average household income for an area, numbers of new homes constructed, rates of increase in both those variables, and relationships between the two. Those kinds of calculations will yield information that is more meaningful than the isolated facts represented by the raw data. Specific statistical concepts with which you should become familiar are presented later in this chapter.

Knowledge of the research problem, a critical viewpoint, knowledge of logic, and an understanding of statistics are essential throughout the data analysis process. The first step in that process is preparing the data for analysis.

DATA PREPARATION

For most types of contemporary business research, data preparation includes editing, coding, and entering into a computer.

Editing

Data editing is inspection of the data to detect errors and omissions. Editing is done to ensure that data are accurate, consistent, complete, and arranged in a way that facilitates coding or classification.

Some editing can be done during or immediately after collection. For example, an interviewer should check the interview guide immediately after an interview to determine whether all items have been covered and whether any obvious inconsistencies exist. If an item has been omitted, the interviewer may be able to schedule a prompt follow-up interview and get the necessary information. If the interviewer notices inconsistencies in a respondent's answers, those items may also be reviewed in a follow-up interview.

When collecting data from a secondary source, you should verify the accuracy and legibility of direct quotations, paraphrases, and the bibliographic reference before you leave the source. Such editing ensures accuracy and saves valuable time by eliminating the need to return to a source for verification.

Data collected by questionnaire must be edited after questionnaires have been returned. Your objective is to detect missing (no answer) and unusable (illegible or obviously inconsistent) responses. In some instances, you may be able to supply the correct information, as when a person provides annual instead of monthly income. In other situations, you may be able to determine the correct answer by a follow-up contact with the survey participant. Frequently, however, missing or unusable answers must be coded and handled as such.

How to deal with missing or incomplete data should not be an arbitrary decision. To protect the validity and reliability of data, the research design should include a decision about how to handle such data.

Coding

Coding is the process of assigning numerals or other symbols to answers so that they can be categorized and interpreted, possibly statistically. Questionnaires and interview guides can be designed to eliminate the need for extensive manual coding. Closed questions, in particular, can be set up so that the responses are numbered with appropriate codes. Open-ended questions must be coded manually to fit into categories defined by the researchers. Any coding system used to establish categories of information must meet four criteria: appropriate, exhaustive, mutually exclusive, and one-dimensional.

APPROPRIATE

As with all aspects of analysis, coding must be directed by the problem and purpose. Those factors, for example, must determine whether age or income ranges should be narrow or wide and how many scale points (values) should be used to measure attitudes. The following codes and ranges might be appropriate to measure annual earned income of students at a state university; but they would likely not be appropriate to measure income of faculty members at that institution because a disproportionate number, probably all, would fall into category 5.

1. $0–4,999.99
2. $5,000–9,999.99
3. $10,000–14,999.99
4. $15,000–19,999.99
5. $20,000 or more

EXHAUSTIVE

The classification set must capture the full range of information. The set used in the previous example will provide little useful information about university professors' salaries. If the majority of responses fall into Category 5, the only information acquired is that the majority of the faculty earns more than $20,000 annually.

Responses to open-ended questions must also be coded to identify the richness of the data. A question about plans for post-secondary education, for example, may originally have been grouped into three sets: college, technical school, no plans for post-secondary education. Closer examination of the data, however, may suggest the need for more classifications to identify the many dimensions of college and technical school education that the responses have indicated: community college, technical school, proprietary trade school, state college, private college, state university, private university, etc.

MUTUALLY EXCLUSIVE

The classifications must not overlap. This standard is met when an answer can be placed in only one category. In an occupational survey, the classifications may be professional, managerial, technical, sales, clerical, and operative. However, a nurse who supervises two assistants in a company health center may have difficulty choosing between the professional and managerial categories. In the previous example of student income ranges, each category is mutually exclusive. A student whose income falls near an extreme end of a category, such as $9,990, should have no difficulty selecting the appropriate category.

ONE-DIMENSIONAL

All items in a classification set must be related to the same concept. In a question asking what kind of automobile the respondent drives, the responses may be compact, midsize, standard size, none. The first three items refer to one dimension, size; but the last item deals with another dimension, current driving status. That item is best handled in a separate category.

Preparing for Computer Analysis

Since virtually all business researchers use computers to analyze numerically coded data, an important step is to prepare the data for entry into the computer. In this step the researcher defines and records the data structure. A data structure is the way the information is positioned on the storage medium, such as a magnetic tape, a magnetic disk, a CD, or a computer hard drive. A record of the data structure is called a codebook or code sheet.

Most statistical programs today are integrated with spreadsheet or database software, permitting direct transfer of data from the spreadsheet or database into the statistical program. A software package such as *Statistical Package for the Social Sciences* (SPSS) permits you to enter data directly into a data editor, which resembles a spreadsheet, or to import the data from a database or spreadsheet. In any case, a codebook should be prepared before

ILLUSTRATION 12-1	CODEBOOK

Variable 1

Name: Case No.
Type: Numeric
Width: 4
Value: 1–2000
Value Label: None
Align: Right

Variable 2

Name: State
Type: String
Width: 2
Value: AA–ZZ
Value Label: 2-letter state abbreviations

Variable 3

Name: Average Monthly Income
Type: Numeric
Width: 1
Value: 1–9
Value Label: 1 = Under $3,000
                   2 = $3,000–$5,999
                   3 = $6,000–$8,999
                   4 = $9,000–$11,999
                   5 = $12,000–$14,999
                   6 = $15,000–$17,999
                   7 = $18,000–$20,999
                   8 = $21,000–$23,999
                   9 = $24,000 or more

the data are entered so that each field of the data editor, spreadsheet, or database can be appropriately identified, data can be entered in the correct form, and data can be interpreted when they are processed.

A codebook for data to be entered directly into the data editor for SPSS might look similar to Illustration 12-1. The codebook identifies each variable (usually equivalent to a column or data field in a spreadsheet or database) by name, type, width, value, and value label.

After the codebook is prepared, the data are entered into the computer. For survey data, you will create a record for each participant or case. A record is all the information related to one case. For data translated into numerical codes, the record consists of a row of numbers entered onto the storage medium in the sequence defined by the data structure.

Some commonly used methods of data entry are optical scanning, manual entry, and direct entry by way of a computer-assisted survey. With optical scanning, survey participants or research assistants use pencils to mark data sheets with the appropriate response codes. The data sheets are then run through a scanner, which "reads" the pencil marks and records the codes onto a magnetic tape or computer disk. In manual entry, an individual keys the responses into the computer, using the numerical codes and sequence defined by the codebook. The data are then saved on disk for use with statistical software. In a computer-assisted survey, the program can be written to collect the data in a format and sequence that conforms to a predetermined codebook.

Since errors can occur during data entry, one preparation step remains before data can be processed: verification.

Verifying

Several techniques are used to ensure that edited, coded data are entered accurately into the computer. One procedure is to print a copy of the entire database and visually scan it for obvious omissions or errors, such as a 6 entered when the maximum code value is 5. Some researchers use two-person teams to orally and visually verify all data. One person reads the codes aloud from the questionnaires or scanning sheets while the second person verifies them on the database printout. For sizable databases, that manual technique may be used on a sample of the records. Verification is a tedious but necessary step to protect the validity of the data.

After much preparation, the data are finally ready for analysis. Most business research employs both nonstatistical and statistical analysis.

NONSTATISTICAL ANALYSIS

Nonstatistical analysis is the application of logical thought processes to extract meaning from the data. Qualitative data can be analyzed in that way only, but quantitative data also require a certain amount of nonstatistical analysis. Classification, analysis, and synthesis are three major forms of nonstatistical analysis.

Classification

As you have already seen in the discussion of data coding, *classification* is a form of data analysis whereby you assign data to categories on the basis of established criteria. Assume you are conducting research to determine whether the general characteristics of the student body at your school have changed during the past 10 years. You could examine enrollments for Year X and Year Y and classify each student by gender, age, work experience, and marital status. You could then compare the student body in Year X with the student body in Year Y on those characteristics and ultimately draw conclusions about whether the general composition of the student body has changed.

When you group your secondary data notes by subject categories, you are also classifying data. In your study of the characteristics of your student population, you may also want to identify new student services that could benefit your students. As you read about student services in secondary sources, you could classify your data by subjects such as services for married students, for mature students, for part-time students, and so on.

For some data, classification may be the only form of analysis you perform. But frequently classification is a preliminary analysis that facilitates further analysis of the data. As you examine the characteristics of the student body, you may decide to survey students about attitudes toward various services. After classifying respondents by gender, you could then determine whether males and females differ in their attitudes toward specific student services.

Analysis and Synthesis

Analysis and synthesis require the application of deduction and induction. In *analysis* you break a large body of information into smaller elements for scrutiny and interpretation. Imagine a gourmet who orders an unfamiliar entree from a restaurant menu and attempts to determine the ingredients while eating the food. That person is engaging in analysis—breaking the whole into parts to discover new information. Similarly, a business researcher who looks at response data from an employee opinion survey breaks the mass of data into parts to identify specific opinions or attitudes.

In *synthesis* you bring together individual facts and assimilate them into a broader finding or conclusion. The gourmet who attempts to duplicate at home the delicacy enjoyed in the restaurant brings together ingredients to synthesize a new recipe. Similarly, assume you have gathered secondary data—published reports—about the effectiveness of flexible benefits programs. You study the facts reported by individual managers who have used flexible benefits programs and summarize the overall success of such programs. The process of pulling together information reported by different individuals in different ways and summarizing that information is a synthesis process.

For most nonquantitative data, logical classification, analysis, and synthesis are the limits of data analysis. Nonetheless, those forms of analysis are critical to successful data interpretation. For quantitative data, statistical processing may also be used to enhance logical analysis and synthesis. Statistics do not replace logic; they complement it.

STATISTICAL ANALYSIS

Statistics is a branch of mathematics dealing with the analysis, interpretation, and presentation of numerical data. Statistical procedures range from relatively simple computations used to describe a data set to complex calculations used to analyze relationships between and among sets of data or to predict behaviors and events.

The primary purpose of this discussion of statistics is to help you recognize possible statistical applications for your research. After choosing a potentially useful application, you should consult a business statistics text or a statistician for specific formulas and interpretations of results.

To comprehend any discussion of statistics, you must understand the relationship of measurement scales to statistical analysis. Such an understanding will help you select appropriate descriptive or inferential statistical applications for your data analysis.

Measurement Scales and Statistical Analysis

As you learned in Chapter 11, a measurement scale is a device used to assign numbers to an element or characteristic that is being analyzed. The type of measurement scale—nominal, ordinal, interval, or ratio—determines what kinds of statistics can be used for data analysis.

Any statistic that can be computed from less powerfully scaled data can also be computed on more powerfully scaled data. Conversely, many statistics that can be computed on more powerfully scaled data cannot be used for less powerfully scaled data. In terms of power, nominal scales are least powerful and ratio scales are most powerful. Consequently, many of the more powerful statistics can be computed only for data measured by an interval or ratio scale.

The first step to effective statistical analysis occurs during the research design stage. While planning the study, you must determine what kinds of data you need, what you want to learn from the data, and what type of measurement is necessary. Those determinations will influence your choice of descriptive or inferential statistics when you reach the data analysis stage.

Descriptive and Inferential Statistics

Descriptive statistics describe and summarize data. The most frequently used descriptive statistics are measures of central tendency (arithmetic mean, median, mode) and measures of dispersion (range, variance, standard deviation).

Measures of central tendency examine how the data are clustered. Assume, for example, that you have collected data about income levels of survey participants. The *mean* is the arithmetic average, computed by adding the reported incomes of all respondents and dividing by the number of respondents. The *median* is the midpoint of the data; half of your respondents have incomes above that point and half have incomes below that point. The *mode* is the most frequently occurring value; more respondents report that income figure than any other figure.

Measures of dispersion show how the data are scattered around a particular point. Although your data may show the mean income of your respondents is $50,000 per year, you may need to know what differences exist among your subjects.

The *range* gives a concise statement of differences, showing the distance between the highest and lowest values. Computing the range, as in the following example, may dramatize the fact that assumptions about an "average" customer may be quite inaccurate with respect to many of your respondents. In the example, no income falls near the mean.

Income

$200,000	
20,000	
13,000	Mean Income = $50,000
10,000	Median Income = $13,000
7,000	Range = $193,000

The *variance* shows the average distance between the mean and the individual values. The variance is computed by determining the difference between the mean and each value and then squaring those differences. The squared differences are added and then divided by the number of observations. Because the deviations are squared, the variance is expressed in "square points," a relatively meaningless number to most people. To convert the variance into a meaningful number, you take the square root of the variance. That figure, the standard deviation, is a measure of dispersion expressed in the same units as the original data.

The *standard deviation* is a helpful statistic if the population has a normal distribution. The standardized normal curve is a theoretical distribution of sample means having these characteristics:

- The highest point of the curve represents the mean of the distribution.
- The curve is symmetrical about its mean.
- The curve has an infinite number of cases; thus, it is a continuous distribution.

If samples are drawn from a normally distributed population, it is expected that 99.7 percent of the observations will fall within plus or minus 3 standard deviations of the mean; 95.5 percent will fall within plus or minus 2 standard deviations; and 68 percent will fall within plus or minus 1 standard deviation. (See Illustration 12-2.)

The concept of the normal curve and standard deviation is essential in selecting statistical analyses and interpreting their results. Parametric statistics, for example, assume that the population from which a sample is drawn is normally distributed, whereas that assumption is not required for nonparametric statistics. Therefore, before selecting a statistical procedure, you must know whether the procedure assumes a normal distribution. If you cannot make that assumption, you must use nonparametric statistics.

When using inferential statistics, researchers make generalizations or forecasts about the population after analyzing data from a sample of that population. Inferential statistics permit you to estimate the degree of confidence that you can have in your inferences and forecasts. Results of analysis with inferential statistics are always interpreted in terms of level of significance, which is an estimate of the probability that the results observed in your sample are due to

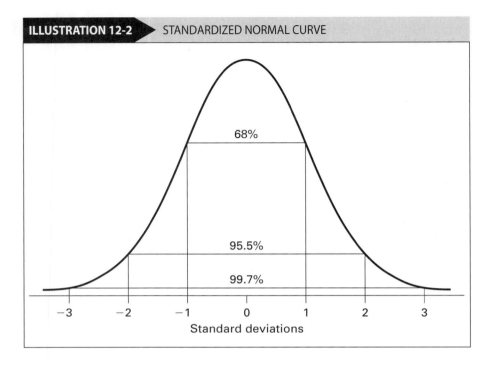

ILLUSTRATION 12-2 STANDARDIZED NORMAL CURVE

chance. A .05 significance level, for example, says that there is a 5 percent probability that your findings are chance findings and that what you observe in your sample is not typical of the population from which it was drawn.

Two primary concerns in business research are analysis of relationships (associations) and differences. Table 12-1 and Table 12-2 are provided to help you select appropriate statistical measurements of association or differences.

To select a measurement of association from Table 12-1, you must do the following:

- Identify two variables (X1 and X2) to be analyzed (for example, income level and importance of supermarket within walking distance).
- Determine the level of measurement for each variable (nominal, ordinal, interval, ratio).
- Identify the measurement in the intersecting column and row for the measurement levels.

To select a measurement of differences from Table 12-2, follow these steps:

- Identify the level of measurement for the variables of interest.
- Decide what you wish to test:
  - The significance of the distribution of a variable within a single sample or the significance of differences in distribution of a variable between groups. For that kind of analysis, select a test from the left side of Table 12-2 (univariate tests). An example of within-group differences

| TABLE 12-1 | MEASURES OF ASSOCIATION | | |

| Measurement of Variable X_1 | Measurement of Variable X_2 | | |
	Nominal (Dichotomous)	Ordinal	Interval or Ratio
Nominal (dichotomous)	Crossbreaks Phi coefficient Contingency correlation*	Rank-biserial correlation	Point-biserial correlation
Ordinal	Rank biserial correlation	Spearman Rank Kendall Tau	Convert X_2 variable to Ranks, and use Spearman or Kendall Tau.
Interval or ratio	Point-biserial correlation	Convert X_1 variable to Ranks and use Spearman or Kendall Tau	Pearson product moment correlation

*Special case when there are more than two categories of each variable.

Source: Glass, G. V. & Stanley, J. C. (1970). *Statistical methods in education and psychology.* Boston: Allyn & Bacon.

would be to determine whether the average supermarket purchases in a single store location differ by age of shopper. An example of between-group variance would be to determine whether the average supermarket purchase at a central-city location differs significantly from the average purchase at a suburban location.

- Whether groups that differ from one another on some defined characteristic also differ with respect to a specific dependent variable. For that kind of analysis, select a test from the right side of Table 12-2. An example of such analysis would be to determine whether managers of central-city and suburban supermarkets differ in their attitudes toward providing discount pricing on bulk purchases. The characteristic defining the group is store location. The dependent variable is the managers' attitudes.

■ Identify whether comparisons are to be for independent or dependent samples. In independent samples, observations on a variable are completely independent of one another; no two observations for a particular variable can be based on the same individual. For example, in a customer preference survey the responses of one customer are independent of responses made by another customer, if precautions are taken to prevent respondents from colluding on answers. With dependent samples (also called paired samples), the data are paired on a unit of analysis. Asking the same

	Univariate Tests		Group Differences—One Dependent Variable	
Measurement Level	**Independent Samples**	**Dependent Samples**	**Independent Samples**	**Dependent Samples**
Nominal	Contingency table analysis (χ^2 test)	McNemar test	χ^2 for independent samples	Cochran-Q
Ordinal	Mann-Whitney Median test Kruskal-Wallis	Wilcoxson signed rank	Kruskal-Wallis— one-way ANOVA	Friedman— two-way ANOVA
Interval and ratio	*t*-test of differences (independent)	*t*-test of differences (dependent)	Linear models	Linear models
	F-test (independent)	*F*-test (dependent)		

TABLE 12-2 TESTS FOR DIFFERENCES

customers to respond to identical survey questions at two different times is an example of using paired samples.

■ Select the statistical test from the intersection of the appropriate column and row in Table 12-2.

Table 12-1 and Table 12-2 are initial aids for selecting statistics. The purpose of this text is not to present the calculations or the interpretation of the statistics. For those kinds of details consult a statistics textbook, a statistical consultant, or the user guide accompanying the computer statistical software of your choice.

USING STATISTICAL SOFTWARE TO ANALYZE DATA

Spreadsheet and statistical software help you prepare reports containing financial and statistical information. Conventional spreadsheets can be used to summarize data, make projections, or prepare data for complex calculations. Spreadsheet software is used to prepare cost projections, operations analyses, cost analyses, and financial reports. Spreadsheets can also be used to create tables, and in some cases, figures or graphs representing the data. Spreadsheets produce data that can be used in other programs or applications. For example, a table produced in *Microsoft Excel* can easily be imported into *Microsoft Word*. Similarly, a figure produced with *Lotus 1-2-3* can be used in *Lotus Word Pro* applications.

Statistical software such as *Statistical Package for the Social Sciences* (SPSS) and Statistical Analysis System (SAS) assist you in processing data in more complex ways. Assume, for example, as the manager of training and development you must write a report summarizing supervisors' and subordinates' responses to a survey of training needs. You must organize the responses in a manner that will be meaningful to a reader. Responses could be grouped into categories such as supervisors' perceptions of training needs and subordinates' perceptions of training needs. However, different readers may interpret the information in a different manner. You may choose to use a statistical technique that shows the relationship of the responses of supervisors and subordinates. If that is the case, you can decide to use statistical software to compute rank order correlations of employee and supervisor ranking of training needs. This analysis of the relationship of supervisors' and supervisees' perceptions of training needs would add a dimension to the analysis that could not be obtained by merely categorizing responses.

Statistical analysis software performs computations very quickly, but you must determine which statistical analysis is most appropriate. Thus, you can see that statistical analysis software relieves you of performing time-consuming, tedious calculations; but it does not determine the appropriateness of the statistical analysis, nor does the software interpret the calculations performed.

Data preparation, nonstatistical analysis, and statistical analysis are interrelated aspects of data analysis. To bring this subject into better focus, consider next the levels or stages of data interpretation through which you must progress.

LEVELS OF DATA INTERPRETATION

Data analysis is a multistage process. In each stage you move further from the objectivity of the raw data and interject the subjectivity that inevitably accompanies data interpretation. When reporting the results of your analysis, you should carefully differentiate the levels of analysis: findings, conclusions, and recommendations.

Findings

Findings are what the data reveal. As you analyze your raw data by statistical or nonstatistical methods, you find out certain things. Findings emerge as a result of data interpretation.

As you present your findings, follow these guides:

- Classify or summarize data; present such classifications or summaries in tables, charts, or graphs whenever appropriate.
- Interpret the data; don't merely repeat the raw data or the summary figures shown in visual aids.
- Show similarities and differences among groups of data. If differences exist, supply possible explanations for those differences.

Assume, for example, that you have asked a sample of FreshMart customers to rate the importance of five new services that you propose to offer. The rating scale used was

1 = Very Unimportant
2 = Unimportant
3 = Neutral
4 = Important
5 = Very Important

The first step in data analysis would be to classify the data by tallying the survey participants' ratings for each service. That process would enable you to report a breakdown of number or percentage of participants rating a specific service in a particular way. You could report, for example, that 58 percent of the respondents considered Thursday afternoon wine-tasting parties to be unimportant. You could also report that respondents tended to value lower overall prices more highly than any other proposed service. That level of analysis, however, would not capture the subtleties of the evaluations. To get a better understanding of customers' attitudes, you would have to reduce the data further.

The next step would be to reduce the data to a summary figure by computing an average rating for each service. Assume you computed the following averages:

Service	Average Rating
Lower overall prices	4.50
Senior discount on Wednesday	4.10
Free delivery of orders within a 10-mile radius of the store	1.75
Free Thursday night wine tasting	.75
Frequent Shopper discount card	3.97

The three highest-ranked items relate to ways in which customers can save money on grocery purchases; the two lowest-ranked items relate to special services for which most stores charge a nominal fee. An appropriate presentation of findings would be similar to the following example.

Average ratings indicate strong customer interest in new services that enable them to save money. Lower overall prices, senior discount on Wednesday, and Frequent Buyer discount cards all received average ratings above 3.95, indicating that FreshMart customers consider those services to be important or very important. In contrast, removing fees from seldom-used services appears to be of little importance to FreshMart customers. Free wine tastings and delivery service within a 10-mile radius of the store were rated unimportant and very unimportant respectively.

Those findings, along with others drawn from the study, should permit you to draw conclusions.

Conclusions

Conclusions are logical inferences based on the findings. As you draw conclusions, you are moving further from the objectivity of the data and relying on your perceptions of what the data mean. To avoid unwarranted subjectivity in conclusions and to state them effectively, follow these guides:

- Conclusions must not be a mere restatement of the findings.
- Conclusions must be objective and flow logically from the analysis. If the data contradict anticipated outcomes, you must put aside your expectations and base conclusions on the available data.
- Conclusions must be relevant to the stated problem and purpose of the report.
- Conclusions must not introduce new material. All relevant data and analysis must be presented before a conclusion can be drawn.
- Several findings may be used to support a single conclusion. You need not draw a conclusion from each major finding. On the other hand, one major finding may lead to more than one conclusion.

The following examples contrast inappropriate and appropriate conclusions related to the survey of FreshMart customer preferences.

Inappropriate Conclusions

Restatement of Findings: FreshMart customers rated services providing lower prices higher than eliminating fees for seldom-used services.

Not Justified by Findings: FreshMart customers will not respond to reduced fees for seldom-used services. Customers want lower grocery prices, not parties or cheaper delivery service.

Not Related to Problem of Report: FreshMart can gain a competitive edge by offering a variety of price-reduction strategies. (This conclusion is not justified if the stated problem is to determine customer preferences for new services and no data were gathered to determine their inclinations to choose a supermarket on the basis of the availability of those services.)

Appropriate Conclusion

Justified by Findings, Not Merely a Restatement of Findings, Related to Research Problem: FreshMart customers are more interested in ways to save money on their grocery purchases than in saving money on peripheral services. FreshMart can satisfy some of the desires of current customers by reducing grocery prices.

Since research is problem oriented, you are usually expected to carry your analysis one step further—to make recommendations.

Recommendations

Recommendations are confident statements of proposed actions based on the conclusions. Recommendations must be context-relevant; that is, they must respond to the purpose of the study and be appropriate for the specific audience. As you write recommendations, observe the following guides:

- Verify that specific conclusions and findings justify each recommendation. Some report writers number summary statements of findings and conclusions so that they can refer easily to such supporting information when they write recommendations.
- State recommendations in imperative sentence structure. Begin each with an action verb.
- State recommendations specifically, including a recommended plan for implementation if appropriate.
- Number the recommendations so that report readers can identify and refer to them easily while reading the report and making decisions about their implementation.
- Suggest additional research to investigate unanswered questions that became evident during the study.

Assume that the purpose of FreshMart's survey was to increase customer satisfaction and loyalty by providing desired services. The following example shows an appropriate way to state your recommendations.

To increase customer satisfaction and loyalty, FreshMart should initiate two new services as soon as possible and determine the feasibility of a third. Specifically, FreshMart should:

1. Cut all prices by 1 percent. This recommendation can be implemented by:
   - Programming point-of-sale registers to compute a 1 percent discount on total order.
   - Training check-out associates to highlight the saving on each receipt and point it out to the customer.
2. Give a 10 percent discount to all seniors on Wednesday. This recommendation can be implemented by:
   - Designing and publishing an attractive newspaper advertisement announcing the new policy.
   - Training checkout associates how to recognize customers who appear to be 60 years of age or older and how to offer the discount to such customers.
3. Investigate the feasibility of issuing a Frequent Shopper discount card. Specific facts needed include:
   - How to identify "Frequent Shoppers"
   - Type of discount that should be offered
   - Cost of providing the card, maintaining records, and fulfilling the discount program

By applying logic and statistics, you should be able to reach defensible conclusions and recommendations. But those conclusions and recommendations must also be ethically defensible.

ETHICAL CONSIDERATIONS

You may be faced with ethical issues at all stages of data analysis. The presumed objectivity of numbers may lead some people to assume that statistical analysis is an objective, amoral process. You may, however, be confronted with ethical questions during statistical analysis. For example, your choice of a significance level may involve ethics. Your findings may be significant at the .10 level, but not at the .05 or .01 level. Is it ethical to present findings as "significant" when there is a 10 percent probability that the observed relationships or differences are chance observations? To avoid this ethical dilemma, most researchers select a significance level before doing the analysis.

During the analysis of findings, you may also have to make choices about whether data should or should not be made public. When you have promised primary data sources that they will not be identified, you have a moral obligation to fulfill that promise. The assurance of confidentiality requires that you present the information in such a way that the data cannot be traced to specific participants. A similar obligation exists even when you have not promised confidentiality. In some situations revelation of sources may cause financial, emotional, or other forms of injury to individuals. When that situation exists, you must decide whether revealing or concealing source identity is the greater good.

Similarly, you may have to decide whether certain data should be included in or excluded from the analysis. You may be tempted to exclude data that will not support your hypothesis or an outcome that you know your manager prefers. Ethical behavior, however, requires objective analysis of all relevant available data. Moreover, while drawing conclusions and making recommendations, ethical researchers test the logic of their conclusions and examine the likely impact of their recommendations. In 2005, allegations that a U.S. government official had asked underlings to manipulate intelligence analyses were leveled when that person was nominated to be the U.S. representative to the United Nations. Such behavior would present an ethical dilemma to an employee. What action promotes the greater good: Obey orders and retain the job? Disobey orders and retain personal integrity, as well as possibly avert disastrous decisions?

A complicated situation arose in the 1990s. Some automobile dealers sold 15-passenger vans to schools to transport students, even though the vans did not meet the safety standards required for school buses and the Federal Motor Vehicle Safety Act says it is illegal to *sell* new vans to schools or day-care centers with educational missions. After the owner of an auto dealership learned of that law, he repeatedly told administrators of a private school to whom he had sold a van that the school should not use the vehicle to transport students. Ironically, the law does not prohibit schools from *using* the vans. Following the death of a child in an accident involving one of those vans, the child's parents began a national campaign for legislation to prevent schools from using such vehicles to transport students. Although technically the school broke no law, its actions were ethically questionable; and a suit brought by the parents against the school was settled before it came to trial.[1] The parents subsequently used those funds to support a campaign against schools' use of 15-passenger vans to transport students.[2] In May, 2005, the U.S. Senate finally passed a bill prohibiting the "purchase, rental, or lease . . . of such vehicles to transport pre-primary, primary, or secondary school students to or from school-related events unless the vehicles meet the same safety standards required for school buses and multi-function school activity buses."[3]

SUMMARY

Data analysis is the process of converting raw data into usable information for decision makers. The process involves reducing raw data into findings, interpreting those findings, drawing conclusions, and making recommendations.

Understanding the research problem, maintaining a critical mindset, and applying logic and appropriate statistical procedures are requirements for data analysis. Before data can be analyzed, they must be edited and coded. They may also be entered into a computer, after which their correct entry must be verified. Analysis may include statistical and nonstatistical procedures.

TOPICS FOR DISCUSSION

1. Define the following terms:
   a. Raw data
   b. Data analysis
   c. Qualitative data
   d. Quantitative data
   e. Induction
   f. Deduction
   g. Mean
   h. Median
   i. Mode
   j. Findings
   k. Conclusions
   l. Recommendations

2. How does knowledge of the research problem assist in data analysis?

3. What is a critical viewpoint? How is it maintained?

4. Give examples of inductive reasoning and deductive reasoning, other than those in the textbook.

5. What are criteria for an effective data coding system?

6. What is the purpose of data verification?

7. For what purposes are descriptive statistics used?

8. For what purposes are inferential statistics used?

9. What are three guidelines for writing findings? conclusions? recommendations?

10. Identify ethical issues that may arise during and after data analysis.

APPLICATIONS

1. As directed by your instructor, continue working on any study for which you wrote a proposal and data collection instruments in earlier assignments. Specifically, follow these steps to complete your assignment.
   - Collect all necessary data for analysis.
   - Select appropriate analysis techniques.
   - Prepare the data.
   - Analyze the data.
   - Write the findings, including visual aids if appropriate.
   - Write the conclusions.

2. The Faculty of Communication Arts (equivalent to a school or department in a U.S. university) at the University of Bangkok, Thailand, has hired several Thai and international lecturers to supplement its professorial staff. These lecturers have contributed to the Communication Arts program with their expertise as artists, designers, advertising producers, and market researchers.

   At a recent meeting of the Academic Committee meeting, the Chairperson, Dr. Chayo Tranadisaikul, announced the university's lecturer development program. Lecturers who hold bachelor degrees were encouraged to pursue a higher degree. Lecturers who have worked for the university at least one year and have received a good teaching evaluation may apply for financial support up to 50,000 baht to attend seminars or short courses that will improve their professional knowledge and teaching skill.

   To assess teaching effectiveness, all lecturers have been required to administer the questionnaire (page 324) at the end of the term.

   The table (page 324) shows the combined results of the evaluation in two classes for A. Kwanta Tamsomdee. (All professors and lecturers in Thailand are addressed as *Arjan,* which is abbreviated A.) Any lecturer whose rating (that is, *Ajarn* mean) exceeds the group mean (mean for all classes in the department) on at least 7 of the 10 items is automatically approved for the 50,000-baht stipend. Compute the mean for this lecturer and determine whether that person should be approved automatically for the professional development stipend. Present your findings, conclusion, and recommendation in a memorandum report to the lecturer with a copy to Dr. Chayo Tranadisaikul.

Teaching Effectiveness Questionnaire

Instructions: Use the following scale to complete this questionnaire.

1 Strongly disagree
2 Disagree
3 Neither agree nor disagree
4 Agree
5 Strongly agree

Indicate your response to each item by circling the appropriate number. When you have completed the questionnaire, please give it to the research assistant who is monitoring the questionnaire administration.

1	I had a clear understanding of what I was expected to learn.	1 2 3 4 5
2	The course syllabus clearly stated what was required in the course.	1 2 3 4 5
3	The instructor encouraged participation and questions from students.	1 2 3 4 5
4	The instructor answered students' questions in a thorough manner.	1 2 3 4 5
5	Course material was presented in an understandable manner.	1 2 3 4 5
6	The instructor appeared well prepared for each class.	1 2 3 4 5
7	Considering the nature of the material, the instructor made the class interesting.	1 2 3 4 5
8	The instructor returned graded tests and homework within a reasonable time.	1 2 3 4 5
9	The instructor was available for consultation outside of class hours.	1 2 3 4 5
10	I would recommend this course and instructor to another student.	1 2 3 4 5

Teaching Effectiveness Questionnaire Response Summary

Item No.	Distribution of Responses						Mean	
	1	2	3	4	5	Total	Arjan(1)	Group(2)
1	2	5	10	23	19	59		3.70
2	2	3	7	15	32	59		4.13
3	3	2	18	20	16	59		3.85
4	2	2	13	21	21	59		4.03
5	2	2	7	28	20	59		4.02
6	2	2	40	10	5	59		2.81
7	2	2	11	22	22	59		3.92
8	2	6	17	17	17	59		3.59
9	3	2	12	24	18	59		4.32
10	3	2	15	24	15	59		3.52

1. Compute class mean.
2. Group mean represents the mean for all instructors in the department.

Based in part on case written by Chonthicha Ungkanungdecha, Senior Marketing Officer at KPMG Phoomchai Holdings Co., Ltd., a subsidiary of KPMG International.

3. The recently organized Downtown Business Association has hired you to conduct a survey to determine what citizens like and dislike about the downtown area. The purpose of the survey was to determine what kinds of people currently frequent the downtown area and what changes might encourage them to visit it more frequently. Your survey strategy was to conduct random interviews on the streets of the downtown area for a one-week period at five time intervals: 8 a.m. to 10 a.m., 10 a.m. to 12 noon, 2 p.m. to 4 p.m., and 4 p.m. to 6 p.m., until you completed 500 surveys. The results of your interviews are summarized below. Analyze the data. Present your findings and conclusions in a report to the Downtown Merchants Association. Use memorandum format. Include at least one visual aid.

Age of Respondents

Age	No.
18–24	111
25–34	151
35–49	166
50–64	52
65 or over	20

Occupation of Respondent

Occupation	No.
Student	92
Professional	73
Clerical Worker	72
Service Worker	61
Technical	42
Manager	35
Blue Collar Worker	31
Sales	28
Other	21
Retired	21
Unemployed	13
No Response	11

Household Income

Income	No.
Less than $15,000	124
$15,000–$24,999	107
$25,000–$34,999	72
$35,000–$49,999	74
$50,000–$74,999	64
$75,000–$99,999	36
$100,000+	20
No response	3

Type of Household

Household	No.
Single, no children	216
Two Adults, no children	109
Two-Parent Household	117
One-Parent Household	58

Place of Residence

Area	No.	Area	No.
Central City	99	Northwest Suburbs	218
Northeast Suburbs	189	Southeast Suburbs	49
Southeast Suburbs	89	Other	35

Reason for Being Downtown When Surveyed (more than one response allowed)

Reason	No.
Working	266
Shopping	70
Other	46
Going to School	44
Running Errands	30
Sightseeing	30
Attending Meeting	22
Going to Library	21
Going to Art Museum	10

Reason for Going Downtown Other Than Work (more than one response allowed)

Reason	No.
Shopping	127
None	119
Eating	100
Other	79
Going to School	46
Sightseeing	41
Going to City Park	37
Going to Library	24
Cultural Events	22
Entertainment/Clubs	17
Going to Art Museum	14
Attend Meeting	13

What People Like about Downtown (more than one response allowed)

Feature	No.
Atmosphere	120
Other	70
Convenience/Proximity	64
City Park	52
Cleanliness	47
Restaurants	42
Stores	37
Nothing	33
Buildings	23
Library	23
Safety	11
Art Museum	10
Entertainment/Clubs	8

What People Dislike about Downtown (more than one response allowed)

Feature	No.
Few Stores	126
Parking	118
Other	87
Street People	65
Atmosphere	51
Boring	45
Nothing	37
Few Restaurants	23
Unsafe	22

One Change That Would Bring People Downtown (Only one response allowed)

Feature	No.	Feature	No.
More Specialty Shops	156	Entertainment/Clubs	31
More Parking	72	More Dining Options	39
Other	80	Department Store	28
More Police/Safety	35	Grocery Store	26
Nothing	33		

4. Executives of companies considering expansion into the international market are often concerned about the level of corruption that exists among public officials in the countries in which they hope to establish a business presence. *Dun and Bradstreet's Guide to Doing Business Around the World* publishes a Corruption Perceptions Index (CPI), which draws on 17 polls and surveys from 10 independent institutions to determine the

perceptions of business people, the general public, and country analysts regarding the level of corruption in 99 countries. Scores on the index range from 10 (highly clean) to 0 (highly corrupt).

The following table summarizes the findings related to countries for which at least 10 surveys were obtained. The standard deviation represents differences in the ratings of sources. Greater variance indicates greater differences of perceptions among those who completed the surveys.

Country Rank	Country	1999 CPI Index	Std. Deviation
1	Denmark	10.0	0.8
3	Sweden	9.4	0.6
5	Canada	9.2	0.5
7	Singapore	9.1	0.9
8	Netherlands	9.0	0.8
9	Switzerland	8.9	0.6
13	United Kingdom	8.6	0.5
14	Germany	8.0	0.5
15	Hong Kong	7.7	1.6
15	Ireland	7.7	1.9
17	Austria	7.6	0.8
18	USA	7.5	1.0
21	Portugal	6.7	1.0
22	France	6.6	1.0
22	Spain	6.6	0.7
25	Japan	6.0	1.6
28	Taiwan	5.6	0.9
31	Hungary	5.2	1.1
32	Malaysia	5.1	0.5
34	South Africa	5.0	0.8
38	Italy	4.7	0.6
39	Czech Republic	4.6	0.8
44	Poland	4.2	0.8
Country Rank	**Country**	**1999 CPI Index**	**Std. Deviation**
45	Brazil	4.1	0.8
50	South Korea	3.8	0.9
54	Philippines	3.6	1.4
54	Turkey	3.6	1.0
56	China	3.4	0.7
68	Thailand	3.2	0.7
71	Argentina	3.0	0.8
72	Colombia	2.9	0.5
72	India	2.9	0.6
75	Ukraine	2.6	1.4
82	Russia	2.4	1.0
96	Indonesia	1.7	0.8

Assume you are the Marketing Director for a company in any country of your choice. Based on management's perception of the significance of corruption among public officials and the type of product or service you wish to introduce into other countries (you decide what your company wants to market abroad), select five countries that your company should investigate as possible target markets. Direct your report to the executive committee of your company. Use memorandum style and include sufficient information about your company and the countries' ratings on the CPI to support your recommendations.

Source: Morrison, T., Conaway, W. W., & Douress, J. J. (2001). *Dun & Bradstreet's Guide to Doing Business Around the World.* Paramus, NJ: Prentice Hall, pp. 495–498.

REFERENCES

1. Davis, M. R. (June 16, 1997). Child's death spurs quest for van safety. *The State,* A1.

2. Crumbo, C. (September 5, 1997). Ads: Vans shouldn't be buses. *The State,* B3.

3. Saferoads (2005, April). *Safety-Related Provisions in SAFETEA 2005.* Retrieved December 1, 2005, from http://www.saferoads.org/federal/2005/SAFETEASummary_Section-by-Section_April2005.pdf

chapter 13

Documenting Data Sources

LEARNING OBJECTIVES

After you have read this chapter, you should be able to:

1. Prepare an annotated bibliography.

2. Construct a list of works cited in your report, using the style recommended by the American Psychological Association, the Modern Language Association, or the University of Chicago.

3. Construct endnotes and in-text citations, using the style recommended by the American Psychological Association, the Modern Language Association, or the University of Chicago.

4. Use standard explanatory abbreviations within the text and the references of your reports.

This chapter illustrates the mechanics of documenting the sources of data you use for your reports. Examples demonstrate the three styles most commonly used in business today: those recommended by the American Psychological Association (APA); the Modern Language Association (MLA); and the University of Chicago Press (CHIC). Each of those organizations publishes a style manual that is available in most bookstores.

WHY YOU SHOULD ACKNOWLEDGE DATA SOURCES

The need to acknowledge data sources is often not understood. Any information that is common knowledge need not be documented. However, ethical experienced writers agree that you should acknowledge your unique sources of information for three reasons:

- The business and academic communities expect honesty in all transactions. When you indicate where or from whom you obtained unique information, you are following a standard academic and business practice.
- The business and academic communities appreciate the ability to build upon previous knowledge. When you indicate where you obtained your

information, you are enabling others to find the data and use it in their business or academic research.

- The business and academic communities respect individual contributions. When you document the sources of data that you acquired from others, including direct quotations and paraphrased material, the readers may infer that any undocumented material is your contribution to the body of work.

In short, appropriate acknowledgement of data sources establishes your credibility as a writer and researcher.

BIBLIOGRAPHY AND FOOTNOTES

Traditionally, source acknowledgments in a report consisted of footnotes placed at the bottom of the page and a bibliography. *Footnotes* cite the exact location of evidence or authority for specific statements. *Bibliographical entries* cite sources as whole entities.

A bibliography should list all references cited in the body of the report; it may also list other pertinent references of potential benefit to the reader. Technically, *bibliography* refers to writings on a particular subject; hence, interviews, speeches, and radio or television broadcasts would not logically be part of a bibliography.

A bibliography is sometimes prepared to direct the reader to useful sources of information about a subject. An *annotated bibliography,* a list of books or other publications with appropriate comments about each entry, is useful in such instances, as shown in Illustration 13-1. Note that the items in the annotated bibliography are printed in bold type merely to separate the citations from the descriptive information. This is not a standard requirement for an annotated bibliography, but it does contribute to readability. Note also that the entries are written in the bibliographic style recommended by *The Chicago Manual of Style.* Subsequent examples will be shown in the style recommended by that source for a reference list, which differs slightly from its style for a bibliography.

APA, MLA, and CHIC reserve the term *bibliography* for a list that includes more than the works actually cited in the text. Current business practice permits—even encourages—variations that effectively combine footnote and bibliographic references. This chapter focuses on those techniques.

REFERENCE LIST, WORKS CITED

For a list that includes only the works cited in the text, the APA, MLA, and CHIC manuals recommend the following practices:

- APA: Use *references* to identify sources cited in the text.
- MLA: Use *works cited* to identify sources cited in the text. *Literature cited* may be used if the list contains only printed sources (that is, no items

ILLUSTRATION 13-1 ANNOTATED BIBLIOGRAPHY, CHICAGO MANUAL OF STYLE

ANNOTATED BIBLIOGRAPHY

Farid, Elashmawi. *Competing Globally: Mastering Multicultural Management and Negotiations.* **Boston: Butterworth-Heinemann, 2001.**

Provides specific information about entering international markets, conducting meetings, making presentations, negotiating, and working with international partners. Focuses on unique business cultures of Arabs, Chinese, Europeans, Indonesians, Japanese, Koreans, North Americans, and Thais.

Fischer, Heinz-Dietrich, and Merrill, John C., ed. *International and Cultural Communication.* **New York: Hastings House, Publishers, 1976.**

A collection of articles exploring "the hope and purpose of international understanding." Topics: communication systems and concepts, the world's media; problems of freedom and responsibility; national development and mass media; international news flow and propaganda; supranational communication efforts, international communication; theory and research in international communication.

Frank, R. Robert. "Nonverbal Communication and the Emergence of Moral Sentiments." In *Nonverbal Communication: Where Nature Meets Culture,* **edited by Ullica Segerstrale and Peter Molnar. Mahwah, NJ: Lawrence Erlbaum Associates, Publishers, 1997.**

Argues that "people are motivated to behave morally not because they have rationally calculated that it is in their material interest to do so, but because they are emotionally predisposed to do so. They have some emotional hardware that they have inherited biologically." (p. 288.)

---

such as films, recordings, or television programs). Use *works consulted* if the list contains items used but not cited in the report.

- CHIC: Use *reference list* to identify sources cited in the text; reserve *bibliography* to identify works for background or further reading.

Observe these general guides when preparing a bibliography, list of references, or list of works cited:

- Alphabetize entries within categories or within the entire list if it is not categorized.
- Use "hanging indentions" for entries. (See Illustration 13-2 and Illustration 13-3.)

ILLUSTRATION 13-2 REFERENCE LIST IN APA STYLE

References

Beijing +10, UN commission on the status of women. (2005, Spring). *Business Woman, 89*, 1.

Downs, Stephanie (n.d.). Web conferencing 101. White paper retrieved December 4, 2005 from http://wp.bitpipe.com/resource/org_984079886_619/macromedia_webconf_101_edp.pdf? site_cd=bp

Fischer, H.-D., & Merrill, J. C. (Eds) (1976). *International and cultural communication.* New York: Hasting House Publishers.

Guanipa, C. (1998). *Culture Shock.* Retrieved July 31, 2005, from http://edweb.sdsu.edu/ people/CGuanipa/cultshok.htm

Hodge, S. (2000). *Global smarts.* New York: John Wiley & Sons, Inc.

Korea in quest of alternative energy sources. (2005, April 16). *KOREA Now, 34,* 28–29.

Leggio, G. (2005, Spring). Culture and identity: Latin American portraits. *Environmental Ethics, 22,* 10–17.

Marx, E. (1999). *Breaking through culture shock: What you need to succeed in international business.* London: Nicholas Brealey Publishing Limited.

Pickett, K. E., Mookherjee, J., & Wilkinson, R. G. (2005, July). Adolescent birth rates, total homicides, and income inequality in rice countries. *American Journal of Public Health, 95,* 1181–1183.

Price, S. (2005, July). Africa opens for business. *New African.*

Rogers, P. S., Ho. M. L., Thomas, J., Wong, I. F. H., & Cheng, C. O. L. (2004). Preparing new entrants for subordinate reporting: A decision-making framework for writing. *Journal of Business Communication, 41,* 370–401.

_____, & Wong, I. F. H. (2005). The MBA in Singapore: A microcosm of communication training for management. *Business Communication Quarterly, 68,* 180–196.

Thomas, D. C., & Inksen, K. (2004). *Cultural intelligence: People skills for global business.* San Francisco: Berrett-Koehler Publishers, Inc.

Travel Insurance Select®. (2004). n.p.: Travel Insurance Services®.

ILLUSTRATION 13-3 ▶ WORKS CITED IN MLA STYLE

Works Cited

"Beijing +10, UN Commission on the Status of Women." *Business Woman.* Spring 2005: 1.

Fischer, Heinz-Dietrich and John E. Merrill eds. *International and Cultural Communication.* New York: Hastings House Publishers, 1976.

Guanipa, Carmen. *Culture Shock.* (1998). 31 July 31, 2005. <http://edweb.sdsu.edu/people/CGuanipa/cultshok.htm>.

Hodge, Sheida. *Global Smarts.* New York: John Wiley & Sons, Inc., 2000.

"Korea in Quest of Alternative Energy Sources." *KOREA Now.* 16 April 2005: 28–29.

Leggio, Gail. "Culture and Identity: Latin American Portraits." *Environmental Ethics,* 22 (2005): 10–17.

Marx, Elizabeth. *Breaking Through Culture Shock: What You Need to Succeed in International Business.* London: Nicholas Brealey Publishing Limited, 1999.

Pickett, Kate. E., Mookherjee, Jessica, and Wilkinson, Richard G. "Adolescent Birth Rates, Total Homicides, and Income Inequality in Rice Countries." *American Journal of Public Health,* 95 (2005): 1181–1183.

Price, Stuart. "Africa Opens for Business." *New African,* June 2005: 8–10.

Rogers, Priscilla S., Mian Lian Ho, Jane Thomas, Irene F. H. Wong, and Catherine Ooi Lan Cheng. "Preparing New Entrants for Subordinate Reporting: A Decision-making Framework for Writing." *Journal of Business Communication,* 41 (2004): 370–401.

--------, and Irene F. H. Wong. The MBA in Singapore: A Microcosm of Communication Training for Management. *Business Communication Quarterly, 68* (2005): 180–196.

Thomas, David C., and Kerr Inksen. *Cultural Intelligence: People Skills for Global Business.* San Francisco: Berrett-Koehler Publishers, Inc., 2004.

Travel Insurance Select®. n.p.: Travel Insurance Services®, 2004.

- Use a solid seven-space line (approximately 1/2 inch) to avoid repeating an author's name. (See Illustration 13-2. Note the entry for Rogers and the entry immediately below it.)
- Be consistent in preparing your list; select one style and follow it consistently throughout your report. Follow the sequence, capitalization, and punctuation illustrated in this chapter or the reference books on which it is based.

The following examples demonstrate the most common types of citations that appear in business reports. The examples are given in APA, MLA, and CHIC styles. Although both APA and MLA suggest underlining the title of a complete work (such as a book or periodical) in a manuscript submitted for publication, most publications that follow those manuals ultimately print such titles in italics. Since you will often be responsible for final publication of your report, this chapter uses italics for all book and periodical titles. If you must cite items that are not illustrated here, refer to the appropriate manual.

Book

One author

APA: Farid, E. (2001). *Competing globally: Mastering multicultural management and negotiations.* Boston: Butterworth-Heinemann.
MLA: Farid, Elashmawi. *Competing Globally: Mastering Multicultural Management and Negotiations.* Boston: Butterworth-Heinemann, 2001.
CHIC: Farid, E. 2001. *Competing globally: Mastering multicultural management and negotiations.* Boston: Butterworth-Heinemann.

Multiple authors

APA: Schultz, D. E., & Kitchen, P. J. (2000). *Communicating globally: An integrated marketing approach.* Lincolnwood, IL: NYC Business Books.
MLA: Schultz, Don E., and Philip J. Kitchen. *Communicating Globally: An Integrated Marketing Approach.* Lincolnwood, IL: NYC Business Books, 2000.
CHIC: Schultz, D. E., and P. J. Kitchen. 2000. *Communicating globally: An integrated marketing approach.* Lincolnwood, IL: NYC Business Books.

No author or corporate author

APA: University of Chicago Press. (2003). *The Chicago manual of style* (15th ed.). Chicago: Author.
MLA: University of Chicago Press. *The Chicago Manual of Style.* 15th ed. Chicago: University of Chicago Press, 2003.
CHIC: University of Chicago Press. 2003. *The Chicago manual of style,* 15th ed. Chicago: University of Chicago Press.

Work in an Anthology or Compilation

APA: Meyer-Dohm, P. (1976). Investment in communication and the development process. In Fischer, H.-D., & J. C. Merrill (Eds.), *International and cultural communication* (pp. 226–235). New York: Hastings House, Publishers.

MLA: Meyer-Dohm, Peter. "Investment in Communication and the Development Process." *International and Cultural Communication.* Ed. Heinz-Dietrich Fischer, and John C. Merrill. New York: Hastings House, Publishers, 1976, 226–235.

CHIC: Meyer-Dohm, P. 1976. Investment in communication and the development process. In *International and cultural communication,* ed. Heinz-Dietrich Fischer and John C. Merrill, 226–235. New York: Hastings House, Publishers.

Article in a Scholarly Journal

One author

APA: Gupta, J. M. (2005). An integrated approach to management communication at the T. A. Pai Management Institute. *Business Communication Quarterly, 68,* 237–246.

MLA: Gupta, Jaba Mukherjee. "An Integrated Approach to Management Communication at the T. A. Pai Management Institute." *Business Communication Quarterly* 68 (2005): 237–246.

CHIC: Gupta, J. M. 2005. An integrated approach to management communication at the T. A. Pai Management Institute. *Business Communication Quarterly,* 68:237–246.

Multiple authors

APA: Toh, S. M., & DeNisi, A. S. (2005). A local perspective to expatriate success. *The Academy of Management Executive, 19,* 237–256.

MLA: Toh, Soo Min, and Angelo S. DeNisi. "A Local Perspective to Expatriate Success." *The Academy of Management Executive,* 19 (2005): 237–256.

CHIC: Toh, S. M., and A. S. DeNisi. 2005. A local perspective to expatriate success. *The Academy of Management Executive,* 19:237–256.

Article in a Magazine

One author

APA: Price, S. (2005, June). Africa opens for business. *New African,* 8–10.

MLA: Price, Stuart. "Africa Opens for Business." *New African,* June 2005: 8–10.

CHIC: Price, S. 2005. Africa opens for business. *New African,* June: 8–10.

Multiple authors

APA: Karnow, S., & Karnow, C. (2005, August). Return to Da Lat. *Smithsonian,* 68–74.

MLA: Karnow, Stanley, and Catherine Karnow. "Return to Da Lat." *Smithsonian* August 2005: 68–74.

CHIC: Karnow, S., and C. Karnow. 2005. Return to Da Lat. *Smithsonian* (August): 68–74.

No author cited

APA: Korea in quest of alternative energy sources. (2005, April 16). *KOREA Now, 34,* 28–29.

MLA: "Korea in Quest of Alternative Energy Sources." *KOREA Now.* 16 April 2005: 28–29.

CHIC: *KOREA Now.* 2005. Korea in quest of alternative energy sources. (April 16): 28–29.

Miscellaneous Sources

You may also obtain useful information from miscellaneous publications, such as brochures, pamphlets, and newsletters. Although such publications may seem relatively simple, they are often protected by a copyright, and you must acknowledge those sources when you acquire unique information from them. Ethical standards also require that you acknowledge certain sources not available to the general public, such as research interviews, questionnaires, and personal communications.

BROCHURE, PAMPHLET

Brochures and pamphlets may be handled as books. Provide all available information.

APA: U.S. Department of Health and Human Services, Office of Communications and Public Liaison, National Institute of Neurological Disorders and Stroke. (2002). *Reflex sympathetic dystrophy/complex regional pain syndrome.* [Brochure] Bethesda, MD: National Institutes of Health.

MLA: U.S. Department of Health and Human Services, Office of Communications and Public Liaison, National Institute of Neurological Disorders and Stroke. *Reflex sympathetic dystrophy/complex regional pain syndrome.* Bethesda, MD: National Institutes of Health, 2002.

CHIC: U.S. Department of Health and Human Services, Office of Communications and Public Liaison, National Institute of Neurological Disorders and Stroke. 2002. *Reflex sympathetic dystrophy/complex regional pain syndrome.* Bethesda, MD: National Institutes of Health.

NEWSLETTER

Newsletters may be handled as magazines. Provide all available information.

APA: Beijing +10, UN commission on the status of women. (Spring, 2005). *Business Woman, 89,* p. 1.

MLA: "Beijing +10, UN Commission on the Status of Women." *Business Woman.* Spring 2005: 1.

CHIC: *Business Woman ,* 2005. Beijing +10, UN commission on the status of women. (Spring): 1.

RESEARCH INTERVIEWS, QUESTIONNAIRES

APA: Kuiper, S., & Booth, R. (2004). [Experiences of salary inequity among female faculty in state universities]. Unpublished survey data.

MLA: Kuiper, Shirley, and Rosemary Booth. Experiences of Salary Inequity Among Female Faculty in State Universities. Unpublished survey data. 2004.

CHIC: Kuiper, S., & R. Booth. 2004. Experiences of salary inequity among female faculty in state universities. Unpublished survey data in authors' possession.

Personal Communications

APA recommends citing personal communications in-text only because the reader cannot verify the information. CHIC recommends citing such communications in-text or in an endnote, but not in the reference list. The basic structures can be used for any type of personal communication: personal interview; letter; memo; e-mail; telephone message, conversation, or interview.

The following examples show suggested styles for the MLA *Works Cited* and for a CHIC endnote:

- MLA: Novak, Deborah. Personal interview. 12 Jan. 2005.
- CHIC note style: Deborah Novak, personal interview with author. January 12, 2005.

Electronic Sources

Protocols for citing electronic media are still being developed. Until all issues have been resolved, the following general guides should help you to cite information obtained from electronic media. In some instances you may not be able to identify parts of a standard reference; however, always provide as much information as you can to assist the reader.

For APA, MLA, and CHIC publication styles, follow the general rules for sequence, punctuation, and capitalization that have already been demonstrated for books, journals, and magazines. Remember, however, that you may have to provide additional information. Two major additions to an electronic citation are the date on which you accessed the source and the path (URL) that brought you there. Keeping detailed records while you are collecting your data will save time when you must cite your references.

The basic facts needed for citing electronic sources are author, year of publication, title, publishing data, date accessed, and type of electronic medium or location on the Internet. If you are unsure, follow an example for printed sources that is most like the document accessed electronically. When in doubt, provide as much information as you can. More information is always better than less.

The following examples demonstrate how to cite some of the most common items accessed electronically. Both APA and MLA recommend inclusion of the date on which you access the source; CHIC recommends inclusion of that date only if the source is time sensitive. For examples of selected items, see Illustrations 13-2 and 13-3. For further information about specific styles, consult the relevant websites or enter the name of the manual in your search engine.

APA: http://www.apastyle.org/elecsource.html
MLA: http://www.mla.org/publications/style_faq
CHIC: http://www.press.uchicago.edu/Misc/Chicago/cmosfaq/
    cmosfaq.html

ONLINE PERIODICAL OR DOCUMENT

APA: Author, F., & Author, S. (year). Title of article or document. In *Title of Periodical, vol.,* page-page. [On-line]. Retrieved month day, year from URL (do not end Internet address with a period)

MLA: Author, First, and Second Author. "Title of Article or Document." *Name of Periodical* vol.no. (year): pages. Day month year of access. <URL>.

CHIC: Author, F., and S. Author. Year. Title of article or document. *Name of Periodical* vol, no. (Month day), URL (accessed month day, year).

REPORT OR DOCUMENT ON AN INTERNET SITE

APA: Author or Owner of Site. (year, month day of publication). Title of part of report or document. *Title of report or document.* Retrieved month day, year, from URL

MLA: Author or Owner of Site. "Title of Part of Report or Document." *Title of report or document.* Month year: pages. Day month year of access. <URL>.

CHIC: Author or Owner of Site. Title of part of report or document. *Title of report or document.* URL (accessed month day, year).

PUBLICATION ON CD-ROM, DISKETTE, OR MAGNETIC TAPE

APA: Author, F., & Author, S. (date). Title of article or portion of document. *Title of Full Work, Vol.:* pages. [Medium]. Retrieved Month day, year, from Name of Source Medium.

MLA: Author, First, and Second Author. "Title of Article or Document." *Title of Full Work.* Publication medium. Edition, release, or version. Place of Publication: Publisher. Date of Publication.

CHIC: Author, F., and S. Author. "Title of Article or Part of Medium Accessed," *Title of Full Work.* Medium, version, date. Place of Publication: Publisher.

FOOTNOTES AND ENDNOTES

Footnotes are citations for specific statements. Traditional footnote style requires a superscript (number placed slightly above the line of type) at the citation point along with a footnote at the bottom of the page. However, contemporary writers usually group notes at the end of a report. When that practice is followed, the list is more appropriately called endnotes.

Observe these guides when preparing footnotes or endnotes:

- Number notes consecutively throughout the manuscript or its chapters.
- Indent the first line of each note.

- Use standard abbreviations (*ibid., op. cit., loc. cit.*) for convenience and economy.
- Be consistent in data sequence, capitalization, and punctuation. Follow the style illustrated in this text or any standard reference book.

IN-TEXT CITATIONS

The American Psychological Association, the Modern Language Association, and the University of Chicago recommend in-text source acknowledgments. This practice requires a complete list for each source referenced but eliminates the need for formal footnotes. The following examples illustrate variations of in-text citations. All citations are from materials listed in Illustration 13-2 and Illustration 13-3.

One Author

APA: According to Marx (1999), "(I)t is a myth that experiencing culture shock is a weakness or a negative indication of future international success" (p. 5).

MLA: According to Marx, "(I)t is a myth that experiencing culture shock is a weakness or a negative indication of future international success" (5).

CHIC: According to Marx (1999, 5), "(I)t is a myth that experiencing culture shock is a weakness or a negative indication of future international success."

Multiple Authors

APA: Experiencing a new culture can be an unpleasant surprise and a frustrating experience similar to working one's way through a maze (Hodge, 2000; Marx, 1999).

MLA: Experiencing a new culture can be an unpleasant surprise and a frustrating experience similar to working one's way through a maze (Hodge 27; Marx 5).

CHIC: Experiencing a new culture can be an unpleasant surprise and a frustrating experience similar to working one's way through a maze (Hodge 2000; Marx 1999).

No Author Cited

APA: New and renewable energy sources such as fuel cells, recycled oil, and power generated from burned waste are expected to supply five percent of Korea's energy needs by 2011 ("Korea in quest," 2005).

MLA: New and renewable energy sources such as fuel cells, recycled oil, and power generated from burned waste are expected to supply five percent of Korea's energy needs by 2011 ("Korea in quest" 28).

CHIC: New and renewable energy sources such as fuel cells, recycled oil, and power generated from burned waste are expected to supply five percent of Korea's energy needs by 2011 ("Korea in quest" 2005).

Personal Communication

APA: The department chairperson acknowledged that staff will likely be cut from the arts programs if the bond issue is not passed (Novak, personal communication).

MLA: The department chairperson acknowledged that staff will likely be cut from the arts programs if the bond issue is not passed (Novak, pers. com.).

CHIC: The department chairperson acknowledged that staff will likely be cut from the arts programs if the bond issue is not passed (Novak, pers. comm.).

A shorter version of in-text citations is used in some business reports. This system requires an alphabetized and numbered source list, prepared in either APA, MLA, or CHIC style. An in-text citation then identifies a source by its number in the source list, followed by a colon and page numbers if a page reference is required. In the following example, 6 refers to the sixth item in the references; 28 refers to page 28 of that source:

- **Text Citation**
  - New and renewable energy sources such as fuel cells, recycled oil, and power generated from burned waste are expected to supply five percent of Korea's energy needs by 2011 (6:28).
- **Source List**
  - Korea in quest of alternative energy sources. (2005, April 16). *KOREA Now*, pp. 28–29.

STANDARD ABBREVIATIONS

To save writing and reading time, the following abbreviations are used in reports. When used, these abbreviations are the same in APA, MLA, and CHIC styles.

c. or ca.	about (from Latin *circa;* used in contexts of time; for example, c.1900)
cf.	compare (from Latin *confer*)
chap. or chaps.	chapter or chapters (followed by numbers)
ed. or eds.	editor or editors
ed. or edd.	edition or editions
e.g.	for example (from Latin *exempli gratia*)
et al.	and other people (from Latin *et alii*)
etc.	and other things (from Latin *et cetera*)
f.	and the following page (for instance, pp. 5f.)
ff.	and the following pages (for instance, pp. 5ff.)
ibid.	the same reference (from Latin *ibidem;* used, especially in footnotes, to repeat an immediately preceding source)
i.e.	that is (from Latin *id est*)
l. or ll.	line or lines continued
loc. cit.	place cited (from Latin *loco citato*)

n.d.	no date (used especially concerning the details of publication)
n.n.	no name (used especially concerning the details of publication)
n.p.	no place (used especially concerning the details of publication)
n. pub.	no publisher (used especially concerning details of publication)
no. or nos.	number or numbers
op. cit.	the work cited (from Latin *opere citato*)
p. or pp.	page or pages
par. or pars.	paragraph or paragraphs
passim	here and there (or throughout)
q.v.	which see (from Latin *quod vide*)
rev.	revised or revision
sec. or secs.	section or sections
sic	thus (usually placed within brackets, not parentheses, to indicate "thus it is in the original document or statement")
trans.	translator or translated
vol. or vols.	volume or volumes

ETHICAL CONSIDERATIONS

The ethical requirements for documentation were mentioned in Chapters 10 and 11. The opening section of this chapter also reminded you that the standard of giving credit where credit is due must be followed in all reporting. The *Publications Manual of the American Psychological Association* reminds writers that the purpose of careful documentation is to ensure the accuracy and integrity of information presented in reports and to protect the intellectual property rights of others whose knowledge you have tapped. Enough said: Ethical writers acknowledge their information sources accurately and as completely as possible.

SUMMARY

When you write a report, you should acknowledge all data sources that contributed to your study. Contemporary writing style suggests use of a brief in-text notation at the point at which you want to acknowledge a source, along with a list of sources at the end of the report.

To ensure a degree of uniformity in such acknowledgements, three organizations have published style manuals: The American Psychological Association, The Modern Language Association, and the University of Chicago. Since the style manuals differ slightly with respect to sequence and punctuation of information included in a citation, you should select one of those styles and use it consistently throughout your report.

Each of those organizations also maintains a website at which you can locate answers to frequently asked questions about documentation. With the convenience of guidance from those websites, the ethical researcher will have no difficulty establishing her or his credibility through proper documentation.

TOPICS FOR DISCUSSION

1. Discuss three reasons why you should provide complete data sources as you write a business report.

2. Compare the APA, MLA, and CHIC styles for citing a book with multiple authors. In what respects do the three styles differ from one another?

3. Compare the APA, MLA, and CHIC styles for citing a journal article with multiple authors and a book with one author. In what respects do the three styles differ from one another for the two types of citations?

4. If you have had the experience of wanting to look up some information that is referred to in a newspaper, magazine, or journal article, were you able to find the source document relatively easily? Why or why not? What techniques did you use to find the source document?

5. In what ways, if any, has your use of the Internet for research changed your procedures for documenting data sources?

6. Compare the online service and the print copy of the manuals cited in this chapter by searching for an answer to a specific question regarding documentation. Which do you prefer? Why?

7. If you have had experience writing a report in a business or non-profit organization, what documentation was expected? In what ways, if any, do business expectations differ from academic expectations?

8. Describe ethical challenges you have faced as you used data from print sources and/or electronic media.

APPLICATIONS

1. Find at least five sources (at least two print and two electronic) on one of the following topics or another topic approved by your instructor. Prepare an annotated bibliography of those sources.
   - Reflex Sympathetic Dystrophy/Complex Regional Pain Syndrome. What is it? How is it diagnosed and treated?
   - How business is reacting to terrorism
   - Investment opportunities in South Africa
   - The future of private enterprise in Russia
   - The value of trip cancellation and/or medical evacuation insurance when traveling abroad
   - Why medical professionals encourage all adults to sign a health-care power of attorney
   - What you should know about nonverbal communication when you travel for business purposes to (a country of your choice)

2. Form a group with three classmates and assign each person one of the manuals cited in this chapter. Each person is to write the following items in appropriate reference list style as recommended by the manual he or she is responsible for. If illustrations are not given in the text, use the respective manual or online service.

   - Shirley Kuiper and Morris P. Wolf, Effective Communication in Business, 10th edition, Cincinnati: South-Western Publishing Co., 1994.
   - Joanne M. Crossman, The Multi-audience Memo and the International Business Interview, *Business Communication Quarterly*, Vol. 66, No. 4, December 2003, pp. 72–77.
   - Dwane Hal Dean, Consumer Reaction to Negative Publicity: Effects of Corporate Reputation, Response, and Responsibility for a Crisis Event, *Journal of Business Communication*, Vol. 41, No. 2, April 2004, pp. 192–211.
   - Book review of *Business Confronts Terrorism* by Dean C. Alexander, accessed on July 31, 2005 at http://www.wisc.edu/wisconsinpress/books
   - Transcript of online interview with Dean C. Alexander conducted by the Washington Post, "Business Response to Terrorism," accessed on December 4, 2005 at http://www.washingtonpost.com/wp-dyn/content/discussion/2005/07/07/DI2005070701112.html?nav=rss_business
   - "Schrempp, 'Friend of SA,' Quits Daimler," London, Jul 29, 2005 (Business Day/All Africa Global Media via COMTEX), accessed December 4, 2005 at http://firstglobalselect.com/scripts/cgiip.exe/WService%3Dglobalone001/globalone/htm/news_article.r?vcnews-id=137256
   - Jerry Joyce and Marianne Moon, *Microsoft® XP Plain & Simple*, 2nd Edition, Redmond, WA: Microsoft Press, 2005.
   - Beth Reiber and Janie Spencer, *Frommer's® Japan, 7th Edition*, Hoboken, NJ: Wiley Publishing, Inc., 2004.
   - Janis Forman and M. Lynne Markus, "Research on Collaboration, Business Communication, and Technology: Reflections on an Interdisciplinary Academic Collaboration," *Journal of Business Communication*, Vol. 42, No. 1, January 2005. pp. 78–102.

3. Each of the following quotations was taken from one of the items given in Application 2. For each quotation, write the item in APA, MLA, or CHIC style as:

   a. A direct quotation with in-text citation

   b. A paraphrase with in-text citation, using the author's name in the paraphrase

   c. A paraphrase with in-text citation, not using the author's name in your paraphrase

"As the nation's capital for more than 1,000 years, Kyoto spawned a number of crafts and exquisite art forms that catered to the elaborate tastes of the imperial court and the upper classes. Kyoto today is still renowned for its crafts, including Nishijin textiles, Yuzun-dyed fabrics, Kyo pottery (pottery fired in Kyoto), fans, dolls, cutlery, gold-leaf work, umbrellas, paper lanterns, combs, Noh masks, cloisonné, and lacquer-ware." (Source: Beth Reiber and Janie Spencer, p. 339)

"Juergen Schrempp unexpectedly quit as CEO of DaimlerChrysler yesterday, raising hopes of deep-rooted change at the German-American car maker he has led for a decade. The shares rose 9%." (Source: Shrempp . . . , n.p.)

"Clearly, interdisciplinary collaborations are one way to bring the perspectives of different disciplines to bear on complex, multifaceted research topics. . . . At the end of the road, the potential rewards—with an emphasis on "potential"—include a richer understanding of complex phenomena but at the cost of time spent learning to work collaboratively across disciplinary boundaries." (Source: Janis Forman and M. Lynne Markus, p. 81)

"Firms responding to the crisis with fairness and compassion for those affected were more highly regarded than firms whose response lacked these elements and attempted to shift the blame for the tragedy." (Source: Dwane Hal Dean, p. 207)

"Communication competence is valued and expected by students' future employers and significantly impacts hiring decisions." (Source: Joanne Crossman, p. 72)

4. Using one of the citation styles presented in this chapter, verify the form of all references you used recently in a report for this course, for another course, or at your place of business. Correct all inconsistencies you detect. (If you have not written a report recently, find one written by someone else and do the same.)

Writing Business Research Reports

You have studied how to plan business research and how to collect and analyze data for a complex report. One aspect of the preparation of a formal business report remains: putting the information into an attractive, functional format that enables readers to absorb the information it contains easily and act on the contents of the report.

Business research reports are often classified as information or analytical reports. An *information* report provides comprehensive data related to a business problem along with interpretation of the data, but it offers no conclusions or recommendations. An *analytical* report includes conclusions and may also include recommendations.

PARTS OF THE FORMAL BUSINESS REPORT

Many relatively lengthy reports are prepared in a formal style such as is presented in this chapter. A characteristic of a formal business report is the inclusion of several parts that are not included in less formal reports. Although you may adapt the parts of a formal report to suit the requirements of your reporting situation, the most comprehensive structure includes the factors listed in Illustration 14-1.[1] Each part is explained in this chapter and demonstrated in Illustration 14-2. (See pages 358–382.)

As you study the explanation of each part, examine its counterpart in Illustration 14-2. Note also the writing style and the inductive structure of the report.

> **ILLUSTRATION 14-1** ▸ PARTS OF A FORMAL REPORT
>
> 1. Report Preliminaries (sometimes called Front Matter)
>   1.1 Cover or binder
>   1.2 Flyleaves
>   1.3 Title page
>   1.4 Transmittal message
>   1.5 Authorization message
>   1.6 Acceptance message
>   1.7 Table of contents
>   1.8 List of tables or figures
>   1.9 Foreword or preface
>   1.10 Acknowledgments
>   1.11 Synopsis or executive summary
>
> 2. Report Body
>   2.1 Introduction
>   2.2 Presentation and discussion of findings
>   2.3 Summary, conclusions, and recommendations
>   (Summary only for an information report; summary, conclusions, and recommendations for an analytical report.)
>
> 3. Report Supplements (sometimes called End Matter)
>   3.1 Endnotes
>   3.2 Bibliography, source list, or references
>   3.3 Glossary
>   3.4 Appendix
>   3.5 Index

Report Preliminaries

The preliminary parts of a formal report help to make the report user friendly. Those parts provide a convenient way to physically transmit the report, establish a context for understanding it, and enable the reader to locate specific information easily. Some preliminary parts may be omitted when justified by the length of the report, the complexity of the topic, or the formality of the situation.

Although the report preliminaries are the first pages the report user sees, many of those parts can be compiled only after you have written the full report. The preliminary parts must accurately reflect the report's content and structure. If you revise your report in any way after you have written the preliminaries, be sure to check the accuracy of all preliminary parts and, if necessary, revise them before delivering the report. For example, be sure that your table of contents accurately shows the final content and pagination of your report.

Cover or Binder

A reader must be able to handle the report document conveniently. Although some readers may prefer that you present unbound pages, perhaps enclosed in an envelope or a file folder, many prefer that you bind the report securely. A cover or binder protects the pages of the report and prevents them from loosening while the reader uses the report. Your report cover should show at least the title of the report; if the title is long, a shortened form may appear on the cover. You may also include a design or illustration to suggest the content of the report and stimulate interest. (See Illustration 14-2, first page.)

Flyleaves

A blank sheet may be placed at both the front and the back of the report to protect other pages and provide a space for readers' comments. Those sheets, called flyleaves, are optional. Since they tend to connote a higher level of formality, include flyleaves only when you think the situation justifies such formality. Note, for example, that most hardcover books contain flyleaves, but many softcover books do not.

Title Page

The title page usually contains four facts: the full title of the report; the identity of the person or agency for whom the report was prepared, including full name and address; the author's identity, including full name, address, and possibly the telephone number or e-mail address; and the submission date. Although inclusion of the author's identity is optional, it may be advantageous to include such information on all reports unless you are instructed not to do so. Such information will help readers provide feedback, such as questions, commendations, or requests for new projects.

The title of the report should provide a concise statement of its content. Include as much *who, what, why, when,* and *where* information as is possible without creating a cumbersome title. To achieve conciseness, avoid using unnecessary words and phrases such as "an analysis of" or "the determination of." A "talking" title may stimulate interest more readily than a purely descriptive title. The following examples contrast a cumbersome, verbose title with a descriptive title and a talking title.

Cumbersome, verbose. A Comprehensive Analysis of Tourism in West Virginia and Actions the Hatfield-McCoy Mountains Coalition Should Take to Increase Tourism in That Region

Descriptive. Increasing Tourism in the Hatfield-McCoy Mountains Region of West Virginia

Talking. What Should the Hatfield-McCoy Mountains Coalitions Do to Increase Tourism in Its Region?

For the title page you may use a traditional format or any creative format that effectively conveys the required information. A nontraditional format is demonstrated in Illustration 14-2, page 359. Notice that no page number appears on the title page. A traditional title page format appears in Illustration 14-3, page 383.

TRANSMITTAL MESSAGE

The transmittal message, in letter or memorandum format, presents the report to your primary reader(s). Generally a letter is used for external reports and a memo for internal reports.

If you have written the report in an impersonal style, the transmittal message gives you an opportunity to speak more personally to your primary contact person and reinforce goodwill. The message may include any comments that will stimulate interest in the report, confirm confidence in you as the researcher and writer, and perhaps lead to further interesting, responsible assignments. Appropriate content for the transmittal message includes some, not necessarily all, of the following: a review of the research problem, purpose, and methodology; highlights of major findings; significant recommendations; comments about the research experience; an offer to discuss the report or assist with future projects.

The transmittal message is often bound within the report, either before or after the title page, but some writers prefer to present it as a separate message accompanying the report. See Illustration 14-2, page 360 for an example of a transmittal message bound within the report.

AUTHORIZATION AND ACCEPTANCE MESSAGES

The authorization message provides evidence of permission to undertake the project, and the acceptance message gives evidence of agreement to do the task. Those messages are often exchanged before the project is undertaken, sometimes orally and sometimes in writing. If written, they may be included in the report as formal notice to secondary readers that the project was appropriately authorized and accepted. However, if the transmittal message includes reference to the authorization, as is done in Illustration 14-2, those messages may be omitted from the report.

If authorization and acceptance messages had been included in Illustration 14-2, they would be similar to the following examples:

Authorization Message

(Appropriate letter or memo format)

Please proceed with the investigation of ways to increase tourism in the Hatfield-McCoy Mountains region.

As we discussed this morning, the members of the Hatfield-McCoy Mountains Coalition must be fully aware of current tourism trends and tourists' perceptions of the Hatfield-McCoy Mountains region. The research proposal you presented to the Coalition convinced us that your agency is the right one to undertake this study. You have my full support.

You agreed to submit a written report of your findings, conclusions, and recommendations no later than September 1. I would appreciate a progress report on August 1.

Acceptance Message

(Appropriate letter or memorandum format)

Thank you for authorizing K-F Research Associates to analyze tourism trends in West Virginia and tourists' perceptions of the Hatfield-McCoy Mountains region. My research team has already begun to collect data.

You will have a report of the research no later than September 1. As you requested, I will submit a progress report on August 1.

You may also occasionally submit unsolicited reports. In such an instance, authorization and acceptance messages do not exist; and the transmittal message must indicate clearly why you are submitting the report.

Contents

In a lengthy report, a table of contents (see Illustration 14-2, page 361) and lists of tables and figures help the reader get an overview of the report and easily refer to specific parts of the report.

The table of contents must list all items that appear after that page: any preliminary pages that follow and all chapter or section headings and subheadings used in the report. Do not list preliminary pages that appear before the table of contents. The number of the page on which each first-level division begins must be included. Many writers include page numbers to mark the beginning of each subdivision as well. Some writers use an outline numbering system, such as the decimal system demonstrated in Illustration 14-1, to identify the entries in the table of contents.

A list of tables or figures follows the table of contents when the report includes visual aids. When only one or two visual aids are used, some writers include them in the table of contents. However, the reader can locate the visual aids more easily if they appear in a separate list. If the list is short and space permits, the list may be included on the same page as the table of contents. The list of tables usually precedes the list of figures; but if few visuals are used, they may be grouped in a list of illustrations.

Preface

A preface should present some special details about the report and create interest. The preface is not as comprehensive as the executive summary, which appears later. Comments about what stimulated the study and its significance are appropriate content for a preface. If that information already is conveyed in the authorization, acceptance, or transmittal messages, you may omit the preface. A preface is most appropriate in an unsolicited report.

The report shown in Illustration 14-2 contains no preface. The following example demonstrates an appropriate preface for that report.

Preface

The decline of coal mining in the Hatfield-McCoy Mountains region requires that community leaders pursue all possible means of promoting new industry in the region. One effective way to improve the economic well-being of the region is to capture a larger share of the state's tourism trade.

This report addresses the challenge of increasing tourism in the Hatfield-McCoy Mountains region and suggests possible routes to that increase.

ACKNOWLEDGMENTS

Include an acknowledgments page when you want to give credit to people who have assisted with the project. When such recognition is included in the transmittal message, the acknowledgments page is omitted. Acknowledgements are often written in the first person, even if the report itself is written in the third person. The following example demonstrates appropriate acknowledgements for the report about tourism.

Acknowledgments

Many people contributed to the success of this study, and I am grateful to all of them. A special thank you goes to several who contributed in unique ways.

Mary Ann Conrad of the Hatfield-McCoy Mountains Coalition is primarily responsible for this project. She entrusted K-F Research Associates with the research assignment and gave valuable advice during the early stages of the project. Her suggestions and perceptive questions helped to clarify the objectives of the project and determine the best ways to accomplish those objectives.

Individuals visiting tourist sites in the Metro Valley and New River-Greenbrier regions willingly provided information about their travel experiences and perceptions of the Hatfield-McCoy Mountains Region. Their candid comments provided the data necessary to gain a perspective on potentially successful promotional strategies. Without their assistance, we would not have been able to produce this report

To all, a hearty "Thank you."

Arlene W. Sherman
Director of Market Research
K-F Research Associates, LLP

Executive Summary

The executive summary, sometimes called a synopsis, immediately precedes the body of the report. In this summary, briefly state the research problem, purpose, research methods, major findings, conclusions, and recommendations. The summary must contain enough information to help a reader decide how much of the full report he or she should read. (See Illustration 14-2, page 363.)

Although an analytical report may be written in inductive (indirect) structure, many readers prefer that the executive summary be written in deductive (direct) structure, beginning with your recommendations. One technique for drafting an executive summary is to reduce each major section of the report to one paragraph. After condensing the report in that way, you can revise the draft by arranging the paragraphs into the desired structure and adding transitions to link the paragraphs into a coherent summary.

Some executives prefer that the summary be no longer than one page. The length and complexity of the report, however, most often govern the length of the summary. Unless instructed to do so, do not feel that you must limit the summary to one page.

Report Body

Whereas the preliminaries provide a context for understanding the report and a summary of its contents, the body of your report must contain all details of the study. Since the report body should be a coherent unit, it begins with the report title, placed about 1 1/2 inches from the top of the first page of the report body.

Write the report body so clearly and completely that a reader will understand its contents even if the person merely skims the preliminary parts. When the report is written in inductive structure, the title is followed by a coherent introduction; a complete presentation, discussion, and summary of findings; and—for an analytical report—conclusions and recommendations. For an information report, the summary marks the end of the report. The body of an analytical report written in inductive structure begins on the first page of the report body in Illustration 14-2—the page immediately after the executive summary.

Introduction

The introduction provides all information necessary to understand the remainder of the report. The introduction establishes the context for interpreting the findings and conclusions.

Typically, the introductory section for a report written in inductive structure includes the background to the problem, a statement of the research problem and purpose, the scope of analysis, and the research procedures. Delimitations, limitations, and definitions of terms may also be included. If you prepared a comprehensive research proposal, you can draw much of the information for the introduction from that document. Do not, however, merely copy the proposal. Use only those parts that are relevant, and write in a style that is appropriate for a final report.

The report headings need not contain the words "introduction" or "problem." Indeed, descriptive headings, such as those used in Illustration 14-2, may increase reader interest.

FINDINGS

The presentation and discussion of findings comprise the major portion of the report. In this section you must present a complete and clear analysis of all data. For coherence, the final paragraph of the introduction or the first paragraph of the findings section should contain a preview of how this section will be organized.

The report need not contain an actual heading called "Findings." Instead, coherence should be achieved through descriptive or talking headings and subheadings that provide clues about the information in each section and lead the reader through the analysis. Use your outline as a guide to ensure that your presentation is complete and organized logically.

The following headings were used in a report entitled "Don't Panic Over Delhi's Deficit."[2] Notice that the headings concisely summarize the content of each major division.

- Is a Revenue Deficit Harmful?
- A Benign Rise
- Setting Realistic Goals
- Focus on the Primary Deficit

SUMMARY

Information and analytical reports should always contain an overall summary of the findings. When the analysis is lengthy and complex, you should also summarize your discussion of the findings at the end of each major section. For an information report written in inductive structure, the summary marks the conclusion of the report. In an analytical report, the summary may occupy a separate section, as is shown in Illustration 14-2, page 374 or may be included in a section with the conclusions and recommendations.

CONCLUSIONS AND RECOMMENDATIONS

When analytical reports are written in inductive structure, the conclusions and recommendations constitute the final section or sections of the report (Illustration 14-2, pages 374–375). However, if the reader's preference or likely reaction justifies your using the deductive structure, recommendations and conclusions may be presented at the beginning of the report. The opening pages of a report presented in that manner are shown in Illustration 14-4.

Conclusions must be logical inferences supported by the data analysis. Recommendations propose actions that are justified by the analysis and conclusions; recommendations may also suggest other research that should be undertaken.

Recommendations are most meaningful when they are related to the stated purpose of the study. Notice, for example, the relationship of the purpose, conclusion, and recommendation in the following example.

Purpose. ...to provide information that would help the Hatfield-McCoy Mountains Coalition promote the area more effectively to resident and nonresident tourists.

Conclusion. Tourists' knowledge of and interest in the area is too low. Confusion within and among some of the state's official tourist publications does little to stimulate interest in the area.

Recommendation. Promote the state parks in the region ....Do not depend on the state to provide adequate publicity about the region's state parks.

Present all information to support the conclusions and recommendations in the data analysis sections. Some writers, perhaps in a mistaken attempt to compose a dramatic ending to the report, introduce new data with the conclusions or recommendations. That practice tends to confuse the reader and destroys report coherence. For example, in the tourism study (Illustration 14-2), a writer might be tempted to withhold the information about coverage of the region in the West Virginia official tourist guide. Such a writer might think that the information would give final, solid justification for the conclusion. However, since the data about coverage in the guide is closely related to tourists' perceptions of the region, it should be—and was—included as part of that analysis.

The conclusions and recommendations indicate completion of the analysis, but some situations warrant use of supplements, which provide supporting information.

Report Supplements

The supplements to a report include any information that may be useful—but not essential—for understanding the analysis, conclusions, and recommendations. Supplements may include endnotes, a bibliography or source list, a glossary, an appendix, and an index.

Source List

A reference list must be included when you decide to group specific source citations at the end of the report instead of using footnotes. Include in the list all sources that contributed data for the study. (See Illustration 14-2, page 376.) Illustration 14-2 also demonstrates how to use in-text citations when you want to acknowledge specific sources within the text. (In the illustrated report, see pages 3, 4, 6, and 10.)

Glossary

A glossary—list of selected words with their meanings—is required only when the report contains terms that may be unfamiliar to some readers. (See Illustration 14-2, page 377.) Including a glossary is advisable when the readership consists of some persons who know the technical terminology and others who do not. That practice provides definitions for readers who need them without cluttering the report with information that is unnecessary for many readers. If the report contains few technical or unfamiliar terms, those terms may be included in the introductory section of the report.

APPENDIX

An appendix includes all items referred to but not displayed in the report body. Similarly, all items displayed in the appendix *must* be identified at some point in the report. Do not use the appendix to "share" interesting but nonessential information. Materials often displayed in an appendix include copies of interview guides (Illustration 14-2, pages 378–379) and questionnaires, tabulations of data (Illustration 14-2, pages 380–382), statistical formulas, graphs, charts, and diagrams. Remember, however, that visual aids intended to clarify, emphasize, or summarize parts of the report should be incorporated into the report narrative unless you are specifically requested to group them in an appendix. See pages 5, 6, 7, and 10 of the illustrated report for effective ways to incorporate figures and tables into the report narrative.

INDEX

An index is a list of key words or topics found in the report. Generally an index is included only if the reader would not be able to locate specific information without that aid. In most situations, a comprehensive table of contents along with clear, concise division headings should be sufficient to direct the reader to specific topics.

The parts for a formal business report should be adapted to meet your specific reporting requirements. Be mindful of your audience, and include all parts that will assist your readers. For example, when you must prepare an information report, you would include all parts except the conclusions and recommendations. In some contexts the report summary may be included in the transmittal message, eliminating the need for a separate executive summary. As you select parts to include in your report, remember that your objectives are to establish rapport with report readers, stimulate interest in the report, and facilitate its use. Include all parts that will help you achieve those objectives.

FORMATTING GUIDES

Lengthy information and analytical reports are most frequently prepared in manuscript format. As you prepare your manuscript, attempt to determine your reader's preference for margins, spacing, headings, and pagination. One way to determine a reader's preference is to ask; another way is to look in the company files to find examples of report styles in use. Some companies and government agencies issue style manuals to their employees and require that all reports follow the approved formats. Some writers find that templates included in word processing software are useful; other writers think those templates give a "canned" look. If you use a template, select one that complements the overall tone and style of the report.

If you cannot determine preferences of a specific reader, use the following formatting guides.

Margins and Spacing

Top, bottom, and side margins should contribute to the appearance and readability of the report. A guide for business report margins appears in Illustration 14-5, page 386.

Although some readers may prefer double-spaced manuscripts, most contemporary business reports are printed in single-spaced, block format. That format is efficient to produce and is attractive to most readers. Whenever you use single spacing, use double spacing (an additional stroke on the Enter key) between paragraphs. The three report templates included in the student/teacher edition of *Microsoft Word* demonstrate effective single-spaced formats. Those templates can be modified slightly to satisfy and simplify your formatting requirements.

Headings

Whether you use a single- or double-spaced format, you should use appropriate division headings to guide the reader through your report. The type style (capitalized, lowercase, bold, underlined, italicized) and placement of the headings must accurately reflect the organization of your report.

Style manuals differ slightly in their guides for style and placement of headings. Some manuals recommend typing the title in all capital letters; others (such as the *MLA Handbook for Writers of Research Papers*[3] and the *Publication Manual of the American Psychological Association*[4] recommend capitalizing only the major words in the title. Although many reference manuals suggest that the title be centered on the first page, effective variations of title placement are shown in the *Microsoft Word* templates.

The American Psychological Association (APA) uses the following scheme to indicate division levels in a report.[5] When a report has fewer than five levels of headings, APA recommends that the centered uppercase heading not be used. Levels 1, 2, 3, and 4 would then be typed as they are shown for Levels 2, 3, 4, and 5 in this example.

LEVEL 1: CENTERED UPPERCASE HEADING

Level 2: Centered Uppercase and Lowercase Heading

Level 3: *Centered, Italicized, Uppercase and Lowercase Heading*

Level 4: *Flush Left, Italicized, Uppercase and Lowercase Side Heading*

Level 5: *Indented, italicized, lowercase paragraph heading ending with a period.*

When the entire report is prepared in block format, all headings except the centered title on the first page should begin at the left margin. Most document designers recommend that you not underline headings because underlining can impair readability. Instead of underlining, headings may be distinguished from the report text and from one another by variations in font style. The following system is used in Illustration 14-2.

TITLE: CENTERED UPPERCASE, BOLD, SANS SERIF TYPE

Level 1. **Uppercase and Lowercase Heading at Margin, Bold, Sans Serif Type**

Level 2. Uppercase and Lowercase Headings at Margin, Bold, Serif Type

Level 3. **Lowercase paragraph heading ending with a period, bold, serif type.**

Level 4. *Lowercase paragraph heading ending with a period, bold, italics, serif type.*

If you have access to a color printer, you can also use colors to differentiate levels of headings.

Pagination

Traditionally, each of the preliminary parts begins on a new page. One exception to that practice concerns the list of tables or figures. If that list is short and space permits, you may place it on the last page of the table of contents. The preliminary pages are generally numbered with lowercase Roman numerals, centered about one inch from the bottom of the pages. Use the following numbering system for preliminary pages:

Flyleaf, if used	No number
Title page	Page i, but no numeral is printed on that page
First page after title page	Page ii
Subsequent preliminary pages	Page iii, etc.

The report body and report supplements are numbered consecutively with Arabic numerals. The numeral 1 is usually omitted from the first page of the report body. If your report is printed one side of each sheet, place numerals for subsequent pages about one-half inch from the top, flush with the right margin; centered, about one inch from the bottom of each page; or flush with the right margin, about one inch from the bottom of the page. If you use two-sided printing, the first page of the report body (after preliminary parts) should be on a right-hand page, with no number printed. Numbers for subsequent odd-numbered pages are on the right side of the page; even numbered pages, on the left side. The pagination feature of your word processing software will give you consistent placement of page numbers.

ETHICAL CONSIDERATIONS

As you finalize a comprehensive report, review the comments about ethical considerations presented in previous chapters. For example, have you verified the need for the research? Have you reported all relevant data? Have you avoided manipulative language? Have you honored the privacy, accuracy, and ownership guides related to data sources? Have you honored your commitments to survey participants to maintain confidentiality? Have you avoided distortion of data in your visual aids? A final question might well be: Does this report represent your best effort to convey information that will promote the good of others as you remain true to your own values and ideals?

SUMMARY

Formal business reports often contain parts that do not appear in less formal reports. The preliminary parts of a formal report should set the stage for the report and enable the reader to access the information easily. The report body must be a complete document that presents all details of the study, from its introduction to its conclusions and recommendations, if those are included. Report supplements may be added to provide additional information that will be of interest to some readers.

Following format guides consistently will contribute to the readability and coherence of your report. Always evaluate templates provided by software manufacturers to determine whether they meet your format standards. If they do, or if you can modify them easily to meet your needs, those templates can simplify the mechanics of formatting a report.

K-F Research Associates, LLP   456 Capitol Way   Phone: 888.888.8888
                                    Charleston, WV 25301   Fax: 123.456.7890

INCREASING TOURISM IN THE HATFIELD-McCOY MOUNTAINS REGION OF WEST VIRGINIA

ILLUSTRATION 14-2 CONTINUED

INCREASING TOURISM IN THE
HATFIELD-McCOY MOUNTAINS REGION
OF WEST VIRGINIA

Prepared for—

Hatfield-McCoy Mountains Coalition
123 Main Street
Chapmanville, WV 25508

Prepared by—

K-F Research Associates, LLP
456 Capitol Way
Charleston, WV 25301

September 1, 2005

ILLUSTRATION 14-2 CONTINUED

K-F Research Associates, LLP   456 Capitol Way   Phone: 888.888.8888
                                   Charleston, WV 25301   Fax: 123.456.7890

September 1, 2005

Ms. Mary Ann Conrad
Hatfield-McCoy Mountains Coalition
123 Main Street
Chapmanville, WV 25508

TOURISM IN THE HATFIELD-McCOY MOUNTAINS REGION

This report is the result of our meeting on June 1 during which you discussed your desire to increase tourism in the Hatfield-McCoy Mountains region. After reviewing my proposal, you authorized K-F Research Associates to conduct a study of tourism in West Virginia and tourists' perceptions of your region. The study focused on ways to increase tourism in the Hatfield-McCoy Mountains region.

Data were gathered from official publications of the West Virginia Division of Tourism and from interviews with 200 visitors to tourist attractions in the Metro Valley and New River-Greenbrier regions. The study shows that you must actively promote your area and try to upgrade its lodging and eating establishments. Supporting details are included in this report.

My researchers and I have enjoyed working with you on this project. If you have any questions about the study, or if you need other market research, please contact me.

Arlene W. Sherman

DIRECTOR OF RESEARCH

ILLUSTRATION 14-2 CONTINUED

TABLE OF CONTENTS

ILLUSTRATION 14-2 CONTINUED

LIST OF ILLUSTRATIONS

Tables

Figures

ILLUSTRATION 14-2 ▸ CONTINUED

EXECUTIVE SUMMARY

K-F Research Associates makes the following recommendations for increasing tourism in the Hatfield-McCoy Mountains region:

1. Develop a radio campaign to promote the region and air it in cities that are within 100 miles of the region, both in West Virginia and in adjoining states. The promotional messages should be short, attention-getting spots that focus on specific attractions as desirable destinations for a one-day or weekend trip.

2. Promote the state parks in the region, particularly to day trippers and campers. Do not depend on the state's Division of Tourism to provide adequate publicity about the facilities and activities available in the region's state parks.

3. Work with merchants in the area to persuade them to advertise more heavily in the state's official tourism guide, thereby giving the region more visibility among potential tourists who study the guide.

4. Work with the Chambers of Commerce in the area to attract a mid- to high-end hotel with restaurant to the area, preferably near its center. Such a facility could be attractive to higher-end travelers who do not want to camp out or sleep in a motel with limited amenities.

5. Try to obtain a matching-funds grant from the Division of Tourism to help defray costs of the promotional campaign.

Visitors to tourist attractions in the Metro Valley and New River-Greenbrier regions, all within 70 miles of the Hatfield-McCoy Mountains region, demonstrated interests that can be satisfied in this region. Yet those tourists have little knowledge of the area and seemed to have little interest in it. Moreover, tourists have a distinctly negative attitude about the quality of eating and sleeping establishments in the area. The Division of Tourism website and official publications do not clearly and consistently define the area and highlight its attractions. Inconsistent presentation of the area likely contributes to the lack of interest in the Hatfield-McCoy Mountains region.

The objective of this study was to provide information that would assist the Hatfield-McCoy Mountains Coalition in its efforts to attract more tourists to its region. Three factors were analyzed:

1. What is the current impact of tourism in the Hatfield-McCoy Mountains region?

2. What kinds of tourists visit nearby areas of the state?

3. What are those visitors' perceptions of the Hatfield-McCoy Mountains region?

The conclusions and recommendations are based on data obtained from the Division of Tourism and 200 tourists interviewed at attractions in adjacent tourist regions.

v

ILLUSTRATION 14-2 ▶ CONTINUED

INCREASING TOURISM IN
THE HATFIELD-McCOY MOUNTAINS REGION
OF WEST VIRGINIA

The Hatfield-McCoy Mountains of West Virginia abound in historical and recreational interest. Yet merchants of the region have expressed concern that tourists are not aware of the many vacation or weekend activities the region offers. The state's 2005 official travel guide shows the state divided into nine regions, one of which is the Hatfield-McCoy Mountains. Yet other official publications show the state divided into eight regions, with the five counties that comprise the Hatfield-McCoy Mountains region included in the Metro Valley region. In fact, a potential tourist who is browsing the website of the West Virginia Division of Tourism will find information about the region only by "stumbling" on it while visiting various links within that site. Such inconsistency in state publications could well distract from the region as tourists plan vacations, weekend getaways, or day trips.

The Hatfield-McCoy Mountain region is located in southern West Virginia. Chapmanville, which marks the center of the region, is approximately 40 miles southwest of Charleston and southeast of Huntington. The area is easily accessible by Interstate 40 and U.S. 119.

The Hatfield-McCoy Mountains Coalition (HMCMC) wants to capture a larger share of West Virginia's tourist trade. HMCMC asked K-F Research Associates, LLP, to determine what the Coalition should do to increase tourism in its area.

Determining Tourists' Perceptions of the Hatfield-McCoy Mountains Region

The research problem was to determine tourists' current perceptions of the Hatfield-McCoy Mountains region and identify ways to increase tourist visits to the regions.

Scope of Analysis

Three factors were analyzed:

1. What is the current impact of tourism in the Hatfield-McCoy Mountains region?

2. What kinds of tourists visit nearby areas of the state?

3. What are those visitors' perceptions of the Hatfield-McCoy Mountains region?

ILLUSTRATION 14-2 CONTINUED

2

Purpose of the Study

The objective of the study was to provide information that would help the Hatfield-McCoy Mountains Coalition promote the area more effectively to resident and nonresident tourists.

Definitions

For this study, a tourist is defined as an individual who travels at least 50 miles one way to a West Virginia destination, other than for commuting to or from a place of employment. The traveler may be a West Virginia resident or a nonresident. Appendix B contains additional definitions that may contribute to understanding the findings.

Methodology

K-F Research Associates used both secondary and primary data to meet the objective of the study.

Secondary data. Secondary sources were limited to official publications of the West Virginia Division of Tourism. These sources suggested content for an interview guide and a checklist used in the study. Secondary sources also provided benchmarks for data analysis and information about two adjoining regions of the state. That information was helpful in analyzing differences among the regions and in formulating recommendations.

Primary data. Primary data were acquired from tourists currently visiting the Metro Valley region and the New River-Greenbrier Valley region of West Virginia. These regions were chosen because they are contiguous to the Hatfield-McCoy Mountains region.

Site selection. The researchers thought that the most reliable comparisons could be made if tourists in the general vicinity of the study area were interviewed. Therefore, all sites selected were within a 70-mile radius of Chapmanville, the approximate center of the Hatfield-McCoy Mountains region. To allow comparisons among similar and dissimilar tourist attractions, an attempt was made to select some sites that are unique to each region and others that are similar to Hatfield-McCoy attractions. Based on those criteria, the following sites were selected.

Metro Valley

- Capitol Market, Charleston
- Clay Center for the Arts and Sciences, Charleston
- Rail excursion to the New River Gorge, out of Huntington
- Jazz-MU-Tazz festival at Marshall University, Huntington
- Tu-Endie-Wei State Park, northeast of Huntington
- Booker T. Washington Memorial, Malden

ILLUSTRATION 14-2 CONTINUED

3

- Cabin Creek Quilts, Malden
- Tri-State Racetrack and Gaming Center, Nitro
- Jenkins Plantation Museum, Lesage
- Blenko Glass Company, Milton

New River-Greenbrier Valley

- Camp Washington-Carver, Clifftop
- Glade Creek Gristmill, Babcock State Park, Clifftop
- Canyon Rim Culture Center, Fayetteville
- New River Gorge National River Visitors Center, Fayetteville
- Daniels Winery, Crab Orchard
- Twin Falls Resort State Park, Mullens
- Coal Heritage Interpretive Center, Bramwell
- Historic Bramwell
- Rivers Whitewater Rafting Resort, Lansing
- History in Our Mountains Museum, Welch

The sample. A purposive quota sampling technique was used. An earlier study of West Virginia tourism (Shifflet, 2001) had reported that 33.2 percent of West Virginia tourists in 2000 were age 18–34; 41.3 percent, age 35–54; and 25.5 percent, age 55 or older. Those age ranges (roughly defined as Gen-X, Baby Boomer, and Senior) and percentages were used to stratify the sample. At each location, 10 interviews were conducted: three with Gen-Xers; five with Baby Boomers; and two with Seniors. This yielded a total of 200 interviews.

Interview technique. Two college students were trained by a K-F staff researcher to conduct the interviews at the 20 sites, alternating days between the two regions. For example, on Day 1, Interviewer 1 randomly selected a site from the Metro Valley region; Interviewer 2, from the New River-Greenbrier region. On Day 2, they switched regions and randomly selected a site from those remaining. This practice continued for 10 days, July 4–13, inclusive. This time period was chosen because it contained a national holiday and a weekend, thereby granting exposure to a broad range of tourists.

Interviewers were instructed to approach adults who seemed to be resting or waiting in an area frequented by tourists. The delimitation that tourists should be resting or waiting was applied because it was thought that such tourists would be more likely to participate in an interview than would those who were actively engaged in or walking toward an activity or attraction.

After greeting the potential interviewee, giving a brief description of the interview, and determining willingness to participate, the interviewer asked two qualifying questions. The first determined whether the potential interviewee was a tourist as defined in this study. The second determined if the person was within the age range of a stratum in the sample whose quota had not been satisfied.

ILLUSTRATION 14-2 CONTINUED

4

If both qualifications were met, the interview continued. This process continued until the quota was met at each location. (Appendix A contains a copy of the interview guide and the checklist each interviewee completed after answering the last question.)

Data analysis. At the end of each day, a K-F associate entered the data into a spreadsheet. Upon completion of the 10 days of interviews, summary statistics were computed.

Delimitations and Limitations

The following delimitations were put on the study.

- Interviews were confined to 20 sites that tend to attract tourists.

- The interviews were restricted to a 10-day period in July.

The following limitations of the study must be acknowledged.

- Tourists in other regions of the state may have different perceptions of the Hatfield-McCoy Mountains region.

- Tourists traveling at another time of year may have different perceptions of that region.

The remainder of this report summarizes some previous research about the economic impact of tourism in West Virginia and the Hatfield-McCoy Mountains region, a profile of the participants in this study, and their perceptions of the Hatfield-McCoy Mountains region as a tourist destination. The report ends with conclusions and recommendations for improving the tourist industry in that region.

Current Impact of Tourism on West Virginia and the Hatfield-McCoy Mountains Region

A study by Dean Runyan Associates (2005) showed that West Virginia received $3.4 billion in travel-generated spending in 2004, up 54.5 percent from $2.2 billion in 2000. The 2004 spending equates to $9.3 million per day. In some regions of the state, tourism is the primary source of earnings and employment.

Approximately 63 percent of tourist dollars ($2.1 billion) were spent on gaming, ground transportation, and food and beverage service. (See Figure 1, p. 5.) Within regions, however, the distribution of expenditures looks considerably different. (See Table 1, p. 5.) Two facts stand out from a study of regional spending:

- The regions that have gaming facilities harvest more tourism dollars than do other regions.

- The Hatfield-McCoy Mountains region garners the smallest share of West Virginia's tourism revenue.

ILLUSTRATION 14-2 ▶ CONTINUED

5

Figure 1. West Virginia Travel Spending, 2004 ($Millions)

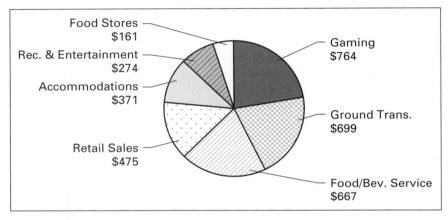

Food Stores $161
Rec. & Entertainment $274
Accommodations $371
Retail Sales $475
Gaming $764
Ground Trans. $699
Food/Bev. Service $667

Source: Dean Runyan Associates, p. 8.

Table 1. West Virginia Tourism Spending, by Region, 2004 ($Million)

Region / Category	Hotel and Motel B&B	Food/ Bev. Serv.	Food Store	Gaming	Grnd. Trans/ Motor Fuel	Rec. Arts, Ent.	Retail Sales	Total
Northern Panhandle	29.5	154.2	31.1	417.7	55.1	16.3	95.9	799.8
Eastern Panhandle	29.7	121.7	26.8	300.1	44.1	19.4	78.6	620.4
Metro Valley	71.8	105.5	22.0	45.8	199.2	47.5	76.3	568.1
New River-Greenbrier	109.6	110.1	26.2	0.0	123.8	91.8	80.5	542.0
Mountaineer Country	38.9	54.3	13.5	0.0	75.5	28.7	42.3	253.2
Potomac Highlands	51.9	50.7	20.2	0.0	42.0	32.6	40.9	238.3
Mid-Ohio Valley	17.2	28.0	7.7	0.0	51.1	15.0	22.8	141.8
Mountain Lakes	18.8	23.3	8.5	0.0	51.2	14.0	19.3	135.1
Hatfield-McCoy Moutains	3.5	18.8	4.9	0.0	56.9	9.2	16.7	110.0
Total	**370.9**	**666.6**	**160.9**	**763.6**	**698.9**	**274.5**	**473.3**	**3,408.7**

Source: Dean Runyan Associates, pp. 16–25.

ILLUSTRATION 14-2 ▸ CONTINUED

6

Especially disconcerting is the low volume of tourist spending for accommodations, food service, and recreation/arts/entertainment. Although rich in history and recreational opportunities, the Hatfield-McCoy region received fewer tourist dollars from those categories than did any other region.

The number of jobs created by tourism is also a significant measure of economic impact. (See Table 2.) In terms of jobs created, the regions ranked in the same order as on the measure of tourist spending, with the exception of the Eastern Panhandle and New River-Greenbrier Valley regions, which switched positions. Again, the Hatfield-McCoy region scored lower than all other regions on this measure, garnering fewer than 3 percent of tourism-related jobs.

Table 2. Direct Employment Generated by Tourism in West Virginia, 2004

Region	Number of Employees
Northern Panhandle	8,280
Metro Valley	6,940
New River-Greenbrier Valley	6,750
Eastern Panhandle	6,330
Potomac Highlands	3,830
Mountaineer Country	3,730
Mid-Ohio Valleys	1,890
Mountain Lakes	1,850
Hatfield-McCoy Mountains	1,190
Total Direct Employment	40,780

Source: Dean Runyan Associates, pp. 16–25.

The Dean Runyan study revealed interesting facts about the total impact of tourism on the state. Another study focusing on day travelers (Longwoods International, 2004) provides insights into a market segment that could prove to be especially profitable for the Hatfield-McCoy Mountains region. Day travelers are West Virginia residents and nonresidents who travel at least 50 miles to a tourist destination but do not include an overnight stay.

The Longwoods study estimated that 39.8 million day trips were taken to and in West Virginia in 2003, 61 percent of which were marketable trips (that is, not for business or to visit friends and relatives.) Those marketable pleasure trips brought in $1.8 billion, or $74.01 per person, in West Virginia that year (Longwoods, pp. 7–17). The Runyan report (p. 10) listed total direct spending by tourists in 2003 at $3.1 billion. So day travelers who came strictly for pleasure accounted for almost 58 percent of that year's tourism spending in the state.

ILLUSTRATION 14-2 ▶ CONTINUED

7

Eighty-four percent (84%) of day visitors were nonresidents; over 50 percent were from West Virginia or from states adjoining or near to the Hatfield-McCoy region. (See Figure 2, left half of chart.)

Figure 2. Origins of Day Trips, 2003

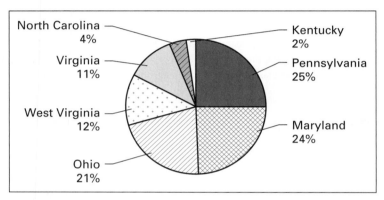

Source: Longwoods, p. 20.

Most day travelers (75%) were influenced to visit West Virginia by previous personal experience or advice from friends and relatives. (See Figure 3.)

Figure 3. Information Sources for Day Tourists, 2003

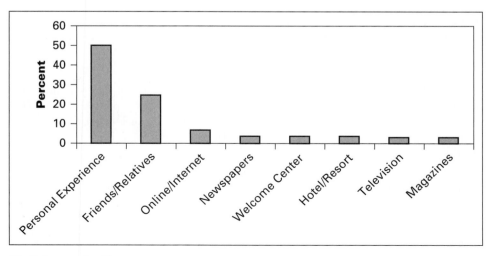

Source: Longwoods, p. 37.

ILLUSTRATION 14-2 CONTINUED

8

Information from the Internet, print media, television, welcome centers, and hotels had minimal impact on day travelers' decisions to visit a West Virginia destination. Of additional interest is the fact that the majority of the trips were planned on short notice: 50 percent within a week of the trip and 20 percent on the day of the trip. Touring attracted 25 percent of day visitors; outdoor activities, 14 percent (Longwoods, pp. 35, 9).

The success of some regions in attracting tourists may be the result of grants offered by the Division of Tourism. The Division offers matching grants of $2,500, $5,000, and $10,000 for development and promotion of tourist-related activities. (See www.wvtourism.com) Although no data were available to indicate the distribution of grant money in previous years, the program has been set up specifically to support advertising that promotes tourism in West Virginia.

What We Learned by Interviewing Tourists

Interviews with 200 visitors (97 males and 103 females) at 20 tourist sites in the Metro Valley and New River-Greenbrier regions yielded data that can help the HMCMC market that region of the state. The findings most relevant to the Coalition in its efforts to promote the region are why travelers visited West Virginia, other West Virginia sites visited on this trip, and the tourists' perceptions of the Hatfield-McCoy Mountains region. (Detailed data are shown in Appendix C.)

Why They Visited West Virginia

The major reasons tourists came to West Virginia were family vacation (48%) and weekend getaway (50%). The major reason given for visiting the specific site at which the tourists were interviewed was that the attraction had been recommended by family or friends (48.7%). The second most frequently cited reason for the visit was an interest in the history and culture of the region (17.3%). Interestingly, nearly 15 percent of the interviewees had chosen to return to the site after having visited it on a previous trip.

Short stays tended to dominate this tourist market. Eighteen percent (18%) of respondents were day tourists, and 38 percent were visiting for 1–3 days. The majority of individuals in the 1–3-day category (69% of that group) indicated they were on weekend getaways, which often include only one or two overnights. Short-term trips accounted for 56 percent of the tourists, compared with 41 percent who planned to stay in West Virginia for 4–7 days, primarily as a personal or family vacation.

Commercial lodging and eating establishments garnered a substantial amount of business from the tourists interviewed in this study. During their stays, the tourists ate most of their meals in commercial restaurants (70%); the second most frequented eating place was a campground (27%). Those who spent one or more nights in West Virginia tended to favor hotel/motel/bed & breakfast lodging

ILLUSTRATION 14-2 ▸ CONTINUED

9

(43%); but campers (27%) and those who rented cabins in state parks (13%) together nearly matched the number who used commercial lodging.

The major activities visitors to the Metro Valley and New River-Greenbrier areas had participated in or planned to take part in were similar to the major attractions to be enjoyed in the Hatfield-McCoy Mountains region. General sightseeing (34%), visiting historical sites (26%), and camping/hiking (16%) were the most frequently mentioned activities. Although gaming is the biggest draw for tourism as a whole in West Virginia, it was not a highly popular activity among the participants in this study.

Other West Virginia Sites They Visited

The interviewees cited many other attractions they planned to visit or had visited. When classified by region, locations in New River-Greenbrier received the most mentions (196), ahead of Metro Valley (140).

Sites in the Hatfield-McCoy Mountains region were mentioned 61 times; that is, 15 percent of sites on these tourists' itineraries were in the Hatfield-McCoy Mountains region. Nearly 27% of interviewees were familiar with the region, yet a far smaller percentage included it on the current trip.

Their Perceptions of the Hatfield-McCoy Mountains Region

On the positive side, 55 percent of the respondents perceived the Hatfield-McCoy Mountains region to be an interesting area of the state. However, that "interesting" aspect seems to be associated primarily with the Hatfield-McCoy feud (95.5%) and the concept of mountaineer pride (54.5%). A majority of respondents perceived the region to be an economically depressed (68.1%) coal-mining (59%) region, in which miners at one time rebelled against mine owners (50%). (See Table 3, p. 10.)

Travelers who have visited or plan to visit the area are obviously much more aware of some of its historical and natural attractions. Those respondents were primarily responsible for the 30 percent to 45 percent awareness of the area's beautiful scenery; hiking, camping, hunting and fishing opportunities; and trails for ATVs, motorcycles, and mountain bikes. They more than other interviewees registered awareness of some of the history and culture associated with the region (items showing less than 30% awareness).

An unsettling fact is that no interviewee associated good restaurants and overnight accommodations with the region. In addition, no interviewees were aware of the availability of three popular forms of recreation or entertainment in the region: golf, auto racing, and festival attendance.

Such perceptions may be justified. The Hatfield-McCoy Mountains section of West Virginia's official tourist guide for 2005 shows advertisements for one bed and breakfast, two small inns, and five motels, all of which could be rated as low- to medium-priced facilities (West Virginia Department of Tourism, 2005). Only one area restaurant, Cow Shed, advertises in the guide. The

ILLUSTRATION 14-2 ▶ CONTINUED

10

perceptions of eating and sleeping facilities appear to be accurate; at least they are not contradicted by the tourist guide.

The Hatfield-McCoy Trail system and various historical monuments and sites are featured in the area's section of the West Virginia guide. In total, however, the guide devotes only 12 pages to the Hatfield-McCoy Mountains region compared with 22 and 32 pages respectively to the Metro Valley and New River-Greenbrier regions.

Table 3. Tourists' Perceptions of Hatfield-McCoy Mountains Region, July 2005

Prompt	Percent of Respondents Who Associated Prompt with Hatfield-McCoy Mountains
A family feud long ago	96
An economically depressed region	68
Coal mining region	59
Mountaineer pride	55
An interesting area of the state	55
Coal Mine Wars	50
Beautiful scenery	45
Good hiking	41
Camping in state park	36
Good hunting and fishing	36
Trails for ATVs, motorcycles, bikes	35
Whitewater rafting	35
Cabins in state park	34
Museums	30
A building made entirely of coal	27
Chief Logan	25
Outdoor drama about a Shawnee princess	25
Historical monuments	23
Chuck Yeager	20
Golf	0
Auto races	0
Festivals	0
Good hotels	0
Good restaurants	0

Source: Primary

ILLUSTRATION 14-2 ▶ CONTINUED

11

Summary

Tourism has a significant impact on the economy of West Virginia, generating more than $3 billion in annual revenues and creating nearly 41,000 jobs. The Hatfield-McCoy Mountains region enjoys about 3 percent of revenues and less than 3 percent of the jobs attributed to tourism.

Day tourism is an especially strong segment of the tourism market, with most of such visitors planning their trips no more than a week in advance. Their previous experiences in West Virginia or recommendations of family and friends are the primary motivators that bring them to the state. Major activities of West Virginia's day tourists are touring (sightseeing) and outdoor activities.

A majority of visitors interviewed for this study were in West Virginia on a day or weekend trip. Tourists visiting areas adjacent to the Hatfield-McCoy Mountains region showed strong interest in the history and culture of those regions, and the number who spent overnight at campsites or in a state park cabin was nearly equal to the number who used commercial lodging. The major activities they participated in were general sightseeing, visiting historical sites, and camping/hiking.

Although the interviewees perceived the Hatfield-McCoy Mountains region to be interesting, and more than 25 percent were aware of the region, fewer than 15 percent of the attractions this group included on their travel agendas were in that region. In general, the interviewees demonstrated low awareness of the region's attractions.

Conclusions

Visitors to tourist areas adjacent to the Hatfield-McCoy Mountains region demonstrated interests that can be satisfied in this region. The scenic beauty, state parks, historic sites, and museums located in the Hatfield-McCoy region should be attractive to visitors who spend a day touring an area. The state parks, wildlife management areas, and Hatfield-McCoy Trail system should be attractive to visitors who want to spend a day or more hunting, fishing, hiking, or biking.

Tourists' knowledge of and interest in the area are too low. Confusion within and among some of the state's official tourism publications does little to stimulate interest in the area and may even distract from it. The relatively low number of pages in the official tourism guide does not present the area as a thriving, vibrant, "must see" region.

Until the area is able to improve its dining and overnight facilities, it would be wise to focus on day travelers and campers. These are highly fertile sectors of the tourism market and ones that should be amenable to exploring a new region of the state.

ILLUSTRATION 14-2 CONTINUED

12

Recommendations

K-F Research Associates recommends that the Hatfield-McCoy Mountains Coalition do the following to stimulate tourism in the region.

1. Develop a radio campaign to promote the region and air it during commuting hours in cities that are within 100 miles of the region, both in West Virginia and adjoining states. The promotional messages should be short, attention-getting spots that focus on specific attractions as desirable destinations for a one-day or weekend trip. Airing such spots during commuting time may stimulate commuters to think about the area as a possible getaway destination.

2. Promote the state parks in the region. Such parks are generally popular with short-term visitors and campers. Developing promotional materials that highlight the parks' attractions and associating them with the larger region should draw more tourists to them. The spillover effect would be to draw attention to nearby historical and recreational attractions. Do not depend on the state to give adequate publicity about the facilities and activities available in the region's state parks.

3. Work with merchants in the area to persuade them to advertise more heavily in the state's official tourism guide. Giving potential tourists more information about the area and making them more aware of the touring and recreational options—such as whitewater rafting, hunting, fishing, trail riding—should increase interest in the area and improve its image.

4. Work with the Chambers of Commerce in the area to attract a mid- to high-end hotel with restaurant to the area, preferably near its center. Chapmanville, which is near the Chief Logan State Park and on U.S. Highway 119, appears to be an ideal location for such a facility. It would be less than an hour's drive from any of the region's tourist sites and could be attractive to higher-end travelers who do not want to camp out or sleep in a motel with limited amenities.

5. Apply for one or more grants from the Division of Tourism to defray part of the costs of the promotional campaign.

ILLUSTRATION 14-2 CONTINUED

13

REFERENCES

Longwoods International (2004). *West Virginia 2003 day trip study.* Available at
http://wvtourism.com

Runyan, Dean Associates (2005). *Economic impact of travel on West Virginia.* Available at
http://wvtourism.com

Shifflet, D. K. & Associates Ltd. (2001). *2000 year end West Virginia overnight leisure travel report.* Available at http://wvtourism.com

West Virginia Division of Tourism (2005). *West Virginia Wild and Wonderful, 2005 Official State
Travel Guide.* South Charleston, WV: Author.

ILLUSTRATION 14-2 CONTINUED

14

Appendix A. Glossary

The following definitions are helpful in understanding the findings of this report.

Accommodation – Spending for lodging by hotel, motel, and bed/breakfast guests, campers, and vacation home users.

Day visitor – A state resident or out-of-state traveler whose West Virginia trip does not include an overnight stay.

Food/beverage services – Table service restaurants, fast-food outlets, and refreshment stands that sell food and beverages for immediate consumption, on or off the premises.

Food stores – Grocery stores, fruit stands, retail bakeries, etc., selling food for consumption off the premises.

Gaming – Revenue generated on wagering at racetracks, via video games and lotteries, and any other publicly approved wagering schemes.

Ground transport – Spending on car rental; gasoline and other vehicle operating expenses; and local transportation, such as taxi, bus, and train.

Recreation – Spending on amusement and recreation, such as admissions to tourist attractions, entertainment venues, and outdoor recreation areas.

Retail sales – Spending for gifts, souvenirs, and other items, excluding spending for food or recreation.

Tourist – Any individual who has traveled a minimum of 50 miles one way from her or his home to visit a site in West Virginia. A tourist may be a West Virginia resident or a nonresident.

Travel spending – Spending by travelers at or near their destinations.

ILLUSTRATION 14-2 ▶ CONTINUED

15

Appendix B. Interview Guide

Perceptions of Hatfield-McCoy Mountains Region

Interview Guide

Location of interview _____

Date of interview _____ Interviewer's initials _____

INSTRUCTIONS: Approach an individual who is seated or standing at a rest or waiting area in the tourist area in which you are conducting the survey. After greeting the individual, explain the study briefly (for example, "I'm trying to find out what people know about one of West Virginia's tourist attractions."). Ask if he or she will answer a few questions about tourism in West Virginia.

- If the person does not want to participate in the interview, offer one of our Hatfield-McCoy brochures and end the conversation cordially.

- If the person agrees, say: Do you live at least 50 miles from this site? (If not, explain that we need participants who have traveled at least 50 miles to reach the site. Offer one of our H/McCoy brochures and end the conversation cordially. If yes, continue.)

- We are trying to stratify our sample by age. Into what age range do you fit?
  18–34 _____   35–54 _____   55+ _____

- Indicate the participant's sex: Male _____ Female _____

QUESTIONS

1. **What is the primary reason for your trip to this location?**
   Family/individual vacation _____
   Weekend getaway _____
   Business trip _____
   Visiting friends _____
   Other_____

2. **Have you visited this area before?**
   Yes _____   How often within the past three years? _____
   No _____

3. **Why did you choose to visit this area? (More than one answer may be given.)**
   Recommended by family or friend _____
   Recommended by travel agent _____
   Required for business _____
   Responded to advertising _____
   Interested in history and culture of area _____

ILLUSTRATION 14-2   CONTINUED

16

4. **What other areas of West Virginia have you visited on this trip?**
   None _____
   Record areas cited.

5. **How many nights have you spent/or plan to spend in West Virginia?**
   None   _____
   1–3   _____
   4–6   _____
   7–9   _____
   10 or more   _____

6. **Where will you spend/have you spent your nights? (More than one answer may be given.)**
   Not staying overnight away from home   _____
   Home of family/friends   _____
   Camping site   _____
   Cabin in state park   _____
   Hotel/motel/B & B   _____
   Other   _____

7. **What activities have you participated in while in this area? (More than one reason may be given.)**
   Visiting friends/family   _____
   Camping/hiking   _____
   Visiting historical sites   _____
   General sightseeing   _____
   Shopping   _____
   Other   _____

8. **Where have you eaten meals on this trip? (More than one choice location may be given.)**
   Home of family/friends   _____
   Private restaurant   _____
   At campsite   _____
   At restaurant in park or other public facility _____

9. **Are you familiar with the Hatfield-McCoy Mountains Region of West Virginia?**
   Yes _____   No _____

10. **(Give the interviewee the list of statements about the Hatfield-McCoy Mountains.) Here is a list of things that come to the minds of some people when they hear "Hatfield-McCoy Mountains of West Virginia." Please check any items that come to your mind when you think of this region.**

COLLECT SHEETS. SAY: Thanks for your assistance. Here's a brochure that will tell you something about the Hatfield-McCoy region. I hope you will visit (it or again) sometime soon. Enjoy your visit to West Virginia.

ILLUSTRATION 14-2 CONTINUED

17

Hatfield-McCoy Mountains of West Virginia

Have you ever visited the Hatfield-McCoy Mountains region of West Virginia? Yes ____ No ____

Please check any items that you currently associate with the Hatfield-McCoy Mountains.

1. A family feud long ago	1.	_____
2. Coal mining region	2.	_____
3. Chuck Yeager	3.	_____
4. Cabins in state park	4.	_____
5. Chief Logan	5.	_____
6. Auto races	6.	_____
7. Golf	7.	_____
8. An interesting area of the state	8.	_____
9. An economically depressed region	9.	_____
10. Good hiking	10.	_____
11. Mountaineer pride	11.	_____
12. Historical monuments	12.	_____
13. Outdoor drama about Shawnee princess	13.	_____
14. Good restaurants	14.	_____
15. Coal Mine Wars	15.	_____
16. A building made entirely of coal	16.	_____
17. Museums	17.	_____
18. Good hotels/motels	18.	_____
19. Camping in state park	19.	_____
20. Good hunting and fishing	20.	_____
21. Beautiful scenery	21.	_____
22. Festivals	22.	_____
23. Whitewater rafting	23.	_____
24. Trails for ATVs, motorcycles, bikes	24.	_____

ILLUSTRATION 14-2 CONTINUED

18

Appendix C. Profile of Interviewees

Factor/Question	Metro Valley	New River-Greenbrier	Total N = 200	Percent of Total
Sex				
Male	48	49	97	48.5
Female	52	51	103	51.5
Age Group				
18–34	30	30	60	25
35–54	50	50	100	50
55+	30	30	60	25
Primary Reason for Trip				
Family vacation	42	54	96	48.0
Weekend getaway	16	34	50	25.0
Day trip	25	10	35	17.5
Business trip	8	2	10	5.0
Visiting family/friends	9	0	9	4.5
Visited Area Before				
Yes	26	19	45	22.5
No	74	81	155	77.5
Why This Area				
Family/friend recommendation	50	99	149	48.7
History/culture of region	13	40	53	17.3
Return trip	20	25	45	14.7
Advertising response	6	23	29	9.5
Travel agent recommendation	8	9	17	5.6
Business requirement	5	8	13	4.2
*Total			**306***	
Other Sites Visited				
New River-Greenbrier	48	148	196	49.4
Metro Valley	111	64	140	35.2
Hatfield-McCoy	15	46	61	15.4
*Total			**397***	

ILLUSTRATION 14-2 ▶ CONTINUED

19

Appendix C. Continued

Factor/Question	Metro Valley	New River-Greenbrier	Total N = 200	Percent of Total
Activities Engaged In				
General sightseeing	54	83	137	33.7
Visiting historical sites	50	56	106	26.0
Camping/hiking	35	29	64	15.7
Entertainment	23	0	23	5.7
Shopping	19	2	21	5.2
Gaming	17	0	17	4.1
Visiting family/friends	8	8	16	3.9
Hunting/fishing	10	13	23	5.7
*Total			**407***	
Nights Spent in WV				
None	28	8	36	18.0
1–3	35	43	78	39.0
4–6	36	45	81	40.5
79	0	2	2	1.0
10+	1	2	3	1.5
Where Lodged				
Hotel/motel/B&B	58	41	99	43.0
Camping site	25	38	63	27.4
Cabin in state park	13	16	29	12.6
Not staying overnight	20	8	28	12.2
Home of family-friends	6	5	11	4.8
Total			**230***	
Where Ate Meals				
Restaurant	83	95	178	69.9
At campsite	30	23	53	20.6
Home of family/friends	8	9	17	6.6
Food service at public facility	9	0	9	3.5
Total			**257***	
Familiar w/Hatfield-McCoy Mts.				
Yes	13	40	53	26.5
No	87	60	147	73.5

Source: Primary   *Total greater than 200 because more than one choice was permitted.

ILLUSTRATION 14-3 TRADITIONAL TITLE PAGE

INCREASING TOURISM IN THE HATFIELD-McCOY MOUNTAINS REGION OF WEST VIRGINIA

Prepared for

Hatfield-McCoy Mountains Coalition
123 Main Street
Chapmanville, WV 25508

Prepared by

K-F Research Associates, LLP
456 Capitol Way
Charleston, WV 25301

September 1, 2005

ILLUSTRATION 14-4 OPENING PAGES OF REPORT IN DEDUCTIVE STRUCTURE

INCREASING TOURISM IN
THE HATFIELD-McCOY MOUNTAINS REGION
OF WEST VIRGINIA

Recommendations

K-F Research Associates recommends that the Hatfield-McCoy Mountains Coalition do the following to stimulate tourism in the region.

1. Develop a radio campaign to promote the region and air it during commuting hours in cities that are within 100 miles of the region, both in West Virginia and adjoining states. The promotional messages should be short, attention-getting spots that focus on specific attractions as desirable destinations for a one-day or weekend trip. Airing such spots during commuting time may stimulate commuters to think about the area as a possible getaway destination.

2. Promote the state parks in the region. Such parks are generally popular with short-term visitors and campers. Developing promotional materials that highlight the parks' attractions and associating them with the larger region should draw more tourists to them. The spillover effect would be to draw attention to nearby historical and recreational attractions. Do not depend on the state to give adequate publicity about the facilities and activities available in the region's state parks.

3. Work with merchants in the area to persuade them to advertise more heavily in the state's official tourism guide. Giving potential tourists more information about the area and making them more aware of the touring and recreational options—such as whitewater rafting, hunting, fishing, trail riding—should increase interest in the area and improve its image.

4. Work with the Chambers of Commerce in the area to attract a mid- to high-end hotel with restaurant to the area, preferably near its center. Chapmanville, which is near the Chief Logan State Park and on U.S. Highway 119, appears to be an ideal location for such a facility. It would be less than an hour's drive from any of the region's tourist sites and could be attractive to higher-end travelers who do not want to camp out or sleep in a motel with limited amenities.

5. Apply for one or more grants from the Division of Tourism to defray part of the costs of the promotional campaign.

The justification for those recommendations is presented in the following analysis.

Current Status of Tourism in Hatfield-McCoy Mountains Region

The Hatfield-McCoy Mountains of West Virginia abound in historical and recreational interest. Yet merchants of the region have expressed concern that tourists are not aware of the many vacation or weekend activities the region offers. The state's 2005 official travel guide shows the state divided into nine regions, one of which is the Hatfield-McCoy Mountains. Yet other official publications show the state divided into eight regions, with the five counties that comprise the Hatfield-McCoy Mountains region included in the Metro Valley region. In fact, a potential tourist who is browsing the web site of the West Virginia Division of Tourism will find information about the region only by "stumbling" on it while visiting various links within that site. Such inconsistency in state publications could well distract from the region as tourists plan vacations, weekend getaways, or day trips.

The Hatfield-McCoy Mountain region is located in southern West Virginia. Chapmanville, which marks the center of the region, is approximately 40 miles southwest of Charleston and southeast of Huntington. The area is easily accessible by Interstate 40 and U.S. 119.

The Hatfield-McCoy Mountains Coalition (HMCMC) wants to capture a larger share of West Virginia's tourist trade. JMCMC asked K-F Research Associates, LLP, to determine what the Coalition should do to increase tourism in its area.

Determining Tourists' Perceptions of the Hatfield-McCoy Mountains Region

The research problem was to determine tourists' current perceptions of the Hatfield-McCoy Mountains region and identify ways to increase tourist visits to the regions.

Scope of Analysis

Three factors were analyzed:

1. What is the current impact of tourism in the Hatfield-McCoy Mountains region?

2. What kinds of tourists visit nearby areas of the state?

3. What are those visitors' perceptions of the Hatfield-McCoy Mountains region?

ILLUSTRATION 14-5 ▶ MARGINS FOR BUSINESS RESEARCH REPORT (IN INCHES)

Type of Page	Top-Bound Manuscript				Left-Bound Manuscript			
	Top	**Bottom**	**Left**	**Right**	**Top**	**Bottom**	**Left**	**Right**
Title Page	N/A*				N/A*			
Transmittal Message	N/A				N/A			
Prefatory Parts								
First page of each part	2	1	1	1	1.5	1	1.5	1
All other pages	1.5	1	1	1	1	1	1.5	1
Body of Report								
First page	2	1	1	1	1.5	1.5	1	1
First page of each chapter	2	1	1	1	1.5	1.5	1	1
All other pages	1.5	1	1	1	1	1.5	1	1
Supplements								
First page of each part	2	1	1	1	1.5	1.5	1	1
All other pages	1.5	1	1	1	1	1.5	1	1

*Not Applicable

TOPICS FOR DISCUSSION

1. What are the purposes of report preliminaries?

2. Why should you bind your report? When should you not bind a report?

3. What information should be shown on a report cover?

4. What information should a title page contain?

5. What should the transmittal message accomplish?

6. What are the functions of authorization and acceptance messages?

7. What are the purposes of the table of contents and the list of tables?

8. When may the preface or acknowledgments be omitted?

9. What should be included in an executive summary?

10. When may an executive summary be omitted?

11. What are the major sections of a report body? What information should be included in each section? Which sections are not included in an information report?

12. What are the purposes of report supplements? What items may be included in the supplements?

13. How do informative or "talking" headings differ from functional or structural headings? Which do you prefer? Why?

14. Describe an effective format for report headings.

15. Explain the pagination systems for report preliminaries, report body, and report supplements.

APPLICATIONS

1. As directed by your instructor, complete any research you began in conjunction with your study of previous chapters in this book. Write the body of a report that presents the results of your research.

2. After completing the body of your research report (Application 1), exchange reports with another student. Each of you is to write the executive summary for the other's report. Evaluate the executive summary that your classmate wrote for your report. Is it a highly effective, marginal, or ineffective summary? In a memo to your instructor explain your evaluation. Attach a copy of the summary to your memo.

3. Complete the report you worked on for Applications 1 and 2. Include the following items:
   - A title page
   - A transmittal message
   - A table of contents
   - An executive summary
   - The report body
   - Source list
   - Appendixes, if appropriate

4. As a collaborative research and writing project, do the following:
   - Interview managers in five companies in your area. Try to get the following kinds of information:
     - What is the average length of reports produced by this company? If no average, what is the page-length range this manager has seen in the company's reports?
     - What major types of internal reports does the manager use or prepare?
     - What major types of external reports does the manager use or prepare?
     - Does the company use a standard template or style guide for its reports? If a company has such a guide, ask for a copy. If the company does not have such a guide, determine the expectations for report structure and format that exist in the company and how those expectations are conveyed to employees.
     - Does the manager prefer that illustrations be integrated into the report or grouped in an appendix at the end?

- Write a report of your findings, showing whether expectations are consistent or inconsistent among those businesses. The working title for your report should be "Report Structures and Formats in Local Businesses." (You may, however, choose another title for your final report.) Be sure to include a full description of the objective of your report, your methodology, your findings, and your conclusions, particularly the implications of your findings for people entering the business world or transferring to a new company. Include any report preliminaries and supplements requested by your instructor.

5. Select a research report that you have prepared for another class or at your job. In a memorandum to your instructor, describe how it is similar to or different from the model given in this chapter. If there are differences, explain how those differences improve or distract from the "user-friendliness" of the report.

REFERENCES

1. This report is a combination of hypothetical and verifiable data, used for illustration purposes only. K-F Research Associates, LLP, is a hypothetical company, and the interview data are hypothetical. However, the author conducted a similar survey among a small sample of adults and projected the findings to the hypothetical sample size of 200. All data about tourism in West Virginia were obtained from studies published by the West Virginia Division of Tourism.

2. Moorthy, V. (2005). Don't panic over Delhi's deficit. *Far Eastern Economic Review, 168:* 8–12.

3. Gibaldi, J. (2003). *MLA handbook for writers of research papers* (6th ed.). New York: The Modern Language Association of America.

4. American Psychological Association. (2001). *Publication manual of the American Psychological Association* (5th ed.). Washington, DC: American Psychological Association.

5. American Psychological Association. (2001). *Publication manual of the American Psychological Association* (5th ed.). Washington, DC: American Psychological Association, 113.

chapter 15

Planning and Delivering an Oral Report

LEARNING OBJECTIVES

After you have read this chapter, you should be able to:

1. Plan an effective presentation by:
   - analyzing the context
   - selecting an appropriate delivery style and level of formality
   - outlining the presentation
   - preparing visual aids
   - rehearsing.
2. Deliver an effective presentation by:
   - managing stage fright
   - using presentation aids without distraction
   - handling a question-answer session with confidence.
3. Apply your presentation skills in a group presentation.
4. Participate effectively in an electronic conference.

After completing a written report, you may utter a sigh of relief. "At last!" you say to yourself. "I've finished that assignment." But in many situations, writing the report is not the final task. You will also be expected to present your information orally to a select audience. That audience may be people at your level, at a lower level, or at a higher level in the organization. In many situations, however, the audience consists of individuals representing different levels in the organization or of persons at the managerial or executive levels.

For that reason, your oral reporting skills will have a significant impact on your career success. In this chapter you will learn how to construct and deliver effective oral presentations.

PREPARING THE PRESENTATION

Effective oral presentations require extensive preparation. In many ways, preparing an oral report is much like composing a written report. The diagram given in Illustration 15-1 will guide you through the preparation steps.

Analyze the Context

The communication context encompasses the internal (psychological) environment and the external (physical) environment. Major aspects of context analysis for an oral report, therefore, are determining the characteristics of the

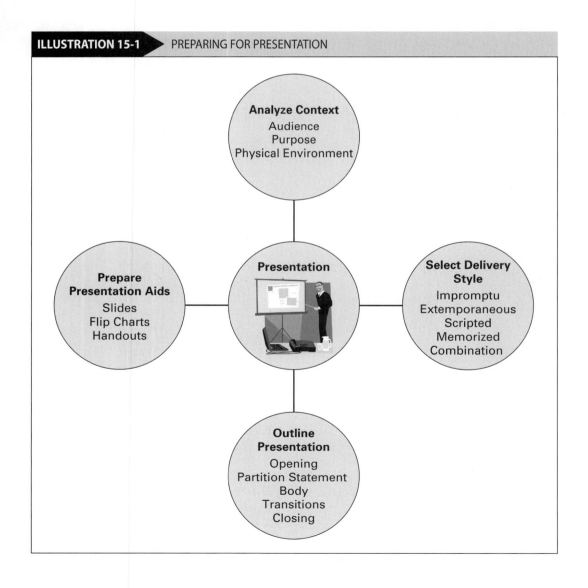

ILLUSTRATION 15-1 PREPARING FOR PRESENTATION

Analyze Context
Audience
Purpose
Physical Environment

Prepare Presentation Aids
Slides
Flip Charts
Handouts

Presentation

Select Delivery Style
Impromptu
Extemporaneous
Scripted
Memorized
Combination

Outline Presentation
Opening
Partition Statement
Body
Transitions
Closing

intended audience and the characteristics of the place in which you will deliver the presentation. Those two factors tend also to define the appropriate degree of formality.

AUDIENCE

Audience analysis is an attempt to assess the psychological environment for the presentation. In this analysis you should try to determine who will attend and their motives for attending your presentation. You can expect to give oral reports to four different types of audiences:

Clients and customers. An oral presentation can be a valuable sales technique. Whether you are trying to interest clients in a silicon chip or a bulldozer, you will present its features and its advantages over the competition. Then, after the sale, you will likely provide detailed oral operating instructions and maintenance procedures to the users.

Colleagues in your organization. If you are the resident expert on a mechanism, procedure, or technical subject, you will instruct your fellow workers, both technical and nontechnical. After you return from an important conference or an out-of-town project, your supervisors will want a briefing—an oral report. If you have an idea for improving operations at your organization, you probably will write a brief informal proposal and then present the idea orally to a small group of managers. Your presentation will help them determine whether it is prudent to devote resources to studying the idea.

Fellow professionals at technical conferences. As you develop in your profession, you might speak about your own research project or a team project carried out at your organization, or you may be invited to speak to professionals in other fields. If you are an economist, for example, you might be invited to speak to real estate agents about interest rates.

The general public. As you assume greater prominence in your field, you will receive invitations to speak to civic organizations and governmental bodies. Since most organizations encourage employees to participate in community service, you will likely be encouraged to give these presentations.

As you analyze your audience, answer questions such as those listed in Illustration 15-2. Answers to such questions will help you define the psychological environment—how receptive your audience is to your message. Assume, for example, that you must present the results of your survey of customer preferences for new services at a local bank. An audience of branch managers who know that the survey was conducted and are eager to increase business in their respective branches will likely be eager to hear your report. Assume further that the managers will meet immediately after your presentation to make a decision based on your recommendations, one of which is to provide Saturday morning teller service. Under those circumstances your audience will likely listen critically, evaluating every bit of information you present, possibly interrupting with questions and asking for immediate clarification of anything they don't understand. Such an audience would likely be attentive even late on Friday afternoon! Add to your assumption one manager's opposition to your recommendation for Saturday morning teller service. In such a

| ILLUSTRATION 15-2 | AUDIENCE ANALYSIS FOR PRESENTATION |

As you analyze your audience, ask yourself . . .

- What is the expected size of the audience?
- Who will attend?
    - Name?
    - Department or area of the company?
    - Position in the company?
    - Male? Female?
    - How long with the company?
- How much do they know about my topic?
    - Little?
    - Much?
- What are their attitudes toward the topic?
    - Indifference?
    - Opposition?
    - Support?
- What are their reasons for attendance?
    - Part of the problem?
    - Expected to be part of the solution?
    - Attending voluntarily?
    - Required to attend?
- What effect will the time of the presentation have on my audience? Will the audience be:
    - Alert?
    - Drowsy?
    - Tired?
- What is the audience expected to do?
    - Receive the information only?
    - Discuss the report?
    - Convey information to other employees?
    - Make a decision at the end of the presentation?
    - Make a decision later? Make individual decisions?
    - Participate in a group decision?

situation, you should anticipate the need for an especially convincing presentation. You should also expect challenging, perhaps even argumentative, questions from that manager and be prepared with appropriate responses.

PURPOSE

Consider the purpose of your presentation, just as you would in writing a report. Are you attempting to inform your audience, or to both inform and persuade them? If you are explaining how solar power can be used to generate energy, you have one type of argument. If you are explaining why solar power is an economical means of generating power, you have another type.

ILLUSTRATION 15-3 ▸ EVALUATING THE PHYSICAL ENVIRONMENT

As you evaluate the physical environment, consider the following . . .
- Where will the presentation be made?
  - Auditorium?
  - Classroom?
  - Part of a divided hotel ballroom?
  - Conference room?
  - Office? Whose office?
- What furniture arrangement will be used?
  - Audience in formal rows facing the speaker?
  - Audience and speaker seated at conference table?
  - Audience and speaker seated in office with no table?
- What presentation aids will be available and where will they be located in the room? What arrangements must be made for their use? Who will make those arrangements?
  - Lectern?
  - Microphone?
  - Chalkboard, grease board, or flip chart?
  - Overhead projector?
  - Computer projector?
  - Slide projector?
  - Electrical outlets?
  - Projection screen?
- What aspects of the physical environment, if any, may distract from your presentation? Can these potential distractions be removed, controlled, or compensated for?
  - Noise?
  - Lighting?
  - Size of room?
  - Kind of seating?
- What aspects of the environment may you be unable to control? Can you adapt your presentation to accommodate such things?
  - Equipment malfunction?
  - Power outage?
  - Insufficient seating?
  - HVAC malfunction?

PHYSICAL ENVIRONMENT

The physical environment also influences the outcome of your presentation. An initially receptive audience can become indifferent or irritable if the physical environment is unsuitable. To define that environment, answer questions such as those listed in Illustration 15-3.

Knowledge about the physical environment, along with an assessment of the psychological environment, can help you plan your presentation strategies.

Consider a presentation to the bank branch managers. If you want to encourage discussion of your findings, conclusions, and recommendations, you should ask for a conference room arrangement with everyone seated around a table. That arrangement tends to foster discussion more readily than does a formal arrangement with the audience seated in rows facing the speaker. If you anticipate serious discussion of the information, use a computer-projected presentation, overhead transparencies, photographic slides, flip charts, or handouts that summarize major points so that your audience can refer to them easily during the discussion. If you want to list or summarize ideas generated during the discussion, be sure the room contains a chalkboard, grease board, or flip chart and appropriate writing instruments. In some instances speakers prefer to use a screen, overhead projector, and transparency pens to guide a discussion. If that is your preference, you should ensure that an electrical plug adapter, an extension cord, a spare bulb for the overhead projector, and some blank transparency sheets are available. While some speakers use this technique effectively, the danger exists that the reduced lighting in the room may cause audience fatigue or inattention.

Recognizing the available options in your physical environment can help you achieve success as a speaker. Selecting the appropriate type of delivery can also enhance your oral report.

Select Delivery Style

Five options are available as you select a delivery mode: impromptu, extemporaneous, textual or scripted, memorized, or combination.

Impromptu delivery consists of speaking spontaneously, without previous rehearsal, with little or no advanced preparation, and without text or notes to assist you. You will seldom use this type of delivery for the major presentation of a report. You may use it, however, for spontaneous interim progress reports on a project. After you have completed your data collection and analysis for the bank customer survey, for example, your supervisor could ask you in a staff meeting for a quick update on the project. Your presentation in response to that request would be an impromptu speech.

Although impromptu speeches are spontaneous, following these guides will help you make effective impromptu presentations:

- Anticipate the major topics that may be discussed at a meeting. Play a "What if . . ." game with yourself. Ask: "What if I am asked to give an update on the bank customer survey?" Answering that question will enable you to consider what information, if any, you will present in the meeting.
- Avoid being surprised. Listen attentively; recognize that the discussion is moving into your area of expertise. You can then anticipate that you may be asked for an impromptu statement.
- Be brief. Cover one or two major points; avoid rambling.

Extemporaneous delivery appears to be spontaneous but involves extensive planning, previous rehearsal, and the use of notes during the presentation. With the notes to aid you and the confidence gained during rehearsal, you can establish and maintain eye contact with your audience and move freely about the presentation area. If you have planned and rehearsed your presentation sufficiently, the information will be accurate, complete, organized, and easy to follow. And if you can think well on your feet, the presentation will have a naturalness that will help your audience concentrate on what you are saying.

The following suggestions will help you master extemporaneous delivery:

- Plan every aspect of your presentation, including use of visual aids and how you will handle questions.
- Write your speech, including notations for visual aids, etc. Read it slowly one or two times to estimate its delivery time. Prepare notes to use during your presentation. Do not memorize the speech.
- Rehearse the presentation until it flows smoothly without giving the impression of being memorized. Use your notes only as prompts to keep the presentation flowing smoothly.
- Become thoroughly familiar with the details that you want to present. Understand them; anticipate points that the audience may question.
- Prepare alternative explanations. Adapt to audience nonverbal feedback or questions that indicate the audience does not understand some part of the presentation.

You may use extemporaneous delivery in both formal and informal settings. This delivery style is justified when you are very familiar with the information and maintaining eye contact with the audience is more important than exact adherence to a prepared script.

Textual or scripted delivery involves reading a manuscript verbatim. This delivery style is appropriate when you are presenting technical or controversial information, and you want to ensure that no errors are made in transmission of that information.

Textual or scripted delivery tends to be used in formal more often than informal contexts. Advantages of such delivery are that you can feel confident about the accuracy of your speech and can give an exact copy of your message to members of the audience—preferably after your presentation—to ensure that they receive an accurate message. A disadvantage, however, is that you will have difficulty maintaining eye contact and may miss significant nonverbal reactions from your audience.

To prepare for textual or scripted delivery, follow these guides:

- Prepare the manuscript and verify its accuracy.
- Mark the manuscript with delivery cues (arrows, bold type, underlining) to indicate variations in speed or emphasis.
- Practice reading your manuscript until you can read it fluently. Avoid reading too quickly.
- Concentrate on precise enunciation. Rapid reading frequently leads to slurring or mispronunciation of words.
- Vary your tone or pitch to appropriately emphasize the content of your report as you would in conversation.

When the context justifies textual or scripted delivery, be cautious about impromptu discussion following the speech. Although discussion may be appropriate, listen attentively and answer cautiously to avoid contradicting what you said during the delivery.

Memorized delivery is presentation of a verbatim message learned by rote. An advantage of memorized delivery is that it allows full freedom of movement and permits you to maintain eye contact with your audience. That delivery style can also promote the audience's confidence in your expertise. A disadvantage, however, is that anxiety may cause you to forget or omit part of the presentation, thereby destroying the coherence of the message and possibly destroying your credibility.

Memorized delivery is appropriate when the volume of information is "memorizable" and you want to foster your audience's confidence in you. Be cautious, however, about appearing pompous or excessively oratorical. Such an impression tends to alienate the audience.

Combination delivery employs a variety of delivery styles in a single presentation. You will find this style suitable for many report presentations. In the bank example, for instance, you could deliver a memorized opening statement that will attract attention and stimulate interest in your presentation; that statement could be followed by an extemporaneous presentation of the major findings, conclusions, and recommendations. Perhaps during the presentation of findings, you may choose to read some statements made by survey participants. And, in answer to a question, you may make an impromptu presentation about further research that you think the bank should conduct.

Your analyses of the psychological and the physical environments will also contribute to decisions about how formal or informal your presentation should be.

In a formal presentation, such as a scripted presentation, you will deliver a carefully structured, controlled message with no immediate verbal feedback from the audience. For formal presentations, you will usually stand at a lectern, facing an audience seated in rows. You may use notes or a manuscript to ensure that you proceed through the presentation as planned. You may also use presentation aids—computer slides, flip charts, pictures, audio recordings, videotapes, handouts—that you have prepared in advance.

A formal presentation leaves little or no room for spontaneous response from the audience; consequently, you must be aware of nonverbal responses to evaluate whether the audience understands your message. If nonverbal feedback signifies that the audience does not understand or is becoming restless, you should modify your presentation. When appropriate, you may permit a question-answer session after a formal presentation. Suggestions for managing question-answer sessions are given later in this chapter.

An informal presentation is also a carefully planned, controlled message; but audience verbal feedback is usually permitted during the presentation. In an informal presentation, your audience will likely be seated at a conference table or in a semicircle to promote interaction among members of the audience. You may also be seated or standing close to the group. You will likely speak extemporaneously, relying on brief notes or presentation aids to direct your speech.

Since members of the audience are permitted to ask questions or make comments, an informal presentation can veer from its intended course. To achieve the objective of your report, you must maintain control of the discussion and refocus audience attention on your topic after each question or comment has been given adequate response.

In a semiformal presentation, you will strike a middle ground between the formal and informal styles, using a combination style of delivery. In the bank example, for instance, you could give a carefully structured report of your findings as you stand before individuals seated at a conference table; and you might request that they hold their questions until you have presented all findings. Then you could entertain questions about the findings before going on to your conclusions and recommendations. During that part of the presentation you could sit at the table and permit free discussion of each of the conclusions and recommendations as you present them. As you plan a presentation, select a degree of formality that complements the topic, the audience, and the physical environment. When the audience is large, a formal presentation may be the most efficient way to present your report. If the findings, conclusions, or recommendations are controversial, you may also choose a formal presentation style so that you can present all information before confronting questions. Deferring questions until the end of the presentation may defuse some issues. When the audience is small, a semiformal or informal style may be effective, especially if you want to promote discussion. When the audience is a mixed group, with various levels of interest in or knowledge about your topic, a formal presentation may be superior to an informal one. The formal style will permit you to control the presentation more closely and be sure that relevant information is presented at a level that is understandable to all members of the audience. For a relatively small, highly motivated, decision-oriented group, an informal style that permits all decision makers to ask questions and evaluate the information is effective.

After choosing a delivery style appropriate for your audience and the context, you are ready to outline your presentation.

Outline the Presentation

A simple yet effective outline structure for an oral report consists of four parts: the opening, a preview or partition statement, the body, and the conclusion. Each must be worded to formulate a coherent speech that accomplishes your reporting purpose, and the parts must be connected by meaningful transitions.

Outlines are extremely useful tools for helping you organize and deliver a presentation. As you prepare, maintain a thorough outline of every element you want to include in the presentation. Organize your outline along the lines presented in Illustration 15-4.

OPENING

The opening of the speech must reach out and grab the listeners' attention. An effective opening draws the audience into the message by showing its relevance to them. Such an opening focuses on the audience, not on the speaker. Some

---

ILLUSTRATION 15-4 ▶ SAMPLE OUTLINE FORMAT

Title of Speech:

Purpose of Speech:

I. Introduction
   A. Strong opening statement to grab the audience's attention
   B. Topic of speech
   C. Relevance of topic
      1. Subpoint 1: reason
      2. Subpoint 2: reason
   D. Preview of the main points to follow

II. Body
   A. Main point 1
      1. Subpoint 1
         a. supporting information
         b. supporting information
      2. Subpoint 2
         a. supporting information
         b. supporting information

   B. Main point 2
      1. Subpoint 1
         a. supporting information
         b. supporting information
      2. Subpoint 2
         a. supporting information
         b. supporting information
   C. Main point 3
      1. Subpoint 1
         a. supporting information
         b. supporting information
         c. supporting information
      2. Subpoint 2
         a. supporting information
         b. supporting information
         c. supporting information

III. Conclusion
   A. Summary of the main points
   B. Relationship of most important point(s) to purpose of presentation
   C. Strong last sentence to close the presentation

---

effective attention-getting openings are quotations, surprising statements, questions, anecdotes, or relevant statistics.

Some speakers have the mistaken idea that all speeches should begin with a joke. A humorous opening is effective only if the humor relates to the speech topic, offends no one in the audience, and is delivered skillfully. Few people have mastered the timing of a stand-up comedian.

Compare the following examples of ineffective and effective opening statements.

Ineffective: Today I'm going to give you the results of the survey of Midland National Bank customers that Mr. Hector asked me to conduct last month. I think you might be interested in some of the results. (Focuses on speaker; tentatively suggests topic may be relevant to listeners.)

Ineffective: What's the slowest-moving line in the world? The line at the teller's window I just chose. I always manage to choose the slowest-moving line. Seriously, folks, I'm here to tell you about your recent customer survey and what it suggests about teller service at your bank. (Trite joke that may offend tellers or bank managers; focuses on speaker; doesn't recognize audience needs.)

Effective: Your customers want innovative bank services that will give them easier access to their accounts. You can give them those services at very little extra cost to your branch. (Focuses on listeners; establishes relevance of message to them.)

Effective: Eighty percent of your banking customers are satisfied with Midland services. That's good news. Today I'd like to suggest how you can turn good news into even better news—how satisfied customers can become extremely satisfied customers. (Pleasing statistic involving the audience; shows immediate relevance of speech to audience.)

PREVIEW OR PARTITION STATEMENT

The partition (preview) statement tells the audience what the speech will cover. This statement should create a mental readiness or "set" that will help the listeners follow your presentation. A partition statement should clearly and interestingly identify the topics to be covered so that the audience will eagerly anticipate the message that unfolds. Compare the following examples of effective and ineffective partition statements.

Ineffective: As I said, Mr. Hector asked me to find out what Midland National Bank customers think about some services that we are considering for our customers. So I basically asked them about five different services. In this presentation I'm going to tell you what those services are, how customers responded to the survey, and some recommendations based on their responses. (Continues to focus on speaker; gives no clue about specific content of message or relevance to audience; provides only a structural overview: questions asked, responses, recommendations.)

Effective: My recommendation will be based on two major findings from our study of Midland National Bank (MNB) customer attitudes toward proposed new banking services. MNB customers showed the strongest interest in new services that give them easy access to their accounts. They showed little interest in incentives for some of our standard consumer banking services. Today I'd like to share with you what we found out about consumer preferences, specifically the services they expressed interest in and the services they were indifferent to. I'll also make some recommendations about how we can satisfy MNB customer preferences. (Heightens interest; tells what will be covered; creates a receptive frame of mind because it suggests relevance to audience.)

BODY

The body of the presentation must adequately develop the points identified in the partition statement. An appropriate sequence of information following the previous effective partition statement would be services preferred by customers, services about which customers were indifferent, and recommendations for providing the preferred services. Development can be achieved by presentation of statistics, examples of customer comments, costs of implementing certain services, and any additional data that will support your recommendations and enable listeners to reach an effective decision.

TRANSITIONS

As you develop the body of your presentation, be mindful of transitions between the main points you must make. Transitions are signposts that tell audience members where you are in the presentation and where you are going. All parts of the presentation should be linked together by simple statements of transition, which demonstrate the organizational pattern you are using. The introductory preview acts as a transition to the body of the presentation. When you move from one main point to another, use a statement announcing the move: "Now that we have looked at point 1, let's look at point 2." Likewise, you should announce demonstrations, examples, digressions, or comparisons and contrasts when they occur: "An example of point 2 occurs when. . . ." Finally, make a clear transition when you begin the conclusion of the presentation: "Now that we have discussed each of the three main points, let's summarize the key elements."

Weak speakers often overlook these simple transitional sentences, but they can be one of your most effective tactics to help the audience follow your points. Because members of the audience do not have the outline of the presentation in front of them, you must verbalize the structure of the outline to keep them on track. Here are several other transition clauses you may find helpful for unifying your presentation.

Enumeration:	"My first main point is . . .
Importance:	"A more important fact is . . ."
Emphasis:	"The main point to remember is . . ."
Addition:	"Another thing to consider is . . ."
Tangents:	"This is off the subject, but . . ."
Return:	"Let me get back to where I was . . ."
Leading:	"The next thing to look at is . . ."
Question:	"What is the next thing to consider?"
Pre-summary:	"I will deal with three main ideas . . ."
Internal summary:	"Let me conclude this section . . ."
Post-summary:	"Let me repeat my main ideas . . ."

Consider the following examples of ineffective and effective transitions.

Ineffective: So that's pretty much what customers thought about services that give them easier access to their accounts. Now let's look at their evaluations of some other kinds of services. (Does not summarize completed part; provides no clue about content of the next part; gives no indication of how the two parts are related.)

Effective: As you have seen, our customers gave "important" or "very important" ratings to the two services related to accessing accounts: Saturday morning teller service, ATMs in more locations. In contrast, MNB customers showed little interest in reduced prices for standard consumer bank services. (Summarizes one part of presentation; links it to the next part of presentation.)

CONCLUSION

The conclusion should clinch the message; that is, it should be what you want the listeners to leave the room with. For an informative speech, the conclusion must help the listeners remember the main points of the message. For a persuasive speech, the conclusion should stimulate action based on the message. Link the conclusion to the body of the speech by a meaningful transition.

Effective ways to end a speech include summaries of the report content, requests or proposals for specific actions, examples or anecdotes that reinforce the message, questions that prompt a response or action, or combinations of those strategies. The closing should be a memorable experience for the audience, not a letdown or an abrupt ending. Compare the following examples of effective and ineffective conclusions.

> **Ineffective:** That's about all I found out. Based on the findings it looks like it might be a good idea to provide Saturday morning teller service. (Does not summarize or recap the report; tentatively hints at action.)
>
> **Effective:** Evidence indicates that MNB customers want easier access to their accounts. The simplest, least costly way to give them that access is to provide Saturday morning teller service at each of our branch banks. None of our competitors currently offers that service. I recommend that we initiate it no later than December 1. Doing so will demonstrate to our current customers—and also to some potential ones—that MNB believes in service. (Summarizes major findings; confidently proposes specific action and likely outcome of that action.)

Outlines vary tremendously because you must adapt them to the situation and the purpose of the presentation. Whatever the case, take care to organize clearly and use a framework that allows you to see at a glance how the presentation is structured. A good outline will assist you in staying organized as you speak, adjusting the presentation to time constraints, adding or subtracting material, and helping you find your place if you become lost during the presentation. Prepare your outline using complete sentences, partial sentences, key phrases, or key words. Experiment with various forms of outlines until you find one that is particularly useful to you.

Your analysis of your audience and purpose will affect the content and form of your presentation. Topics, for example, can be arranged to accommodate the audience's needs. You might have to emphasize certain aspects of your subject or ignore others altogether. Using meaningful and memorable language will add to the effectiveness of your presentation.

Evaluate Your Language

If people doze off while reading a report you have written, you probably will not know it, at least until they complain to you later or you realize that the report failed to accomplish its purpose. But if they doze off while you are speaking to them, you'll know it right away. Effective presentations require memorable language.

To help make your language more memorable, follow these three techniques:

- **Involve the audience.** People are more interested in their own concerns than in yours. Talk to the audience about their problems and their solutions. In the introduction, establish a link between your topic and the audience's interests. For instance, in the presentation to the Toledo City Council about waste management, you might begin like this:

  "Picture yourself on the Gafney City Council two years from now. After exhaustive hearings, proposals, and feasibility studies, you still don't have a waste-management plan that meets federal regulations. What you do have is a mounting debt: the city is being assessed $1,000 per day until you implement an acceptable plan."

- **Refer to people, not to abstractions.** People remember specifics; they forget abstractions. When you want to make a point memorable, describe it in human terms.

  "What could you do with that $365,000 every year? You could buy almost 200 personal computers; that's a computer for almost every classroom in every elementary school in Arcadia Township. You could expand your school-lunch program to feed every needy child in the township. You could extend your after-school programs to cover an additional 3,000 students."

- **Use interesting facts, figures, and quotations.** Do your research and find interesting information about your subject. For instance, you might find a brief quotation from an authoritative figure in the field or a famous person not generally associated with the field. (George W. Bush on waste management?)

Ideas within your presentation must be linked logically and clearly. Transitional words or phrases help the audience understand a discussion by pointing out the direction of the presentation.

Now that you have structured your presentation, developed your outline, and incorporated transitional words and phrases, you must find ways to enhance it further. Visual aids are the tools to accentuate the information you want to share.

Prepare Visual Aids

Because we live in a visually oriented society, we expect to see as well as hear information. Therefore, effective speakers show as well as tell their points. Two broad categories of visual aids are available to enhance presentations. One category, direct viewing visuals, includes such things as real objects, models, flip charts, diagrams and drawings, photographs, and handouts. The second category, projected visuals, includes transparencies, slides, videotapes, and computer presentations.

Always remember that visual aids are just that—*aids*. Adding visuals to a poorly researched, poorly organized presentation will not salvage it. Visual aids should be used to attract and hold attention, clarify meanings, emphasize or elaborate main ideas, or prove a point. Several factors must be considered in selecting the appropriate visual aid:

- **The constraints of the topic.** Some topics will limit your choice of visual aids. For example, if you were explaining how a large robot operates, you would probably use a videotape of the robot in operation. A scaled-down model of the robot may not be as effective, since the scope and movement of the machinery may be a persuasive point. Similarly, a drawing or photograph of the robot would be the least effective visual aid.
- **The availability of the equipment.** If the speaking site does not have an overhead projector, you could not use transparencies. Similarly, if the site does not have an electrical outlet near the lectern, you would not be able to use a projected visual.
- **The cost of the visual.** If your budget is very small, you may be limited to something like a transparency, flip chart, or handout. Remember, however, that even low-cost visuals can and must be used purposefully.
- **The difficulty of producing the visual.** If you have only two days to prepare for your presentation, it may be impossible to assemble a prototype of an anti-theft device for a motorcycle or to process slides of a manufacturing operation.
- **The appropriateness of the visual to the audience.** The type of audience and the nature of the presentation affect the choice of visual aids. Some charts, graphs, and diagrams may be too technical for anyone but specialists to grasp. Detailed and complicated tables and charts that require considerable time to digest should be avoided. Generally the best visuals are simple to use and to comprehend.
- **The appropriateness of the visual to the speaker.** Visual aids require skill for their effective presentation. A person must be able to write legibly and draw well-proportioned diagrams to use a flip chart. Projected visuals require skill in handling slides, videotape, film, or computer equipment. If you do not feel comfortable with a particular visual medium, do not use it.
- **The appropriateness of the visual to the time limit.** The speaker should carefully check the time required to display and explain a visual aid to make sure the main ideas of the presentation will not be neglected. Any visual aid that needs too much explanation should be avoided.

After you have planned and organized the content of your presentation, developed your notes or outline, and prepared your visual aids, you are ready to rehearse your presentation.

Rehearse the Presentation

Some of history's greatest speakers—such as Abraham Lincoln and Winston Churchill—were known to practice extensively before delivering a speech.[1] You should rehearse your presentation until you are confident that you can handle all aspects with finesse. Rehearse not only the verbal content of the message, but also your posture, gestures, and use of presentation aids. In addition, anticipate possible questions and rehearse appropriate answers. As you rehearse, time your presentation to be sure it fits into the time that you have been allotted.

During rehearsal, experiment with different ways of managing your notes or manuscript. Some speakers use cards for extemporaneous speeches; others write their notes on sheets of paper. Whatever method you prefer, you should practice so that your notes or manuscript are unobtrusive. The following hints can help you develop those skills:

- **For Notes or Manuscripts.** Print in large, legible letters that you can easily read from your delivery position. Highlighting the key points with colored ink will help you focus on those statements. Include symbols or verbal signals in your notes or manuscript to indicate when you must use a presentation aid.

- **For Note Cards.** Record only key points on cards. Do not use too many cards; try to limit yourself to one card for the opening, one for each main point in the body, and one for the closing. Number the cards. Arrange them in numerical sequence with a rubber band around them. Remove the band just before your presentation. Hold the cards in the palm of your hand or place them on the lectern. If you hold them in your hand, slip each card to the back of the deck as you complete its use. If you place the cards on the lectern, put the used cards in a stack next to the deck. Some speakers staple their cards in sequence inside a file folder and place the opened folder on the lectern.

- **For Note Sheets.** Avoid this technique if you will not have a lectern on which to rest the sheets. If you do use the technique, use a type size that is large enough to be read easily from an erect standing position. Number the sheets and arrange them numerically. Slide each sheet unobtrusively to the side as you complete its use. You may find that placing your finger on each point as you discuss it will keep you from losing your place in your speech.

- **For Manuscripts.** Use different colors of ink, arrows, bold type, or underlining to highlight key points and to provide signals for emphasis: raising or lowering your voice, pausing, speeding up. Use a type size that is large enough to be read easily from an erect standing position, and use only the upper half of the pages. This technique promotes better eye contact. It keeps you from dropping your head and eyes to read to the bottom of the page.

If possible, rehearse before an audience—even if it's only one person, such as a helpful family member or roommate—who will provide honest feedback about the message content and your delivery style. When possible, rehearse in the room in which you will give the presentation.

If you cannot rehearse before an audience, make an audio recording or a videotape of your rehearsal so that you can do a critical self-analysis. As you evaluate your rehearsal, consider all aspects of structure that were presented in the previous section and the presentation guides that will be given later in this

---

ILLUSTRATION 15-5 ▶ ORAL REPORT CHECKLIST

Oral Report Checklist

Will the **Introduction** of your presentation:
get the audience's attention at the beginning? _____
make a solid connection between your audience and the topic? _____
preview the main points you want to make in the presentation? _____

Will the **Organization** of the presentation:
contain several main ideas or issues? _____
use clear and convincing supporting material? _____
make transitions from one point to the next clearly? _____
use graphics effectively to reinforce and explain the main points? _____

Will the **Conclusion** of your presentation:
summarize the main points effectively? _____
briefly recap your stated purpose? _____
close with a memorable ending? _____

---

chapter. Illustration 15-5 presents a short checklist to help you prepare a successful report presentation.

PRESENTING THE ORAL REPORT

To make an effective oral presentation, you must control three factors: stage fright, the vocal and verbal aspects of a presentation, and the nonverbal aspects of a presentation.

Controlling Stage Fright

It is estimated that nearly 75 percent of people suffer from fear of public speaking. For some the fear is experiencing discomfort at the thought of making a speech, which they overcome by thorough preparation. For others, the fear may be so strong that they become physically incapable of speaking when they appear before the audience.[2] Some years ago a *Wall Street Journal* writer characterized public speaking as one of top executives' greatest fears.[3] Many speakers, even those with many years of experience, are often nervous before they go "on stage." So if you experience some stage fright, you are in good company.

A small amount of tension before a presentation can be beneficial. The tension that accompanies anticipation of an important event can make you alert and prompt you to prepare thoroughly for your speech. But excessive nervousness is often an indication that you are focusing on the wrong things:

Instead of attending to your audience and your message, you may be placing attention on yourself and others' reactions to you. To avoid stage fright, follow these guides.

- **Justify your presentation.** The fact that you have been asked to give a presentation justifies your speech. Remind yourself that you have been asked to present the information because you possess information that others need.
- **Bolster your self-confidence.** Remind yourself of previous successful communication experiences. Make a list of all you know about the topic that your audience likely does not know. List reasons why your audience needs the information you must convey. Remember that the audience is not there to look at you; it is present to hear what you have to say.
- **Trust your audience.** Most audiences are empathetic, receptive, and friendly. They become bored or antagonistic only after a speaker has demonstrated incompetence or lack of respect for the audience. If you attract favorable attention with your opening words and show that you respect your audience's intelligence and needs, you will likely be respected in return.
- **Prepare for the presentation.** Prepare so thoroughly that you know your information, can vary your presentation to meet audience needs, and can enjoy the opportunity to *communicate* important data to others. Think of the presentation as an opportunity to have an informed, animated conversation about a topic that you are knowledgeable of and think is important.
- **Arrive early.** Allow enough time to become comfortable with the room and to check such things as seating arrangements or equipment that will influence your presentation.
- **Use stress reduction techniques just before your presentation.** Some stress reduction techniques that speakers use successfully are shown in Illustration 15-6. Those techniques tend to focus the audience's attention on you, give you a few seconds to collect your thoughts before delivering your opening statement, and promote speaker-audience rapport.

In addition to controlling stage fright, effective speakers demonstrate control of the vocal and verbal aspects of speech.

Controlling Vocal and Verbal Aspects

The vocal aspect of speech communication relates to the quality of sounds that come from your mouth; the verbal aspect relates to the clarity of words that come from your lips.

Vocal quality is controlled by the inhalation, phonation, and resonation phases of speech. *Inhalation* is the process of taking air in through your mouth and nostrils for temporary storage in your lungs. That air is the "fuel" that powers speech and supplies oxygen to your brain. When you breathe deeply, using your diaphragm muscles, you take in a larger supply of fuel than when you breathe shallowly.

ILLUSTRATION 15-6 ▶ STRESS REDUCTION TECHNIQUES

Before assuming your speaking position . . .

- Take a few deep breaths. This technique tends to relax the body and supplies necessary oxygen for clear thinking.
- With arms hanging loosely at your side, clench your fists and then relax the fingers. Imagine and feel the tension flowing out of your body through the tips of your fingers.
- Swallow a few times and wiggle your jaw to relax the muscles that control your throat and jaw.
- Pause before beginning your presentation. Sweep your eyes over the audience. Select one person at whom you will look directly and imagine beginning a conversation with that individual. Smile, unless the topic is so serious that a smile is inappropriate.
- Begin your speech with a confident tone. Conveying confidence helps establish rapport with your audience. Once you "connect" with the audience, you will likely be confident throughout the presentation.

Practice breathing exercises frequently to improve control of inhalation and exhalation. The following exercises will help you control your breathing:

1. Place your hand lightly in the region of the diaphragm, the area between your lower ribs and waistline. Inhale gently but firmly so that the air seems to flow to the area where your hand is resting. As you inhale, that area should move outward; as you exhale, it should move inward. In contrast, when you breathe shallowly, you will feel little or no movement in the abdominal region. Instead, you will feel short, panting movements in the upper chest.
2. Inhale deeply. See how far you can count on one breath. Talk rapidly, but *enunciate* each word distinctly. Work toward a goal of 45 to 60. Men should be able to reach higher counts than women, because men generally have larger chest cavities.

Sound is produced in the *phonation* phase. As you exhale, pushing the air out of your lungs, the air passes through your larynx, commonly called the voice box. The voice box has membranous surfaces called vocal folds. Those folds vibrate as air passes over them, producing sound or vocal pitch. If the folds vibrate quickly, which occurs when the throat muscles are tense, the sound is high-pitched. When the folds vibrate slowly, which occurs when the throat muscles are relaxed, the sound has a lower pitch. In general, a lower pitch is more pleasing to audiences than is a high pitch. Therefore, relaxing the vocal folds during speech is an important speaking skill to master.

The following exercises will help to relax your throat and shoulders. Practice them often, and do one or more in private—not in front of the audience—shortly before giving your speech.

- Drop your head gently forward; slowly rotate it toward your left shoulder, then backward, then toward the right shoulder, then forward again. Do this exercise slowly and smoothly, not jerkily, until you feel the muscles of your shoulders and throat relax.

- Yawn. Feel your throat muscles relax.
- Think "forward" so that you try to project the sound beyond the region of your throat. Do not force from the throat. Instead, imagine the sound flowing outside your body, to a spot on the wall. Read the following paragraph, directing your tone to that one spot.

"I am seeing my grandmother at the back of the room. I am talking to Granny and only to Granny. But Granny does not hear very well, and I must project my voice or she will miss my message. Listen, Granny—hear what I say. My voice is clear, the room is quiet—hear me, if you will."

- Say "one" in the lowest tone you can produce with a clear, controlled, unstrained voice. Move up the musical scale, saying "two, three, four, . . ." until your voice feels slight strain. Move down the scale as far as you can without strain in your voice. Repeat. Through frequent practice, you should be able to extend your vocal range and reduce vocal strain.

After passing through your voice box, the air enters the resonating cavities of your head. In this *resonation* phase vocal timbre (quality) is determined. The cavities act as echoing chambers. If sound is permitted to resonate freely in the cavities, a rich, warm sound is produced. But if the cavities are constricted or closed, a strident or nasal sound is produced.

To produce rich, pleasing sounds, use these techniques.

- Swallow to relax your throat muscles; flare your nostrils to open the nasal passages, and protrude your lips slightly as though preparing to utter the letter O.
- Create a mental image of roundness instead of flatness. This practice tends to open the cavities and permit full resonation of sound.
- Relax your lips and cheeks, and keep your lips covered. Do not expose your teeth in a tight smile. This practice tends to produce a nasal sound.
- Try to keep the throat and resonating cavities open as you practice sentences given in Illustration 15-7.

Although you can create sound by inhalation, phonation, and resonation, you do not form words until the *modification* or *articulation* stage of speech. In this stage you use your lips, teeth, tongue, and palate to form vowels, diphthongs, and consonants—the components of words. A vowel is any sound that continues indefinitely so long as there is breath to support it (for example, *a-a-a-a, e-e-e-e,* etc.) A diphthong is a combination of two vowels that blend rapidly seeming to produce one sound (for example, *ei* sounding like long *i; ie* sounding like long *e*). A consonant is a sound that stops or interrupts itself no matter how much breath is available (for example, *k, p, l*).

Understandable speech results from precise articulation of all word components. One way to improve articulation is to practice the pronunciation and enunciation of difficult letter and word combinations. The sentences given in Illustration 15-7 can also be used to improve articulation.

| ILLUSTRATION 15-7 | RESONATION AND ARTICULATION PRACTICE |

To develop a rich, resonant sound and crisp, clear enunciation, practice saying these sentences aloud.

- Fight fiercely and boldly for firm beliefs but not biases.
- Wet your whistle with water at the well.
- Teresa thought that she and Patty had parted ways too abruptly.
- Many men and women experience stress in modern America, and they must spend some time in mental institutions.
- Must we meet Millie at the milliner?
- Cal can scheme to shoot skeet; but his twin is a twit whose tales are always tame.
- Evaluate the effect of Edward's efforts to study serious spending habits of students.
- After you had discussed those details with your doctor, was your affect toward such affectations altered abundantly?
- What was the incidence of unjustifiable incidental charges entered on your invoice? Was this the first such incident?

Understanding the four phases of speech will help you realize that, through practice, you can control and improve the vocal and verbal qualities of speech. Through that control, you can improve the understandability of your oral presentations. You can also improve communication by gaining greater control of the nonverbal aspects of your presentations.

Controlling Nonverbal Aspects

The major nonverbal communication factors that require control during an oral presentation are your appearance, posture, gestures, and facial expressions.

Appearance. The first impression that your audience forms of you is derived from your appearance. If you want to be judged as a competent, professional person, you must present yourself as one. In a formal context a suit, dress shirt, and tie are recommended for a man, and a conservative suit or dress is recommended for a woman. In less formal settings a man may safely wear a sports jacket and slacks, and a woman may wear a skirt and blouse. Be sure your clothes are comfortable and that the colors complement you. In addition, wear a neat hairstyle that complements your features but draws no excessive attention to itself. Jewelry, if worn, should not be distracting. In all situations avoid gaudiness and extremes.

Dress in such a way that people do not notice specific items that you are wearing but get an overall impression that you are well groomed. Especially for women, a general, safe guide is that if you would wear the garment for leisure, sport, or an after-five party, do not wear it for a presentation.

Posture. Your posture should suggest that you are in control of the presentation. Avoid slouching or rigidity as you stand or sit before your audience.

Slouching tends to connote indifference or carelessness; rigidity tends to connote nervousness. In contrast, sitting or standing erectly tends to signify self-confidence, interest, alertness, readiness, and enthusiasm.

As you stand, place your feet 10 to 12 inches apart, parallel to one another; rest your weight evenly on both feet; let your hands hang loosely at your sides; keep your spine erect, shoulders back, and stomach in. That position permits you to inhale and exhale properly for effective speech. From that stance you can also use your hands easily and naturally for gestures and move gracefully to a new position.

If you sit in front of your audience, move comfortably to the back of the chair, permitting it to support your back and feeling the edge of the seat behind your knees. Place both feet flat on the floor, one slightly in front of the other, to keep yourself balanced and to prevent yourself from slouching or twisting in the chair.

Gestures. Effective speakers do not remain stiffly in one position throughout a presentation. Use gestures—body movements—to complement your words. You probably use gestures spontaneously during interpersonal communication; try to achieve that same spontaneity in your more formal presentations. One way to improve gestures is to use them deliberately while practicing, but do not think about gestures during the actual delivery. If you practice your presentation several times, concentrating on specific gestures, they will tend to become spontaneous and provide appropriate emphasis during the presentation. Although some gesturing can improve your presentation, excessive body movement can become distracting. Use gestures purposefully to emphasize or clarify, not merely to release excess energy.

A clenched fist brought down on the lectern may be used to emphasize or to express anger; arms raised quickly, to express surprise; fingers raised sequentially, to enumerate; finger pointing, to single out a person or object; arms and hands moved, to suggest size, shape, or motion. If, however, your audience is an international one, be aware that gestures have different connotations in different cultures. Illustration 15-8 lists some gestures that are common in the United States but may be offensive in another culture.[4]

Facial Expressions. Facial expressions convey emotions with remarkable accuracy. When you give an oral report, your facial expressions should suggest your enthusiasm for the topic. Moreover, your expressions should show your interest in your listeners and your desire to communicate with them. Those feelings will be conveyed if you develop a positive mental attitude toward your topic and your audience. In contrast, if you are nervous and unsure about your presentation, those feelings will likely be registered in your facial expressions. Therefore, an excellent way to control facial nonverbal communication is to be thoroughly prepared for and confident about your presentation.

Eye contact is essential for effective communication. Lack of such contact suggests discomfort, uncertainty, or embarrassment. Through eye contact you convey your interest in and concern about the audience. In addition, by maintaining that communication link with your audience, you can detect the reactions of individuals to your message. You will see enthusiasm,

ILLUSTRATION 15-8	PRESENTATION GESTURES: POSSIBLE CROSS-CULTURAL MEANINGS	
Action	**U.S. Use/Meaning**	**Meaning in Another Culture**
Pointing with index finger	Emphasis; identification of person in a group, such as pointing to someone in the audience who raises a hand to ask a question	Considered rude in many cultures, especially in Asian countries
Thumbs-up	"That's great"; agreement; sometimes used during an informal discussion	Obscene in many countries, including Nigeria, Australia, and some Middle Eastern countries; no meaning for many Southeast Asian cultures
Crooked finger	"Come here"; sometimes used to signal that a member of the audience should come to the front of the room	Obscene in Asian cultures
Speaker's eye contact with listener/ audience	Connecting with listener; considered essential in U.S. presentations; among urban youths may be considered an invitation to fight	Impudence, disrespect in many Asian and Latin American cultures
Lack of eye contact	Speaker's lack of confidence during presentation; disrespect or disinterest in interpersonal conversation	Respect for authority figure in many Asian and Latin American cultures
Smiling	Friendliness	Japan: sadness, happiness, apology, anger, confusion Korea: shallowness, thoughtlessness Puerto Rico: "Thank you"; "you're welcome"; "excuse me, please"

understanding, interest—or their opposites. When you get negative feedback through eye contact, you have an opportunity to adjust your presentation to meet the needs of your audience. Eye contact will then tell you whether your adjustments are effective.

To maintain eye contact you must actually look at and see the eyes of individuals. Do not look over their heads or at their foreheads, pretending to make contact. Your audience will readily detect that sham. Try to give equal coverage to all of the audience. Avoid focusing on one side of the room or only on the persons who are providing positive feedback.

You can improve the effectiveness of your oral reports through careful preparation and rehearsal of your speech. That kind of preparation tends to reduce stage fright and helps you manage the verbal and nonverbal aspects of your presentation. In addition, you can increase the impact of many oral reports by using presentation aids.

USING PRESENTATION AIDS

Presentation aids are any audio or visual tools you use to supplement your spoken message. A microphone, for example, is an audio tool that can improve your presentation in a large room, enabling everyone to hear you well. A large poster displaying a chart is a visual aid that helps you explain or dramatize data.

To be effective, presentation aids must be incorporated smoothly into your speech. The guides shown in Illustration 15-9 will help you use most audio and visual aids effectively.

USING PRESENTATION SOFTWARE

Today many presenters use graphics *software* programs, such as *Microsoft PowerPoint*®, *Lotus Freelance*®, and *Corel Presentations*®. The programs contain tutorials and templates that make it easy to learn and use the packages. These programs enable you to produce professional-looking visuals if you use them wisely. You can easily add graphics and audio and video clips to produce professional slide shows. You can also print audience handouts and speaker notes from the slides you prepare.

You can begin crafting your presentation by using the outline feature in each package. This feature helps you divide your topic into main points and subpoints. The outline feature prompts you to develop each heading. You can then convert the outline into headings and bullet points. Each main topic becomes a slide heading; subheadings become bullet points. The purpose of the bulleted text is to prompt you as well as visualize the information you want the audience to remember. All three presentation software packages let you use automatic-build slides. This means that bulleted points are added one at a time for a dramatic introduction of your ideas.

Next, you may want to use a design template (master slide) provided in the software package or develop your own. A master slide has common graphic elements, such as your company or organization's name or logo. Select appropriate colors for good contrast. Generally, light text on a dark background is preferred. Also use a readable type size. Projected text is most readable in 32-point type, although there may be some occasions where 24-point type is acceptable. Also, to ensure that conversion issues are not a problem from one machine to another, you will want to use standard fonts common to Windows-based machines. Times New Roman and Arial are almost always available.

ILLUSTRATION 15-9 ▸ GUIDES FOR USING PRESENTATION AIDS

To use presentation aids effectively...

- Prepare the aids in advance; use them in your rehearsal to help you become more confident when using them.
- Check the room in which you will give your presentation to be sure it can accommodate your aids.
- Check all equipment before the presentation to be sure it is operating properly. Be sure that sound equipment, such as a microphone or tape recorder, operates effectively, projecting sound neither too softly nor too loudly.
- Keep the visuals simple. If necessary, prepare and display several aids instead of crowding too much information into one exhibit.
- Number all visuals; mark your notes or manuscript to indicate when they will be used.
- Do not use too many visuals. Each visual should add something to the presentation, not detract from it.
- Be sure each visual aid is large enough for your audience to see and detect the detail you want noticed.
- Avoid displaying a visual aid, or any part of it, until you need it in your presentation.
- Do not block your audience's view of the visual aid; use a pointer if necessary.
- Address the audience, not the aid. As you explain portions of the exhibit, face your audience as much as possible.
- Do not remove the visual before the audience has had an opportunity to examine the information.
- Remove the aid from view when it is no longer relevant to your presentation.
- Avoid talking about something on a visual aid after you have put it aside.
- Turn the equipment off when the projection is finished so that the light and noise will not distract your audience.
- Use your natural speaking voice when using a microphone. Avoid standing so near to the microphone that it picks up sibilant speech sounds or noises from the movement of your papers. An appropriate distance for most microphones is 6 inches from the speaker's mouth.
- Designate a specific person to signal you if the microphone volume is too loud or too soft or a visual is not visible. Make necessary adjustments before your audience becomes distracted.
- Avoid distributing handouts until you need them in the presentation. Restrict their use to information that cannot be presented in other kinds of visual aids or to summarize your message.
- If you prepare a summary handout, inform the audience at the beginning of the presentation that you will distribute that summary at the end.

Be aware that it is easy to overload an audience. Slides, therefore, should have no more than six to seven lines per slide. If you crowd the slide, the audience strains and the impact of the presentation is reduced. Each slide, including text and title, should cover no more than three-fourths of the screen.

When used judiciously, graphics can add interest and aid comprehension within your presentation. This is especially the case when inserting clip art (computerized artwork), graphs, and photographs to your slides. Clip art libraries may include hundreds of symbols such as automobiles, electronic equipment, people, animals, buildings, flowers, etc. To be effective, clip art, graphs, and photographs should be used sparingly, relevant to your topic, and in proper scale. Since business report presentations are often expected to convey a businesslike appearance, make certain that a particular piece of clip art or a specific graph or photograph will help you convey your information more effectively. Do not use such additions merely to demonstrate your familiarity with presentation software.

You may have heard the expression "Death by PowerPoint." This phrase captures many viewers' attitude about the number of poorly developed presentations they are subjected to in business and nonbusiness settings. To avoid killing *your* audience, remember these principles[5]:

- Visuals should enrich the message, not become the message. The speaker's discussion of relevant content should be the focus of audience attention.
- An effective slide show reflects more than just technical features of the software. The overriding goal is effective communication of easy-to-grasp *content* that facilitates extemporaneous delivery by a well-rehearsed, confident speaker.
- The value of slides should be weighed against the need for audience interaction. Slide presentations tend to flatten discussion, sacrifice the richness of dialogue, and reduce audience involvement.

Presentation software outlines and templates should never direct or control your presentation. An effective presentation must begin with a worthy *message* that you are able to formulate and support, can organize and effectively deliver, and can inspire listeners to attend to.[6] Following the guides given in Illustration 15-10 will enable you to use presentation software in such a way that it enhances your presentation of significant content.[7]

In addition to planning the content of your presentation, preparing your visual aids, and rehearsing your presentation, you must decide whether you will encourage your audience to participate by asking questions.

MANAGING QUESTION-ANSWER SESSIONS

Some speaking situations require that the speaker give the audience an opportunity to ask questions. At other times, the speaker may simply want to involve the audience by following a presentation with a question-and-answer session. As you plan your presentation, you should decide the ground rules for questions. Before you begin the presentation, you or the person who introduces you should tell the audience how questions will be handled. Generally, the time allowed and the formality of the situation influence your management of a question-answer session. However, you must always be prepared to answer a question that cannot be forestalled. If the CEO asks a question, you may be wise to answer it when he or she asks, no matter what ground rules you have established.

ILLUSTRATION 15-10   GUIDES FOR CONSTRUCTING PRESENTATION SLIDES

As you plan and prepare your presentation slides . . .

- **Develop an outline for your presentation.** The outline may be based on a written report, but your presentation must never be a verbatim delivery of the written report.
- **Mark the outline to indicate points where a picture, chart, or clip art will enhance the message.** Meaningful placement of visual effects can reinforce ideas, illustrate complex concepts, or relieve the tedium of worded slides.
- **Develop a design or select a template that sets the tone for your presentation and ensures consistency.** The opening slide should establish your identity and the nature of your organization or tone of your message. Some authorities suggest that in a business presentation, the first slide should contain *only* the company's logo.
- **Develop simple, precise, engaging text that introduces or supports your points.** The slides must not contain your full message. Your task is to explain.
- **Write grammatically and logically parallel bullet lists.** Ungrammatical lists and unrelated ideas lead to confusion and misreading.
- **Minimize slide density.** Use type size of 24 points or larger; slide titles of four words or less; maximum of seven words per line and seven lines per slide.
- **Use special effects in moderation.** All animation and sounds should complement the text and tone of the presentation. Excesses annoy audiences.
- **Provide visual as well as oral transitions.** Show the audience where you are going. Use a preview slide at the beginning and divider slides as you move from one point to another and into the Q-A session.
- **Incorporate flexibility and audience interaction into your presentation.** Divider slides can indicate your willingness to open the floor for discussion; a nonlinear design will let you adapt your presentation to audience needs; links to documents or web sites can provide up-to-the-minute information; stories, metaphors, anecdotes, and demonstrations can enliven the presentation.

Informal Presentations

In informal presentations you may permit or encourage the audience to interrupt your presentation as questions arise. If you permit that questioning strategy, you must be able to redirect the discussion to your topic after the question has been answered.

The following techniques will help you redirect the discussion to your topic:

- Graciously remind the audience of the topic that was being discussed before the diversion: "Thank you for your comments. They were stimulated by the statement that customers want teller service on Saturdays. Let's return to that point briefly before we look at other services our customers requested."
- Solicit other questions on the topic to assure the audience that relevant questions or comments are welcome: "Before we examine other options to expand customer services, does anyone have another question or comment about Saturday morning teller service?"

- Summarize the discussion and show its relevance to the last point or the next one to be discussed: "You seem to agree that Saturday teller service is not your first choice. Let's look at other options suggested by our customers."
- Politely stop a person who is monopolizing the question session: "You've asked some good questions. The last one is more closely related to the next topic that I want to cover. Let's hold that one for awhile."

Formal Presentations

For a formal presentation, you will usually ask people to hold their questions until the end of the presentation. If you have allowed time for questions, you can be embarrassed if no one asks a question; conversely, your listeners may be dissatisfied if they are not given enough time for questions. The first rule in managing a formal question-answer session is to allow a realistic amount of time, as is dictated by the content of your message and the context in which it is given.

The following techniques will help you manage specific problems that arise in formal question-answer sessions:

- Anticipate specific questions. You can usually expect questions related to the most complex or controversial parts of your presentation. Be prepared with answers to expected questions.
- "Plant" a question with one member of the audience. Sometimes people are reluctant to ask questions. Ask one person in the audience to ask a specific question if the session begins slowly. That question and its answer may stimulate questions from other people.
- Ask a question yourself. If the questioning begins slowly or lags, suggest a question by saying, "Some of you may be wondering why . . ." As you answer that question, someone may be stimulated to ask another.
- Do not let one person monopolize the session. Politely suggest that you will continue the discussion later ("Let's discuss that over a cup of coffee.") Turn to receive a question from someone else.
- When the allotted time has elapsed, politely thank the audience for its participation and interest. Offer to be available later (give time and place) for further discussion. Do not hold an audience beyond the stated time. Some members may have other commitments.
- If questions lag before the allotted time has elapsed, thank the audience for its participation and interest and dismiss the group. Continuing a discussion that has become redundant can alienate the audience. Most people appreciate the consideration of being given some free time rather than being held for a redundant discussion.

The previous guides for presentations have suggested that you will give a solo performance. Although you will often present reports alone, you will also be required to participate in group presentations during your career.

PARTICIPATING IN TEAM PRESENTATIONS

Oral reports are often developed and delivered by teams of presenters. This is especially true if the presentation requires the input of people with different expertise. For example, individuals from accounting, marketing, and human resources all may be involved in a team presentation regarding the creation of a team to manage a new business account. The best team presentations are "seamless." That is, each segment supports the presentation's overall purpose and is linked to but does not repeat the material in the other segments. In addition, performances are coordinated as each person acts according to a carefully developed plan intended to maintain the focus of the final presentation.

The preceding preparation and presentation guides apply to both individual and team reports. In addition, however, you should master specific techniques required for effective team presentations.

A team presentation should be a carefully orchestrated performance that gives the impression of a single unified report rather than a series of individual speeches. The following guides will help you achieve coherent team presentations:

- As the report is prepared, individuals should be given responsibility for specific parts of the presentation. Ideally, each person will assume primary responsibility for a part about which he or she is most knowledgeable.
- All members of the team should be familiar with the total report, not only with the parts for which they have primary responsibility.
- One team member should act as coordinator to introduce the presentation and the presenters and to moderate the discussion. The coordinator may also be responsible for summarizing the report.
- As an individual completes a section of the report, that person or the coordinator should introduce the next presenter and topic. If you are using presentation software, a divider slide can accomplish that task and take attention away from the physical movements of the speakers as they change positions.
- Team members should be seated quietly while the current presenter stands before the audience. That procedure permits the audience to focus on the current speaker and topic. The seating arrangement should permit a person to sit down gracefully when finished and allow the next presenter to take the speaking position before the audience.
- All aspects of the presentation—spoken parts, use of presentation aids, seating arrangements—should be rehearsed until the group achieves a smooth, comfortable performance. Time the total presentation, including introductions, speaker movements, and Q-A session to be sure that it conforms to the allotted time.

Most oral report presentations are made with the audience and speaker occupying the same room. However, today's electronic technology permits electronic conferencing, techniques by which you can present an oral report to people at a distant location and receive immediate feedback from them.

PARTICIPATING IN ELECTRONIC CONFERENCES

A conference is a meeting called to exchange data and opinions or to solve problems. Conference agendas frequently include oral reports or presentations, followed by discussion and problem-solving sessions.

A traditional conference setting includes all participants in one room, frequently seated around a table. Today, however, electronic technology permits individuals who are separated geographically to conduct a conference as effectively as if they were assembled in the same room. A major advantage of such conferences is that companies can save the travel time and expense required to bring people from many locations together at one site. Regularly scheduled electronic conferences can become an efficient way to accommodate the need for communication among people who are separated from one another geographically.

A *teleconference* is a concurrent telephone conversation among conferees at different locations. Conferees may be alone at their respective telephones or assembled in a room equipped with speaker phones.

A *videoconference* uses both audio and video transmission. To be fully effective, this type of conference requires that television cameras and viewing screens be operating at all sites for conferees. Because of cost, however, video-conferencing often uses one-way video and two-way audio transmission. In such a situation, video cameras are located at a primary conference location with video receivers and audio transmitters/receivers at secondary locations. Whatever technology is employed, the lighting, video, and sound systems, along with the seating arrangements, must permit all conferees to participate fully in the meeting.

Another form of conferencing, the web conference, efficiently integrates audio and video conferencing, along with electronic access to and transfer of files. This type of electronic conference is likely to grow as employees and managers become more dependent upon the Internet as a form of rapid, interactive communication. It may soon replace the teleconference and videoconference because of its flexibility, convenience, and low cost relative to face-to-face meetings. Meeting participants can remain at their desks, using their own computers, instead of going to a specially equipped room. A web conference permits real-time participation of members, both vocally (by telephone or computer sound system) and by chat-room capabilities.

One *web conference* service that is available commercially[8] lets the conference host control the pace of a presentation and participation of the conferees. This system permits sharing of presentation and document files; lets the host annotate a panel while presenting and enable conferees to modify documents in real time; let conferees speak or mute them (a convenient feature to block out static or a domineering conferee); and record the entire meeting to be played back at another time or sent to conferees by e-mail or file transfer. The potential for team collaboration or employee training across great distances makes this type of conferencing almost mandatory to make efficient use of time and talent when employees are scattered geographically.

When suitable technology for an electronic conference is available, managers have found that they can be as effective as face-to-face conferences.[9]

| ILLUSTRATION 15-11 | GUIDES FOR LEADER OF ELECTRONIC CONFERENCE |

Before the Conference

- Notify conferees by telephone or in writing about the objective of the conference.
- Arrange a time that is suitable for all participants.
- Announce purpose and time early enough to allow participants to prepare.
- Distribute a written pre-conference overview or discussion guide to focus the conferees' attention and increase the efficiency of the conference.
- Familiarize yourself with the equipment. Be sure that you know your responsibilities for ensuring that the technology complements the presentation and responses.

During the Conference

- Look at the camera and do not stray from the microphone. Pay attention to signals from audio or video technicians to be sure that the transmitted sound and pictures contribute to your presentation.
- Verify that all participants are online and can hear.
- Introduce yourself. Ask others to identify themselves when they respond to anything during the conference.
- Remind the group of the ground rules to be observed.
- Keep your presentation, or major parts of it, short.
- Provide for frequent verbal feedback.
- Ask for responses from other conferees if the topic requires such input.
- Listen attentively when conferees ask questions or discuss your report. Lack of visual cues or limited cues require that you listen more attentively than when you have full access to your audience's nonverbal responses.
- Give an oral summary at the end of the conference.

After the Conference

- Send each conferee a written summary of the conference within a day or two.
- Attend to any action items for which you are responsible.

Effectiveness is greatly influenced, however, by the conferees' preparation, as it would be for any meeting. In addition to the guides already given in this chapter, follow the guides given in Illustrations 15-11 and 15-12. Although some of those guides may apply only to one type of electronic conference, observing those that apply in your particular conference mode will help you participate effectively as a leader/presenter or conferee in an electronic conference.

ETHICAL CONSIDERATIONS

Some might argue that speakers who deliver wordy, imprecise messages requiring additional inquiry to clarify meaning are acting unethically. Such messages waste time and resources of both speakers and audience members. But they are not unethical unless the intent is to deceive.

ILLUSTRATION 15-12	GUIDES FOR PARTICIPANTS IN ELECTRONIC CONFERENCE

Before the Conference

- Familiarize yourself with the objective of the conference.
- Prepare notes or assemble reference documents.
- Arrive at your receiving site early enough to ensure that you are present when the connection is made and are familiar with any equipment you will use.

During the Conference

- Listen purposefully to the conference leader and all speakers. Lack of visual cues or limited cues require that you listen more attentively than when you have full access to your audience's non-verbal responses.
- Take notes on the presentation so that you can respond when the leader calls on you.
- Do not interrupt while others are speaking.
- Identify yourself and speak distinctly when you respond.
- Make your responses clear and concise.
- Relate your comments to specific parts of the discussion guide if you were given one.
- Listen attentively to the leader's summary. If you disagree with or do not understand any part it, ask for corrections or clarification.

After the Conference

- Read the written summary promptly. If you disagree with or do not understand any part of it, ask for corrections or clarification.
- Attend to any action items for which you are responsible.

In creating a presentation, your goal should be to ensure a common frame of reference between you and your audience; you want your audience to see and hear how important you consider each idea to be. Your goal is not to mislead the audience; rather it is to understand the needs, values, and attitudes of your audience so you can make them identify with your point. This analysis must be based on a respect for and sensitivity to the audience's position.

Speakers may be tempted to make their points more forceful by exaggerating a point, omitting something crucial, or providing deceptive emphasis. Consider the case of a speaker attempting to convince employees to accept a change in insurance benefits. The speaker emphasized a small benefit but de-emphasized a major reduction in total coverage. Some members of the audience missed the main point. Others recognized the deception, however, and before long the speaker's credibility was lost. A speaker is effective only when he or she is believable. If audience members suspect that they are being manipulated or misled, or if they find any part of the presentation untruthful, the total presentation fails.

Conveying an accurate picture is no simple undertaking. Words have imprecise and inconsistent meanings in our minds. But words do not present the only difficulties in delivering effective presentations. Perhaps as important are the items you select for presentation and the emphasis you give them.

Managing the question-answer session also offers some interesting ethical dilemmas. If it is a team presentation, share the responsibility for answering the questions. Avoid having one person dominate the session. However, if you sense that a team member is hesitant or may be about to convey inaccurate information, tactfully step in to answer the question. You can do so by interjecting a statement such as, "I've worked closely with this part of the project . . . ," If you do not know the answer to a question during or after a presentation, freely say so and promise to have the answer within a specific period of time. Much credibility is lost when a speaker attempts to "bluff" through an answer.

The best approach to making an ethical presentation is to present your information honestly, fairly, and without deception. Be aware of your own biases and prejudices so that you do not unconsciously distort data. Remember that the goals of an ethical communicator include telling the truth, labeling opinions so that they can be distinguished from facts, being objective, writing and speaking clearly, and giving credit when you use others' ideas or words.

SUMMARY

Effective oral presentations begin with comprehensive preparation. That preparation includes analysis of the context, selection of delivery style, outlining the presentation, devising effective transitions between parts, preparing visual aids, and rehearsing the presentation until you have perfected all aspects of delivery.

Effective delivery of an oral presentation requires control of stage fright, the vocal and verbal aspects of speech, and nonverbal communication cues. In addition, you should develop skill in using presentation aids to give additional audio or visual impact to your oral reports.

The ready availability of presentation software requires a concentrated effort to make every slide or panel meaningful. Begin with a worthy message. Avoid the temptation to overload slides and to use unrelated sounds or trite clip art.

Group reports require careful coordination of all aspects of the presentation. Group members must be knowledgeable about all parts of the report, not only those for which they have specific responsibility. Both individual and group reports may be presented in an electronic conference mode as well as in face-to-face contexts.

TOPICS FOR DISCUSSION

1. Explain the purpose and methods for doing an analysis of the speech context, including the audience and physical environment.

2. Explain how the style of presentation is related to the audience and the physical environment. Give examples to demonstrate your understanding of the relationship.

3. Describe the major characteristics of each of these types of delivery:
   - Impromptu
   - Extemporaneous
   - Textual/scripted
   - Memorized
   - Combination

4. Describe the desired characteristics of these aspects of a presentation:
   - Opening
   - Partition statement
   - Body
   - Transitions
   - Conclusion
   - Memorable language

5. Discuss factors that must be considered when selecting a visual aid.

6. Describe effective rehearsal techniques.

7. Describe effective techniques to reduce stage fright. If you use any techniques that are not described in this chapter, share them with your classmates.

8. Explain what occurs in each of these phases of speech and their relevance to your developing a pleasing delivery style:
   - Inhalation
   - Phonation
   - Resonation
   - Modification

9. For each of the following categories, give examples of specific nonverbal behaviors and how they can enhance or detract from an oral presentation:
   - Appearance
   - Posture
   - Gestures
   - Facial expressions

10. Compare the advantages and disadvantages of the following media for oral reports:
    - Computer presentation software
    - Transparencies
    - Flip chart
    - Objects
    - Handouts

11. Discuss recommendations for preparing a presentation using presentation software packages. Share with your classmates characteristics of effective and ineffective use of presentation technology that you have seen.

12. Explain how to manage question-answer sessions effectively.

13. Identify behaviors or techniques that contribute to effective team presentations.

14. Identify behaviors or techniques that contribute to effective participation in an electronic conference.

15. If you have had experience participating in a web conference, describe the experience for your classmates.

APPLICATIONS

1. Plan an informative speech (about five minutes long) for delivery to your classmates. Select a topic with which you are comfortable and knowledgeable. Try to select a topic that is not familiar to your classmates. Examples of appropriate topics include an unusual hobby, a unique travel experience, a creative idea for a new product or service, your position on a controversial issue, an "unforgettable person" whom you know. Answer the following questions and prepare a preliminary outline:
   • Audience for the speech?
   • Reasons the audience may need the information?
   • Relevant audience interests and needs?
   • The purpose of the speech?
   • What the audience already knows?
   • Additional information to be researched?
   • Resources for information?
   Structure your speech to include an attention-getting beginning that draws the audience into your presentation; a partition statement that clearly and interestingly defines your main points; interesting, adequate development of the points; meaningful transitions, and a memorable conclusion. Follow any additional guides for preparation or delivery that your instructor may give.

2. Write a memo to your instructor in which you evaluate a speech presented by one of your classmates. In your evaluation include specific strengths or weaknesses related to:
   • Opening of speech
   • Partition statement
   • Body of speech
   • Transitions
   • Conclusion
   • Verbal and vocal aspects of delivery
   • Nonverbal aspects of delivery
   • Handling questions (if applicable)

3. Interview a person who gives presentations frequently. For example, you may want to talk to a salesperson, a teacher, a member of the clergy, or

someone else who regularly talks to large groups of people. Ask that person how he or she organizes, constructs, practices, and actually delivers his or her presentations. In a memo, share your findings with your instructor.

4. Prepare and deliver a five-minute presentation in which you demonstrate effective use of presentation software. Use a topic of your choice or one assigned by your instructor. Include at least one of each of the following types of slides in your presentation:
   - A title slide
   - A slide containing text with bulleted items
   - A slide containing clip art or a picture
   - A slide containing a pie chart, bar chart, or line graph
   - A slide using animation effects

5. Change one of the reports you have prepared in this course into an oral report. Deliver the report extemporaneously. Use visual aids to support major points.

6. This application will give you experience thinking on your feet. You will need a container to gather topics. Each member of the class writes two impromptu topics on pieces of paper and puts the papers into the container. Each speaker then draws a topic from the container. After three minutes of preparation, each speaker gives a three-minute presentation to the class on that topic.

7. After giving the impromptu presentation mentioned in Application 6, conduct additional research to get information needed for a 7- to 10-minute presentation on the same topic. Develop an outline and at least three visual aids to accompany the presentation. As directed by your instructor, deliver the presentation.

8. Select one of the topics below. Gather enough information for a five-minute presentation. Outline your presentation. Prepare three interesting and relevant opening statements, previews, and concluding statements for the presentation. Select the best opening statement, preview, and conclusion and incorporate them into your outline, along with appropriate transitions between main points. Plan the kinds of visual aids that would assist you in creating interest in and understanding of your topic. Identify at least two visual aids you might use in your speech. Draw a rough sketch showing what each aid would look like. Also indicate the means by which you would present the aid.
   - Advantages and pitfalls of payday loans
   - What you can learn from urbandictionary.com
   - Importance of beginning your retirement fund now
   - Business adoption of "green" (environmental friendly) construction
   - Costs of owning a companion animal (pet)
   - Psychological benefits of owning a companion animal (pet)
   - What you can learn by "googling" yourself
   - Terrorism and Human Resources Management

- Questionable behavior of corporate or government officials during the past decade
- Women in military combat

9. Using the topic you selected in Application 8, pair up with a classmate. Exchange your speech outlines and sketches of visual aids. Offer constructive criticism to one another.

10. Incorporate any valuable suggestions received from your classmate in Application 9. Complete your preparation and rehearsal for the presentation. Deliver the presentation at a time and place chosen by your instructor.

11. Select an article from a recent issue of a professional journal such as *Journal of Business Communication, Journal of Business and Technical Communication,* or *Academy of Management Executive.* In a memo report to your instructor, identify each of the following:
    - Attention-getting device(s)
    - Intended audience and audience adaptation(s)
    - Preview or partition statement
    - Main points
    - Conclusion

12. In a memo to your instructor, identify the changes you would make in the structure or content of the article used in Application 11 if you were to present the same information to members of your class; to a group of business people; to the media.

13. Attend a presentation by a guest lecturer on your campus, a meeting of a business or professional organization (such as Rotary, Kiwanis, or Business and Professional Women), or a student chapter meeting of a professional association. In a memo to your instructor, critique the speaker in terms of the following categories:
    - Introduction:
        - How clear were the topic and the purpose of the speech?
        - What attention-getting devices did the speaker use?
        - How effective were the devices in building rapport and interest?
    - Body:
        - Were the main points clearly organized?
        - What kind of information did the speaker use to support the main points?
        - What visual aids did the speaker use? Were they incorporated into the presentation effectively?
    - Conclusion:
        - What concluding devices did the speaker use?
        - How effective were the devices in ending the presentation?
    - Language:
        - Did the speaker use memorable language? Give examples.
        - Was the level of formality appropriate for the audience and context?

REFERENCES

1. Ramki, --. (2003). *Speak freak*. Retrieved August 2, 2005, from http://www.speakfreak.com

2. Nicoli, T. *Public speaking package*. Retrieved August 2, 2005, from http://www.tomnicoli.com/public-speaking-pkg.shtml

3. Proodian, R. (1981, September 28). One challenge many executives fear: A speech. *The Wall Street Journal*, p. 26.

4. Adapted from Dresser, N. (1996). *Multicultural Manners*. New York: John Wiley & Sons, Inc., pp. 11–33.

5. DuFrene, D. D., & Lehman, C. M. (2004). Concept, content, construction, and contingencies: Getting the horse before the PowerPoint cart. *Business Communication Quarterly, 67*: 84–88.

6. Jones, G. H. (2004) Message first: Using films to power the point. *Business Communication Quarterly, 67*: 88–91.

7. These guides are a synthesis of two sources: DuFrene, D. D., & Lehman, C. M. (2004). Concept, content, construction, and contingencies: Getting the horse before the PowerPoint cart. *Business Communication Quarterly, 67*: 84–88; guides that appeared in Kuiper, S., & Kohut, G. F. *Contemporary business report writing, 2nd edition.*

8. Webex™ integrated audio conferencing. Retrieved August 4, 2005, at http://www.webex.com

9. Rosetti, D. K., & Surynt, T. J. (1985). Video teleconferencing and performance. *The Journal of Business Communication, 22*: 25–31.

chapter 16

Writing the Business Plan*

LEARNING OBJECTIVES

After you have read this chapter, you should be able to:

1. Tell what a business plan contains.
2. Explain the two principal objectives of a business plan in terms of its purposes of convincing and persuading.
3. Understand why entrepreneurs need a business plan.
4. Apply your knowledge of business research and analysis to write a business plan.

Creating a business plan is a special situation in business writing. The business plan is a document that describes in detail the business concept in an entrepreneur's mind: an unsatisfied need on the part of potential customers that creates an opportunity for the entrepreneur, what the entrepreneur will offer to meet that need, why and how the entrepreneur's offering will draw customers away from the alternatives available to them. The business plan also describes the various resources he or she will employ to realize the business concept and the expected financial results, usually projected under several scenarios.

ENTREPRENEURS AND THE BUSINESS PLAN

Entrepreneurs and consultants alike often say that a business plan serves as a road map to "help your business get where you want it to be." Use of this metaphor has become a cliché, but it expresses an important truth about the business plan's use and importance. It misleads on an equally important truth, though. Unlike a road map, the business plan doesn't wait in a display rack for your purchase. Instead, the business plan waits for you to create it.

Special Challenge of the Business Plan

The business plan combines vision and often novelty with concrete information to offer a thorough, coherent argument for the proposed business. Therefore, in

*This chapter was contributed by William R. Sandberg, Ph.D., Associate Professor of Management, Moore School of Business, University of South Carolina.

creating a business plan you will draw on the business research and communication skills learned in the preceding chapters and present the results with a dual purpose: first, to *convince* readers that your business concept is valid and you are prepared to pursue it; and second, to *persuade* them to play a part in making it real. Seen in this light, your business plan is primarily a sales document; and its readers are various markets you have targeted, each for its own reason.

When thinking of a sales document, most people bring to mind an advertisement or brochure that touts the benefits of a company's product or service. They may imagine unfailingly positive statements, glowing descriptions, extravagant claims, and the heavy use of superlatives (the *most, best, biggest, finest*, etc.) to describe products and services. However effective such presentations may be in some sales situations, they are disastrous in a business plan.

Think about industries in which you have worked or that you have studied. Just about any company faces competitive threats from rivals; just about any business strategy commits resources on the basis of assumptions or estimates that may be wrong; just about any innovation encounters resistance from those who have invested in the previous technology or arrangements; and just about any group of customers may change their preferences within a product category or their spending priorities across categories. In short, no new business venture faces only opportunity and promise; it also faces threats and problems. A business plan that emphasizes the venture's bright prospects and downplays (or worse, omits) its risks warns a reader that the entrepreneur is uninformed, imperceptive, or dishonest—or that he or she underestimates the reader's business sense. Any of these judgments will prove fatal to the entrepreneur's hopes to convince and persuade the reader. Instead, the business plan should present your business concept to the best effect by recognizing its risks and the problems you will encounter, coupled with the steps you will take to reduce the risks or counter the problems. The readers whose opinions count most in your future will be more impressed by the plan *and by you* if you do so.

Your plan's readers will fall into two general audiences: people who might work with you to implement it as your fellow managers or employees, and people who can provide the financial resources or other means to accomplish it. Among the second group may be bankers from whom you hope to borrow funds, professional investors who may buy an interest in your business, and the managers of other companies that you seek as either suppliers or customers. Members of these audiences have different reasons for reading the business plan, concentrate on different aspects of it, and make different uses of what they read.

Many of the readers also read business plans submitted by other entrepreneurs who seek from them the same resources or cooperation that you want; consequently, these reader will compare you to those other entrepreneurs as well as consider your idea in some absolute sense. Almost every reader has many other claims on his or her attention. Your business plan must arrest and sustain that attention, thoroughly present the necessary information, and yet not overtax his or her scarce time. Thus the business plan presents not only a special but also an unusually complex situation in business writing.

Why Write a Business Plan?

You may never write a business plan except as a course assignment. Writing a business plan is not among most employees' responsibilities. On the other hand, almost anyone who starts a business, even as a solo effort, would benefit from writing a business plan. Through the necessary research you may discover overlooked opportunities or competitive threats to your idea, or simply clarify your thoughts. For example, you may modify your business concept to focus on a slightly different need or group of potential customers, or conceive of a more effective way of meeting the original need. A related benefit of writing a business plan is the chance to discover fatal flaws in your concept through research and analysis rather than through costly trial and error. Consultants and professors in entrepreneurship regularly hear entrepreneurs describe their failures in terms such as "If I had only known . . ." or "I didn't expect. . . ." Often a business plan would have revealed the problem.

Entrepreneurs and small-business owners sometimes rationalize their failure to write a business plan by arguing that no one can expect to implement a plan as written. New opportunities, unseen threats, uncontrollable changes in a company's markets or its supply sources, and other possibly unimaginable conditions will arise, they say, and quickly invalidate the plan. In this way of thinking, the effort and expense devoted to a business plan become wasted resources, and the entrepreneur would have been better off concentrating on production, sales, or raising capital.

Here again the skeptics miss the potential value of a business plan. Just as your research and analysis can discover both opportunities and problems before you launch the business, they also give you a richer, more instinctive understanding of the key factors on which your success will depend. When events surprise you or performance does not meet your expectations, that understanding will improve your chances of solving the problems and saving your company. In the face of a crisis during your company's early years, you will be stretched to your physical and mental limits to keep the company going while identifying and implementing the changes needed to save it. By the point of crisis, you no longer have the luxury of stepping away from daily pressures to rethink your strategy or undertake extensive research. Instead, you need to have the information and understanding already in your mind and recorded in usable form.

If you start a business that requires more than just your own money and individual effort, you will probably *have to* write a business plan; and that document is likely to be among the most important you ever produce. The people you approach for critical resources or cooperation—potential partners, investors, lenders, members of your management team, major suppliers or customers, and others—will use the business plan to evaluate both you and your venture. Many of them will insist on receiving it before fully considering your proposition to participate or cooperate in the venture. Sometimes their evaluation will be analytical and carefully thought out on the basis of information you provide, and at other times it will be subjective and perhaps quick-triggered on the basis of how well you seem to understand your own business concept and plans. In either case, the business plan will be pivotal in their evaluation of the business concept and of your qualifications to carry it out and, therefore, in their response to your proposition.

COMPONENTS AND CONTENTS OF A BUSINESS PLAN

There is no standard template that all business plans must fit. Among experts who advise entrepreneurs, write entrepreneurship textbooks, or themselves regularly invest in new ventures, there is widespread agreement on what should be covered and how arguments should be made but no consensus on the sequence of a business plan's components or their precise titles. These experts and most of the people who will read your business plan look for a clear, logically compelling presentation of your business concept, the resources needed, and the expected financial results. Through experience they have learned that each business venture is unique and that, within limits, there are many effective variations on a "standard" business plan. The key to successful presentation of your business plan is to cover what readers expect and to organize the material so that your arguments (for the proposed venture's prospects, your qualification to lead it, and the reader's commitment to participate or cooperate in the desired ways) are effective. In this section of the chapter, you will learn about each component, what it should contain, and how its arguments can be made effective. The titles of the components employed here are generic; in any business plan you will want to create titles that focus on *your* business concept. The components appear in a sequence that should always be effective, but it is possible that slightly different sequences could be more effective for a particular business plan.

At the end of this chapter, you will find *KidSmart*™, a business plan prepared by entrepreneurial MBA students who sought venture capital investors to fund their company. This business plan was the 2003 global champion in the prestigious MOOTCORP® Competition of the McCombs School of Business at the University of Texas at Austin, dubbed by *Business Week* "the Super Bowl of world business-plan competition." "Comment balloons" throughout the document illustrate and expand on the material presented in this chapter.

Preliminary Components

The business plan begins with several components whose purpose is to aid the reader in quickly sizing up the proposed venture, understanding the entrepreneur's ideas, and finding more detailed arguments and information in the plan's main body. The preliminary components are brief and typically are produced late in the process of writing a business plan. Those facts do not justify the casual attitude of some entrepreneurs to writing these components. Like every other component of a business plan, they are included for good reasons and can either help or frustrate your efforts to secure resources and support for your venture.

COVER PAGE

The cover page is the business plan's first page. (See *KidSmart*™, p. 451). As such its purpose is similar to that of title pages you have used on other business reports. The cover page should include the following items:

- The company's name, address, and telephone number
- Its Internet and/or e-mail address
- The company's logo or other identifying image
- The name, address, telephone, and e-mail address of the company's contact person
- The date of the business plan (to distinguish it from earlier or later versions) and its copy number (so you can track how many copies you have issued, and to whom)
- A statement that prohibits copying of the business plan

The layout of the cover page allows some flexibility within certain conventions. The company name and logo should appear in the upper half of the page. Position the logo or other image where it achieves the best visual effect, whether above or below the company name; you may place the logo between the company's name and its address and contact information if doing so creates a more powerful visual impression without obscuring the information. If the contact person's address and phone number are identical to the company's, you may list him or her with the company information to avoid repeating these details. (Again see *KidSmart*™ cover page, p. 451.) The plan's date should be centered in the lower quarter of the page, followed a few lines lower by the copy number.

Because the cover page influences a reader's first impression of the company, you must create a professional appearance on several dimensions. First, the page should look good: relevant information organized and attractively displayed. A business plan is a serious document from which the reader hopes to extract essential business information. The cover page is the first visual clue of the writer's care and competence. Second, avoid the temptation to economize by using clip art or your own artistic rendering of a logo or other image; either approach appears amateurish. Because flashiness may or may not be appropriate in the industry you are entering, you should study the logos and other visual images of successful firms in that industry to see what tone they set, then craft a similar yet distinctive logo or imagery for your company. If you have the financial means to be launching a company that will appeal to investors, lenders, and others, you ought to be able to afford the professional services of a graphic designer or artist. If you cannot afford this modest cost, you probably cannot afford the business venture either. It is better to omit a logo than to use one that presents you as bizarre, lacking business judgment, or severely undercapitalized.

TABLE OF CONTENTS

The business plan's second page should be a table of contents, so labeled, that shows an outline of the principal section headings and the page on which each section begins. (See *KidSmart*™, p. 452.) The table of contents should include secondary headings and their page numbers, indented below their principal headings, if the plan's sections typically exceed four or five pages in length. (In that case you also should consider trimming the length of the business plan or some of its sections!)

The table of contents should include all appendices, identified by title and page number. Do not treat the appendices as one undifferentiated lump named "Appendix," or readers will abandon their effort to find the supplementary information.

Remember that you *want the reader to persist* in reading your plan. The moment the reader loses interest and sets aside your document, you have failed to secure the loan, investment, contract, management talent, or other resource you sought from him or her. The table of contents plays a crucial role in facilitating the reader's navigation through your business plan. Research has shown that venture capitalists read business plans by skipping from section to section, seeking topics or information that would address the interests, concerns, or questions that come to mind as they read.[1] Other readers may respond to different topics or information than venture capitalists, but there is every reason to believe that they too skip through the plan. You can ease their task, and thereby sustain their interest in your plan, by using page tabs to locate principal sections.

EXECUTIVE SUMMARY

On the page immediately following the table of contents, the executive summary usually is the first component to be read. (See *KidSmart*™, Section I.) In no more than two pages, the executive summary offers a quick look at the entire business plan. It is *not* an introduction to the business plan nor an identification of the topics covered. Instead the executive summary expresses the essence of the business concept, how the entrepreneur will pursue it, the expected results, and the proposition placed before the reader. Your aim at this point is to win the reader's further interest and, if possible, his or her tentative acceptance of your logic as you build your arguments throughout the plan.

Many entrepreneurs believe that their business concept, strategy, marketing plans, financial projections, and other vital information cannot be compressed into two pages. Yet the executive summary must accomplish precisely that, while capturing readers' attention and motivating them to dig deeper into the business plan. In writing the executive summary you must exercise selective judgment, distinguishing the most important points from the necessary but lesser details in your business plan. Your success in doing so will depend on both your skill as a writer and your conceptual understanding of your own business idea: If you cannot distinguish the keys to success in this idea, you are likely to fail in its execution. Savvy readers appreciate this point and use the executive summary as a quick screening device, often reading no further before abandoning interest.

With so much at stake, you must devote more attention per page to the executive summary than you are likely to give to the writing of any other section. In spite of its position at the beginning of the document, the executive summary should be the last component you write. Begin it only after you have completed the entire business plan. Write the executive summary from scratch so it accurately presents the business plan's main points in a fresh, inviting way. For two reasons you should avoid recycling sentences or paragraphs from the body of the plan. First, the reader may notice and be put off by such verbatim repetition when the same text appears in the body. By that point in the plan, you want the reader to experience a comfortable familiarity with your reasoning but not a sense of *déjà vu*. The more important reason, though, is what you lose by taking this writing shortcut. Cutting and pasting to create the executive summary avoids the difficult but rewarding job of articulating your two arguments—for the venture's viability and your qualification to launch it, and for the action you want each reader to take. Exhausted by writing the complete plan, steeped in its logic, and eager to place it in the hands of important readers, the entrepreneur often neglects to connect the pieces of his or her arguments so a first-time reader will follow them. A reader who does not follow the arguments will not tentatively accept them.

Body: Concept and Product

The body of a business plan consists of critical components that all experts agree must be included as well as other components that may not always appear, although their usual contents may be folded into another component. The sequence of components within the main body will vary according to the priorities of the business venture and its plans, or according to the preferences of the expert giving advice; but the components should fall into an order that logically develops the entrepreneur's arguments and the proposition offered to readers.

Some experts recommend that the business plan begin with a "general company description" or similarly titled section. The information presented there is basic. It elaborates what was presented on the cover page (company name, location, etc.); tells whether the company is organized as a sole proprietorship, partnership, or corporation; identifies the company's industry and products; explains its objectives; and recounts its history, if any. The value of including this section lies primarily in ensuring that the plan does not omit this important information. Its primary drawback is the risk of starting the business plan's body with a dry recitation of dull, unimaginative information when the entrepreneur has the opportunity to explain the business concept. Most of the information routinely included in the "company description" either appeared on the cover page or can be presented later, in covering the organizational plans or management team, without losing credibility in the reader's eyes. With these considerations in mind, you may begin the business plan's body by explaining the business concept.[2]

THE BUSINESS CONCEPT

Recall that the business concept identifies an unsatisfied need on the part of potential customers, what the entrepreneur will offer to satisfy that need, and how this offering will draw customers away from the alternatives they currently use. (See *KidSmart*™, pp. 3–4.) In this section of the business plan you must concisely and convincingly detail your business concept. What you write here will establish the context for everything that follows in your business plan. For example, the subsequent sections on the organizational plan and management team will detail the human resources required to start and build this company, not merely as a generic example of its line of business but specifically as a company that pursues the kind of uniqueness and serves the types of customers you identify here. Readers will keep in mind the requirements implied by your business concept and will assess your organizational plan and management team against them.

Explaining the Business Concept. Your description of the concept should specify the company's product or service, the types of customer on which it will focus, the benefits customers will derive from the product or service, and its means of distribution. Rather than emphasize the features of your product or service, you should explain the venture largely in terms of the customer needs it will fill through them. For example, an air charter service shouldn't be described merely as renting airplanes and the services of pilots; instead its mission might be to provide rapid aerial transportation to locations not served by scheduled carriers plus flyover services for aerial photography and the location or evaluation of sites for property development. An effective description of the air charter's business concept would include both the physical (for example, the rental of airplanes and pilots' services) and the needs met by its services (for example, the motives that would lead business or pleasure travelers to use private aircraft). You would identify the groups of customers that are your primary focus (for example, executives plus sales and service personnel with local companies who need to reach industrial customers in territory not conveniently served by airlines, state economic development officials and representatives of companies they are assisting in plant location decisions). Finally, your business concept should tell how your product or service will reach its customers (for example, direct mail and personal meetings with executives of the companies known to need better air connections, similar contacts with state and local government agencies that undertake industrial recruitment).

Keeping in mind the value of visual images, you should include photographs or quality drawings when they will clarify your business concept. For example, students proposing a fashion design boutique included sketches of dresses and suits by their designer (a member of their team). The sketches clarified the fashion concept underlying the proposed venture and conveyed a sense of the designer's talents. Whether to present illustrations in this section or later, in a detailed description of the product, is your decision. Consider whether the product or service is so novel that readers will need help to grasp the concept (if so, illustrations belong in this section); or less novel and more closely comparable to existing products (if so, the illustrations could wait).

Primary Customer. Which customers will respond to your efforts? Not every person or organization that is part of the market is equally attracted to the benefits you will offer, able to pay the price you will charge, or reachable through the distribution channels you will use. Your business plan will describe the primary customer in greater detail in its section on the market, but here you should describe the chief differences between your key customers and other buyers of the product/service who are less likely to respond to your appeal.

Uniqueness of the Product/Service. Entry into an industry and the market it serves is challenging under most conditions but is especially difficult and unpromising if a venture will merely imitate the companies that already are in place. Therefore, it is extremely important that you state clearly the points that will set your venture apart from its rivals. In some markets customers may understand the benefits of features without elaboration on your part, but you should not take this understanding for granted in writing your business plan. You seek to persuade investors, lenders, and others who may not thoroughly understand the products and market you describe. Whereas the features may be obviously different from those of rival products or services, you will want to link those differences directly to the benefits they create for customers.

THE PRODUCT (OR SERVICE)

You have explained the product's role in your business concept. Now you should elaborate on the product itself—its design, features, and use. (See *KidSmart*™, pp. 5–7.) The benefits you outlined earlier are created through product features or applications. Readers will want clear explanations of how the necessary capabilities are embodied in your product. Similar issues arise as they consider services you propose to offer. What will enable you to provide customer benefits that competitors cannot? Have you rethought a familiar service so it can be performed uniquely? If so, have you demonstrated its effectiveness?

Development of the Product/Service. When the product or service already is well established, this topic may be omitted. It *is* needed, though, if you intend to modify the product or service in some new way. If your business concept rests on improving a technology or its application, your company probably will have to develop and test a prototype product or service before beginning commercial operations. If so, you should report on the prototype's state of development and the steps required to bring the product to readiness. The same is true of any improved production process that the venture would use.

A new type of service faces parallel challenges: The business plan should report the development of the service and any pilot operations. This would be true, for example, of a pioneering use of self-service in a business that has not seen that concept. Customers would have to learn how to perform the functions typically performed by an employee, and the adoption of self-service might require the redesign of the typical site of interaction with customers.

Proprietary Status. Note any protection available to the venture for its product, service, or business concept. Possible sources of protection include patents, copyrights, trademarks, and licensing agreements. Consider also trade secrets and the types of complexity that make imitation difficult—not all proprietary information and processes are based on legal protection.

Sources of Materials, Components, Supplies. Even though a detailed operational plan follows later in the business plan, readers may want to know at this point how the venture will acquire needed materials or other process inputs. Pay particular attention to any input that is critical to the venture's strategy or that is not generally available. For example, a fashion designer whose products required especially fine woolen or silk fabrics explained how a reliable supply of those fabrics would be assured, whereas one whose products were cut from a commodity fabric did not need to detail her sources. Most restaurants would need only to ensure readers that reliable restaurant food suppliers served their area, but one specializing in fresh seafood while operating in Nebraska would need to identify its sources of supply.

Potential Extension or Diversification. Describe directions for growth that derive from the initial strategy of your venture. These might include additional lines of product or service that could be sold to your primary customers or other customer groups that might become reachable from your position in your primary market or segment. This topic is optional as not all ventures have such prospects at their inception. It is better to remain silent on product or service diversification than to offer far-fetched notions.

Body: The Industry and the Market

Your next aim is to demonstrate that an entrepreneurial opportunity exists. (See *KidSmart*™, pp. 7–13.) An assessment of the possible opportunity rests on two fundamental questions:

- Do enough people or organizations have an unmet need *and* the ability to pay for a solution?
- Is it possible to overcome or evade existing competitors in entering, capturing, and holding the market you seek?

How you sequence the sections on the industry and the market will depend on which elements of your business concept hold the keys to understanding your venture and to its success. For instance, if the unmet need results from insufficient industry capacity, or if you propose an improvement in the production process, then your argument depends primarily on characteristics of the industry (the producers or providers of the product/service) and the individual firms it comprises. On the other hand, if the unmet need is one that incumbent firms have not noticed or that customers themselves have yet to recognize, your argument depends primarily on the characteristics of the market (the buyers and their needs). Your coverage of industry and market should open with the subject that is more central to the uniqueness of your business concept.

From this portion of the business plan the reader should learn not only about the industry and the market, but also about your insight into them. It is a grave error to treat this portion or its sections as a series of separate essays. Instead you must present an integrated portrait of industry and market that develops and sustains your key findings and conclusions about them and about your venture's place in them. Lead the reader to your conclusions by stating them at the outset in concise, summary form, then building the argument for them throughout the section. Success in your argument does not arise from repetition of the same points or from the accumulation of assertions, but from careful construction of the argument through the introduction and logical integration of ever more information pointing to your conclusions.

Although a business plan certainly is not a business research paper, your work on the industry and market must adopt many of the values and conventions associated with that type of writing. You will need to find, integrate, and use numerous sources of information. The sources will range from published accounts in business or general news media to your own specialized research. For example, you may interview industry participants or representative customers to determine their satisfaction with existing products, their interest in an alternative such as you will offer, their sensitivity to price versus other factors, or other issues. Combine what you glean from public sources with your own investigation. It is crucial to the quality of your arguments that you push beyond the standard sources (for example, *Standard & Poor's*, *Moody's*, or *Hoover's*), useful though they are for a starting point, to write your own creative analyses.

THE INDUSTRY

Your industry analysis should show a thorough understanding of the overall industry and an assessment of the potential for profit within that industry.

Industry Description. Tell how large the industry is, its stage of development (for example, introduction, growth, maturity, decline), and its potential for growth beyond this point. In doing so you should introduce quantitative data from authoritative sources whenever possible. Don't use hyperbole! In describing a particular industry it may be relevant to refer to the number of establishments operated by its firms (for example, number of pizza restaurants); their physical output (for example, tons of steel, number of housing units built); number of customers served (for example, number of tax returns prepared); dollar volume of sales; or other measures. The appropriate and customary choices will vary from one industry to another, and your study of the industry should make these choices obvious.

Describing the industry also includes detailing its geographic concentration, if any, and the patterns of difference between regions. This discussion is likely to include both quantitative and qualitative information. For example, you might report that production capacity in your industry is concentrated in the upper Midwest and New England, supporting the statement with data on plants and their capacity, but also quote industry analysts' opinion that the most forward-looking competitors are young companies on the West Coast. Similarly diverse sources and approaches may describe trends, entry barriers, and other patterns in the industry.

Competitive Forces. The pivotal point in this section should be your assessment of the industry's potential for profit. Many effective assessments rely on the "five forces model" of Michael Porter[3] to examine the impact of:

1. Rivalry among firms already in the industry
2. The threat of new entrants
3. The competitive threat of other products that may substitute for those of the industry
4. The bargaining leverage of the industry's suppliers
5. The bargaining leverage of the industry's customers

The stronger the effect of any force, the lower the industry's potential profitability. Therefore, your choice of which forces to emphasize in your analysis must depend on their strength. Your venture's greatest competitive barriers or pressures on profitability will arise from them. Many entrepreneurs do not adequately research their industry to assess its five forces. Instead they offer a few generalizations—but no documented support—or fail to connect what they do find to the industry's profitability.

Closely related to the industry's long-run profit potential is a discussion of the gross margins on sales that prevail in the industry. Such information gives you a clearer idea of the volume needed to break even and serves as a reality check on your own financial projections. Typical gross margins may depend on the market segments in which companies sell or on the technologies they use, so you must be careful not to settle for the first statistic you find.

THE MARKET

Along with the industry, you must describe and discuss your venture's market. Not every possible customer of your industry is of equal significance to your venture. Some customers are content with the offerings of established companies; others will have unmet needs that your venture is unprepared to resolve. Your venture's strategy probably cannot be tailored to satisfy everyone; instead it must match the benefits you can deliver with customers who will respond to them. They are your target market. Your task in the business plan is to define this select group and estimate its likely response. (See *KidSmart*™, p. 11.)

You should describe the primary and any secondary target markets of the venture. Use a mixture of quantitative and qualitative data. For example, you can draw a demographic or psychographic portrait of the individual, household, or organization that typifies a target market from qualitative data or observation; then enrich it with hard numbers. At the same time you should discuss the customer needs that your venture will serve. Even though you have identified those needs in describing the business concept, you should elaborate on them in this section and provide evidence that they are unmet to a significant degree within the target markets.

This section is the probable home for any original market research—your own surveys, observations, etc. Rather than present such material in a separate section, it is better to integrate it. Explain briefly how you carried out the research; an appendix is the ideal vehicle for a detailed description of your methods and complete results, if relevant.

THE COMPETITORS YOU WILL FACE

You have broadly described the industry and detailed the market segments your venture will target. The stage is set for your analysis of the specific competitors your venture will face. They will be your rivals, and their effectiveness in pursuing the same market segments or in repelling your entry can decide your venture's fate. Readers will know that correctly identifying an unmet need does not ensure that your venture will succeed in that market. They will want proof that you understand this reality and evidence that your plan will withstand the competitive efforts of your rivals.

Identify and discuss your rivals in detail. You should compile the following information and assessments of each rival for your target markets:

- The company's product line
- The features and customer benefits it provides
- Principal competitive methods
- Price to consumers (and to intermediaries, if applicable)
- Strengths and weaknesses as a competitor

This information lends itself to presentation in a table within your text. You should use the text to highlight the most important competitors and the opportunities or threats posed by the competitors. Make your discussion focused and important rather than trying to summarize all the information; the table will take care of the latter need.

Sometimes it is impossible or impractical to name specific competitors, especially if they are indirect rather than direct competitors for your target market. In such a case you should identify the category or type of competitor. If your venture were a lawn care company, for example, you might identify "casual yard services" comprising teenagers who earn extra money by mowing lawns in their neighborhood—it would be futile to try to name them, but overlooking the category would omit a possible source of competition for your company.

Body: Venture Strategy and Plans

From the foundation laid in analyzing the industry and market, you are ready to build the strategy your venture will pursue. Drawing information and conclusions from previous sections, you can argue convincingly for the type and source of competitive advantage on which you will rely in the market you have targeted and the strategic goals you will seek. Then will come the detailed treatments of your plans for marketing, operations, and management. (See *KidSmart*™, pp. 13–16.)

This chapter's coverage of the three plans is less extensive than its discussion of venture strategy. That difference does not mean that the plans are unimportant or that they should necessarily be shorter portions of the business plan. Instead, the difference reflects two considerations. First, a company's detailed plans for marketing, operations, and management are particular to that firm. Here your objective is tactical: You must ensure that each plan effectively carries out the venture strategy by building and maintaining the necessary competitive advantages. To do so, each plan must be consistent both with the venture strategy and within itself. Do not fritter away resources on activities that are unrelated to the keys to success for your company. The specifics of your plans, though, are beyond the scope of this chapter's coverage. Second, in the words of Kathleen Allen, "It is much easier to develop tactics than to develop strategies."[4] Entrepreneurs are prone to answering investors' questions about strategy by detailing tactics while neglecting the strategy they carry out.

Although tactics are important, professional investors recognize that the venture is likely to fail if the entrepreneur does not articulate a well-considered strategy to guide the venture.

Venture Strategy: Differentiation or Cost Advantage?

Now that you have detailed the target market and principal competitors your venture will encounter, you are prepared to state its strategic goals (the competitive position and capabilities it will pursue) and the advantages on which it will rely. Earlier you described conceptually the uniqueness of the venture's product or service. Now you should explain concretely how your product or service will differ from those of your rivals and/or how its costs will be lower. Go into more detail than in that earlier, somewhat basic explanation. Relate the venture's advantage to (a) its attainment through your strategy (for example, the resources on which your venture relies, how they will be organized or deployed); and (b) the customer needs it will meet.

For example, the business plan for a gun club described the shooting ranges and equipment to be included in the club's facilities. It linked them to the types of hunters and weapons that each one would suit, then contrasted these features and benefits to those available at other gun clubs in the geographic market. (The business plan had described the rivals earlier in this section.)

If your venture's strategy relies on its cost advantage against rivals, you should spell out how the advantage can be achieved. A cost advantage often is not easily described before presenting a description of the manufacturing or operational plans, which follow later in the business plan. Even so, an entrepreneur whose venture will depend on a cost advantage must take extra pains at this point in the document to describe the aspects of the venture's operations that will provide the advantage. The uniqueness of the activities performed, how they are performed, or how they are coordinated with one another is as important to the cost advantage strategy as the unique benefits created for customers are to the differentiation strategy. Cost advantages are notoriously difficult for new ventures; consequently, your readers will require substantial evidence to accept your argument.

Marketing Plan

In the section on the market, you identified your target market and quantified its potential as much as possible. You also have explained the advantage(s) on which your strategy depends. Now you should tell how your company's marketing plans will implement that strategy with respect to the target market. (See *KidSmart*™, pp. 16–22.) Your readers will look for thoroughness and savvy. Your marketing plan should be comprehensive and detailed, crafted with insight into the workings of the channels and customers with which you will deal. This section should include the following information:

- The distribution channels through which the product/service will be sold
- The sales methods employed by the venture for each channel
- Advertising and promotion directed to each channel

- Advertising and promotion directed to final purchasers
- Alliances with other companies or organizations to advance the venture's marketing
- Other methods

You should organize this section to emphasize the marketing efforts that are crucial to the venture's success, especially those on which the business concept's uniqueness depends. The sequence of topics within the section is not fixed by any template; instead you should develop your description logically around what you deem to be the most important aspects of the marketing plan. The arguments you make are unique to your venture, and so is the ideal structure of this section.

OPERATIONAL PLAN

The content of an operational plan will be quite different for a manufacturing company than for a service company. Even so, the plan's purpose remains constant—it explains how the company produces what it sells. For a manufacturer the operational plan should detail the manufacturing process, the plant that will house it, the types of production equipment and labor it requires, its raw materials and their procurement, how the production process will be controlled for efficiency and quality, and any special considerations such as environmental impact or process certification that will affect the company's operations. A service provider's operational plan should detail the organizational process by which the service is performed. For example, an auto repair business uses a special facility and equipment, manages the flow of vehicles through its various functions, may organize work around specialized workers or all-purpose teams, ensures its quality of service while minimizing waste of materials, and complies with environmental requirements in disposing of fluids and batteries. Even a labor-intensive service that uses little equipment has a production process, and so a counseling service's operational plan would cover its processes and facilities (for example, private and/or group sessions, appropriate space and furnishings for them), the scheduling of appointments, methods to ensure quality, and similar details.

Like the marketing plan, the operational plan is not fixed to a single template. You should concentrate on a logical presentation that emphasizes the activities and tactics that most directly affect the venture's strategy and competitive advantage. The structure of this plan should follow the most effective flow of topics to build your argument for the venture strategy's viability. At the same time you will indirectly advance the idea that you are qualified to launch the venture.

MANAGEMENT PLAN

Your objective in the management plan shifts to establishing your qualifications and those of the management team you have assembled thus far. You will need to think carefully about the duties and composition of the management team before you write this section. At the time when you are creating the business plan, it is not likely that the complete management team has been brought together, or even identified. It is advisable in your preparation, though, to detail the skills required, the responsibilities to be borne, and how the team's managerial activities are to be organized into positions. From that analysis emerge the proposed management structure and the specification of their skills and backgrounds. Only then can you confidently prepare to staff your management team. (See *KidSmart*™, pp. 24–26.)

Readers may study the management plan early in their consideration of a business plan. But venture capitalists and other serious investors typically look first at the executive summary, the business concept, and the venture strategy; then they turn to the management plan. These investor-readers explain that they want to know what the team must accomplish before they evaluate its qualifications. Therefore you should open this section by briefly restating the key management roles and requirements under the strategy. They are the basis for what you will highlight in presenting the background, knowledge, and skills of the management team.

Next you should identify the management team. The body of the business plan is not the place for complete biographies. (You should include résumés in an appendix.) In a short paragraph devoted to each person, state his or her position, qualifications, and duties. Resist the temptation to inflate someone's qualifications. Such misrepresentation is unethical and may constitute fraud. Professional lenders, investors, and other readers will see through your ruse, either immediately or during subsequent "due diligence" investigation of your proposed venture; and even the appearance of such misrepresentation will ruin your chance to enlist their support. It may also blacken your reputation among the close-knit community of venture investors and lenders in your vicinity. If a member of your management team lacks the necessary qualifications, change the team or leave the position vacant. In that case, state your plan for filling the vacancy and, if necessary, how its duties will be covered in the interim.

Many of the venture's needs for management talent can be met through its board of directors or through an advisory board. Identify the directors, providing a short profile of each that emphasizes his or her qualifications and unique contribution to the venture. Then do the same for members of your company's advisory board, if you have one. Conclude your coverage of necessary talent by identifying the providers of professional services required by the venture (for example, legal, accounting, insurance).

Readers will also want to know how you will ensure an adequate supply of qualified employees. Their concerns will not normally extend to the identity of these employees but will focus on their recruitment, selection, training, and retention. You should explain your plans with emphasis on skilled or other critical positions.

Body: Risks, Contingencies, and Future Development

Any experienced business manager or investor (or military officer, or airline passenger) has learned that few projects (or campaigns, or vacation itineraries) work out exactly as planned. Simple or routine operations may offer few surprises as they take place, but with complexity or novelty come complications and unanticipated changes. Earlier in this chapter you learned why business plans are helpful even though they will not remain unchanged throughout their implementation. Now you will learn about how to deal with the reality of changed conditions.

Readers of the business plan will have their own doubts about its assumptions or about how smoothly you will be able to implement it. Those doubts can prove fatal to your arguments to convince them of the plan's validity and your qualifications to execute it and to persuade them to support your efforts. On the other hand, you can neutralize the doubts or even turn them to your advantage if you:

- Recognize risks your venture will encounter
- Spell out the contingent (that is, conditional or standby) plans for dealing with those risks should they materialize
- Lay out further plans for the company's development beyond the stage covered in detail by the business plan

RISKS AND CONTINGENCIES

Readers will look for evidence of your understanding of the venture strategy and the conditions the company will face. Your ability to distinguish between important and trivial risks will be taken as evidence of your readiness to launch and manage the venture, as will your insightful and specific explanation of those risks. Readers will look for similar evidence in your contingent plans for limiting or offsetting their impact. If you define and explain the risks in specific terms, your plan for dealing with each risk can be presented in a paragraph or two. This section is *not* meant to be an alternative version of your business plan. Instead, think of each portion as though it were a supplementary "what if" comment on some key element of your plan. (See *KidSmart*™, pp. 32–33.)

In preparing to discuss risks and contingencies, you must overcome the temptation to write an imitation of the annual reports or prospectuses of corporations that you may have read. These documents, written to satisfy securities regulations and legal precedents, contain much *boilerplate* (standardized) language on business risks that, taken literally, would discourage most investors from owning the companies' stock. Virtually anything that could go wrong is presented as a possibility, sometimes softened by a statement that management believes the problem can be overcome. Remember that the objective of the annual report or prospectus increasingly is to avoid lawsuits alleging that management misled stockholders, and that those documents never were intended as candid treatments of a company's strategy or the steps that might counter the associated risks and problems. (You may want to protect yourself by including an investor's disclaimer as described in the section "Producing and Presenting the Business Plan.")

FUTURE DEVELOPMENT

Readers will want to know about your venture's prospects after it accomplishes the strategy and objectives laid out in the business plan. Whether you choose to present this information as part of the "risks and contingencies" component or as a separate component will depend on its ability to stand alone. If your ideas for future development involve new products or some other significant departure from the original plan's strategy, present this material as its own major section of the main body. Explain what milestones or conditions would trigger this new phase of your company's development; otherwise readers may suspect that you have not settled on a primary strategy and are proposing alternatives to be trotted out whenever troubles arise. Describe the opportunities you have in mind, giving basic information on their size or the evidence of their existence. (See *KidSmart*™, pp. 33–35.) You should not attempt to project market or financial results of the future possibilities, as they are too speculative at present.

Unlike your discussion of risks and contingencies, which is essentially defensive, your discussion of the company's future development should build on the success of your venture to exploit opportunities it will create. Avoid giving the impression that this next phase would be a clean break from the strategy and activities that went before, or readers will suspect that it would pose the same risks and uncertainties as starting from scratch while giving up the chance to take advantage of its early risk-taking and achievement. Such a suspicion would cause readers to discount your capability as an entrepreneur—in effect, you could convince them of the venture's viability while also convincing them that another person must be found to launch it. At that point, you have lost the argument to persuade readers to support your plan. If they support the venture, it will be with another entrepreneur as its leader.

Body: Financial Plan

The purposes of the financial plan are to detail the venture's financial needs, how the funds will be used, the financial performance expected in the next few years, and how investors and lenders will recoup their money. (See *KidSmart*™, pp. 26–32.) Nearly all readers will be keenly interested in this section. Those who invest will become owners, those who lend funds will become creditors, and those who agree to provide supplies or other resources on standard terms typically will become trade creditors. Each of these parties has an obvious interest in the venture's financial status. Other readers will have other reasons for their interest in the financial plan. A company that considers making your company a supplier will want assurance of its financial stability: Will your company be able to meet its contractual commitments? Even if your company possesses the necessary technical skills and equipment, for example, its reliability as a supplier will depend on its ability to obtain raw materials and other purchased resources on a timely basis and to finance production and shipment of its goods before it receives payment. Readers whom you recruit for your management team will want assurance as well, both of the company's ability to pay their salaries and of its ability to survive and grow. These various readers will focus on different aspects of the financial plan, but each of them will use it to assess the company's soundness and evaluate your qualifications to lead it.

Entrepreneurs often produce financial plans that are unrealistic or incomplete. A lack of realism sometimes results from the entrepreneur's upbeat, optimistic attitude toward the business idea and his or her skills. Entrepreneurs have above-average confidence in their own abilities and insights, and so they naturally become excited about the opportunities they have uncovered. Thus unrealistic financial plans partly reflect an honest difference of perception between an entrepreneur and unbiased observers. They also may reflect entrepreneurs' failure to understand the competitive requirements or conditions of the market and industry they intend to enter. Experienced readers who are interested in the proposed venture will research these requirements and conditions, using public information as well as their own sources and judgment, with particular attention to financial assumptions or results that depart from an industry's typical experience. You should keep in mind the following truth: A new company almost never matches, let alone surpasses, the operational efficiency and materials costs of successful incumbents in its industry. A financial plan that shows your company enjoying higher gross margins (lower costs of goods sold), lower costs of raw materials or manufactured components, or any other operating advantage over incumbent firms will cause skepticism among your readers. At the very least, they will want to know exactly why and how your company will be able to achieve these advantages even as it is learning its way in the industry. Only a fundamentally different way of organizing or carrying out operations has a chance to convince your readers, and even then they will see great risks in your proposed innovation.

Unrealistic or incomplete financial plans also result from entrepreneurs' lack of financial and accounting skills. Most entrepreneurs count on their knowledge of a market, personal contacts or selling abilities, technical acumen, or novel idea; they are not often experts in finance or accounting. You should honestly assess your competence in the latter subjects and, if there is any doubt in your mind, hire a professional to assist in preparing your financial plan.

Even reasonable financial plans may meet with doubt among readers if you fail to explain the assumptions that underlie them. Merely generating detailed, monthly financial projections running years into the future will not impress readers: They use spreadsheets too, and know that a computer's output is only as good as its input data and assumptions. Entrepreneurs frequently project robust growth rates in sales, stable or declining unit costs of production, or other optimistic trends that yield impressive results when plugged into a spreadsheet program. Without solid evidence or compelling arguments for the assumptions you built into the financial plan, experienced readers will discount your results and, in all likelihood, reduce their regard for your qualifications to lead the venture. You will have lost ground in both objectives of convincing them.

Pro Forma Financial Statements

The financial plan should present the following information:

- The sources and uses of funds received from investors and lenders
- *Pro forma* (formal, conventional) statements of sales and income, cash flow, balance sheets
- Expected returns to investors and coverage of any debt obligations

You should present the pro forma statements in two ways to satisfy readers' different needs. Summaries of yearly results or balances will provide quick access to your financial plans for all readers and will be sufficient for some. Readers will expect at least three years of statements and may want more. As a second way of presenting the information, monthly statements of the same accounts will satisfy other readers' need for greater detail, especially with respect to the first two years of operation. Their desire for monthly data stems from the danger that a young company will run out of cash during its slow season or while gearing for rapid growth, and consequently fail for insolvency before it can achieve the satisfactory results projected for the longer period. Your financial plan should guard against this possibility, for your sake as well as your investors' or lenders'. (See *KidSmart*™, Exhibits 11–15 on pp. 27–31.)

PROPOSED DEAL STRUCTURE

In one sense the business plan has been building to this portion of the financial plan ever since its first page. In spite of the potential advantages of writing a business plan even if you are not seeking outside capital, most entrepreneurs do not discipline themselves to do so until they encounter investors' or lenders' insistence on reading the plan. Even after demonstrating the existence and extent of an unmet need, the practicality of pursuing this opportunity with his or her particular strategy, and the lucrative returns that await the venture, the entrepreneur must attract the necessary backing. One part of this effort is convincing readers that he or she is the right person to launch the venture. Another key to persuading readers to support the venture is offering an acceptable deal.

Remembering that the business plan is primarily a sales document, you should describe the deal in terms of its benefits to the readers who would provide the capital. You are asking them to bear some of the venture's financial risk, and in return you must offer payoffs that induce them to accept your proposition. The venture's profitability will mean nothing to its investors unless they share in the rewards. How you structure the financial deal will determine how the rewards are divided; the exit strategy you propose for these investors will tell how and when they may expect to receive their rewards. Both parts of the deal—the division of rewards and the method and timing of their realization—must appeal to investors. (See *KidSmart*™, p. 32.)

State clearly what you offer and the price you ask. For equity investors, your proposition is to sell them a proportional stake in the company, represented by ownership of its stock. For lenders, your proposition is to borrow funds for a certain period in return for their repayment with interest according to a specific schedule. The pro forma financial statements will not spell out the terms in sufficient detail to satisfy potential investors or lenders, and so you must include concise summary tables of the proposed capital structure. As illustrated by the *KidSmart*™ plan (Exhibits 15 and 16, p. 31), the summaries should show the several categories of investors and the amounts they contribute in return for their shares of the company. A similar distinction is needed among different types of lenders if the proposed capital structure includes debt.

Professional investors differ in how long they prefer to own the shares of companies they back. Because many such investors specialize in identifying promising young companies rather than in holding a portfolio of established companies, they will want to sell their stock within a few years of investing in your company. For these investors the exit strategy is a crucial consideration: Are you asking them simply to trust that the company's strong performance and rosy prospects will ensure a market for its stock? Or have you laid out a plan for converting their investment into cash? Professional investors will insist on the latter and will expect a credible scenario for bringing it about. Possible exit strategies may include the sale of their stock during a subsequent offering of shares to the public or the sale of the entire company to a larger, established company. The exit strategy should mesh logically with the venture strategy and discussion of the company's future development that you have included in earlier sections.

Appendices

You may have heard people refer to the tag-end portion of a report or term paper as an appendix. For a lengthy or complex report such as a business plan, it's more likely that you will include a set of *appendices* (the plural). The distinction emphasizes that each appendix stands on its own, has its own title and number, and appears on a numbered page so it may be found by the reader without wading through all the others. A reference to each appendix must appear in the business plan's main body at the first point where its material is relevant, and possibly at subsequent points where it also applies. Otherwise the reader will never know that the appendix exists or where to find it, and your effort in creating it will be wasted. Worse is the impact on the quality of your business plan, as the persuasive power of the appendix is lost.

Appendices are appropriate for supplementary material. Their contents should deepen the reader's understanding of your business concept and plan or elaborate on information included in the main body. For example, appendices often contain the résumés of the company's managers or directors, letters of reference or from satisfied customers, photos of the company's facilities, press coverage of the company or its founders, or published research.

Do not use appendices to present charts, tables, or graphs that depict data or concepts you present in the body, or to provide photographs that are keys to understanding your product or service. The reader does not want to flip back and forth between the body and the appendices while trying to understand your argument. Place such materials in the body, either separately (*KidSmart*™ Exhibits 11–14, pp. 27–30) or sharing a page with text.

PRODUCING AND PRESENTING THE BUSINESS PLAN

You probably have written term papers in several courses, perhaps in high school and almost certainly in college. Therefore you know teachers' advice to students: Work with an outline to organize your thoughts; use notes to prepare your arguments and supporting material; write drafts of sections and later tie them together; ask knowledgeable friends to criticize the drafts; revise your work through multiple drafts; proofread and edit, etc. The same advice pertains to your work in writing a business plan and is even more critical to your success. In seeking support for your business venture there is no equivalent to "just good enough for a B." Unlike a college course in which you may know exactly how many points you need for a passing or satisfactory grade, in your pursuit of capital, management talent, or key suppliers and customers there is no way to do "just enough" in a business plan to secure your goal. Your aim is to win the readers' support by demonstrating the attractiveness of your business concept and strategy as well as your own fitness to lead the venture, and halfway measures are not good enough.

Just as many students seek shortcuts to a "just good enough" term paper, entrepreneurs are tempted to avoid the hard work of writing their business plan. Widely distributed, inexpensive computer programs promise the ease of "fill-in-the-blanks" software to produce your business plan. Entrepreneurs who see the business plan as busywork imposed by a lender, for instance, are drawn to this shortcut; failing to appreciate the business plan's significance to its readers, they also fail to devote the necessary effort to its creation. In completing the software's sentences they exercise as little imagination and express as little innovative potential as a student might in taking the typical "objective" exam. This approach to writing a business plan almost invariably smothers the reader's interest in either the venture or the entrepreneur. Hire someone to assist in organizing and polishing your business plan if you need help, but avoid the computer programs' seemingly easy way out of the hard work.

Producing the Business Plan

Throughout this chapter you have learned about the contents of a business plan and how to argue effectively for your venture and your leadership of it. Now the chapter's focus turns to the business plan's physical appearance. You will need to accomplish a balancing act to make it look professional without being too "slick."[5] To achieve the desired appearance and thereby create the desired impression, you should consider these guidelines:

- Use a binding that allows the plan to lie flat when opened. Do not merely staple the pages as you might a course assignment. Avoid excess, though, such as elaborate or expensive binding, that looks fussy or extravagant. A conservative, business-like image is your aim. A plastic spiral binding and plastic or heavy stock covers are satisfactory.
- Use a common type size and style, such as 12-point Times Roman.
- Print on only one side of each page.
- Use large enough margins to allow space for readers' notes. Block paragraphs and 1.0 or 1.5 spacing between lines will leave room for notes while using space economically.
- Maintain a consistent style and voice throughout the business plan. Do not cobble together the work of several writers whose styles are different. The effect on readers can be jarring and gives the impression of poor integration even when the arguments and ideas are carefully organized.

The success of your business plan hinges in part on its ability to maintain readers' interest. To that end you must ease their task in reading and navigating it. Your challenge begins with managing the business plan's length. Whereas experts once suggested 40 pages or more as a representative length, today's readers seem to appreciate briefer presentations. Twenty-five pages is a reasonable target for your plan's main body, including its embedded exhibits of all types. Entrepreneurs sometimes bind their plan's appendices separately and offer that volume to readers who express an interest in further discussion after reading the main body. For example, the KidSmart founders brought such a volume, containing more than a dozen appendices, to their follow-up meetings with venture capitalists. Here are three other guidelines to ease your readers' task:

- Use index tabs to divide the plan's principal sections.
- Use boldface headings to identify sections and subsections.
- Number all pages.

Presenting the Plan to Investors and Others

Entrepreneurship textbooks counsel care and selectivity in distributing your business plan. Take time to learn a venture capitalist or other investor's

ILLUSTRATION 16-1	STANDARD INVESTORS' DISCLAIMER

READER NOTIFICATION AND WARNING

This Plan has been created for internal planning and for preliminary review by sophisticated investors. While a good faith effort has been made to ensure the reliability and accuracy of all the information contained herein, the ABC Company and its representatives make no warranties as to the absence of errors in this document, or as to the magnitude and/or certainty of any potential investment returns. Furthermore, since the XYZ industry is unique, the ABC Company's earnings potential is highly uncertain. Moreover, its core business operations may unexpectedly encounter insurmountable obstacles to eventual market acceptance from unanticipated sources. Even careful, well-informed, experienced investors can and do regularly lose their entire investments in well-conceived startup businesses run by competent management. Therefore, prospective investors should NOT invest any funds in the ABC Company unless they are fully prepared to lose their entire investment.

Finally, it should be noted that this is not an offer to purchase securities. Such an offer, if made, will only be made pursuant to a definitive investment agreement prepared for such an offer.

I acknowledge that I have read, understand, and fully accept these representations and warnings.

Name _____

Signature _____ Date _____

interests before submitting your plan, and send it only to those whose stated investment interests appear to include your type of venture. (Many directories of venture capital or angel investor groups state each group's investment criteria by industry, technology, company size, stage of development, geography, etc.) Professional investors are a networked community, as are many local investors, and your indiscriminate distribution of a business plan may give you an unwanted reputation among them. Moreover, it unproductively circulates more copies of your plan, needlessly increasing the risk of lost confidentiality.

If you send a "cold" (unsolicited) copy of the business plan, it is wise to include an *investors disclaimer*. This statement is the business plan's equivalent to the boilerplate warnings found in prospectuses, although it is less exhaustive or specific. (Such protective language would appear in later documents presented during negotiations with interested investors.) Illustration 16-1 presents a standard disclaimer prepared by the advisor to KidSmart.

SUMMARY

A business plan describes in detail an entrepreneur's business concept and the resources needed to launch a venture to realize it. The plan also presents the expected financial results and proposes a deal to prospective backers. In writing a business plan, the entrepreneur has the twin purposes of convincing readers that the business concept is viable under his or her leadership and of persuading them to provide the desired support. A business plan is usually required in order to obtain outside funding but is useful even to the entrepreneur who seeks no investors.

There is no template that all business plans must fit, but most successful plans include these components: cover page, table of contents, and executive summary; discussion of the business concept and product; discussion of the industry, market, and competitors; the venture strategy and plans for marketing, operations, and management; discussion of risks, contingencies, and future development of the company; the financial plan and proposed deal structure, including an exit strategy for investors; and appendices containing supporting materials. Throughout the business plan the entrepreneur must present not only information but also the arguments to convince and persuade readers. To those ends the chapter offers guidelines for the production and presentation of a business plan.

Vocal Smoke Detector

WE'RE TALKING SAFETY™

Contact Person:
Matt Ferris, President

KIDSMART™ BUSINESS PLAN

TABLE OF CONTENTS

3

I. EXECUTIVE SUMMARY

Long-Term Vision and Mission[1]

KidSmart (dba Smart Safety Systems, Inc.) will market and develop a new line of innovative products to protect children from residential safety threats. The Company's initial products will focus on reducing the perils of residential fires to children under the age of 14. Within ten years, KidSmart seeks to become the leading developer and marketer of a wide range of specialized safety products for children ages 14 and under.

[1]In a few lines the plan explains what the venture will be, both immediately and well into the future.

The Problem: Residential Fire Safety Among Children[2]

In 2000 alone, United States fire departments responded to nearly 380,000 residential fires or one every 83 seconds. While these fires accounted for only 20% of all reported fire incidents, they caused 80% of all fire-related deaths and injuries, many of which were to children. Each year more than 40,000 children under the age of 14 are seriously injured in US household fires and an additional 1,200 more[3] die. The total societal cost of these deaths and injuries is a staggering $5.5 billion. One of the leading causes of these deaths and injuries is the inability of a properly functioning smoke detector to awaken young children because they have extremely deep R.E.M. sleep patterns. Furthermore, even when the child is awakened, studies show that many deaths and injuries could be avoided. According to the National Safe Kids Campaign, over 40% of residential fire-related deaths among children result from panic and irrational behavior, such as hiding under the bed or in the closet.

[2]This paragraph identifies *and* quantifies the problem.

[3]"More" is redundant after "additional."

The Solution: The *KidSmart* Vocal Smoke Detector[4]

The *KidSmart VSD™* is designed to solve the "wake-up" problem by combining a "Wake-up Command" in the parent's voice, such as "Sally, wake up!", to force children out of R.E.M. sleep. Additionally, a temporal tone siren has been incorporated, which alternates with the verbal "Wake-up Command." KidSmart's tests have shown that, even when sleeping, children respond to verbal commands in the parent's voice because of the ability of the brain to orient and focus on one's own name or a familiar voice in the midst of a crowd or even while sleeping. The *KidSmart VSD™* also solves the "irrational behavior" problem by allowing parents to record personalized, lifesaving instructions to their children on how to escape from the house in the event of a fire. These instructions are automatically played back when the alarm is triggered. A typical message might include: "Sally, wake up! There's a fire in the house—do like we practiced and climb out the window. We'll meet you outside." According to child psychologist Dr. Jeremy Shapiro, a consultant to Underwriters' Laboratories, "a familiar voice, especially that of a parent, can

[4]The solution is bolstered by the company's research and by an independent expert.

4

help a child overcome panic in unfamiliar or traumatic situations." **The KidSmart VSD™ is the only product in the smoke/fire detection market that incorporates these two patented features, which together overcome the two main causes of serious injury or death to young children in fires.[5]**

The **KidSmart VSD™** incorporates two additional features to provide maximum protection to young children. First, the **KidSmart VSD™** will have a test button and set of instructions so that parents can easily conduct fire drills with their children. Second, the **KidSmart VSD™** will utilize a 10-year lithium battery that will automatically generate a vocal warning of "Unit Needs Replacement" when the power source approaches six months of remaining useful life. Because of these lifesaving features, the **KidSmart VSD™** won a *Best of Innovations Award* at the 2003 Consumer Electronics Show in Las Vegas, Nevada, and a *New Product Award* from the Inventors Club of America. It has also recently been featured in *The New York Times* and on *Good Morning America, CNN,* and a host of other media outlets.

START-UP & GROWTH[6] STRATEGIES

KidSmart's start-up strategy is to sell the **KidSmart VSD™** to target middle- and upper-middle-class parents with children ages 2 to 14 years. Currently, KidSmart's market potential is $1.6 billion and growing by $165 million each year. The **KidSmart VSD™** will be positioned as a product specifically designed to awaken children and to increase the likelihood of their survival during a residential fire. KidSmart believes that alleviating fears about their children's safety will be of significant value to parents of young children and will allow the Company to charge a premium price for the **KidSmart VSD™.** The packaging and promotion of the **KidSmart VSD™** will be designed to allow potential consumers to easily identify and understand the product's primary differentiating features. The distribution of the **KidSmart VSD™** will be through child safety and specialty retail stores and catalogues and eventually neighborhood hardware stores. To minimize upfront capital costs, manufacturing of KidSmart's products will be outsourced.

INVESTMENT OPPORTUNITY[7]

KidSmart's founders have already invested $80,000 in developing the KidSmart technology and have committed an additional $50,000 to commercialize the **KidSmart VSD™.** To initiate product launch, KidSmart is seeking $750,000 in additional start-up capital for a 20% stake of the Company in order to bring the product to market later this year.

II. PRODUCT

KidSmart's initial product, the **KidSmart Vocal Smoke Detector™** (VSD), offers an innovative, patented (Patent # 5,349,338) verbal warning system that will wake a child and replay personalized instructions to him or her on how to escape from the house during a fire. KidSmart hopes that the introduction of this lifesaving product will prevent many of the thousands of injuries and deaths that occur each year in households equipped with traditional smoke alarms.

THE *KIDSMART VSD*™'S KEY PRODUCT FEATURES

Patented Verbal Wake-up Command System to Awaken the Child—The ability to awaken a sleeping child is especially critical in a fire hazard. According to the United States Fire Administration, nearly 70% of all fires occur between 10 p.m. and 6 a.m. To ensure that the KidSmart detector will wake a sleeping child, the **KidSmart VSD™** features two distinct alarm mechanisms: a *familiar voice* verbal "Wake-up Command" followed by a temporal tone siren. KidSmart's patented verbal "Wake-up Command" allows a parent to record a command such as "Timmy, wake up!!!" that will be followed by and alternate with a distinctive temporal tone siren, which has been designed in accordance with the National Fire Alarm Code (NFPA 72[8]). In tests conducted to date, KidSmart's "Wake-up Command" has awakened 100% of all the children on which it was tested within 30 seconds of sounding (see Exhibit 1). This is due to what is known as the "cocktail party effect," i.e., the phenomenon whereby individuals have the ability to hear someone say their name and focus on that conversation,[9] even from a distance and above the din of a crowd. Independent tests are being conducted by both the United States Naval Academy Fire Department and the Sleep Laboratory of Victoria University in Australia to further document the effectiveness of this type of alarm system.

Personalized Verbal Escape Instructions to Reduce Children's Panic Responses—Another patented feature of the **KidSmart VSD™** is that it allows parents to record individualized escape instructions for their children that are played during a fire emergency. According to Dr. Shapiro, a child psychologist and Underwriters' Laboratories Standard #217 committee member,[10] children act more rationally in high-stress situations when they hear a reassuring, familiar voice. The **KidSmart VSD™** will take advantage of this phenomenon to effectively calm and direct the child into a safe and rational escape behavior.

Testing and Instructional Capabilities to Ensure Proper Response—In order to further enhance the safety performance of the **KidSmart VSD™**, KidSmart has integrated a testing circuit into its design. Thus, by merely pressing a

[8]**What is this? Always write out a possibly unfamiliar term before using its acronym.**

[9]**Awkwardly worded. The quotation marks eliminate the need for "what is known as," and the explanation is not smooth.**

[10]**Another well-placed invocation of independent authority to validate the product's operating concept.**

6

button, parents can both test the functionality[11] of the unit and, more importantly,[12] perform drills with their child by simulating an actual fire alarm. Furthermore, given the importance of education in overall fire prevention, an instruction manual with child-specific fire safety tips and suggestions for personalized recorded messages will be included in the packaging for each unit. In addition, all **KidSmart VSD™** owners can receive regular opt-in e-mails with updated "fire safety tips" for children.

> [11]Readers may react unfavorably to this overused, often vaguely understood buzzword. Note its frequent appearance in this portion of the plan.

> [12]Picky grammarians will properly prefer "important."

Extended Life Battery System to Guarantee Detector Functionality— According to the Consumer Product Safety Commission, over 16 million smoke detectors in the United States do not work simply because the battery has either died or been removed by the homeowner. KidSmart has outfitted the **KidSmart VSD™** with an extended life, 10-year lithium battery as well as an early warning system to notify homeowners when the battery begins to weaken. The unique audio features of the **KidSmart VSD™** allow it to emit a verbal "Unit Needs Replacement" warning when the battery approaches six months of remaining life. With the verbal warning system and the 10-year lithium battery standard in the **KidSmart VSD™**, there should be no reason for a homeowner to be unaware of a non-functioning smoke detector.

KidSmart VSD™ Pricing

The **KidSmart VSD™** will be sold to retailers at $40.00 per unit, with a suggested retail price of $79.95. In KidSmart's independent research, as well as in actual purchasing behavior, consumers have demonstrated a willingness to pay "premium" prices for additional smoke-detector functionality, validating KidSmart's "premium" pricing strategy (*see Exhibit 2*[13]). Given its multiple features, including the exclusive use of voice technology, combination ionization and photoelectric sensors, a testing/drill function, dual alarm mechanisms and an extended life battery system, KidSmart can easily charge $79.95 because, with the purchase of the **KidSmart VSD™**, parents not only buy a fire detection product, they buy peace of mind.

> [13]The business plan placed Exhibit 2 three pages after this passage, potentially reducing its impact. The exhibit specifically describes rival products to make an essential point: KidSmart's product offers unique benefits that will justify the premium price.

Follow-On Products[14]

KidSmart Wireless™—Building on the unique benefits of the **KidSmart VSD™**, KidSmart is concurrently developing a whole-house solution, **KidSmart Wireless™**. The **KidSmart Wireless™** base system will include three detectors, but can be easily scaled to accommodate up to twelve different sensing devices connected by wireless links. For each separate sensing device, a parent will be able to record different escape instructions based on the location of the initial alarming sensor. For example, if the unit in the front living room is activated first, all vocal units in the system can be programmed to instruct occupants to escape via the rear stairway.

> [14]Note that the follow-on product will build on the initial product and serve the same market. Moreover, it is under development rather than lying in the indefinite future.

The latest trend in state building codes is the requirement for an interconnected or wired system of smoke detectors in new construction.[15] When one detector is activated, the signal is distributed via copper wire, causing all other connected detectors to sound. The benefits of this design are realized in the form of quicker response times, fewer serious fires, and lower average property damage. While interconnected systems seem to perform better than collections of individual detectors, their cost of installation is significant since a licensed electrician must actually[16] run the wiring and install each detector. The Canadian Mortgage and Housing Corporation[17] estimates the average cost for a four-unit interconnected system to be approximately $315 and $490 for an eight-unit interconnected system.[18]

KidSmart Wireless™ will deliver the same benefits and functionality of these systems, as well as the patented verbal alarms and instructions of the *KidSmart VSD*™, for approximately the same cost. Furthermore, the plug-and-play functionality of *KidSmart Wireless*™ will allow homeowners to easily add multiple sensing devices that can be located throughout the house. Moreover, the *KidSmart Wireless*™'s escape instructions can be customized to vary the escape route depending on which sensor is activated first, a significant benefit not available on any current wired systems.

PRODUCT RECOGNITION

Given its ability to save lives, the *KidSmart VSD*™ has won numerous awards including the *Inventors Club of America New Product Award* and the prestigious *Best of Innovations Award* from the 2003 Consumer Electronics Show, as seen in *Exhibit 3*. In addition, the *KidSmart VSD*™ has received an overwhelmingly positive response from both potential consumers and the media alike as shown in *Exhibit 4*. Additional media opportunities continue to present themselves and will prove pivotal in increasing consumer awareness of the many benefits found in the *KidSmart VSD*™ that aren't offered by the competition.

III. THE SMOKE DETECTOR MARKET[19]

MARKET SIZE, GROWTH & SEGMENTATION[20]

Since the 1970s, the percentage of U.S. households with at least one smoke detector has increased nine-fold[21], from 10% in 1975 to over 94% in 1997. This dramatic growth can be attributed to increased public awareness of fire safety, as well as federal, state, and local government legislation mandating the installation of household smoke detectors. While this growth has been dramatic, there is also a strong trend toward installing multiple smoke

---

[15]This passage sets up the problem and regulatory pressure to which the wireless system will respond. Thus the business plan builds up the potential value of the follow-on product.

[16]What is the need for this word? The reader understands that someone must actually (as opposed to hypothetically) install the wiring and the unit.

[17]An independent source of the alternative's cost allows KidSmart to position its future product against it.

[18]Poorly, confusingly stated. The $315 figure should appear in closer relation to the four-unit system. Consider saying "…estimates average costs of $315 for a four-unit and $490 for an eight-unit interconnected system."

[19]The KidSmart plan consistently focuses on segments rather than on the broadest possible definition of the market. Readers recognize that a newcomer cannot normally serve all possible buyers equally well, and they expect entrepreneurs to identify specific segments, and then tailor the competitive strategy to the needs of those segments.

[20]This title confuses the reader because the immediate section does not address segmentation. The section's second paragraph could become the introduction to a section on Market Segmentation that would comprise the three subsequent subsections on various segments.

[21]The increase appears to have been eight-fold, or 84 divided by 10.

8

Exhibit 1

KidSmart VSD™ **Test Results**

Subject Number	Gender	Age Years	Time to 1st movement (in seconds)	Time to Alertness (in seconds)	Time to exit bed (in seconds)	Sound Level (in db)
Familiar Voice Alarm Testing						
1	M	8	0.78	13.27	15.38	80
2	F	12	3.89	9.11	17.47	77
3	F	9	1.68	19.62	23.59	85
4	M	4	1.27	17.84	29.44	81
5	M	2	11.63	27.59	na	81
6	F	2.5	1.79	11.21	26.52	78
7	M	7	2.43	24.59	29.34	80
8	M	2.5	9.01	15.53	24.46	80
9	F	3	4.79	8.21	21.45	82
10	F	8	2.27	18.72	27.74	84
11	M	11	1.24	12.66	26.70	84
12	M	5	0.86	15.49	21.38	76
13	M	7	2.12	8.35	14.41	76
14	F	4	7.81	10.63	27.29	84
15	F	6	1.68	22.27	28.48	84
Average			**3.55**	**15.67**	**23.83**	**80.9**

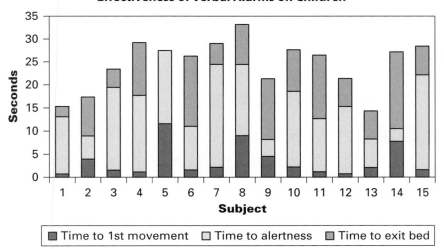

Effectiveness of Verbal Alarms on Children

Legend: ■ Time to 1st movement □ Time to alertness ■ Time to exit bed

Exhibit 2

***KIDSMART VSD*™ Product Advantages**

Smoke Alarm Brand & Type	"Wake-Up" Alarm in Parent's Voice	Customizable Verbal Instructions	Test Capability for Fire Drills	Multiple Alarm Types	Extended Life Battery	Dual Sensing	Price
Fyrnetics Smoke Alarm	NO	NO	NO	NO	NO	NO	$ 6.93
Kidde Smoke & Fire Alarm w/ Exit Light	NO	NO	NO	NO	NO	NO	$13.85
Firex Dual Sensor	NO	NO	NO	NO	NO	YES	$27.00
First Alert 10 YR Lithium	NO	NO	NO	NO	YES	NO	$37.99
Firex Model CCPB - 4021L	NO	NO	NO	NO	YES	YES	$41.99
Kidde 900 Smoke & CO	NO	NO	NO	YES	NO	YES	$56.69
KidSmart VSD™	YES	YES	YES	YES	YES	YES	$79.95

459

Exhibit 3

2003 Consumer Electronics Show

11

Exhibit 4

Consumer Reaction to the *KidSmart Vocal Smoke Detector*™[22]

"I read an article in the Arizona Republic newspaper about your smoke alarm this morning. I have a 19-month-old daughter and I would love to know where I could buy one of these for our home. We had an electrical fire before she was born, and smoke detectors saved our lives that time. *I want to make sure our house is as safe as possible for my daughter.* Thank you!"

Leah
Phoenix, Arizona

"I am a childcare provider and would like to know when your product will reach the market. I am looking forward to purchasing one. I think this is a creative idea for parents and providers alike. If you have a mailing list please put my information on it."

Jane
Fairfield, California

"How do I go about ordering one of your KidSmart Smoke Detectors? **Your idea is incredible**. I work with kids with special needs and this would be perfect for them. Our *extremely loud and traumatic detectors now frighten them so badly they freeze* and getting them to follow directions outside is challenging to say the least. I can only imagine their caretakers at home are faced with the same problems. **Excellent idea all around!!!**"

Marlene
Baltimore County Public Schools
Towson, Maryland

"I think your vocal smoke detector is a great product! *I am going to write about it in the Swedish version of Plaza Woman* and I would like to know how to order your product …Thank you."

Marina W.
Writer—Plaza Woman
Sweden

"We are very interested in more information on your KidSmart Smoke Detector. Also are they available in Australia? As parents with four children and in particular a little girl frightened of any sirens, this product interests us greatly."

Deidre
Sydney, Australia

[22]A reader might wonder how KidSmart received these comments. Also, does "Marlene" speak for a public school system, or merely work for one? Marina is a writer, but what is "Plaza Woman"?

12

detector units in the home. In fact, fire safety officials recommend at least one smoke detector within 15 feet of each bedroom and a minimum of one detector on each level of the dwelling. Based on these criteria, *Exhibit 5* provides a visual representation of recommended smoke detector placement in a multi-story home. Currently, however, the U.S. Consumer Product Safety Commission (CPSC) estimates that only 41% of U.S. households have two smoke detectors, and a mere 13% have three or more smoke detectors, leaving room for substantial future growth. Based on US[23] Census data, NFPA[24] guidelines for smoke detector placement and an average retail price of $18.95 per unit, the current smoke detector market potential is approximately $3.5 billion.

> [23]Most style guides call for "U.S." The plan's rendering of the abbreviation is inconsistent even within this paragraph.

> [24]The second unexplained mention of NFPA.

Currently, the U.S. smoke detector market is divided into two primary segments, the consumer mass market and the commercial market segment. Each of these segments is dominated by a single firm; FirstAlert and Kidde, respectively.

THE CONSUMER MASS MARKET

The typical detectors in the consumer mass market are priced between $7.00 and $20.00, offer limited features, and utilize a single 9-volt battery as the primary power source. In the late 1990's[25], a slightly improved product, offering a 10-year lithium battery, was introduced for between $30.00 and $45.00 per unit. Total consumer mass market sales are about 28 million units each year. The majority of these products are manufactured by FirstAlert, Kidde Safety Systems, Inc., and Maple Chase.

> [25]Correct identification of a decade does not include an apostrophe.

FirstAlert, the major player[26] in the consumer mass market, produces smoke and carbon monoxide detectors, as well as a variety of other safety products, including automatic night lights, radon detectors, and infrared motion detectors. Their smoke detector product line includes three segments: Basic, Premium, and Ultimate with retail prices ranging from $8 to $55 per unit.

> [26]The term may strike some readers as too casual.

From a manufacturing and distribution standpoint, FirstAlert is able to sell its basic products at low prices as a result of economies of scale achieved through offshore manufacturing[27] and high volume distribution. Its products are typically sold through "big-box" retailers such as Wal-Mart, Home Depot, Lowe's, Ace Hardware, Kmart, Sears, and Costco.

> [27]It's unclear why offshore manufacturing creates economies of scale. Volume, not location, is the key to such economies. Offshore manufacturing may offer cost advantages that are independent of scale.

Kidde and Maple Chase, FirstAlert's two main rivals, have also followed a low price strategy and use similar manufacturing, pricing and distribution strategies as FirstAlert. Currently, FirstAlert's parent company, American Household (formerly Sunbeam), is emerging from bankruptcy after losing its foothold in many of its major retailers[28].

> [28]Elaboration is in order, if only in a sentence or two. Has the parent company's bankruptcy affected FirstAlert's competitive strength? Did FirstAlert "lose its foothold" as well?

THE COMMERCIAL MARKET[29]

FirstAlert's low-price, residential smoke detector is not adequate for commercial use, leading to the development of a separate, commercial smoke detector market. One firm, Kidde Safety Systems, Inc., has emerged as the dominant firm in this segment, amassing a 70% share, while its largest competitor has only a single-digit market penetration. Compared to the consumer segment, products in the commercial segment typically are of a larger, bulkier, more heavy-duty design, and are usually wired into the building's electrical system. Prices begin at $50 per unit, and professional installation is usually required.

CREATING A NEW CHILD-ORIENTED CONSUMER MARKET SEGMENT[30]

KidSmart plans to create a new consumer market segment that focuses exclusively on smoke detectors designed for children's unique needs, thereby minimizing strong competitive reactions from FirstAlert, Kidde, and Maple Chase. KidSmart's market research at various retail outlets provides strong evidence that such a child safety segment exists; and through the use of its strong patent, KidSmart anticipates that it will be able to avoid direct competition with the "Big Three" in this new segment. One survey, conducted at a leading retail store, revealed that 130 of 163 people surveyed expressed a high interest in the *KidSmart VSD™*, many requesting follow-up information and several offering to buy the product on the spot (*see Exhibit 6*[31]). Equally important, recent consumer data from the USDA shows that on average, parents in the U.S. spend between $4,000 and $10,000 each year on their children[32]. As KidSmart's survey indicates and consumer data supports, parents realize that $79.95 is a small price to pay for the safety of their children.

IV. GOALS & STRATEGIES[33]

KIDSMART'S LONG-TERM GOALS

KidSmart will develop and market a series of products to protect children from residential safety threats. KidSmart's flagship product, the *KidSmart Vocal Smoke Detector™*, will focus on reducing the deaths and injuries to children ages 14 and under in household fires. Within ten years, the Company seeks to become the leading developer and marketer of a wide range of specialized child safety products.

KIDSMART'S STARTUP & GROWTH STRATEGIES

KidSmart will initially target the *KidSmart VSD™* at[34] middle- and upper-middle-class parents of children ages 2 to 14. The *KidSmart VSD™* will be

[29]Apparently KidSmart will not pursue the commercial market. Its mention is justifiable to avoid giving the impression that the entrepreneurs are unaware of this market.

[30]Here the founders acknowledge and rebut likely concerns about KidSmart's competitive position. Readers are not blind to competitive threats, and the entrepreneur is wise to recognize and address them in both the venture strategy and in the business plan's discussions.

[31]Exhibit 6 does not show 130 responses of any type. And what is "high interest"?

[32]The wide range of this "average" creates doubt that the plan expresses it accurately. The rhetoric relies on the notion that $79.95 is a trifle by comparison to all spending on a child; a better comparison might reflect spending on recreation or other nonessential items that might be redirected to this product.

[33]This section will reiterate elements of earlier sections, but such repetition is necessary in order to state the venture's strategy. Readers cannot be expected to construct the strategy as they go along; an explicit statement is needed.

[34]*Target* means "to make a target of." It takes a direct object. Therefore "at" is incorrect.

14

Exhibit 5

Example: Smoke Detector Placement

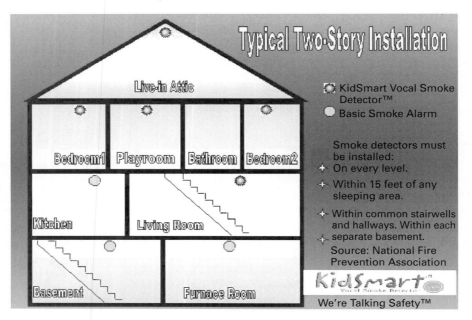

positioned as a child-safety product designed to increase the likelihood of a child's survival during a household fire. The **KidSmart VSD™** will be sold in a newly created child safety segment of the smoke detector market for two primary reasons. First, KidSmart is intent on appealing to parents' concern for their child's safety in a residential fire and using its patented, lifesaving features to put that fear at ease. Second, KidSmart will not attempt to introduce any lower-priced smoke detectors that do not incorporate its unique, patented features in order to avoid direct competition with the large competitors in this industry.[35]

KIDSMART'S GEOGRAPHIC EXPANSION STRATEGIES

After successfully introducing the **KidSmart VSD™** in the United States, management will take the steps needed to move the **KidSmart VSD™** into international markets. In light of considerable interest from the Canadian media and several discussions with potential **KidSmart VSD™** customers at the 2003 Consumer Electronics Show, expansion into Canada is considered the most logical near-term extension outside of the United States. Especially since it is clearly evident[36] that Canadian citizens easily understand how the product works and find value in its patented, familiar voice technology.[37]

[35]This sentence is confusing. The double negative contributes to that confusion.

[36]Redundant

[37]This is not a complete sentence, but a dependent clause introduced by an adverb. Better to incorporate it in the preceding sentence.

15

Exhibit 6
KidSmart VSD Price Sensitivity Analysis

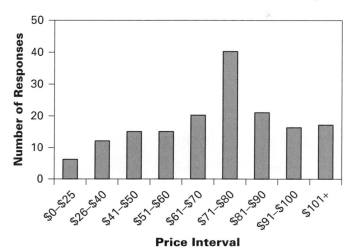

Survey Findings

163 Participants
Average Price: $73.46

Mode: $80
(27 responses[38])
60% favor[39] price > $70
$100 & up: 30 responses

KIDSMART'S FOCUSED VALUE CHAIN STRATEGY

To minimize upfront capital costs, manufacturing of the **KidSmart VSD™** will be outsourced to an independent manufacturer. In that context, KidSmart has already received quotes from an offshore manufacturer and is exploring additional alternatives in more geographically proximate[40] locations. Given the **KidSmart VSD™**'s high margins, KidSmart's primary criteria for selecting an outsourcing partner are:[41] (1) the ability to produce high-quality products and (2) the ability to scale[42] rapidly if needed. Distribution will be through specialty retail stores and catalogues and neighborhood hardware stores[43] with eventual migration toward mass market outlets if product demand supports such moves. All finished products will be shipped from the manufacturer directly to the Company's distribution warehouse, where it[44] will be inventoried until orders have been placed. KidSmart's focused value chain on the next page[45].

KIDSMART'S COMPETITIVE ADVANTAGES[46]

KidSmart has several major competitive advantages that will ensure[47] its success for the future including[48]:

- A feature-laden[49] and truly superior product

16

Exhibit 6–A

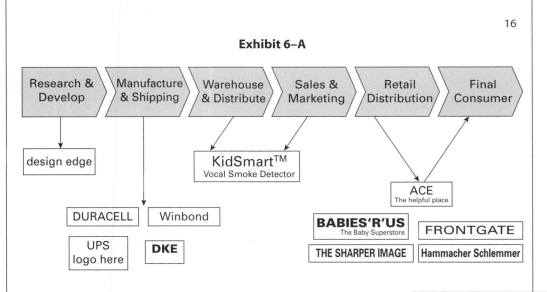

design edge

DURACELL   Winbond

UPS logo here   **DKE**

KidSmart™
Vocal Smoke Detector

ACE
The helpful place

BABIES'R'US
The Baby Superstore

FRONTGATE

THE SHARPER IMAGE   Hammacher Schlemmer

- A strong patent covering our familiar voice[50] technology
- An exclusive license[51] for use of the familiar voice technology
- Documented support from child psychologists and fire-safety experts
- A product and pricing strategy that affords the Company access to specialty retailers unavailable to Kidde and FirstAlert

V. MARKETING & SALES

TARGET MARKET

KidSmart's initial target market will be families with incomes over $50,000 per year who have children under the age of 14. This group, as seen in *Exhibit 7*,[52] includes 33 million households; represents a target market potential of $1.6 billion; and is growing by 10% each year. KidSmart will position the ***KidSmart VSD*™** as a unique product designed to significantly increase the safety of their children.

DISTRIBUTION STRATEGY

KidSmart will initially sell and distribute its suite[53] of products[54] primarily through specialty retail outlets and catalogues and neighborhood hardware stores. These channels, based on their customer mix, can support the Company's pricing strategy and help enable[55] KidSmart to avoid direct competition with mass merchandisers. If demand warrants, KidSmart may eventually move the ***KidSmart VSD*™** to more mass market channels, while selling KidSmart Wireless™ and other follow-on products through its specialty channels.[56]

[50]A hyphen (familiar-voice) would avoid the impression that the voice technology is familiar. In fact, the technology is novel while the voice is familiar.

[51]Why must it be licensed, and from whom? Will a founder receive fees or royalties from the company, and does the company not own the technology?

[52]A word is missing.

[53]An odd word choice.

[54]The wording suggests the immediate offering of the full product line at the company's birth. That would contradict earlier mentions of plans to expand the product line.

[55]Flabby wording, and weak in comparison to earlier, muscular language.

[56]The founders display savvy by recognizing that different versions and price points for its products may require different channels to reach each targeted market segment.

17

Management has chosen to implement a three-phased distribution strategy[57] to bring the **KidSmart VSD™** to market.

Phase I: Test Marketing & Internet Sales

Management has secured an agreement with an Ace Hardware store in Pleasanton; California; to test market the **KidSmart VSD™** (see *Exhibit 9*). Pleasanton meets many of the middle- to upper-middle-class target market demographics for the **KidSmart VSD™**. The first round of commercial units is anticipated to be available for sale by mid-summer 2003. This test market will allow KidSmart to solicit consumer response and test a variety of marketing campaigns. While KidSmart is finalizing the agreements necessary to implement Phase II of its distribution strategy, it will sell directly to consumers via the KidSmart website. Although this website is still in its developmental stage, a beta version has been developed at **www.kidsmartdetector.com** and will be fully operational no later than June 2003. To effectively service its customers and provide the needed support for its product(s), KidSmart has also established a toll-free number at **(877) 4-SMART-0** to handle calls concerning customer returns, warranty issues, and product questions.

Phase II: Sales Through Specialty Retail Stores and Catalogues

In Phase II of its marketing strategy, KidSmart will distribute the **KidSmart VSD™** through specialty retail stores. Given KidSmart's emphasis on child safety, specialty retail stores that carry products targeted to young children and homeowners, such as the Discovery Store, Radio Shack, and Brookstone are perfect candidates for the **KidSmart VSD™**. These stores have been selected for Phase II,[58] because each has already contacted KidSmart and indicated a willingness to carry the **KidSmart VSD™** as soon as it is available. To enhance sales in these stores, KidSmart will provide each outlet with interactive Point of Sale (POS) materials including the ABC and NBC specials detailing the inability of traditional smoke detectors to awaken sleeping children, as well as both networks' follow-up specials featuring the **KidSmart VSD™** as the solution to this problem. This[59] is important since KidSmart's market research indicates that consumers who are aware of the problem are willing to pay a premium of $10 or more over our $79.95 suggested retail price.

KidSmart will also introduce the **VSD™** into certain specialty catalogues, including Parenting Concepts, Hammacher Schlemmer, Frontgate and Sharper Image. The innovative nature of the **KidSmart VSD™** and its "unique"[60] features provide a natural complement to the offerings of these vendors, many of which already carry child safety and household products. KidSmart has established three primary criteria for catalogue selection; specifically,[61] the catalogue must focus on the **KidSmart VSD™**'s target customer, regularly feature child and/or safety products[62] and be published at least quarterly (*see Exhibit 8*).

---

[57]Readers will respect the founders' judgment in viewing distribution strategy in phases rather than as simultaneous or undifferentiated activities.

[58]Unnecessary but harmless punctuation.

[59]Use of "this" risks vagueness. Better wording would mention the POS materials.

[60]Why quotation marks? Their use suggests "scare quotes," which imply a writer's skepticism or sarcasm.

[61]A colon would provide stronger separation and prepare the reader for a series described by what precedes the punctuation. "Specifically" would become unnecessary.

[62]A comma following products would make clear the beginning of the third term in the series.

By utilizing catalogues as part of its initial distribution channel, KidSmart can take advantage of the brand recognition and credibility that have already been established by each of its catalogue partners. Moreover, KidSmart will be able to acquire sales on a national level without having to make the investment in a national sales force.[63]

[63]Readers may wonder how KidSmart will achieve the retail presence discussed two paragraphs earlier without investing in a national sales force. Therefore, the savings implied here seem to be illusory.

Phase III: National Mass Market Distribution

Eventually, KidSmart will distribute the **KidSmart VSD™** through one or more mass market channels, such as Home Depot or Ace Hardware. To gain entry into these "Big Box" retailers, the Company plans to either joint venture with one of the larger players in the industry or enter into a relationship with a distributor who already sells to these chains in order to leverage their[64] existing relationships and gain low-cost shelf space. As the **KidSmart VSD™** moves to the mass market, the Company will introduce the **KidSmart Wireless™** and related follow-on products to its existing specialty retail and catalogue partners.

[64]A hopelessly unclear pronoun, "their" could refer to "one of the larger players," "a distributor," or "these chains [the larger players] again." The pronoun should be singular if it refers to "one of" or "a distributor."

[65]This exhibit is hard to follow. Wouldn't the number of income-qualified households with children be more relevant than the number of children? It's the household, not the children, that purchases the product. Also, the exhibit omits some steps in arriving at its estimates.

Exhibit 7

Target[65] Market

U.S. Census Population Estimates In millions	
	2003
Households with Children 18 & Under	32.9
Target Household Percentage	51.6%
Children Households with $50K Income	**17.0**
U.S. Children	
5 to 9 years	19.2
10 to 14 years	20.8
Total 5 to 14 years	**40.0**
Target Market Potential by Children	20.6
Retail Price of KidSmart VSD™	$ 79.95
Estimated Target Market Size	**$ 1,649.9**
Annual U.S. Births	4.0
Target Household Percentage	51.6%
Annual incremental market	**$ 165.0**
Source: 2000 U.S. Census projections	

19

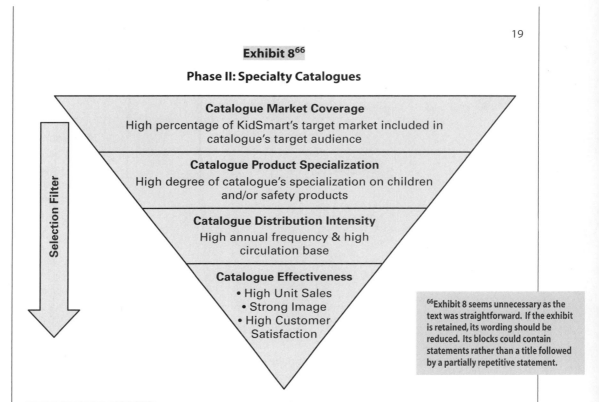

Exhibit 8[66]

Phase II: Specialty Catalogues

Selection Filter

Catalogue Market Coverage
High percentage of KidSmart's target market included in catalogue's target audience

Catalogue Product Specialization
High degree of catalogue's specialization on children and/or safety products

Catalogue Distribution Intensity
High annual frequency & high circulation base

Catalogue Effectiveness
• High Unit Sales
• Strong Image
• High Customer Satisfaction

CONSUMER EDUCATION[67]

Consumer awareness and the clear conveyance of the **KidSmart VSD™**'s benefits for children will be paramount[68] to our success. KidSmart intends to create a unique fire safety education program in cooperation with the National Fire Prevention Association (NFPA)[69] to be presented to young children at school. This program will detail recommended fire safety procedures as well as the role the **KidSmart VSD™** can play in a complete and efficient fire safety plan. Children will view this program both live and via school broadcast television and be given educational materials related to child fire safety. The children will be instructed to deliver these materials to their parents and to discuss what they learned and to ask questions about their family's fire preparation plan. This will educate our target customers regarding their households' fire safety deficiencies and promote the **KidSmart VSD™** at the same time.

PRODUCT DEMONSTRATIONS

KidSmart will continue to demonstrate the **KidSmart VSD™** to potential customers in a variety of ways, including retail demonstrations and circulation of marketing collaterals at applicable industry conferences. In addition to attending the National Fire Prevention Association (NFPA)[70] Annual Education

[66]Exhibit 8 seems unnecessary as the text was straightforward. If the exhibit is retained, its wording should be reduced. Its blocks could contain statements rather than a title followed by a partially repetitive statement.

[67]This section responds creatively to an important question for KidSmart. Even so, readers may wonder how the company will secure NFPA's cooperation, who will teach the program, and how the costs will be covered.

[68]Wrong word. The writers may mean "of paramount importance to …"

[69]Here is the identification of NFPA that should have accompanied its first mention.

[70]Now that the acronym has been identified, there is no need to repeat its full name.

20

Exhibit 9

Phase I: Test Market

 © The Helpful Hardware People™

Bill Anderson
Assistant Manager
Kolln Ace Hardware
600 Main Street
Pleasanton, CA 94566
925-426-1500

November 14, 2002

Mr. Matt Ferris
President
KidSmart Corporation
322 Beechwood Drive
Athens, GA 30606

Dear Matt:

After my discussions with your team regarding the KidSafe Vocal Smoke Detector, and after receiving approval from the store owner this past Friday, we would be willing to sell your product in our Pleasanton, California, store. I agree with your team's assessment of the demographics in the Pleasanton area and believe the product has the potential to achieve substantial sales.

I will offer the following:

- An entire end-cap display in the most high-traffic area of the store, dedicated to the product and its literature.
- The product itself will be located at eye-level.
- I will train my sales team on the benefits of the item and require them to inform customers of its benefits.

In consideration for offering this shelf space and promotion of the KidSafe Vocal Smoke Detector, I will require payment terms of net 60.

Additionally, the owner would be willing to put you in touch with other Ace Hardware stores in the area and introduce you to the National Products Distribution Manager at our headquarters in Oak Brook, Illinois.

I look forward to receiving your product.

Sincerely,

Bill

Bill Anderson

21

Exhibit 10

Media Coverage

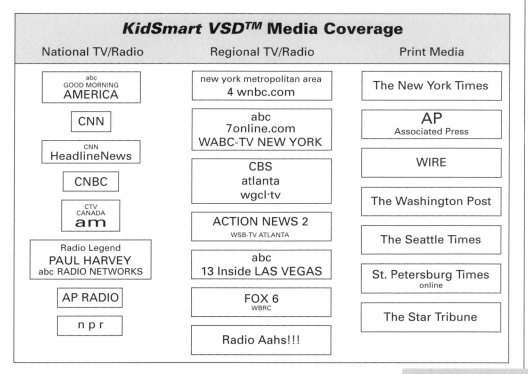

KidSmart VSD™ Media Coverage		
National TV/Radio	Regional TV/Radio	Print Media
abc GOOD MORNING AMERICA	new york metropolitan area 4 wnbc.com	The New York Times
CNN	abc 7online.com WABC-TV NEW YORK	AP Associated Press
CNN HeadlineNews	CBS atlanta wgcl·tv	WIRE
CNBC	ACTION NEWS 2 WSB-TV ATLANTA	The Washington Post
CTV CANADA am	abc 13 Inside LAS VEGAS	The Seattle Times
Radio Legend PAUL HARVEY abc RADIO NETWORKS	FOX 6 WBRC	St. Petersburg Times online
AP RADIO	Radio Aahs!!!	The Star Tribune
n p r		

Conference in Atlanta, November 16–20, 2002, management also demonstrated the **KidSmart VSD™** at the Consumer Electronics Show (CES) in Las Vegas, January 9–12, 2003, where it won a *Best of Innovations Award* in the Home Appliances category. KidSmart will also have a booth at the New Product Exposition at the National Hardware Show in Chicago on August 10–13, 2003. This will be in coordination with the **KidSmart VSD™**'s product launch through specialty retail catalogues[71].

Free Magazine, Radio, TV and Newspaper Publicity[72]

The **KidSmart VSD™** has already been featured on/in[73] numerous television, radio and print media as seen below, and KidSmart anticipates that such goodwill promotion will continue (*see Exhibit 10*[74]). Most recently, KidSmart has been approached by ABC–Milwaukee and NBC–Dallas to develop special reports on the **KidSmart VSD™**'s ability to awaken sleeping children. KidSmart

[71] KidSmart does well to plan a coordinated campaign but should clarify how the product demonstration in Chicago fits into its launch through catalogues.

[72] This brief paragraph enhances KidSmart's credibility to readers. It suggests widespread recognition of the fire-safety problem, belief in the effectiveness of the company's solution, and effectiveness on the part of its founders in securing such publicity.

[73] Awkward. Either *in* or *by* would suffice.

[74] Exhibit 10 originally displayed logos. It was colorful but of limited effect.

22

is currently trying to schedule these reports to coincide with the availability of the *KidSmart VSD™* for Phase II distribution.

VI. MANUFACTURING & DISTRIBUTION

KidSmart's Outsourcing Manufacturing Strategy

KidSmart plans to outsource all manufacturing of the *KidSmart VSD™*. Despite its many unique product features, the *KidSmart VSD™* is built from fairly standardized components[75], including a digital voice chip, a speaker and a dual smoke-sensing unit. Based on the company's proof-of-concept prototype, DK Electronics has quoted KidSmart a price per unit of $15.69 FOB Taiwan. Harbor fees and ocean freight costs add another $0.093 to per-unit cost, and a separate import charge of 1.7%[76] will be applied to that total. Initially, shipments will take 30 to 45 days from dock-to-door; however, as volume increases, it should be possible to negotiate more favorable terms with DK Electronics. Management has elected to maintain QC[77] in house and to negotiate terms for the return of defective batches of 2% or more.

Ability to Scale Rapidly—Given the overwhelmingly positive[78] response of consumers to the *KidSmart VSD™*, the Company believes that initial demand for the unit may exceed our conservative estimates[79]. DK Electronics has the resources and capacity to meet "runaway"[80] demand should the latter occur and has agreed to produce 50,000 units within 45 days of initiating production. Once production has commenced, DK Electronics possesses the capacity to manufacture an additional 100,000 units every 30 days.

Potential to Lower Costs—It may also be possible to lower future costs through more cost-effective designs. For example, the 28-second voice chip is the most expensive component in KidSmart's proof-of-concept prototype, and the heat sensing thermistor is the second most expensive component in that unit.[81] However, discussions with fire safety industry participants[82] have suggested the maximum message length should be less than 15 seconds to discourage delay, and that the thermistor should be replaced by the much more reliable and affordable ionization technology. Design engineers suggest these two changes alone could decrease unit costs by up to 35%, and that KidSmart should expect a final unit cost of under $12.

Supplier Partnerships—KidSmart's management has already partnered with Duracell to design an optimal power system for the *KidSmart VSD™*. This partnership will allow KidSmart to utilize the most effective power consumption configuration and to ensure that the *KidSmart VSD™* will

[75]A reassurance that this innovative product will be readily and reliably produced, and at a competitive cost.

[76]Explain what this is and who levies it. Is it a tariff?

[77]Ought to spell out *quality control*.

[78]Hyperbole.

[79]Business plans routinely describe their projected sales as "conservative." Readers discount this word unless convinced by evidence and argument that the figures truly are conservative.

[80]A second instance of odd quotation marks. Rapidly rising would be better wording. Specifying the agreement with DK Electronics is concrete reassurance to readers.

[81]Rare instance of poor writing in this plan. It's awkward and more detailed than necessary. Better to say "the most expensive components in KidSmart's proof-of-concept prototype are the 28-second microchip and the heat-sensing thermistor."

[82]Vagueness won't help and may hurt. Better to tell what sort of "participants" by role or position, imparting credibility to their opinions.

function properly throughout its 10-year life and provide ample warning as the battery begins to weaken.

Logistics & Distribution

KidSmart will initially inventory all units at its Company headquarters in Atlanta, Georgia. However, by the beginning of 2005, unit sales will be large enough to warrant the leasing of a separate warehouse for product storage and distribution. All units will be shipped by KidSmart to its retail distributors FOB Atlanta.

Product Certification

While current Federal and State laws require "approved" smoke detectors to be installed throughout public buildings, no regulations exist regarding smoke detector certification for private residences. Thus, the *KidSmart VSD™* could be sold to the public without any type of certification. However, because of the *KidSmart VSD™*'s "child safety" product image, KidSmart plans to seek UL (Underwriters Laboratories, Inc.) approval for the *KidSmart VSD™* under *Standard 217* for single and multiple station smoke detectors.

In light of the recent studies proving traditional detectors are ineffective at waking children, UL is currently exploring how it should change its standards to address this problem. KidSmart has been solicited by the UL with regard to these new standards and is participating in these discussions. Furthermore, the NFPA recently revised the National Fire Alarm Code (NFPA 72), stating that the alarm signal must be distinctive in sound from other signals and consist of a "three-pulse" temporal pattern. NFPA 72 was the former basis for UL 217, so by meeting the following criteria, KidSmart can assure that the *VSD™* is in compliance with all regulations:

- Three successive "on" phases of .5 seconds each and separated by .5 seconds of "off" time.
- At completion of third "on" phase, 1.5 seconds of "off" time before cycle is repeated.
- Total cycle time shall last 4.0 seconds and have a minimum duration of three minutes.[83]

[83]Confusing. The cycle is four seconds, not three minutes. Apparently operation continues for at least three minutes during which each cycle lasts four seconds.

The requirement of temporal tones on all new detectors will certainly be an improvement. At the same time, KidSmart is exploring the possibility of working with the UL to create a new standard[84] requiring a recorded voice command for detectors sold for use in children's bedrooms. In fact, Dr. Shapiro is both an advisor to KidSmart and a board member of the UL 217 initiative. This certification process should take between 8 and 16 weeks and cost between $10,000 and $20,000. Once it has UL certification, KidSmart will secure product

[84]Vague: Is KidSmart in discussion with UL or merely "exploring" on its own the possibility of such collaboration? The wording nine lines earlier seemed more definite.

24

liability insurance[85] for the *KidSmart VSD™*. The preliminary quote that KidSmart has received is for $11,700 per year for $5 million dollars in coverage.

VII. THE MANAGEMENT TEAM

KidSmart's founding management team and advisors possess the full range of business skills necessary to bring the *KidSmart VSD™* to market. To ensure the success of the *KidSmart VSD™* in a retail environment, KidSmart plans to hire a CEO with consumer product experience prior to the mass market introduction of the *KidSmart VSD™*.

Matt Ferris, President. Initially, Matt will coordinate the overall operations of the company and act as the company spokesperson. Matt has managed an ACE Hardware store for several years and has considerable experience operating a small business. Furthermore, Matt's relationships within the neighborhood hardware store arena[86] will prove invaluable in the success of KidSmart. Matt will also be involved in the sales and marketing of the *KidSmart VSD™* and will be one of two full-time employees at startup.

Kerry Moher, VP of Marketing. Kerry has extensive experience in consumer product marketing and understands the creativity and commitment needed to succeed in a start-up environment. In Kerry's last position, he was responsible for developing and successfully launching three new products: Impatica for PowerPoint™, Impatica for Director™ and Impatica On Cue™. His market research skills have helped to define the opportunities available in the underserved specialty smoke detector segment. As VP of Marketing, Kerry will be responsible for promotion and pricing strategies and will assume a full-time role upon startup.

Doug Ghertner, VP of Operations. Doug will be responsible for creating the manufacturing and distribution alliances that will be essential in maintaining on-time delivery of the *KidSmart VSD™* and ensuring a positive experience for the customer. Doug has considerable experience in establishing strategic alliances with Fortune 100 companies and in creating and managing operational teams. Also, Doug's experience in developing and successfully establishing a new business division within his most recent employer[87] will be critical to our success.

Bruce Black, VP of Finance. Bruce has extensive experience with startups, having arranged over $212 million of equity financing for private firms. Bruce was extensively involved in securing private placement financing with venture and strategic investors and has cultivated an extensive network of influential lawyers, investment bankers, entrepreneurs, and venture capitalists across the Southeast who will provide gainful advice and contacts as KidSmart grows.

[85]The founders are wise to mention the insurance and its cost, but readers may want a more detailed discussion of the company's potential liability.

[86]*Arena* seems odd to describe the hardware store industry. Better to describe Matt's relationships and why they will be helpful.

[87]Seeming coyness may be necessary for reasons that are not apparent to readers. If interested in the business plan, they'll certainly want to know more about the founders.

25

Exhibit 10–A

Sources & Uses of Cash: First Round			
Sources		**Uses**	
New Money (Internal)	$ 50,000	Industrial Design Costs	$ 60,000
New Money (External)	750,000	Injection Mold & Tooling	50,000
		Underwriters' Labs Approval	15,000
		Initial Product Marketing	250,000
		New Product Development	125,000
		Working Capital	300,000
Total Sources of Cash	**$800,000**	**Total Uses of Cash**	**$800,000**

Exhibit 10–B

Shareholder	% Ownership	Investment	Post-Money Valuation
Management	50.0%	$ 50,000	$1,500,000
Initial Investors	*25.0%*	*750,000*	*750,000*
Directors & Advisors	5.0%	—	150,000
Option Pool	20.0%	—	600,000
Totals	**100%**	**$800,000**	**$3,000,000**

BOARD OF ADVISORS[88]

Brent E. Routman, Inventor. Brent Routman is a co-inventor of the *KidSmart VSD™* product, and will provide high-level strategic advice and intellectual property law assistance for the company. Brent is an attorney with one of the nation's 10 largest intellectual property law firms, Merchant & Gould, Minneapolis, Minnesota. He serves as the Chairman of the Patent Division of the American Bar Association Section of Intellectual Property Law and is slated to be President of the Hennepin County (Minneapolis) Bar Association in 2004.

Devin Green, CEO, ESP Systems. Devin's leadership with ESP Systems is helping to revolutionize several labor-intensive industries through the use of a wireless electro-selective prompting technology. Prior to joining ESP Systems, Devin was an associate with Bank of America Capital Investors, the private equity arm of Bank of America, where he selected and structured over 50 buy and sell-side early-stage, private company financings.

[88]The founders have assembled a small but valuable advisory board. Given their own youth and limited experience, the team needed guidance; the readers will welcome the assurance of such advice. Note the advisors' strength in intellectual property law and new venture strategy/management.

26

Exhibit 10-C

KidSmart Five Year Pro Forma Projections ($ In Thousands)					
Sales	2003	2004	2005	2006	2007
Target Market Potential by Children	20,637	20,653	20,554	20,479	20,388
KidSmart VSD™ Market Share	0.03%	0.25%	1.50%	3.50%	5.50%
KidSmart VSD™ Unit Sales	5.4	50.7	308.3	716.8	1,121.4
Source: 2000 U.S. Census projections					
Average Wholesale Price($)	$ 40.00	$ 40.00	$ 30.00	$ 27.50	$ 25.00
Projected Revenues	$ 214.0	$ 2,028.0	$ 9,249.2	$ 19,710.7	$ 28,034.2
Growth %	*NA*	*847.7%*	*356.1%*	*113.1%*	*42.2%*
COGS	65.6	621.8	3,781.5	8,791.1	13,753.8
COGS Margin	*30.7%*	*30.7%*	*40.9%*	*44.6%*	*49.1%*
Gross Profit	148.4	1,406.2	5,467.8	10,919.6	14,280.4
Gross Margin	*69.3%*	*69.3%*	*59.1%*	*55.4%*	*50.9%*
Sales & Marketing	290.3	909.6	2,664.2	5,353.4	6,647.4
% of Sales	*135.6%*	*44.9%*	*28.8%*	*27.2%*	*23.7%*
General & Administrative	67.2	176.8	638.8	1,115.8	1,465.7
% of Sales	*31.4%*	*8.7%*	*6.9%*	*5.7%*	*5.2%*
EBITDA	(219.1)	218.5	2,049.8	4,277.9	5,917.1
EBITDA Margin	*−102.4%*	*10.8%*	*22.2%*	*21.7%*	*21.1%*
Net Income	$ (136.1)	$ 112.4	$ 1,193.4	$ 2,520.5	$ 3,494.5
Net Margin	*−63.6%*	*5.5%*	*12.9%*	*12.8%*	*12.5%*

Dr. Charles W. Hofer, Regents Professor and President, The Strategic Management Group. Dr. Hofer offers over 30 years of start-up and strategy experience and is the only business school faculty member to be named a Regents Professor in the state of Georgia. He has assisted over a dozen successful new venture startups and completed extensive work with AT Kearney and General Electric Corporation.

Nicholas P. Johns, Attorney. Nick practices Intellectual Property law with an emphasis on microelectronics, software, and communications for the law firm of Merchant & Gould. He has also worked as a design engineer in research and development for Guidant Corporation and possesses a degree in Electrical Engineering from the GMI Engineering Management Institute.

VIII. FINANCIALS

CAPITAL STRUCTURE

To date, KidSmart's founders have invested $80,000 and have committed an additional $50,000 to further the refinement of the *KidSmart VSD*™. To

27

Exhibit 11

KidSmart

Proforma[89] *Annual Income Statement*
(in thousands)

[89]Note that "proforma" should be two
words, as on page 26.

Sales	FYE 2003	FYE 2004	FYE 2005	FYE 2006	FYE 2007
US Children ages 5 to 13 in target market	20,637	20,653	20,554	20,479	20,388
Share%	0.03%	0.25%	1.50%	3.50%	5.50%
Units Sold	5.4	50.7	308.3	716.8	1,121.4
Price per Unit	$ 40.0	$ 40.0	$ 30.0	$ 27.5	$ 25.0
Total Revenues	**$ 214.0**	**$ 2,028.0**	**$ 9,249.2**	**$ 19,710.7**	**$ 28,034.2**
Cost of Goods Sold					
Unit Costs	64.2	608.4	3,699.7	8,601.0	13,456.4
User Fees	0.1	1.3	7.8	18.1	28.3
Warranty Costs	1.3	12.2	74.0	172.0	269.1
Cost of Goods Sold	65.6	621.8	3,781.5	8,791.1	13,753.8
Gross Margin	**148.4**	**1,406.2**	**5,467.8**	**10,919.6**	**14,280.4**
Operating Expenses					
Sales & Marketing					
Travel & Trade Shows	26.5	64.5	161.9	344.9	490.6
Advertising	165.0	547.0	1,479.9	3,153.7	4,205.1
Promotion & Direct Mail	65.0	180.0	647.4	1,379.7	1,401.7
Salaries	33.8	118.1	375.0	475.0	550.0
General & Administrative					
Salaries	47.7	137.5	450.0	845.0	1,130.0
Insurance	5.9	11.7	69.4	147.8	210.3
Rent	6.6	13.2	84.0	86.5	88.3
Utilities	4.9	10.2	26.4	27.2	27.7
Other Expenses	2.1	4.2	9.0	9.3	9.5
Product Development	10.0	101.3	115.0	172.5	250.1
Operating Expenses	**367.4**	**1,187.7**	**3,418.0**	**6,641.7**	**8,363.3**
Depreciation & Amortization	7.8	31.1	60.8	77.1	93.0
Pre-tax Income (Loss)	**(226.9)**	**187.4**	**1,989.0**	**4,200.8**	**5,824.2**
Provision (Benefit) for Income Taxes	(90.8)	75.0	795.6	1,680.3	2,329.7
Net Income (Loss)	**(136.1)**	**112.4**	**1,193.4**	**2,520.5**	**3,494.5**
Breakeven Unit Sales	13.2	42.8	192.7	436.0	656.7

initiate startup, an additional investment of $750,000 will be needed for
product design and certification, product inventory, working capital, and future
product development. Initial discussions have placed the cost of obtaining
a production event prototype at $60,000, and an additional $65,000 will be
consumed at startup for manufacturing molds, tooling and UL approval. The
KidSmart VSD™'s initial marketing launch will require another $250,000

28

Exhibit 12

KidSmart

Pro Forma Cash Flow Statement
(in thousands)

	FYE 2003	FYE 2004	FYE 2005	FYE 2006	FYE 2007
Net Income:	(136.1)	112.4	1,193.4	2,520.5	3,494.5
Plus:					
Depreciation & Amortization	7.8	31.1	60.8	77.1	93.0
Net Increase in Deferred Tax Asset	(90.8)	132.0	223.9	294.9	216.5
Total Cash From Operations	**(219.1)**	**276**	**1,478**	**2,892**	**3,804**
Less:					
Accounts Receivable (Increase)/Decrease	(140.0)	(100.0)	(626.5)	(1,185.5)	(789.7)
Inventory (Increase)/Decrease	(116.0)	(51.7)	(644.8)	(722.3)	(681.8)
Prepaid Expenses (Increase)/Decrease	(5.9)	—	(28.8)	(39.2)	(31.2)
Plus:					
Accounts Payable (Decrease)/Increase	80.0	185.4	152.4	561.3	89.4
Accrued Expenses (Decrease)/Increase	1.2	—	1.8	0.1	0.1
Accrued Salaries (Decrease)/Increase	7.4	5.1	21.9	20.6	15.0
Total Working Capital Sources/(Uses)	**(173.3)**	**38.8**	**(1,124.2)**	**(1,365.1)**	**(1,398.2)**
Net Cash Provided By (Used in) Operations	(392.3)	314.3	353.9	1,527.4	2,405.7
Investments					
Less:					
Total Capital Expenditures	(25.0)	(8.0)	(66.0)	(64.4)	(57.2)
Investments	(150.0)	(205.0)	(54.8)	(34.6)	(44.3)
Net Cash Provided By (Used in) Investing	**(175.0)**	**(213.0)**	**(120.8)**	**(99.0)**	**(101.4)**
Financing					
Plus:					
Issuance of Convertible Preferred Stock	750.0	—	—	—	—
Issuance of Common Stock	50.0	—	—	—	—
Net Cash Provided by (Used in) Financing	**800.0**	**—**	**—**	**—**	**—**
Net Cash Flow	232.7	101.3	233.2	1,428.4	2,304.3
Net Cash Position	232.7	334.0	567.2	1,995.6	4,299.8

of capital, and the remainder of funds will fund working capital and new product development.

KidSmart is offering a 25% equity stake in the Company for these funds. In addition, 25% of the Company's shares will be held in an option pool to be distributed as awards to management for reaching certain milestones and goals. KidSmart will also employ working capital loans to fund any seasonal demand for its products.

29

Exhibit 13

KidSmart

Pro Forma Balance Sheet
(in thousands)

Assets Current Assets	Post Closing	FYE 2003	FYE 2004	FYE 2005	FYE 2006	FYE 2007
Cash	800.0	232.7	334.0	567.2	1,995.6	4,299.8
Accounts Receivable	—	140.0	240.0	866.5	2,052.1	2,841.8
Inventory	—	116.0	167.8	812.6	1,534.9	2,216.7
Deferred Taxes	—	90.8	—	—	—	—
Prepaid Expenses	—	5.9	5.9	34.7	73.9	105.1
Total Current Assets	—	**585.3**	**747.6**	**2,281.0**	**5,656.5**	**9,463.4**
Fixed Assets						
Tooling & Molds	—	50.0	50.0	87.5	96.3	103.0
PP&E	—	25.0	33.0	99.0	163.4	220.5
Intellectual Property	—	100.0	305.0	322.3	348.1	385.6
Less: Accumulated Depreciation & Amort.	—	(7.8)	(38.9)	(99.7)	(176.8)	(269.8)
Net Fixed Assets	—	**167.2**	**349.1**	**409.1**	**430.9**	**439.4**
Total Assets	—	752.5	1,096.7	2,690.0	6,087.4	9,902.8
Liabilities						
Current Liabilities						
Accounts Payable	—	80.0	265.4	417.8	979.0	1,068.5
Accrued Expenses	—	1.2	1.2	3.0	3.0	3.1
Accrued Salaries & Payroll Taxes	—	7.4	12.5	34.4	55.0	70.0
Income Taxes Payable	—	—	41.3	265.2	560.1	776.6
Total Current Liabilities	—	**88.6**	**320.4**	**720.3**	**1,597.2**	**1,918.1**
Equity						
Convertible Preferred Class A	750.0	750.0	750.0	750.0	750.0	750.0
Common Stock	50.0	50.0	50.0	50.0	50.0	50.0
Retained Earnings	—	(136.1)	(23.7)	1,169.7	3,690.2	7,184.7
Total Equity	**800.0**	**663.9**	**776.3**	**1,969.7**	**4,490.2**	**7,984.7**
Total Liabilities & Equity	800.0	752.5	1,096.7	2,690.0	6,087.4	9,902.8

PRO FORMA FINANCIALS

KidSmart's pro forma financial projections are based solely on the potential domestic sales[90] of its primary product, the *KidSmart VSD*™. KidSmart expects to grow revenues to over $28 million on unit sales of approximately 1.1 million by 2007, which is only 5.50% of KidSmart's primary target market in that year.

[90]Conservative restriction of projections to domestic sales.

Exhibit 14

KidSmart
Pro Forma Monthly Cash Flow Statement

	Jul-03	Aug-03	Sep-03	Oct-03	Nov-03	Dec-03	FYE 2003	Jan-04	Feb-04	Mar-04	Apr-04	May-04	Jun-04	Jul-04	Aug-04	Sep-04	Oct-04	Nov-04	Dec-04	FYE 2004
Net Income:	(17,740)	(16,735)	(25,109)	(36,966)	(23,704)	(15,878)	(136,131)	5,683	829	75	2,428	5,388	7,474	5,554	9,464	13,624	20,784	20,455	20,675	112,433
Plus:																				
Depreciation & Amortization	583	1333	1333	1417	1500	1667	7,833	1667	1667	2083	2083	2083	2542	2675	3092	3092	3092	3508	3508	31,092
Net Increase in Deferred Tax Asset	(11,827)	(11,157)	(16,739)	(24,644)	(15,802)	(10,585)	(90,754)	3,788	553	50	87,982	3,592	4,982	(6,491)	6,309	9,083	(5,238)	13,637	13,784	132,031
Total Cash From Operations	(28,983)	(26,558)	(40,514)	(60,194)	(38,006)	(24,796)	(219,052)	11,138	3,048	2,208	92,493	11,064	14,998	1,738	18,865	25,799	18,638	37,600	37,967	275,555
Less:																				
Accounts Receivable (Increase)/Decrease	—	—	(16,000)	(20,000)	(38,000)	(66,000)	(140,000)	(35,000)	(11,000)	(9,000)	(11,000)	(14,000)	(15,000)	65,000	(10,000)	(10,000)	(10,000)	(20,000)	(20,000)	(100,000)
Inventory (Increase)/Decrease	—	(180,378)	4,810	8,418	18,038	33,069	(116,043)	36,076	37,879	(80,569)	42,088	45,095	(132,277)	51,107	54,113	(123,258)	60,126	66,139	(108,227)	(51,708)
Prepaid Expenses (Increase)/Decrease	(4,875)	975	975	975	975	(4,875)	(6,850)	975	975	975	975	975	(4,875)	975	975	975	975	975	(4,875)	(4,875)
Plus:																				
Accounts Payable (Decrease)/Increase	—	180,378	(150,378)	30,000	—	20,000	80,000	(30,000)	5,000	125,252	(125,252)	2,000	183,378	(180,378)	—	180,378	(185,378)	15,000	195,378	185,378
Accrued Expenses (Decrease)/Increase	1,075	75	50	—	—	—	1,200	—	—	—	2,813	—	—	2,292	—	—	—	—	—	5,104
Accrued Salaries (Decrease)/Increase	6,667	—	—	—	—	729	7,396	—	—	—	—	—	—	—	—	—	—	—	—	—
Total Working Capital Sources/(Uses)	2,867	1,050	(160,543)	19,393	(18,987)	(17,077)	(173,297)	(27,949)	32,854	36,658	(90,376)	34,070	31,226	(61,004)	45,088	48,095	(134,277)	62,114	62,276	38,774
Net Cash Provided By (Used in) Operations	(26,117)	(25,508)	(201,057)	(40,801)	(56,993)	(41,873)	(392,350)	(16,812)	35,902	38,866	2,117	45,133	46,223	(59,266)	63,953	73,893	(115,639)	99,713	100,243	314,329
Investments																				
Less:																				
Total Capital Expenditures	(25,000)	—	—	—	—	—	(25,000)	—	—	—	—	—	—	(8,000)	—	—	—	—	—	(8,000)
Investments	(20,000)	(90,000)	—	(10,000)	(10,000)	(20,000)	(150,000)	—	—	(50,000)	—	—	(55,000)	—	(50,000)	—	—	(50,000)	—	(205,000)
Net Cash Provided By (Used in) Investing	(45,000)	(90,000)	—	(10,000)	(10,000)	(20,000)	(175,000)	—	—	(50,000)	—	—	(55,000)	(8,000)	(50,000)	—	—	(50,000)	—	(213,000)
Financing																				
Plus:																				
Issuance of Convertible Preferred Stock	750,000	—	—	—	—	—	750,000	—	—	—	—	—	—	—	—	—	—	—	—	—
Issuance of Common Stock	50,000	—	—	—	—	—	50,000	—	—	—	—	—	—	—	—	—	—	—	—	—
Net Cash Provided by (Used in) Financing	800,000	—	—	—	—	—	800,000	—	—	—	—	—	—	—	—	—	—	—	—	—
Net Cash Flow	728,883	(115,508)	(201,057)	(50,801)	(66,993)	(61,873)	232,651	(16,812)	35,902	(11,134)	2,117	45,133	(8,777)	(67,266)	13,953	73,893	(115,639)	49,713	100,243	101,329
Net Cash Position	728,883	613,375	412,318	361,516	294,523	232,651	232,651	215,839	251,741	240,608	242,725	287,858	279,081	211,815	225,768	299,662	184,022	233,736	333,979	333,979

31

Exhibit 15

KidSmart Rapid Growth Projections
($ In Thousands)

Sales	2003	2004	2005	2006	2007
Target Market Potential by Children	20,637	20,653	20,554	20,479	20,388
KidSmart VSD™ Market Share	0.1%	2.0%	7.5%	15.0%	22.5%
KidSmart VSD™ Unit Sales	15.5	413.1	1,541.5	3,071.8	4,587.4
*Source: 2000 U.S. Census projections					
Average Wholesale Price($)	$ 40.00	$ 40.00	$ 30.00	$ 27.50	$ 25.00
Projected Revenues	**$ 619**	**$ 16,522**	**$ 46,246**	**$ 84,474**	**$ 114,685**
Growth %	NA	2568.7%	179.9%	82.7%	35.8%
COGS	190	5,066	18,907	35,792	50,780
COGS Margin	30.7%	30.7%	40.9%	42.4%	44.3%
Gross Profit	429	11,456	27,339	48,682	63,906
Gross Margin	69.3%	69.3%	59.1%	57.6%	55.7%
Sales & Marketing	362	3,797	10,335	19,159	24,505
% of Sales	58.5%	23.0%	22.3%	22.7%	21.4%
General & Administrative	293	1,576	5,003	9,076	12,116
% of Sales	47.4%	9.5%	10.8%	10.7%	10.6%
EBITDA	**(301.0)**	**5,458.8**	**10,750.8**	**19,159.9**	**25,959.2**
EBITDA Margin	−48.6%	33.0%	23.2%	22.7%	22.6%
Net Income	$ (192.6)	$ 3,250.0	$ 6,407.8	$ 11,440.3	$ 15,507.0
Net Margin	−31.1%	19.7%	13.9%	13.5%	13.5%

Exhibit 16

Investor Returns ($ in Thousands)

Stake Holders	Cash Investment	Investment Timing	Exit Stake	Exit Valuation	IRR	CoC Return
Management	$ 130	Q3–03	50.6%	$ 78,851	260%	606.5 x
Initial Investors	*$ 750*	*Q3–03*	*18.8%*	*$ 29,204*	*108%*	*38.9 x*
1st Round Investors	*$ 5,000*	*Q1–04*	*25.0%*	*$ 38,939*	*67%*	*7.8 x*
Directors & Advisors	NA	NA	5.6%	$ 8,761	NA	NA
Total	**$ 5,880**	**NA**	**100.0%**	**$ 155,755**	**93%**	**177.0 x**

KidSmart's projections also assume that the wholesale price of the *KidSmart VSD*™ declines by 38% over the next five years[91]. However, even with this projected decline, KidSmart still expects to realize gross margins of over 50% in 2007. These projections also assume no reductions in unit cost over the five years, but KidSmart does expect to negotiate significant volume purchase discounts as unit volume grows and its outsourced manufacturing partner(s)

[91] Further conservative assumptions. The projections allow for possible effects of competition by building in a declining wholesale price. Profits under the plan's scenario come from increased unit sales rather than higher prices and in spite of no reduction in unit costs.

32

enjoy increasing economies of scale. With these attractive margins and its efficient organizational structure, KidSmart projects that it will become EBITDA positive by its seventh month of operations, and net cash flow positive after only eight months of operations.

Exit Strategy & Investor Returns

KidSmart intends to provide its investors'[92] liquidity at the end of 2007 through a strategic sale of the company. Primary targets include traditional smoke detector industry participants, as well as child safety product manufacturers such as Graco, Evenflo, and Safety First. These potential acquirers all operate in mature markets and should be willing to pay a premium multiple for a profitable source of growth in a related industry. Additional acquirers from the security monitoring industry and home networking industry will also be contacted.

At a 6x 2007 EBITDA multiple, KidSmart should command a purchase price of nearly $36 million. This corresponds well with a price of $35.6 million based on a 2007 P/E multiple of 10×. Ignoring the development of new products, international sales, and potential cost reductions, these projections indicate KidSmart's initial investors should realize a 12× cash on cash return, or a 64% IRR, from their investment in KidSmart.

While the Company's future products and international expansion offer tremendous growth potential, management believes that the greatest opportunity for upside will occur should consumers pull the ***KidSmart VSD***[TM] to the mass market even quicker than anticipated. Should this happen, KidSmart will seek an additional $5 million to finance this rapid growth. With sales of nearly $115 million and EBITDA of nearly $26 million, our initial investors would enjoy a 40× cash-on-cash return from their initial investment. (See Exhibits 15 and 16[93].)

IX. KEY RISKS AND CONTINGENCIES

KidSmart faces three primary risks: (1) uncertainty surrounding UL approval for vocal alarm with recordable functionality, (2) problems with outsourcing manufacturers, and (3) competitive reactions from traditional smoke detector manufacturers.

Uncertainty surrounding UL approval for vocal alarm with recordable functionality. Underwriters Laboratories expects to revise Guideline 217 in the near future. However, UL's current standard makes no provisions or

> [92]**Should be a plural and not a possessive. Delete the apostrophe.**

> [93]**Earlier references to exhibits appeared in italics.**

33

requirements for a vocal alarm with recordable functionality. If this guideline is not revised or is revised against that functionality, KidSmart could experience difficulties receiving product certification. Management believes this scenario to be unlikely due to the positive response in the fire safety community regarding the *KidSmart VSD™* and their significant influence in setting these guidelines through the NFPA. KidSmart is also working closely with UL, psychologists, and child behaviorists to study the benefits of familiar-voice alarms, and hopes to create a new UL standard that might require the use of KidSmart's technology on all smoke detectors sold for use in children's bedrooms.

KidSmart may encounter problems with its Outsourcing Manufacturers.
KidSmart will initially employ a strategy of outsourcing manufacturing in order to minimize fixed costs. Should demand for the *KidSmart VSD™* prove to be substantially more than our primary supplier can meet or should our primary supplier fail to meet certain quality standards, KidSmart will need to be able to change manufacturers. To mitigate these risks, KidSmart will contract excess demand above our primary manufacturer's capacities to one or more back-up,[94] suppliers and will maintain relationships through ongoing requests for quotes to ensure competitive pricing and sufficient volume.

[94]Improper comma.

Our "Child Safety" Market Segment May Be Targeted by Strong Competitors. KidSmart's initial strategy will be to carve out a profitable children's safety segment of the smoke detector market while growing the total market through the sale of additional detectors for children's rooms. KidSmart's strong patent precludes traditional industry competitors from producing units employing "familiar-voice recordings of any type."[95] However, if traditional industry[96] is able to develop alternate types of wake-up alarms that work with children, KidSmart could experience significant pricing and margin pressures.

[95]Is the quotation from the patent? Identify its source.

[96]Vagueness harms understanding. If the reference is to incumbents in the smoke alarm business, say so.

X. FUTURE GROWTH

As the *KidSmart VSD™* penetrates the children's market, KidSmart will expand in two different ways: (1) the introduction of new products, and (2) international sales.

FOLLOW-ON NEW PRODUCTS

KidSmart's first new product will be an alternate current[97] (A/C) hard-wired version of the *KidSmart VSD™* as well as several combination hazard

[97]The correct term is alternating current.

34

detectors based on the Company's core patented technology. These include:

KidSmart Toxic Gas Detectors™ (TGD)[98]—KidSmart has already applied for provisional patents covering the extension of its core technology into toxic gas detectors[99]. For instance, carbon monoxide (CO) is the leading cause of poisoning deaths in the United States. According to the *Journal of the American Medical Association,* "there are approximately 2,100 unintentional deaths from carbon monoxide (CO) every year in the U.S."[100] In addition, more than 10,000 CO injuries occur annually from this colorless, odorless, and tasteless poison. Mounting evidence also points to radon gas in homes as another important public-health problem. The Environmental Protection Agency estimates that radon poisoning causes between 15,000 and 21,000 deaths annually, and the American Lung Association has identified radon poisoning as a leading cause of lung cancer, second only to cigarette smoking. KidSmart intends to offer CO and radon detection capabilities in connection with its core technology as standalone units, combination detectors, and as plug-and-play add-ons to the ***KidSmart Wireless™*** system. These units will also be offered with a choice of power options including lithium batteries and hardwired models.

KidSmart PoolWatch[101]***™***—Each year, more than 450 children under the age of nine drown in residentially owned pools. Another 6,500 children are medically treated in hospitals and emergency rooms for near-drownings. A study by the Consumer Product Safety Commission found that in California, Arizona, and Florida, drowning was the leading cause of accidental death in and around the home for children under the age of 5 years. Nearly half of the child victims were last seen in the house before the pool accident occurred. KidSmart will leverage its wireless smoke detector system to provide a whole-house alert when a mounted sonar device detects a significant disturbance in the water of a residential pool. The pool disturbance will then trigger the transmission of the owner's pre-[102]recorded message to each ***KidSmart VSD™*** base detector, ensuring owner notification regardless of their location inside the home[103]. This product will be sold as an add-on, but also in stand[104] alone form to the more than 7 million American residential pool owners.

KidSmart SIDS Alert™—According to the National Institute of Child Health and Human Development, more than 2,700 children under the age of one year die from SIDS (Sudden Infant Death Syndrome) each year. Recent research has documented a significant relationship between a parent's voice saying the child's name and the abrupt reversal of an ALTE, acute life-threatening episodes which are highly correlated with SIDS[105]. While the Institute is

[98]Note that this paragraph offers brief documentation of the problems of CO and radon gas.

[99]Evidence that the follow-on product is more than a pipe dream.

[100]Readers may wonder whether quoted article is recent. Is the quotation an editorial statement by the journal, or from one of its articles?

[101]Once more the founders sketch the problem while including some documentation.

[102]Unnecessary.

[103]Reads awkwardly. Consider saying "ensuring its broadcast throughout the house."

[104]Close space.

[105]ALTE is defined as a plural noun yet introduced by a singular article (an).

35

conducting further testing, KidSmart is pursuing a provisional patent of its technology for a product that would trigger a parent's recorded message to their[106] child in the event of an ALTE.

[106]Avoid using a plural pronoun with a singular noun as its antecedent.

INTERNATIONAL GROWTH

The worldwide opportunity for the *KidSmart VSD*™ is enormous. The European market alone is $2.9 billion and growing by 8% annually. European households are 26% less likely to have an installed smoke detector than their United States counterparts and those that do, only possess 0.7 smoke detectors per residence vs. the United States average of 1.3. The ever-increasing population of Asia, combined with their penchant for novel inventions,[107] also presents a unique opportunity for the KidSmart technology. Initial response from Canadian consumers, fire safety officials, and media representatives show a significant demand for our initial product and provide evidence of support for the VSD™ in this $464 million market. While, KidSmart does not hold any international patents on its primary technology, the international target market opportunity could be more than triple the size of the Company's domestic market opportunity. Management expects to begin international expansion to Canada immediately upon product certification and overseas within 12 months of starting operations[108].

[107]This broad, facile generalization doesn't bear the burden of argumentation. Are Asians indeed so fond of novel inventions? All Asian cultures, or certain noteworthy ones? Evidence?

[108]One of the business plan's weakest moments, this idea reads like an afterthought on an essay exam written under time pressure. It was not covered in the financial plan. Neither the organizational nor logistical plans provide for overseas expansion.

TOPICS FOR DISCUSSION

1. In what respects is the business plan intended to convince? To persuade?

2. Unlike many business reports or documents, the business plan is intended for both internal and external readers. How does this dual audience affect the job of writing a business plan?

3. Why is the writing of a business plan beneficial to many entrepreneurs even if they are not "required" to write one?

4. Why is the executive summary so important? How should the entrepreneur take account of that importance in writing it?

5. What elements should your explanation of the business concept include?

6. Under what circumstances is it necessary to discuss the development of your product or service?

7. What portions of the industry analysis require intellectual creativity on your part? What portions seem likely to be more routine?

8. Why is your assessment of the industry's potential for profit the pivotal point in your industry analysis? Supposing that a potential investor and a potential lender both read your business plan, which one do you think would be more keenly interested in the industry's profit potential?

9. Why should your discussion of the competitors facing the venture be linked to your identification of its target market? How would your business plan be weakened if you analyzed competitors without logically linking that analysis to your target market?

10. Explain in your own words Kathleen Allen's reasoning when she writes, "It is much easier to develop tactics than to develop strategies." How does this truth affect the task of writing a business plan?

11. Why are the marketing plan and operational plan "not fixed to a single template"?

12. Why are financial plans often unrealistic or inaccurate?

13. Explain the role of assumptions in the writing and reading of the financial plan.

14. In what ways must the exit strategy for investors be consistent with the venture strategy and the company's plans for future development?

15. What do you see as the advantages and disadvantages of using "business plan" software to prepare your own business plan?

16. The *KidSmart*™ business plan does not use exactly the structure and section headings described in this chapter. Study the plan. Locate the parts that are comparable to those discussed in the chapter. Do you think the presentation is effective as given? What changes in content or structure do you suggest?

Applications

1. Think of a business concept; then briefly describe it as you would in a business plan.

2. For the business concept you imagined in Application 1, explain how your business plan would cover its development.

3. Interview someone who has started a full-time business within the past five years. Write a report describing that entrepreneur's planning prior to launching the business, including the role (if any) of a written business plan in that process. Compare and contrast the entrepreneur's approach to planning in those days to his or her approach today.

4. Research the sources of assistance in your city for would-be entrepreneurs who want or need to plan a new business. Evaluate and compare two of them in terms of their likely value to a first-time entrepreneur. Write a two-page report of your findings.

5. The Carnegie Library of Pittsburgh maintains a Business Plans and Profiles Index (http://www.carnegielibrary.org/subject/business/bplansindex.html) from which you may obtain sample business plans. Select one and study it. Write a two-page evaluation of its executive summary in terms of its effectiveness in presenting the plan. Also write your own, improved executive summary of the plan.

References

1. Sandberg, W. R., Schweiger, D. M., & Hofer, C. W. (1988). "The use of verbal protocols in determining venture capitalists' decision processes." *Entrepreneurship Theory and Practice 13*, 2 (Winter): 7–20.

2. For a thorough but brief explanation of how to develop a business concept, see Allen, K. R. (2003). *Launching new ventures: An entrepreneurial approach*. Houghton-Mifflin Company, Chapter 5.

3. For the original source, see Porter's *Competitive Strategy* (New York: Free Press, 1980). Numerous textbooks in strategic management and entrepreneurship summarize his model and techniques.

4. Allen (2003), page 241.

5. Allen (2003), page 243.

chapter 17

Writing Policies, Procedures, and Instructions

LEARNING OBJECTIVES

After you have read this chapter, you should be able to:

1. Explain the functional importance of policies, procedures, and instructions.
2. Explain legal considerations related to development of an employee manual.
3. Demonstrate specific techniques for writing unambiguous policies, procedures, and instructions.
4. Identify levels of social responsibility that should be evidenced in policies, procedures, and instructions.

A common writing task that you will encounter in your career is writing policies, procedures, and instructions. These writing assignments may be as simple as a memo that tells employees how to apply for a parking permit, a letter that describes the procedures for returning merchandise to a mail order company, or a memo that informs employees of a new policy regarding staggered lunch breaks. In contrast, your writing tasks may be as complex as preparing a brochure listing the steps required to select the benefits you want from the Human Resources Department's website, a section of an employee manual detailing steps for reporting sexual harassment, or a complete employee manual presenting all guidelines covering employment with your company.

Whether the document is short or long, it falls into the category of a report: It is an organized, objective presentation of information used in the decision process. Employees, managers, and clients of your company will base significant decisions on instructions, procedures, and policies that you write. Although the discussion and examples given in this chapter will focus on policies, procedures, and instructions written for employees, the principles discussed apply also to such documents written for customers and clients.

IMPORTANCE OF POLICIES, PROCEDURES, AND INSTRUCTIONS[1]

Well-written policies, procedures, and instructions contribute to organizational efficiency and effectiveness. Although these documents have common characteristics, they differ in why they are written and how they are used. *Policies* define an organization's view on specific issues or problems and indicate how the organization will handle problems when they arise. *Procedures* are general guidelines for accomplishing a task or objective; they sometimes also describe *who* does *what* and *when*. Some tasks, such as explaining how to get approval for a community-service project, may require general procedures only. In contrast, *instructions* provide detailed step-by-step directions for completing a task. Explaining to an employee how to use the company's website to select employee benefits requires step-by-step instructions.

Policies help to define the culture of an organization by explaining the desired behavior of the individuals associated with the organization. Whether they are for a unit within the organization or for the organization as a whole, policies usually describe the nature of the employment relationship, including the benefits and obligations of the relationship. Those benefits and obligations may be as mundane as parking policies or as substantive as rules about accepting gifts from suppliers or giving gifts to potential clients. Without established, published policies, decisions are made on an *ad hoc* basis, resulting in uncertainty and confusion among employees and clients. With established policies, managers and employees need to spend little time determining what is permissible and what is not; they can devote their energies to accomplishing the work of the organization.

Because policies have substantial impact on employees' lives, they should be established fairly, communicated clearly, and applied consistently. The best way to ensure fairness and consistency is to commit the policies to writing and ensure that all employees have access to the policies. A well-written employee manual serves that purpose. The manual assists managers in day-to-day supervision. It simplifies decisions about acceptable and unacceptable behavior and promotes consistency in handling violations. The manual also helps employees by promoting fair treatment. Some policy statements also explain how to implement the policy. In such instances, the policy is merged with procedures. For example, many employee manuals contain a procedure statement immediately after the statement of each policy.

Instructions are written for people who do not know how to do what you want them to do; most are written to ensure safe and effective performance of a process or use of a product. Well-written instructions contribute to efficiency and protect the employer and employee. Instructions should help an employee do the job correctly and safely the first time it is done. For example, clear and accurate instructions for removing worn tires and installing new tires on a customer's automobile—if followed—help the technician perform the task in the most efficient manner and protect her or him from injury. Those properly followed instructions can also protect the employer by reducing employee compensation claims for on-the-job injuries and avoiding liability suits by car owners should accidents occur.

Although policies, procedures, and instructions differ in content and purpose, certain general writing guides apply to all of these documents.

Guides for Policies, Procedures, and Instructions

Policies, procedures, and instructions can be difficult to write because language is easily misinterpreted. For that reason, these documents are often drafted, reviewed by experts, and revised many times before they are released. However, the basic guides for writing these items are similar to those you followed for all reports discussed in previous chapters of this book: Analyze your audience; identify the context; define your goal; and use a writing style and document design that complement the audience, context, and goal.

Analyze Audience

Identify specifically who will read your document. Identifying "employees" as the audience may be insufficient. For example, when your company adds a 401K plan to its benefits roster, the policy regarding participation and amount that may be dedicated to the plan must be written in such a way that all employees can understand why and how to participate in the plan. Those employees may range from executives with MBA degrees to shop workers who have not completed a high school education.

To define your audience more fully, ask yourself the following questions. How will the audience perceive what I write? What is the audience's attitude toward the message? Will the audience perceive the message as a genuine benefit to employees or as an attempt by management to manipulate or control them?

For example, when the U.S. Internal Revenue Service approved the "medical spending account," a major state university offered that benefit to its employees. The major feature of the medical spending account is that, at the employee's request, the employer withholds pre-tax dollars that are set aside to cover out-of-pocket medical expenses. Usually the employer contracts with an external agency to process claims against the account. The employee has full discretion to specify the amount to be withheld (up to federal limits) and submits receipts for reimbursement. This procedure permits the employee to pay for certain medical expenses with tax-free money. However, when the benefit was offered, some employees resisted the program, declaring that it was a way for the business manager to "hang onto our money a little longer." Although the person who wrote the policy and the procedures for participating described the plan clearly, that writer failed to consider the climate of suspicion (context) that prevailed on the campus at that time.

Identify Context

The context in which a document is read influences its use and interpretation. Determine when, where, and how your employees will use the document. Is the document intended as a reference tool to be consulted only when a specific question arises? Do you want the user to read the document carefully before acting, or do you expect the person to read the document while performing a step-by-step procedure? How will cultural and international differences affect the interpretation of a policy or the understanding of the language used to define steps in a process?

Define Goal

Before writing a policy, a procedure, or a set of instructions, ask yourself what you want the reader to do or be able to do after reading the document. Link your goal to your analysis of audience and context: *Who* must be able to do *what*, in *what way*, to *what extent*, and under *what circumstances*?

Consider the case of writing policies and procedures to apply for a reserved parking space. You should identify all types of employees who are affected by the policy, when they are most likely to read the policy and procedures, everything you want them to do in the process, and whether it is important for employees to complete all steps of the process. For example, if your company provides preferred parking for employees who carpool, those who do so would have to complete certain parts of the application procedure that others would not be required to complete. The policy must clearly identify the criteria to qualify for preferred parking, and the procedure must indicate clearly which steps must be completed by employees who want to be considered for preferred parking.

Use Appropriate Writing Style and Document Design

As you write your document, always ask what you can do to make the information easy to use and understand. The writing style and document design should contribute to those goals.

WRITING STYLE

Strive to achieve clarity, consistency, completeness, and gender equity. For clarity, use simple declarative sentences with active verbs and limited modifiers. Avoid ambiguous terms, such as "reasonable" or "excessive." Also avoid "legalese" or excessively formal language. (For example: "All full-time employees are hereby notified that they should not pursue employment that may unduly interfere with their timely arrival at the Company and pursuit of Company expectations.") Illustration 17-1 demonstrates unambiguous policy and procedure statements. Notice that the text clearly accomplishes several things:

- Gives the rationale for the policy
- Identifies to whom the policy applies
- Identifies standards that are to be met
- Lists consequences of violating the policy

In addition to writing policies and procedures clearly, you should pay careful attention to consistency. Throughout the document, use the same words to describe the same thing. For example, wage rates can be described

ILLUSTRATION 17-1   POLICY REGARDING ELECTRONIC COMMUNICATION

7. Electronic Communication

7.1 General Policy

The company's computer, telephone, and voice mail systems are intended for the sole purpose of supporting the company's business needs. Use of those systems is a privilege, not a right. All employees are expected to use those systems only for business-related purposes.

7.2 Confidentiality of Information

Business-related information contained in the electronic systems, including e-mail, is considered confidential and should be disclosed to authorized employees only.

No employee has a personal privacy right in any matter created, received, or sent through electronic or voice mail or in files and data residing on her or his assigned computer, disks, computer system, or voice mail.

7.3 Software Ownership and Use

Only company-authorized software is permitted on the company's computers. Installation of non-company computer programs is allowed only with the express permission of the information systems manager.

All software, files, and/or data loaded into the company's computer network become the property of the company. Such files or software may be used only in ways consistent with their licenses or copyrights.

No games of any type, other than those that were included on the system when installed, are permitted.

System users are not to abuse Internet access privileges.

The company's system is not to be used to violate the law by downloading or distributing pirated information.

The company's system is not to be used to download or transmit material that is offensive, obscene, vulgar, or threatening.

7.4 Monitoring of Use

The company will monitor the electronic communication system to ensure that it is being used for business purposes. The company may inspect computer files on any of its computers or terminals without notice and at any time.

Responsibility and authority to inspect computer files, computer terminals, electronic mail, and voice mail is vested in the president and CEO or her/his designate.

7.5 Violation

Improper use of the company's electronic information systems may be grounds for discipline, including immediate discharge.

as "base rate," "hourly rate," "straight-time rate," or other descriptors. However, as a writer you should choose one term and use it consistently throughout the document.

A third style consideration is completeness. Whenever a policy or procedure is modified, all related policies and procedures should be reviewed to ensure that they are complete and consistent with the modifications. A change in one policy could well require a review of the entire employee manual.

A final style consideration is gender equity. Avoid the outdated practice of referring to the employee as *he*. When it is logical to do so, use plural nouns and pronouns (*employees . . . they*). If the sentence logically requires a singular noun (*employee, associate*), refer to the noun with two singular pronouns, such as *her or his, he or she*.

DOCUMENT DESIGN

Most people resist reading policy manuals and instructions. Therefore, you must use your best skills to make the document user-friendly. The following format strategies will help you create a visually appealing document:

- Use headings and subheadings to identify each section. Use words in those headings that clearly describe the content (for example, General Policy, Violation).
- Single space the document text, but use white space effectively.
  - Double or triple space between sections (for example, before main headings).
  - Double or triple space after main headings.
  - Double space before and after secondary headings.
  - Double space between steps and items in long lists.
- Place visual aids where the reader needs them.
  - Integrate visuals with text (at appropriate point, say "See Figure X" or "See Illustration X").
  - Make visuals easy to see and understand; separate from text with white space, ideally the equivalent of a triple line space.
  - Do not begin a policy, an instruction, or a paragraph at the bottom of one page and complete it at the top of the next page. Each should be separate from others so that old policies can be removed and pages containing the new policy can be inserted easily.

When policies are grouped together into an employee manual, document design criteria should be applied consistently throughout the manual.

EMPLOYEE MANUALS

An employee manual, sometimes called a personnel policy manual, provides a single source for all policies and procedures related to the employer-employee relationship. The manual is an important tool to ensure consistency in supervisory decisions and to inform employees of their rights and responsibilities with respect to employment with the organization. When disputes about employee treatment arise, the employee manual is often cited as the guide for resolution of those disputes. However, if the manual is written carelessly, it may weaken the employer's case in such disputes.

Therefore, when you are responsible for drafting policies or helping to develop an employee manual, it is essential to be aware of legal considerations and apply writing standards that will not compromise the company's position but will, instead, enable the users to be well-informed, confident employees.

Legal Considerations

Employment rules differ among jurisdictions. In general, however, U.S. employment law assumes an "at-will" relationship; that is, either party may terminate employment at any time without cause, and the employer may change the terms of employment without notice. In some states, statements in employee manuals have been held to modify the at-will assumption, whether or not the employer intended such modification. Other states have held that policy manuals are general guidelines that do not alter the at-will status.

To avoid misunderstandings and potential legal difficulties about the employment relationship, some states have enacted legislations specifying exactly how the employment status is to be described in the manual. For example, in 2004 South Carolina enacted a law that requires conspicuous display of a disclaimer. Specifically, if a company wants to maintain "at-will" employment status, it must place the disclaimer on the first page of the employee manual in underlined capital letters. The disclaimer must also be signed by the employee. (See Illustration 17-2.)

An employee manual should contain three types of policies:

- Requirements of employment (for example, rules, regulations, standards)
- Benefits of employment (for example, vacations, holidays, insurance)
- Statements to satisfy legal requirements or to protect the organization against legal action (for example, overtime pay, sexual harassment, family and medical leave provisions)

The American Bar Association offers the following guides for employee manuals:

- Avoid creating a contract. Limit the handbook to an explanation of company rules, procedures, and benefits. In the introductory section include a disclaimer that specifically indicates the manual does not create a contract.
- Maintain an at-will relationship. In the introductory section, state that the employment relationship is at-will. Avoid terms, such as "just cause," or "proper cause," when describing discipline or termination policies and procedures. Also avoid reference to probationary, orientation, or training periods. Such terms may suggest that after the period has lapsed, the employee is protected beyond the at-will status.
- Establish benefits clearly. Make sure the language clearly indicates *what* benefits apply (for example, vacation, holidays, insurance, retirement);

ILLUSTRATION 17-2 FORM FOR EMPLOYEE'S ACKNOWLEDGEMENT OF EMPLOYEE MANUAL[2]

EMPLOYEE ACKNOWLEDGMENT REGARDING SIGNATURES AND CONTENT OF DISCLAIMER PAGES

My signature below acknowledges that I have reviewed and signed the following documents:

- The Disclaimer Page that appears in the newly issued Employee Handbook (with an issue date of August 31, 2005) that has been given to me.
- A duplicate of the Disclaimer Page that my employer has retained.

I acknowledge that I have had the opportunity to compare the content of those two documents and that the two documents are identical in contents.

_____

Employee Signature   Date

_____

Employee Name (Please Print)

who is entitled to them (for example, full-time employees only; full- and part-time employees); and *when* the employee qualifies for the benefit (for example, on first day of employment, after six months, after one year). Avoid phrases that guarantee benefits.

- List/explain work rules and procedures. Clearly identify expectations and procedures to be followed with respect to reporting to work, taking breaks, approval for overtime, and any conduct during work that may be reason for discipline. Be sure that any sections about discipline do not erode the at-will concept. (For example, "just cause" and "progressive discipline" may erode that relationship. The employee may claim the cause was not just or that he or she was not granted progressive discipline.)
- Set forth required policies. Be sure the manual includes policies and procedures required by federal or state law.
- Consider union contract conflict. Clarify the degree to which the employee manual does or does not apply to employees who are covered by a union contract. Such clarification can be provided in the introduction or at the beginning of specific sections of the manual.

- Define modification authority. Notify the employee that the employer reserves the right to modify all aspects of the manual at its discretion; also indicate that it cannot be modified except by certain individuals within the company, and then only in writing.
- Provide a receipt form. Ask employees to sign a form acknowledging receipt of the manual. Avoid phrases that can be interpreted to create a contract (for example, "agrees to abide by," "promises to review").
- Instruct supervisory personnel. Advise supervisors not to modify the manual (except as authorized) and not to make statements that suggest guarantees of employment or benefits.

Although you may follow those guides as you write employee policies and develop an employee manual, you should always have the document reviewed by legal counsel to ensure that it consistently upholds the at-will employment relationship. Moreover, the employee manual should be reviewed and revised periodically. In a dynamic, international business environment, a manual that was written five or ten years ago may no longer meet the company's needs. The following situations, in particular, are warning signs that the manual should be reviewed:

- New laws. Employment law changes constantly. The manual must reflect the most current law.
- Company growth. As a company grows, its employment practices change. For example, sick-leave policies and procedures for a workforce of 30 or 40 employees would differ considerably from policies and procedures for a force of 3 or 4 employees. Similarly, company growth may change manufacturing and sales operations, resulting in the need for new safety procedures or travel policies.
- Changes in benefit plans. The changing nature of the labor force has prompted employers to make significant changes in benefits plans, requiring changes in the employee manual.
- Changes in company goals and philosophy. Internationalization, mergers, acquisitions, and downsizing are current business phenomena that often result in a change in managerial philosophy and practice.

Writing and Assembling the Manual

If the employee manual is not functional, it will not be used. Therefore, you must apply all you have learned about document design to assemble a manual that is user-friendly.

Policies can be presented effectively in the general structure of introduction, body, and conclusion. The introduction should present the rationale for the policy and identify to whom it applies. The previous example about use of electronic communication systems (Illustration 17-1) and the policy about sexual harassment shown in Illustration 17-3 include the rationale as the first sentence in the paragraph headed "General Policy." The body of the policy describes conditions addressed by the policy and related procedures. The final section, disciplinary action for violations, concludes the policy.

ILLUSTRATION 17-3 ▶ POLICY REGARDING DISCRIMINATION OR HARASSMENT

9. Discrimination or Harassment

9.1 General Policy

The company endeavors to maintain a work environment that nourishes respect for the dignity of each individual. Acts of discrimination by supervisors or co-workers, including sexual or racial harassment, are strictly prohibited and may result in disciplinary action, depending on the circumstances, up to and including termination.

9.2 Supervisor and Employee Conduct

Unwelcome racial or sexual conduct that interferes with an individual's job performance or creates an intimidating, hostile, or offensive environment is strictly prohibited. All employees, including both supervisory and nonsupervisory personnel, are prohibited from engaging in unwelcome sexual conduct or making unwelcome sexual overtures, either verbal or physical. Such prohibited conduct includes, but is not limited to, offensive and unwelcome sexual flirtations, advances, or propositions; repeated verbal abuse of a sexual or racial nature; graphic or degrading comments about an individual or his or her appearance; the display of sexually suggestive objects or pictures; or any offensive or abusive physical contact.

Women are not the only persons who experience sexual harassment; men also experience sexual harassment, and harassment can occur between persons of the same sex.

9.3 Supervisor Conduct

Each supervisor is responsible for maintaining a discrimination-free environment. Supervisors are strictly prohibited from implying or stating that submitting or refusing to submit to sexual advances will have any effect on an individual's hiring, placement, compensation, training, promotion, or any other term or condition of employment.

9.4 Procedure for Employees

When possible, the person experiencing discrimination or harassment should clearly explain to the offending party that the behavior is causing discomfort. Ask that it cease immediately. If it continues, employees should immediately report any incident that they believe to be discrimination or harassment to their supervisor or the Director of Human Resources.

9.5 Investigation

Complaints of discrimination or harassment will be promptly investigated by the complaining employee's supervisor and/or the Director of Human Resources. The investigation should be conducted as impartially and confidentially as possible. At the conclusion of the investigation, the supervisor and/or Director of Human Resources should advise the complaining employee of the results of the investigation and the disciplinary action to be taken, if any.

9.6 Discipline

Any employee who is found to have engaged in harassment of another employee will be subject to disciplinary action, up to and including termination.

To facilitate location of and reference to specific policies, most writers use a numbering system similar to that shown in this chapter's illustrations. Typically, the first-level heading carries a whole number (in Arabic style), with the subheadings identified by decimal units. Such a system also permits easy cross-referencing of related sections in the manual, another desirable user-friendly feature.

A partial table of contents for the employee manual of a university is shown in the following example.[3] Notice that not all possible numbered units are included. This practice allows for flexibility in revising the manual. For example, military leave is currently covered under Section 2.12. However, if the policy needs to be expanded and highlighted more prominently, the Human Resources unit could easily create a separate section, perhaps 2.16, for that policy. This university added section 2.9 in 2004, expanding upon weather conditions (that were formerly under 2.11) and recognizing other emergency conditions.

2.0 Attendance and Time Off
2.1 Absenteeism and Lateness
    2.11 Campus Closed—Charging Time
    2.12 Leave of Absence
    2.13 Family Leave
    2.14 Sick Leave
    2.15 Vacation
2.3 Bereavement (Death in the Family)
2.5 Holiday Schedule for Employees
2.7 Hours of Work
2.9 Hazardous Weather/Emergency Conditions Plan

In addition to using a flexible numbering system, you should adopt a page size and binding that facilitate use of the manual. If the manual is most likely to be referenced at a desk, an 8 1/2-by-11-inch size may be appropriate. But if the employees are going to use the manual in a cramped workspace, such as an automobile or truck, a smaller size (such as 8 by 5 inches) may be more appropriate. Typically, the pages are placed in a loose-leaf binder, which enables the employee to easily remove an outdated policy or procedure and replace it with the revised version.

Because manuals must be updated frequently, it is wise to begin each policy or procedure on a new page. When that practice is followed, the pages related to an outdated policy can be removed and replaced freely, without requiring reformatting of other sections of the manual. To ensure that all employees and supervisors have access to the latest version of a policy, the revision date should be put in a conspicuous place, such as the bottom of the last page of each section that is changed or, if the entire manual is revised, on its cover.

In addition to writing policies that will be placed in the employee manual, you may be asked to write procedures for the implementation of the policies and instructions for performance of specific tasks. All writing and document design guides that apply to policies apply also to procedures and instructions. In addition, some specific guides will help you write effective procedures and instructions.

Procedures and Instructions

Both procedures and instructions address how to do something. As you write these documents, keep in mind that you are trying to tell the reader how to do something that he or she is currently unable or only partially able to do. Therefore, writing procedures and instructions requires a keen analysis of the process or task that you are addressing. You must analyze exactly what you want the person to do and the exact sequence of those acts.

Writing effective instructions and procedures requires the following:

- Clear, simple writing
- A thorough understanding of all technical details of the procedure
- The ability to put yourself in the place of the person who will use your instructions
- The ability to visualize the task in great detail and capture that awareness on paper
- The willingness to test your instructions on the kind of person for whom they were written

Writing Procedures

Procedures describe a system or process in general. They are less detailed than instructions, which are intended to show a single person how to carry out a single task. Procedures may be written effectively in the following general structure, including each element that is applicable to the situation:

- Introduction. Rationale for and importance of the procedure
- Scope. Who and what activities are affected by the procedure
- Definitions. Terms readers need to know to follow the procedure
- References. Related documents readers may need to consult to follow the procedure
- Responsibilities. Tasks required of key individuals who are involved in the procedure
- Attachments. Sample forms and explanatory material alluded to in the procedure

Some items in that list may be omitted if they have already been included in a policy that accompanies the procedure. (See Illustration 17-4.) Some items may also be combined, as is shown in Illustration 17-5. It is, however, important that you review the procedure—and the policy that may accompany it—to ensure that you have included all necessary factors to enable someone to complete the procedure efficiently and effectively.

ILLUSTRATION 17-4 ▶ POLICY REGARDING COMMUNITY SERVICE

10. Community Activity

10.1 General Policy

The company believes that a workforce that is active in the community is a more valuable workforce. Accordingly, the company will reimburse employees for costs related to their memberships in clubs and civic organizations if such membership is deemed to benefit the employee, the company, and the community.

10.2 Policy of Non-Discrimination

The Company will not reimburse any expenses incurred for membership in or activities associated with organizations that discriminate on the basis of race, sex, religion, color, national origin, or any other factors prohibited by law.

10.3 Requests for Reimbursement

When any employee joins a social club or civic or fraternal organization or association, he or she may make a written request for partial reimbursement of membership expenses. The request must be approved by the employee's supervisor and the Director of Human Resources.

The request should include the following information.

- The name, nature, and purpose of the organization
- Any positions the employee holds or has held in the organization
- A description of the benefits to the Company
- The exact nature of the cost (that is, initiation fee, monthly dues, etc.)

If approved, the maximum reimbursement will be 75 percent of the initiation fee and monthly or annual dues.

Writing Instructions

Instructions should contain the following: an introduction; warnings, cautions, or danger notices; technical background or theory governing the task; materials necessary to perform the task; and discussion of steps in performing the task. All of those parts contribute to the coherence of the document and to the successful completion of the task.

INTRODUCTION

The introduction should orient the reader to the task. You may define the task and describe where, when, and why it is performed. If only individuals who have a certain skill level should perform the task, the level of expertise required should also be identified. A general overview of the task or the theory

ILLUSTRATION 17-5   PROCEDURE FOR REIMBURSEMENT OF RELOCATION EXPENSES

11. Reimbursement of Relocation Expenses

11.1 Purpose

The Company will reimburse a new employee for relocation expenses when such reimbursements are considered essential to successful recruitment of the job candidate. Partial or full reimbursement may be allowed.

11.2 Scope

Relocation expenses may be reimbursed for the moving of household goods and personal effects for the employee and the members of her or his household. The reimbursement will cover the cost of packing, crating, and transporting the goods and personal effects from the former home to the new home. Travel and lodging expenses incurred during travel from the former home to the new home may also be covered.

Nonreimbursable expenses are meals while moving from the old residence to the new residence; meals, travel, and lodging expenses for pre-move house-hunting trips; and stays in temporary quarters while getting settled into the new residence.

11.3 Definitions

Relocation expenses must comply with deductible moving expenses as defined by the Internal Revenue Service, unless those expenses are specifically excluded under Sec. 11.2.

11.4 Procedure

11.4.1 Direct Expenditure Voucher

Reimbursements for relocation expenses must be processed on Form DEV, Direct Expenditure Voucher.

11.4.2 Required Documentation

A copy of the moving company invoice is required for partial or full reimbursement.

If full reimbursement for moving is allowed, two quotes must accompany the DEV and invoice. Only the lower amount will be reimbursed, even if the company with the lower quote is not used.

If partial reimbursement is allowed, the amount to be paid must be specified by the employee's supervisor, as indicated in Sec. 11.4.3.

ILLUSTRATION 17-5 CONTINUED

11.4.3 Responsibilities

- The **employee** is responsible for obtaining the two quotes from licensed movers, providing the copy of the moving company's invoice, and completing form DEV.

- After reviewing all materials, the **employee's supervisor** shall insert the appropriate code to indicate the account to be charged, enter the amount of reimbursement, sign the form to indicate authorization, and submit the required documentation to the Human Resources Division for review and approval.

- **Human Resources** shall forward all approved requests to the Accounting Division for payment. Unapproved requests shall be returned to the employee's supervisor with an explanation of the reasons for non-approval.

- **Accounting** will make reimbursement directly **to the employee** at the address indicated on the DEV.

governing the procedure can help a reader understand the desired outcome and identify when an error has been made.

The introduction may also include a description of the conditions under which the task should be performed and the time required. Imagine, for example, the frustration you would experience if, in the middle of a process, you were to discover that you do not have time to complete it.

WARNINGS AND SPECIAL NOTES

Alert the readers to the possibility of damaging the equipment, making an error, or hurting themselves. Warnings or safeguards should be identified clearly (perhaps with standard icons for warning or caution) and should provide an explanation of the reason for the warning—what will happen if the caution is disregarded. Warnings are sometimes given at the beginning of the document and again at crucial points within the procedure.

TECHNICAL BACKGROUND OR THEORY

For some instructions, the technical theory or background is critical. For example, instructions for making a curved-front wall cabinet include the following statement: "To cut the tongues on the panels, bury a dado blade in an auxiliary fence attached to your rip fence."[4] To understand those instructions, the reader needs some background in woodworking and use of power tools.

EQUIPMENT AND SUPPLIES

Complete instructions include a list of things that must be gathered before the reader starts the process. These are typically given in a simple vertical checklist that helps the reader assemble the necessary items and avoid the frustration of discovering at some point in the process that some materials required for the task are missing.

DISCUSSION OF THE STEPS

As you describe the steps in performing the task, number and name each step. Be sure to limit each step to one action and order the steps into the required chronological sequence. For each step, include the following:

- Purpose and function of the step in relationship to other steps
- Warnings, cautions, and notes, along with reasons
- Conditions under which the step is performed
- Time required for the step
- Specific materials required for the step

As you write instructions, pay special attention to the following writing and document design factors:

1. Structure and format. Base your choice about structure and format on the following considerations:
   - Fixed-order steps must be performed in the order presented. Use vertical, numbered lists.
   - Variable-order steps can be performed in any order. Use vertical, bulleted lists.
   - Alternate steps present two or more ways to do something. Use bulleted lists with OR inserted between the alternatives or a lead-in line that indicates you are presenting alternatives.
   - Nested steps are substeps of a complicated procedure. Indent the substeps further and sequence them as *a*, *b*, *c*, etc.
2. Supplementary information. For clarity, you may have to present supplementary information, such as the mechanical principle involved or how something should look before and after the step is completed. Clearly distinguish supplementary information from the specific instructions that make up the step. You can do this by placing the supplementary information in a separate paragraph or by printing the instruction step in bold type.
3. Writing style. You want the reader to identify himself or herself as the person who performs the task. For that reason, instructions make heavy use of imperative verbs and the pronoun "you." The writing style in this chapter tends to emulate the style that should be used for procedures and instructions.
4. Graphics. Use illustrations generously to help the reader visualize the process and its outcome. Place every illustration strategically to complement the instruction to which it is related.

The instructions shown in Illustration 17-6 demonstrate many of the principles discussed in this section. The instruction manual begins with a description of the parts with which the operator must be familiar, followed by

ILLUSTRATION 17-6 INSTRUCTIONS FOR OPERATING A PAPER SHREDDER

ROYAL rs90

STRIP CUT

Paper Shredder

PARTS DESCRIPTION

UPPER HOUSING

Wall Outlet AC

1. Slide Switch
2. Power Cord (Min. 6Ft.)
3. Shredder Feed Opening (Upper Housing)
4. Wastebasket (Not included)
5. "OVERLOAD" Indicator
6. Paper guides
7. Outlet Slot (Lower Housing)

LOWER HOUSING

INSTRUCTION MANUAL

1

ILLUSTRATION 17-6 ▶ CONTINUED

IMPORTANT SAFEGUARDS

When using electrical appliances, basic safety precautions should always be followed including the following:

1. Read all instructions before using this shredder.
2. This product should be operated from the type of power source indicated at the bottom of unit. If you are not sure of the type of power available, consult your dealer or local power company.
3. Remove all packaging and literature before using the appliance.
4. Follow all warnings and instructions marked on the product.
5. Close supervision is necessary when any appliance is used by or near children.
6. Unplug from outlet when not in use, before servicing and cleaning. Grip plug and pull, to unplug from outlet. **Do not** pull on cable.
7. Avoid contacting moving parts.
8. **Do not** operate any appliance with a damaged cable or plug or after the appliance malfunctions, or is dropped or damaged in any manner.
9. The use of attachments not recommended or sold by ROYAL CONSUMER BUSINESS PRODUCTS may cause fire, electric shock or injury.
10. **Do not** use outdoors.
11. **Do not** place this product on an unstable cart, stand, or table. The appliance may fall, causing serious damage to the product or injury to persons.
12. **Do not** allow anything to rest on the *Power Cord* (2). **Do not** position this product where persons will walk on the cord.

13. If an extension cord is used with this product, make sure that the total of the ampere ratings on the products plugged into the extension cord **do not** exceed the extension cord ampere rating.
14. **Never** push objects of any kind into this product through *Feed Opening* (3) as they may touch dangerous voltage points or out parts that could result in a risk of fire or electric shock. **Never** spill liquid of any kind on the product.
15. **Do not** attempt to service this product other than that stated within the service manual which may expose you to dangerous voltage points or other risks. Refer all servicing to service personnel.
16. **Do not** operate in the presence of explosive and/or flammable fumes.
17. **Do not** use this product near water.
18. Unplug this product from the wall outlet and refer servicing to qualified service personnel under the following conditions:
    A. When the *Power Cord* (2) or plug is damaged or frayed.
    B. If liquid has been spilled into the product.
    C. If the product has been exposed to rain or water.
    D. If the product **does not** operate normally when the operating instructions are followed. Adjust only those controls that are covered by the operating instructions since improper adjustment of other controls may result in damage and will often require extensive work by a qualified technician to restore the product to normal operation.
    E. If the product has been dropped or the cabinet has been damaged.
    F. If the product exhibits a distinct change in performance, indicating a need for service.

2

3

ILLUSTRATION 17-6 ▶ CONTINUED

HOW TO OPERATE

1. Plug cord into *AC* wall outlet.

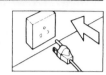

2. Locate unit on solid waste basket and check for properstability.
See "PARTS DESCRIPTION"

3. Push *Slide Switch* (1) to "AUTO" position.

4. Put paper(s), **no more than 3 sheets** together, into the *Shredder Feed Opening* (3). The Sensor will detect paper and automatically start the shredder and then stop it once paper has finished.

5. Empty the wastebasket periodically in order to maintain proper service condition of the machine.

6. "FWD" continuous operation is **not recommended for over 15 minutes**.

NOTE:
This paper shredder is capable to shred 9.5" computer paper continuously.
Important:
When shredding continuous computer paper, turn the paper guide in up-right position for smooth cutting.

4

FOR OVERLOADING

The built-in thermostat safeguarding the machine from overloading when:

1. shredding beyond the shredder sheet capacity; or
2. the shredder has been operating for an extended period of time beyond the machine operation time limit of 15 minutes

WHEN PAPER JAM

When a paper jam occurs and the motor being stalled:

1. Immediately push the Slide Switch (1) to "REV" position.

2. Remove the jammed paper from the shredder.

3. Push the Slide Switch (1) to the "OFF" position and wait for at least 15 minutes before operate again in order to cool down the machine.

Remark: If the user leaves the jammed shredder unattended for 1~2 minutes, the thermostat will cut off the power and the Overload Indicator (5) will light up. In this case, the user might observe smoke coming out from the shredder unit due to the stalled motor heating up the grease inside.
Please note that this is a normal phenomenon and the smoke is safe to human being.

WHEN OVERHEATING

When the thermostat render the shredder to stop because of overheating, turn the unit off and leave it to cool down for at least 15 minutes before operate again.

> **IMPORTANT:** Push the Slide Switch to "REV" position immediately after the motor being stalled.

5

ILLUSTRATION 17-6 ▶ CONTINUED

ATTACHMENT OF THE ADAPTOR RACK

Overturn the unit, then follow the procedures to attach the Adaptor Rack as shown in the diagrams below.

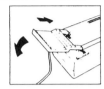

MAINTENANCE

1. Always use the machine at "AUTO" position.
2. Clean the outside of the shredder by wiping it with a damp cloth. Stubborn mild stains can be removed by using a soft damp cloth and detergent. Be sure to remove any detergent residue with a damp cloth.
3. **Never** use any harsh or abrasive cleaners.
4. **Never** operate the shredder **more than 15 minutes** continuously otherwise the thermal protector will render the unit unserviceable.
5. **Do not** insert too many sheets of paper at one time and always feed the paper in straight, **never** at an angle.
6. **Do not** operate shredder with a damaged AC cord, or after it has been dropped or damaged in any manner, return shredder to the nearest authorized service facility for examination or repair.
7. While operating, **never** put your fingers into the *Shredder Feed Opening* (3) or outlet for any reason. **Do not** insert any sharp or pointed tools into the *Feed Opening* (3).
8. **Do not** insert any materials other than dry paper products. For example, **do not** insert any metal products, wet paper, carbon sheets, film, oil paper, or anything that may leave a residue on the cutters.
9. **Do not** use the shredder where there is the possibility of loose clothing or jewelry being caught in the *Shredder Feed Opening* (3).
10. **Do not** try to disassemble or adjust any portion of the machine. There are no user serviceable parts.
11. **Never** try to shred more than 3 papers at the same time, overloading the machine will only cause you troubles and shorten the machine durability.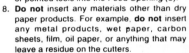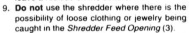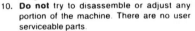

6

7

ILLUSTRATION 17-6 CONTINUED

SPECIFICATIONS

TYPE	: Personal Type
PAPER SIZE	: A4 paper - 8 1/2" x 11" (210mm)
	Computer paper - 9.5" (242mm)
CAPACITY	: Max. 3 single sheet A4 papers/ 1 ply 9.5" continuous computer paper
CUTTING SPEED	: 3 second / page (A4)
REDUCTION GEAR RATIO	: 1:105 (Motor to driving shaft)
CUTTER'S DIAMETER	: 32mm
MOTOR SPINDLE SPEED	: 5,500 r.p.m. (Full Loading)
FEATURES	: Automatic paper detection; Forward / rewind selection; Adaptor Rack to fit with various size wastebaskets
DIMENSIONS	: 310mm(L) x 151mm(W) x 68mm (H)
WEIGHT	: 2.6kg

8

RS90AOM0196A
IBSM2-03

765 U.S Highway 202
Bridgewater, NJ 08807

cautions to ensure safe use of the shredder. The step-by-step instructions are numbered to indicate the sequence that should be followed and are interspersed with notes and cautions that the operator should observe while using the shredder. Pictures and diagrams have been inserted at appropriate locations to clarify the instructions. Formatting techniques include use of bold type for emphasis, numbered lists for clarity and order, reverse-color headings to highlight main sections of the instructions, and boxed subheadings to differentiate them from main headings.

Although instructions and procedures serve similar purposes—contributing to safe, efficient, and effective job performance—procedures are written with less specificity than instructions. The next section discusses ways to write procedures.

ETHICAL CONSIDERATIONS

One management theorist has developed a pyramid of social responsibility. He contends that a business has four types of social responsibilities, which may be conceptualized as ranging from foundational (bottom of the pyramid) to optional (top of the pyramid). (See Illustration 17-7.)[5] Those responsibilities are the economic responsibility to satisfy the needs of customers, employees, and owners; the legal responsibility to obey the law; the ethical responsibility to meet public expectations that have not been codified into law; and the philanthropic responsibility to foster a better world for all.

One purpose of an employee manual is to help establish the organization's climate. Therefore, the employee manual should clearly establish the social responsibility standards that the company expects of and will practice

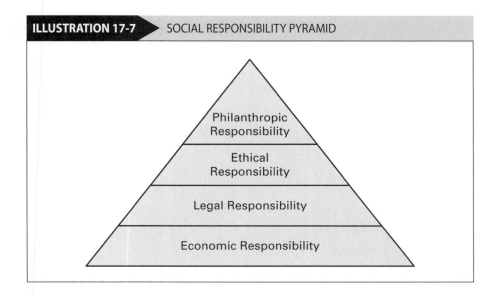

ILLUSTRATION 17-7 ▸ SOCIAL RESPONSIBILITY PYRAMID

Philanthropic Responsibility

Ethical Responsibility

Legal Responsibility

Economic Responsibility

with its employees. A formal code of ethics is often included in the manual to set forth the general ethical standards of the company. Within specific policies and procedures, the company's ethical stance can be further explained and reinforced. For example, policies related to the employment relationship clearly fit into the economic responsibility and legal responsibility levels of the pyramid. The discrimination and harassment policy shown in Illustration 17-3 clearly sets forth the company's stance with respect to acts of discrimination: They are "strictly prohibited." This policy conforms to the legal and ethical responsibility levels of the pyramid. Similarly, the community service policy shown in Illustration 17-4 evidences that the company recognizes an ethical commitment at the top level of the pyramid—a commitment to the community.

Writing clear, complete instructions may also be approached as an ethical responsibility to employees and customers. The purpose of job instructions and procedures for applying certain policies is not only to improve employees' efficiency, but also to protect their health, safety, and economic well-being. Similarly, clearly written, easy-to-follow user instructions assist customers in using a product with pleasure, health, and safety.

SUMMARY

To write policies, procedures, and instructions effectively, you should analyze your audience; identify the context in which your audience will use the policy, procedure, or instructions; define what you want the reader to do after having read the document; and use a writing style and document design that complement your audience, context, and goal.

Policies, along with procedures for their implementation, are often assembled in an employee manual. The manual is intended to define the rights and responsibilities of the employment relationship, both for employees and their supervisors. A well-written employee manual fosters efficiency and fairness in the employer-employee relationship. Legal counsel should review all policies to ensure that they do not violate the "at-will" principle of employment. Manuals should be updated periodically to ensure that they reflect the current policies and procedures of the organization. The manual should also reflect the ethical commitments of the organization.

Instructions are written to ensure that employees and customers perform specific tasks in a safe, efficient, and effective way. As you write instructions, you must be able to envision every step in the task and be able to translate that image into clearly written, orderly steps of performance.

TOPICS FOR DISCUSSION

1. What is the common purpose of policies, procedures, and instructions? How do they differ from one another?

2. Assume that you must write a personnel manual for men and women who volunteer to act as leaders of a Boy Scout or Girl Scout troop. Identify specific factors that are relevant to:
   - Audience analysis
   - Identification of context
   - Definition of goal
   - Choice of writing style and document design

3. Identify and give an example of three types of policies that should be included in an employee manual.

4. Identify and explain the importance of nine legal guides for the construction of an employee manual.

5. Discuss conditions that would warrant revising an employee manual.

6. Why should an organization's attorney review all new and revised policies before they are adopted?

7. Describe writing and formatting techniques that make an employee manual user-friendly.

8. Describe an effective structure for procedures.

9. Identify and describe basic guides for writing and document design that you should follow when you write instructions.

10. Identify the four levels of the pyramid of social responsibility. Give an example of a possible organizational policy that is related to each level.

APPLICATIONS

1. Obtain samples of employee manuals from two different organizations, either by contacting the company directly or from its website. Write a memorandum to your instructor, explaining which manual is more effective. Base your judgment on a critical review of the following factors:
   - Writing style: Is it clear, simple, easy to understand? Does it protect the company from legal liability? What other elements of writing style are strong or weak?
   - Document design: Is the format consistent throughout the manual? Does the format contribute to user-friendliness? Are the illustrations useful? Are they placed in appropriate places throughout the document? What other elements of document design are strong or weak?

2. Select a specific policy, such as a policy on sexual harassment, substance abuse, or family leave. Compare how the two companies (Application 1) present the policy in the manual. What are the similarities? What are the differences?

3. Review the two manuals (Application 1) for evidence of the company's code of ethics and stance on ethical issues. For each company, identify at

least one policy that fits into each of the levels on the pyramid of social responsibility. In a memorandum, report your findings to your instructor.

4. Search the Internet for companies that prepare employee manuals. Select two of those companies. Compare and contrast the services offered. Based on the information provided, which company would you choose to prepare a manual? Why?

   Assume that your instructor is the Director of Human Resources for your company. Write a report, in memorandum format, recommending the choice of a company to prepare an employee manual.

5. Obtain a copy of the travel reimbursement policy for your college or place of employment. Evaluate the policy on the following factors:
   • Clarity; identification of types of travel and associated costs that will be reimbursed
   • Procedures for gaining approval to travel on company time for company business
   • Procedures for handling submitting requests for travel reimbursement
   • Penalty for violations of the travel policy
   In a memorandum, report your findings and conclusions to your professor.

6. Select any assignment that you have been given in writing for this class or another class that you are currently taking. Evaluate the extent to which the assignment adheres to the guides for instructions presented in this chapter.
   • If the assignment is clearly written as a set of instructions, write a memorandum to the professor commending her or him for the clarity of the instructions. Point out specific strengths.
   • If the assignment was not written clearly, rewrite it as a set of instructions, following the guides presented in this chapter. Present the original instructions and your version to your instructor for this course. Attach them to a memo explaining the major changes you have made.

7. Select a set of instructions that came with any item you purchased recently (for example, lawn mower, gas grill, computer printer, digital camera). Evaluate the extent to which the instructions demonstrate the guides presented in this chapter. As directed by your instructor, present your analysis in an oral presentation to your class or in a memorandum to your instructor.

8. Select a broad employee-related topic to explore on the Internet (for example, parking policies, military leave, family leave, tuition reimbursement, etc.). Select a website from your search results; navigate it to find information about the topic you entered into your search engine. Keep a log of the steps you take to find your answer. In a memo to your instructor describe whether the site is an example of well-written instructions. Why or why not? What made it easy or difficult to navigate?

REFERENCES

1. Unless otherwise stated, the discussion in this chapter and all illustrations are based on information derived from the following sources:
    *   Hartsfield, W. E. (1986 with periodic updates). *BLR encyclopedia of employee handbooks*. Madison, CT: Business & Legal Reports, Inc.
    *   McMillan, E. J. (2003). *Model policies and procedures for not-for-profit organizations*. Hoboken, NJ: John Wiley & Sons, Inc.
    *   Macy, J. R. Avoiding booby traps in drafting employee manuals. Retrieved August 7, 2005, from http://www.abanet.org/genpractice/compleat/w96man.html
    *   Sample employment practices. Retrieved August 7, 2005, from http://www.sampleemployeehandbook.com
    *   Shuler, F. G. Jr., and Justice, A. E. Jr. (2000). *Model employee policies for South Carolina employers—With legal commentary* (4th ed.). Columbia: South Carolina Chamber of Commerce.
    *   McMurrey, D. A. Online technical writing: Instructions. Retrieved August 10, 2005, from http://www.io.com/%7Ehcexres/tcm1603/acchtml/instrux.html

2. Adapted from memorandum of advice issued by Malone & Thomson LLC, Columbia, SC, June 9, 2004.

3. Information retrieved on August 7, 2005, from http://www.gatech.edu (This site is easy to navigate and is an example of well-written instructions. After reaching the home page, just follow the links that will lead you to the specifics you want, for example: Employment, Office of Human Resources, Policies & Procedures, Classified Employee Handbook, specific policy.)

4. Curved-front wall cabinet. *Worksmith, 26* (156), 34.

5. Carroll, A. B. (1991). The pyramid of corporate social responsibility: Toward the moral management of organizational stakeholders. *Business Horizons, 34*(4), 39–48.

Promoting and Raising Funds for Nonprofit Organizations

LEARNING OBJECTIVES

After you have read this chapter, you should be able to:

1. Describe the nonprofit sector of the economy, including career opportunities in that sector.
2. Write several kinds of messages to keep the public informed of a nonprofit agency's activities.
3. Write persuasive messages to increase public support.
4. Write goodwill messages to maintain public support.
5. Prepare a news release or op-ed column.
6. Recognize qualities of a well-written grant and write a small-grant application.
7. Report to a grantor how the funds were used.

As is true of a for-profit business, primary concerns of a nonprofit organization are maintaining a steady flow of income, building and nurturing positive relationships with clients and the public, and ensuring that the organization operates efficiently and demonstrates accountability. Consequently, employees of nonprofit agencies apply many of the same writing and reporting skills that successful business employees have mastered.

However, because of the noncommercial relationship that a nonprofit agency has with its supporters and clients, some kinds of writing tasks are unique to a nonprofit agency. Much of the external communication, for example, focuses on obtaining funds to carry out the agency's mission. Since obtaining funds often rests upon public awareness and appreciation of the agency's services, a large proportion of the agency's communications are promotional and goodwill messages.

To work effectively in a nonprofit organization, you should understand the role nonprofits play in the economy and become skilled in the types of writing that are essential to an agency's continued existence.

THE NONPROFIT ARENA

Many career opportunities exist in the nonprofit arena. Nonprofit organizations range from small local humanitarian or humane organizations, such as a pet adoption agency, to large national and international associations, such as the Society for Prevention of Cruelty to Animals (SPCA). In the United States, more than 1.25 million organizations met the qualifications for nonprofit or tax-exempt status with the Internal Revenue Service in 1998. Over half of those (approximately 730,000) were scientific, literary, educational, artistic, or charitable organizations that provide services to the public and met 501(c)(3) status.[1] The number 501(c)(3) refers to the section of the U.S. Internal Revenue Code that specifies the conditions for tax-exempt status for these kinds of organizations.

In 2001 the U.S. nonprofit sector employed approximately 12.5 million individuals, representing 9.5 percent of the nation's labor force. The nonprofit sector comprises six subsectors. (See Illustration 18-1.) Health services and education/research together accounted for nearly 74 percent of nonprofit employment; but even the small sectors (that is, foundations; arts and culture; civic, social, and fraternal organizations) offer many employment opportunities. Those three sectors, encompassing many small agencies, together contributed more than 760,000 jobs to the nation's economy. Between 2000 and 2010 the health services industry is expected to add 28 million jobs; social and human services, 1.2 million.[2]

So you can see that opportunities abound for you to serve society by bringing your special skill set to a nonprofit organization. Nearly every kind of professional skill can be applied in nonprofits. Health care skills continue in strong demand; but educators, social workers, psychologists, art and music therapists, general managers, office managers, art historians, retail managers, information systems specialists, writers—the list is endless—all find job opportunities in nonprofit organizations. A search of http:\\www.salary.com will reward you with job descriptions and salary ranges for many positions in nonprofit organizations.

ILLUSTRATION 18-1 ▶ EMPLOYMENT IN THE NONPROFIT SECTOR, 2001

Nonprofit Subsector	% of Nonprofit Sector	Total Jobs
Health Services	41.9	5,237,500
Education/Research	21.9	2,737,500
Social and Legal Services	18.3	2,287,500
Religious Organizations	11.8	1,475,000
Civic, Social, and Fraternal Orgs.	3.9	487,500
Arts and Culture	1.9	237,500
Foundations	0.3	37,500
Total	**100%**	**12,500,000**

The terms *nonprofit* and *not-for-profit* are often used synonymously. A distinction that is sometimes made is that *not-for-profit* refers to an activity, whereas *nonprofit* refers to an organization that is formed for public or mutual benefit, not for making a profit. For example, hunting wild game is generally a not-for-profit activity, pursued primarily for relaxation or skill development. In contrast, the National Rifle Association (NRA) is considered a nonprofit organization. It was established in 1871 "to promote and encourage rifle shooting on a scientific basis" and today presents itself as "the premier firearms education organization in the world."[3]

Although many people think of nonprofits as charities, by contrasting the primary purpose of the SPCA with that of the NRA, you can understand that a nonprofit may or may not be a charitable organization. Further, a nonprofit corporation is not prohibited from making a profit; however, the law places limitations on how it can make money and how it can use its profits. If a nonprofit derives profits from activities unrelated to its purpose, it must set up a separate corporation for the profit-making activity or risk losing its tax-exempt status. Note, for example, that the Society for Prevention of Cruelty to Animals maintains both a nonprofit web site (SPCA.org) and a site that suggests for-profit activities (SPCA.com).

Common writing tasks in a nonprofit agency include informational messages, promotional messages, goodwill messages, and requests for funds. In addition, a director of a nonprofit organization will likely find herself or himself responsible for writing policies, procedures, and instructions, which were discussed in Chapter 17.

INFORMATIONAL MESSAGES

Typical informational writing includes copy for general advertising, brochures, newsletters, and annual reports. Whenever you write these communications, try to answer the typical journalistic questions: *Who? What? Why? When? Where? How?* You should also apply principles of document design (presented in Chapter 4), along with careful decisions about the physical distribution of each item.

General Advertising

General advertising may range from a 2- × 4-inch ad in a newspaper or telephone directory to a 10- × 22-foot billboard. It may also include radio or television spot announcements. The major purpose of general advertising is to keep the community aware of the agency's name and services and how to gain access to those services. Consequently, the agency's name (who) along with its address and telephone number (where) must be prominent. Such advertising must also be eye-catching and describe the agency's mission or services (why, what) in concise, simple language. The "three-second" test is often applied. A reader should be able to grasp the message in three seconds—the time it takes to drive by a billboard or notice a newspaper advertisement.

ILLUSTRATION 18-2 ▸ BILLBOARD OR NEWSPAPER ADVERTISEMENT

sexual trauma services of the midlands

...the healing place

Hope and Healing for Survivors of Sexual Assault

24-hour hot line: 803-555-RAPE

2001 Green Street, Columbia, SC 29205
803-555-5555

The example shown in Illustration 18-2[4] could be adapted to a small print-media advertisement or a large billboard. It clearly identifies the agency and its services, along with its location and telephone numbers. Most people could read and comprehend the message in three seconds.

Brochure, Newsletter, Annual Report

A brochure is used when an agency wants to convey more detailed information about its operations—or part of its operations—than can be presented in a typical advertisement or billboard message. For example, a pet adoption agency might prepare a brochure that describes what it expects of potential clients who want to adopt a pet and what the clients can expect of the agency. Such a brochure could be used as a mailer to attract new clients, or it could be given to potential clients when they inquire about pet adoption.

To write an effective brochure, begin by answering these questions:

- Who is concerned about this topic?
- What *must* readers know?
- What do readers *want* to know about this topic?
- Should readers receive this information in a single story or brochure? Should it be presented in a set of shorter, more focused stories or brochures?
- Will the audience view the brochure as a benefit? Does it contain information the audience will want to keep?
- How can I transmit the information most effectively? What tone, style, and level of complexity best complement the content and audience?

As you write the text for the brochure, consider the average reading level of your audience and the circumstances in which the receivers will read the brochure. In general, brochures should be written in vigorous, relatively simple language because most readers will not spend a lot of time trying to discern the message that you are trying to convey.

A newsletter contains information of interest to a specific group. Newsletters are typically sent on a scheduled basis, such as monthly, bimonthly, or quarterly. The content often reports recent events or accomplishments of the agency and describes upcoming activities. The following guides will help you plan and publish an effective newsletter:

- Include a statement of purpose. This statement should orient new readers to your organization and the publication.
- Choose a unique title that reflects your organization and will not be confused with another publication or infringe on trademarks or copyrights.
- Decide on the size of the publication. Generally, shorter is better, both for individual articles and for the newsletter as a whole.
- Decide on frequency of publication. Be realistic in terms of time and money available for production. Infrequent high-quality publications are more effective than frequent, mediocre publications.
- Maintain your schedule. If your publication appears erratically, readers will not depend on it as a reliable source of information.
- Devise an issue date and number scheme and follow it consistently.

When writing the articles for your newsletter, answer the following questions in addition to those that were listed for writing a brochure:

- If the topic is about an event that will occur or has occurred, when will/did the event happen?
- If the purpose of a story is to elicit action, how and when should the reader act?

Articles in brochures and newsletters must have headings (also called headlines). The headline is the first part of a story to catch the reader's attention; therefore, it should draw—even pull—the reader to the article. Here are some guides to help you write effective headings.

- Use action verbs and logical phrase structure.
- Develop a headline around a key idea in the text.
- Avoid using words with double meanings.
- Capitalize the first word and proper nouns only.

Ineffective word choice:
American Trips Up in 2005
Economics Drives Drop in Black Fertility Rate[5]

Effective word choice:
Americans Travel More in 2005
Drop in Black Fertility Rate Linked to Economics

- Use meaningful formatting when a headline is more than one line. Some publishers make the second line shorter to lead the reader to the beginning of the article; other publishers center all lines of a headline above the story.

Ineffective format:
Annual Fundraising
Concert Scheduled for April 13

Improved format:
Annual Fundraising Concert
Scheduled for April 13

OR

Newberry Opera Benefit
Scheduled for
April 13, 2007

- Avoid awkward phrases if you must divide a multiple-line headline.
- Avoid hyphenating words in a headline.

Ineffective format:
Partnership Benefits Animals in
Richland and Lexington Counties

Improved format:
Richland, Lexington County Animals
Benefit from Partnership

- Use a type size that is larger than the text body. Avoid extreme contrasts unless the content of the article requires a dramatic headline.

Inappropriate type size:

Microchip Fee Added to Cost of Pet Retrieval

Under the ordinance passed by City Council,
pet owners will have to pay . . .

Improved type size:

Microchip Fee Added to Cost of Pet Retrieval

Under the ordinance passed by City Council,

pet owners will have to pay . . .

Most newsletters have a standard nameplate and masthead that must be considered during page layout. The top of the first page is usually reserved for the nameplate, which contains the name of the newsletter and publication data, such as date and/or number of the issue. The nameplate may also include the organization's logo or other identifying information. Since the nameplate sets the tone for the newsletter and remains the same for many issues, it should be designed carefully to convey the desired image of the organization.

Each issue of a newsletter should also contain a masthead, which presents business information about the organization. The name and address of the organization, its Board of Directors, calendar of upcoming events, and/or names of staff members are some items that could be included in the masthead. The masthead may be placed at any location in the newsletter (often at the side of one of the pages); however, it should appear in the same location in each issue of the newsletter.

After you have planned the contents of the newsletter, you should rank the articles in terms of importance. Then use the guides for page layout described in the document design section of Chapter 4.

Today, many agencies publish electronic newsletters. (Go to http:\\www.globalvolunteers.org to view an example of an effective electronic newsletter.) These guides will help you produce a reader-friendly electronic newsletter:

- Be kind to readers with slow Internet connections. Use graphics sparingly.
- Choose colors carefully, remembering that some colors may be unattractive or distracting on the screen. If your organization already has identifying colors and logo, use those in the electronic newsletter to maintain consistency with your agency's other publications.
- Be considerate about line length. Be sure to accommodate small screens when formatting columns and paragraphs.
- Use blank space or other visual effects (such as ### or *****) to separate articles if yours is a plain-text e-mail newsletter.

The guides given for designing a newsletter or brochure also apply to the design of an annual report. As the name suggests, an annual report is issued once a year to report a nonprofit agency's major accomplishments during the past year, its current financial status, and plans for the coming year. The report tends to be written in a more formal style than a newsletter and is directed toward readers who have a legitimate interest in the business and program activities of the agency. Many grantors require a grant recipient to provide an annual report to demonstrate responsible use of funds.

Content for the annual report must provide an accurate picture of the agency's operations. If the agency suffered some setbacks during the year, those, along with its accomplishments, should be reported. As you design pages and write headlines for an annual report, provide a strategic, yet honest, balance of positive and negative information.

Most corporate annual reports feature the CEO's letter on the first or second page. Similarly, an annual report for a nonprofit agency often includes a report or letter from the Board President, the agency's Executive Director, or both.

ILLUSTRATION 18-3 ANNUAL REPORT OF NONPROFIT AGENCY

sexual trauma services of the midlands

2004/2005 Annual Report

President's Report *Sally Boyd*

Last February I got a call from STS's Executive Committee asking that I step in for a few months as interim president (having served as president of the board in the past). Shortly after Jay Dowd's term had begun in July 2004, he moved from Columbia to take a position at Francis Marion but valiantly tried to continue as board president. While his commitment to the agency has never flagged, he determined after several months that the distance was too much and requested to be replaced. Many thanks, Jay, for your fine leadership--STS is the better in many ways thanks to your years of service! From March through June 2005, working closely with Vice President Janet Heuer (in whose capable hands the board leadership now resides) I served as interim president.

During this period we grappled with issues surrounding board/staff responsibility, reaching solutions that are leading our agency toward new strength. Some staff turnover has given our executive director an opportunity for realignment of workloads and approaches, resulting in additional strength. New staff members are bringing a wealth of experience, expertise, and passion to their work. Funding continues to be a major challenge, and the board and executive director continue to collaborate in seeking the solutions that are most feasible and productive for the agency's continued health.

A major highlight during my interim term was a very successful golf tournament at Golden Hills Country Club in April--netting over $16,000, it was the most lucrative fund-raiser in the agency's history. In addition to bringing in significant dollars, it involved about 100 golfers and 26 sponsors, spreading the agency's visibility over significant new territory. Board member Randy Senn headed it up, ably assisted by STS staff and numerous volunteers, including many of Randy's colleagues at SCANA. Special thanks go to Randy, who has agreed to a repeat performance next spring in hopes that this will become a signature annual event.

My brief period "back on board" with this agency renewed my commitment and support for the work done here. On a daily basis the staff take on a burden they approach from the perspective of bringing hope. The board is populated with dedicated supporters bringing a variety of skills and insights. And the volunteers are the backbone of the agency's work. Particularly rewarding was the opportunity last spring to honor the operators at Palmetto Richland whose volunteer service handling hotline calls is absolutely essential to the agency's ability to respond. And an informal birthday reception (the 22nd) I hosted in June brought in $2000 in birthday gifts, thanks to the generosity of STS's friends. I appreciate having had the opportunity to work closely with the agency again, and I will continue to support Carol and her staff, Janet and the board, and all the volunteers and

Director's Report *Carol M. Wyatt, M.Ed., LISW-CP*

"I am here. You are here." These are words that years ago were uttered at the opening of therapy groups I facilitated. It was a powerful declaration of shared community and of taking ownership of ourselves present among others collectively searching for hope, help, understanding, and common goals. It was also recognition that the individual is there first, responsibly, and is also part of a "we." Sexual Trauma Services came into being as a nonprofit as Rape Crisis *Network* because we recognized that we needed to be part of a "we" - a system response to sexual assault and abuse. We recognized that we could not do and should not do what we needed to do for survivors alone. That is still true today, and is in fact never more crucial than ever that we conduct our work with the same declaration – STS is here and *WE* are here. -Continued on Page 2-

These articles set the tone for the report. They typically focus on some major accomplishments of the agency. If reports by both the board president and the executive director are included, the articles should not be redundant. Together, they should convey the major accomplishments or challenges of the past year.

Placement of the nameplate and masthead for an annual report are shown in Illustration 18-3. Examples of a president's report and an executive director's report also appear in that illustration. Notice that each writer reports about different aspects of the agency's operations. Notice also that the writing styles differ slightly, representing the individuals' personalities and their relationships to the agency.

Persuasive Messages

Two types of persuasive messages used in a nonprofit organization are periodic appeals for funds and promotion of special events.

Periodic Fundraising Appeals

A fundraising appeal is similar to a sales letter. The first step is to decide upon a theme around which you will construct the letter. Choosing a theme helps you focus on the basic objective of the letter—to obtain contributions. When writing this kind of message, the AIDA approach is often used. (See Illustration 18-4.)

A fundraising letter directed to a select audience is often printed in standard business letter format, or even in a personal letter style. The objective of targeted letters is often to add the recipients to the "large donor" list. The receivers must, therefore, be treated as a special audience. A personalized fundraising appeal is shown in Illustration 18-5.

When a letter is to be sent to a large mailing list, it may be impractical to use a standard letter format that includes a letter address and greeting. A deviation from standard formats can be used effectively as a creative attention-getting device. For example, instead of using a letter address and greeting, you can use those locations for an opening statement that will establish the theme and attract attention.

A successful fundraising letter centered on the theme of "Hope" is shown in Illustration 18-6. Notice the deviation from standard letter format and use of the AIDA structure.

ILLUSTRATION 18-4	A-I-D-A STRUCTURE FOR PERSUASIVE LETTER
Attention	Attract the reader to the message.
Interest	Pique the reader's curiosity; prompt further reading.
Desire	Stimulate reader's will to act.
Action	Request concrete action; make action easy.

ILLUSTRATION 18-5 ▸ PERSONALIZED FUNDRAISING LETTER

PetSave

1705 S. Rosewood Blvd.   TELEPHONE: 352-555-5957
Bedford, IN 47421

July 1, <year>

Ms. Meredith McDaniel
1234 S. Rosewood Blvd.
Bedford, IN 47421

Dear Meredith:

Hunger, thirst, fear for life. That's what abandoned animals are feeling during the heat of summer. While many of us pamper our four-legged friends, hundreds of animals merely survive.

Last year you showed compassion for such animals by contributing $250 to PetSave. We hope you will continue to help us rescue those animals and bring them into a friendlier environment.

We are asking previous donors to increase their contributions to PetSave by 10 percent this year, if possible. May we count on you to bring joy and love to these naturally loving creatures? Just complete the enclosed form and mail it, along with your check, in the enclosed envelope.

Sincerely,

Debra Leagones

Debra Leagones

Enclosures: Payment form, envelope

Yes, I want to make life easier for the abandoned animals in our community.

Please select your method of contributing to Pet Save.

☐ Charge $ _____ to _____ Visa _____ MasterCard _____ American Express

Card Number _____ Exp. Date _____ Signature _____

☐ Check enclosed $ _____

☐ Pledge of $ _____ per month for _____ months (Please send a monthly reminder.)

ILLUSTRATION 18-6 WIDE-APPEAL FUNDRAISING LETTER

sexual trauma services
of the midlands
...the healing place

2001 Green Street
Columbia, SC 29205
803-555-5555

<Date>

**Even in a mountain of despair
there must be a stone of hope.**

Those words of Dr. Martin Luther King still inspire us.

Survivors of sexual assault often see no hope, only despair.

> "Theresa" had told no one in 24 years about her abuse, and breaking the silence was her **stone of hope** in a mountain of despair.

> "Clare" blamed herself for her assault, but she finally recognized her **stone of hope** and believed in herself when other group members shared their experiences.

Each day at Sexual Trauma Services of the Midlands we strive to empower individuals whose lives have been forever altered by sexual assault and abuse. We offer **hope** and a way out of the abyss of pain and suffering.

But we cannot do it alone.

We need *your* help if we are to bring hope to the lives of those in our community who are touched by sexual assault. When we offer help to survivors and their families, we climb with them and help them find *their* **stone of hope.**

Last year STSM served nearly 2,000 individuals. Thirty-four percent of them were under the age of 18. The climb to recovery is a long one, but with *your* help we can offer **hope** to survivors and their families.

**Please be generous in your gift today so that tomorrow's
survivor may also find that stone of hope.**

Janet Heuer

JANET HEUER, TREASURER, BOARD OF DIRECTORS

Promotion of Special Events

Promotional pieces for special events differ slightly from general advertising. Whereas general advertising is intended to keep the nonprofit's name and purpose before the public, special events advertising must draw attention to a specific activity, usually designed to increase community support for the agency.

Some special events may be put on primarily to increase goodwill in the community. An example of such an event would be a dinner to honor current supporters, such as volunteers or large donors. Others may be set up primarily to increase the support base, either by attracting new contributors or encouraging larger contributions from current donors. An example of such an event is a night at the theater or an auction conducted for the benefit of a nonprofit agency.

Nonprofits often use more than one form of advertising to promote an event. Combinations of flyers, posters, news releases, notices in the newsletter or newspapers, radio and television spots, or personal invitations to the event are common. The immediate objective of special events advertising is to get optimal participation in the event. A longer-term objective is to increase public awareness of the agency and enlarge its base of supporting constituents. To accomplish those objectives, the event planner and communication director must determine whom to target and what kinds of communication will best stimulate those supporters to attend the event.

To encourage participation in a special event, you should again approach the message as a sales message. It must attract attention, pique interest, stimulate desire, and encourage action. An example of copy placed in a newspaper and used on posters is shown in Illustration 18-7.

Goodwill Messages

Goodwill is the positive feeling stakeholders have toward your nonprofit organization. In an environment in which keen competition for resources exists, all stakeholders—clients, employees, suppliers, and donors—need to be assured that their contributions to your agency are appreciated and that you treat all constituents with fairness and dignity. Thank-you letters and other types of goodwill messages should be used faithfully to promote goodwill in the community.

Thank-You Messages

Business etiquette requires that you express gratitude for favorable things people have done. Every donor should receive a prompt thank-you message. Other examples of favors that require a thank-you message include recommendations, introductions, volunteer services, or considerate actions of a client or supplier. The following guides will help you maintain goodwill by composing effective thank-you messages:

- Send the message promptly, preferably within a day or two of the act that merits thanks. All circumstances related to the act will be fresh in the

ILLUSTRATION 18-7   POSTER

minds of your receiver and you. Prompt, accurate thanks may reinforce the value of the act and stimulate similar action in the future.

- Be specific in your thanks. Identify the specific act or contribution that is being acknowledged. The U.S. Internal Revenue Services requires that if a donor receives something of value in return for a cash payment to a non-profit organization, the organization must indicate the portion of the contribution that represents that value and the proportion that is tax deductible. For example, if a donor pays $500 to attend a fundraising event at a theater, the reasonable value of the theater ticket and refreshments would be considered the value received by the donor; the remainder may be considered a charitable contribution.

- Personalize the message. Even a standard letter of thanks can be personalized with a brief handwritten comment by the executive director or a board member.

- Limit the content of the message. Use this message solely to generate goodwill, not to promote a cause. The message should be brief.

Here is an effective structure for a thank-you letter. Notice that the letter focuses on the statement of thanks and the act that deserves thanks. The writer mentions nothing to promote the agency. The focus remains on the recipient, not the agency.

- Thank the receiver.

  Thank you for selecting and directing the human resources project we requested of your students.

- Explain why the receiver has merited appreciation or gratitude.

  As I watched Drew and Heather's outstanding presentation, I tried to compute how much such a consulting project would have cost the agency had we hired professional consultants. Your students did a truly exceptional job, which is testimony to your fine instruction.

- Reinforce goodwill with a positive, future-oriented statement.

  I hope we will be able to avail ourselves of such valuable consultancy again in the future. Your contribution and that of your students is truly appreciated.

Other Goodwill Messages

Other goodwill messages include messages of welcome, introduction, congratulation, and celebration of holidays or special events. The following brief examples can guide you as you prepare these types of messages.

Welcome messages help a newcomer to the organization or community feel at home. Greeting the newcomer creates a climate for establishing a new professional relationship. Such a message might be sent to a new employee, a new member on your board, or a new arrival in the community whose professional interests complement those of your agency.

This basic structure works well for a message of welcome.

- Greet the newcomer cordially and sincerely.

> It's a pleasure to welcome you to the Board of Directors for City Art Museum. You have much to offer the agency, and we look forward to working with you.

- Indicate the likely association your organization may have with this individual.

> The Board has elected you for a two-year term, beginning on July 1, 2008. We currently meet at 5:30 p.m. on the second Monday of each month; consequently, your first meeting will be on July 14.

- Close with a statement of goodwill.

> As you pursue your own career, your time and talent are valuable resources. We truly appreciate your willingness to share those resources as we promote the mission of City Art Museum.

Introductions are messages that acquaint people with one another. In nonprofit agencies, a person who is well known in the community may write a letter of introduction for a member of the agency's staff, particularly when the staff member is approaching people or organizations for money or other contributions to the agency.

Whether the introduction is written or oral, this message structure is useful.

- Identify the person being introduced and describe the person's business relationship to you.

> This letter introduces to you Patricia Huguenin, who has been the Executive Director for The Children's Bureau for nearly five years. As a member of the Bureau's board, I have admired her dedication to the welfare of children.

- Explain the reason for the introduction.

> Pat will soon be contacting you on behalf of The Children's Bureau. The Bureau recently received a matching-funds contribution from a local donor. That donor has promised to give $25,000 to bolster the Bureau's operating fund if the agency can match the contribution with another $25,000 from other donors. Ms. Huguenin will ask for an opportunity to describe some of the work of Children's Bureau—and to ask for your financial assistance.

- Offer appreciation for courtesy or assistance.

> I hope you will take time to talk to Pat and perhaps even introduce her to other civic-minded persons who can help The Children's Bureau.

A fine way to maintain a link with your loyal supporters is to recognize their accomplishments. Outstanding achievements or honors and happy events such as appointment to a new position, appointment to the board of a business or nonprofit agency, opening of a new facility, anniversaries, or retirement celebrations are opportunities for messages of congratulation.

This message structure is effective for offering congratulations.

- Open with a personalized statement that is congratulatory.

  Congratulations, Martha, on your appointment as Dean of the School of Social Work at State University.

- Indicate why the congratulations are merited.

  Your distinguished academic record, ability to attract research funding, and generous contributions of time and talent to local nonprofit organizations made you the perfect choice for this position. You obviously have both the expertise and the energy to undertake this demanding work.

- Close with a confirmation of goodwill.

  As President of the Board of Women's Haven, I appreciate the contributions you have made to this organization. I'm sure State University will benefit greatly from your appointment to this position.

Holidays and special events are opportunities to build goodwill for your agency. Some organizations use these messages as low-key promotional pieces. An effective structure for a special-event message follows:

- Relate the receiver to the occasion being celebrated.

  What better time to wish you happiness than in this spring season—a time when all of nature seems to be reborn, and our spirits rise.

- Convey good wishes, linked to a low-key promotion if appropriate.

  Along with Za-Za's Pizza, we invite you to join us in a Spring Fling. Za-Za's is offering half-price pizzas and beverages from 5 p.m. until 7 p.m. on March 20. You can also buy tickets ($5 each) to enter a drawing for a Bose Surround Sound CD/Radio donated by Fine's Electronics. All proceeds from ticket sales will go to Community Cupboard to buy food for needy people in our community.

- Close with reinforcement of goodwill.

  Give yourself a Spring Fling! Eat some delicious Za-Za's pizza and help Community Cupboard at the same time. We look forward to seeing you on the 20th.

Most nonprofit organizations use print and broadcast media to get their message into the community. The next section provides guides for using the media effectively.

MEDIA TIPS

As an employee of a nonprofit agency, you will soon learn the value of a positive relationship with the media. News stories can give you valuable free publicity. If you cultivate a favorable relationship with the press, you will increase the odds of getting your news published.

The following guides will help you cultivate a promising relationship with print and broadcast media:

- Contact the media often. Not all of your news releases or public service announcements will be published or aired, but reporters and producers will become aware of your agency and its services if you put out frequent news items.
- Never lie to the media. If you don't know an answer to a question, say so; but offer to find out and get back to the reporter later.
- Don't let a reporter force you into saying something you don't want to say. If you are not authorized to release certain information, say something like, "We are still gathering information about that. It would be premature for me to speak at this time." You can also "turn" the question. Turning is slightly rewording a question and providing information that you *do* want to get out. For example, if a reporter asks you to verify that your agency is in a dangerously tight financial position, you can say something like, "Most nonprofits are continually looking for funds. We have just submitted a major grant to a foundation, and we intend to continue our services to the community."
- Remember that your story is competing with many others. Your story must be interesting enough to capture the attention of a reporter, editor, or news director.

You can bring information about your agency to the attention of the media by using news releases, press calls, op-ed articles, and public service announcements.

News Release

A news release is an approved statement issued to newspapers and broadcast media. Although most news releases are informational, they sometimes have persuasive aspects as well. You should use news releases to announce upcoming events and to inform the press about significant accomplishments of your agency.

For example, if your agency buys a building that has to be renovated to serve your needs, a news story could include facts about the purchase (for example, where, when), how the new location will improve your ability to serve the community (why), and perhaps your need for volunteer labor to refurbish the building (what). When the building is ready for occupancy, your agency might issue a news release announcing the upcoming grand-opening celebration.

Effective news releases require appropriate timing and succinct writing.

Timing the Release

If your release is about an upcoming event, it should be sent a week or more in advance. Give reporters time to put your event on the calendar and see how it fits with other stories. This practice increases the likelihood of your getting some news coverage. If your lead time is short, you may fax the release or send it by e-mail. Whether by mail, fax, or e-mail, target the person most likely to be interested in the story. An untargeted release may be put into a general "in" basket and receive no attention at all.

Writing the Release

Before writing the release, list the points you wish to make. Remember that you must attract attention! The first paragraph should succinctly address *who, what, where, when,* and *why*. It must stimulate the interest of the person reading the release, whether or not that reader is familiar with your agency.

The next paragraphs should expand on the most interesting facts touched on in the first paragraph. Information about people involved with the event or its location may be especially newsworthy. Although you may have to present some background information about your agency, remember that you need not tell everything. As you write the material, be clear and concise.

News releases vary in format. (General guides are given in Chapter 7.) One style, sent by e-mail, is demonstrated in Illustration 18-8.

Press Call

If a news release is sent several days prior to an event, you should follow it with a press call. In a press call you reinforce your relationship with the reporter by providing an opportunity to ask questions, clarify an issue, or get more background on your agency. The press call should help the reporter develop a sense of why he or she should cover news about your organization in general and this event specifically.

These guides will help you make an effective press call:

- Ask for a reporter or desk editor by name. Try to deal with the same person each time you call so that you can establish a relationship.
- Review what you will say before you place the call. Be clear and succinct, but be prepared to supply more details if the reporter asks. Rehearse before placing the call.
- Identify yourself and your agency immediately and refer to the news release that was sent earlier. Be prepared to fax another copy immediately if the release has been lost or misplaced.
- Be sensitive to the person. If the reporter seems to be rushed, keep the call short. If the person seems ready to talk, be prepared to chat amiably and informatively.
- Leave your telephone number so that the reporter can reach you with follow-up questions.

> **ILLUSTRATION 18-8** ▶ E-MAIL NEWS RELEASE*
>
> From: Jo5pts@aol.com
>
> Date: 2005/06/01 Tue PM 03:30:06 EDT
>
> To: (concealed list of press contacts)
>
> Subject: NEWS MEDIA ADVISORY
>
> ### St. Pat's in Five Points to Contribute over $40,000 to Charity
>
> The Five Points Association will be hosting a news conference in Five Points Fountain Plaza on **Thursday, June 9, at 10 a.m.** to distribute over $40,000 in proceeds to local charities from St. Pat's in Five Points. On hand to assist with distributing these gifts will be Columbia's own colorful, vibrant, and entertaining Kudzu Queens.
>
> The success of St. Pat's in Five Points has allowed for thousands of dollars to benefit local charities over the celebration's 23-year history. This year, funding allocations were determined by a Charitable Advisory Committee of the Five Points Association.
>
> As a result of outstanding turnout for this year's festival, twelve charitable organizations and four local public schools will receive funds from St. Pat's in Five Points earnings, each of which will be presented with their contribution at the Thursday news conference.
>
> ***Interview Opportunities:***
> ~Members of the St. Pat's in Five Points planning committee
> ~Representatives from charities receiving funds from St. Pat's in Five Points
>
> ***Visual Opportunities:***
> ~Charity organization receiving their checks, in front of the beautiful Five Points Fountain
> ~Interactions between nonprofits and Charitable Advisory Committee
> ~Five Points' very own Kudzu Queens!
>
> *Five Points will again play host to the ever-improving St. Pat's in Five Points on March 18, 2006.*

*Used by permission of St. Pat's in Five Points Committee.

Some news releases are sent to provide information for a story. Others are sent to announce a coming news conference or event that you want the reporter to attend. If the latter situation is true, call again on the morning of the event to remind the reporter of time, place, and purpose of the news conference.

Although not all news releases or news calls result in a story about your agency, frequent contact with media representatives will create greater awareness of your work in the community and eventually lead to greater press coverage.

Op-Ed Article

Occasionally an employee of a nonprofit submits an op-ed article to a newspaper in an attempt to heighten community awareness of an issue that impacts the agency. The term *op-ed* has been coined to identify the page that appears *op*posite the *ed*itorial page in a newspaper. Many newspapers reserve that page for opinions other than those of the newspaper and its editorial board. A newspaper may feature one or more syndicated journalists on a regular schedule and devote the remainder of the page to commentary by local citizens.

When you write an op-ed piece, apply the principles you have learned about persuasive messages. The article must focus on a theme or issue that captivates the attention and interest of the editor, prompting that person to act by publishing the piece. Your hope is that your comments will promote desire and action among the community readers. An op-ed piece constructed around the theme of the need to understand sexual assault as a crime of violence is shown in Illustration 18-9.

Public Service Announcement

Occasionally a nonprofit agency uses a public service announcement (PSA) to raise consciousness, educate, announce an event, or generate funds. These announcements are written to be aired on radio or television. Some PSAs are used as general advertising; others are used to publicize a specific event or issue. In either case, these "spots" resemble sales messages. The listener must not only learn what is being offered but must also be stimulated to recall that information and act upon it when needed.

The primary difference between a news release and a PSA is length and, consequently, the amount of information that can be included. PSAs are typically written for 60-second, 30-second, or 10-second "spots." The message must be clear and concise, use simple language, and make a strong impact in a short time span.

The following examples demonstrate the approximate amount of information that can be included in a 60-, 30-, or 10-second spot. They also demonstrate the clear, concise language that is necessary.[6]

60-SECOND PSA (APPROXIMATELY 150 WORDS)

Liven up those hot summer days with a visit to *A Body of Work: From Degas to Diebenkorn* at the Columbia Museum of Art.

A Body of Work features approximately 70 artworks that showcase figural work created primarily in the 20th century. Sixty artists are included with works in a variety of media, including oil on canvas, watercolor, lithograph, and etching on paper.

The Columbia Museum of Art has launched this exhibit to highlight some of the museum's rarely seen artworks and to bring a fresh perspective to a long history of figural art. This is the first time that an exhibition of this breadth has been organized from the museum's permanent collection.

A Body of Work will run from July 29 through October 2. Museum hours are 10 a.m. to 5 p.m., Wednesday, Thursday, and Saturday; 10 a.m. to 9 p.m. on Friday; and Sunday, 1 to 5 p.m.

ILLUSTRATION 18-9 ▸ OP-ED ARTICLE

There's That Sexual Place. . . .

I was walking into my office last week as four women casually strolled through the parking lot upon leaving a nearby restaurant, obviously having enjoyed a leisurely lunch. As they passed my office ahead of me, one of the four women uttered the words, "There's that sexual place: ooh, ooh. Don't you want to stop in *there?*" There was some friendly shuffling and pushing toward the doors of Sexual Trauma Services of the Midlands.

I was somewhat surprised, but not totally. I have seen similar reactions before, but never quite so disturbing. My immediate thought was, I hope you never have to use our services.

As I entered my office, I pondered what I had witnessed and felt deep sadness: sadness that women would feel so uncomfortable about a word, idea, or issue that has likely touched one of them in one way or another. A fact about sexual violence is that one in four women will feel the effects of sexual abuse during her lifetime, either directly or indirectly (through its impact on a friend or family member). I also felt sadness that these women would not have thought about the women—each one someone's mother, daughter, sister, or grandmother—who have walked through those doors and been served by STSM. I felt sad that they seemed not to care about young boys who are assaulted, or men who were molested as children and only began to deal with the aftermath when they became adults. The experience reminded me of all men and women, girls and boys who suffer in silence, rather than be connected with "that *sexual* place."

I have a dream that one day we will talk about prevention and risk reduction for sexual abuse the way we talk about the risks of smoking or the importance of eating healthy foods. I dream that parents and children will talk comfortably about something they must not shy away from. I dream that schools will accept the responsibility to supply their students with knowledge about sexual abuse and skills that will empower them to make healthy decisions. I dream that people who need hope and healing will come without embarrassment to "that *sexual* place."

30-SECOND PSA (APPROXIMATELY 75 WORDS)

On July 29, the Columbia Museum of Art will launch *A Body of Work: From Degas to Diebenkorn.* This exhibit features approximately 70 artworks by 60 artists, mostly 20th century, showcasing figural work in a variety of media, including oil on canvas, watercolor, lithograph, and etching on paper.

This is the first time that an exhibition of this breadth has been organized from the museum's permanent collection.

The exhibit will run through October 2.

10-SECOND PSA (APPROXIMATELY 25 WORDS)

On July 29 Columbia Museum of Art will launch *A Body of Work: From Degas to Diebenkorn.* This important exhibit showcases figural work from the museum's permanent collection.

One of the most technical forms of writing undertaken in a nonprofit organization is grant writing. The next section of this chapter discusses important aspects of that writing task.

GRANT WRITING

(This section contributed by Lulis del Castillo-Gonzalez, certified grant writer, Columbia, SC.)

In the nonprofit sector, a variety of financial sources cover operational and project expenses. Grants are an oft-used (and oft-overlooked!) option for nonprofits. Grants are awarded to nonprofit agencies by religious organizations; community and civic groups; private foundations; county, state and federal governments; and local United Way agencies, to name a few.

The requirements for grants from each of these sources and the reports required by each vary considerably. It would be impossible to describe all of the types of grants that are available for nonprofits, but some commonalities run across all applications for money from private or public sources. Those commonalities are discussed in this section.

Factors in successful grant writing include knowing where to seek grants, how to write and submit grants, and how to write reports for grantors.

Where to Seek Grants

Many sources of money are available for the nonprofit organization. Keep in mind, though, that many nonprofit agencies compete for these precious funds. Most nonprofit agencies have some established funding sources, such as United Way, that cover a portion of operational expenses; but those agencies are still required to file applications on a recurring basis. If your agency serves a specific population, such as abused women or children, cancer patients, or victims of natural disasters, resources exist that fund such specific services. State and municipal governments often provide funding to nonprofit organizations but still require the submission of requests to city or county boards or appropriate departments of state governments. In addition to these more established sources of income, the nonprofit agency often turns to foundations or corporations to supplement budgetary needs or fund new projects.

When looking for a grant source, it is important to match the grantor's priorities with those of your agency or proposed project. The annual report of a corporation or foundation will indicate funding priorities as well as the types of projects the entity has funded in the past. If you are looking for novel sources of funding, an Internet search will identify many resources. Your local public library will likely have several foundation directories that list foundations by region or program interest and give eligibility and application instructions. Some foundations will only consider organizations that the foundation has invited to apply for funding. Others will request letters of inquiry, and still others will provide applications upon request or on their websites.

Many directories are also available for sale or as an online subscription. Although these directories are excellent resources, they are expensive and often out of reach for the nonprofit organization. However, even the smallest nonprofit can usually gain access to such information in the reference section of a university or public library.

Applying for a Grant

Different types of grants require different types of applications. Illustration 18-10 shows various types of requests, ranging from simple to complex, and the components of each.

Letter of Request

Corporations such as Wal-Mart, Target, Dell Computers, or Kmart provide funding or in-kind donations (merchandise or services) in communities where their stores are located. A simple phone call or visit can often secure one of these donations, but some vendors request letters indicating your need and use of the donation. Each corporation has its own funding priorities; and your agency's needs must match up with those of the corporation in question. If you are unsure whether your proposed idea falls within the funding priorities, a phone call or letter of inquiry is recommended.

Religious organizations and community groups usually require completion of a small application form or a simple letter of request. It is often advantageous to have board members or agency supporters contact people within these organizations to act as an advocate for your agency when you submit your application or letter of request. Sometimes, these organizations require that a member nominate your agency before you may request grant monies. Illustration 18-11 shows a letter of request written by a church member to an organization in the church of which she is a member. This letter resulted in a contribution of approximately $6,000.

Letter of Inquiry

The guidelines of private foundations differ widely. Some foundations clearly describe their guidelines on their applications or websites. If you are unsure whether your project or agency falls within the guidelines, the contact person listed can probably answer most of your questions. Some foundation grants

ILLUSTRATION 18-10   TYPE OF REQUEST AND REQUIREMENTS FOR SUBMISSION

Request	Submit	Components
Request for in-kind donation or cash contribution	Letter of Request	1. Agency description 2. Description of need 3. Request of items
Request for grant application	Letter of Inquiry	1. Brief agency overview 2. Need statement 3. Project description 4. Budget
Request for Funding	Grant Proposal	1. Executive summary 2. Agency description 3. Need statement 4. Proposed project description 5. Goals and objectives 6. Project budget 7. Attachments

Request for Proposal (RFP)	Full Proposal	1. Cover page
		2. Budget description
		3. Budget narrative:
		    Personnel
		    Contractual services
		    Travel
		    Other
		4. Program narrative:
		    Description of organization
		    Interagency coordination
		    Volunteer coordination
		    Problem definition
		    Project description
		    Project objectives
		    Performance indicators
		    Project evaluation
		    Project continuation
		    Sources of income
		    Time frame
		Grant terms and conditions
		Audit requirements
		Signature page
		Appendix (supporting documents)

ILLUSTRATION 18-11 LETTER OF REQUEST FOR GRANT FROM COMMUNITY ORGANIZATION

2001 Green Street   Columbia, SC 29205   803-555-5555

SEXUAL TRAUMA SERVICES
of the Midlands

<Date>

Ms. B. R. Hayes
3000 Katrina Drive
Columbia, SC 29206

...the healing place

Dear Ms. Hayes:

Please consider this nomination of Sexual Trauma Services of the Midlands (STSM) for funding by the Trinity Community Mission Committee. As an STSM board member, I support this agency's efforts to expand a much-needed program in its array of services to survivors of sexual assault and sexual abuse. We hope to increase the availability of services to children and adolescents by changing the position of Child and Adolescent Services Coordinator from part-time to full-time status.

STSM, a private non-profit United Way agency, is one of 17 rape crisis centers in South Carolina. Its mission is to provide crisis intervention, advocacy, and support services for female and male—child, adolescent, and adult—survivors of sexual assault and abuse. Our service area covers Richland, Lexington, and Newberry Counties. In the year 200Y, STSM staff and volunteers assisted over 2,000 primary and secondary victims of sexual assault and abuse. This represents a 49% increase over our 200X numbers. Additionally, group services were provided to another 251 survivors and their family members—a 239% increase in those services. Through the Division of Education, more than 4,000 persons across our service area of Richland, Lexington, and Newberry Counties participated in public education presentations about the incidence and impact of sexual assault and current prevention and intervention strategies. STSM performed these services, free of charge, with a mere seven full-time and two part-time employees.

An area that compels us to seek additional funding wherever we can is the rising number of victims under age 18. This year, 530 cases of sexual assault have been reported to our offices with 223 of these involving children age 17 and under. Child sexual abuse is a reality that plagues the lives of victims, families, and the entire community. Without treatment, the aftermath of abuse can progressively undermine and overwhelm the intellectual, emotional, physical, and spiritual aspects of the victims' lives and of family functions.

Please be assured any funds received from your program will benefit victims of sexual trauma under the age of 18 as we endeavor to expand those services. Although there are other agencies in this community who work with children's issues, children in the 12–17 age group have almost no help available from professionals who understand the issues of sexual trauma. We believe Sexual Trauma Services of the Midlands is addressing a critical community need and is worthy of support by Trinity's Community Mission Program.

Carol Wyatt, our Executive Director, can be reached at 555-5555. She is ready to provide any additional information you may need. I look forward to your response.

Sincerely,

Shirley Kuiper

Shirley Kuiper
President, Board of Directors

require only the completion of a short application form with agency and project descriptors. As is true of most grants, certain sections are commonly required. Content for those sections is similar to that included in a letter of inquiry.

A letter of inquiry is often the preliminary step to writing a full grant. This inquiry is frequently presented as a two- or three-page document along with a cover letter. Alternatively, it may be written as a multi-page letter. Whatever presentation style you use, the letter of inquiry is a concise statement that usually contains the following sections:

- Brief agency overview
- Need statement
- Project description
- Budget

The agency overview should contain your agency history, including a summary of your agency's achievements, especially as they relate to the specific project for which you are requesting funds. The letter should also include a brief statement of need and a description of your proposed project and anticipated outcomes, a time frame, and the estimated cost. If you are requesting funding for the same project from other sources, or will have matching funds for the grant, be sure to state this fact, presenting details in the budget section.

In a cover letter briefly identify your project, refer to the enclosed project description, and list a contact person at your agency, in case the grantor would like additional information. Finally, request that the potential grantor send you an application form.

Grant Proposal

If you have located a possible source of funding and are ready to apply for a grant, follow the application instructions carefully. A reviewer often initially reads a grant application before passing it along to a committee or panel for a decision. Since this first reader is most likely not an expert in your field, you should make your case clearly and concisely, avoiding jargon and acronyms. Most grant proposals include the following sections:

- Executive summary or abstract
- Agency description
- Need statement
- Proposed project description
- Goals and objectives
- Project budget
- Attachments

The initial reviewer will often read only the executive summary; therefore, you must provide a clear idea of the need and your proposed solution. Much as a cover letter for a job application should entice the reader to look at your complete résumé, this summary should grab the reader's attention by stating why *your* agency is best suited to fulfill the identified need in the community. Within one page, you should be able to establish your organization or agency's reputation, convey the very real need for funding, and make a case for your proposed solution.

Your agency description must tell the grantor who you are and what you do. This is where you should emphasize the achievements of your agency as well as demonstrate your sound fiscal and management qualifications. Although it is essential to promote your agency's capacity, do not criticize other nonprofits; rather, if possible, make a case for proposed collaboration with other community agencies. Funders are attracted to collaborations because such alliances show that you are willing to cooperate with others and make the best use of available resources.

In your statement of need, clearly describe the problem that exists in your community. Provide evidence of need specific to your situation and the community you serve. In this section, you can include statistics that help to make your case, but make certain that your proposal is accurate, with up-to-date and appropriate statistics. Avoid manipulating statistics in order to exaggerate the need.

Your project description must express to the grantor your proposed solution for the problem described in the previous section and clearly define who will benefit from your project. You need to make a case for your agency and why *you* are the best equipped to fulfill this community need. Unless you have been asked to do otherwise, include the project goals and objectives in this section. Be as specific as possible with your goals, and ensure that you have clear, measurable objectives. If requested, include a proposed timeline for your project. Describe how you will evaluate the project effectiveness upon completion and describe how you anticipate sustaining the project in successive years.

The project budget can be as simple as a one-page statement of the expected project expenses. Some grantors, however, request very complex budgets that clearly explain personnel costs with fringe benefits, insurance, and taxes, as well as proportional ongoing expenses that will be charged to this specific project (such as utility cost, printing, copying, general office supplies), travel expenses, and any contractual services you will be purchasing. You may also be asked to submit a list of other business and foundation donors with their contribution levels.

Attachments that should be supplied are specified in the instructions. Include *only* those that the grantor has requested, such as letters of support, IRS Letter of Determination, lists of board and staff members, and agency budgets. Most funding sources ask that you *not* include videotapes, photographs, résumés or staff bios, annual reports/publications, news articles, books, magazines, or newsletters.

A website that can be extremely useful for nonprofit organizations is located at http://www.npguides.org. An excellent example of an RFP from a private source and a grant written in response to that RFP can be downloaded from that site.

FULL PROPOSAL

County, state, and federal grants usually have much longer and more cumbersome requirements than those required by private foundations. Government grants are advertised through a Request for Proposal (RFP). The RFP provides guidelines, which state eligibility requirements, availability of funds, due dates, and restrictions. The RFP will usually also describe the grant evaluation process. Responses to RFPs are difficult to complete and are highly competitive. Some nonprofits hire certified grant writers to handle this type of writing.

The first step is to review carefully the lengthy RFP, noting the sections that should be included in your grant application, information to include in each section, page length, font type and style, margins, guidelines on binding or stapling, and number of copies to submit. Be sure to follow all instructions *exactly* as delineated in the submission procedures. It is essential that you complete all pages accurately and that you provide clean copies of any forms you send. (An excellent example of an RFP from a public agency and a grant written in response to that RFP can be downloaded from http://www.npguides.org).

As in all grants, you must make the case for your agency and for the project that you are submitting. These grants usually require that you state clear goals and objectives as well as a timeline in which each activity is to occur. These goals and objectives should be realistic and measurable. If you are awarded a government grant, you will usually be required to make periodic reports to the granting agency.

Finally, after you have completed your grant proposal, whether it is a simple or complex application, check it for clarity and accuracy, including typographical and spelling errors. Before submitting the proposal, proofread it, and then ask somebody outside of your agency to proofread it. If clarification is needed, an outside person will be able to indicate which areas are unclear or could be improved. Try to write on a ninth-grade to twelfth-grade level. Submit your proposal on bright white paper, with the cover letter on agency letterhead. Do not bind your proposal (unless specifically requested by the grantor), and include as many copies as requested on the application form.

Following these basic guidelines will help you secure funding for your agency. Grant writing is an acquired skill; if you are unsuccessful in your first attempts, ask for feedback from the granting sources on how to improve your grant. Ask if you can resubmit it at a later date, or submit it to a different funding source. Keep trying and remember that it is not about you, but about those individuals your agency is trying to help.

To maintain a flow of funds from private and public sources, you must also meet all reporting requirements.

Reporting to Grantors

Most funding sources require—or at least appreciate—periodic reports from recipients of funds. As is true of requests for money, reports to grantors range from simple to complex.

Most funding sources that require no more than a letter of request or completion of a simple grant application are not extremely demanding about reports. These kinds of donors are often satisfied with a thank-you letter and a copy of the agency's financial report to demonstrate its accountability. Some granting organizations ask for no report, but you can—and should—build goodwill by voluntarily keeping such donors informed about the activities of your agency. Placing donors on your mailing list to receive periodic publications, such as the newsletter and annual report, will keep you on the donor's "radar screen" and demonstrate your appreciation for even the smallest contribution.

Foundations and local government agencies tend to require much more detailed reports. For example, when you receive a grant from a foundation, the terms may stipulate that at the end of the grant period you are to give a full accounting of how the money was spent. Such a requirement, obviously, requires that you keep accurate records and ensure that all money is spent as specified in the grant. A foundation may also ask to visit your agency for an on-site audit. During such a visit you will be expected to produce documentation as to how grant moneys have been spent, including any expenditures for equipment or materials. Foundations often request quarterly and year-end progress reports on the funded project. If a foundation has pledged support for more than one year, it may make delivery of continuing funds contingent on satisfactory completion of year-end reports.

If your funds were granted in response to a proposal that you submitted, progress toward the goals and objectives that were specified in the proposal should be highlighted in your report. If you are not meeting those goals, be honest: Give the grantor reasons for the situation. An honest explanation will help the funding agency understand the existence of obstacles that may prevent project completion and may make it more inclined to continue funding the project or allow diversion of funds to another purpose.

Grantors that administer federal funds require extensive and complex reports, often on a quarterly basis. These reports are sometimes referred to as "rewriting the grant." In the rewrite process you must show how the funds already received were used and any anticipated changes in needs. For example, your original proposal may have asked for travel funds for one of your staff members. If that staff member did not travel as much as anticipated, but instead conducted more project-related business by long-distance telephone, you may ask for permission to divert funds from the travel category to an office expense category when you "rewrite the grant." If the diversion of funds is not granted and you do not use the funds for the originally specified use, you will be required to "leave the money on the table"; that is, forego that money. Consequently, a major task of the grants manager is to track expenditures related to each grant and anticipate the need to ask permission to divert funds to uses other than those originally specified.[7]

ADMINISTRATIVE WRITING

As is true in the management of any organization, several documents are used to record official actions taken at meetings of the board or committees, to direct the normal operations of the agency, and to report actions or outcomes to the board or other stakeholders. Uses of and styles for these documents are similar in nonprofit and for-profit organizations. Some, such as a meeting agenda and minutes of a meeting, are relatively short and uncomplicated. Others, such as policy manuals and procedures can be quite lengthy, complex, and technical.

For assistance with agendas, minutes, routine reports, and nonroutine reports, refer to Chapters 5 and 6 of this book. Guides for writing policies, procedures, and instructions appear in Chapter 17.

ETHICAL CONSIDERATIONS

Communicating within and for a nonprofit organization presents several ethical challenges. For example, employees of nonprofits often have access to sensitive personal information about clients and donors. Obviously, such information must not only be protected by storage in secure files, but employees must refrain from communicating the information in any way that would enable the reader or listener to identify specific individuals. Even an "example" in a news release or interview must be presented in such a way that it protects client and donor confidentiality.

Perhaps the greatest temptation for grant writers or employees who write promotional materials for a nonprofit is to exaggerate such things as ability to deliver services, program success, or financial need. Whether writing a PSA about a fundraising event, a grant proposal, or a report to the Board of Directors, remember—Tell the truth, the whole truth, and nothing but the truth. This maxim applies to both budgets and narratives. For example, if you do not have proof that you "serve more clients annually than any other trauma center in the state," say instead that you have "one of the largest annual caseloads in the state."

If major changes occur in your agency's ability to deliver proposed services or if you want to use some of the money for something not originally included in a grant, notify the grantor immediately; explain the situation. Many grant makers are willing to accept alternatives to the original proposal so long as the changes still meet their general funding objectives and they are confident that the money will be used responsibly. By notifying the granting agency, you are demonstrating your adherence to ethical standards.

Nonprofit managers sometimes debate the ethics of reporting the value of in-kind contributions (that is, contributions of goods or services), both as receipts and as part of the cost of providing services to the community. However, an argument can be made that if you do not report the value of volunteer services, you do not accurately report the total cost of providing your client services. The ethical dilemma is sometimes not whether to report the value of such contributions, but how to value them. One Internal Revenue Service guideline is that if you would have hired someone to perform the work done by a volunteer, you may consider the "reasonable value" of that work as income and the service as part of your operating expense. For example, if a skilled plumber donates his services to repair a faulty drain in your restroom, you may count the reasonable value of his labor as income, and recognize the equivalent value as an operating expense. Although the figures offset each other, these kinds of reports can show that the actual costs of your operations are greater than your cash outlays. Since most grant givers are interested in the total costs of your operation, and some even require an "in-kind match," working with your accountant to record the value of in-kind contributions may improve the accuracy of your fiscal responsibility reports.

SUMMARY

Although some of the communication forms discussed in this chapter are not exclusive to nonprofits, mastery of them is essential for effective management of a nonprofit agency. For example, a large business may have a communication division whose task it is to write news releases, make press calls, hold press conferences, and coordinate the publication of brochures, newsletters, and annual reports. Similarly, the human resources division may be responsible for maintaining an up-to-date employee manual, and a technical writing team may be responsible for writing operating procedures. But many nonprofits are relatively small, and an executive director or director of development is often expected to write such documents—or to know when to enlist the help of a skilled volunteer or a contract writer.

If you aspire to a career in the nonprofit arena, you will have to become especially skilled in writing promotional and goodwill messages. Much of a nonprofit's success depends upon keeping its name before the public and increasing its support base. You must become proficient in several types of writing that a for-profit enterprise may never encounter, particularly the many kinds of documents associated with fundraising. The quality of appeal letters, grant applications, grant proposals, and reports to grantors may well dictate the financial health of a nonprofit agency.

TOPICS FOR DISCUSSION

1. Discuss the role of nonprofits in the U.S. economy. If you have had employment or volunteer experience with a nonprofit agency, describe to your classmates the mission of that agency and your estimate of its value to the community.

2. What should a writer consider when preparing general advertising copy?

3. What should a writer consider when writing copy for a newsletter, brochure, or annual report?

4. Describe types of persuasive messages (purposes, suggested structures) commonly used by nonprofits.

5. Describe types of goodwill messages (purposes, suggested structures) commonly used by nonprofits.

6. Identify behaviors that should lead to a favorable relationship with the media.

7. Discuss guides for an effective news release, press call, and public information message.

8. In what ways does an op-ed column differ from a news release?

9. Why is grant writing so critical to the life of most nonprofit organizations?

10. Discuss ways to find out about available grants and improve your chances of receiving grants. If you are familiar with some techniques or strategies that are not included in this textbook, share that information with your classmates.

11. Differentiate the following items used in the process of asking for grant money: letter of request, letter of inquiry, grant proposal, full proposal.

12. Why is it wise to send a report about fund usage to grantors, even when they don't require one?

APPLICATIONS

1. Select a local nonprofit agency. After visiting the agency or its website, write a profile of the organization. Include such information as its mission, services offered, size of staff, number of clients served annually, volunteer opportunities, annual budget, major sources of revenue, and any other facts that will give a picture of the agency's impact in the community. As directed by your instructor, present this information in a memorandum or in an oral report.

2. Based on the information you gathered for Application 1, write a fundraising appeal letter for the agency.

3. Form groups of three or four students. Each student should obtain a newsletter or an annual report from a nonprofit agency. (At least one sample should be an electronic newsletter or annual report.) Discuss the strengths and weaknesses of each document obtained by the group members and select the one that best meets the criteria presented in this chapter. Summarize your findings in a memorandum to your instructor.

4. Assume you are the chair of a committee planning a benefit for PetSave, an agency that rescues and finds homes for abandoned and abused animals. The benefit will be held on February 19, <year> at the restored opera house in your city. Features of the evening include a wine and cheese reception from 6:30 to 7:30 p.m. in the lobby of the opera house; a performance by a famous musician (select one whom you would like to hear); and an optional dinner before the performance. All proceeds go to PetSave, and donations are tax deductible to the extent allowed by the IRS. Tickets may

be purchased online (supply a fictitious web address) or by telephone (supply a fictitious number). Credit card payments are accepted.

Pricing options available to donors:

- $1,000 for six tickets, dinner for two, special seating, wine and cheese reception, and private reception with performer after the concert
- $500 for four tickets, special seating, wine and cheese reception, and private reception with performer after the concert
- $250 for two tickets, special seating, wine and cheese reception, and private reception with performer after the concert
- $50 for one ticket and wine and cheese reception
  a. Design an announcement suitable for mailing to your donor list. Include information about the performer and any other data that will attract attention and stimulate desire to attend the benefit concert.
  b. Write a news release about the event.
  c. Write a 60-second, 30-second, and 10-second public service announcement about the event.

5. Each year Dr. William Dean, an entrepreneurship professor at a nearby university, offers free consulting services to nonprofit agencies. The consulting work is done by MBA students under the guidance of the professor. In a brief request for proposals (RFP), which are to be a maximum of two pages, the professor gives the following guides: (1) Describe the agency, its background, brief history, current status. (2) Identify the key person with whom the students will have the greatest contact. (3) Identify key issue(s), problem(s), or assignment(s) you would like the team to address over the next four months. Be as specific as possible. You will be able to adjust and modify the project after meeting with the team. (5) Explain why this issue or these issues are important to you and to the agency. (6) Provide other information you think the team should be aware of as it considers your agency and project along with other options available to them.

Assume you are the executive director of PetSave (see Application 4). The executive committee of your board of directors suggests that you should apply for these services. They suggest two possible projects: a marketing project analyzing community awareness of your agency or a human resources project exploring ways to evaluate employees in a nonprofit organization.

Select one of the projects. Write a proposal for services, based on the information requested in the RFP. Prepare it in appropriate, readable manuscript style as a file that will be sent by e-mail to the professor.

6. Assume the services requested in Application 5 were successfully performed. Your agency wants to maintain goodwill with the professor so that he might select you again for free consulting services. Write an appropriate thank-you letter to Dr. Dean.

7. Assume that Dr. Dean (Applications 5 and 6) has received an award from the State Alliance for Nonprofit Organizations (SANO). You had nominated him for the award, citing the many *pro bono* hours he had devoted to helping PetSave develop a five-year business plan as well as his work

with the student consulting team that had helped your agency. He received the award at SANO's annual "Hero Recognition Dinner," at which the alliance presents two awards to community members who have assisted nonprofits in significant ways. Write a letter of congratulation to Dr. Dean.

8. Using the Internet, identify a funding source that you think would be interested in providing money for an agency such as PetSave (or choose another nonprofit that you are interested in). Write a letter of inquiry regarding funding for a new project the agency wants to undertake. Include a brief agency overview, a need statement, a project description, and a proposed budget.

9. Contact a local nonprofit agency. Ask for a copy of a letter of request or an executive summary for a grant that was successfully funded. In a memorandum to your instructor, analyze the strengths of the letter or executive summary and explain why you think it contributed to the agency's success in receiving the grant.

10. Refer to Illustration 18-11. Write a brief letter to the grantor reporting how the $6,000 grant was used. Assume the money was spent on the program described in the letter of request, but identify one or two specific costs that were covered by the grant (for example, printing brochures, hiring a part-time therapist for teens, buying supplies for the children's art therapy program, etc.).

REFERENCES

1. *The New Nonprofit Almanac and Desk Reference.* (2002). New York: Jossey-Bass, p. 6.

2. *Employment in the nonprofit sector.* Retrieved August 10, 2005, from http:\\www.IndependentSector.org

3. Information obtained on November 15, 2004 from www.nramembership.org

4. All references to Sexual Trauma Services of the Midlands and illustrations using that name appear with permission and approval of the Executive Committee of that agency.

5. *The State,* January 20, 2005, p. D3.

6. Adapted from news release retrieved August 11, 2005 from http://www.colmusart.org

7. Additional useful sources about grant writing and identifying grant sources include:
    *   Bauer, D. G. (1999). *The "How To" grants manual: Successful grant-seeking techniques for obtaining public and private grants* (4th ed.). Phoenix: The American Council on Education and the Oryx Press.

- Eckstein, R. M. (ed.). (2005). *750 web sites for grant seekers* (1st ed.). Loxahatches, FL: Research Grand Guides, Inc.
- Hall, M., & Howlett, S. (2003). *Getting funded: A complete guide to writing grant proposals* (4th ed.). Portland, OR: Continuing Education Publications, Portland State University.
- Morris, J. M., & Adler, L. (eds.). (1998). *Grant seekers guide* (5th ed.). Wakefield, RI: Moyer Bell.
- Wells, M. K. (2005). *Grantwriting beyond the basics: Book 1: Proven strategies professionals use to make their proposals work*. Portland, OR: Continuing Education Publications, Portland State University.

Index

Note: Page numbers in *italic* type indicate tables or illustrations.